Encyclopedia of Cultural Anthropology

The Encyclopedia of Cultural Anthropology was prepared under the auspices and with the support of the Human Relations Area Files (HRAF). A research agency founded at Yale University in 1949, HRAF is a not-for-profit international consortium of 21 Sponsoring Member institutions and some 300 participating Associate Member institutions in 30 countries. In accord with its primary mission to facilitate the comparative study of human culture, society, and behavior, HRAF produces and distributes a full-text database on the cultures of the world known as the Human Relations Area Files.

Encyclopedia of Cultural Anthropology
Editorial Advisory Board

Encyclopedia of Cultural Anthropology

SPONSORED BY:

Human Relations Area Files at Yale University

EDITORS:

David Levinson
Melvin Ember

Volume 2

A Henry Holt Reference Book

Henry Holt and Company
New York

A Henry Holt Reference Book
Henry Holt and Company, Inc.
Publishers since 1866
115 West 18th Street
New York, New York 10011

Henry Holt® is a registered trademark
of Henry Holt and Company, Inc.

Published in Canada by Fitzhenry & Whiteside Ltd.,
195 Allstate Parkway, Markham, Ontario L3R 4T8.
Distributed outside the United States and Canada
by Macmillan Publishers, London, England: ISBN 0-333-671-473

Library of Congress Cataloging-in-Publication Data
Encyclopedia of cultural anthropology /
edited by David Levinson and Melvin Ember.
p.   cm.
Includes bibliographical references and index.
1. Ethnology—Encyclopedias.   I. Levinson, David.
II. Ember, Melvin.
GN307.E52   1996   95-37237
305.8'03—dc20   CIP

ISBN 0-8050-2877-3

First Edition—1996

Designed by Chestnut Hill Enterprises, Inc.

Printed in the United States of America.
All first editions are printed on acid-free paper. ∞

10 9 8 7 6 5 4 3 2 1

Project Staff

AMERICAN REFERENCE PUBLISHING COMPANY, INC.
Lakeville, CT 06039

Publisher   Richard Gottlieb

Managing Editors   Laura Mars
                       Karen Christensen

EDITORIAL/PRODUCTION

Alexcia Fales
Lee Kennedy
Diane Marchionna
Penni Martorell
Betsy Trotta

Rodelinde Albrecht, Proofreader
Judy Davis, Indexer
Chestnut Hill Enterprises, Inc., Design/Typesetting

E

ECOLOGY

See: *Behavioral Ecology; Cultural Ecology; Historical Ecology*

ECONOMIC ANTHROPOLOGY

Economists are known for their qualification "all other things being equal," while anthropologists have made a discipline of the fact that things are never equal. This has been the crux of the best-known debate in economic anthropology—between substantivists and formalists, a debate that has never been resolved because the parties to it never agreed sufficiently on their assumptions to be able to engage each other meaningfully. Others who did not enter the debate were less committed to its rhetoric and assumptions and could profit from the issues it highlighted and use the insights to define a practice they called economic anthropology, although different people stress disparate dimensions of it. This suggests sufficient consensus about topics, if not approaches, that people can share a label. Because whatever else they do, all people do something that strikes European and American anthropologists as being economic by some definition or another, economic anthropology is as old as the tradition of fieldwork in anthropology. The substantivist-formalist debates concerned these definitions.

Bronislaw Malinowski (1922) rejected the notion of self-interested economic decision-making by individuals in favor of a view of economic activity as social. Several years later, three anthropologists published works that took a different stance (Firth 1939; Goodfellow 1939; Herskovits 1940). They did not reject the idea, favored by economists, that a single psychology of choice underlies all economic, allocative behavior in which people must decide how to use limited resources (e.g., time, effort, or money) to achieve objectives (e.g., prestige, glory, or profits). These works introduced parlance from economics into anthropology.

The economic historian Karl Polanyi (1957) distinguished between the substance of economics, the means by which people provision themselves, and the emphasis on individual allocative choices, the formal notion of economics. From that time formalists and substantivists joined the debate. Formalists emphasized methodological individualism, the doctrine that all social phenomena are the culmination of individual actions and can best be explained in terms of individual motivations. Like economists, formalists assumed that individual allocative choices, each made in the best interests of the individual, culminate in well-ordered systematic institutions. They looked to economics for theory and rhetoric to justify it. Substantivists argued that cultural and social systems defined not only the possibilities among which individuals could choose but also the motivational structures in terms of which they could make choices. If people do not organize experience to distinguish between leisure and work, as people in the industrial societies do, then it makes no sense to speak of "preference for leisure." If people do not distinguish risk as a dimension of their experience, it makes no sense to speak of "risk avoidance." Thus, individuals were functions of and defined by collective social and cultural forces. Substantivists looked to Émile Durkheim and his followers, who articulated this sociological view, for their theory and rhetoric of justification.

Scott Cook (Schneider and LeClair 1968) argues that the substantivists rejected economic analysis not because it was inappropriate but because they abhorred the market as an antihuman institution and wished that it did not exist. They were in the thrall of an ideology, he argues, that romanticized the "savage" and held such nonmarket (and hence uncorrupted) beings to be altruistic and noble as opposed to their Western brothers and sisters entrapped in the inhuman business of buying and selling themselves, others, and their goods.

There is certainly a substantial romantic dimension to the whole sociological enterprise, a longing for a lost past of community closeness among families in agricultural villages versus the harshness of anomic alienated life among hostile strangers in industrial cities. This view recognized neither the harsh realities of rural life nor the gratifications of urban life but mythologized both. The substantivists, Cook argues, were an extension of the same romantic movement.

Frank Cancian (in LeClair and Schneider 1968) suggests that the combatants in the debate never really addressed the issues at stake. The formalists argued that economics is the study of allocation of scarce means to alternative ends according to the theories of economists. Substantivists argued that such theories only apply in market economies. Formalists replied that the means and ends need not be material, they could be such immaterial entities as prestige. This did not delimit any particular field of action as economic. While some were interested in allocative processes and others in institutions, all said they were interested in whether economic theory was applicable to non-Western societies. Neither, however, delimited a field of economic anthropology.

Cancian argues that the whole debate did not concern whether to import economic theory to anthropology but focused on the idea that some said that maximization was a fruitful approach to human behavior, while the other group thought institutions were variable and economic institutions were sufficiently different across cultures that only in some did the principle of maximization hold. Formalists, he argues, had successfully applied some economic concepts to non-Western issues and substantivists had studied social concomitants to different types of exchange. Because of their mutual caricatures and what Cook calls the "split level" dialogue in which neither could engage the other, the task of operationalizing theoretical propositions or building theories about institutions had been lost. Cancian concludes, with Polanyi, that the economy is an instituted process and, with LeClair, that economics is the study of economizing. In other words, we should study how

people operate within their own institutional configurations.

Formalists and substantivists parodied each other's work and ideas. Harold Schneider (1968) chides substantivists for their preoccupation, which economists did not share, with social and cultural dimensions of economic systems. Marshall Sahlins (1972) equates formalism with the importation of neoclassical microeconomic models, and substantivism with developing analyses appropriate to their various societies. It is the difference, he says, between taking primitive economies as underdeveloped versions of Western businesses and honoring them for what they are. Sahlins quotes the formalist Manning Nash citing Cook in support to the effect that substantivism had been found to be simply confusion and error. Sahlins continues that while many of the arguments seemed to make sense, the effect had been to confirm everyone's original positions, while the audience to the debate had become bored or ready to go to work doing anthropology.

Cook (1974) characterizes Sahlins's approach as one that gives analytical precedence to culture over behavior. Sahlins, he says, thought that culture determines behavior. Cook believes that some combination of "ethnoeconomics" and Marxian theory would be most productive but admits that the problems of applying such ideas to noncapitalist economies would not disappear just because the ideas were not imported from the discipline of economics. If neoclassical economics was invented to explain capitalist systems, so was Marxism; if neoclassical economics was ethnocentric, so was Marxism, as Maurice Godelier (1967) points out. Rather than simply rejecting such ideas at the beginning, the task of economic anthropology, Cook argues, is to try out various ideas developed in Western thought to test their usefulness in understanding non-Western economies in order to refine, clarify, elaborate, or reject them on the basis of experience.

In his studies of domestic production among Oaxacan metate producers and their relationships to an embracing capitalist system, Cook (1982) came to appreciate a number of limitations of both the substantivist and formalist approaches in economic anthropology. He summarizes them as a tendency to reduce explanations of complex processes of interrelated and contradictory variables to descriptions of isolated events; a failure to develop any theoretical means for seeing through observable behavior to underlying dynamics; a focus on individuals; and an emphasis on systems of exchange.

Formalists chided substantivists for not understanding economics or economists. Substantivists chided formalists for being ethnocentric and thinking all societies were sufficiently like their own to be characterized in the same terms. The fact remains that anthropologists are not economists, that reading a couple of introductory texts could not make anthropologists into economists, and that there never was any need for anthropologists to be economists. This substantivist-formalist debate is now dead, not because it was ever resolved in favor of one side or the other or because there was a successful synthesis, but because it became fruitless, as both Cancian and Cook point out. Other things are not equal, and it is the job of anthropology to describe how this is so and explain why it is so.

With its claim to four fields of biological, sociocultural, linguistic, and prehistoric comprehension of the human species, every discipline concerning humanity becomes relevant to anthropology. On the other hand, this very insistence on holism defines anthropology as a discipline separate from others with its own distinctive approach to issues and problems.

Although it would be impossible to get anthropologists to agree on underlying premises or programs of research, three postulates underlie most anthropological work: holism, comparativism, and ethnography. Holism means seeing any characteristic in terms of all others. Thus, instead of analytically separating the political from the economic, or literature from commerce, anthropologists see them as dimensions of larger systems. Comparativism means that instead of seeing societies as unique, anthropologists conceive of them in terms of what we know about other social orders at different times and places. Thus, instead of thinking of chieftaincy or exchange in a particular society, we think in terms of chieftaincy or exchange across a wide variety of societies to find their dimensions of similarity and difference. Ethnography means that we try to know our subject matter from the point of view of everyday life by participating in and observing the lives of the people we wish to understand.

Together, these three postulates define a discipline that is different from any other. Economic anthropology, as part of anthropology, shares these postulates and has continued to develop accounts of economic phenomena independently of economics as a discipline, just as we have developed accounts of politics, history, and literature separate from those disciplines dedicated to the study of more narrow phenomena than anthropology.

Economic anthropology today is not best thought of as economics in non-Western settings but rather as anthropological approaches to economics in any setting. Given the holistic and comparative dimensions of anthropology, this means that the notion of economics is considerably broader than it might be in the discipline of economics. At least, anthropologists do not strive to hold other things equal, but rather to understand the range of variation, the reasons for it, and the consequences of it.

People provision themselves and make allocative decisions. To meet their material needs, people produce, distribute, and consume goods. Economic anthropology describes the ways in which people produce, distribute, and consume goods, how these systems are organized, how they operate, how they got that way, how they relate to other systems, how people behave and make decisions in terms of such systems, and the consequences of people's actions (often unintended and unrecognized) for the systems. Economic anthropology includes the objectives of theorizing and describing the processes of allocative decisions, their institutional contexts and their consequences, the operation of the economic institutions and their dynamics, how they affect people, and how people's actions affect their institutions. Different anthropologists have addressed different problems in different ways from different theoretical frameworks.

To look for simple causal chains, to argue that one factor or variable in some simple way causes or determines another is to ignore the complexities of real economic systems. A complementary goal of economic anthropology is to describe the systems of consumption, production, and exchange in locally meaningful terms which are universally relevant and useful for understanding any economic system at any time and any place. To understand how various economic systems organize production, distribution, and consumption, we have to understand what the system is, what its parts are, and how the parts relate to one another.

Stuart Plattner (1989) collected works on hunters and gatherers, horticulturalists, precapitalist states, peasants, the international system, markets, cities, industrial agriculture, the informal economy, women and economic institutions, common property, and Marxism. This reflects the interest in different types of socioeconomic orders; different kinds of exchange; and issues of the time, such as common property and gender studies.

Some of the questions of economic anthropology derive from concerns that were introduced from economics with the substantivist-formalist debate. One is an interest in decision-making derived from economists' assumptions around methodological individualism and the importance of allocative decisions. Rather than examining decisions as such, anthropologists have analyzed the values, means, goals, and institutional structures that inform and underlie and constrain decisions. Because, as Plattner (1989) points out, economic anthropologists never stopped doing empirical work but just abstained from further argument about how to do it, a body of research from economic anthropologists of all theoretical persuasions suggests that to develop the "internal" perspective and understand decisions from the actor's point of view, we need to develop locally relevant cultural accounts. Because this approach does not address the questions of how the system became the way it is, why it stays that way, and how it is changing from that way, the relationships among parts of the system, the relationship of the system to larger and smaller ones, and the relationships of individuals and systems, other anthropologists emphasize the institutional relationships and the dynamic interactions of elements within systems and among systems at local, national, and international levels.

To answer these questions in a comparative framework, anthropologists have more or less accepted a set of categories for comparative description. To understand a set of kinship terms, we plot them on a universally applicable genealogical diagram; to understand different economies, we need external reference points.

We can understand the organization of social units in terms of the how people are organized to produce things, and secondarily, how they are organized to consume and distribute things. A view of economies as systems directs us to analyze how each unit or component in the system operates, how it relates to the other units, and how they operate together. In any human system, not all systems will operate smoothly; some of the parts will operate at cross-purposes to others.

Another component goal of economic anthropology is to examine these complex relationships, both in particular and in general; and in the process, develop the concepts necessary to understand and analyze economies. Because of the complex interrelationships among economic, political, and ideological forms, our discussion ranges over a number of issues that at first glance do not appear "economic," but without which, economic systems do not make sense.

The three universal dimensions to economic systems are production, consumption, and exchange. Cook was correct in that more attention has gone to defining forms of exchange than forms of production. Social relations are formed around production processes and these determine the possibilities for exchange and definitions of the good life that inform consumption. The three generally recognizable forms of exchange are reciprocity, redistribution, and market.

Reciprocity is based on symmetrical exchanges. It is often seen in systems of labor exchange in which a household will send one member to work for another household for a day in exchange for the promise that the receiving household will later return a day of the same kind of labor. Everyone exchanges with everyone else and all the exchanges are reciprocal.

Redistribution is also based on the logic of reciprocity, but it is more organized. In redistributive exchange, every unit contributes to a central one which gives each contributor something different from what they contributed. For example, fishermen in a shore-based community may receive a regular supply of yams from gardeners inland if they provide a central figure with fish. The gardeners contribute yams and receive fish. All participants are indebted to the central figure for the gifts they receive, and to fulfill that obligation, they continue to contribute to the central figure and thus the system perpetuates itself. A system in which all receive as much as they put in is called symmetric. A system in which the central figure keeps some of the goods to support a household, relatives, or friends is called asymmetric.

Reciprocity also underlies market exchange, although the exchanges are more indirect. Instead of an exchange of fish for yams directly or through a re-distributing intermediary, people set prices for their products according to the relationships of supply and demand and exchange money for goods. In such systems of exchange, a yam grower sells yams for money and uses the money to purchase fish. The relative prices of yams and fish are set by the supply and demand of each, but in exchange the buyer and seller reciprocate. Because political relations may determine exchange relationships, buyers and sellers may not be on equal footing and the reciprocity may be neither "fair" nor "just."

While one form of exchange may predominate in a given society, as the market does in the United States, there are usually other forms of exchange as well, for instance, redistribution by taxation and reciprocity in gift exchanges. We can distinguish between use value and exchange value. Use value is the use that people have for something; it is qualitative and cannot be compared with other use values. For example, shovels are useful for shoveling but not for eating. Chopsticks are useful for eating but not for shoveling. They have different and incomparable use values. Exchange value is quantitative and allows things to be compared in terms of the ratio of one another when people exchange them. For example, we might find that one may trade a hundred chopsticks for one shovel.

The one thing that all useful objects have in common is that someone made them; they are the products of labor. Exchange values are the ratios of amounts of labor that it took to produce the objects being exchanged. For example, to make a chopstick, it takes 1/100th of the labor to make a shovel. These concepts of value allow us to compare very different economic systems in similar terms. We can always compare systems of production, consumption, and exchange in terms of the labor involved in producing the goods exchanged, produced, and consumed.

In market systems, the price is not always a good guide to value, because prices are set by supply and demand. Thus, there may be little labor in a product that is in great demand but in short supply and which, therefore, has a high price. In systems where markets organize exchange, they will also organize production. So if the object has little value relative to its price, many people will start to produce it in order to take advantage of the differential. As they do this, the market will be flooded with the product, and its supply will increase relative to its demand and the price will

fall. As the price falls, there is less differential between price and value, and price may fall below value so that only the most efficient producers, those that produce the object in the least amount of labor time, remain. Through such processes, price oscillates around value in systems in which markets organize both production and exchange.

There are two well-defined ways in which production can be organized: by firms and by households. Firms operate in market terms, so wherever there are firms, there are markets. Firms purchase commodities, including labor, on the market. They use these inputs to produce other commodities that they sell on the market. Their goal is to recapture the amount of exchange value that they used to purchase the original commodities plus an increment to it, which is called profit. Firms make decisions in terms of market variables and profits.

Instead of buying labor on the market, households use their own labor, like family farms in the United States. Even though everything these farms produce may be sold on markets, households do not make decisions in terms of profits but in terms of the balance between their needs and the effort required to produce goods they can use or sell. As they produce more of the necessary total value, their need for more decreases; as they work more to produce that amount, they do not want to work more. When it is no longer worth their effort, households stop production.

Some of the factors that determine how hard people work include technology, soil fertility, irrigation systems, the prices of their products, and the distance to markets. Some factors that determine need in households are taxes; debts; interest on debts; costs for replacing and improving machines, livestock, buildings, and tools; medical costs; costs for education and taking care of children; and costs for supporting the members of the household. As with exchange, while one type of production may predominate, it does not rule out the other. Firms predominate in the United States, but this does not rule out production by households.

The holistic view of anthropology suggests that production, consumption, and exchange are related systemically: each affects the other. The question we must ask of any society is how these are related to each other. The dimension of holism takes us well beyond the traditional field of the economic to consider worldviews, ideologies, and political systems. The comparative view defines three kinds of political order: egalitarian, rank, and stratified.

There may never be complete equality. At least some people are young, inexperienced, and not fully capable; others are older, more experienced, and more capable; still others are very old, very experienced, very wise but perhaps less physically capable. When anthropologists talk about "egalitarian people" they mean it in the sense of having the same number of positions of prestige within each of the recognized age and gender categories as there are people capable of filling them (Fried 1967).

Rank societies make invidious distinctions. There may be six hardworking gatherers but only one who is given a title or special clothing or deference. The definition of the ranked political form is a society in which there are fewer positions of prestige than people capable of filling them. The main feature of both rank and egalitarian political orders is that everyone has equal access to important resources.

What distinguishes these two forms from stratified forms is that in stratified forms there is not equal access to resources. Wherever there is unequal access to resources there are ways to enforce differential access and worldviews that make it seem reasonable. These different forms of production (household and firm), exchange (reciprocity, redistribution, market), and polity (egalitarian, rank, and stratified) define different political-economic systems.

The interaction of kinds of production and kinds of exchange define the six different economic types, as shown in Table 1.

| | Production | |
	Household	Firm
Exchange		
Reciprocity	1	2
Redistribution	3	4
Market	5	6

Table 1. Types of production with types of types of exchange define six different economic types.

Since firms are in business to make money, and money is really important for organizing exchange only in market exchange, it follows that if exchange is not organized by the market, there will not be any firms. Thus, two forms disappear from our table: 2, and 4. When firms and markets are established, households

become of secondary importance in production, though they do not disappear. They simply are not powerful enough to organize the system as a whole. Thus, form 5, "market, household," drops out of our table, leaving us with forms 1, 3, and 6 or household production with reciprocity and redistribution and firm production with the market.

Table 2 shows the intersection of these economic forms with the three political forms.

| | Political Form | | |
Economic Form	Egalitarian	Rank	Stratified
Household/reciprocity	1	2	3
Household/redistribution	4	5	6
Firm/market	7	8	9

Table 2. Economic and Political Forms

The firm/market economic form does not occur in egalitarian and rank political forms; only in stratified forms, so political/economic forms 7 and 8 disappear from our table. Likewise, the household/reciprocity economic form does not occur in stratified societies as a major form, so form 3 disappears.

There can be stratification with certain kinds of redistribution, so form 6 stays in the table. Wherever rank is a political form, reciprocity tends to be organized as redistribution rather than directly. Thus, form 2 drops out of our table. By the same token, where there is redistribution, there is not egalitarian political organization but either rank or stratified. Thus, form 4 does not exist.

This leaves us with four of the nine possible forms of political-economic systems that we actually find: household/reciprocity/egalitarian (Table 2, cell 1), household/redistribution/rank (Table 2, cell 5), household/redistribution/stratified (Table 2, cell 6), firm/market/stratified (Table 2, cell 9).

To understand how these features of political and economic systems relate to each other in concrete historic and ethnographic cases, to understand why only some of the possible forms are found in history and ethnography and how people operate in and affect them are the major objectives of economic anthropology.

E. Paul Durrenberger

See Also: Reciprocity; Redistribution

COOK, SCOTT. "Structural Substantivism: A Critical Review of Marshall Sahlins' Stone Age Economics." *Comparative Studies in Society and History* 16 (1974): 355–379.

——. *Zapotec Stoneworkers: The Dynamics of Rural Simple Commodity Production in Modern Mexican Capitalism.* Washington, D.C.: University Press of America, 1982.

FIRTH, RAYMOND. *Primitive Polynesian Economy.* 1939. Reprint. New York: Norton, 1975.

FRIED, MORTON H. *The Evolution of Political Society.* New York: Random House, 1967.

GODELIER, MAURICE. *Rationality and Irrationality in Economics.* New York: Monthly Review Press, 1975.

GOODFELLOW, D. M. *Principles of Economic Sociology.* London: Routledge, 1939.

HERSKOVITS, MELVILLE J. *Economic Life of Primitive Peoples.* New York: Knopf, 1940.

LECLAIR, EDWARD E., JR., and HAROLD K. SCHNEIDER, eds. *Economic Anthropology: Readings in Theory and Analysis.* New York: Holt, Rinehart and Winston, 1968.

MALINOWSKI, BRONISLAW. *Argonauts of the Western Pacific.* 1922. Reprint. New York: Waveland Press, 1984.

PLATTNER, STUART, ed. *Economic Anthropology.* Stanford, Calif.: Stanford University Press, 1989.

POLANYI, KARL, C. W. ARESNBERG, and H. W. PEARSON, eds. *Trade and Market in Early Empires.* New York: Free Press, 1957.

SAHLINS, MARSHALL. *Stone Age Economics.* New York: Aldine, 1972.

EDUCATIONAL ANTHROPOLOGY

Educational anthropology is the subfield of sociocultural anthropology concerned with the study of both formal and nonformal education. It is relatively new, having become an academic subfield in the 1970s.

HISTORICAL BACKGROUND

Social History

The history of educational anthropology before 1970 is largely social, rather than academic. The first part of this social history lasted from 1900 to 1960; the second period covered 1960 to about 1970. During the first period, anthropologists refuted "false theo-

ries" about the learning disabilities of immigrant, minority, and lower-class children in U.S. public schools and native children in colonial territories. They suggested alternative explanations for the children's difficulties in school, proposed "solutions" to the school problems, and conducted research to provide better knowledge for solving the school problems.

Ironically, one theory that Franz Boas, Bronislaw Malinowski, and other anthropologists needed to refute came from anthropology. Anthropologists concerned about the school problems of immigrant, minority, and lower-class children—and the problems of the native children in colonial territories—accepted the evolutionary theories of Lewis Henry Morgan (for example, Nina C. Vandenwalker) and Herbert Spencer (for example, Edgar L. Hewitt) and thought that the children came from lower cultures. Therefore, these children had difficulty learning things taught to them in higher Anglo-American culture. Another theory posited that the children's learning difficulties arose from their biological inferiority. Evidence of their inferiority was said to be found in their stature, weight, head size, teeth, and IQ test scores, which differed from those of mainstream Anglo-white Americans. The geographical habitats and occupations of the nonmainstream populations were also given as a reason for their school problems.

Boas and Malinowski were among the anthropologists who addressed these issues. Boas (1928), who has been called the father of modern American anthropology, was a professor at Columbia University. He expressed his views on the educability of non-Anglo populations and rejected the cultural evolution explanation. Instead, he stressed cultural relativity, arguing that there was not yet enough anthropological data to rank cultures as superior or inferior. He also rejected biological, geographical, and occupational explanations. Boas used both physical and cultural anthropological data to argue that differences in stature, weight, head size, and teeth were not due to biological differences. With cross-cultural data from Russia, Italy, the United States, and other countries, he suggested that the differences were due to differences in socioeconomic backgrounds, because children of the well-to-do classes in the diverse cultures tended to develop more quickly than those of the poor of the same cultures and that the children of the affluent classes attained certain physiological stages earlier.

Malinowski, a Pole who was naturalized as a British citizen, addressed similar problems of formal education of colonial people in Africa. He presented his views at two international conferences, one in Pretoria, South Africa (1934), and the other at Fisk University in the United States (1940). Like Boas, he criticized the schools for undermining the cultural integrity of the natives. He argued that differences in IQ test scores between Africans and Europeans were not due to racial or genetic differences; rather, Africans did poorly on IQ tests because they were given inferior education.

Anthropologists then provided an alternative explanation of the school problems of immigrants, minorities, and colonial people. They said that the problems were caused by "cultural discontinuities." Children of the lower classes, immigrants, minorities, and native people acquired their own cultural heritage at home and community, but they encountered a different culture at school. Under these circumstances, they experienced learning difficulties in school. Anthropologists proposed a twofold solution to the problem of cultural discontinuities: a cultural relativistic approach to schooling and multicultural education.

Ethnographic research designed to provide better knowledge for solving these school problems began in the 1950s. Among the pioneers were G. D. Spindler and Jules Henry, who conducted research in the United States, Theodora Brameld in Puerto Rico, Laurence Wylie in France, and Margaret Read in Africa. In addition, anthropological interest in education grew in the 1950s, partly because of a conference (1940) jointly sponsored by the American Anthropological Association and the School of Education and the Department of Anthropology at Stanford University and funded by the Carnegie Corporation of New York. The conference resulted in important work by Spindler (1955).

Several events marked the second phase of the social history of educational anthropology. Toward the end of the 1950s, anthropologists began to encourage teaching their discipline at the precollege level. The American Anthropological Association set up a curriculum study committee to develop and disseminate appropriate curriculum materials. The efforts with which U.S. anthropologists in the 1960s addressed educational and other social issues marked another event. To determine how the field of anthropology might aid in finding solutions of these problems, in 1965 the American Anthropological Association sponsored the Culture of the Schools Study Project. For the project, anthropologists prepared a bibliography on education, organized conferences, and commissioned papers on specific educational concerns. Conference proceedings and commissioned papers were later published (Wax et al. 1971).

Anthropologists were also drawn into education by the need to correct the misuse of the culture concept by educational researchers and interventionists who characterized lower-class and minority children as "culturally deprived." This term meant that those children did not have certain "traits" found among their mainstream white, middle-class peers. Anthropologists objected to the trait definition of culture (Valentine 1968), supported the claims of minority groups that their children were failing in school because of "cultural discontinuities," and started to conduct ethnographic studies among various minority groups and in schools to demonstrate the discontinuities and to find remedies for them.

These events culminated in the formation of the Council on Anthropology and Education in 1970 by anthropologists concerned with educational issues and nonanthropologists interested in applying anthropological ideas to educational problems. The council has twelve committees with interests in the study of school and culture, cognitive and linguistic studies, the teaching of anthropology, minority affairs, and preparation of teachers. In 1978 its newsletter became the journal *Anthropology and Education Quarterly*.

Academic History

Educational anthropology developed as an academic subfield of sociocultural anthropology in the 1970s. The conceptual origins of educational anthropology can be traced to culture-and-personality, the main area in anthropology where anthropologists systematically studied childrearing practices, cultural transmission, or "primitive education" among the people they studied, exemplified by Margaret Mead's study among the Manus and John Whiting's study of the Kwoma. Culture-and-personality contributed to the birth of educational anthropology in three ways: the founders of educational anthropology were culture-and-personality anthropologists (for example, F. O. Gearing, Jules Henry, John D. Herzog, and Spindler); educational anthropologists follow culture-and-personality anthropologists in defining "education" broadly as cultural transmission; and educational anthropology inherited from culture-and-personality studies a strong comparative perspective.

There appear to be two reasons for the emergence of educational anthropology as an academic subfield in anthropology in the 1970s. One was the activities of the Council on Anthropology and Education and its publications; the other was the need to respond to theoretical, methodological, and policy claims of conventional educational researchers about culture and the experiences of nonmainstream white children (*Educational Anthropology at Stanford* 1977; McDermott and Hood 1982; Spindler 1982). One of the things that anthropologists objected to was the practice of divorcing educational processes from their sociocultural context.

Education is now studied by anthropologists in such countries as Australia (Funnel and Smith 1981), Belgium (Leman 1991), Great Britain (Delamont and Atkinson 1980), France (Henriot-van Zanten 1987), Israel (Lewis 1979), and the Netherlands (Eldering 1989).

METHODOLOGICAL CONSIDERATIONS

The principal methodology in educational anthropology is ethnography, or fieldwork. As in classical socialcultural anthropology, participant observation and interviews play a prominent role (Ellen 1984; Wolcott 1987). Although ethnographers of education cannot establish a long period of residence among their subjects, as in classical ethnographic research, they do maintain a long period of association with the school populations. Anthropologists may take up residence in communities with studies of school populations. The ethnographic approach allows educational anthropologists to establish good rapport, obtain otherwise difficult data, and collect data on actual behavior or educational events in their natural setting. They strive to describe fully the educational situation based on direct observation and an intimate understanding of the participants' point of view. Analysis of such data results in a better understanding of specific problems of cognition, language and communication, community-school relations, educational evaluation, and other dimensions of schooling.

THEORETICAL INTERESTS

In 1991 about forty educational anthropologists were asked what they considered to be the major concerns of their subfield. Some mentioned theoretical issues surrounding the following: cultural transmission/acquisition, cultural continuities in schooling, culture and cognition, and language and education. No overall theory of education was mentioned. From the survey and a sampling of their publications, it is evident that educational anthropologists have developed a number of analytical frameworks or heuristic models. As J. Singleton (1974) points out, however, they are united by the common assumption that formal education is a particular form of cultural transmission.

One example, the instrumental activities model proposed by Spindler (1976), explains both how cultures change and how individuals choose among alternatives in a period of social change. Another example, Gearing's transactional models, explains how culture is generally transmitted. Gearing (1976) assumes that knowledge (inside and outside of formal education) flows freely between teachers and students, unless there are social barriers. From this perspective, the learning difficulties experienced by some school populations arise from the difficulty of transmitting knowledge across social boundaries. In the 1980s some anthropologists (Wolcott 1991) began to suggest that children play a more active role in their education, that culture is not only transmitted by adults but actively acquired by children themselves.

Ecological analysis of education is based partly on ecological psychology and partly on cultural ecology. J. F. Hansen (1979) suggests that unlike psychologists, educational anthropologists go beyond the behavioral impact or physical settings to examine the role of history, cultural assumptions, and values. Some try to show how the relationship between community and school, the perspectives, interests, and strategies of diverse groups, and the differential access of the groups to economic and political resources and to postschool rewards (e.g., jobs) affect classroom learning. John U. Ogbu (1981) has proposed a cultural-ecological model to fill the gaps in other frameworks by integrating microlevel and macrolevel analyses of schooling. Thus, the aim of this framework is to integrate economic, political, cognitive, and behavioral structures into a single frame of analysis.

The most active conceptual issue in educational anthropology concerns minority education. The question is basically an old one in the anthropological tradition: whether the school adjustment and performance of minority children are due to cultural discontinuities. This is both a conceptual and a substantive issue. Other analytical frameworks include those focusing on language and communication in school settings and the learning theory of Russian psychologist Lev Vygotsky.

SUBSTANTIVE STUDIES

Anthropologists study a wide range of substantive issues in education. The study of the evolution of education is based on data from physical anthropology, neuroanatomy, neurolinguistics, primatology, and ethnographic studies of hunter-gatherer societies. Biological studies indicate that the changes in the brain that differentiate humans from nonprimates and non-human primates are important in the evolution of human learning. The humans differ in having evolved with larger brains and more extraneurons of the nervous system that form the basis of information-processing capacities. Studies of sociocultural adaptations of primates and hunter-gatherer peoples indicate that sociocultural adaptations are closely tied to biological changes, that they determine what the young ones have to learn to become contributing members of their groups or communities, and how they learn what they have to learn. A contributing member is one who possesses the attributes to ensure biological and social survival of his or her social group or community (Bogin 1994; Fishbein 1976; Herzog 1976). Some anthropologists, such as H. C. Wilson (1972), suggest that formal schooling evolved in response to technoeconomic evolution; others, such as Y. A. Cohen (1971), believe that it evolved in response to the evolution of the state policy.

The sociocultural milieu or culture of the schools is another topic of research. Researchers have described the social organization of the school and the relationship between its various segments and the power structure in the wider community, and the organization of everyday life of the classrooms. Researchers have analyzed the school as a microcosm of the larger community, showing how the status and power hierarchy, sacred symbols, ethnic conflicts, and the value of productivity are reflected in the school. They have examined how schooling functioned to transmit national symbols and analyzed school rituals and economic activities of student associations.

The linkage between education and other societal institutions in society is recognized as important but has received only limited attention, most of which has focused on economic linkages. An example is a study focusing on the relationship between the changing nature of the economy in the United States and some innovations or changes in the curriculum of the public schools. Some educational anthropologists think that schools are organized to emphasize the skills that contribute to a bureaucratic, automated, and skilled workforce. Others study how children are taught to work under the corporate economy through the "hidden curriculum"; they try to show a correspondence between the behavioral requirements of the workplace (e.g., punctuality, obedience to authority, and dependability), and the task orientation of the classroom (e.g., conformity to a schedule and maintenance of order). K. A. Wilcox (1982) carried out ethnographic studies of upper-middle- and lower-class children, respectively, to test the hypothesis of neo-Marxists, namely, that schools socialize children from different social strata to fit into the kinds of occupational roles that they are expected to assume in adult life. Her study appeared to confirm that hypothesis. One linkage that has not received much attention is political linkage, probably because anthropologists in general do not study modern political systems.

Anthropologists pay more attention to culture than to social stratification in their analysis of education, but they have studied stratification and education from a functionalist perspective (Warner 1944), a neo-Marxist perspective (Leacock 1969), and interpretive perspective (Gumperz and Gumperz 1994). W. L. Warner assumed that education is the route to upward mobility and that school sorts schoolchildren according to their individual abilities to be trained. E. B. Leacock (1968) takes the opposite view; she found in her study of New York City schools that lower-class children were taught to be obedient, an attribute compatible with their future jobs, while the teaching of middle-class children emphasized independence, an attribute required in the jobs that upper-class children were destined to have when they left school. J. C. Gumperz and J. J. Gumperz reject the functionalist and neo-Marxist analyses. Instead, they focus on the interpretation of the structure and content of school curriculum and upon teacher-student interaction in the classroom to show how inequality in the wider society is replicated in the classroom. Ogbu (1978, 1994) suggests that analysis of social stratification and education should also consider how opportunity structure in the wider society is experienced, perceived, interpreted, and responded to through education by members of various strata.

The topic that draws by far the biggest theoretical interest and debate concerns cultural discontinuities in schooling. As S. U. Philips (1976) explains, cultural discontinuities in education occur where children with different cultural backgrounds attend schools or are educated in a different culture (i.e., receive their education in a culturally different learning environment from the one familiar to them at home). In such a learning situation, the children from the different cultural backgrounds have difficulty acquiring the content and style of learning presupposed by the curriculum materials and teaching methods. As noted, cultural discontinuities occur when non-Western children attend Western-type schools and when immigrant, minority, and lower-class children attend schools controlled by middle-class members of the dominant group in an urban industrial society like the United States.

The majority of educational anthropologists accept the notion that cultural discontinuities are the root of the nonmainstream white children's learning difficulties in school (Erickson 1993). Ethnographic studies have documented discontinuities in home/community-school relationships, language and communication, cognition, and teaching and learning styles (Jacob and Jordan 1993). A major problem is that the proponents of this hypothesis do not explain why cultural discontinuities do not adversely affect all groups but only some. For example, both African Americans and Asian Americans face cultural discontinuities in the public schools, but primarily African Americans are adversely affected. Ogbu (1992, 1993) suggests that to understand why African Americans are more adversely affected would require distinguishing between two kinds of cultural differences. One kind of cultural difference exists between two populations from different geographical areas who have come into continuous contact with one another. Such differences often result in misunderstandings, for example, between immigrants and members of the host society. The misunderstanding may be temporary. In addition, immigrant minorities consider the difference barriers as something to be overcome, and they try to overcome them by learning how to behave or talk like members of the mainstream in school and other selected places. They think that they will achieve the goal of their emigration by knowing how to behave

and talk like members of the dominant group. In doing so, however, they do not imagine that it requires them to give up their culture and language.

The other type of cultural differences exists between two populations that are members of the same society with differential power relations. The cultural differences arose historically as a part of coping mechanisms of members of the subordinate group. The latter also considers the cultural differences to be symbols of group identity to be maintained, but even when they consider the cultural differences as barriers because they are stigmatized by the dominant group, they tend to think that in order to learn how to behave or talk like members of the dominant group in school and other designated areas, they first have to dispose of their stigmatized ways, which is not easy. Judging from their past experiences in the opportunity structure, they do not have as much strong instrumental incentive to cross-cultural boundaries as do the immigrants. This type of cultural differences tends to be oppositional and persistent. The two types of cultural differences or discontinuities appear to have different educational consequences.

Other topics studied by educational anthropologists include education and social change, the school experience of natives of erstwhile colonial territories, informal education, and nonformal education.

APPLIED ANTHROPOLOGY IN EDUCATION

Applied anthropology in education takes many forms. In the 1960s, some anthropologists worked with educators or wrote to counsel them on cultural differences. The American Anthropological Association encouraged the incorporation of anthropology into the public school curriculum in the 1960s. A recent study indicates that anthropology is now taught at precollege level in many parts of the United States and Canada (Erickson 1993).

Anthropologists are also involved in three change-oriented efforts: multicultural education (Mukhopandhyay and Moses 1994), bilingual education (Pease-Alvarez 1994), and teacher education and translation of culture from ethnographic data to various educational programs (Brenner 1994). Some anthropologists collaborate with teachers in research to provide cultural data for designing culturally meaningful curricula, to teach style, and to improve interpersonal and intergroup relations in and out of the classroom; others work with teachers to translate existing ethnographic findings into similar educational programs and to prepare teachers for culturally diverse school populations.

FUTURE DEVELOPMENTS

The subfield of educational anthropology has grown rapidly since 1970. It has established its identity as an academic subfield of anthropology: in the United States, it is well represented in the governing body of the American Anthropological Association, which sponsors many intellectually stimulating sessions, and the quality of its journal, *Anthropology and Education Quarterly*, is well recognized. Within the educational establishments the methodological, theoretical, and pedagogical contributions of educational anthropology are both evident and taken very seriously.

Educational anthropologists look to the future with considerable optimism for several reasons. One is that education presents many opportunities for research and application. Another is that in educational research there are immense opportunities for theoretical and methodological contributions to both sociocultural anthropology and education. The younger generations of educational anthropologists have much going for them. They are trained in an established academic field and are not ambivalent about their status within anthropology. They have a grasp of the relationship between education and anthropology and between education and culture. They expect to continue developing their field, making important theoretical and methodological contributions not only within educational anthropology but also to sociocultural anthropology.

JOHN U. OGBU

BOAS, FRANZ. *Anthropology and Modern Life.* 1928. Reprint. New York: Dover, 1986.

BOGIN, B. "Evolution of Human Learning: Anthropological Perspectives." *International Encyclopedia of Education,* 2nd ed. Oxford: Pergamon Press, 1994.

BRENNER, M. E. "Translating Culture from Ethnographic Information to Educational Programs." *International Encyclopedia of Education,* 2nd ed. Oxford: Pergamon Press, 1994.

COHEN, Y. A. "The Shaping of Men's Minds: Adaptations to the Imperatives of Culture." In *Anthropological Perspectives on Education,* edited by M. L. Wax, S. Diamond, and F. O.

Gearing. New York: Basic Books, 1971.

DELAMONT, S., and P. ATKINSON. "The Two Traditions in Educational Ethnography: Sociology and Anthropology Compared." *British Journal of Sociology of Education* 1 (1980): 139–152.

Educational Anthropology at Stanford. Stanford, Calif.: School of Education, Stanford University, 1977.

ELDERING, L. "Ethnic Minority Children in Dutch Schools." In *Different Cultures, Same School: Ethnic Minority Children in Europe.* edited by L. Eldering and J. Kloprogge. Berwyn, Pa.: Swets North America, 1989.

ELLEN, E. F., ed. *Ethnographic Research: A Guide to General Conduct.* New York: Academic Press, 1984.

ERICKSON, FREDRICKSON. "Transformation and School Success: The Politics and Culture of Educational Achievement." In *Minority Education: Anthropological Perspectives,* edited by E. Jacob and C. Jordan. Norwood, N.J.: Ablex, 1993.

FISHBEIN, H. D. *Evolution, Development and Children's Learning.* Pacific Palisades, Calif.: Goodyear, 1976.

FUNNEL, R., and R. SMITH. "Search for a Theory of Cultural Transmission in Anthropology of Education: Notes on Spindler and Gearing." *Anthropology and Education Quarterly* 12 (1981): 275–303.

GEARING, F. O. "Where We Are and Where We Might Go From Here: Steps Toward a General Theory of Cultural Transmission." In *Educational Patterns and Cultural Configurations: The Anthropology of Education,* edited by J. I. Roberts, and S. Akinsanya. New York: David McKay, 1976.

GUMPERZ, J. C., and J. J. GUMPERZ. "Changing Views of Language in Education: Anthropological Perspectives." *International Encyclopedia of Education,* 2nd ed. Oxford: Pergamon Press, 1994.

HANSEN, J. F. *Sociocultural Perspectives on Human Learning: An Introduction to Educational Anthropology.* Englewood Cliffs, N.J.: Prentice-Hall, 1979.

HENRIOT-VAN-ZANTEN, A. *L'Ecole et l'espace local. Les enjeux des zones d'education prioritaires.* Lyon: Presses Universitaires de Lyon, 1990.

HERZOG, JOHN D. "The Socialization of Juveniles in Primate and Foraging Societies: Implications for Contemporary Education." In *Educational Patterns and Cultural Configurations: The Anthropology of Education,* edited by J. I. Roberts, and S. Akinsanya. New York: David McKay, 1976.

JACOB, E., and JORDAN JACOB, eds. *Minority Education: Anthropological Perspectives.* Norwood, N.J.: Ablex, 1993.

LEACOCK, E. B. *Teaching and Learning in City Schools.*

New York: Basic Books, 1969.

LEMAN, JOHN. "The Education of Immigrant Children in Belgium." *Anthropology and Education Quarterly,* 22 (1991): 140–153.

LEWIS, A. *Power, Poverty and Education: An Ethnography of Schooling in an Israeli Town.* Forest Grove, Ore.: Turtledove Publishing Company, 1979.

MALINOWSKI, BRONISLAW. "Native Education and Culture Contact." In *Educational Patterns and Cultural Configurations: The Anthropology of Education,* edited by J. I. Roberts and S. Akinsanya. New York: David McKay, 1976.

McDERMOTT, R. P., and L. HOOD. "Institutional Psychology and the Ethnography of Schooling." In *Children In and Out of School: Ethnography and Education,* edited by P. Gilmore, and D. M. Smith. Arlington, Va.: Center for Applied Linguistics, 1982.

MOORE, A.. *Realities of Urban Classrooms.* Garden City, N.Y.: Doubleday, 1967.

MUKHOPANDHYAY, C. C., and Y. T. MOSES. "Anthropological Perspectives on Multicultural Education." *International Encyclopedia of Education,* 2nd ed. Oxford: Pergamon Press, 1994.

OGBU, JOHN. "Black Education: A Cultural-Ecological Perspective." In *Black Families,* edited by H. P. McAdoo. Beverly Hills, Calif.: Sage Publications, 1981.

——— . "Understanding Cultural Diversity and Learning." *Educational Researcher* 21 (1992): 5–14.

——— . "Variability in Minority School Performance: A Problem in Search of an Explanation." *Minority Education: Anthropological Perspectives,* edited by E. Jacob and C. Jordan. Norwood, N.J.: Ablex, 1993.

——— . "Anthropological Perspectives on Education and Social Stratification." *International Encyclopedia of Education,* 2nd ed. Oxford: Pergamon Press, 1994.

PEASE-ALVAREZ, L. "Anthropological Perspectives on Bilingual Education." *International Encyclopedia of Education,* 2nd ed. Oxford: Pergamon Press, 1994.

PHILIPS, S. U. "Commentary: Access to Power and Maintenance of Ethnic Identity as Goals of Multicultural Education." *Anthropology and Education Quarterly* 7 (1976): 30–32.

SINGLETON, J. "Implications of Education as Cultural Transmission." *Education and Cultural Process: Toward an Anthropology of Education,* edited by G. D. Spindler. New York: Holt, Rinehart and Winston, 1974.

SPINDLER, G. D. "From Omnibus to Linkages: Cultural Transmission Models." In J. I. Roberts and S. Akinsanya, eds. *Educational Patterns and Cultural Configurations: The Anthropology of Education.* New York: David McKay, 1976.

WARNER, W. L. *Who Shall Be Educated? The Challenge of Unequal Opportunity.* New York: Harper and Brothers, 1944.

WAX, M. L., S. DIAMOND, and F. O. GEARING, eds. *Anthropological Perspectives on Education.* New York: Basic Books, 1971.

WILCOX, K. A. "Differential Socialization in the Classroom: Implications for Equal Opportunity." In *Doing the Ethnography of Schooling: Educational Anthropology in Action,* edited by G. D. Spindler New York: Holt, Rinehart and Winston, 1982.

WILSON, H. C. "On the Evolution of Education." In *Learning and Culture,* edited by S. T. Kimball and J. Burnett. Seattle: University of Washington Press, 1972.

WOLCOTT, HARRY F. "On Ethnographic Intent." In *Interpretive Ethnography of Education: At Home and Abroad,* edited by G. D. Spindler and L. Spindler. Hillsdale, N.J.: Lawrence Erlbaum Associates, 1987.

——— . "Propriospect and the Acquisition of Culture." *Anthropology and Education Quarterly* 22 (1991): 274–278.

ELITE STUDIES

Elites have often been a desired object of research in cultural anthropology, but in practice have been a rather underdeveloped area of study for reasons that have primarily to do with the methodological constraints and moral preferences of the discipline. By definition, elites tend to be exclusive, often to the point of secrecy, which, of course, presents severe problems of accessibility for anthropologists in pursuit of their "signature " research practices of ethnographic fieldwork and participant-observations. It is just very difficult to find elite communities and groups that might serve as the analogue of the village, the neighborhood, or the workplace in which anthropologists have traditionally resided to observe and participate in the everyday lives of their subjects.

Further, anthropologists have usually been granted an equal, specially protected, or even elevated social status by the subjects who have hosted them, and these acts of indulgence and courtesy have created the relationships necessary for the inside stories of cultural life that anthropologists typically produce. Work with informants of elite status is likely to be predicated on reverse assumptions about the social standing of the anthropologist in relation to his or her subjects, or on very limited "windows" of accessibility, firmly controlled by the elite subject, accustomed to managing relations with an often excluded public.

Another major reason for the underdevelopment of elite studies has to do with the moral-ethical preferences of most anthropologists who generally conform to (and perhaps have been particularly exemplary of) the left-liberal leanings of the majority of middle-class academics over the past several decades. That is, given the very human portraits of their subjects that anthropologists provide, there has been a definite sense of a moral responsibility to make the powerless, marginalized, and silenced subjects of history and society heard and to explore the sources and markings of difference in social life outside dominant ideas of what seems natural and common-sensical.

Of course, the whole historic project of anthropology's painstaking creation of an ethnographic archive of systematic cultural diversity among the world's peoples has been devoted to relativizing and calling into question taken-for-granted dominant ideas. Elites—those who operate and control the major institutions of modern societies—were the promoters of the dominant ideas, and as such were more the implied object of critiques than the subjects of anthropological study. When anthropologists did transfer their interests to research within their own societies, they correspondingly tended to focus on the marginalized, the poor, the victimized, and the unassimilated, whose lives could most strikingly call into question the assumptions of middle and upper classes, rather than groups within these latter classes themselves.

From time to time, there have been explicit calls for the study of elites and elite cultures (Nader 1969; Marcus 1983, Marcus and Fischer 1986), especially when it becomes obvious that the conditions of everyday life of common people in modern societies cannot be fully understood without equally intimate studies of conditions of power and privilege. The obstacles to actually conducting ethnographic research on elites have been very difficult to overcome until recently, but, in the modern tradition of anthropological work, there have been two distinct ways in which anthropological research has focused on elite individuals and groups, without this interest being explicitly labeled as such.

First, in their study of small-scale, so-called tribal societies and in larger traditional societies, anthropologists have often focused their ethnographies on chieftainship, kingship, core political institutions and rituals, and the questions of leadership and the sources of social distinction generally. The long-standing anthropological interest in the characteristics of traditional societies that could be classed as hierarchical versus egalitarian has in fact been concerned with processes of elite formation in such societies. Thus, there are now classic genres of ethnographic work, for example, on African kingship, Polynesian chieftains, Melanesian "big men," Indian high castes, and so on, that are constantly being reinterpreted by contemporary research (Feeley-Harnik 1985; Marcus 1989; Dumont 1970). From the point of view of the colonial or world capitalist system contexts in which this research has been done, this has very much been the study of elites within encapsulated societies, as if they were free of such larger contexts. In these societies key symbols, rites, and cosmologies were focused on clearly marked elite groups and involved participation by large segments of particular populations. Whether or not anthropologists worked directly with chiefs or achieved leaders in these societies, attention to elites and their spheres of activity provided crucial access to cultural processes generally.

A second focused interest in elites arose circumstantially during the 1950s and 1960s, a period of rapid decolonization in large parts of Asia and Africa and, in parallel, of the rise of theories and programs of political and economic development in the newly dubbed "Third World." Mainstream anthropology became intensively concerned with questions of nationalism and nation-building and how their tribal subjects, previously viewed as insulated, were being integrated into larger nation-state entities through processes of modernization. Along with sociologists, economists, historians, and political scientists, and others who turned to development studies, anthropologists, under the influence of the social theory of Max Weber, undertook studies of the conditions for the emergence of entrepreneurs, the transformation of traditional elites into bureaucratic officials and modern politicians, and the role of education and literacy in modernization (Geertz 1963). While not explicitly defined as elite studies, many of the ethnographic studies of local-level development were after all about the conditions of elite formation through which economic and political development would be achieved. Whereas economists, for example, provided analyses of major institutions, anthropologists provided important studies of informal political cultures by which such "rational" institutions operated imperfectly.

The tradition of the concern with development projects continues in anthropology but in a much more critical vein (Ferguson 1990), as has the ethnography of local-level elites, although few monographs of the quality of Paul Friedrich's (1986) study of political elites in a Mexican village have appeared. The successors to development studies have been the emergence of the Marxist-inspired, critical study of the modern capitalist world system, pioneered by Immanuel Wallerstein (1974), and the revitalization of the relationship between anthropology and history, especially in the intensive reexamination of the colonial and postcolonial histories of places and peoples in which anthropologists had traditionally been interested and that they tended to treat as insulated from such histories. At the heart of Wallerstein's framework are questions about the processes by which crucial elites emerge along with the development of capitalist markets in various places at various historic moments, thus encouraging a systematic interest among anthropologists in elite formation.

The revival of the anthropological interest in historical studies has also been fueled by the powerful critiques of European colonialism as both a social system and a system of ideas, pioneered by Third World scholars in U.S. academia, who operated with new analytic tools derived from trends in the discipline of literary studies, such as Edward Said's *Orientalism* (1978). The influence of this critical work in literary studies on anthropologists has led them into complex investigations of colonial systems of domination and their legacies in the formation of postcolonial societies. In a de facto way, this trend has been focused on elite processes without being labeled as such.

Still, for all this substantial and indirect concern with elites in recent important trends of anthropological work, detailed monographs on specific elite cultures, comparable to classic genres of the ethnographic archive on particular peoples and regions, are rare. Notable exceptions are Abner Cohen's (1981) study of the elites of Sierra Leone, Michael Fischer's (1980) study of Shi'ite clerics before the Iranian revolution, Gary McDonogh's (1986) study of the old families of Barcelona, Larissa Adler de Lomnitz and Marisol Pérez-Lizaur's study (1987) of a single powerful Mexican family, George Marcus's (1992) study of contemporary American dynastic families, and Takie S. Lebra's (1993) study of the contemporary Japanese aristocracy.

While these works are clearly self-identified as ethnographies of elites, they do not fit into any substantial body of work in anthropology explicitly on elites, nor do they inform in a systematic way the trends of anthropological work where there has at least indirectly been concern with elite cultures. They do demonstrate that with creative adaptations and expansions of the model of ethnographic fieldwork (Lebra 1993; McDonogh 1986; Marcus 1992), commitment to the "signature" traditional methodology of anthropology should not be a bar to the study of elite subcultures. Besides, the study of elites is just one category of subjects sensitive to their privacy for which anthropologists will need to adapt their traditional methods as they inevitably find themselves working amid the institutions and processes of modernity in contemporary societies worldwide.

Most of these ethnographic works are also notable for their choice of the sort of elite subjects, ones that anthropologists would be most comfortable with, given their classic interests. That is, these monographs are largely concerned with traditional elites in modern societies, and all but one deal with elite cultures organized around families, concepts of status honor, and relations of kinship-frames for the study of culture with which anthropologists have great experience. Thus, while they might be viewed as exemplary works that demonstrate the potential of anthropological studies of elites, they do not treat the most consequential kinds of elites in modern societies—professionals, experts, scientists, corporate and financial managers, policy intellectuals, and so on, those people generally shaped by institutional processes themselves. There is no recognizable framework here from past work, as with contemporary traditional elites, dynasties, modernized aristocracies, and the like on which to comfortably found anthropological study.

There is also as yet no established institutional frame of reference, for example, a distinctive anthropology of business or corporations in which intensive ethnographic studies of elites would have systematic significance. This situation is changing, however, with the emerging vigorous participation of anthropology in the field of science and technology studies, in which ethnography as a method of inquiry has long been popular. This is perhaps the first fully legitimatized nontraditional area of study for anthropologists in which there is little or no obvious connection with past styles and situations of research. (Anthropologists can, of course, lend a badly needed cross-cultural perspective to science studies, but the focus is on institutional communities with very uneven rootings in the villages, households, and kin groups that are the comfortable milieus of past anthropological thought.) In addition, albeit not explicitly classed as "elite studies," anthropological research in this domain is inherently about the careers and lives of the most important kind of contemporary elites (Traweek 1989; Marcus 1994).

Such a field that focuses anthropological attention on professionals, experts, and knowledge elites in contemporary societies also affects the kind of moral/ ethical position that has served to inhibit anthropological attention to elites. There is at least some kinship between the communities of scientists and the kinds of academic/intellectual communities of which anthropologists are a part. Thus, in some sense, participation in science studies sensitizes anthropologists to the fact that elites, far from being another distanced subject of anthropological study, are actually part of the field or community that shapes anthropology as a specialized field of knowledge itself. Elite studies, concerned with professionals, expertise, and intellectuals, is thus part of anthropology's self-critique and understanding.

A further implication of this embedding of anthropology itself in elite cultures is that even research among the most victimized and powerless subjects reveals that the conditions of research itself are embedded in the discourses and practices of elite communities (of knowledge production). Further, the lives of the relatively powerless are likely to be bound up with what goes on among particular elite groups, and any study of the former is likely to be incomplete without equally resolute attempts to provide ethnographic treatments of the latter. For example, while not directly associated, what goes on in the seminar rooms of policy experts has much to do with what happens in certain local populations or urban communities. While they are more experienced in working in the latter, anthropologists need to approximate the same closeness of observation and analysis in working in the former. This may not lead to a distinctive area of research known as elite studies, but it should make attention to elite communities necessary as an integral part of the "landscape" of almost any ethnographic project in contemporary societies. Thus, by necessity, the moral inhibition on an intensive focus upon elites is likely to be broken purely by the circumstances of defining complex objects of study for contemporary anthropology. The inherent elite character of research on contemporary technoscience has opened the way.

Therefore, while the study of elites may become much more prominent in the anthropology of the future, it will unlikely do so under the explicit label of elite studies. In this regard, it should be appreciated that the study of elites as a distinct field, not only in anthropology but in other social sciences, derives specifically from a tradition of sociological theory originating in the nineteenth-century writings of the Italian thinkers Vilifred Pareto and Gaetano Mosca (Marcus 1983). This kind of theory was an alternative to the large institutional perspectives provided, for example, by Marxist theory, of great changes occurring in Europe toward industrial capitalism. Produced on the agrarian margin of Europe, Pareto's and Mosca's writing focused the dynamics of social change on elite groups, their structure, culture, power, and replacement. Consequently, most of anthropology's past explicit concern with elites has followed the primarily sociological character of this historic intellectual tradition. While the small-group level at which this theory has been developed suits the ethnographic method of anthropology, it has skewed anthropological research on elites toward questions of social architecture rather than cultural content or meaning, that is, toward the mapping of elite groups, their internal structure, their degrees of effective power in society, their practices for displaying status, maintaining continuity and exclusivity, and so on.

Anthropology has perhaps been best at showing how formal institutional orders can be understood by the operation of informal elite communities that guide and control them. In addition, a prominent issue in defining these communities inevitably concerns the variant public and private faces of any elite. It is little wonder that research on elites has inevitably confronted questions of conspiracy, lack of or degree of accountability, and norms of inequality that tinge any consideration of elites in modern liberal states sensitive to a legitimate rationale for any manifest inequalities or hierarchies in society.

These are, of course, basic questions about elites, but they do not cover the internal idioms or quality of relationships in elite cultures, which are features of special interest to anthropological inquiry. There is nothing in classic social theory that could provide deep perspective on these aspects of elite groups. Over the past two decades, such perspective has been provided by certain varieties of French poststructuralist theory, especially the work of Michel Foucault (Dreyfus and Rabinow 1983). This work provides a comprehensive theory of how power pervades the cultural formations of society in language and the production of various kinds of knowledge that have historically shaped modern institutional orders.

While not in any way framed in terms of elite cultures as such, this kind of theory, which materializes "micropractices" of power for study, in combination with the classic sociological questions about elites in modernity, produces the analytic resources for the shaping of anthropological studies of elites that go beyond narrow definitions of this field and the attendant inhibitions that have held it back in past work. It is just such resources that are currently at work in the anthropological interest in science and technology studies. It is also here that a long-inhibited desire in anthropology to know the powerful and the privileged, as intimately and closely as any classic subject of study, is being fulfilled.

GEORGE E. MARCUS

SEE ALSO: Caste; Colonialism; World System Theory

COHEN, ABNER. *The Politics of Elite Culture.* Berkeley: University of California Press, 1981.

DREYFUS, HUBERT L., and PAUL RABINOW. *Michel Foucault: Beyond Structuralism and Hermeneutics.* Chicago: University of Chicago Press, 1983.

DUMONT, LOUIS. *Homo Hierarchicus: An Essay on the Caste System.* Chicago: University of Chicago Press, 1970.

FEELEY-HARNIK, GILLIAN. "Kingship." *Annual Review of Anthropology.* Stanford, Calif.: Annual Reviews, Inc., 1985.

FERGUSON, JAMES. *The Anti-Politics Machine: Development, Depoliticalization, and Bureaucratic Power in Lesotho.* New York: Cambridge University Press, 1990.

FISCHER, MICHAEL. *Iran: From Religious Dispute to Revolution.* Cambridge: Harvard University Press, 1980.

FRIEDRICH, PAUL. *The Princes of Naranja.* Austin: University of Texas Press, 1986.

GEERTZ, CLIFFORD, ed. *Old Societies and New States.* Glencoe, Ill.: Free Press, 1963.

LEBRA, TAKIE S. *Above the Clouds: States Culture of the Modern Japanese Nobility.* Berkeley: University of California Press, 1993.

LOMNITZ, LARISSA ADLER DE, and MARISOL PÉREZ-LIZAUR. *A Mexican Elite Family: 1820–1900.* Princeton, N.J.: Princeton University Press, 1987.

McDONOGH, GARY. *Good Families of Barcelona.* Princeton, N.J.: Princeton University Press, 1986.

MARCUS, GEORGE E. "Chieftainship." In *Developments in Polynesian Ethnology,* edited by Alan Howard and Robert Borofsky. Honolulu: University of Hawaii Press, 1989.

———. *Lives in Trust: The Fortunes of Dynastic Families in Late Twentieth Century America.* Boulder, Colo.: Westview Press, 1992.

MARCUS, GEORGE E., ed. *Elites: Ethnographic Issues.* Albuquerque: University of New Mexico Press, 1983.

———. *Science, Technology, and Culture: Conversations, Profiles, Memoirs.* Chicago: University of Chicago Press, 1994.

MARCUS, GEORGE E., and MICHAEL FISCHER. *Anthropology as Cultural Critique: An Experimental Movement in the Human Sciences.* Chicago: University of Chicago Press, 1986.

NADER, LAURA. "Up the Anthropologist—Perspectives Gained from Studying Up." In *Reinventing Anthropology,* edited by Dell H. Hymes. New York: Pantheon, 1969.

SAID, EDWARD. *Orientalism.* New York: Pantheon, 1978.

TRAWEEK, SHARON. *Beamtimes and Lifetimes.* Cambridge, Mass.: Harvard University Press, 1989.

WALLERSTEIN, IMMANUEL. *The Modern World-System.* New York: Academic Press, 1974.

EMIC/ETIC DISTINCTIONS

The neologisms "emic" and "etic," which were derived from an analogy with the terms "phonemic" and "phonetic," were coined by the linguistic anthropologist Kenneth Pike (1954). He suggests that there are two perspectives that can be employed in the study of a society's cultural system, just as there are two perspectives that can be used in the study of a language's sound system. In both cases, it is possible to take the point of view of either the insider or the outsider.

As Pike defines it, the emic perspective focuses on the intrinsic cultural distinctions that are meaningful to the members of a given society (e.g., whether the natural world is distinguished from the supernatural realm in the worldview of the culture) in the same way that phonemic analysis focuses on the intrinsic phonological distinctions that are meaningful to speakers of a given language (e.g., whether the phones /b/ and /v/ make a contrast in meaning in a minimal pair in the language). The native members of a culture are the sole judges of the validity of an emic description, just as the native speakers of a language are the sole judges of the accuracy of a phonemic identification.

The etic perspective, again according to Pike, relies upon the extrinsic concepts and categories that have meaning for scientific observers (e.g., per capita energy consumption) in the same way that phonetic analysis relies upon the extrinsic concepts and categories that are meaningful to linguistic analysts (e.g., dental fricatives). Scientists are the sole judges of the validity of an etic account, just as linguists are the sole judges of the accuracy of a phonetic transcription.

Besides Pike, the scholar most closely associated with the concepts of "emics" and "etics" is the cultural anthropologist Marvin Harris, who has made the distinction between the emic and etic perspectives an integral part of his paradigm of cultural materialism. Pike and Harris continue to disagree about the precise definition and application of emics and etics (Headland et al. 1990). The most significant area of their disagreement concerns the goal of the etic approach. For Pike, etics are a way of getting at emics; for Harris, etics are an end in themselves.

From Pike's point of view, the etic approach is useful for penetrating, discovering, and elucidating emic systems, but etic claims to knowledge have no necessary priority over competing emic claims. From Harris's perspective, the etic approach is useful in making objective determinations of fact, and etic claims to knowledge are necessarily superior to competing emic claims. Pike believes that objective knowledge is an illusion, and that all claims to knowledge are ultimately subjective; Harris believes that objective knowledge is at least potentially obtainable, and that the pursuit of such knowledge is essential for a discipline that aspires to be a science.

As is apparent, the debate over emics and etics raises a number of fundamental ontological and epistemological issues. It is not surprising, therefore, that controversy continues to surround even the definitions of emics and etics. Although the terms are part of the working vocabulary of most cultural anthropologists, there are no standard definitions that have won universal acceptance. A survey of introductory textbooks in anthropology reveals that the terms "emic" and "etic" are glossed in highly disparate fashion. The situation is even more obscure outside anthropology, where the concepts have been widely diffused and widely reinterpreted. The terms "emic" and "etic" are current in a growing number of fields—including education, folklore, management, medicine, philology, psychiatry, psychology, public health, semiotics, and urban studies—but they are generally used in ways that have little or nothing to do with their original anthropological context.

Despite that diversity and disagreement, it is possible to suggest a precise and practical set of definitions by focusing on emics and etics as epistemological concepts. From that perspective, the terms "emic" and "etic" should be seen as adjectives modifying the implicit noun "knowledge." Accordingly, the distinction between emics and etics has everything to do with the nature of the knowledge that is claimed and nothing to do with the source of that knowledge (i.e., the manner by which it was obtained).

Emic constructs are accounts, descriptions, and analyses expressed in terms of the conceptual schemes and categories that are regarded as meaningful and appropriate by the members of the culture under study. An emic construct is correctly termed "emic" if and only if it is in accord with the perceptions and understandings deemed appropriate by the insider's culture. The validation of emic knowledge thus becomes a matter of consensus—namely, the consensus of native informants, who must agree that the construct matches the shared perceptions that are characteristic of their culture. Note that the particular research technique used in acquiring anthropological knowledge has nothing to do with the nature of that knowledge. Emic knowledge can be obtained either through elicitation or through observation, because it is sometimes possible that objective observers can infer native perceptions.

Etic constructs are accounts, descriptions, and analyses expressed in terms of the conceptual schemes and categories that are regarded as meaningful and appropriate by the community of scientific observers. An etic construct is correctly termed "etic" if and only if it is in accord with the epistemological principles deemed appropriate by science (i.e., etic constructs must be precise, logical, comprehensive, replicable, falsifiable, and observer independent). The validation of etic knowledge thus becomes a matter of logical and empirical analysis—in particular, the logical analysis of whether the construct meets the standards of falsifiability, comprehensiveness, and logical consistency, and then the empirical analysis of whether or not the concept has been falsified and/or replicated. Again, the particular research technique that is used in the acquisition of anthropological knowledge has no bearing on the nature of that knowledge. Etic knowledge may be obtained at times through elicitation as well as observation, because it is entirely possible that native informants could possess scientifically valid knowledge.

Defined in that manner, the usefulness of the emic/etic distinction is evident. Answers to the most fundamental anthropological questions—including the origins of humanity, the characteristics of human nature, and the form and function of human social systems—are part of the worldview of every culture on the planet. Like all human beings, individual anthropologists have been enculturated to some particular cultural worldview, and they therefore need a means of distinguishing between the answers they derive as enculturated individuals and the answers they derive as anthropological observers. Defining "emics" and "etics" in epistemological terms provides a reliable means of making that distinction.

Finally, most cultural anthropologists agree that the goal of anthropological research must be the acquisition of both emic and etic knowledge. Emic knowledge is essential for an intuitive and empathic understanding of a culture, and it is essential for conducting effective ethnographic fieldwork. Furthermore, emic knowledge is often a valuable source of inspiration for etic hypotheses. Etic knowledge, on the other hand, is essential for cross-cultural comparison, the sine qua non of ethnology, because such comparison necessarily demands standard units and categories.

JAMES W. LETT

SEE ALSO: Cultural Materialism

HARRIS, MARVIN. "History and Significance of the Emic/Etic Distinction." *Annual Review of Anthropology*, vol. 5 (1976): 329–350.

———. "The Epistemology of Cultural Materialism." In *Cultural Materialism: The Struggle for a Science of Culture.* New York: Random House, 1979.

HEADLAND, THOMAS N., KENNETH L. PIKE, and MARVIN HARRIS, eds. *Emics and Etics: The Insider/Outsider Debate.* Newbury Park, Calif.: Sage Publications, 1990.

LETT, JAMES. "The Importance of the Emic/Etic Distinction." In *The Human Enterprise: A Critical Introduction to Anthropological Theory.* Boulder, Co.: Westview Press, 1987.

PELTO, PERTTI J. "Units of Observation: Emic and Etic Approaches." In *Anthropological Research: The Structure of Inquiry.* New York: Harper & Row, 1970.

PIKE, KENNETH L. *Language in Relation to a Unified Theory of the Structure of Human Behavior.* 1967. 2nd ed. The Hague: Mouton, 1967.

ENVIRONMENTAL ANTHROPOLOGY

Environmental research in anthropology has been a part of the discipline from its very beginnings. It is often referred to as the ecological approach in anthropology, but "environmental anthropology" is a more inclusive term than "cultural ecology." The ecological or environmental approach in anthropology includes topics as diverse as primate ecology, paleoecology, human adaptability studies, ethnoecology, agrarian ecology, pastoral ecology, geographic information systems and remote sensing, landscape ecology, and a number of other areas, many of them interdisciplinary in scope and methodology.

Franz Boas led the way in the United States with his original study of Eskimo adaptations to life in the Arctic, *The Central Eskimo* (1888), which stresses the interrelationship between geographical and cultural factors. This focus on geographical factors came from a tradition that goes back at least to Greco-Roman times in so-called geographical determinism and/or environmental determinism. These views varied but tended to emphasize that environmental factors, such as latitude, played a major role in the character of people: "Mountains produce isolation and cultural stability, while lowlands promote racial and cultural mixture and migration; topography that promotes isolation and overexhuberant flora [as in tropical forests] inevitably produces political and cultural stagnation" (Thomas 1925). While these views have been shown to be inadequate simplifications many times, they recur because of their simple appeal to the ethnocentrism present in all societies.

A not dissimilar view is represented by a view that the environment, while not determining human society, exercises a powerful limitation on human possibilities. This view, exemplified in the work of Thomas Malthus and most of Boas's work, presented the role of environment as passive. In other words, certain things could not occur because they were environmentally not feasible (e.g., stone houses in an environment that lacked stone). Most of these views were characterized by a kind of cultural determinism that privileged culture as the factor that explained the constitution of society. This view has once again gained prominence in anthropology under the guise of postmodernism, which relegates environment to a trivial factor in the construction of culture and history.

The view that the environment, or a culture, exercised a determining influence on human society was matched by a no less important body of scholarship that emphasized the interaction of human beings with the physical environment. This "adaptational" body of knowledge gained impetus with the development of evolutionary theory. This adaptationist/evolutionary approach mediated between the two other views and offered an alternative to their tendency toward determinism. This tradition, based on Darwinian concepts of evolution and adaptation, became a significant trend in anthropology in the late 1950s.

CULTURAL ECOLOGY

Significant progress came from the development of what came to be known as "cultural ecology," an approach proposed by Julian H. Steward, whose emphasis on behavioral considerations and on the comparative method make this approach among the most robust in the study of environmental anthropology. It serves to focus attention on the interaction between social organization, subsistence requirements, and those aspects of environment that matter to people (Steward 1955; Netting 1977). This version of environmental anthropology is still practiced, with modifications, in both archaeology and cultural anthropology. It is now more quantitative, more inclusive of biological variables, and more historical than when it began to be practiced in the 1950s and 1960s.

ECOSYSTEM ECOLOGY

Other approaches followed cultural ecology that expanded the scope of environmental research in anthropology. Whereas cultural ecology seemed to be concerned with cultural areas as a unit of analysis, the approach proposed by A. P. Vayda and R. Rappaport (1976) emphasize that humans are but a compartment in much larger ecological systems. The ecosystem concept accords the physical environment a more prominent place than any other biological concept or theory. This attention to abiotic factors is an important contribution in itself that complements evolutionary ecology's greater emphasis on biotic interactions (Schulze and Zwölfer 1987). Ecosystems are said to have distinctive structure and function and these systems can be studied as systems through which energy flows and matter cycles. As such, humans participated in this process, affecting flow and cycling in distinctive and important ways (Moran 1990). During the important multidisciplinary studies sponsored by the International Biological Program between 1964 and 1974, a large number of biological anthropologists, and a modest number of cultural anthropologists, took part in studies of human adaptability to a variety of ecosystems with the objective of arriving at a better understanding of the genetic, physiological, and cultural ways in which humans adapt to their habitats (Jamison et al. 1978; Baker and Little 1976; Baker 1978; Moran 1979).

The ecosystem approach was attractive to anthropologists for a number of reasons. It endorsed holistic studies of humans in their physical environment. It emphasized structural, functional, and equilibrium considerations that suggested common principles with biology and the possibility of modeling. In archaeology the ecosystem approach found form in the use of catchment analysis and regional surveys rather than the traditional study of particular sites (Butzer 1990) and gave impetus to a move toward macropaleoecology (Jochim 1990). The impact of the ecosystem approach in social and cultural anthropology was notable in increasing the degree of quantification thought desirable, which took the form of energy flow analysis (Thomas 1973), time-allocation studies (Johnson 1974; Gross 1990), and analysis of choice-making (Wilk 1990; Barlett 1982).

This approach led environmental research in anthropology away from a focus on cultural areas to a concern with "population" as the appropriate unit of analysis. These studies emphasized the plasticity of our species and the important role of physiological and behavioral adaptation—in contrast to the important role that was presumed by geneticists. For example, it was long thought that the Inuit had unique genetic adaptations that facilitated cold adaptation. Instead, the Inuit repertoire of adaptations was found to be largely cultural, emphasizing appropriate clothing, housing, diet, and management of exposure (Jamison et al. 1978).

EVOLUTIONARY ECOLOGY

In the latter part of the 1970s and a good part of the 1980s, anthropologists with environmental interests took a number of directions. One of the most notable ones was to focus on biocultural processes using concepts from evolutionary ecology. Evolutionary ecology refers to the study of evolution and adaptive design in ecological context (Smith and Winterhalder 1992). Its explicit goal is to explain the diversity of behavior that is encountered in human systems. To do so it gives a central place to the process of natural selection in an environmental context. Instead of emphasizing units of analysis such as ecosystems and populations, this approach focuses on individuals as the locus of evolutionary change. This view has been expressed in a number of books expounding theories of cultural evolution and cultural transmission. For example, according to R. Boyd and P. Richerson (1985), cultural evolution is a Darwinian process in the sense that information about how to behave is transmitted from individual to individual, but differs from biological evolution in that cultural inheritance is a system for the inheritance of acquired variation (Cavalli-Sforza and Feldman 1981).

ETHNOECOLOGY

Another direction taken by researchers was to focus on ethnoecology or ethnoscience, the study of how people categorize their environment. This has now become a fairly standard set of techniques available to all environmental anthropologists and is highly recommended in the early stages of any study. This approach focuses on "the words that go with things," trying to understand how a population segments by name certain environmental domains and examines the criteria that are used to arrive at that particular structure. This permits assessment of whether morphology or function are more important or whether color, age, height, or some other characteristic is used by a population. Data collection in the ethnoecological tradition aims at eliciting native terms for plants, animals, insects, soil types, and so on. It is a linguistics-derived tradition concerned with the "labels" that go with things and the distinguishing characteristics between them. It provides an excellent starting point for environmental research by providing a locally relevant set of terms and the meaningful differences between items. Unfortunately, only a handful of studies have tried to test the degree of correspondence between verbally elicited terms and observed behavior (Johnson 1974; Moran 1977). This approach is important for testing theories of cognition and perception (Berlin 1992).

HISTORICAL ECOLOGY

An even more recent development is the variety of forms of what is coming to be known as "historical ecology" (Crumley 1994). While concern with history in anthropology is ancient, many environmental anthropologists had taken notice that a concern with history had not been a notable part of environmental research. Influenced in part by "environmental historians," such as D. Wooster (1988), who looked to anthropology for insight into the history of resource use, contemporary historical ecologists focus on the role of individuals and communities in constructing not only their history but also their environments. This emphasis is interactional, like the adaptationist approach, but tends to give greater weight to the transformative powers of people in changing the environment, rather than their simple adaptation to it. They tend to be critical of discussions that present a false dichotomy between "natural" and human-influenced landscapes that they see as glorifying a nonexistent pristine nature. No spot on earth has escaped human action and landscapes that seem "natural" are often those that have experienced the most intense human uses (Balee 1989).

GLOBAL ECOLOGY

Global ecology is closely linked to what may very well become the environmental anthropology of the twenty-first century—one concerned with our history and evolution and with the consequences of these experiences to our present and future prospects on this and other planets. As the twentieth century draws to a close, it is increasingly clear that to address the seriousness of the environmental crises all around us at local and global scales will require systemic and comprehensive methods. Natural and physical scientists began intensive research in the 1980s on global environmental change and were joined in the 1990s by a growing community of environmental anthropologists concerned with the human dimensions of these changes. It is now generally acknowledged that humans are the biggest source of change on the planet through their use of resources, rates of population growth, and the exponential rate of growth in both of these dimensions.

Environmental anthropology builds on the past experience of anthropologists working on human use of environment but it must perforce go beyond those approaches. An environmental anthropology for the twenty-first century must build on the comparative approaches proposed by Steward if analysis of global environmental changes is to be informed by local and regional divergences in causes and effects. This poses a major challenge to research methods, in that generally agreed-upon ways of selecting sample communities or sites and what data is to be collected across highly variable sites must be undertaken despite differences in environment, culture, economy, and history. Efforts are currently under way at a number of international centers to arrive at these shared standards (Turner and Turner 1994; Moran 1992, 1994).

Solutions to contemporary problems will require the integration of experimental and theoretical approaches at various levels of organization. No single approach will be adequate to the complex tasks ahead. Approaches of the past, emphasizing equilibrium and predictability, were necessary to test null hypotheses, but they do not serve well as representations of real landscapes and hide the dynamic processes of patches within ecosystems. Dynamic, stochastic ecosystem models are necessary to address questions of global environmental change, and environmental anthropologists need to use such approaches to engage issues of ecosystem restoration, agroecology, and biosphere design and maintenance.

One of the tools that will need to be used with growing frequency by environmental anthropologists is geographic information systems (GIS) and techniques of remote sensing and satellite data imaging. Remote sensing from such satellite platforms as AVHRR of the National Ocearnographic and Atmospheric Administration (NOAA), Landsat TM 4 and 5 (from NASA), and the French satellite SPOT provide information of considerable environmental richness for local, regional, and global analysis (Conant 1978, 1990). For analysis of global processes or large continental areas, such as the Amazon Basin, NOAA's AVHRR is most appropriate because of its coarser resolution and daily coverage. Although this satellite was designed for meteorological studies, it has been used to monitor vegetation patterns over very broad spatial areas. Because of its large scale, anthropologists to date have had little participation in work with this data, but this may change in the near future.

Available since 1972, data from Landsat's Multispectral Scanner (MSS) is relatively inexpensive to obtain from the EROS Data Center in Sioux Falls, South Dakota. The pioneering work of Francis Conant and Priscilla Reining depended on MSS data (Conant 1978; Reining 1973). Use of MSS is valuable in particular for fairly dichotomous processes or categories, such as forest versus nonforest, grassland versus bare soil or desert, and water versus dry land. Efforts at making fine distinctions, such as those between mature moist forest and advanced stages of secondary growth could not be achieved with MSS data, and many scholars gave up on this effort (Woodwell et al. 1987).

Recent assessments of deforestation using single-band 30-meter resolution data suggest that earlier estimates of deforestation overestimated deforestation by as much as 50 percent (Skole and Tucker 1993) because of the coarseness of the AVHRR satellite data and the confounding of forest with secondary growth of more than a few years. Use of the Landsat 4 and 5 Thematic Mapper (TM) sensor provides not only 30-meter spatial resolution but also spectral data from the visible to the thermal infrared. This work has permitted detailed work at the field level at a number of sites in the Amazon Basin and elsewhere (Moran et al. 1994; Mausel et al. 1993; Brondizio et al. 1994). Discrimination of age classes in secondary growth following deforestation in Amazonian moist forests has been achieved, as well as discrimination between subtle palm-based agroforestry management and flooded forest in the estuary. Others have been able to study shifts in agricultural fields and issues of intensification in indigenous systems (Behrens et al. 1994; Guyer and Lambin 1993), and erosion in Madagascar (Sussman et al. 1994).

LANDSCAPE ECOLOGY

As is the case with historical ecology, landscape ecology takes a view of the environment wherein people, other species, the physical environment, climate forces, and other processes interact in dynamic ways with consequences for each of the other components. Environmental anthropology is engaged in this multidisciplinary and interdisciplinary effort to understand the processes of global environmental change at a variety of scales from local to global. Such an approach takes as a given that the human species is a major force in bringing about both "positive" and "negative" environmental changes on landscapes. It is concerned with temporal changes and spatial changes. It is concerned with a range of scales from local to community to regional and even to global scale. It is concerned with understanding what behaviors lead to degradational patterns, to reduced or increased vulnerability, to reduced or greater inequality in income, and to patterns of increased or decreased forest cover and biodiversity.

RESEARCH QUESTIONS

Environmental anthropology still works with communities but more often than not it is concerned with clusters of communities across a region or number of regions. More likely than not environmental anthropology is team-executed rather than an individual enterprise, requiring collection of complex data across a number of disciplines. It is also multiscale, multitemporal, and multinational. Environmental anthropology, even more than earlier versions of environmental research in anthropology, is more concerned with addressing urgent environmental issues than in questions of purely disciplinary interest.

Questions that environmental anthropologists are currently addressing include helping to improve the resolution and prediction capabilities of Global Circulation Models (GCMs) so that questions about the directions of rates of change and human motives and actions can be incorporated in modeling efforts; helping to identify distributional effects, such as how change affects different groups of people; issues of environmental equity, such as the siting of toxic dumps and nuclear waste; issues of the patterned behavior of members of a society and the environmental consequences of this habitual behavior; modeling the risk to people of different alternatives to use of resources and to ensure sustainable use; understanding the role of institutions in bringing about changes in individual behavior; and clarifying under what conditions the tragedy of the commons can be avoided.

The scope of environmental anthropology is not dissimilar from earlier approaches known variously as cultural ecology, ecological anthropology, ethnoecology, human ecology, and so on. It differs from these in its greater concern with questions of more than disciplinary interest and its greater commitment to interdisciplinary questions of urgent significance to life in the biosphere.

EMILIO F. MORAN

SEE ALSO: *Adaptation; Biological Anthropology; Cultural Ecology; Historical Ecology*

BAKER, P., ed. *The Biology of High Altitude Populations.* Cambridge: Cambridge University Press, 1978.

BAKER, P., and M. LITTLE, eds. *Man in the Andes.* Stroudsburg, Pa.: Dowden, Hutchinson, and Ross, 1976.

BALEE, W. "The Culture of Amazonian Forests." *Advances in Economic Botany* 7 (1989): 1–21.

BARLETT, PEGGY F. *Agricultural Choice and Chance.* New Brunswick, N.J.: Rutgers University Press, 1982.

BEHRENS, C., M. BAKSH, and M. MOTHES. "A Regional Analysis of Bari Land Use Intensification and its Impact On Landscape Heterogeneity." *Human Ecology* 22 (1994).

BERLIN, BRENT. *Ethnobiological Classification.* Princeton: Princeton University Press, 1992.

BOYD, R., and P. RICHERSON. *Culture and the Evolutionary Process.* Chicago: University of Chicago Press, 1985.

BRONDIZIO, E., et al. "Land Use Change in the Amazon Estuary." *Human Ecology* 22 (1994).

BUTZER, KARL. "A Human Ecosystem Framework for Archeology." In *The Ecosystem Approach in Anthropology: From Concept to Practice,* edited by Emilio F. Moran. Ann Arbor: University of Michigan Press, 1990.

CAVALLI-SFORZA, LUIGI L., and M. W. FELDMAN. *Cultural Transmission and Evolution: A Quantitative Approach.* Princeton, N.J.: Princeton University Press, 1981.

CONANT, FRANCIS. "The Use of Landsat Data in Studies of Human Ecology." *Current Anthropology* 19 (1978): 382–384.

———. "1990 and Beyond: Satellite Remote Sensing and Ecological Anthropology." In *The Ecosystem Approach in Anthropology: From Concept to Practice*, edited by Emilio F. Moran. Ann Arbor: University of Michigan Press, 1990.

CRUMLEY, C., ed. *Historical Ecology*. Santa Fe, N.Mex.: School of American Research Press, 1994.

GROSS, D. "Ecosystems and Methodological Problems in Ecological Anthropology." In *The Ecosystem Approach in Anthropology: From Concept to Practice*, edited by Emilio F. Moran. Ann Arbor: University of Michigan Press, 1990.

GUYER, J., and E. LAMBIN. "Land Use in an Urban Hinterland: Ethnography and Remote Sensing in the Study of African Intensification." *American Ethnologist* 95 (1993): 836–859.

JAMISON, P., et al. *The Eskimo of NW Alaska*. Stroudsburg, Pa.: Dowden, Hutchinson, and Ross, 1978.

JOCHIM, M. "The Ecosystem Concept in Archaeology." In *The Ecosystem Approach in Anthropology: From Concept to Practice*, edited by Emilio F. Moran. Ann Arbor: University of Michigan Press, 1990.

JOHNSON, A. "Ethnoecology and Planting Practices in a Swidden Agricultural System." *American Ethnologist* 1 (1974): 87–101.

LITTLE, M., et al. "Ecosystem Approaches in Human Biology." In *The Ecosystem Approach in Anthropology: From Concept to Practice*, edited by Emilio F. Moran. Ann Arbor: University of Michigan Press, 1990.

MAUSEL, P., et al. "Spectral Identification of Successional Stages Following Deforestation in the Amazon." *Geocarto International* 8 (1993): 61–71.

MORAN, EMILIO F. "Estrategias de Sobrevivencia: O Uso de Recursos ao Longo da Rodovia Transamazonica." *Acta Amazonica* 7 (1977): 363–379.

———. *Human Adaptability*. North Scituate, Mass.: Duxbury Press, 1979.

———. "Minimum Data for Comparative Human Ecological Studies: Examples From Studies in Amazonia." *Advances in Human Ecology* 2 (1992): 191–213.

MORAN, EMILIO F., ed. *The Ecosystem Approach in Anthropology: From Concept to Practice*. Ann Arbor: University of Michigan Press, 1990.

———. *The Comparative Study of Human Societies: Toward Common Standards for Data Collection and Reporting*. Boulder, Colo.: L. Rienner, 1994.

MORAN, EMILIO F., et al. "Integrating Amazonian Vegetation, Land Use, and Satellite Data." *BioScience* 44 (1994): 329–338.

NEAL, J., M. LAYRISSE, and F. SALZANO "Man in the Tropics: The Yanonama Indians." *Population Structure and Human Variation*, edited by G. Harrison. London: Cambridge University Press, 1977.

NETTING, ROBERT. *Cultural Ecology*. Menlo Park, Calif.: Cummings, 1977.

REINING, PRISCILLA. *ERTS Image Analysis: Site N. of Segon, Mali, W. Africa*. Springfield, Va.: NTIS, 1973.

SCHULZE, E., and H. ZWÖLFER, eds. *Potentials and Limitations of Ecosystem Analysis*. Berlin: Springer-Verlag, 1987.

SKOLE, D., and C. J. TUCKER, "Tropical Deforestation and Habitat Fragmentation in the Amazon." *Science* 270 (1993): 1905–1910.

SMITH, E., and B. WINTERHALDER, eds. *Evolutionary Ecology and Human Behavior*. New York: Aldine de Gruyter, 1992.

STEWARD, JULIAN H. *The Theory of Cultural Change*. Urbana: University of Illinois Press, 1955.

SUSSMAN, R., G. M. GREEN, and L. K. SUSSMAN. "Satellite Imagery, Human Ecology, Anthropology, and Deforestation in Madagascar." *Human Ecology* 22 (1994).

THOMAS, F. *The Environmental Basis of Society*. New York: Century, 1925.

THOMAS, R. B. *Human Adaptation to a High Andean Energy Flow System*. University Park: Pennsylvania State University, 1973.

TURNER, B. L., and MEYER TURNER. "Global Land-Use/Land-Cover Change: Towards an Integrated Study." *Ambio: A Journal of the Human Environment* 23 (1994): 91–95.

VAYDA, A. P., and R. RAPPAPORT. "Ecology, Cultural-Noncultural." In *Human Ecology*, edited by P. Richerson and J. McEvoy. North Scituate, Mass.: Duxbury, 1976.

WILK, R. "Household Ecology: Decision Making and Resource Flows." In *The Ecosystem Approach in Anthropology: From Concept to Practice*, edited by Emilio F. Moran. Ann Arbor: University of Michigan Press, 1990.

WOODWELL, G., et al. "Deforestation in the Tropics: New Measurements in the Amazon Basin Using Landsat and NOAA Advanced Very High Resolution Radiometer Imagery." *Journal of Geophysical Research* 92 (1987): 2157–2163.

WOOSTER, D., ed. *The Ends of the Earth: Perspectives on Modern Environmental History*. Cambridge: Cambridge University Press, 1988.

ESKIMO/INUIT

SEE: North America, Eskimo/Inuit

ETHICS

In the introduction to her powerful book, *Death Without Weeping: The Violence of Everyday Life in Brazil* (1992), Nancy Scheper-Hughes confronts some of the most difficult circumstances surrounding anthropology. She notes that many young anthropologists have been influenced by French philosopher Michel Foucault's writings on the relationship between power and knowledge. Foucault argues that ideas are not neutral but rather that those with power are most likely to control the creation of knowledge. As a result, these anthropologists reject ethnographic research as a flagrant intrusion into the lives of "vulnerable and threatened people," seeing the anthropological interview as reminiscent of the "inquisitional confession" (Ginsberg 1988), and observations as a vehicle for turning *subjects* into *objects* of our "discriminating, incriminating, scientific gaze" (Horowitz 1967). Consequently, some young anthropologists have rejected traditional ethnography for quantitative methods and more distanced and formalized analyses. Others focus on themselves rather than on the apparent subjects of the study.

This critique generates crucial questions of professional ethics. Are field workers invariably engaged in exploiting people they study? Do subjects benefit from anthropological research? Such penetrating questions have shaped the debate on professional ethics and have taken on particular prominence since the eruption of the Project Camelot controversy in 1965.

THE ETHIC OF POWER

The ethic of power raises questions about the sponsorship and use of anthropological research. In the World War II era working for the United States government was considered a patriotic duty. Distinguished scholars like Ruth Benedict, Margaret Mead, and Gregory Bateson produced analytical papers for the government. Carolyn Fluehr-Lobban (1991) writes that Benedict worked on wartime secret conferences in support of the European underground and anti-Nazi partisan movements. Given the almost universal support for the Allied cause, those who contributed to the war effort were proud of their involvement and received the kudos of their colleagues.

This unanimity changed dramatically during the United States war in Vietnam. The death of Project Camelot in 1965 was one of the first salvos announcing that the social sciences had entered a new era. Increasingly, anthropologists began to scrutinize what projects they worked on, who were the sponsors, and what use would be made of their data.

Project Camelot, sponsored by the United States Army, was a six-country comparative study on the social, political, and economic causes of unrest in the Third World. The Army provided $6 million for the study—a sum never before available for any social science project. According to the lengthy unclassified 1964 study document, "U.S. Army Project Camelot," the findings would include recommendations to nation wide governments on how best to deal with potential uprisings. In addition, the United States Army would assist these allies in dealing with the root causes of popular discontent.

When approached for cooperation by an anthropologist representing the project, social scientists condemned Camelot for serving United States military interests and turned over the project document to the Chilean government. International controversy and an investigation by the United States Congress resulted in the Army's canceling the project. The debate about Camelot's legitimacy, however, raged in the social science community long after the project's demise.

Some scientists argued that Camelot would have yielded invaluable comparative data. For them Camelot represented a coming of age for social science when it would be taken as seriously by government policymakers as were the physical sciences. Yet, other scientists condemned Project Camelot as support for Pentagon counter insurgency policies, pointing to a long history of United States intervention in Latin America as evidence that social science should not serve military priorities.

The debate became more heated when, in 1970, during the height of the controversy over the Vietnam War, several anthropologists were accused of engaging in secret counter-insurgency activities in Thailand. These allegations led the American Anthropological Association (AAA) to adopt the Principles of Professional Responsibility (PPR) in 1971 which underscored anthropologists' primary responsibility to research subjects. The PPR emphasized independence from government restrictions and condemned clandestine research. The Principles stood unamended until the mid-1980s, when the employment picture for anthropologists changed dramatically and large numbers entered employment outside academia. These applied anthropologists feared their conduct could be sanctioned as unethical if they sought government contract research. The revision of the PPR, voted upon in 1990, deleted all mention of clandestine research and emphasized responsibility not only to those studied, but also to employers and sponsors. While one's sponsorship should be public knowledge, the revision stated, freedom of research should not be abridged.

The revised code recognized the new realities confronting anthropologists employed in the government and industrial sectors. Nonetheless, the major professional organizations remain cautious about anthropologists conducting research for the U.S. intelligence agencies or the Department of Defense. There are still fundamental reservations about anthropologists becoming the "servants of power." This tension will continue as anthropologists are pulled between influential sponsors and vulnerable communities which must be protected against powerful interests.

THE ETHIC OF RECIPROCITY

In her response to the critics of ethnography, Scheper-Hughes (1992) sets forth an alternative interpretation which, while recognizing the limits of anthropological analysis, emphasizes a commitment to a "good enough ethnography." She underscores what might appropriately be called the ethic of reciprocity; that is, the exchange of favors and gifts. Scheper-Hughes believes that the community members she studied in Northeast Brazil wanted her to record their life story. Her written account would be payment for their cooperation.

"Don't forget me; I want my turn to speak. That one has had your attention long enough!...Seeing, listening, touching, recording, can be, if done with care and sensitivity, acts of fraternity and sisterhood, acts of solidarity. Above all, they are the work of recognition."

In Scheper-Hughes's investigations and in countless others throughout the years, the ethic of reciprocity has facilitated the building of vibrant, yet occasionally troubled, relationships. Listening attentively to informants and recording their words affirms such informants' importance. A prime example is found in the work of Barbara Myerhoff, who gave attention and dignity to a neglected and combative community of elderly Jews in Venice Beach, California. Their lives and culture are preserved in her book and award-winning film, both from 1978, entitled *Number Our Days* (Myerhoff 1994). Prior to this study Myerhoff had spent months recording the words of Ramon Medina Silva, a Huichol shaman-priest, who lived with his wife, Lupe, in the Sierra Madre Occidental of Mexico. Fearful that his culture would be lost, Ramon was determined to create an accurate account of Huichol religious beliefs and thus responded enthusiastically to Myerhoff's overtures. His life experiences were documented in her book *Peyote Hunt* (1974).

Nevertheless, there is mounting evidence that not all subjects feel compensated for their time, information, and trust. As anthropological writings have become accessible to literate communities, some reactions have been quite severe. We know from Scheper-Hughes, for example, that many people in the Irish community she studied for her first book, *Saints, Scholars, and Schizophrenics* (1982/1979), felt betrayed. They chastised her for publicizing their foibles and secrets.

Many Native Americans, such as Vine Deloria, Jr., in his book *Custer Died for Your Sins*, originally published in 1969 (Deloria 1988), decry the portrait painted by anthropologists of tribal life and culture. They define anthropologists as exploiters who take much and return little to those they study. This critique has challenged all would-be fieldworkers and forced archaeologists, for example, to reexamine their relations with native peoples of the American Southwest. In the book edited by Ernestine L. Green, *Ethics and Values in Archaeology* (1984), T. J. Ferguson presents the transformation of archaeological ethics and relationships. Modern agreements in American Indian archaeological programs call for the training of local

peoples in professional skills and require that non-Indian archaeologists respect native cultural traditions. Under such carefully forged agreements, archaeologists become partners in the work of uncovering a people's past.

A second dimension of reciprocity revolves around the appropriateness of anthropologists engaging in advocacy to policymakers on behalf of research subjects. Anthropologists such as David Maybury-Lewis are engaged in the struggle for the survival of threatened indigenous groups. Maybury-Lewis in *Advocacy and Anthropology* (Paine 1985), urges his colleagues to confront national governments and international agencies. Without inside help, he argues, indigenous peoples are doomed to ever-growing encroachment upon their lands and way of life. Cultural Survival, an organization founded by Maybury-Lewis, has been engaged in a decades-long battle to empower local leaders to argue in their own distinctive voices.

Others, like David Price, who was encouraged and assisted by Maybury-Lewis, are far more dubious. Price, in his book *Before the Bulldozer* (1989), argues that national and international organizations have their own economic development agendas and that they often manipulate anthropologists. Other anthropologists agree with Price's position and argue that indigenous peoples should lead their own struggles. For these critics, advocacy by anthropologists represents a continuation of a colonial mind-set toward native peoples. The controversy over the legitimacy and efficacy of anthropological intervention is among the most divisive issues confronting the field.

THE ETHIC OF RESPECT

The ethic of respect is a third component of anthropological ethics. It requires anthropologists to respect the integrity of the subjects' culture and to avoid undue interference. It implies that researchers should seek to be "invisible people" who observe and question, and have the least possible impact on those around them. Yet this level of invisibility seldom is possible. At the extreme, if anthropologists witness violence, should they be forthcoming under interrogation? Joan Cassell and Sue-Ellen Jacobs in their *Handbook on Ethical Issues in Anthropology* (1987) present such a case. A researcher denies to regional police having any knowledge of a murder despite her eyewitness observation of the event. She decided not to intervene in the community's own methods of conflict resolution and gave precedence to the ethic of respect over the

obligation she would have felt under any other circumstance.

The debate over informant and community anonymity reveals yet another complexity in the ethic of respect. While anthropology has traditionally required confidentiality to protect those studied, some informants have demanded that the researcher disclose their identities so they may reap the emotional and practical rewards of recognition. Cassell and Jacob discuss an anthropologist who gathered sensitive health material in an African American community. Prior to publication this anthropologist met with community members who contested confidentiality and questioned why she had disguised the names of the city, the health center, and the local residents. Given the possible future release of sensitive information, the anthropologist decided to disguise the name of the city and the health center but to acknowledge the help of specifically named residents in her footnotes.

Jay Szklut and Robert Roy Reed, writing in *Ethics and the Profession of Anthropology* (Fluehr-Lobban 1991), have asked for a reassessment of "The Principle of Community Anonymity in Anthropological Research." The authors suggest several specific steps: ask the informants what they prefer; consider the needs of future publication; consult with colleagues; and, most importantly, consider how disguising or revealing the research site affects an anthropologist's ability to present an accurate account supported by significant data.

Questions about the ethic of respect reach an acute level when the researcher faces the death of informants. Should he or she carefully record their last days, hours, and minutes in his or her field notes? Does the ethic of respect provide for any privacy, any truly personal space? Myra Blue-Bond Langner confronted these disturbing questions as a graduate student studying a pediatric oncology clinic.

Blue-Bond Langner felt such intense personal conflict that she questioned the worth of her own research. Ultimately, she knew that the ethic of respect did not preclude her from continuing her work. The young patients had accepted her as the anthropologist who studied children, the anthropologist who was "there for them." They believed she would not turn away from them no matter how much pain they endured. She presented these struggles in her book *The Private Worlds of Dying Children* (1978).

THE ETHIC OF ACCOUNTABILITY

The ethic of power, the ethic of reciprocity, and the ethic of respect are but three stages on which appropriate professional conduct is played. Another arena involves the ethic of accountability. In 1919 Franz Boas wrote to the *Nation* magazine accusing four colleagues of unethical behavior during World War I. According to Boas, the four had emphasized their scientific credentials when introducing themselves to foreign governments—actually they were gathering intelligence for the United States. According to Fluehr-Lobban's discussion (1991), this was "the first clear-cut case wherein unprofessional behavior was raised in the AAA organizational framework." Boas's letter elicited a negative response from the Executive Council of the Anthropology Society of Washington. The Council condemned his disclosure on the grounds that it might publicly impugn the motivation of all anthropologists. The attack on Boas preempted the opportunity to debate the issue of ethical accountability.

To this day, those who protest unethical actions risk the ire of their colleagues even when raising the most serious issues. Despite codes of behavior, anthropologists who demand accountability often have little recourse. In one instance, presented by Cassell and Jacobs (1987), a graduate student engaged in two years of fieldwork sent letters to her adviser describing her observations. Upon her return, she learned that he had published some of her material without attribution, breaking a cardinal ethical rule of faculty-student interaction. She hesitated to challenge him, however, for fear he would retaliate by impeding progress on her dissertation. When she did confront him, he answered that she would not have received her research grant without his assistance. The use of some of her material was his just reward and he urged her to get back to the dissertation and forget such "petty matters."

What mechanisms exist to enforce accountability? Too frequently, abuses are overlooked because formal action is divisive and publicity might reflect badly on all department faculty members and other colleagues. Ethical whistle-blowers are reluctant to come forward for fear they will be labeled as troublemakers and find future opportunities closed to them. For example, all codes of ethics in anthropology condemn plagiarism, but there is no clear path to enforcement and no guarantee of protection. Janet E. Levy, a past chairperson of the AAA Committee on Ethics, made an astounding observation in the February 1994 *Anthropology Newsletter* when she reported that no member had ever been sanctioned for an ethical violation. She urged a reevaluation of the association's ethical code and its grievance procedures which she labeled as highly ineffective in ferreting out and sanctioning offenders. This is an ongoing ethical issue that anthropologists have yet to confront fully.

MYRON PERETZ GLAZER

BLUE BOND LANGNER, MYRA. *The Private Worlds of Dying Children*. Princeton: Princeton University Press, 1978.

CASSELL, JOAN and SUE-ELLEN JACOBS, eds. *Handbook on Ethical Issues in Anthropology*. Special Publication of the American Anthropological Association 23 (1987).

DELORIA, VINE, JR. *Custer Died for Your Sins: An Indian Manifesto*. Norman, Okla.: University of Oklahoma Press, 1988.

FERGUSON, T. J. "Archaeological Ethics and Values in a Tribal Cultural Resource Management Program at the Pueblo of Zuni." In *Ethics and Values in Archaeology*, edited by Ernestine L. Green. New York: The Free Press, 1984.

FLUEHR-LOBBAN, CAROLYN, ed. *Ethics and the Profession of Anthropology*. Philadelphia: University of Pennsylvania Press, 1991.

GINSBERG, CARLO. "The Inquisitorial Interview." Paper presented at the Annual Meeting of the American Anthropological Association, 1988.

HOROWITZ, IRVING LOUIS, ed. *The Rise and Fall of Project Camelot*. Cambridge, Mass: MIT Press, 1974, revised edition.

MYERHOFF, BARBARA. *Number Our Days*. N.Y.: Meridian, 1994.

———. *Peyote Hunt: The Sacred Journey of the Huichol Indians*. Ithaca, N.Y.: Cornell University Press, 1974.

PAINE, ROBERT, ed. *Advocacy and Anthropology*. St. John's, Newfoundland: Institute of Social and Economic Research, 1985.

PRICE, DAVID. *Before the Bulldozer: The Nambiquara Indians and the World Bank*. Cabin John, Md.: Seven Locks Press, 1989.

SCHEPER-HUGHES, NANCY. *Saints, Scholars, and Schizophrenics. Mental Illness in Rural Ireland*. Berkeley: University of California Press, 1979.

———. *Death Without Weeping: The Violence of Everyday Life in Brazil.* Berkeley: University of California Press, 1992.

ETHNICITY

The term "ethnicity" is of recent origin and refers to that which pertains to, or belongs to, an ethnic group and the study of ethnic groups and ethnic relations. It also refers to both seeing oneself and being seen by others as part of a group on the basis of presumed ancestry and sharing a common destiny with others on the basis of this background. The common features that ethnic groups share may be racial (color), religious, linguistic, occupational, or regional. Often a combination of such features marks the contents of such identities. A belief in shared ancestry marks ethnic groups, although categories and groups formed by individuals on some other basis, such as deafness, homosexuality, or being members of a celibate Catholic religious order, may resemble them. First-generation religious sects are not an ethnic group, but they may produce one.

The term "ethnic group" was rarely used in anthropology prior to the mid-1950s. It appeared, in part, as a substitute for the words "race" and "tribe" and as a synonym for "cultural group." Its substitution for race was due to its association with Nazism. The preference for "ethnic group" as a term over "tribe" resulted from the association of the word "tribe" with colonialist views of Africans as essentially different from Europeans and the nationalist view in Africa that eschewed nations' internal divisions as deleterious to the newly formed state. Use of the new terminology made divisions like those between Hausas, Yorubas and Igbos in southern Nigeria comparable to the split between Walloons and Flemings in Belgium.

In the 1950s and 1960s there was a gradual realization of the existence of intracultural variation and of the fact that communal structure, individual self-identity, and acceptance of cultural norms often did not coincide. This led to the perception that, like the relationships of race, language, and culture, there is no one-to-one relationship between ethnic identity and culture. This lack of coincidence between ethnic identity and culture comes out in examples used by Frederik Barth (1969) and his colleagues. Practices that confirm a man's status as a Pathan in one area change when he moves to live among Baluch or Kohistanis or when he goes to south India as a migrant. The Pathans in those places must adapt to different environments, occupations, and political circumstances. A Pathan moneylender in Madras must live by a different code than a herdsman in the Hindu Kush of Afghanistan, but both may be considered Pathans. Alternatively, some individuals may live by two or more codes of conduct at different times in their lives depending on their situation.

Implicit in Barth's work is the notion that members of an ethnic group, who share a common label or group appellation, have a claim to a shared common cultural heritage. The word "claim" is operative here. Pathans should act like Pathans. African Americans should conform to a certain pattern of behavior that is different from that of middle-class whites. In the United States, where most Jews are of East European, Yiddish-speaking, Ashkenazic background, Sephardic Jews and others who did not conform to this pattern have had to constantly validate that they, too, were Jews. Immigrants would sometimes find in the United States or in Israel that while they were (unmarked) Jews in Romania or Morocco, in their new homes they had become Romanians or Moroccans. The relations between different groups sharing a single ethnic identity is sometimes called "internal ethnicity."

The identity of particular ethnic groups is composed of elements that may differ markedly from those that mark others groups due to the unique history of each group. Thus, the Druze in Lebanon, Syria, and Israel share a particular religion and a history of persecution and dissimulation, but they are similar to their national neighbors in language and secular culture. The Basques of the Pyrenees are marked off from their neighbors by their language but share a religion, Catholicism, with many of those neighbors. Slavery and race were important factors in the creation and persistence of diverse African-American ethnic groups in the Western Hemisphere.

Ethnic arena is a useful concept for describing situations in which individuals may have several different identities and where ethnic boundaries are often unclear, as in many of today's Western societies. For example, an American of mixed Greek and "Yankee" English descent visiting her Greek relatives or going to the Greek Orthodox church will be in

a Greek arena. When working in her job as manager of a large bank she may fall into a "neutral" unmarked arena, and be marked as a "Yankee" or "Old American" when participating in a meeting of the Daughters of the American Revolution. Identities thus become circumstantial. The ethnic arena permits individuals opportunities to play out roles as members of a particular group, to perform rituals and other symbolic acts relating to the history of the group, and to validate their membership in other ways.

Ethnic identity is a product of interaction between people with different origins and identities. Presumably a small group of isolated persons that is completely isolated geographically from other populations would not be an ethnic group. In addition, people who are classed together do not necessarily form communities on the basis of what outsiders perceive as their commonality. Even when there are ethnic groups, some individuals classified as group members remain outside the group. Thus there may be "people of color" or blacks who are not part of an African American community or people whose parents were Jews who do not participate in a Jewish community or identify themselves as Jews.

Ethnic groups appear and disappear. One can assume neither their ephemerality nor their permanence. Group persistence over time is, according to Edward Holland Spicer (1980), part of what he called an "oppositional process." He was particularly concerned with the way in which ethnic groups choose particular symbols for preservation, while being flexible with regard to other aspects of their culture. With regard to some groups, this consists of retaining use of a particular language for domestic purposes, such as Welsh, Catalan, or Kurdish; in other cases, religion forms a focal element. In still other instances, maintenance of an economic or ecological adaptation is related to the persistence of the ethnic identity (such as the Gypsies or Rom). In the particular cases that Spicer studied in detail, he did find that group labels for the in-group and the dominant group, maintenance of a sacred language (even if not used for everyday purposes), memory of holy places and events, sacred laws, special songs and dances, and maintenance of communities and/or voluntary organizations all played a role in group endurance.

The disappearance of ethnic groups, or what has been called the processes of structural and identificational assimilation, is marked in different ways. One model is that of "passing," which is the term used by African Americans for those individuals who have fair skin and pretend to be white. Such individuals deny they have any African ancestry, but this denial of an identity is not characteristic of all forms of assimilation. Many individuals retain knowledge of their origins. The groups into which they or one of their parents were born simply cease to be significant for their present lives, while another identity related to another parent or a spouse becomes more salient. For instance, many Germans, Britons, and Americans may have French Huguenot descent, but do not belong to any Huguenot organization or participate in any Huguenot arena, except for genealogical purposes. While for some the memory of such ancestry will be forgotten as the family name changes, others will cherish the memory for a long time after its importance has disappeared. This latter phenomenon has been called "symbolic ethnicity."

Because ethnicity is almost by definition a sign of heterogeneity, interethnic relations must always be considered. Ethnic groups are generally stratified by wealth, power, and status. Labeling groups as "ethnic," "tribal," or "communal" may in some context be a sign of low status. For a long time the term "hyphenated American" was a stigma in the United States, where the goal was to become "100 percent American." In the 1960s the children of fairly recent immigrants succeeded in diluting this goal by attaching the rubric WASP (White Anglo-Saxon Protestant) on the previously dominant groupings. This implied that the "100 percent Americans" were really just another ethnic group. In Israel different labels have been used for Jewish and non-Jewish ethnic groups. Non-Jews (largely Arabs) were called *mi'utim* (minorities), while Middle Eastern Jewish groups were *'edot hamizrah* (eastern groups), but no such label was applied to Jews of European origin. Both Jews of Middle Eastern origin and Arabs have challenged the use of such labels. Thus, the rubrics applied to various categories of people indicate the nature of ethnic stratification.

Ethnicity plays an important role in most systems of ranking and stratification. In some native North American societies, members of other groups, such as war captives, were incorporated in the group as slaves, but in other instances they were adopted as full members of the group. In many preindustrial agrarian and urban societies there was discrimination against peoples conquered in warfare, as well as those who did not belong to the majority religion. The castes

of South Asia bear the marks of ethnic stratification. In the class systems of colonial, industrial, and postindustrial societies, racial, religious, and "national" markers often differentiate those with power and privilege from those who form the bulk of the lower classes.

In studying ethnic groups and stratification, social scientists have variously emphasized different aspects in relationship to political and economic action. Some focus on the cultural configuration as an essence that gives rise to the peculiar characteristics of the group in its vocational preferences, as opposed to the differing characteristics of other groups. In this view the employment of Mohawks as workers in high steel construction is explained on the basis of a culturally programmed desire for male high-risk activities, such as being a warrior or a firefighter. Jewish entry into the learned professions is seen as a secular version of the prestige given to Talmudic scholars. Thus, assuming that the labor market is competitive, the different percentages of members of one ethnic group in one industry or specialty are seen as a product of that group's culture.

Other social scientists, including both Marxists and non-Marxists, see ethnic groups as political or economic interest groups. Use of a common identity as a means for the mobilization of individuals for political action or economic activity is simply one more resource that a group has for achieving success. Proponents of this view will emphasize such features as segmented labor markets. Those who support such political and economic views do not give much weight to the presumed common cultural patterns of the group or appeals to group loyalty. They may even view these with suspicion as a kind of "false consciousness." The present circumstances of the group are more important in this view than past history.

Some theorists of ethnicity are concerned more with consciousness than with the material underpinnings of ethnic solidarity. An approach that evolved from postmodernist theories stresses the consciousness of memory and/or common destiny held by group members. This is so, even if the "memories" are seen as fabricated, because all human descriptions of the past are viewed as self-constructed and reinvented. Anthropologists and others who use this approach are more concerned with the contemporary uses of history than in tracing the accuracy of the history used. Ethnic entities, as well as nations, in this viewpoint are constantly being invented and imagined. The key is how the identity is formulated

today and how it is manipulated. Whereas the political and economic approaches require the use of statistical data, this perspective focuses on the rhetoric of ethnicity, resembling psychoanalytic studies of identity. The identities of the individual, revealed in autobiographical texts or novels, are used by Michael M. J. Fischer (1986), one exponent of this approach, as his primary data.

Ethnicity is a descriptive concept that lends itself to a wide variety of theoretical interpretations. Evolutionary, sociobiological, and materialist analyses have been usefully applied to the explanation of ethnic phenomena. Likewise, psychological and hermeneutical approaches have been fruitful in understanding the relationships of individuals to their group affiliations.

WALTER P. ZENNER

SEE ALSO: Assimilation; Caste; Colonialism; Diasporas; Ethnocentrism; Ethnogenesis; Genocide; Middleman Minorities; Nationalism; Pluralism; Race Relations; Racism; Tribes

BARTH, FREDERIK, ed. *Ethnic Groups and Boundaries.* Boston: Little, Brown, 1969.

BONACICH, EDNA. "The Past, Present and Future of Split-Labor Market Theory." In *Research in Race and Ethnic Relations: A Research Annual*, edited by Cora Bagley Marrett and Cheryl Leggon. Greenwich, Conn.: JAI Press, 1979.

FISCHER, MICHAEL M. J. "Ethnicity and the Post-Modern Arts of Memory." In *Writing Culture: The Poetics and Politics of Ethnography*, edited by James Clifford and George E. Marcus. Berkeley: University of California Press, 1986.

ORING, ELLIOTT, ed. *Folk Groups and Folklore Genres: An Introduction.* Logan, Utah: Utah State University Press, 1986.

———. *Folk Groups and Folklore Genres: A Reader.* Logan, Utah: Utah State University Press, 1989.

SPICER, EDWARD HOLLAND. *The Yaquis: A Cultural History.* Tucson: University of Arizona Press, 1980.

ZENNER, WALTER P. "Jewishness in America." In *Ethnicity and Race in the U.S.A. Toward the End of the Century*, edited by Richard D. Alba. Boston: Routledge and Kegan Paul, 1985.

———. "Common Ethnicity/Separate Identities: Interaction Among Jewish Immigrant Groups." In *Cross Cultural Adaptations*, edited by Y. Y. Kim and W. Gudykunst. Newbury Park, Calif.: Sage, 1988.

ETHNOARCHAEOLOGY

Ethnoarchaeology refers to ethnographic field work carried out with the express purpose of enhancing archaeological research by documenting aspects of sociocultural behavior likely to leave identifiable residues in the archaeological record. The term has been in use for almost a century, although concept and praxis have flourished only since the 1960s. During the 1960s and 1970s, and into the 1980s, archaeologists debated the utility and limitations of ethnographic research in relation to study of the prehistoric past. Particular note was taken of the need to select appropriately comparable contexts, of the likelihood that hominids predating anatomically and (probably) behaviorally modern forms (which appeared by about 40,000 years ago) behaved differently from humans being studied today, and of the probability that many modern situations have no prehistoric counterparts, just as many adaptations of the past have either changed radically or disappeared entirely. More recently, many archaeologists concede that when the choice of research venue is adequately justified (in relation to the archaeological problem to which it pertains), ethnoarchaeological research can contribute much to the stock of models from which archaeologists draw possible analogs in developing inferences and reconstructions, as well as suggest new approaches to the design of research methods (for example, in defining sample areas and sizes and data-recovery procedures, and exploring ranges of variation within and between populations). Much of the early systematic and explicitly ethnoarchaeological work was carried out under the assumption that twentieth-century observations can shed light on comparable adaptations of earlier populations occupying the same regions. Even today, this "direct historical approach" drives some ethnoarchaeological research.

Some of the early (and seminal) studies were carried out by archaeologists with long-term experience in the prehistory of particular culture areas (e.g., Patty Jo Watson in Iran and Richard Gould in Australia). Archaeologists with interests in specific socioeconomic adaptations and their origins and development have worked in analogous settings (e.g., Lewis Binford's concern with [premodern] Pleistocene hominids' subsistence and settlement strategies led him to study the settlement and food-procurement and storage systems of Alaska's cold-adapted Inuit; Frank Hole's interest in early pastoralism caused him to live with nomads in Iran, one of the Middle Eastern countries in which animals were first domesticated and where nomadic pastoralism continues to be a distinctive and widespread adaptation). Such studies do not assume that their host populations are "survivals" or "relics" of earlier times (since all cultural groups change); rather, they are based on a presumption that both environment and subsistence adaptation constrain behavioral responses.

Many of these and other ethnoarchaeological projects have incorporated archaeological components; for example, John Yellen (1977) excavated recently occupied !Kung San camps (in Botswana), Roger Cribb recorded features of abandoned nomads' campsites in Turkey, and Watson (1979) noted archaeological analogs to objects whose everyday uses she detailed in rural Iran. These and other studies are noteworthy for their visual documentation of objects, structures, sites, and their spatial distributions; indeed, the 1970s interest of archaeologists in "activity areas" (loci where concentrations of artifacts can be used to reconstruct activities that can, in turn, shed light on aspects of social and economic organization) was paralleled and followed by some ethnoarchaeological work incorporating detailed scale maps of sites and their contents. Such published data reflect a more general pattern: archaeologists have taken to the ethnographic field to obtain information of kinds not often systematically recorded in ethnographic publications.

Much ethnoarchaeological work reflects a bias in favor of hunter-gatherers (most notably in Africa, Alaska, and Australia) and small-scale farming communities (in, for example, Latin America and the Middle East). Comparatively little research has, to date, been done in urban or industrialized settings, or with specialists in activities not directly related to subsistence (although, for example, J. Mark Kenoyer has worked with Pakistani bead makers; Carol Kramer and Daniel Miller have worked with potters in, respectively, urban and rural settings in India, and several other projects have dealt with potters elsewhere; Brian Hayden and colleagues have worked with Mexican *metate* manufacturers; Nicholas David and others have documented iron production in Africa, and Lee Horne studied Bengali brass casters). Much recent ethnoarchaeological work has been carried out by U.S. anthropologists (although, as the foregoing indicates, it has not been limited to the Americas); many researchers, inspired by the "New Archaeology" of the 1960s and 1970s, focus on aspects of social and economic organization and subsistence and settlement systems. The interests and theoretical orientations of some Europeans differ; examples of the influence of structural and symbolic trends in sociocultural anthropology on archaeologists (and on ethnoarchaeological research) can be found in several publications (e.g., Hodder 1982; Rencontres Internationales 1993).

Several other edited collections (e.g., Gould 1978; Kent 1987; Kramer 1979; Longacre 1991) reflect the range of research topics pursued, and, like other collections, their bibliographies are an important source of additional information. Here it can be noted that subjects on which ethnoarchaeological fieldwork has focused are diverse and wide-ranging. For example, the work of Dean Arnold (in Mexico and Peru), Philip Arnold (in Mexico), Nicholas David (in West Africa), Warren DeBoer and Donald Lathrap (in Peru and Ecuador), Margaret Hardin (in Mexico and Zuñi Pueblo), William Longacre and others (in the Philippines), and Michael and Barbara Stanislawski (among Hopi) has dealt with various aspects of ceramic production, distribution, and use and relationships between social organization and frameworks within which craft skills are acquired. Brian Hayden (among highland Maya in Guatemala and Mexico) and Ian Hodder (in various African localities) have collected detailed household data pertaining to material expressions of such disparate matters as socioeconomic and ethnic variation. Polly Wiessner and Roy Larick, also working in Africa (with San and Maasai, respectively), have focused on some of the ways in which group affiliation is signaled by differences in such items of material culture as projectile points and ornamented headbands. Lee Horne, interested in relationships between social and spatial organization, mapped an Iranian village and documented the size, socioeconomic status, and genealogical links of its households, and the (sometimes dispersed) locations of their structural properties.

Archaeologists' long-standing interest in prehistoric demography (because population size relates to such matters as the nature of and changes in household organization, land use, and economic and political organization) have led some to document relationships between household size and composition and room and house size (e.g., Kramer, in Iran),

and household size, house area, seasonality, and duration of occupation (e.g., Yellen, in Botswana). In a somewhat different kind of demographic study, focusing on livestock management strategies, Claudia Chang has documented demographic parameters of (Greek) sheep and goat herds in relation to the sizes and seasonality of use of their pens, substantial structures that would leave some archaeological trace but, like so many other areas in which important activities are carried out, would not necessarily fall within the boundaries of the sorts of sites archaeologists most typically investigate (because they leave prominent remains). This and other ethnoarchaeological studies point to the need to explore such "off-site" areas as fields surrounding mounded sites, or water sources and slopes near caves and rock shelters.

Many ethnoarchaeological studies have been of short duration. Quite a number have been embedded in longer-term archaeological projects, with important ethnographic observations sometimes being made almost serendipitously (by virtue, for example, of an archaeologist living near or among indigenous people who comment on the function of archaeological finds, or whose material culture resembles artifacts or structures encountered during the course of archaeological fieldwork). Other field programs, of varying duration, have involved the use of a systematic but sometimes superficial "blitzkrieg" strategy in which questionnaires or interview schedules and translators play a major role in data acquisition. In such circumstances, large data sets generated can provide standardized, quantifiable information, but researchers may encounter prospective informants skeptical of investigators' lack of linguistic skills, hostile toward native research assistants (who may belong to opposing social or political factions, or different castes), or reluctant to answer questions about such potentially sensitive matters as household income, family members' ages, or religious beliefs and practices. Short-term projects, particularly those carried out for only a few weeks or months, also run the risk of not collecting information about the range of behavior characteristic of the full seasonal round of activities that will leave tangible traces.

As all anthropologists know, no group of humans carries out all its essential activities in a single place, and diverse activities (such as those related to food and craft production, trading expeditions, marriage and funeral ceremonies, and religious rituals) are also

ETHNOARCHAEOLOGY

often differentially distributed over a period of many months. Thus, just as no single archaeological site can be deemed "representative" of an entire prehistoric system or "culture," no set of ethnoarchaeological observations based on a single household, made in a single season, can be considered truly representative of the larger sociocultural system of which it is a part. Although much useful information has come from short-term and localized research programs, those few that have an explicit commitment to longitudinal observations merit special mention. They are a particularly welcome and rich source of information since archaeology, whose data are worldwide and represent more than three million years of hominid behavior, is the study of cultural change.

Comparatively few ethnoarchaeological projects reflect a long-term commitment to a particular place. (Analogs in ethnography might be field schools, such as Harvard's in Mexico, or "restudies" involving return visits, such as those made by Margaret Mead to various field sites.) In one longitudinal study, William Longacre and several students worked in the Philippines starting in the mid-1970s, and their work with Kalinga potters and pottery has been the subject of many articles and several dissertations and books (Longacre and Skibo 1994). Initially designed to acquire empirical information about relationships between social organization and learning frameworks relevant to earlier archaeological work on ceramic styles and prehistoric social organization carried out in the U.S. Southwest, this project has expanded to include (among other things) studies of vessel function and use attributes, spatial and social organization of ceramic distribution, and ceramic change.

Three other examples of long-term ethnoarchaeological programs noted here are based in Africa. Two of them grew out of ethnographic projects, the third out of archaeological work. The work of John Yellen (an archaeologist) with the !Kung San of Botswana began as one component of Harvard's by then decades-long ethnographic involvement with that group; his research yielded new information on hut and settlement morphology, settlement location, seasonality, duration, and residue-generating activities and social organization of camps, and it complements earlier detailed work on !Kung subsistence with studies of butchering and culinary practices (Yellen 1991). The work of Glenn Davis Stone (an archaeologist) with the Kofyar of Nigeria builds on and

complements two decades of ethnographic research by Robert Netting, using detailed data on household histories and locations, ethnicity, and agrarian practices to document relationships between social and spatial proximity, and settlement patterns and farming strategies (Stone 1991). Nicholas David (also an archaeologist) began his ethno-archaeological work in Cameroon in the 1970s, when, during the course of an archaeological project, he collected extensive information from local potters; more recent work, carried out with Judith Sterner and students there and in nearby Nigeria, favors structural and symbolic perspectives and has dealt with style and ethnicity, potters and their wares, iron metallurgy, and mortuary behavior (David et al. 1991).

Such attention to mortuary behavior is salutary because much of the archaeological record for socioeconomic variation and change derives from burials. Whereas some sociocultural anthropologists have provided rich information on treatment of the dead, most ethnographic fieldwork in small-scale communities is carried out in comparatively brief intervals during which comparatively few members of the host group die. More ethnoarchaeological research on mortuary behaviors, particularly on their ideological underpinnings, variations in treatment of the deceased, and locations and morphology of mortuary sites, would be useful to archaeologists. Much additional work could also be done on artifact use-life, recycling, and modes of discard and site formation, relationships between kinship and spatial organization of structures and activities, material correlates of socioeconomic differentiation and hierarchical organization, and change in any of the innumerable areas of human activity that have tangible correlates. Increasing attention to processes of settlement abandonment (Cameron and Tomka 1993) and site structure (Gamble and Boismier 1992; Kroll and Price 1991) is a promising development, as is the occasional integration of ethnoarchaeological observations and controlled experimental work, such as has been carried out on cooking pots by James Skibo, who, as a member of the Kalinga project, recorded vessels' uses and later identified distinctive chemical "fingerprints" of the residues of particular food groups.

The ethnoarchaeological research cited here, and many other studies, have vastly enriched archaeologists' understandings of human behavior, and expanded the spectrum of possible courses of action in

398

archaeological data recovery, analysis, and interpretation. The need for ethnoarchaeological fieldwork grows increasingly urgent as traditional communities and sociocultural adaptations throughout the world are either literally obliterated or totally transformed by their contact with industrial societies. Also important is the need for archaeologists explicitly to bring their ethnographic observations and newly gained insights back to the archaeological record and, in so doing, to specify their views of the relationships between present and past.

CAROL KRAMER

CAMERON, CATHERINE M., and STEVE A. TOMKA, eds. *Abandonment of Settlements and Regions: Ethnoarchaeological and Archaeological Approaches.* Cambridge: Cambridge University Press, 1993.

DAVID, NICHOLAS, KODZO GAUVA, A.S. MACEACHERN, and JUDY STERNER. "Ethnicity and Material Culture in North Cameroon." *Canadian Journal of Archaeology* 15: 171–177, 1991.

GAMBLE, C. S., and W. A. BOISMIER, eds. *Ethnoarchaeological Approaches to Mobile Campsites.* Ethnoarchaeological Series, 1. Ann Arbor, Mich.: International Monographs in Prehistory, 1992.

GOULD, RICHARD, ed. *Explorations in Ethno-archaeology.* Albuquerque, N.M.: School of American Research, 1978.

HODDER, IAN, ed. *Symbolic and Structural Archaeology.* Cambridge: Cambridge University Press, 1982.

KENT, SUSAN, ed. *Method and Theory for Activity Area Research: An Ethnoarchaeological Approach.* New York City: Columbia University Press, 1987.

KRAMER, CAROL, ed. *Ethnoarchaeology: Implications of Ethnography for Archaeology.* New York: Columbia University Press, 1979.

KROLL, ELLEN M., and DOUGLAS PRICE, eds. *The Interpretation of Archaeological Spatial Patterning.* New York: Plenum Press, 1991.

LONGACRE, WILLIAM A., ed. *Ceramic Ethnoarchaeology.* Tucson: University of Arizona Press, 1991.

———, and JAMES SKIBO, eds. *Kalinga Ethnoarchaeology: Expanding Archaeological Method and Theory.* Washington, D.C.: Smithsonian Institution Press, 1994.

RENCONTRES INTERNATIONALES D'ARCHÉOLOGIE ET D'HISTOIRE D'ANTIBES. *Ethnoarchéologie: Justification, problèmes, limites.* XIIe Rencontre Internationale d'Archéologie et d'Histoire d'Antibes.

Juan-les-Pins: Association pour la Promotion et la Diffusion des Connaissances Archéologiques, 1993.

STONE, GLENN DAVIS. "Settlement Ethnoarchaeology." *Expedition* 33 (1991): 16–23.

WATSON, PATTY JO. *Archaeological Ethnography in Western Iran.* Viking Fund Publications in Anthropology, 57. Tucson: University of Arizona Press, 1979.

YELLEN, JOHN. *Archaeological Approaches to the Present.* New York: Academic Press, 1977.

———. "Small Mammals: !Kung San Utilization and the Production of Faunal Assemblages." *Journal of Anthropological Archaeology* 10 (1991): 1–26.

ETHNOBIOLOGY

SEE: Ethnobotany; Ethnozoology

ETHNOBOTANY

Plants are the irreplaceable basis for animal life. Organisms that cannot make their own food (as can plants) must eat plants or eat creatures that feed on plants. Human society is thus profoundly dependent on the plant kingdom, without which all civilization, science, and anthropology itself would have been impossible. Ethnobotany is the study of the total complex of relations that has ever ensued between human beings and plants. Although monographs in ethnobotany often involve only the study of plants and people in specific local or regional contexts, such as the ethnobotany of a specific society or the medicinal uses of a particular plant species to certain indigenous peoples, ethnobotany is a universalizing field, for no peoples are known who do not rely on, utilize, name, and classify plants in their everyday milieus.

A MULTIDISCIPLINARY FIELD

Ethnobotany represents an emergent field of knowledge, not only a merely technical skill practiced worldwide by farmers, diviners, curers, shamans, and other specialists in the culture-bound uses of local plants. Ethnobotanists today constitute a heterogeneous group of scientists, many of whom are trying to find a common ground for discourse. Ethnobotany should be given a scientific status, whereby basic and applied research would be recognized as different yet interdependent aspects of the same field.

Although ethnobotany is truly multidisciplinary, its specific practitioners have tended to exhibit backgrounds in only one discipline, usually biology (with specialties in systematic botany, plant ecology, mycology, or agricultural sciences and forestry), pharmacology (with a specialty in pharmacognosy or ethnopharmacology), chemistry (with a specialty in phytochemistry), and anthropology (with specialties in cultural anthropology, linguistics, or archaeology). Ethnobotany itself, depending on definition, encompasses or overlaps with several other multidisciplinary specialties, including economic botany, ethnopharmacology, paleoethnobotany, and ethnomycology.

Economic botany deals generally with the uses of plants and their products in human societies; a recent emphasis has been quantitative ethnobotany, which involves increasingly sophisticated techniques to determine the proportion of useful plants by category of use to given peoples in local habitats. Ethnopharmacology (sometimes called medical botany) focuses more specifically on the medicinal plants used in nonindustrial, non-Western societies and the potential applications of these to humankind generally. Paleoethnobotany (sometimes called archeobotany) is concerned with ancient plant remains subjected to human behavior and the information these can supply concerning the sociocultural systems with which they were associated. Ethnomycology is the study of the role of fungi as food, medicine, and hallucinogens in human societies. Also affiliated with ethnobotany proper is the linguistic and cognitive study of indigenous systems of plant nomenclature and classification, to which modern cultural anthropologists and anthropological linguists have most contributed.

The work of ethnobotanists takes place in the field, library, herbarium, and laboratory. Among their extremely diverse pursuits, ethnobotanists study the effects of past human activities on current vegetational forms and landscapes, investigate the myriad uses of specific plants to certain peoples and societies, search for new drugs from plant compounds in nature, research folk ways of naming and classifying plants, examine the distribution and utility of little-known landraces of cultivated food plants, and seek evidence for the evolution and antiquity of domesticated plants under artificial selection. Each of these research pursuits has shown its own notable successes, both of an applied and a basic sort, yet clearly none alone or even all together can represent the potential scope of ethnobotany as a field of inquiry.

If defined broadly, ethnobotany existed in all the earliest civilizations that left written records. Ethnobotanical records of ancient Sumer in the form of cuneiform tablets indicate an interest in keeping accounts of stores of domesticated plant products (such an interest itself may have stimulated the rise of writing in the first place). The old and new testaments of the Judeo-Christian Bible contain numerous references to plants and agriculture. Because plants were the source of the main medicines used for most of human history, many of the earliest medical writings deal extensively with plant pharmacopoeias. The Ebers papyrus from Egypt mentions the use of pond scum to treat leg ulcers (modern pharmacology extracts antibiotic compounds from a wide variety of microorganisms). Dioscorides, a Greek physician, wrote a treatise on medicinal plants that continued to be used for almost two thousand years. The Florentine Codex of the Aztecs listed scores of plants appropriate for treating fever, of which nearly two-thirds contain known bioactive principles that are probably febrifugic. The European pharmacopoeias written by herbalists and alchemists, known as the medieval herbals, were usually based on the doctrine of signatures, wherein plants supposedly indicated the signs of their usage by some external morphological feature; often any biological activity inherent to the plant was imaginary in this metaphysical scheme. But one medieval herbal prescribed a poultice of moldy bread to be applied to infected wounds: modern medicine, of course, treats many infections with penicillin, which is extracted from bread mold.

More recently, ethnobotanists have recorded many uses of plants among peoples that live most intimately with the natural environment. Many of the most important drugs in modern medicine are derived from plants or are based on chemical structures found in plants that have been brought to the attention of modern medicine originally through ethnobotanical research. Aspirin was first derived from the bark and leaves of the willow tree, an important febrifugal to many North American Indian groups. Curare, a blowgun poison of lowland South America extracted from a liana, acts by blocking neurotransmitters to skeletal muscle. This prevents monkeys that have been shot for food by blowgun hunters from becoming entangled in the tree canopy upon rigor mortis. This same property of curare saves thousands of human lives today by reducing the trauma of abdominal surgery. Because it only affects skeletal muscle, but not the heart, curare and synthetic compounds based on it have been used to relax all the voluntary muscles of the body, facilitating surgery in the abdominal cavity and avoiding extensive damage to the abdominal muscles. Quinine was originally extracted from the bark of the Cinchona tree, probably used by Quechua-speaking indigenous peoples of the lower eastern slopes of the Peruvian Andes. Quinine has been deployed effectively in the treatment of malaria, a disease that afflicts hundreds of millions of people yearly in the tropics. A more recent example of miracle drugs discovered through ethnobotanical clues concerns vincristine and vinblastine, the only effective treatments for childhood leukemia, which are extracted from the rosy periwinkle (*Vinca rosea*). Although not traditionally used for leukemia, the periwinkle's place in the traditional medicine of Madagascar and Jamaica did alert ethnobotanists to the possibility that it contained active principles. Extensive testing of these active ingredients followed and led to the discovery of the two compounds that revolutionized the treatment of childhood leukemia, formerly considered nearly incurable.

Although ethnobotany, therefore, exhibits a scientific basis, it does not constitute an academic discipline, for degree-granting programs in ethnobotany, generally speaking, have yet to be created. (Ethnobotany as a field, however, is emphasized in the doctoral program in biology at the Institute of Economic Botany of the New York Botanical Garden, among other institutions). Ethnobotany is a young science. The term ethnobotany itself was coined only in the 1890s, at about the same time that academic anthropology was being established in the United States. Unlike anthropology, however, ethnobotany never developed a unique body of subdisciplines, axioms, paradigms, and theories. This basic lack of academic institutionalization for ethnobotany reflected, in part, its extremely diverse disciplinary roots in the nineteenth century. The growing importance of ethnobotany in the modern world probably lies partly in the absence of a well-defined niche in higher education. Because ethnobotany is so broad in scope and because it so directly impinges on human affairs, it will probably never become an academic discipline of the sort known today.

Given a recent emphasis by university administrations and granting agencies on interdisciplinary programs of research, however, ethnobotany has been influencing many fields. At the same time, ethno-botany continues to draw eclectically upon several disciplines and subdisciplines, including cultural anthropology, which has left its own distinctive mark.

CULTURAL ANTHROPOLOGY AND ETHNOBOTANY

Cultural anthropology together with anthropological linguistics have supplied much of the evidence concerning non-Western systems of plant classification and nomenclature in ethnobotany. In addition, cultural anthropology has led to a better understanding of plant management and landscape alterations by local peoples in many ethnographic settings. Many scholars now think that diverse landscapes of the earth, once believed to be pristine, are in fact anthropogenic, as revealed in recent ethnographic work with living floras and associated peoples. Such research interests as well as ethnobotany itself were not, however, always so prominent in cultural anthropology. The environment was most often taken to be a noncultural given in earlier work, and plant names were just another feature of the lexicon.

The little ethnobotanical work carried out in cultural anthropology prior to World War II was typically ancillary to descriptions of the habitat and economic conditions of local peoples. Much of the work of early U.S. ethnobotanists such as Melvin R. Gilmore, Volney Jones, J. Walter Fewkes, and J. H. Harshberger, not all of whom were anthropologists, was directed almost entirely to collecting and describing useful plants of North American Indians. Whether they were originally trained in anthropology or botany, early ethnobotanists tended to perceive "aboriginal botany," as ethnobotany was sometimes called then, as being merely the extensive cataloguing of the uses of plants to indigenous or "primitive" peoples. Ethnobotany was a highly descriptive endeavor, therefore, displaying a conspicuously weak theoretical frame of reference. As such, the concerns and results of early ethnobotanists were virtually irrelevant to the main developments of cultural anthropology as well as of botany itself before World War II.

In his famous ecological study of the Shoshonean peoples of the Great Basin Plateau, "Basin-Plateau Aboriginal Sociopolitical Groups" (published by the Smithsonian Institution in 1938), J. H. Steward (1938) includes two minor appendices, one on "native names of plants" that includes data on the medicinal, food, and technological uses of local plants to the Shoshone, and the other on "miscellaneous uses of plants" that includes information on medicinal plants, plants used in manufacturing, plants used in smoking, and names of some plants not used. The relationship between the Shoshone and the plants of their habitat did not constitute the principal focus of this pioneering work in human ecology, even though it is clear from the appendices that the foraging Shoshone were extremely dependent on their botanical environment.

Shortly after World War II, ethnobotany changed course with the emergence of new theoretical concerns, particularly those having to do with human categorization of natural objects, in cultural anthropology. A landmark work that pointed to ethnobotany as a particularly important area for anthropological research was Harold Conklin's still unpublished but classic 1954 doctoral dissertation at Yale, which concerned the Hanunóo people and their plants on Mindoro Island, Philippines. Conklin explicitly indicated that earlier ethnobotanical works, even when authored by anthropologists, were more botanical than ethnological and that his principal concern would be "not with the taxonomic botanical data, but with Hanunóo folk botanical knowledge and its organization" (1954).

Ethnobotanists trained primarily in anthropology and those trained mainly in botany parted ways in terms of their research interests at this time. Anthropological ethnobotanists, such as Conklin, became far better known for their approaches to linguistic and cognitive phenomena than for the study of plants and their local material uses; botanical ethnobotanists, such as Richard Evans Schultes of Harvard, in contrast, were generally much more interested in explicating the systematics and biologically active principles of the useful plants that they studied in the context of local peoples and habitats.

The new ethnobotany from the perspective of cultural anthropology, pioneered by Conklin, reflected concerns of the paradigm of ethnoscience, which involved an attempt to record as accurately as possible how non-Western peoples perceive and classify the world around them so that predictions could be made as to how to think and behave as a native in given sociocultural contexts. Describing as rigorously as possible the non-Western classifications of plants, animals, kinship, disease, and other semantic domains was one of the principal vehicles for representing non-Western modes of thought itself.

Ethnobotany in this context became concerned with delimiting the similarities and differences between Western taxonomic botany and folk taxonomic botany of selected peoples. Conklin found that the Hanunóo language encoded 1,625 specific plant "types" (terminal folk taxa) for a total flora of only 1,100 botanical species (1954). In other words, Conklin found that the Hanunóo taxonomically overdifferentiate the local flora in relation to Western science, at least partly because certain domesticated species each receive more than one and sometimes many folk-specific names, whereas in Linnaean taxonomy each species has but one valid name. Recent comparative work by cultural anthropologist Cecil Brown suggests that the mean upper limit to monomial, generic plant names ("one-word" expressions such as "oak," "pine," and "maple" in folk English) in natural languages is about 500.

The linguistic and cognitive concerns of Conklin would reach fruition in the work of Brent Berlin. Unlike many earlier ethnobotanists trained in anthropology, however, Berlin worked closely and coauthored books and articles with ethnobotanists originally trained in botany. Rigorous plant collecting and identifying procedures pioneered by botanists were combined with careful, linguistically sound techniques of data elicitation advanced by anthropologists. This research resulted in the most important collaborative work on ethnobotany of the 1970s, the *Principles of Tzeltal Plant Classification* by Berlin and his botanical colleagues (1974). It also laid the groundwork for a more general convergence of botanists and anthropologists in ethnobotanical research, even if the principal topical concerns of Berlin's and his colleagues' work were still much more similar to those of Conklin than to those of Schultes.

Berlin's work propounds the general theory that a common, underlying pattern unites all ethnobotanical classifications. In particular, folk classifications tend to exhibit a taxonomic hierarchy of ranked categories (or ranks) of not more than five in number. Moreover, the categorical distinctions within any logically complete ethnobotanical classification of a people stems from shared perceptions of gross discontinuities in the morphology of plants in the local habitat. In principle, it is held that all (or at least the great majority) of plant taxa in a given language can be differentiated and classified according to morphological criteria.

According to this theory, the highest level of discrimination, the plant kingdom itself, which in a hypothetical but plausible dialect of folk English would be "plants," is typically divided into major morphological categories, called life forms, such as "tree," "vine," and "herb." Immediately subordinate to such categories are monomial, folk-generic names for plants, such as "oak," "pine," and "maple," which are kinds of "trees" in this dialect. Immediately included as members of the folk generic term "oak" would be terms such as "live oak," "water oak," and "gray oak," which represent binomial folk-specific terms in this dialect. Beyond the kingdom name ("plants"), life-form terms (such as "tree"), folk-generic terms (such as "oak"), and folk-specific terms (such as "live oak"), there is a fifth rank, that of the folk varietal. Folk-varietal names for plants are a subset of folk species and are typically rare in any language. They tend to be used only in reference to domesticated plants of considerable economic importance. In this regard, research by several cultural anthropologists, including Cecil Brown, indicates that folk-varietal names are practically absent in the plant vocabularies of foraging peoples.

THE MATURING SCIENCE

Whereas botany and anthropology had diverged in their approaches to ethnobotany immediately after World War II, a rapidly evolving convergence of these disciplines has been underway since the early 1980s. This is evidenced in part by further major research in which botanists and cultural anthropologists collaborated, as with Felger and Moser's study of the ethnobotany of the Seri foraging people of northern Mexico (1985) and Breedlove and Laughlin's exhaustive account of the ethnobotany of the Tzotzil people of Zinacantán in southern Mexico (1993). The growing convergence of botany and cultural anthropology was also exemplified by the founding of the Institute of Economic Botany at the New York Botanical Garden in 1981, which brought together professional anthropologists and botanists within a single institutional framework that was dedicated to core concerns of ethnobotany as here defined. In 1993 the Ciba Foundation held a major international symposium in Brazil on ethnobotany, at which trained professionals in botany, chemistry, cultural anthropology, and pharmacology sought a common ground for discourse on the subject.

The growing importance of ethnobotany as a multidisciplinary field in the 1990s is also seen in graduate programs: an increasing number of botany students are taking courses in cultural anthropology even as more and more students of cultural anthropology are registering for courses in plant ecology and systematic botany. These recent developments suggest that ethnobotany is coming of age as a full-fledged field of inquiry, a development with immediate consequences for agriculture, medicine, education, and the environment. Ethnobotany is affecting the current development of cultural anthropology more now than at any time in its past. Ethnobotany is also establishing itself as one of the most important sciences for the present and future well-being of humankind itself.

WILLIAM BALÉE
J. CHRISTOPHER BROWN

SEE ALSO: Ethnomedicine; Ethnopharmacology; Food and Diet, South America, Tropical Forest

ALCORN, JANIS B. *Huastec Mayan Ethnobotany.* Austin: University of Texas Press, 1984.

ANDERSON, EDGAR. *Plants, Man, and Life.* Berkeley: University of California Press, 1952.

ANDERSON, EDWARD F. *Plants and People of the Golden Triangle: Ethnobotany of the Hill Tribes of Northern Thailand.* Portland, Oreg.: Dioscorides Press, 1993.

BALÉE, WILLIAM. *Footprints of the Forest: Ka'apor Ethnobotany: The Historical Ecology of Plant Utilization by an Amazonian People.* New York: Columbia University Press, 1994.

BERLIN, BRENT, DENNIS E. BREEDLOVE, and PETER H. RAVEN. *Principles of Tzeltal Plant Classification: An Introduction to the Botanical Ethnography of a Mayan-Speaking People of Highland Chiapas.* New York: Academic Press, 1974.

BREEDLOVE, DENNIS E., and ROBERT M. LAUGHLIN. *The Flowering of Man: A Tzotzil Botany of Zinacantán.* Smithsonian Contributions to Anthropology, 35 (1993). Washington, D.C.: Smithsonian Institution Press.

CONKLIN, HAROLD. *The Relation of Hanunóo Culture to the Plant World.* Ann Arbor, Mich.: University Microfilms, 1954.

DUKE, JAMES. *Medicinal Plants of China.* Algonac, Mich.: Reference Publications, 1985.

ETKIN, NINA L., ed. *Plants in Medicine and Diet.* Bedford Hills, N.Y.: Redgrave Publishing Co., 1986.

FELGER, RICHARD S., and MARY BECK MOSER. *People of the Desert and Sea: Ethnobotany of the Seri Indians.* Tucson: University of Arizona Press, 1985.

FORD, RICHARD I., ed. *The Nature and Status of Ethnobotany.* Anthropological Papers, Museum of Anthropology, University of Michigan, no. 67. Ann Arbor: University of Michigan, 1978.

HEISER, CHARLES B. *Of Plants and People.* Norman: University of Oklahoma Press, 1985.

MILLIKEN, WILLIAM, ROBERT P. MILLER, SHARON R. POLLARD, and ELISA V. WANDELLI. *The Ethnobotany of the Waimiri Atroari Indians of Brazil.* Kew, U.K.: Royal Botanic Gardens, 1992.

PLOTKIN, MARK J. *Tales of a Shaman's Apprentice: An Ethnobotanist Searches for New Medicines in the Amazon Rain Forest.* New York: Viking, 1993.

SCHULTES, RICHARD EVANS, and ROBERT F. RAFFAUF. 1990. *The Healing Forest: Medicinal and Toxic Plants of the Northwest Amazonia.* Portland, Oreg.: Dioscorides Press, 1990.

STEWARD, J.H. "Basin-Plateau Aboriginal Sociopolitical Groups." *Bureau of American Ethnology,* Bulletin 120. Washington, DC: Government Printing Office, 1938.

WASSÉN, S. HENRY. *A Medicine-Man's Implements and Plants in a Tiahuanacoid Tomb in Highland Bolivia.* Göteborg: Goteborgs Etnografiska Museum, 1972.

WASSON, R. GORDON. *Soma: Divine Mushroom of Immortality.* Ethno-Mycological Studies, no. 1. New York: Harcourt Brace, 1968.

ETHNOCENTRISM

The concept of ethnocentrism combines the belief that one's own culture is superior to other cultures with the practice of judging other cultures by the standards of one's own culture. The concept was introduced to the social sciences by the sociologist William Graham Sumner in his book *Folkways,* first published in 1907, and remains a central concern of cultural anthropology. One of the primary missions of anthropology has been to combat ethnocentrism by documenting the rich diversity of human behavior and culture around the world and by pointing to the appropriateness of different behaviors and customs in different social, political, economic, and environmental circumstances.

Ethnocentrism is a human universal in that it is displayed at least sometimes by members of all cultures. People in many cultures tend to describe the beliefs, customs, and behaviors of their own culture in stereotypically positive terms, whereas customs and beliefs of other cultures are described in stereotypically negative terms. When considered from a cross-cultural perspective, ethnocentrism is best viewed as a continuum, with some cultures displaying little ethnocentrism, others expressing some, and still others a great deal. In addition, a single culture may be more ethnocentric in regard to some groups and less ethnocentric in regard to others. In general, ethnic groups that are culturally and linguistically similar, that live near one another, and that interact regularly are less ethnocentric toward each other than are groups without such close ties. Even in situations of peaceful contact, however, ethnocentrism may not be completely absent.

In situations of conflict between cultures, ethnocentric beliefs of superiority are often tied to feelings of mistrust and fear and to actions that are designed to limit contact with members of the other group and to discriminate against them. In situations of violent cultural conflict, ethnocentrism is accompanied by xenophobia, discrimination, prejudice, physical separation of the groups, and extreme negative stereotyping. Ethnocentrism seems to be a component of all situations of violent conflict between groups, although the presence of ethnocentrism does not necessarily predict that violence will follow. One very common pattern of ethnocentrism in the world involves neighboring groups of different levels of economic development, and ethnocentrism is a major cause of problems between the Western industrialized portion of the world and developing nations in the Third World.

As a universal feature of human life that is present in all ethnic-conflict situations, ethnocentrism has occasioned numerous explanations for its presence and persistence. One common explanation is that ethnocentrism is a rational choice made by members of an ethnic group that is competing with other ethnic groups for scarce resources, such as political power or territory. Many other explanations emphasize the sociopsychological aspects of ethnocentrism and suggest that it reflects aggression displaced from the in-group to an out-group or a projection of feelings of low self-worth or weakness on to others. Evolutionary explanations suggest that ethnocentrism is a biologically determined response to external threats against the group. Last, explanations based in sociobiology point to the kin-group basis of cultures and to the role ethnocentrism plays in aiding the reproductive success of group members when in competition with members of other groups for limited resources. All of the explanations are essentially conjecture that awaits careful testing, a difficult task because ethnocentrism is so common around the world.

Regardless of why ethnocentrism occurs, it is clear that one major way ethnocentric stereotypes of other peoples are spread and reinforced is through the mass media. Before the advent of radio and television, reports by explorers, missionaries, and government agents played the major role in shaping and reinforcing preconceived ideas of the so-called inferior or bizarre ways of life of other cultures. Ethnocentric descriptions are now reinforced by cultural tourism and the stereotypical portrayal of different peoples in literature and the popular press.

DAVID LEVINSON

BREWER, MARILYNN B., and DONALD T. CAMPBELL. *Ethnocentrism and Intergroup Attitudes.* New York: John Wiley, 1976.

GRANQVIST, RAOUL. *Stereotypes in Western Fiction on Africa: A Study of Joseph Conrad, Joyce Cary, Ernest Hemingway, Karen Blixen, Graham Greene, and Alan Paton.* Umea Papers in English No. 7. Umea, Sweden: Umea, 1984.

LEVINE, ROBERT A., and DONALD T. CAMPBELL. *Ethnocentrism: Theories of Conflict, Ethnic Attitudes, and Group Behavior.* New York: Wiley, 1972.

REYNOLDS, VERNON, VINCENT FALGER, and IAN VINE. *The Sociobiology of Ethnocentrism.* London and Sydney: Croom Helm, 1987.

SMOOHA, SAMMY. "Jewish and Arab Ethnocentrism in Israel." *Ethnic and Racial Studies* 10 (1987): 1–26.

SUMNER, WILLIAM GRAHAM. *Folkways.* New York: Dover, 1959.

WIARDA, HOWARD J. *Ethnocentrism in Foreign Policy: Can We Understand the Third World?* Washington, D.C.: American Enterprise Institute, 1985.

ETHNOCIDE

Ethnocide is the destruction of one people's culture by another, more powerful people. The word is derived from the Latin *caedere* (to kill) and the Greek *ethnos* (nation). Etymologically it has essentially the same meaning as, but is usually distinguished from, genocide (from the Greek *genos,* meaning race), which is used to denote the physical destruction of a human group. Although ethnocide has been going on throughout history, it is difficult to analyze, and several terms (for example, deculturalization, integration, assimilation, cultural genocide) have been used to describe its different aspects. In anthropological terminology it is equivalent to enforced acculturation.

The word "ethnocide" first appeared in print in 1965 in a book by French anthropologist Georges Condominas, who used it to describe French colonization in Vietnam. It was popularized by the radical French anthropologist Robert Jaulin, who highlighted it in several books he wrote and edited during the 1970s. Jaulin studied the Bari in Colombia and described their physical, social, and cultural destruction, which resulted from the invasion of their lands by oil companies and missionaries. He viewed ethnocide as the result of the denial of "others" (indigenous peoples) by "us" (white civilization), a thesis that led him to the view that colonialism and ethnocide would only end when "we" had been psychologically transformed and learned to accept the "other" both within ourselves and in foreign cultures. The word was quickly adopted into Spanish *(etnocidio).* It was first published in English in 1972 in a work edited by Walter Dostal and was soon popularized by those who opposed the destruction of indigenous peoples, particularly Amerindians. This movement surged in the late 1960s and 1970s and attacked some governments, missionaries, and extractive industries, all of which were accused of ethnocidal policies. Ethnocide was used as an emotive term to engender outrage and sympathy. When the word was first used, its importance lay perhaps as much in helping to define this movement as in explaining the destruction.

The association of ethnocide with genocide and homicide suggests that it should be thought of as a criminal offense, but it does not figure in any laws. It has also been suggested that it should be viewed as a process, with no requirement for the identification of a perpetrator or any deliberate intention to commit a wrongdoing. The word "ethnocide" does not appear in most dictionaries, although it has been used in preparatory drafts of a United Nations declaration on the rights of indigenous peoples. It appears to be restricted to the technical terminology of anthropology.

Ethnocide usually refers to the enforced merging of small-scale indigenous or tribal societies into industrialized civilization. Industrialized society is seen as the perpetrator of ethnocide and indigenous peoples are the victims. Ethnocide results in the disintegration of the culture and values of the victim group and their assimilation culturally, socially, and eventually genetically, through miscegenation, generally into the most deprived stratum of the dominant society. This is not, however, the inevitable fate of all indigenous peoples and many have survived and adapted to sustained assaults on their culture for generations. Ethnocide is related to racism and colonialism in that it arises when the dominant society perceives itself as civilized and the indigenous people as savage or primitive. This ethnocentric position is justified on the grounds that the ethnocide benefits the so-called "primitives" in religious, moral, or economic senses, or effectively pacifies and stops them defending their territory. It is also often argued that the "primitives" must catch up with the "civilized" society and that change is inevitable. Every living culture is continually changing as people develop ideas and interact with neighbors and visitors, but the difference between change that is enforced by the more powerful people and that which is desired by the weaker group can be subtle and open to different interpretations.

Many ethnocidal practices are aimed at children. It has long been recognized that an effective way to promote acculturation is to remove children from their parents and give them aspirations that cannot be met through their way of life, for example, putting them in schools where they are immersed in another culture, prevented from speaking their own language or consuming the foods their parents eat, and where their own customs are denigrated. Many such schools often punished children for speaking their own languages, and when progressive teachers (often missionaries) responded to criticisms in the 1970s and began teaching local languages and knowledge, indigenous parents complained in a few locales. Knowing that the traditional culture would be picked up at home, parents actually wanted the school to teach the dominant culture, not their own.

These examples illustrate some of the problems in defining particular cases as ethnocidal. Difficulties may arise in showing that change is genuinely enforced and that it comes from outside the victim group. Among a certain group of African pastoralists, it is a tradition that the men spend some of their teenage years as warriors, living separately from their families. During this time they often steal the livestock of their elders. To stop this, some old people support government attempts to ban traditional warriorhood. (This unusual illustration turns on its head the axiom that the old are custodians of traditional culture.)

The line between what is mere encouragement and what is full-scale coercion is often debatable. In many parts of Amazonia, for example, indigenous parents whose children do not attend the mission school may be denied credit in the mission's store. If traditional weapons are no longer made, the Indians may be dependent on the store as the only source of ammunition for hunting. Thus, it could be said that the children are forced into schooling. On the other hand, the mission may argue that families without school-age children are less likely to repay any credit given at the store and that it is simply encouraging, not enforcing, schooling.

The distinction between ethnocide and genocide is also often debatable. The United Nations Convention on Prevention and Punishment of the Crime of Genocide (1948) defines genocide as the deliberate infliction of "conditions of life calculated to bring about [a group's] physical destruction in whole or part." The destruction of natural environments from which indigenous people derive their subsistence, either by extractive industries (logging, prospecting, mining) or simply by colonists (farming, cattle ranching), clearly entails denying their "conditions of life." With their resource base destroyed, the only way they will be able to procure food is as beggars, laborers, servants, or prostitutes. This obviously constitutes ethnocide; some would argue that it is also genocide.

STEPHEN CORRY

SEE ALSO: *Assimilation; Colonialism; Cultural Survival Inc.; Culture Change; Ethnocentrism; Ethnogenesis; Genocide; Indigenous Peoples; National Culture; Racism; Tribes.*

BODLEY, JOHN H. *Victims of Progress.* Menlo Park, Calif.: Benjamin/Cummings, 1982.

CONDOMINAS, GEORGES. *L'Exotique est quotidien,* Paris: Plon, 1965.

DOSTAL, WALTER, ed. *The Situation of the Indian in South America: Contributions to the Study of Inter-Ethnic Conflict in the Non-Andean Regions of South America.* Geneva: World Council of Churches, 1972.

JAULIN, ROBERT. *Le livre blanc: Introduction à l'ethnocide.* Paris: Seuil, 1970.

ETHNOGENESIS

Ethnogenesis is an inchoate but important concept in cultural anthropology. It has been used metaphorically by many scholars to refer to a people who seem to come into being as a definable group, aggregate, or category at some point in history. As such the concept may refer to history (what is written about a people) or to historicity (what people say about their pasts, their origins, their sense of being and becoming). The concept of syncretism—the blending of distinct, even contrasting, systems of culture to form a novel system—is a salient feature of ethnogenesis, when the phenomenon dealt with is a definable or stipulated people, rather than an institution or set of institutions. Ethnogenesis does not refer to the origin of traits, complexes, or themes.

CONCEPTS

The concept may apply to how people appear in history (e.g., the Black Carib of Central America or the Black Arawak of Guyana), to how or what people speak as their native language (e.g., blends of languages such as Haitian Creole or Krio of Sierra Leone, West Africa), or to the overall culture that seems to have emerged (e.g., the Amazonian Quechua or "Sacha Runa"). However the concept of ethnogenesis is deployed, the symbolic criterion of contrast—one language, appearance, or culture as distinct from another—is a key feature.

Ethnogenesis may emerge during a social movement, when people consciously forge (or try to forge) their futures by making specific reference to their common heritage, in order to create or enforce a particular desirable or undesirable destiny. A desirable destiny may be a "land without evil," as was conceived, for example, by the Tupi-Guaraní Amazonian people at the time of the sixteenth-century European conquest of the Americas. An undesirable destiny may be potential or perceived genocide at the hands of power wielders, or the perception of perpetual bondage, as represented by the European system of black and indigenous slavery from the sixteenth century to self-liberation movements or emancipation.

Norman E. Whitten (1976) argued that ethnogenesis is the complementary dimension of ethnocide, which is the conscious effort by power wielders within a nation-state to obliterate a people's lifeways. The complementary features of ethnocide and ethnogenesis, he argued, reflect the historic and contemporary struggle between hegemony and resistance to hegemony. These concepts are subsumed by the idea of ethnicity: the reciprocal patterns of a group, aggregate, or categorical identity and the rejection of others with supposed other identities. Systems of ethnicity flow through complexes of history and historicity. All such systems can be seen as intercultural, and reflect the complementarity of ethnocide and ethnogenesis.

Ethnogenesis is also a concept that has been applied in various ways to the emergence of nations or even to complexes of cultural features that extend well beyond national boundaries and form the basis for a distinct cultural heritage. To illustrate the concept of nationalism, consider the emergence of the idea of a "German people" with a distinct race, language, and culture. This concept fits the Western European image of one people, one language, one culture, one nation (indivisible, under one God). Such ethnogenetic nationalist underpinnings have often designated the king and/or queen of a nation as ascending to divine status. The cultures of the Ashikaga, Momoyama, and Tokugawa periods of Japan in the fifteenth through seventeenth centuries, and the culture of the kingdom of Castile and Aragon in 1492 are excellent illustrations of this ethnogenetic phenomenon.

We frequently find that the collision of nation-state nationalist ethnogenesis and ethnic-bloc ethnogenesis mark critical junctures of cultural histories. The concept of "ethnic bloc" is taken from politics, and is analagous to a "political bloc." Stated simply, as Clifford Geertz (1973) has demonstrated, we expect the strongest ethnic reaction against nation-state nationalism to become manifest at the very moment of the consolidation of nation-state power. This is in part because of ethnocidal policies enacted in order to enforce cultural hegemony during the consolidation of such nation-state power. It is also because, at that moment, people who do not entirely share nation-state ideologies of culture, personality, and society consciously begin to enact counterhegemonic strategies, increasing their own sense of distinct history and altered destiny. One need only look to the contemporary Balkans, to the former Soviet Union, or to the racism and its racialist demise in South Africa to see modern illustrations of this way of conceptualizing ethnicity and cultural history.

The Latin American doctrine of *mestizaje,* or racial and cultural mingling, is an excellent example of complexes that extend beyond the boundaries of nation-states, but are nonetheless contrasted with other imputed systems. The central idea in *mestizaje* is that people of "mixed" Hispanic and indigenous descent in the Americas constitute a desirable heritage of culture and genotype that should override other cultural and phenotypic manifestations. In such an ideological amalgamation, the cultures of the people who are polarized to either the indigenous or the African-American antipode are excluded from the emerging civilization of the nation-states of the Americas.

Ethnogenesis is part and parcel of religious movements as well, especially in their millennarian manifestations. Christians are different from Jews because the latter do not accept Jesus as a messiah who reformed Judaism. Followers of the teachers of Islam acknowledge Jesus as an important prophet but one superseded by Mohammed. A cultural and symbolic history of Judaism, Christianity, and Islam demonstrates a flow of common culture that is cut and contrasted by ethnogenetic processes which are profoundly millennarian and yet profoundly ethnocidal and even genocidal as well.

Ethnogenetic processes are symbolic and, as such, value laden (a value is something cultural that constitutes the desirable in a system of human action). Cultural processes that are ethnogenetic can move people to action. Symbols themselves are either verbal or nonverbal signs that convey meaning; they are the building blocks and reference points of culture. When symbols come into being vis-à-vis contrasting systems of ethnicity, the stage is set for the proliferation of both ethnocidal and ethnogenetic processes.

An example of such a process is the emergence in the Spanish, Italian, French, and English languages around 1500 of the concept "race." At this time the idea of distinct systems of biocultural being—black, Indian, white—empowered a vast system of colonial

values of white supremacy, and black and Indian subservience. In Latin America this system of ethnic polarities is said to be mediated by *mestizaje,* even to the point of bringing into being a "cosmic race" that transcends colonial and other distinctions.

Such ideology of transcendence not withstanding, the racial paradigm that has been of fundamental importance in the western Hemisphere from about 1500 on looks like this:

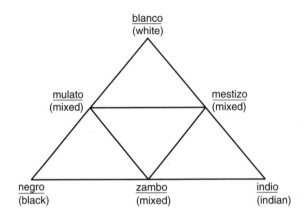

Here, according to some conceptualizations, white genes mingling with Indian genes produced a "half-breed" race of mestizos. White genes mixed with those of black Africans produced mulattos, analogous to the cross between a horse and a donkey that produces a mule. And black African and Indian mixes produced the zambo, or black Indian, a cultural status that is prevalent in colonial accounts of dangerous people. Obviously, given such a set of symbols that emerged in history nearly 500 years ago, cultural stereotypes and ethnic formations came to reflect, accept, and reject one another during the entire modern epoch in the West.

ILLUSTRATIONS IN THE LATE TWENTIETH CENTURY

The Amazonian Quechua of South America

Quechua is the language that was used by the Imperial (and near-divine) Inca in the mid- to late-fifteenth century to gain hegemony over many Andean people and to establish the vast empire that ranged from what is now northern Chile through Bolivia, Peru, and Ecuador to southern Colombia. The Inca were notoriously unsuccessful in conquering the upper Amazonian areas (the Antisuyu) to the northeast. Andean people themselves, however, did trade with the unconquered people in what is now called Upper Amazonia.

The northern dialects of Quechua are known as Quichua, and the Amazonian Quechua speak Quichua dialects. Two ethnogenetic sites for the emergence of Amazonian Quechua are those of the Quijos region of Ecuador, from the Quijos valley to the headwaters of the Napo River, and the Canelos region of Ecuador, where the Pindo and Puyo rivers flow into the Pastaza River. In both of these areas Quechua came to be spoken soon after the Spanish conquest, if not before. In the Canelos region, the language spoken syncretized with the pottery styles of the Tupi people of the Amazon to create a definitive and self-identifying "Runa" (which means human beings in Quechua), from what previously had been a congeries or collection of warring and intermarrying Zaparoan and Jivaroan cultures.

In 1992 approximately 2,000 Amazonian Quechua people of Ecuador marched from Puyo, at the base of the Andes, to Quito, the capital of the republic of Ecuador. They were joined by 5,000-8,000 more Andean Quechua-speakers. This march was a strong assertion of ethnogenetic identification, and the Quechua language was the symbolic base of the representation of Amazonian-Andean indigenous solidarity. The march also had strong millennarian qualities, and spokespeople during and after the march asserted the ethnic-bloc nationalism of their enduring indigenous culture.

The Garífuna and Mískito of Central America

The Arawakan-Spanish *cimarrón* (English maroon, French *marrón*), enters our western lexicons at about the same time as the word "race" enters. It refers to runaway people, both black and indigenous (and "mixed") who fled slavery and established fortified communities and even small-scale states on the edges of colonial territories. A significant variant of *cimarrón* is "Seminole," the native Americans of Florida whose name and image have been appropriated as a sport mascot by the Florida State University in Tallahassee, Florida.

The Garífuna are a Maroon people who came into history in the 1700s in the Lesser Antilles of the Caribbean. They are called Black Carib because of their appearance, and because they spoke a dialect of Arawak which was called Carib (meaning cannibal) by the Spanish who wished to wage "just wars" against

them and to enslave them to white masters. Their movement from the Lesser Antilles to Central America is well documented. Within their own historicity they appropriated the term Garífuna in the early twentieth century to refer to themselves as a multinational people with distinct ethnic characteristics.

The modern Garífuna are a contemporary people of Central America who speak English, Spanish, and Garífuna, the latter being based on Taíno (the language spoken by the people whom Columbus found in the Americas), or Taíno-like Arawak from the Lesser Antilles and creolized by Carib, African, and European elements. In the diagram the Garífuna would occupy the zambo position in colonial, Creole-Spanish language and culture. Today they live in Nicaragua, Honduras, Belize, and Guatemala. Male Garífuna travel widely in the world in search of livelihood, and send remittances to their matrifocal residential households in their respective communities in these four nations. In addition, there are sizable Garífuna populations in Los Angeles and New York City.

The Mískito (Mosquito) are a people of Central America with a similar background to the Garífuna. Their name comes from the English word "musket." The Mískito fought against Spanish hegemony in Nicaragua from the 1600s through much of the twentieth century. In the seventeenth and eighteenth centuries they were helped by British buccaneers sponsored by the English Crown. With newly acquired muskets, the Mískito emerged in colonial history in the seventeenth century and were able to exert indigenous dominance over other people of the Atlantic coast of Nicaragua, Honduras, and Costa Rica. They captured runaway black slaves, gave refuge to *cimarrones*, and intermarried with their captives and refugees. Their gene pool became quite diverse, representing indigenous and African polarities, and all of the genetic traits in between, including the Spanish-Creole category of zambo.

Fighting on the side of the British, they ranged as far as Jamaica, where they once helped to put down rebellions of Jamaican Maroons, contributing thereby to the expulsion of some of those Maroons to Nova Scotia in the Canadian Maritimes. During the epoch of the Sandinista revolutionary government of Nicaragua, the Mískito fought for their own indigenous ethnic-bloc rights, and won significant concessions from the government for rights to their territory.

During that government and continuing today, however, Mískito who appear to power wielders as "Indians" are classed as "indigenous people" with territorial rights, while those who appear "black" are classed as ethnic or West Indian and are regarded as immigrants. Today the Mískito speak Spanish, English, Mískito, and a distinct Creole of the Mosquito Coast. Their leaders have traveled to international conferences and have been at the forefront of indigenous movements for self-liberation in the Americas.

African-American Maroon Societies

History, as in Stedman's journal (1988), and historicity, as in Richard Price's book *First-Time* (1983), document the ethnogenetic processes of the Saramaka people of the interior of Suriname. These processes are applicable to people throughout the Americas. Today, in Surinam and Guyana (French Guiana) alone, there exist six nations of self-liberated black people—the Saramaka, Matawai, Kwinti, Djuka, Paramaka, and Aluku—who emerged from the creativity of African-American self-liberation and cultural ethnogenesis. Each of these peoples fought for fifty to more than one hundred years against the Dutch and French to win their independence.

Then, in the mid-1980s as Surinam entered a phase of avowed socialist nationalism, the sheer existence of peaceful and autonomous black people seemed to threaten the sovereignty and territoriality of an increasingly oppressive military regime, genocidal and ethnocidal policies against these nations were executed. Nonetheless, the various nations of African-Americans still exist in Surinam and Guyana and are complemented by cognate ethnogenetic cultures such as the Black Arawak of Guyana. The Guianas of South America continue to offer vivid if awful evidence of the complementarity of ethnocide and ethnogenesis.

Elsewhere marronage-sponsored ethnogenesis created the pluralist structures of many regions in the Americas, and linked these regions to one another and to the entire Atlantic basin. For example, the Trelawny Maroons of the Cockpit region of eastern Jamaica were defeated in a war in the late eighteenth century. The defeated were shipped to Nova Scotia, Canada, where they arrived just in time to help white forces put down an uprising of African Americans in the Halifax region. The Trelawny Maroons also built the battlements of Halifax, perhaps with the help of Black Nova Scotians.

From Halifax in 1800, many black people together with white women from England were shipped to Freetown, Sierra Leone (and to Liberia) by the British navy. There they joined other liberated black slaves from England and African Americans from Eastern Canada who had been relocated by the navy in 1780s. In Sierra Leone today, the Krio (from "Creole") descendants of the Maroon Creoles of the Americas form the "state elite" groupings among their African congeners, and it is they, with a population of only 2 percent, who are in control of this African nation.

With the concept ethnogenesis, we sidestep sterile arguments over pristine or authentic cultures versus acculturation as negative ascription, and we eschew the racialist polarity between studies of "Indians of the Americas" and "bona fide African American." We also have a concept with which to uncover cultural processes in complex nations, and to conjoin oral and written history within a framework of dynamic ethnic studies and multiculturality.

Norman E. Whitten, Jr.

Geertz, Clifford. *The Interpretation of Cultures.* New York: Basic Books, 1973.

Gonzalez, Nancie L. *Sojourners of the Caribbean: Ethnogenesis and Ethnohistory of the Garifuna.* Urbana: University of Illinois Press, 1988.

Hill, Jonathan, ed. *History, Power and Identity: Ethnogenesis in the Americas 1492–1992.* Iowa City: University of Iowa Press, 1996.

Porter, Arthur. *Creoledom: A Study of the Development of Freetown Society.* London: Oxford University Press, 1963.

Price, Richard. *First-Time: The Historical Vision of an Afro-American People.* Baltimore: Johns Hopkins University Press, 1983.

Stedman, John Gabriel. *Narrative of a Five Years Expedition Against the Revolted Negroes of Surinam.* Translated from the original 1790 manuscript, edited, and with an introduction and notes by Richard Price and Sally Price. Baltimore: Johns Hopkins University Press, 1988.

Sturtevant, William. "Creek into Seminole." In *North American Indians in Historical Perspective,* edited by Eleanor Leacock and Nancy Oestreich Lurie. New York: Random House, 1971.

Whitten, Norman E., Jr. *Sacha Runa: Ethnicity and Adaptation of Ecuadorian Jungle Quichua.* Urbana: University of Illinois Press, 1976.

Whitten, Norman E., Jr., and Arlene Torres, eds.

To Forge the Future in the Fires of the Past: Blackness in South America and the Caribbean. New York: Carlson Publishing, 1995.

WILLIAMS, BRACKETTE F. *Stains on My Name, War in My Veins: Guyana and the Politics of Cultural Struggle.* Durham, N.C.: Duke University Press, 1991.

ETHNOGRAPHIC FILM

Anthropologists have argued for years about the definition of ethnographic film and video. As Sol Worth (1961) suggests, any film is anthropological if an anthropologist chooses to examine it as such. Of particular interest to anthropologists are films made by members of the society depicted because, as cultural documents, they reveal aspects of the world of their makers. More problematic to evaluate are films made by members of one society about another. In form, they usually represent the culture of the filmmakers, but if the behavior filmed was not scripted or directed, there is also something of the culture of the subjects on film. In documentary films, however, there is always a double-voicing, in Mikhail Bakhtin's sense. Uncertainty about whose position is being represented, the author's or the subject's, clouds responsibility for what is said or done, blurring distinctions such as objectivity and subjectivity.

Ever since the invention of motion pictures in the late nineteenth century, filmmakers have used film to document the lives of people from cultures other than their own (for example, Felix-Louis Regnault's 1895 film of a Wolof woman making a clay pot and Alfred Haddon's (1898 Torres Straits films). In common parlance, "ethnographic film" has come to mean any documentary film about non-Western people. Anthropologists have at least two criteria: footage should be of spontaneous, nonscripted human behavior unless scripted by the participants themselves, and decisions about what to film should be informed by an ethnographic study of the people in the film. As more and more ethnographic filmmakers work in their own culture, however, and as indigenous and Third World people and people of diaspora gain access to film and video technology, it has become harder to define ethnographic film. This effort is productive because it reminds us that the production, distribution, and consumption of media are sites where representations may be contested and that film not only reflects and represents culture, it influences the construction of social identity.

In the 1930s tensions had already arisen within ethnographic filmmaking that are still of concern today: the blurring of documentary and fiction genres and the achievement of a balance between aesthetic, emotional, or narrative pleasure and analysis. Ethnographic film was then best known as a popular medium, exemplified by the epic struggles in the films of Merian Cooper and Ernest Schoedsack (*Grass*, 1925), Robert Flaherty (*Man of Aran*, 1934), and Knud Rasmussen (*The Wedding of Palo*, 1937).

At that time, anthropologists had already begun using single-concept films in teaching, to focus on a craft, ceremony, or dance, for example. Gregory Bateson and Margaret Mead experimented with film as a research tool, recording Balinese social interaction in order to help them understand that culture's ethos. Their later films, *Karba's First Year* (1950), *Childhood Rivalry in Bali and New Guinea* (1952), and *Trance and Dance in Bali* (1951), included an authoritative, analytical narration. As anthropology moved away from its scientific roots, Mead and Bateson's filmmaking descendants identified more with "realism" than with science.

The work of other early filmmakers raised additional issues of current interest to ethnographic filmmakers. In *Man with a Movie Camera* (1929), Dziga Vertov introduced a reflexive element that undermined his film's impression of reality and raised the question of whether films simply reflect social reality or if films themselves can become part of the construction of that social reality. Filmmakers like Chris Marker and more recently Trinh T. Minh-ha have carried on this critical social commentary. Basil Wright in *Song of Ceylon* (1934) linked traditional life and religion with colonialism in a style much like a visual poem. Anthropologists still argue about whether or not poetic montage is appropriate in ethnographic film because poetry is probably more a cultural response of the filmmaker than a reflection of the culture of the people filmed; one could also argue that most film is the result of cultural conventions. The stark social realism of the images in Luis Buñuel's *Land Without Bread* (1932), which is accompanied by a musical score and narration that undermines this sense of reality, is often cited as an early example of surrealism, although this impression may have more to do with his narrative films and his association with Salvador Dali.

Jean Rouch, whose ethnographic filmmaking began in the late 1940s, also has a surreal element in some of his films. In his most famous film, *Chronicle of a Summer* (1960), made with Edgar Morin, Rouch adopted Vertov's terminology, cinema verité, or the cinema of reality. He used reflexive and at times humorous, multiple, and spontaneous strategies to get at people's inner experience and attitudes, and this style continues to influence new generations of filmmakers. Rouch's reputation as an ethnographic filmmaker had already been made with *Les Maîtres Fous* (1953), a controversial film of a West African possession cult whose culture appeared to be a response to colonialism, and *Moi, un Noir* (1957), the first of Rouch's many narrative films, that deals with traditional ethnographic subjects and blends the lives of the actors with the roles they are playing.

Ethnographic film evolved most rapidly in the 1960s with the invention of lightweight sound-synchronous technology. John Marshall's film record of the Ju/'hoansi in the former protectorate of South-West Africa, now Namibia (250 hours shot in the 1950s and an equal amount since), is the most extensive record of any small-scale society. His first film, *The Hunters* (1958), a heroic epic of a giraffe hunt, is reminiscent of Flaherty's *Nanook of the North* (1922). Robert Gardner, who had once worked with Marshall, made another epic in 1963, *Dead Birds,* on Dani warfare in West New Guinea, now Irian Jaya, a province of Indonesia. Gardner's subsequent films—most notably *Deep Hearts* and *Forest of Bliss*—challenged the definition of ethnographic film by spawning controversy over the relationship between ethnography and art. Gardner argues that a poetic approach can often capture the essence of human life better than more didactic approaches.

During the 1960s Marshall produced what he called "sequence films"—*A Curing Ceremony, A Joking Relationship, Argument About a Marriage,* and *The Meat Fight.* He used dozens of sequences of Ju/'hoansi social interaction, each of which were filmed in great detail, beginning at the start of an encounter or event and continuing through to a resolution or separation. Footage of these small events was edited into short films to allow teachers flexibility when illustrating concepts in lectures. Marshall, who was also the cinematographer on Frederick Wiseman's first documentary, *Titicut Follies* (1967), persuaded Wiseman to let him film sequences that he later combined in a portrait of prison life—a strategy Wiseman continued to use in the later twentieth century in his films on American institutions. Marshall also used this se-

quence approach to make films on the Pittsburgh police, for example, *Three Domestics* (1970).

Napoleon Chagnon and Timothy Asch, while filming the Yanomamö of southern Venezuela, also filmed sequences—for example, *A Father Washes His Children, A Man and His Wife Weave a Hammock,* and *Yanomamö Myth of Naro.* Sequence filming allows maximum use of footage for research and for making short, educational films, but still provides excellent footage for longer films. Asch was committed to altering the ad hoc way ethnographic film was used in university instruction; he did so by collaborating closely with anthropologists and by integrating film with written ethnography and lectures. Asch's collaboration with Linda Connor and Patsy Asch led to the first joint distribution of a written monograph and videotapes by a major academic publisher, Cambridge University Press: *Jero Tapakan: Balinese Healer* 1986 and four films on Jero's life and practice).

There are many notable collaborations that have produced ethnographic films and monographs: James Woodburn wrote about the Hadza and collaborated, with Sean Hudson, on the film *The Hadza* (1966); Richard Cowan along with Eduardo Calerón, Douglas Sharon, and F. Kaye Sharon made *Eduardo the Healer* (1978) and coauthored *Eduardo el Curandero* (calerón et al. 1982); Douglas Sharon wrote a more scholarly text, *Wizard of the Four Winds* (1978); Barbara Myerhoff wrote *Number Our Days* (1979) and then collaborated with Lynn Lippman to make a film of the same name. Contemporary interactive technologies allow us to integrate image and written texts but also permit alternate texts to exist side by side, encouraging anthropologists to digitize all their research data on film and to use their expertise to suggest varied pathways through cultural media.

While synchronized sound (sync-sound) had a profound effect on documentary filmmaking from the early 1960s, particularly among those experimenting with cinema verité, it was not until 1968, when Asch went to Venezuela and David and Judith MacDougall went to Uganda, that the full impact of sync-sound on ethnographic filmmaking became evident. The MacDougalls challenged the use of narration with their films of the Ugandan Jie: *Nawi* (1970), *To Live with Herds* (1973), *Under the Men's Tree* (1974). They created complex films solely using images with translations of the indigenous voices in subtitles. The evocative trilogy, *Turkana Conversations* (filmed in

1973–1974 and completed in 1977–1981), attests to their success. The MacDougall films, while offsprings of a long tradition of narrative filmmaking, do not dramatize the lives of those filmed, nor do they follow an Aristotelian structure of inquiry, but instead the films emphasize participant observation. Colin Young coined the phrase "observational cinema" to describe these kinds of films. While filming the Kenyan Boran, David MacDougall found he also needed to be provocative in order to get people to articulate the more taken-for-granted aspects of their culture. In their Australian projects, the MacDougalls' work took on a more interactive style even as they continued to structure their films around images and dialogue. David MacDougall's 1993 Sardinian film, *Time of the Barman*, is an exemplar of their interactive style. The practice of subtitling reflected a move away from "objectifying film subjects" toward an interest in meaning and a desire to know what people were saying. The development of sync-sound equipment made this possible.

Although many ethnographic documentaries (e.g., National Geographic television programs) tended to rely on narration, in 1970 Brian Moser introduced a television series, *The Disappearing World*, for Grenada TV that was influenced by the observational cinema of the Macdougalls and by other students of Colin Young, who was then the director of the National Film School in Britain. The series was made in response to concern over the destruction of traditional cultures and was an attempt to preserve remnants of the richness of human cultural diversity on film. These films were intended for the general public. Moser's commitment to collaboration with anthropologists meant that many of his films also became popular in university classrooms because they enriched and were enriched by written ethnography. Some, like Charles Nairn's *The Kawelka: Ongka's Big Moka* (1974), complemented publications written by the anthropologists who worked on the film (Andrew and Marilyn Strathern, in this case); other subjects, such as *The Shilluk* (by Chris Curling and anthropologists Walter Kunijwok and Paul Howell, 1976) were chosen to support and illustrate classic ethnographies.

Melissa Llewelyn-Davies, the anthropologist on two of the *Disappearing World* films directed by Chris Curling, *Masai Woman* (1974) and *Masai Manhood* (1975), later directed ethnographic films for the British Broadcasting Company. In *The Women's Olamal* (1984) and *Memory and Dreams* (1993), Llewelyn-Davies used an observational style but included her own voice in the film, talking with Masai women in a way that conveyed trust and a desire for mutual understanding. What distinguishes Llewelyn-Davies's Masai films (and those Jean Lydell made with Joanna Head among the Hamar, e.g., *Two Girls Go Hunting*, 1991), is an intimacy with those filmed that came from years of contact.

Jorge Preloran also developed a unique style. He recorded hours of tape until he had a life history that he then illustrated with film (*Imaginero* 1969; *Zerda's Children*, 1978), thereby producing inexpensive yet powerful biographies of people in his own country of Argentina and elsewhere in South America. In the late eighties Perloran taught a woman from Ecuador named Zulay, to edit film, and she helped him edit a film about her life, *Zulay Facing the 21st Century*, 1991. He filmed Zulay both in Ecuador and Los Angeles. His wife, Mabel Preloran, herself an anthropologist, worked with Zulay and together they created a commentary for the film. Close collaboration between those depicted in films and filmmakers has become increasingly important since the decline of colonialism.

Ian Dunlop, in his films made in Papua New Guinea with Maurice Godelier (*Towards Baruyu Manhood*, 1974), and in his many films on Australian Aboriginal artists and communities, sought to show respect for his subjects by making long, detailed films, particularly of ritual, in a realist tradition, in an attempt to minimize cultural distortion.

Gary Kildea, working with anthropologist Jerry Leach, brought humor and originality to their film *Trobriand Cricket* (1976), which is about how the English game was transformed in a New Guinean context. His later films, *Celso and Cora* (1983), an intimate portrait of street vendors in Manila, the Philippines, and *Valencia Diary* (1992), about the intersection of national politics with peasant concerns in a migrant community on Mindanao Island in the Philippines, follow the evolution of friendship between himself (an Australian filmmaker) and the people he encounters. His films locate human problems within a historical and geographical context without narration or formal interviews. Kildea's films, like many by the MacDougalls, Marshall, Preloran, and Rouch, are biographies.

While written ethnography traditionally obliterated individuals and particular encounters in its general analysis of a society, film is a particularizing medium; it can help students grasp the relationship between theory and experience. For example, Chagnon and Asch made *The Feast* (1970), which follows in detail a political feast between two Yanomamö villages, to illustrate Marcel Mauss's theory of "The Gift" (Mauss 1967). Chagnon and Asch's film *The Ax Fight* (1975) combines the observation of particular events with analysis. The film is often cited as an early example of reflexivity: the audience sees an unedited, ten-minute sequence and then hears the voices of the filmmakers trying to make sense of what they are seeing. Reflexivity disrupts narrative pleasure by reminding the viewer that they are watching a film, and that films are not a substitute for reality. In *The Ax Fight* reflexivity calls attention to the filmmakers's experiences during the fight but also to the way kinship models and film conventions are used to analyze the fight and reedit the sequence.

Jero on Jero: A Balinese Trance Seance Observed (1981), made by Asch with Linda Connor and Patsy Asch, filmed a Balinese healer watching herself on film for the first time and commenting on what she saw. The use of videotape to record feedback is a potentially rich method of enquiry. It is a way to avoid structuring questions that might influence answers, to share footage with the people filmed, and to test interpretations.

With a few exceptions, such as William Geddes's *The Land Dyaks of Borneo* (1966) and *Miao Year* (1969), earlier ethnographic films were not made by anthropologists, but in the late twentieth century technology made it possible for anthropologists with minimal training to make a videotape and to use that tape for a multitude of purposes, including the study of participant feedback and teaching. Feedback can be an invaluable tool, particularly in the analysis of events in which people are too involved to stop and answer questions.

Throughout the 1960s and 1970s Rouch made detailed films about Dogon ritual in a poetic, trance-like style. He also made improvisations in films such as *Jaguar* (1967), in which he and his African subjects explored "what if" adventures. This film is narrated by the protagonists while they watch footage of themselves leaving their village and traveling to the city. *Petit a Petit* (1969) is a parody, the same men portraying anthropologists who have come from Africa to study Parisians. In *Madame L'eau* (1993) they go to Holland to observe windmills. These films, made over a span of forty years, are what Rouch calls "ethno-fictions," and represent a playful space between two cultures.

Robin Anderson and Bob Conolly have made three documentaries in the highlands of Papua New Guinea. Their films move from a naive look at the impact of Australian colonial expansion in *First Contact* (1984) to devastating critiques of the struggle toward capitalism. In Anderson and Conolly's films *Joe Leahy's Neighbours* (1988) and *Black Harvest* (1992), a man named Leahy is caught between the colonial privilege of his father and the local custom of his mother and his home. Lengthy experience in the region and an opportunity to examine in detail the tensions inherent in rapid cultural change helped Anderson and Conolly make films valuable for anthropology students.

In the *Navaho Film Themselves* project of the early 1970s, John Adair and Sol Worth gave the Navaho cameras to see if their footage would reveal new aspects of Navaho cognition. A quite different, political stimulus has led to the adoption of video technology by indigenous peoples around the world who wish to establish communication among their own communities and between those communities and the dominant cultures that surround them (e.g., groups like the Kayapo of Amazonas, Brazil, or the Yanomamö of Venezuela, as well as individuals like Zacharias Kunukthe, an Inuit Eskimo). These and other personal, autobiographical explorations provide rich data for anthropologists. Although lacking the "critical distance" implied by "ethnographic film," they provide insights into human experience that more "objective" studies miss. They also demand a shift in perspective to understand the multiple contexts in which the film is recorded and in which it is seen.

Early filmmakers were concerned with the romance of exotic places or with careful scientific recordings. Filmmakers in the 1960s explored realism and the impact of new technology; in the 1970s they developed observational cinema, reflexivity, and unnarrated films. In the 1980s they explored voice, subjectivity, and objectivity; in the 1990s, they perhaps documented their own experiences, mixing genres, the ways to represent memory and history, and dreams and meaning. These issues, along with ethical considerations, remain current for students today. Filmmakers have also found different ways to deal with the ethical questions that arise when one person represents the life of another. Films have the power, literally, to harm their subjects. The national film board of Canada made a film, *Sons of Haji Omar*, from footage Timothy and Patsy Asch took with Asen Balikci in Afghanistan. Unknown to them, the film was sold to the BBC. The BBC added a patriotic commentary at the head and tail of the film about the invasion of Afghanistan and then said that the people in the film had joined the rebel forces. It is unlikely there was any evidence that this was true but even if it were, the lives of the Afghan nomads who allowed the Asches to film were endangered because the film included their names, the names of their family and where they lived. Filmmakers apparently need to be cynical about all media, and find ways to ensure that footage they took does not get used without their supervision and control. There are many more subtle ways in which someone's life can be negatively effected, even just the effects of resulint fame. Short of actually injuring someone films may also exploit or misrepresent their lives.

It is not surprising that the greatest innovations and challenges to ethnographic film are coming from newly empowered people whose parents grew up under colonial regimes around the world. The Black Audio Collective in England exemplifies a more meditative, surreal, yet politically critical voice; in *Of Great Events and Ordinary People,* Raul Ruiz, a Chilean living in Paris, casts an ironic exile's eye that denies the limit of the frame because what is not there, his country, is as important as what is; Trinh T. Minhha offers a critique of film conventions and of the dominance of the filmmaker's gaze, bringing to the conscious level the colonial and gender-power relations that previously made a hegemony of much of ethnographic filmmaking. Their works, among others, signal a shift in the position of cultural authority.

TIMOTHY ASCH
PATSY ASCH

SEE ALSO: Photography; Visual Anthropology

ASCH, TIMOTHY. "The Ethics of Ethnographic Filmmaking." In *Film as Ethnography,* edited by Peter Ian Crawford and David Turton. Manchester: Manchester University Press, 1992.

——— . "The Story We Now Want to Hear is Not Ours to Tell: Sharing Visual Communication Skills with the Yanomamo." *Visual Anthropology Review* 7 (1991): 102–106.

ASCH, TIMOTHY, and PATSY ASCH. "Images That Represent Ideas: The Use of Films on the !Kung to Teach Anthropology." In *The Past and Future of !Kung Ethnography: Critical Reflections and Symbolic Perspectives,* edited by Megan Biesele, Robert Gordon, and Richard Lee. Hamburg: Helmut Buske Verlag, 1987.

——— . "Film in Anthropological Research." In *Cinematographic Theory and New Dimensions in Ethnographic Film,* edited by Paul Hockings and Yasuhiro Omori. Osaka: National Museum of Ethnology, 1988.

ASCH, TIMOTHY, JOHN MARSHALL, and PETER SPIES. "Ethnographic Film: Structure and Function." *Annual Review of Anthropology* (1973): 179–187.

BATESON, GREGORY, and MARGARET MEAD. *Balinese Characters: A Photographic Analysis.* New York Academy of Sciences, Special Publications 2, 1942.

BARNOUW, ERIK. *Documentary: A History of the Non-Fiction Film.* New York: Oxford University Press, 1983.

BENEDICT, RUTH. *The Chrysanthemum and the Sword.* Boston: Houghton Mifflin, 1946.

CALERÓN, EDUARDO, RICHARD COWAN, DOUGLAS SHARON, and F. KAYE SHARON. *Eduardo el Curandero: The Words of a Peruvian Healer.* Richmond, Va.: North Atlantic Books, 1982.

CONNOR, LINDA, PATSY ASCH, and TIMOTHY ASCH. *Jero Tapakan: Balinese Healer.* New York: Cambridge University Press, 1986.

COLLIER, JOHN JR., and MALCOLM COLLIER. *Visual Anthropology: Photography as a Research Method.* Albuquerque: University of New Mexico Press, 1986.

CRAWFORD, PETER I., and JAN K. SIMONSEN. *Ethnographic Film Aesthetics and Narrative Traditions.* Aarhus, Denmark: Intervention Press and Association the Nordic Anthropological Film Association, 1992.

CRAWFORD, PETER I., and DAVID TURTON, eds. *Film as Ethnography.* Manchester: Manchester University Press, 1992.

DEVEREAUX, LESLIE, and ROGER HILLMAN, eds. *Alternative Visions.* Berkeley: University of California Press, 1994.

HEIDER, KARL G. *Films for Anthropological Teaching,* 8th ed. Washington, D.C.: American Anthropological Association, 1994.

———. *Ethnographic Film.* Austin: University of Texas Press, 1976.

HOCKINGS, PAUL, ed. *Principles of Visual Anthropology.* New York: Aldine de Gruyter, 1975.

LOIZOS, PETER. *Innovation in Ethnographic Film: From Innocence to Self-Consciousness 1955–1985.* Manchester: Manchester University Press, 1993.

MAUSS, MARCEL. *The Gift.* N.Y.: W. W. Norton, 1967.

MYERHOFF, BARBARA. *Number Our Days.* New York: E. P. Dutton, 1979.

NICHOLS, BILL. *Representing Reality.* Bloomington: Indiana University Press, 1992.

———. *Ideology and the Image.* Bloomington: Indiana University Press, 1981.

ROLLWAGEN, JACK R., ed. *Anthropological Filmmaking.* N.Y.: Harwood Academic Publishers, 1988.

RUBY, JAY, ed. *The Cinema of John Marshall.* Philadelphia: Harwood Academic Publishers, 1993.

RUBY, JAY, and BARBARA MYERHOFF. *A Crack in the Mirror: Reflexive Perspectives in Anthropology.* Philadelphia: University of Pennsylvania Press, 1982.

SHARON, DOUGLAS. *Wizard of the Four Winds: A Shaman's Story.* New York: Free Press, 1978.

SINGER, ANDRE, and LESLIE WOODHEAD. *Disappearing World.* London: Boxtree Press with Grenada Television, 1988.

SORENSON, RICHARD, and CARLETON GAJDUSEK. *Research Films for the Study of Child Growth and Development and Disease Patterns in Primitive Cultures.* Bethesda, Md.: National Institute for Neurological Disease and Blindness, 1963.

STOLLER, PAUL. *The Cinematic Griot: The Ethnography of Jean Rouch.* Chicago: University of Chicago Press, 1992.

STRATHERN, ANDREW. *The Rope of Moka: Big-men and Ceremonial Exchange in Mount Hagen, New Guinea.* Cambridge: Cambridge University Press, 1971.

STRATHERN, MARILYN. *Women in Between: Female Roles in a Male World, Mount Hagen, New Guinea.* New York: Seminar Press, 1972.

TRINH, T. MINH-HA. *Woman, Native, Other: Writing Postcoloniality and Feminism.* Bloomington: Indiana University Press, 1989.

WORTH, SOL. *Studying Visual Communication.* Philadelphia: University of Pennsylvania Press, 1961.

WORTH, SOL, and JOHN ADAIR. *Through Navajo Eyes.* Bloomington: Indiana University Press, 1972.

ETHNOGRAPHY

Writing about customs or, more generally, the description of cultures based on firsthand observation and participation in fieldwork. In the United States today, many anthropologists would agree that cultural anthropology entails three premises: holism, comparative perspective, and ethnographic description. Many would agree that our knowledge of humanity rests on the description of various life ways and that fieldwork is an indispensable element in the education of cultural anthropologists and in the collection of the basic information upon which other conclusions are based. Fieldwork is the process of observing and participating in life ways of people. Anthropologists report the results as ethnography. Much else is debated such as how to do fieldwork, what its process entails, how best to report findings, and even whether we can learn anything by fieldwork.

In Britain, ethnography is usually distinguished from ethnology as descriptive from theoretical analysis. In the United States, the distinctions are less clearcut. The central place of ethnography and its major tenets were first articulated in Britain by Bronislaw Malinowski and in the United States by Franz Boas.

Malinowski established one widely emulated, quoted, and read example of ethnography in his writings about his two years of fieldwork in the Trobriand Islands, which he commenced in 1915. His writings include *Argonauts of the Western Pacific* (1922), *Crime and Custom in Savage Society* (1926), *The Sexual Life of Savages* (1929), and *Coral Gardens and Their Magic* (1935). Malinowski's description of the process of fieldwork in the introduction of *Argonauts of the Western Pacific* is often cited as a model of fieldwork. His journals were published in 1989, some twenty-seven years after he died.

Malinlowski learned the language of the Trobrianders and explored their everyday life from a vantage point similar to their own. He observed and recorded quarrels, work, errands, jokes, family scenes, festivals, stories, voyages, and other events. He wrote that his goal was to understand the point of view, comprehend their lives and their visions of their world, and grasp their subjective feelings as well as their mentality, behavior, customs, codes, and institutions.

The experience of a year among whalers and Eskimos in 1883, while he was on a geological expedition, convinced Boas of the value of fieldwork. He moved from Germany to the United States, became a museum curator and professor, and is now known as the founder of anthropology in the United States. A prolific writer of articles and books, he is known especially for his work on the Kwakiutl of the Pacific Northwest coast as well as for his attacks on universal theories, his insistence on detailed data, and as the teacher of a generation of U.S. anthropologists. He advocated the study of specific cultures in their particular historical contexts, an approach called "historical particularism." In his critique of the comparative method, he suggested that to understand general processes, anthropologists should understand the historical processes of individual societies and compare them. Through the understanding of detailed particular processes, he argued, one could develop an understanding of general historical processes.

Through the influence of Malinowski and Boas, ethnographic fieldwork became central to anthropology in Britain and the United States. One of the problems of ethnography has always been point of reference. There is little reason to do ethnographic description for its own sake. If we want to compare ethnographic observations, we need a common vocabulary. The terms of the common vocabulary, however, may have scant relationship to the categories or concepts the people themselves use.

Much of this discussion goes back to an old argument about whether there is something special about humans that makes human life intrinsically inappropriate to scientific study. The nineteenth-century German philosopher, Wilhelm Dilthey, argued that because people act in terms of purposes, any explanation of human action must be in terms of an understanding of their purposes. This could be developed only by putting oneself in the position of the actor and understanding from that point of view. This was contrasted to an external point of view in which the actor's point of view and purposes are not considered relevant.

This became especially problematic to the U.S. anthropologist Ward Goodenough when he began to analyze census data he had collected on the island of Truk in 1947 and to compare his results with those of another anthropologist, J. L. Fischer, who had done a similar census not more than three years before. They disagreed on the numbers of patrilocal (newlywed couples living with the groom's father's group) and matrilocal (newlywed couples living with the bride's mother's group) residences. The problem was not that the categories "matrilocal" and "patrilocal" were badly defined, or that people had moved, or that the anthropologists disagreed about who lived with whom. The problem was that the imported categories were not very straightforward to use in classifying very complex matters such as residence. A case that appeared patrilocal at first sight might turn out to be matrilocal when the anthropologist knew more of the story.

Goodenough suggested that the problem arose from using categories that were not appropriate to the local situation. Trukese did not decide whether they would be matrilocal or patrilocal, they decided residence on the basis of where land was available to them, where their children's lineage mates lived, and where the husband had political responsibilities. Goodenough advocated an ethnography in terms of such locally relevant categories and concepts instead of external ones.

In 1954 a linguist, Kenneth Pike, suggested that the distinction linguists were making between the description of verifiable real sounds using the universal International Phonetic Alphabet (phonetic analysis) and the locally relevant distinctions speakers of the language could actually "hear" (phonemic analyses) was the same as the distinction between descriptions of reality anthropologists offered from an external point of view and their descriptions of locally relevant and salient categories, criteria, and forms. This was the wider metaphoric use of the emic/etic distinction. The anthropologist Marvin Harris (1968) connects these developments to older currents of thought.

Anthropologists talk with, live among, and observe individuals for finite periods of time to describe their cultures. How can one guarantee the connection between the work of the anthropologist and his or her descriptions of cultures? One solution to the problem of reliability was to follow the methods of immediate constituent linguistics, which Pike represented, to develop similarly reliable practices for anthropological fieldwork.

This call for the description of locally relevant categories led a movement of "new ethnography" or "ethnoscience." Much of the literature of this movement is collected in Stephen A. Tyler's book, *Cognitive Anthropology*, published in 1969. Tyler characterized anthropologists up to that time as being so concerned with constructing unitary systems to explain cultures internally or their development through time that they spent much of their effort classifying ethnographic observations into typologies and defining abstract definitions of types and subtypes. This led, paradoxically, to more particular rather than universal thinking, as anthropologists tried to match various inappropriate general schemes to their particular ethnographic experience.

Based on the assumption that each people comprehends and experiences emotions, things, events, and behavior according to its own distinctive scheme, the new ethnography focused on discovering these schemes; its goal was to describe how the people of the culture think. Much effort went into developing methods and procedures for describing how people think, largely based on analogies to immediate constituent analysis (developed for describing languages), which was then current in linguistics, for instance, careful, orderly, and structured eliciting techniques such as frames for collecting cultural data from individual informants. A description of a culture should specify what a person would have to know to act appropriately in that culture or to consider the actions of others usual.

The new ethnography also raised the question of validity. Were anthropologists, for all their detailed procedures, actually describing what they said they were describing? Were they describing culture, or simply various individual opinions? Perhaps there is massive variability and people manage to get along as well as they do, not because they share cultures but because they systematically misunderstand one another.

Some of the new-ethnography group continued to address questions of validity and imported methods from educational testing and measurement rather than from linguistics. This group assumes that with better methods it is possible to transcend the problems of validity and reliability posed by the attempt to describe cultures and develop procedures for doing so. It is paradoxical that the most reflexive of anthropologists, these methodologists, acutely aware of every move in the construction of their object of study and representations of it, should not be known as reflexivists, but that the term should be reserved for those whose reflections are of themselves rather than of what they do.

A second response to the problem of validity is to suppose, on the contrary, that the problem cannot be transcended. If one takes this stance, one does not develop methods but dismisses such concerns as uninformed and develops a reflexivism that is no less intense or critical than the self-reflections of the methodologists yet collapses the focus onto the individual anthropologist rather than the people and cultural systems one has tried to understand.

In 1973, only four years after Tyler's book was published, Clifford Geertz collected fifteen of his essays into a book titled *The Interpretation of Cultures*. Disagreeing with the cognitive approach, he centered on formal models and discovery procedures, and argued that what ethnographers actually do is not specified by their methods but is an exercise in "thick description"—descriptions of events with sufficient background to make them comprehensible from the point of view of the people involved. He uses the term "interpretation" in his title because, he argues, every dimension of the construction of descriptions and background knowledge rests first on the interpretations of the people and second on the ethnographer's interpretations of those interpretations. The proponents of new ethnography, Geertz argued, in their attempts to develop formal models of how people see their worlds, did not pay attention to the central dimension of culture: meaning.

Culture, for Geertz, is the totality of local meanings in terms of which people understand, think about, talk about, and describe behavior, institutions, events, and processes. Culture is public—in the actions people interpret, in their discussions, rituals, and behavior. It is thus as accessible to ethnographers as to the people and thus can ethnographers describe it without having to do anything as mysterious as "getting into the minds" of the people. The descriptions ethnographers construct of cultures, meanings, are not necessarily the same descriptions the people the ethnographers study would make. They are the descriptions of foreigners—ethnographers—rather than part of the local culture itself.

Conceptual structures are complex, overlapping, interrelated, inexplicit, and strange to the ethnographer who is trying to understand and explicate them. Geertz makes an analogy to reading the faded ink of an ambiguous and garbled manuscript full of omissions in a foreign language; he uses the term for the interpretation of texts, "hermeneutics," to characterize ethnography. He warns, though, that such an approach can and has divorced the analysis of cultures from the informal logic of everyday life. He reiterates that culture is public—in what people do—and this is what ethnography must understand. Ethnography cannot be divorced from what people do, say, and experience, lest it become empty. A good interpretation, he warns, should take us into the heart of the thing interpreted, not to an admiration of the elegance or cleverness of its author. He also cautions that ethnographic interpretations must stay close to the "hard surfaces of life"—the economic and political realities of everyday life and the biological and physical realties of life.

Ethnography, Geertz says, interprets the flow of local social discourse and fixes it as a historical document. Such interpretations are in their own terms, he warns, and thus self-validating, and sometimes validated by the authority of the person who imparts them. Thus externally generated general schemes and classifications are not appropriate.

According to Geertz, theory is not used to predict, but as an aid to ethnographic interpretation, to suggest what is important and how things may be related to one another. Rather than situating observations in terms of governing laws, ethnographers make their observations intelligible in local terms. The objective is to draw large conclusions from small well-contextualized facts.

Meanwhile, at about the same time, in 1970, the movement toward a more precise methodology for ethnography was consolidating. Pertti and Gretel Pelto said that those anthropologists who were in graduate school in the 1950s learned about the contributions of their predecessors to description and theory, but not how they practiced ethnography. Their teachers told them they would learn about it only by doing it themselves. They were neither concerned with nor taught about rules of evidence, questions of representativeness, validity, or reliability. In *Anthropological Research: The Structure of Inquiry,* they argue that the goal of ethnography is to produce information that is both useful and credible, but since the commitment to the kinds of emotional understandings that grow during the process of ethnographic research is not sufficient to assure either usefulness or credibility,

anthropologists should integrate both qualitative and quantitative methods. They point out that relying on intuitive understandings may result in imposing alien definitions and feelings quite different from those of the people. Even if intuitive hermeneutical approaches can describe inside views, they may be biased, unaware, or inaccurate. They argue for clear definitions of basic concepts and use of quantitative measures when feasible and argue for the operationalization of the research process in anthropology.

Some anthropologists selected parts of Geertz's program and neglected other parts. For instance, moving from the idea that ethnography is interpretive or hermeneutic, various anthropologists discussed a distinct hermeneutic or interruptive anthropology as a way of doing ethnography as opposed to Geertz's notion that that is the way any ethnographer works. In doing so, they ignored the embeddedness of life and culture in political and economic forms and the biological basis for culture. This development rested much on the authority of the ethnographer, thus ignoring another of Geertz's warnings. It was ironic that this group, who sometimes announced that they followed Geertz, in fact illustrated the pitfalls he warned against. The problem with interpretive anthropology is that, as Geertz admonished, the source of the knowledge is neither shared nor sharable experience but private intuition; one has to rely only on the authority of the writer.

This concept of ethnography led to a related development that focused on the activity of interpretation itself and treated ethnography as literature because, as James Clifford and George Marcus say in the preface to their 1986 collection, *Writing Culture,* ethnographers *write.* This led to the importation of concepts and vocabulary from the discipline of literary criticism and to some confusion between ethnography and literary criticism. In literature, there is no confusion between novelists, those who write novels, and literary critics, those who write about literature. Somehow in anthropology, there seemed to be a confusion between ethnography, the writing of interpretations, and writing about it and conflating the two into a single activity governed by the insights of literary criticism rather than anthropology. Although ethnographers write, writing is one medium (film and video are others), not the content, of their work. Physicists also write and interpret experience, but no physicist has confused literature with physics.

These developments in turn led to a critical reassessment by Melford Spiro in his *Anthropological Other or Burmese Brother,* published in 1992. The title refers to a disparity in the goals and assumptions of classical and modern anthropology. The classical anthropology of Boas and Malinowski envisioned a theoretically oriented, empirically grounded, comparative science devoted to understanding and explaining human diversity. Such a science would rest on the assumption that people of different cultures can understand each other, an assumption that underlies the work of anthropologists from Malinowski through Geertz.

Some who followed the literary critics claim that this understanding is impossible because it is an artifact of one culture, and specific to it. That is, ethnography, even science, is, like Navaho witchcraft, a dimension of a single culture and no different from any other cultural construct. Because science is "Western" and a creation of historic culture, it has no more explanatory power than any other cultural construct. Explanation is impossible. They argue that cultures are so different that people of different cultures cannot understand one another. Cultural diversity is not an opportunity to discover by contrast and understand the human condition but a barrier to comprehension.

According to Spiro, classical anthropology holds that culture can be understood and explained. Modern anthropology assumes that culture determines social and psychological patterns and that there are no transcultural standards of judgment, and no way of knowing is privileged. Classical anthropology holds that science transcends time and culture, not in its findings, but in its way of asking and answering questions and in the continual testing of ideas against what one can see and experience.

Spiro wonders how an ethnographer can understand a group different from her or his own, if it is true that cultures are incommensurable and everything is culturally determined. Under such assumptions it is impossible to communicate about one's own group to others, and those who pretend to do so are either not convinced of their own arguments, or are incapable of representing other cultures. Furthermore, there is no reason to describe or interpret exotic, even different cultures, for the sake of showing variability. The purpose of theory is not to make better descriptions of local diversity, as Geertz suggests, but to provide answers to fundamental questions about human existence.

Spiro counsels that skepticism is appropriate for all inquiry and drives science. The constructive response is not to reject inquiry but to get on with programs of research to assess generalizations and theory against what we can observe empirically. He argues for the rejection of subjectivity in favor of a practice that is replicable and public rather than egocentric and private.

In modern anthropology Spiro sees the rejection of science and the possibility of generalizing about the human condition. If this is ruled out, how can anthropologists expect others to take them or their work seriously? He argues that it was interpretive or hermeneutic or symbolic anthropology that led to modern anthropology by confusing three senses of cultural relativism: descriptive, which understands variability among human groups in terms of differences in cultures; normative, which argues that one cannot translate cultural standards and that all judgments are ethnocentric; and epistemological, which argues that everything human is cultural and cultures are endlessly variable. The weak form of epistemological relativism is that all cultures have something in common given by the common genetic history of our species, the psychic unity of humankind. The strong form is that all cultures are particular, and there is no psychic unity, therefore one can never explain anything and can only interpret individual cultures. In rejecting the possibility of universal explanations, these people reject science as a means for doing ethnography because the basis of scientific explanation is the idea that when something occurs it is systematically related to other events and objects, and hence predictable. The object of science is reliable (i.e., replicable) and public knowledge as opposed to the private and nonreplicable knowledge of the interpretivists.

The scientific method formulates explanatory theories and uses empirical and logical procedures that can lead to verification or falsification. In science, the concept of "cause" is not restricted to material conditions but includes purposes, motives, intentions, and meanings. Because motives, intentions, and purposes are causes, one needs to study meanings and offer interpretations, but one should be sure they are valid interpretations.

Spiro states that the long-held opposition between interpretation and explanation is a false dichotomy and distinguishes between "discovery," which is always intuitive, and "verification," which is public. Scientific methodology provides a means for validity and reliability.

Whereas some anthropologists started writing about writing, many continued studies of people and the tradition of the Peltos endured throughout. The cognitive-anthropology approach continued and developed more sophisticated methods, and anthropologists learned more about the methods of other social-science disciplines. In 1988, H. Russell Bernard published *Research Methods in Cultural Anthropology* as a practical guide for doing scientific research in anthropology. Neither he, nor the Peltos, nor Spiro, nor any of the other proponents of scientific anthropology have ever denied the relevance of humanistic approaches, because they realize that the search for understanding is always interpretive and humanistic. Nevertheless, they maintain that the testing of ideas against empirical data is the realm of science.

Just as some anthropologists based their work on the branches of Geertz's work rather than on the trunk, and developed an interpretive ethnography devoid of political and economic facets, some methodologists have concentrated so hard on questions of validity and reliability that they seem to have forgotten the questions that raised these issues, the questions of cultural description and comparison, of formulating and testing theories about culture and people. There may be a third position between the rigor of the methodologists and the confessional literature of reflexivism, a kind of anthropology that recognizes the impossibility of certainty, yet gets on with the work of ethnography and the construction and testing of theories as best we can in a context of science and humanism.

The whole concept of ethnography relies on an accessible community of people with whom an anthropologist can live to learn about their culture. As anthropologists from the 1950s started to expand their work from people living on small islands like the Trobrianders with whom Malinowski lived, the Trukese Goodenough described, or "tribal" groups such as those of the Native Americans Boas studied in the Pacific Northwest, to peasants in Mexico and other Latin American countries, as well as in China and other large and complex societies, it became apparent that ethnography was not the only or even always the best way to learn about a people or its culture. Many cultural phenomena in such societies are not localized. A banking system, for instance, is not something one can best learn about simply by living and working with local bankers. For one thing, their private lives may not be relevant to the question; for another, the system transcends communities and even nations, and it is that system one must learn about. By the same token, anthropologists learned that to understand rural peasant communities, they had to comprehend how the communities fit into larger national political and economic systems and the histories of those larger systems. This was not something they could do with the traditional community-based methods of ethnography. Thus anthropologists began to expand their methods beyond ethnography, however they defined it, to include history and national and even international systems they could only understand statistically and in terms of much larger systems than communities.

Even when these studies are global in scope, anthropologists tend to rely on locally community-based ethnography to build their analyses of overarching structures, processes, and histories.

Ethnography was the fundamental component of anthropology at the time it was founded as an academic discipline. Anthropologists would take the theories of the great thinkers of Europe and the United States to the ends of the earth to determine how well they characterized the lives and cultures of ordinary people, whether in Europe, the United States, or elsewhere. Since that time, there have been many debates and disputes about how best to do ethnography—whether to take an outside or inside view, and whether to use well-defined or intuitive methods—but ethnography remains one of the three components of the discipline of anthropology.

To get an idea of what fieldwork is like, one would do well to read Malinowski's introduction to *Argonauts of the Western Pacific*, a classic model for anthropologists, as well as his journals to get a more private view of what it felt like to him to do fieldwork. Malinowski's day is long gone, however, and today we do anthropology in an age of computers and international airplane flights, in a world that comes into peoples' homes via satellite television wherever they may be, a world that is no more than two or three days distant from any other part of the world. To understand ethnography in this more modern context, one can do no better than to read Miles Richardson's essay, "The Myth-Teller," in his book *Cry Lonesome and Other Accounts of the Anthropologist's Project* (1990).

E. PAUL DURRENBERGER

SEE ALSO: *Cross-Cultural Research; Cultural Relativism; Culture; Fieldwork; Humanistic Anthropology; Statistical Methods; Writing Culture*

BERNARD, H. RUSSELL. *Research Methods in Cultural Anthropology*. Newbury Park, Calif.: Sage Publications, 1988.

CLIFFORD, JAMES, and GEORGE E. MARCUS, eds. *Writing Culture: The Poetics and Politics of Ethnography*. Berkeley and Los Angeles: University of California Press, 1986.

GEERTZ, CLIFFORD. *The Interpretation of Cultures: Selected Essays by Clifford Geertz*. New York: Basic Books, 1973.

HARRIS, MARVIN. *The Rise of Anthropological Theory: A History of Theories of Culture*. New York: Thomas Y. Crowell, 1968.

MALINOWSKI, BRONISLAW. *Argonauts of the Western Pacific*. Reprint, New York: E. P. Dutton, [1922] 1961.

PELTO, PERTTI J., and GRETEL H. PELTO. *Anthropological Research: The Structure of Inquiry*. 2d ed. (First published in 1970). Cambridge: Cambridge University Press, 1978.

RICHARDSON, MILES. *Cry Lonesome and Other Accounts of the Anthropologist's Project*. Albany: State University of New York Press, 1990.

SPIRO, MELFORD. *Anthropological Other or Burmese Brother: Studies in Cultural Analysis*. New Brunswick, N.J.: Transaction Publishers, 1992.

TYLER, STEPHEN A., ed. *Cognitive Anthropology*. New York: Holt, Rinehart & Winston, 1969.

ETHNOHISTORY

For most of the twentieth century, there has been a consensus of opinion on what constitutes ethnohistory. Today, that consensus no longer holds beyond agreement that ethnohistory is a method, not a discipline. What some hesitatingly call ethnohistory, others think of simply as history. Ethnohistorians themselves, as well as outsiders, might find this state perplexing, but it reflects a broader shift in the relationship between anthropology and history. In the first half of the twentieth century, on both sides of the Atlantic, each of these disciplines virtually excluded the other; but since about 1980, the two have converged markedly. The implications of this profound shift in historiography are broad-ranging for ethnohistory. To understand why requires discussion first of the connection between anthropology and history, then of the history and current scope of the methodology commonly known as ethnohistory—for which, for reasons explained below, a better label might be anthropological history.

ANTHROPOLOGY AND HISTORY

Until the middle of the twentieth century, the boundaries between anthropology and history were sharp and virtually impermeable. When A. R. Radcliffe-Browne (1929) wrote that history "does not really explain anything at all," he spoke for a generation and more of structural-functional anthropologists in Great Britain and elsewhere, who paid little attention to historical process. Although American cultural anthropology before the middle of the century is not so easily generalized, Alfred L. Kroeber (1935) considered it "anti-historical in tendency," and Robert H. Lowie (1915) revealed a particular antipathy to the historicity of oral traditions when he said that one cannot accord them "any value whatsoever under any circumstances whatsoever" because "we know them to be true." As for other historians, as argued elsewhere (Krech 1991), most concentrated on narrative, most were hostile to social scientific theory, and few were interested in the history of indigenous people among whom anthropologists, to the exclusion of most other scholars, worked.

There were, however, exceptions in both anthropology and history; neither discipline has ever been entirely monolithic in theory, methodology, or subject matter. In Great Britain, the exceptions included social anthropologists interested in social change and history, of whom E. E. Evans-Pritchard is the best known. In America, several cultural anthropologists of Lowie's generation and the following one (including Kroeber) wrote at length about acculturation and other processes of cultural change. In France, historians of the Annales school maintained comparative interests in institutions and society, which brought them far closer to then-current anthropological concerns than their colleagues, for many of whom the description of political events or biography represented the most important objective of historical research.

The exceptions prepared the ground for an expanding conversation between history and anthropology. The pace of this dialogue has picked up notably in recent years, during which time sea changes in historiography have affected both disciplines. In anthropology, analyses incorporating history have increased greatly in number each year. In history, various "new" histories have undermined the historicist political and biographical narratives which had dominated historiography. Today, anthropologists regularly use traditional historical materials and methods to make sense of the problems that interest them, and historians habitually employ traditional anthropological methodologies like ethnographic and informant work to make sense of theirs. Evans-Pritchard (1962) remarked that he would accept F. W. Maitland's dictum that "anthropology must choose between being history and being nothing" if he could add that "history must (also) choose between being social anthropology and being nothing." Evans-Pritchard was prescient; he forecast one of the major trends in the late-twentieth century scholarship.

ETHNOHISTORY, 1900–1980

These changes in the relationship between anthropology and history have affected ethnohistory; this term, in fact, was in use by the end of the first decade of the twentieth century. In 1909 Clark Wissler spoke of reconstructing prehistoric cultures by combining "ethno historical" with archaeological evidence. By "ethno," Wissler referred to an ethnic group, most likely an American Indian tribe or some other indigenous small-scale society that held his attention. He evidently equated ethnohistorical evidence with documentary data, and most of the documents which pertained to the groups in which he and other anthropologists of his generation maintained interest were produced by nonnative people.

Many whose interests were the analysis of cultural change in American Indian societies favored Wissler's approach to ethnohistory—the use of documents to speak about the past. In the late 1940s and 1950s, that approach underwent two important impetuses. The first involved the institutionalization of ethnohistory, which occurred principally through a succession of academic organizations, beginning with the Ohio Valley Historic Indian Conference, which initially convened in 1954. It soon changed its name to the American Indian Ethno-historic Conference, then, in 1966, to the American Society for Ethnohistory. The official journal of these organizations is *Ethnohistory*, which in 1955 proclaimed devotion to research on "the documentary history of the culture and movements of primitive peoples, with special emphasis on the American Indian." In "documentary," the journal stated what it privileged as evidence. "Primitive" and "American Indian" narrowed the focus of research to culturally distant people in whom anthropologists were then almost exclusively interested. The agenda remained Wissler's.

For anthropologists and historians alike, the methodology of ethnohistory in those years involved documentary sources to talk about the past of the Miami, the Shawnee, the Paiute, and other societies located mainly in the New World, especially North America. It was amply illustrated in the pages of *Ethnohistory*. Lowie's earlier skepticism about oral history did not die; rather, it resurfaced forty years later when Erminie Wheeler-Voegelin (1954)—one of the founders of the American Society for Ethnohistory and editor of *Ethnohistory* for its first decade—proclaimed that memory ethnographies were not useful for any period before the childhood of informants from whom they were elicited. For many at this time, relevant ethnohistorical materials were mainly documentary.

The emphasis on documentary evidence was also prominent in the second stimulus to affect ethnohistory—arguments before the Indian Claims Commission during the 1950s. The debates, which concerned land claims, provided the context for much of the ethnohistorical research in the United States. The judicial settings in which legal arguments unfolded privileged documents produced by the literate nonnative in historical testimony, rather than oral, indigenous sources. Sources, and ethnohistorians, responded with document-based history.

Most of the proposed definitions of ethnohistory between 1950 and 1980 stressed the wide-ranging use of data obtained in the field, archive, and museum in order to write what John Ewers (1961) called a "thorough, delicately balanced" history of a particular society or group, and Wilcomb E. Washburn, a historian, "history in the round" (1961). For historian James Axtell (1981), the goal was "to gain knowledge of the nature and cause of change in a culture." From history came "cautious accuracy" and from anthropology "imaginative theorization," as Washburn said, as well as culture "defined by ethnological concepts and categories," in Axtell's words. Ideally, these methodological skills and intellectual forces fused in the ethnohistorian. Nancy O. Lurie (1961) commented that the ethnohistorian must take proper precautions against the antiquarian virus (to which historians were thought to be particularly prone) and seek "valid culture and social generalizations, 'laws' if you will" (presumably the forte of anthropologists).

In what became an influential and lasting definition, William C. Sturtevant (1966) defined ethnohistory as the study of "the history of the peoples normally studied by anthropologists." For Sturtevant and many others, conventional anthropology focused mainly on remote, exotic people and presumed that explanation required theory, typology, and generalization; conventional history dealt primarily with nonexotic Western people and unique or particular events, and favored narrative over explicit generalization.

Throughout the years, there has been relatively little disagreement over what are the principal products of ethnohistory, and only minor debate over what labels to assign them. One major product is "historical ethnography," which is a timeless or synchronic reconstruction of a culture or society at some past time. A second type has been most often called "folk history," which amounts to historiography as conceptualized by people in a particular, usually nonliterate, society. A third, "specific history," amounts to a diachronic historical study of a specific society or ethnic group written either from the earliest or most recent moment in time (known as a "downstream" direction), or by relying heavily on projecting and writing from the present to the past in an "upstream" direction—the so-called direct historical method. When conceptualized "downstream," specific history often amounts to traditional narrative history of events in the past of a tribe or other ethnic group (Krech 1991).

THE LABEL OF ETHNOHISTORY: SOME PROBLEMS

Today, historical ethnographies, specific histories, and folk histories continue to appear, although their authors may call them by other names. The debate over what to label different ethnohistorical products, however, is of less consequence than whether all should be considered ethnohistory. Definitions of ethnohistory still preoccupy ethnohistorians. Some who write ethnohistory consider as "insufficient, if not faulty" ethnohistory as "the reconstruction of the history of a people who previously had no written history." For them, in contrast, as Edward Schieffelin and Deborah Gewertz (1985) have argued, that ethnohistory "must fundamentally take into account the people's own sense of how events are constituted, and their ways of culturally constructing the past." Their appeal is for folk history as the only type of ethnohistory.

This exclusionary position can be explained in part as a result of problems spawned by the changing relationship between anthropology and history. One problem is in Sturtevant's definition; what was conventional in both disciplines in 1960 is no longer conventional today, when anthropologists are as likely to study urban Westerners as people earlier percieved as remote and exotic, and when historians increasingly work on history from the bottom up or history from below—what Bernard S. Cohn called "protological history." Thus, an anthropologist whose interests are historical may find himself or herself writing the history of an urban Western community, and a historian may write about people whose cultures and societies had once been the exclusive focus of anthropologists. The difficulty is evident: Are both writing ethnohistory?

A related problem stems from the lack of consistency in applying the label ethnohistory. This dilemma is less apparent on a particular continent, where conventions about what to call the method and product of historical research are more likely to be shared, than between continents, where they are not and where essentially the same kind of historical study receives different names. What is ethnohistory in North America is social or cultural history, ethno-ethnohistory, or just plain history somewhere else. For example, a historical study readily called ethnohistory in North America would seldom be labeled ethnohistory in Africa. That may be due to the influence of Jan Vansina (1960), an Africanist and oral historian, who stated that "history in illiterate societies is not different from the pursuit of the past in literate ones," and that "there is therefore no need to coin a special term, such as ethnohistory, just for this reason." If one is persuaded by Vansina, then one is tempted to ask, in case after case, on continent after continent, why records, materials, data, and processes that may be called ethnohistorical are not simply labeled historical.

In one sense, this problem is exacerbated by a growing awareness that ethnohistory, unlike other "hyphenated" histories, may in practice exclude certain types of people and societies. There are many hyphenated histories, including demographic, economic, labor, social, family, political, diplomatic, urban, cultural, intellectual, psycho-, quantitative, and oral; or the history of ideas, of science, of women, of mentalities. Most qualifiers refer to a cultural or social abstraction; some indicate a method. In theory, they do not exclude certain kinds of societies—one can do quantitative, oral, family, or cultural history anywhere. But can one say the same for ethnohistory?

To answer this question one must understand what is meant by the prefix "ethno-" in ethnohistory. As in ethnography, ethnology, ethnic group, its derivation is from *ethnos* (nation, in Greek). An ethnic group today is usually thought of as a distinctive people who may or may not form a nation. Thus, ethnohistory applies in theory to the history of any ethnos or ethnic group, but there has always been a problem. In classical Greek, *ethnos* became a term for tribal people, for barbarians, a term for the Other. These features were retained in English forms like ethnic, which came to mean (in the adjectival form) of or relating to a non-Christian or non-Jewish "heathen" people. In ethnohistory today ethno- has not shaken its tribal or pagan referent. Tribal groups have ethnohistory, "minority" groups may have it, but never or rarely do the majority groups. So, in practice, ethnohistory is exclusionary (Krech 1991).

This did not go unnoticed by ethnohistorians, but it was not until the 1960s that the full implications of restricting ethnohistory to certain types of societies, which has marked scholarship since Wessler's day, came in for scathing critique. In that decade Henri Brunschwig (1965) likened ethnohistory to a weed and stated flatly that there were no "people without history." Brunschwig, who not surprisingly approved of Vansina's stand that the history of literate and nonliterate societies was not so different to demand history and ethnohistory respectively, posed the unsettling question, "Is it then 'people without written

history' that is meant by 'people without history,' and will Blacks, wounded by this title, be relieved to be named people with ethnohistory?" Hubert Deschamps (1968) answered by proposing that reserving ethnohistory for people considered "primitive" would be "resented as an unjust discrimination by Africans." In recent years others have raised similar questions (Krech 1991).

ETHNOHISTORY OR ANTHROPOLOGICAL HISTORY?

The dilemma is genuine. Why apply a special name to the history of some but not all ethnic groups? Why restrict it especially to those whose cultural distance from the typical historian has always been the greatest? In North America, some ethnohistorians confine ethnohistory to American Indians. Others extend it to other so-called minorities. Only a few would use it equally for "dominant" ethnic groups. As a rule, Westerners, especially those who are urban-dwelling or who belong to "majority" groups, possess history, not ethnohistory. Restricting ethnohistory to particular groups is invidious; the charge of unfairly ghettoizing people with ethnohistory comes easily. This is a serious flaw.

Another problem is that much self-described ethnohistory is old-fashioned chronological narrative history. The term "ethno-" applies to it only in that it is of the Cherokee or some other ethnos in which anthropologists traditionally had stated vested interests. Without question, the most common genre is the history of a specific society or group: a historical narrative that chronicles (part of) a tribe or nation's past. It usually places particular emphasis on interethnic, particularly indigenous-European relations.

At the same time, the number of historians incorporating anthropology into their histories and the number of anthropologists writing history of some sort have exploded, and define major trends in both disciplines. Literally hundreds of works have appeared (Krech 1991). Either a new definition of ethnohistory or a new label to replace ethnohistory is needed.

At the heart of ethnohistory, today no less than in the past, is the combination of method and theory current in history and anthropology, and the focus on history or historiography in or of some ethnic group. The former—the combination of method and theory of both disciplines—should be the least problematic part of this statement. For many, the ethno- prefix in ethnohistory has become synonymous with anthropological. There has been a tendency to argue, as Robert Carmack (1972) has, that ethnohistory's aims "are those of cultural anthropology in general, and have to do with theories of culture." It is, however, disciplinary chauvinism to insist that theory in ethnohistory has always been or should be drawn solely from anthropology, since history has an equal claim on Karl Marx, Max Weber, and other social theorists and their descendants. Strictly speaking, especially by today's standards, theory in both disciplines is not likely to derive from either, but from semiotic, structuralism, Marxism, linguistics, sociology, cultural studies, literary criticism, political economy, and world-system theory, among other sources.

If the combination of anthropological and historical methodology is not problematic, the second part of the definition of ethnohistory is: the focus on history or historiography in or of some ethnic group. Here is the heart of the problem with the label ethnohistory, the problem that stems from the exclusion of certain ethnic groups from ethnohistory in practice. One solution is for ethnohistory to be applied to all ethnic groups, regardless of their perceived status in nation-states. A second and perhaps preferable solution is to abolish the label ethnohistory altogether and call the permutations of anthropological and historical method and theory when applied to history of, or historiography in, an ethnic group something else. "Anthrohistory" might appeal to some, but there is no need for neologisms. Either "anthropological history" or "historical anthropology" would suffice; and in contrast to the label ethnohistory, neither is susceptible to stigmatization. Which discipline is nominal and which dependent may be a matter of taste, but anthropological history, like ethnohistory, keeps the focus on the historical study undertaken. If the traditional boundaries of ethnos disappear as the critical criterion, then it should be a fairly straightforward matter to decide that an anthropological analysis is also historical or a historical one is also anthropological.

ANTHROPOLOGICAL HISTORY TODAY

Anthropological historians, thus, distinguish themselves by combining method and theory in the two disciplines and by their focus on the history of, or historiography in, some ethnic group. If this is accepted, then it would seem contrary to agree that anthropological history should be reserved for a cognate of other ethnoterms such as "ethnobotany" or "ethnoscience,"

as some argue ethnohistory should. But while there is no reason to be so exclusionary, the emphasis on indigenous conceptions of history is longstanding and an important part of anthropological history. In the mid-1960s Sturtevant spoke of ethnohistory as the perceptions of a society's past entertained by its members, not by anyone else. Others called this "folk history." Here, ethnohistory is regarded as cognate with ethnoscience, ethnobotany, and ethnozoology, among other terms. Perhaps because nobody paid much attention, Raymond D. Fogelson (1989), who has championed taking seriously the historically and culturally constructed worlds of Cherokees and other native North Americans, "in exasperation" coined "ethno-ethnohistory."

Since 1980 the interest in ethno-ethnohistory or folk history as a type of anthropological history has escalated, with several scholars, in addition to Fogelson, qualifying as pioneers in this shift. Richard Price (1983) is one. His analysis of the presentist, fragmented, perspectival, guarded, dangerous historical thought of the Saramaka is remarkably sensitive from a number of standpoints, not least of which is ethical. Another pioneer is Marshall D. Sahlins, whose emphasis on the conflicting interests and interpretations brought to particular structures of conjunctures (like the death of Captain Cook), whose forceful analysis of the cultural structure of Polynesian societies, and whose view that cultural structure is either open or closed to history and that each orders the other, have prompted much discussion.

An increasing number of scholars interested in the history of small-scale societies agree on the importance of ethno-ethnohistory as one type of anthropological history. They are linked more broadly to those for whom culture, ideationally conceptualized as symbolic system or text, or in some manner structured, holds center stage in historical analysis. A number of anthropological historians are concerned explicitly with reading metaphor, metonym, and other tropes in historical texts, with the "logics" of texts. Their interest is in discovering meaning in the actions and expressions of people who encountered each other on beaches and whose nncultures clashed. They have questions about the historicity, cultural structure, and perspectival nature of history, myth, and other categories.

Many anthropological historians have recently investigated the historical thoughts of a variety of indigenous peoples, both in and outside the West, as well as conceptions of time, inventions of culture, the cultural specificity of ways of "knowing" or "making history." They concern themselves with cultural and historical constructions of presentist histories, with how to capture an "authentic" native voice in texts that reflect ambivalent colonial discourses, and related issues. They debate, especially over authenticity and what constitutes history. The reflexive quality of much recent anthropological history is striking. To decipher historical thought, one must appreciate how history is produced. Anthropologists like Edward M. Bruner (1986) pay attention to narratives that have dominated whole eras to effectively structure the telling of American Indian history. Historians like Greg Dening (1988) caution us to understand how history "is both a metaphor of the past and a metonym of the present." Others argue for awareness of the perspectival and contested nature of histories, or of the variety of inventions of traditions (Hobsbawm and Ranger 1992). Today more than ever before, there is a greater concern for how the past is perceived: as foreign or structurally familiar terrain, forever behind or always to be reencountered, or in some other way.

The specific history or historical narrative—the most common form of anthropological history—is often driven by data rather than by explicit theory. It relies more often than not on documents, instead of on oral testimony; it assumes that a descriptive chronological narrative is awaiting "release" from the archives; and it is sensitive to native culture, not perspective. It does not offer a people's historiography, but does offer one version of their history. Some narratives soar as sensitive explorations of culture and motivations but simultaneously eschew theory as intrusive (Peires 1989). The best may not engage pretentiously with theory but is marked by strong narrative style and careful weighing and interpretation of evidence. James H. Merrell's (1989) sensitive exploration of the convergence of Catawba and white culture and society and Axtell's (1986) elegant essays and sustained inquiry into what he has called contests of cultures are examples.

Theory drives the specific history and other forms of anthropological history. Many anthropologists and historians are principally interested in the historical analysis of—to borrow Eric R. Wolf's metaphor—the fields of force or social and cultural processes linking societies to one another in an interconnected political economy, processes ultimately world-historical or world-systematic in scope. They are concerned with what Wolf (1982) calls "a manifold of social and cultural processes at work," or the "fields of force" and "chains of causation and consequence" that have affected societies in the past and continue to today. Their language reveals a collective preoccupation with ecology, demography, mercantilism, market economy, world-system, political economy, control of productive resources, internal colonialism, modes and relations of production, commoditization, hegemony, dependency, underdevelopment, articulation with global capitalism or the state, dialectical and colonial relations. The works which explore these issues tend to emphasize economy, politics, demography, and ecology; to be materialist, positivist, and implicitly or explicitly comparative; and to trace intellectual heritage ultimately from Marx, through critical engagement with a range of thinkers. Some are concerned mainly with demographic process, ecology, materialism, economic exchange, and cultural adaptation—the analysis, for example, of an alpine community as self-sufficient and in ecological equilibrium until certain nutritional changes both altered demography and effected links to the outside (Netting 1981); or the comparative analysis of the impact on traditional Native American economies of market economies linked to Europe, and the subsequent development of dependency in indigenous societies (White 1983); or the analysis of fundamental ecological transformations in colonial New England and their larger (European) economic and political context (Cronon 1983).

The "force-fields" exhaustively explored by Wolf and others revealingly explicate technoeconomic change, political economy, and political and economic differentiations as a function of capitalist development. As others have pointed out, however, this scheme suffers in part from paying insufficient attention to agency and oppositions to colonial relationships. Relations between center and periphery were not unidirectional; history does not simply involve recounting the impact of the West on the non-West, the center on the periphery, the metropolis on the satellite.

Anthropological historians vary in their emphasis placed on local culture mediating or structuring outside forces, or on human agency overriding systemic power; they differ in the degree to which these are read into various neo-Marxian agendas. Some consciously seek to analyze both the impact of the world-system on a society or region, as well as agency and counterhegemonic processes, and make no assumptions about the outcome of incorporation into capitalist systems. The degree to which theory is engaged directly remains a matter of disciplinary preference; anthropologists tend toward a self-consciously comparative and explicit in-text engagement, while historians tend to privilege narrative and burden endnotes with theoretical remarks. But these are tendencies to which there are increasing exceptions.

To write histories of the non-West—not histories of the West's impact on the non-West—historians and anthropologists, taking cues from P. Bourdieu, M. Foucault, A. Giddens, E. P. Thompson, R. Williams, and others, have put indigenous peoples as active agents into their histories. Thus, the expansion of a capitalist market's determinative influences are mediated and affected by indigenous peoples acting creatively and often in a resistant manner in the unfolding dialectic between world-systemic forces must be considered, or that peasants have resisted coercion and hegemony whose origin can be traced to external capital relations. In some hands, these emphases can be fairly minor, and the world-system continues to be the principal focus. In others (e.g., studies of indentured laborers in Sumatra, coffee planters in Brazil, or villagers in Newfoundland or early modern Germany), a clear weight is placed on comprehending cultural values together with external relations, discourses of power and relations of power with capitalist development, and actions and motivations of resisters or revolutionaries with structures of colonialism. Other works richly contextualize the structural connections between market economic forces and class formation, differentially mediated by resistance; emphasize the internal differentiations of peasantry; explore the systems of relations within which peasant intellectuals and others operate and engage in political discourses; or focus on specific transformations in gender ideologies in the carrying articulations between local cultural and global forces. There are clear links to the earlier-mentioned work by Sahlins, but also to those poetics of oppressive history and subtleties of culturally encoded collective consciousness. In her most comprehensive work, Jean Comaroff (1985) insists upon viewing the Tshidi of South Africa as "determined yet determining to their own history; as human beings who, in their everyday production of goods and meanings, acquiesce yet protest, reproduce yet seek to transform their predicament." Krech (1991) provides further discussion of these and related points.

PAST AND FUTURE

For the first half of the twentieth century, ethnohistory, the history of small-scale ethnic groups whose history had hitherto been ignored by historians and anthropologists, filled the gap between anthropology and history. The history of these societies—ignored by historians because of their scale, location, and ethnicity, and by anthropologists because history was anathema to ethnography and science which valorized anthropology—was made visible by ethnohistory. Today, the label of ethnohistory may be suspect because ethnos itself is doubtful, but not its methodology. When we use the term anthropological history, the doubts disappear. It involves, as it has always to its most open adherents, the combination of method and theory current in history and anthropology, and the focus on history or historiography in or of some ethnic group. There is no reason to think that it will not flourish.

SHEPARD KRECH III

AXTELL, JAMES. *The European and the Indian: Essays in the Ethnohistory of Colonial North America.* Oxford: Oxford University Press, 1981.
———. *The Invasion Within: The Contest of Cultures in Colonial North America.* Oxford: Oxford University Press, 1986.
BRUNER, EDWARD M. "Ethnography as Narrative." In *The Anthropology of Experience,* edited by Victor Turner and Edward M. Brunner. Urbana: University of Illinois Press, 1986.
BRUNSCHWIG, HENRI. "Un faux problème: l'ethno-histoire." *Annales: Economies, Sociétés, Civilisations* 20 (1965): 291–300.
CARMACK, ROBERT. "Ethnohistory: A Review of Its Development, Definitions, Methods, and Aims." *Annual Review of Anthropology* 1 (1972): 227–246.
COHN, BERNARD S. *An Anthropologist Among the Historians and Other Essays.* Delhi: Oxford University Press, 1991.
COMAROFF, JEAN. *Body of Power, Spirit of Resistance: The Culture and History of A South African People.* Chicago: University of Chicago Press, 1985.
CRONON, WILLIAM. *Changes in the Land: Indians, Colonists, and the Ecology of New England.* New York: Hill and Wang, 1983.
DENING, GREG. *History's Anthropology: The Death of William Gooch.* New York: University Press of America, 1988.

DESCHAMPS, HUBERT. "Histoire et ethnologie: l'ethnohistoire." In *Ethnologie Generale,* edited by J. Poirier. Paris: Gallimard, 1968.

EVANS-PRITCHARD, E. E. "Anthropology and History." In *Social Anthropology and Other Essays.* New York: Free Press, 1962.

EWERS, JOHN. "Symposium on the Concept of Ethnohistory: Comment." *Ethnohistory* 8 (1961): 262–270.

FOGELSON, RAYMOND D. "The Ethnohistory of Events and Nonevents." *Ethnohistory* 36 (1989): 133–147.

HOBSBAWM, ERIC J., and TERENCE RANGER, eds. *The Invention of Tradition.* Cambridge: Cambridge University Press, 1992.

KRECH, SHEPARD, III.. "The State of Ethnohistory." *Annual Review of Anthropology* 20 (1991): 345–375.

KROEBER, ALFRED L. "History and Science in Anthropology." *American Anthropologist* 37 (1935): 539–569.

LOWIE, ROBERT H. "Oral Tradition and History." *American Anthropologist* 17 (1915): 597–599.

LURIE, NANCY O. "Ethnohistory: An Ethnological Point of View." *Ethnohistory* 8 (1961): 78–92.

MERRELL, JAMES H. *The Indians' New World: Catawbas and Their Neighbors from European Contact Through the Era of Removal.* Chapel Hill: University of North Carolina Press, 1989.

NETTING, ROBERT M. *Balancing on an Alp: Ecological Change and Continuity in a Swiss Mountain Community.* Cambridge: Cambridge University Press, 1981.

PEIRES, J. B. *The Dead Will Arise: Nongqawuse and the Great Xhosa Cattle-Killing Movement of 1856–1857.* Bloomington: Indiana University Press, 1989.

PRICE, RICHARD. *First-Time: The Historical Vision of an Afro-American People.* Baltimore: Johns Hopkins University Press, 1983.

RADCLIFFE-BROWN, A. R. *Method in Social Anthropology.* Chicago: University of Chicago Press, 1958.

SAHLINS, MARSHALL D. *Islands of History.* Chicago: University of Chicago Press, 1987.

SCHIEFFLIN, EDWARD, and DEBORAH GEWERTZ. "Introduction." In *History and Ethnohistory in Papua New Guinea,* edited Deborah Gewertz and Edward Schiefflin. Sydney: University of Sydney, 1985.

STURTEVANT, WILLIAM C. "Anthropology, History, and Ethnohistory." *Ethnohistory* 13 (1966): 1–51.

VANSINA, JAN. "Recording the Oral History of the Bakuba: I. Methods." *Journal of African History* 1 (1960): 43–53.

WASHBURN, WILCOMB E. "Ethnohistory: History in the Round." *Ethnohistory* 8 (1961): 31–48.

WHEELER-VOEGELIN, ERMINIE. "An Ethnohistorian's Viewpoint." *Ethnohistory* 1 (1954): 166–171.

WHITE, RICHARD. *The Roots of Dependency: Subsistence, Environment, and Social Change among the Choctaws, Pawnees, and the Navajos.* Lincoln: University of Nebraska Press, 1983.

WOLF, ERIC R. *Europe and the People Without History.* Berkeley: University of California Press, 1982.

ETHNOLOGY

Ethnology is the study of culture. Combining the Greek *ethnos*, race or people, and *logia*, science or theory, ethnology translates literally as "theory of peoples." The "theory" referred to is the effort to explain similarities and differences among the world's cultures, that is, ethnology is intrinsically comparative and explanatory. As an aspect of anthropological endeavor, ethnology is often distinguished from ethnography—the description of societies and cultures—but they are two sides of the same coin. Ethnologists require valid ethnographic descriptions, based on expert field research, if they are to develop explanations and evaluate them, and ethnographers require a knowledge of ethnology if their descriptions are to be of any value to the community of scholars.

HISTORICAL NOTES

Ethnology has different meanings in different countries where anthropology has undergone local elaboration. Often, its meaning is restricted to the distribution in time and space of specific customs, such as rituals and ceremonies, folktales, art styles, crafts, and a wide range of folk beliefs and practices that characterize the "little traditions" (Redfield 1960) of the less formally educated or less powerful sectors of society. Such beliefs and practices are frequently overlooked in histories that emphasize learned, literate traditions found in ruling houses, academies, temples, colonial administrations, and other elite institutions. In this sense, ethnology might be viewed as a branch of history specially concerned with documenting the often-disparaged ("pagan," "uncivilized," "naive") arts, beliefs, and practices of hinterlands and small communities.

In some countries, there is a political aspect to this limitation on the scope of ethnology. Under some political regimes, the comparative, cultural relativist, and explanatory strengths of ethnology are viewed as politically dangerous. This is appropriate, since contemporary ethnology is capable of challenging orthodoxies and undermining claims of one group to cultural superiority over another. In such settings, the ethnologist must be cautious of scholarly activities that could be deemed punishable as sacrilege or treason.

Ethnology as culture history, important to modern anthropology from the outset, originated the first powerful theoretical paradigm in ethnology—diffusion. R. H. Lowie (1937), for example, made it the core of his definition of culture: "By culture we understand the sum total of what an individual acquires from his society—those beliefs, customs, artistic norms, food-habits, and crafts which come to him not by his own creative activity but as a legacy from the past, conveyed by formal or informal education."

Whether by migration and displacement or by borrowing across cultural boundaries, culture traits have clearly spread widely in the past, just as they do today. They have origins and histories. Patterns of cultural similarity and difference in the world today can be better understood by tracing flows of migration and borrowing that began centuries, and in some cases millennia, ago. That such histories can provide illuminating explanations of cultural distributions may be the most widespread idea in modern ethnology.

Voget (1975) has shown that in the early twentieth century this approach, which he calls "culture historicism," laid the foundation for modern ethnology. Diffusionists ranged from those who believed that all world civilizations originated in Pharaonic Egypt, such as E. G. Smith and W. J. Perry in England, to "culture tradition" (Kulturkreis) theorists like Friedrich Ratzel, Leo Frobenius, and Fritz Graebner in Germany who sought less global, more regional culture traditions, such as the postulated Malayo-Nigritian tradition linking East Africa to Southeast Asia. Under Franz Boas in the United States, the search for cultural traditions became even more localized, with strong empirical skepticism limiting speculative historical reconstructions.

Voget (1975) identifies four major contributions of the diffusionists to modern ethnology: entrenchment of fieldwork as the essential means of data collection; establishment of the concept of culture as

the central concern of ethnology; documentation of a "geography of culture" that remains useful to this day; and insights into culture process, such as the relation between culture and environmental adaptation, or the invention and dissemination of culture traits.

As ethnological theory, diffusion quickly came up against several criticisms. One was that social and cultural traits have an intrinsic patterning that is not the simple result of diffusion but must be understood in its own right. In England, the development of the idea that society is an integrated whole—roughly analogous to the functional integration of organs in a living body—led A. R. Radcliffe-Brown (1923) to argue for a functionalist social anthropology, which he took to be entirely distinct from ethnology. As theory, social anthropology accounts for the existence of social traits in terms of their place in, or functional relation to, the social whole. In a pastoral society, for example, the trait of patriliny can be understood only in the context of its relationship to herd management, marriage exchanges, debt-credit relations, raiding, domestic authority, political hierarchy, and other features of society. Such a context-specific, functionalist explanation may be completely nonhistorical, in the sense that a trait or feature of society can be understood without reference to where it came from.

In the United States, a different line of thinking led to a similar conception of culture as pattern (Benedict 1934) or configuration (Kroeber 1944). Focusing on culture as a belief system, rather than on society as a system of roles and statuses, this theoretical approach viewed culture as less like an organism than a work of art—a mosaic whose elements exist in a relational matrix expressive of a local aesthetic or set of values. In this theory, diffusion plays the role of supplying many of the elements of which any culture is composed, but only in the sense of a cafeteria of possibilities, from which elements are selected, reshaped, and patterned according to cultural standards of appropriateness. Robert Redfield's (1941) definition of culture as "an organization of conventional understandings" nicely summarizes this approach.

In the United States, however, this subordination of diffusion to pattern was not seen as a departure from ethnology. Rather, this and other theoretical approaches, including British social anthropology, were eclectically brought under the umbrella of ethnology, as in George P. Murdock's editorial in the first issue of the journal *Ethnology* (1962): "The title of our journal is a word of long and respected standing in the sciences that deal with man, and in most countries it connotes quite accurately the field in which we shall specialize. *Ethnology* will encompass anything that Americans class as cultural anthropology, and that the British imply by social anthropology, as well as whatever they and anthropologists of other nationalities understand by the title itself. . . . Our interest in ethnography will extend from simpler societies, through folk and peasant cultures, to historical and contemporary civilizations. . . . We shall define ethnology in the broadest sense to embrace, for example, technology, pre-industrial economics, primitive or comparative art and religion, pre-scientific medicine and psychotherapy, social and political organization, value systems, culture and personality, and culture change." Although Murdock no doubt laid down a claim to a large territory in an effort to enhance the broad appeal of his new journal, he nonetheless fairly characterized the inclusive scope of the term "ethnology" as it is used in the United States. Indeed, his last sentence lists a range of topics that were frequent chapter headings for ethnographies published throughout the world during much of the twentieth century.

A further criticism of diffusion is that it gives too great a role to individual creativity and historical accident. A feature of culture could be the brainstorm of an exceptional individual, a random discovery, an accidental borrowing from a contiguous culture—it need have no further rationale for its existence or prevalence. This applies equally to American configurationists and to British social anthropologists insofar as what matters does not seem to be which features a culture or society possesses so much as their integration into a pattern or system.

By contrast, many related theories explain the existence of cultural beliefs and practices by reference to their purpose in a framework of human needs. Bronislaw Malinowski (1939) developed a version of functionalism quite distinct from Radcliffe-Brown's, finding function not in the relations of elements in a system, but in the ways that beliefs and practices met basic human needs, of which he provided a detailed list. Various branches of ecological anthropology (Netting 1986) and cultural materialism (Harris 1979; Johnson and Earle 1987) likewise found

the explanation of cultural traits in their adaptive significance, and a predominant paradigm in the culture-and-personality (Whiting and Whiting 1975) school saw culturally specific personality traits as the outcome of a process of adaptive socialization that produced adults who would be prepared to do the things needed for the survival of their families and communities.

Such theories root cultural process in the satisfaction of human needs, and hence lay a biological basis for culture. Theories of culture may also be mentioned that relate cultural patterns to the structure of the brain or the mind (Levi-Strauss 1969), because that structure, whether linked to language or to other modes of information processing, is presumably laid down in human DNA. Insofar as cultural patterns, such as binary oppositions in mythology or kinship systems, can be traced back to such "cognitive imperatives" (D'Aquili 1972), a biological basis for aspects of culture is also being sought.

Further developments in ethnology expanded quite naturally out of the research program begun by the diffusionists. Cross-cultural research originated in the efforts of ethnologists to organize the collection of ethnographic data by developing standardized trait lists, or "cultural element" lists (Driver and Kroeber 1932). By using these lists to collect similar data on many cultures, ethnologists had an increasingly comparable set of cross-cultural data to work with. Some early diffusionists foresaw a day when enough good ethnographic data would be collected that theory-driven scientific exploration would become possible (Boas 1988). Cross-cultural research fulfilled that expectation, eventually using careful hypothesis-construction, representative sampling, and measurement of variables to test thousands of hypotheses and discover a host of theoretically important cross-cultural regularities.

Another line of ethnological theory grew out of the diffusionists' emphasis on cultural descriptions that faithfully represent the "native's eye view" (Lowie 1937). The tendency of early reporters to describe other cultures in blatantly ethnocentric terms was repudiated in favor of careful studies of their folk categories and theories. The theoretical approach of ethnoscience (Tyler 1969) formalized this goal by developing research methods, based on comparative linguistics, for eliciting native "words for things" and their frameworks of meaning. The goal of these field methods and subsequent data analyses was to reduce as far as possible any impact the fieldworker might have in distorting the data away from a faithful representation of the native's cultural world.

A further development from the same seed of cultural relativism and respect for the native's eye view, although strongly opposed to the scientific commitments of ethnoscience, has been the application of critical theory (Marcus and Fischer 1986) to ethnology. From the beginnings of modern ethnology, it has been apparent that respect for other cultures implies abandoning the stance that the ethnologist's own culture is superior or privileged over any other culture. What would it mean, however, to take this implication seriously? We would have to admit that all truth is culturally constructed and therefore relative. Every ethnographic description is anchored in the cultural time and space—not to mention the individual idiosyncrasy—of the ethnographer. Because in the great majority of cases ethnographers come from the well-educated and comparatively affluent precincts of the world elite, their ethnographic descriptions of rural and urban poor people are also tainted by class bias. The ethnologist must not accept these data uncritically, but rather unmask the biases—of gender, class, and ethnicity, among others—that have intrinsically and unavoidably shaped those data.

CONTROVERSIES

Ethnology has from the beginning been characterized by deep, intractable controversies. No single internally consistent theory unifies the field. Although knowledge of world cultures has grown vastly in the twentieth century, and understanding of cultural similarities and differences has certainly progressed, the enthusiasm for debate about the larger significance of this knowledge and understanding continues undiminished. The issues being debated also continue to shift according to the fashions of the moment, but for reasons that may or may not derive from the culture of Euro-American scholarship, new debates are often merely refurbished versions of ancient oppositions that seem to resist every effort at resolution. Insofar as participants fail to recognize that current debates have timeless philosophical roots, they tend to craft their arguments parochially, asserting narrow solutions and rejecting alternative solutions out of hand.

To see this in action one can begin with perhaps the most fundamental such opposition, that between nature and culture. It is known that through cultural transmission human beings have added a revolutionary process to that of biogenetic transmission of information encoded in DNA. The debate becomes polarized over whether culture is a handmaiden of human biology, a kind of complex prosthetic, to use Sigmund Freud's (1932) metaphor, that extends the human mastery of nature to meet needs for food, reproduction, and defense of territory; or whether culture is something not only qualitatively new on the scene but utterly independent of biology, indeed liberating human beings from the shackles of instinct and animal needs.

Theorists who see human society and culture as part of a toolkit underlying human adaptive success tend to criticize opposition theorists for depicting culture as a realm of freedom, creativity, and irrational flights of fancy—as in art, poetics, mythology, and cosmology—while ignoring those domains where the real work of culture, like provisioning food, reproducing species, and defeating enemies, is done. Indeed, they insist that art and mythology often themselves play adaptive roles.

By contrast, theorists who see culture as liberated from biological necessity will criticize the opposition for biological reductionism, the effort to explain culture as an outcome of processes operating at a lower, biological level of nature. They see this as a misguided effort to locate a sphere of biological processes independent of the meaning people assign to their biology and to all so-called material aspects of their world, a world that can only exist for humans as an interpreted space.

A vast portion of ethnological debate clearly owes its energy to the nature-culture dialectic. Where one theorist sees economic life being driven by scarcity of need-filling resources, the other sees scarcity as a matter of cultural definition of appropriate standards of consumption. Where one sees a health system as an adaptive effort to cope with biological suffering, another sees a moral structure defining individuals' positions in a social and spiritual universe. Where one sees patriliny as a means for regulating access to life-sustaining land and mating opportunities, another sees a mythical charter offering meaning and order in place of insignificance and chaos.

The second powerful generator of debates in ethnology concerns the relation between the individual and the community. On the one hand, we have the image of the individual as a center of will and responsibility, actively shaping the world according to a personal agenda, and, on the other hand, the image of the individual as inseparable from a sustaining matrix of relationships. The former emphasizes individual freedom, the latter emphasizes community definition of the individual. The debate is often cast in terms of the contrast between Western individualism and the social embedment of the individual reputedly found in most of the rest of the world.

Theorists of the individual pole identify agency as the central concern, focusing on what individuals want and how they make rational choices, decisions, and strategies to satisfy those wants. They criticize the opposition for reifying the supraindividual level, arguing that concepts like community, society, and culture (Kroeber 1917) cannot be shown to exist apart from the minds and activities of individuals. They describe the individual's environment, whether natural, social, or cultural, as a context, or set of constraints, that the individual takes into account in making choices. Here, individual is figure and context is ground.

Theorists of the community pole reverse polarity, making context figure, arguing that it is the autonomous individual who cannot be shown to exist apart from a defining nexus of social relations and cultural commitments. Individual freedom of action is an illusion. Individuals cannot choose beliefs or courses of social action apart from the wishes of their families and communities, not to mention the coercive authority of cultural conventions and the larger political society.

The identification of society as a discrete level of analysis in British social anthropology, and of culture in American ethnology, reflects the community pole of the individual-community dialectic. Theoretical debates attempting to validate process, choice, and agency—generally in opposition to structure—reflect the individual pole. Debates arise, for example, over whether individuals must marry and work where their families tell them to or are able to construct their own lives through personal choices; or over whether individuals are rational decision-makers or followers of scripts provided for them by their cultural community; or, as suggested, over whether individualism is a Western cultural artifact, not found in the family-centered and socially centered cultures of Asia and elsewhere, or is in fact a human universal.

A third generator of debates in ethnology is, for want of a better label, the science-humanism dialectic. Although it is common in modern academic institutions to draw a sharp bureaucratic division between the sciences and the humanities, ethnology (in the broadest sense) has not migrated to one or the other of these two great camps, but remains in both, sometimes in a fence-sitting and conciliatory fashion, sometimes harshly split internally.

Ethnologists on the science side view scientific method as a path to a superior form of knowledge whose peculiar strength derives from adherence to clearly defined procedures accepted by the scientific community. Although formal derivation of hypotheses and explicit methods of measurement are important, perhaps the most crucial emphasis is on hypothesis testing, the process of deciding whether or not propositions about the shape of the world are supported by evidence. By following the rules, scientists aim to build a store of knowledge that is cumulative (cannot be shown to be wrong by future research) and effective (can lead to successful efforts to change the world by designing interventions such as new technologies or public policies). Such knowledge is held to be preferable to knowledge based on opinion, belief, or faith.

The humanistic side is less easy to define, but its emphasis is on meaning and understanding. It accepts that meaning, and therefore understanding, are situated in cultural contexts that vary by time and place and community, and ultimately reside in deeply personal and often idiosyncratic interpretations of the world. Pathways to meaning are diverse and always open to challenge. Opinion, belief, and faith are all potentially valuable aspects of understanding. Knowledge is not necessarily accumulated in this process: Current knowledge may be less profound than that held by great thinkers of ancient times. Scientists delude themselves that their knowledge is any greater than that achieved by humanistic means—which include introspection, inspiration, contemplation, and exegesis—and indeed often sacrifice authentic understanding in favor of statistical significance.

Although the two camps are so far apart in ethnology that they often simply ignore each other, many important debates have a strong flavor of science versus humanism. Efforts to explain culture in cause-and-effect terms, such as explaining sociocultural evolution as caused by population growth or technological progress, are strongly linked to the scientific outlook, even where hypothesis testing is not prominent. Critics of such theories often point out that no simple cause, or even short list of causes, can explain something as complex and variable as sociocultural evolution, in effect abandoning causality in favor of detailed, contextualized, many-layered accounts of particular cultures and their own particular histories.

Several general points can be made about the three primary dialectics of nature-culture, individual-community, and science-humanism. First, they identify oppositions that are never resolved by debate or new information: each has a life of its own that extends far beyond ethnology. Second, debates are rarely explicit about the degree to which these dialectical oppositions underlie them; on the contrary, debaters usually mask their participation in such dialectics by a rich array of rhetorical devices and in many cases would view these dialectical oppositions as sophomoric and outmoded issues with no place in modern ethnology. Proponents of each view are liable to be surprised by the inability of their opponents to see the obvious value of their own position. Third, the important debates in ethnology are never just about these dialectical oppositions, but instead uses them to energize debate and clarify differing positions on matters of substantive importance to the further development of ethnological understanding.

A final point concerns the likelihood that these three oppositions are not independent but linked into broad ethnological world views. Certainly, they may be independent. For example, some theorists on the nature side of nature versus culture dialectic argue for individual decision-making as key to cultural adaptation, while others argue for the adaptive functions of community-level processes like ritual systems, thus reproducing the individual versus community dialectic. Elman R. Service (1985), however, has argued that at least in American ethnology, debates have frequently tended to cluster anthropologists into two broad groups that he labels Moiety A and Moiety B. These are summarized in Figure 1.

Such are the divergences between these two moieties that Service (1985) writes, "controversies seem to come down to mutual incomprehension.... Not only do they sometimes talk right past each other, often they are not talking toward one another at all."

Moiety A	Moiety B
Natural Science	Humanities
Determinism	Free-willism (Individualism)
Evolutionism	Relativism
Social Structure	Culture
Generalization	Particularism
Comparative Method	Holism
Environmentalism	Mentalism
Organismic Analogy	Language Analogy

Figure 1. Ethnological Moieties

SHARED UNDERSTANDINGS

That ethnology has survived several generations of disputes and continues as a vital field of knowledge is testimony to a submerged unity of values and assumptions not always evident at the surface where the storms of controversy rage. Foremost among these is respect for cultural diversity. At core is the simple belief that all cultures are the valid expressions of the peoples who participate in them and deserve the respect accorded the right to self-determination of any human community. Although this belief is sometimes severely strained in light of cultural practices—genocide, infanticide, genital mutilation—that an international community may consider abhorrent, it does not break because the basic principle is too important. Too many times in history, someone else's "abhorrent" cultural practices have been singled out by dominant external powers to justify repression. Ethnologists are profoundly suspicious of any use of power to force local communities to abandon deeply held cultural commitments, seeing in it the potential for ethnocide—cultural destruction.

Related to this is a further core assumption of ethnology, that culture is intrinsic to individual identity. No human individual exists apart from a human community, beginning with early family life and extending outward through growth and development, through socialization and enculturation. Inherent in each person's self-structure are knowledge systems, moral judgements, behavioral expectations, and ways of interpreting that, if stripped away (as in brainwashing) leave the individual devastated. Although it may be that individuals continually revise their cultural identities and in that sense reinvent themselves throughout life, this is a process that must remain under individual control. Hence, freedom of cultural affiliation is part of any ethnologist's list of basic human rights.

A third core value of ethnology is holism, the idea that cultural beliefs and practices do not exist as isolated traits or features, but instead as interrelated parts of (more or less) integrated wholes. Insofar as ethnology is a social science, it examines the broad range of activities that economists, geographers, political scientists, and sociologists would divide up between them, not to mention overlapping interests of historians and psychologists. Insofar as it is a humanistic subject, ethnology likewise spans topics that art history, mythology, literary criticism, hermeneutics, philosophy, and religious studies would parcel out separately.

We need not assume an emergent whole greater than the sum of its parts in order to defend ethnological holism. Suffice it to remember that what we call society and culture are lived daily by members of specific communities. Seemingly distant connections, between ecology and religion, say, or politics and aesthetics, are experienced continuously by individuals, who do not compartmentalize religion to the Sabbath or aesthetics to moments of private contemplation. Ethnology, by accepting this lived interconnection of all things cultural, has been able to discover and describe these connections ethnographically.

Another way of describing ethnological holism is, ideally, as an appreciation of the value of diverse theoretical and methodological approaches to the study of culture. Although, in practice, ethnology is rent by debates exposing disagreements so profound that virtually no real dialogue takes place, the ideal of tolerance of different viewpoints—a variant, in fact, of tolerance of cultural differences—is embraced by most ethnologists and helps keep the field from flying completely asunder.

Central to ethnology is the idea that culture makes sense, that cultural similarities and differences can be explained. The starting point for such explanations is always cross-cultural comparison. The very idea of cultural similarities and differences implies at least two cultures (often, implicitly, the author's own and some other), or else "similar" and "different" would have no referents.

All the controversies reviewed have been played out on a field where it was assumed that explaining culture matters, which amounts in effect to saying that culture is important, not trivial or ephemeral, which follows from the positive values of respect for cultural diversity and the right of the individual to cultural affiliation. But the importance of ethnology also reflects a darker reality. Repeatedly throughout history, as in the present, the fault lines along which warfare and mass cruelty break out have been cultural. It would be naive to assume that such devastating cleavages are a thing of the past, or linger only in pockets of ignorance in an increasingly enlightened world. It is far more likely that ethnic boundaries will continue to be the places where the social fabric tears under stress. Ethnology, by documenting and explaining cultural diversity, is one of the few tools we have to help us anticipate ethnic conflict, minimize its impact, and repair multicultural tolerance and respect when they have been damaged.

ALLEN JOHNSON

SEE ALSO: Critical Anthropology; Cross-Cultural Research; Cultural Materialism; Diffusion; Ethnography

BENEDICT, RUTH. *Patterns of Culture.* New York: Houghton Mifflin, 1934.

BOAS, FRANZ. "The Central Eskimo." *6th Annual Report, Bureau of Ethnology.* Washington, D.C.: Smithsonian Institution, 1888.

D'AQUILI, E. *The Biopsychological Determinants of Culture.* Module in Anthropology 13. Reading, Mass.: Addison-Wesley, 1972.

DRIVER, H. E., and A. L. KROEBER. "Quantitative Expression of Cultural Relationships." *University of California Publications in American Archaeology and Ethnology* 31 (1932): 211–256.

FREUD, SIGMUND. *Civilization and Its Discontents.* London: Hogarth Press, 1932.

HARRIS, M. *Cultural Materialism.* New York: Random House, 1979.

JOHNSON, A. W., and T. EARLE. *The Evolution of Human Societies.* Stanford, Calif.: Stanford University Press, 1987.

KROEBER, ALFRED L. "The Superorganic." *American Anthropologist* 19 (1917): 163–213.

———. *Configurations of Culture Growth.* Berkeley: University of California Press, 1944.

———. *The Nature of Culture.* Chicago: University of Chicago Press, 1952.

Lévi-Strauss, Claude. *The Elementary Structures of Kinship.* Boston: Beacon Press, 1969.

Lowie, R. H. *The History of Ethnological Theory.* New York: Rinehart, 1937.

Malinowski, Bronislaw. "The Group and the Individual in Functional Analysis." *American Journal of Sociology* 44 (1939): 938–964.

Marcus, George E., and Michael M. J. Fischer. *Anthropology as Cultural Critique.* Chicago: University of Chicago Press, 1986.

Murdock, George P. "Editorial." *Ethnology* 1 (1962): 1–4.

Netting, Robert M. *Cultural Ecology.* Prospect Heights, Ill.: Waveland Press, 1986.

Radcliffe-Brown, A. R. "The Methods of Ethnology and Social Anthropology." *South African Journal of Science* 20 (1923): 124–147.

Redfield, Robert. *The Little Community and Peasant Society and Culture.* Chicago: University of Chicago Press, 1960.

Service, Elman R. *A Century of Controversy.* New York: Academic Press, 1985.

Tyler, S. *Cognitive Anthropology.* New York: Holt, Rinehart and Winston, 1969.

Voget, Fred A. *A History of Ethnology.* New York: Holt, Rhinehart & Winston, 1975.

Whiting, B., and J. W. M. Whiting. *The Children of Six Cultures.* Cambridge, Mass.: Harvard University Press, 1975.

ETHNOMEDICINE

Disease is a universal feature of the human condition. All people have had to cope with this challenge to well-being and to life itself. In each and every culture there is a complex domain of information that allows patients and caretakers alike to deal with the biological, social, and psychological realities of sickness and injury. This information describes how members of any given society diagnose, explain, and treat the afflictions that befall them. Just as cultures vary, so do their theories about disease and its treatment. For example, most members of Western society treat headache with rest, application of a compress, and ingestion of analgesic compounds, but for the same complaint, the Aztec of Central Mexico sniffed dried botanical irritants and made incisions in the patient's nose, face, and scalp. The consequent loss of blood and the violent sneezing in response to the irritants was considered therapeutic; it was thought that headaches arose from an overabundance of blood in the cranium (Ortiz de Montellano 1990).

Ethnomedicine can be defined as the information specific to a given culture that allows its members to diagnose and categorize illness and trauma, explain their onset or cause, and to seek appropriate therapies for the restoration or the maintenance of a critically ill patient.

Ethnomedicine falls within the larger field of medical anthropology which explores environmental, biological, and cultural factors as they impact on disease patterning and how people respond to it. Within ethnomedicine are a number of more specialized concentrations; for example, the study of the use of materia medica, or the treatment of mental disorders. Furthermore, ethnomedicine is but one of many branches within ethnoscience, a field that explores how people perceive and categorize information in various domains such as plants, trees, or soils. The prefix "ethno" means that the information and behaviors under discussion are relevant to a particular culture and domain.

Ethnomedicine has traditionally been used by anthropologists as an umbrella term to encompass the health-related beliefs and practices of indigenous peoples, peasants, and those in urban societies who practice alternative healing strategies such as spiritism. As such, ethnomedicine has traditionally referred to any system whose theory and practice fell outside the Western biomedical model. Growing awareness of the biases of ethnocentricity has led to the realization that Western biomedical science is simply the "ethnomedicine" of Western physicians (Rubel and Hass 1990). While this understanding is both valid and timely, there are significant differences between the beliefs and behaviors of peoples who follow the Western biomedical model and those who follow other ethnomedical traditions.

Perhaps the most obvious of these differences is that Western biomedicine has become pancultural and is essentially the same regardless of where it is learned or practiced. Ethnomedicine, on the other hand, is more geographically and culturally constrained. While sand paintings and healing chants are appropriate curative strategies for the Diné (Navaho) of Arizona, such practices would be unacceptable to members of a neighboring Hispanic community. The services of a physician, however, now crosscut cultural boundaries, and both the Diné and the Hispanic patient would be treated by a physician in much the same way.

Ethnomedical systems typically exhibit great historical depth. That is, they are shaped by tradition and reflect long-honored beliefs and practices. For instance, the custom of the Mayan Indians of Guatemala of burning incense and giving offerings of food during a healing ritual (Orellana 1987) is certainly a carryover from aboriginal culture. On the other hand, the Western biomedicine model has much less historical depth despite its vast global diffusion.

Ethnomedical systems are deeply embedded in the fabric of a culture's daily life and in their religious worldview. Little if any division separates health-related behavior from normative social codes and even belief in the supernatural. All aspects of life are interrelated, unlike that in Western society, where medicine has developed into a separate entity. In the West, the study of health and disease has become so compartmentalized that it now lies far from the realms of religion and social relations; these last two facets of daily life play prominent roles in ethnomedical disease theory. For instance, a simple display of greed such as the hoarding of wealth is frequently considered sufficient cause for disease to strike. Similarly it may be thought that by freely sharing similar wealth a person may elicit health and good fortune. Other forms of disruptive or antisocial behavior are thought to incur a costly sanction of sickness or trauma from the deities, spirits, or sorcerers. Such behavioral and perhaps superstitious disease theories are a ubiquitous feature of ethnomedical systems worldwide, and enjoy great antiquity as well. They are noticeably absent, however, in contemporary biomedicine.

Many other differences are seen between contemporary biomedicine and ethnomedical systems. Some of the more noticeable contrasts that set contemporary biomedicine apart from ethnomedicine are the degree of technical complexity, relative efficacy, depth of experimental research, legal accreditation and legal supervison, length of practitioner training, disparity of knowledge between healer and patient, relative cost, and liability for failure. This should not be understood to mean, however, that biomedicine is bias-free. It is as laden with cultural meaning as any ethnomedical system. But its history is tied to the emergence, application, and diffusion of the Western scientific method.

The literature on ethnomedicine is vast (e.g., Nichter 1992). Anthropologists and other researchers have long collected ethnographic data and earlier ethnohistoric materials that detail how members of a given culture attempted to maintain health, and how, faced with sickness or injury, they explain such misfortune and seek its reversal. Interest has also been paid to many related domains from birthing, childcare, and nutrition, to aging and coping with the losses that death brings. Additional study has focused on cultural change and the rise of medical pluralism, in which once-independent medical systems are subsequently juxtaposed within a single geographic setting. Syncretism, or the borrowing and remolding of foreign medical traits, typically follows. As diverse as the literature on ethnomedicine is, a careful reading of it reveals several findings that deserve special comment here.

When viewed from a comparative perspective, ethnomedical systems take on a similar appearance; each is functionally much like the next. While the specific health-related theories and practices of one system may vary greatly from another, each performs a similar set of functional roles. This is true of all people, irrespective of historical time or geographic setting.

These functional roles are diverse yet interrelated. Ethnomedicine functions, first and foremost, as an explanatory tool. This is a particularly important aspect of any medical system; illness demands interpretation. Through explanation and labeling of the problem at hand, the patient can alleviate stress and anxiety as well as gain hope for endurance and, ideally, recovery.

Interpretation of illness is a culturally informed process, one in which patient, healer and a community of others make use of locally appropriate disease theories to account for the misfortune at hand. These theories typically make a distinction between immediate and ultimate cause. The former provides details on the specific nature of the problem, and the latter offers a rationalization as to why this problem occurred. An immediate cause would be the intrusion of a foreign object into a patient's body; the ultimate cause would be the anger of a spirit or sorcerer because of a patient's inappropriate behavior. Disease theories may emphasize naturalistic origins such as exposure to cold and dampness, or they may attribute misfortune to the workings of a "personalistic" agent like a god, an ancestral ghost, or a vengeful human (Foster 1976). Such personalistic disease theory is prevalent in cultures that lack institutions of social control such as courts, a police force, and codified laws. Interestingly, though, it is also prominently seen in some state-level societies, but typically only those in which religion permeates daily life, as was the case with the ancient Aztec.

The degree to which a person is responsible for sickness as well as for the efficacy of the cure is also explained by ethnomedical disease theory. There is variance though more so a continuum in the degree to which individuals are thought to control their own fate. At one pole, an external interpretation of events is emphasized. At this pole, external factors such as a god or destiny are held accountable for the onset of sickness or the maintenance of good health. These external agents are also held responsible for the success or failure of therapies. The opposite pole in this continuum is internal in nature, and responsibility for any outcome is traced directly to the individual.

In all societies there is a theory of illness control. When developmental diseases predominate over acute infectious disorders, the locus of control commonly shifts to the individual; the illness is considered the victim's fault. On the other hand, an external orientation is typically seen in cultures in which disease is truly ubiquitous. When the condition is life-threatening and effective therapies rarely exist, the people of a culture will frequently resort to powerful external agents such as deities (Logan 1991).

After comparing the disease theory of cultures worldwide, anthropologists have concluded that in the explanation of disease, there are a number of casual perspectives or themes that appear with great frequency. These themes crosscut time periods, geographic space, and ethnic boundaries. Most common among these are object or spirit intrusion (e.g. poisoning), structural loss or displacement (e.g. "soul-loss" or fallen fontanelle), the need to maintain balance between opposing qualities (e.g. between hot and cold), and exposure to powerful forces (evil eye or airs). These usually are considered immediate causes of illness. The most frequently seen "ultimate" causes are breaches of normative social codes, acts associated with greed, lack of deference, failure to propitiate spirits or deities, excessive or compulsive behavior, infidel-ity, theft, and numerous other transgressions. It is now clear that ethnomedical systems play a truly important yet latent function; that disease theory is an ancient and effective form of social control. It also helps those caught in largely unchangeable and insufferable conditions to cope with those conditions. In the slums of Brazil, for example, the death of an infant may not be followed by grief and mourning, for many believe that certain children are born without God's divine will to live. It is inevitable, it is thought, that a certain number of children will die (Scheper-Hughes 1992).

In addition to the functional roles of explanation, diagnostic labeling, social control, and coping, all of which are ultimately derived from the disease theories of a given culture, ethnomedical systems are also broadly therapeutic. They provide solutions to many biomedical needs, as well as those more social and psychological in nature. There is a wealth of evidence to attest to how sophisticated and empirically sound ethnomedical systems truly are.

Indigenous people have vast knowledge concerning the natural resources around them. It is not uncommon for them to have plant-based lexicons with a thousand or more entries; several hundred of these will have medicinal uses. This knowledge is the result of a long history of human-plant interaction. The discovery of plants with therapeutic compounds was rarely a random occurrence (Johns 1990; Logan and Dixon 1994). Rather, it was a process of guided selection. The taste, odor, and appearance of plants attracted human inquiry and inspired experimental use. A plant that had no insect predators or served as a food for animals did not escape human notice. Many discoveries were linear, in that knowledge of one species with distinctive characteristics, a bitter taste for example, led to the parallel use of other species having similar attributes. Many discoveries of medical importance also arose from the exploration of a suite of plants employed as food or flavoring (Etkin and Ross 1991).

Of the scores of botanical remedies used by peoples adhering to a specific ethnomedical tradition, a significant number produce physiological effects specifically desired by a given culture. The aforementioned Aztec treatment for headache, for example, was judged effective because the procedures employed produced the desired biological reaction. Similarly, if local cultures value cleansing as a therapeutic tool, then ingestion of strong purgative agents would regularly be seen. It must be noted, however, that while such practices conform to the dictates of ethnomedical disease theory and in any particular culture may be considered effective, they may not actually be therapeutic save for a placebo effect (Moerman 1983) At times the procedures may prove to be deleterious or possibly fatal (Nations 1986). The treatment of the folk-illness of *empacho* is a case in point. To eliminate the congealed ball of food thought responsible for this illness, some parents administer lead-based powders to the sick child. And while these minerals do cause evacuation of the bowel, this ingestion can cause severe, even terminal, lead poisoning (Baer et al. 1989). Both deleterious and nonessential practices can also be found in Western biomedicine (Glasser and Pelto 1980). Not all therapy is beneficial even though it conforms to the mandates of a culture's disease theory.

It is clear, however, that many ethnomedical beliefs and healing procedures carry empirical benefit. The removal of infected tissue, the resetting and immobilization of fractured bones, and the suture or cauterization of open wounds have been employed by indigenous peoples worldwide (Majno 1975). Psychiatric and behavioral disorders, as well as biomedical pathologies of largely psychosomatic origin, have been successfully treated with the manipulation of powerful symbolic imagery, as in the use of cut-paper figurines to absorb malevolence from a patient's body (Dow 1986). Similar success has been achieved by Brazilian spiritist healers who perform unorthodox and invasive surgeries without anesthesia, antiseptics, or, in most cases, medical training, while they themselves are in a trance (Greenfield 1987). Interestingly, patients in Mexico who were serviced by spiritist healers perceived greater improvement and returned more quickly and fully to their normal social roles than those treated solely by Western physicians (Finkler 1985).

Nowhere is the empirical nature of ethnomedicine more clear than in the complex domain of medical botany (e.g. Lewis and Elvin-Lewis 1977). As we have mentioned, plants have long been useful in the care of human health. Even primates employ plants to free themselves from parasites and to heal infection (Strier 1993). Many botanically derived remedies contain phytochemicals that combat disease-causing agents from viruses and bacteria to protozoans and intestinal worms. Other remedies are employed, and frequently with positive effect, to reduce swelling and fever, to coagulate blood, to reverse allergic reactions,

and to facilitate birth or the avoidance of pregnancy. Some ethnomedical therapies lower blood pressure and serum cholesterol levels. Others hold promise as therapeutic agents against cancer and the AIDS virus HIV (Farnsworth 1990).

Western society has certainly gained from the ethnomedical knowledge of indigenous peoples, and this gain has been sizeable, both medically and financially. Of the millions of prescriptions dispensed annually in the United States, at least 50 percent contain compounds of natural origin (Farnsworth 1990). The profits earned from the sale of the consequently developed drugs have been enormous. Complex ethical questions of cultural piracy and the intellectual property rights of indigenous peoples surface here, of course. Nevertheless, in the twentieth century, while these questions were beginning to attract greater scholarly and public notice, native peoples worldwide are being displaced, their forests clearcut, and because of these disruptions, their children were failing to inherit the valuable medical and cultural knowledge of plants that their elders possess.

Equally important in the late twentieth century was the finding that folk illnesses are not simply disorders of psychiatric origin, as was once generally assumed, but that they also represent underlying organic pathologies. Their occurrence in a population is highly patterned, and that patterning is just as real as that seen for cardiovascular disease, diabetes, or other afflictions.

Most revealing in this respect is the research of Rubel et al. (1984) into the folk illness known as fright-sickness or, more commonly in the Americas, *susto*. In fright-sickness, the loss of one's soul is held responsible for illness or even death. The victims of soul-loss have been shown to harbor internal feelings of failure in their social-role performance (e.g. father, husband, provider). The disorder involves several clinically diagnosed diseases, and it crosscuts lines of economic class, ethnicity, and age (see Logan 1993). Similar epidemiological patterning has been recorded for several other endogenous maladies. These include *pibloktoq*, a condition among Eskimos characterized by excitement and sometimes by mania usually followed by depression, and occurring chiefly in winter and usually in women, and other forms of hysteria (Simons and Hughes 1985), the degenerative neural disease of *kuru* (Gajdusek 1973), and several other conditions that are widespread throughout Latin America, notably hot-cold imbalance (Weller et al. 1983), fallen fontanelle (Trotter et al. 1989), and the digestive disorder of *empacho* (Weller et al. 1993). It is now clear that folk illnesses, are never random in their occurrence. Rather they exhibit patterning based on a large number of variables ranging from age, gender, and diet to social role performances, degree of acculturation, and relative economic deprivation.

Early studies of ethnomedicine, while certainly pioneering for their day, were nonetheless marked by a number of methodological and theoretical shortcomings. All too frequently, for example, ethnomedical beliefs and practices were described as if all members of a given community, region, or culture adhered to a uniform and unvarying code of health-related behavior. Such homogeneic reporting masked important variability in ethnomedical knowledge, the avenues of therapy employed and their respective outcomes, case-specific reconstructions of illness casuality, and patterning in the occurrence of folk-illness across lines of age, gender, social status, and so on. An additional weakness of early anthropological investigations of ethnomedicine was that they were almost universally qualitative in nature. Readers gained no insight into magnitude, frequency, efficacy, severity, underlying risk, or causal agents. Ethnomedicine was presented in a way that revealed little of the true complexity that underlay sickness and health-seeking behaviors.

While these and other shortcomings can still be found in studies of ethnomedicine in the late twentieth century, it is promising to note, however, that an increasing number of publications are problem-oriented and methodologically rigorous concerning sampling, operationalizing test variables, and employing statistical analyses to assess the validity of correlations in quantitative data. An instructive case is Rubel et al.'s (1984) aforementioned pioneering study of *susto*. Other exemplary cases can be found inquiring into therapeutic decision-making (Young 1981), confidence levels in the efficacy of folk remedies (Browner et al. 1988), the therapeutic outcome of symbolically based healing strategies (Finkler 1985), and factors that enhance the risk of folk illness morbidity and mortality (Carey 1990).

Less headway was achieved in the late twentieth century in a similar refinement in theory. In fact, the field of ethnomedicine has been woefully short of uni-

fying theoretical perspectives to guide the formation of hypotheses and testing. While a few notable exceptions can be found, as in Johns' (1990) innovative research on the evolution and chemical ecology of medicinal plant use, a surprisingly large number of recent publications still hold to antiquated and mostly erroneous theoretical assumptions. An all-too-frequently-seen example is the use of analogy as an interpretive tool. Humoral medicine, commonly known as the hot-cold theory of disease in which health is believed to follow from a balance between hot and cold elements in the body, does not persist simply because adults need to maintain harmony in social relations or because infants experience polar extremes during abrupt weaning, as some researchers have suggested (see Logan 1977).

The question is how best to achieve further growth or refinement in theory; in other words, what types of interpretative perspectives will help us generate novel and testable hypotheses with which we can explain patterning in ethnomedical data? These are complex questions and invite different and potentially competing responses. Nonetheless, an effort should be made to draw from current theory in other areas of anthropological inquiry and apply it to ethnomedical data in order to assess its ability to explain and predict.

For example, might certain types of ethnomedical data conform to the predictions of the biological theory of evolution? As suggested in greater length elsewhere (Logan 1993), Darwinian theory may prove to be very useful in analyzing health-related beliefs and practices. It may offer similar utility in the explantion of epidemiological patterning in the occurrence of folk illnesses.

Two brief illustrations are given below. These must be phrased as exploratory questions, since empirical tests have not yet been conducted to assess their validity.

Chagnon and Irons (1979) were among the first to predict that cultural success translates into somatic and reproductive success. Their prediction has received considerable cross-cultural support. When this prediction is applied to ethnomedical data, an interesting question surfaces. Might those in a given sample who exhibit the highest rates of folk-illness morbidity and mortality also be found to be ranked lowest in cultural performance of locally valued behaviors?

The findings of Rubel and his colleagues on the sickness of *susto* suggest that this hypothesis may indeed be correct.

Trivers and Willard (1973) have predicted that parents differently invest in their offspring on the basis of gender. In rigidly stratified societies, parents of low social rank will typically favor daughters over sons, since it is assumed that females in such families enjoy a greater likelihood of marrying and becoming parents themselves than their male siblings. This prediction has received cross-cultural support (e.g. Cronk 1989). Might the patterning in infant mortality observed by Marilyn K. Nations and L.A. Rebhun (1988), as well as Nancy Scheper-Hughes (1992) conform to the predictions of Trivers and Willard? Do those infant deaths in Brazilian slums involve significantly more males than females? Insight from evolutionary biology suggests that female survival would be favored.

While other illustrations could be provided, the point should be clear that researchers working in the area of ethnomedicine should try to incorporate theories from other, related, fields into their research. Darwinian theory has already provided such a fruitful source.

Ethnomedical research holds considerable relevance for the applied health sciences as well. Practitioners trained in the Western scientific paradigm, be they physicians, epidemiologists, or nursing and public-health personnel, cannot achieve optimal results when, as is frequently the case, the meanings of disease and trauma for their clientele are poorly understood or even totally ignored. This observation is not new (e.g. Paul 1955). Unfortunately, even in the late twentieth century, it has yet to gain wide recognition among health professionals despite the idea's maturity within medical anthropology (Foster 1982). Among other factors, the relative lack of methological rigor in ethnomedical reporting has made it difficult for workers in the health sciences to recognize that ethnomedical data are relevant to their professional goals.

While physicians who service Spanish-speaking populations may dismiss *susto* as a relic of traditionalism and hence merely psychosomatic, it should be recalled that Rubel et al. (1984) discovered that *asustados*, or victims of soul-loss, are actually the sickest of the sick. It is precisely these patients who most need medical attention. Similarly, Nations (1986) reports that epidemiologists in Brazil may miss up to 20 percent of the infant deaths because the researchers are largely uninformed about local beliefs about disease and dying among children. Patient compliance and hence therapeutic outcome can be improved when local ethnomedical beliefs and practices are integrated into orthodox medical care. A particularly clear case involves alcohol counseling and recovery programs for Native Americans (Blum, et. al. 1992). It was found that the greater the respect for and involvement of the local culture in the administration of a recovery program, the greater the success in attaining program goals.

Anthropologists have demonstrated both the richness and relevance of ethnomedical systems worldwide. Yet success in this endeavor may have perpetuated a picture in which ethnomedical particulars overshadow the despair, disease, and death among the ethnic and marginal cultures from whom we collect our field data. There is a serious risk of allowing ethnomedical text to foreclose dialogue about the underlying variables that invariably produce poor health. While it is important to record and interpret the details of a given ethnomedical system, it is equally important to disclose how economic and political realities affect the beliefs, practices, and quality of life of those who have freely given us their cultural knowledge and personal histories.

Michael H. Logan

See Also: Ethnopharmacology; Ethnopsychiatry; Medical Anthropology

Baer, Roberta D., Javier Garcia de Alba, Luz Maria Cueto, Allen Ackerman, and Sharon Davison. "Lead Based Remedies for Empacho: Patterns and Consequences." *Social Science and Medicine* 29 (1989): 1373–1379.

Blum, Robert W., Brian Harmon, Linda Harris, Lois Bergeisen, and Michael D. Resnick. "American Indian-Alaska Native Youth Health. *Journal of the American Medical Association* 267 (1992): 1637–1644.

Browner, C.H., Bernard R. Ortiz de Montellano, and Arthur J. Rubel."A Methodology for Cross-Cultural Ethnomedical Research." *Current Anthropology* 29 (1988): 681–702.

Carey, James W. "Social System Effects on Local Level Morbidity and Adaptation in the Rural Peruvian Andes." *Medical Anthropology Quarterly* 4 (1990): 266–295.

CHAGNON, NAPOLEON A., and WILLIAM IRONS, eds. *Evolutionary Biology and Human Social Behavior: An Anthropological Perspective*. North Scituate, Mass: Duxbury Press, 1979.

CRONK, LEE. "Low Socioeconomic Status and Female-Biased Parental Investment: The Mukugodo Example." *American Anthropologist* 91 (1989): 414–429.

DOW, JAMES. *The Shaman's Touch: Otomi Indian Symbolic Healing*. Salt Lake City: University of Utah Press, 1986.

ETKIN, NINA L., and JOHN P. ROSS. "Should We Set a Place for Diet in Ethnopharmacology?" *Journal of Ethnopharmacology* 32 (1991): 25–36.

FARNSWORTH, NORMAN F. "The Role of Ethnopharmacology in Drug Development." In *Bioactive Compounds From Plants*. D.J. Chadwick and J. Marsh, editors. New York: John Wiley and Sons, 1990, pp. 2–21.

FINKLER, KAJA. *Spiritualist Healers in Mexico: Successes and Failures of Alternative Therapeutics*. New York: Praeger, 1985.

FOSTER, GEORGE M. "Disease Etiologies in Non-Western Medical Systems." American Anthropologist 78 (1976): 773–782.

———. "Applied Anthropology and International Health: Retrospect and Prospect." *Human Organization* 41 (1982): 189–197.

GAJDUSEK, D. CARLETON. "Kuru in the New Guinea Highlands." In *Tropical Neurology*. John.D. Spillane, editor. New York: Oxford University Press, 1973, pp. 377–383.

GLASSER, MORTON, and GRETEL PELTO. *The Medical Merry-Go-Round*. Pleasantville, New York: Redgrave, 1980.

GREENFIELD, SIDNEY M. "The Return of Dr. Fritz: Spiritist Healing and Patronage Networks in Urban Industrial Brazil." *Social Science and Medicine* 24 (1987): 1095–1108.

JOHNS, TIMOTHY. *With Bitter Herbs They Shall Eat It: Chemical Ecology and the Origins of Human Diet and Medicine*. Tucson: University of Arizona Press, 1990.

LEWIS, WALTER Hepworth, and MEMORY P. F. ELVIN-LEWIS. *Medical Botany: Plants Affecting Man's Health*. New York: John Wiley and Sons, 1977.

LOGAN, MICHAEL H. "Anthropological Research on the Hot-Cold Theory of Disease: Some Method-ological Suggestions." *Medical Anthropology* 1 (1977): 87–112.

———. "New Perspectives on an Old Disorder: Fright-Sickness in Oaxaca." *Anthropology* 14 (1987): 167–181.

———. "New Lines of Inquiry on the Illness of Susto." *Medical Anthropology* 15 (1993): 189–200.

LOGAN, MICHAEL H., and ANNA R. DIXON. "Agriculture and the Acquisition of Medicinal Plant Knowledge." In *Eating on the Wild Side: The Pharmacologic, Ecologic and Social Implications of using Noncultigens*, N.L. Etkin, ed. Tucson: University of Arizona Press, 1994.

MAJNO, GUIDO. *The Healing Hand: Man and Wound in the Ancient World*. Cambridge: Harvard University Press, 1975.

MOERMAN, DANIEL E. "Physiology and Symbols: The Anthropological Implications of the Placebo Effect." In *The Anthropology of Medicine*. L. Romanucci-Ross, D.E. Moerman, and L.R. Trancredi, editors. New York: J.F. Bergin, 1983, pp. 156–167.

NATIONS, MARILYN K. "Epidemiological Research on Infectious Disease: Quantitative Rigor or Rigormortis? Insights from Ethnomedicine." In *Anthropology and Epidemiology*. Craig R,. Janes, et al., editors. Dordrecht, Holland: D. Reidel Publishing Company, 1986, pp. 97–123.

———, and L.A. REBHUN. "Angels With Wet Wings Won't Fly: Maternal Sentiment in Brazil and the Image of Neglect." *Culture, Medicine and Psychiatry* 12 (1988): 141–200.

NICHTER, MARK, ed. *Anthropological Approaches to the Study of Ethnomedicine*. Philadelphia: Gordon and Breach Science Publishers, 1992.

ORELLANA, SANDRA LEE. *Indian Medicine in Highland Guatemala: The Pre-Hispanic and Colonial Periods*. Albuquerque: University of New Mexico Press, 1987.

ORTIZ DE MONTELLANO, BERNARD R. *Aztec. Medicine, Health and Nutrition*. New Brunswick: Rutgers University Press, 1990.

PAUL, BENJAMIN D., ed. *Health, Culture and Community: Case Studies of Public Reactions to Health Programs*. New York: Russell Sage Foundation, 1955.

RUBEL, ARTHUR J., and MICHAEL R. HASS. "Ethnomedicine." In *Medical Anthropology: A Handbook of Method and Theory*. T. M. Johnson and Carolyn F. Sargent, editors. New York: Greenwood Press, 1990.

RUBEL, ARTHUR J., CARL W. O'NELL, and ROLANDO

COLLADO-ARDON. *Susto: A Folk Illness*. Berkeley: University of California Press, 1984.

SCHEPER-HUGHES, NANCY. *Death Without Weeping: The Violence of Everyday Life in Brazil*. Berkeley: University of California Press, 1992.

SIMONS, RONALD C., and CHARLES C. HUGHES, eds. *The Culture-Bound Syndromes: Folk Illness of Psychiatric and Anthropological Interest*. Dordrecht, Holland: D. Reidel Publishing Company, 1985.

STRIER, KAREN B. "Menu for a Monkey." *Natural History*, December 1993, pp. 34–42.

TRIVERS, R. L., and D. E. WILLARD. "Natural Selection of Parental Ability to Vary the Sex Ratio of Offspring." *Science* 179 (1973): 90–92.

TROTTER, ROBERT T. II, BERNARD R. ORTIZ DE MONTELLANO, and MICHAEL H. LOGAN. "Fallen Fontanelle in the American Southwest: Its Origin, Epidemiology, and Possible Organic Causes." *Medical Anthropology* 10 (1989): 211–221.

WELLER, SUSAN C. "New Data on Intracultural Variability: The Hot-Cold Concept of Medicine and Illness." *Human Organization* 42 (1983): 249–257.

WELLER, SUSAN C., LEE M. PACHTER, ROBERT T. TROTTER II, and ROBERTA D. BAER. "Empacho in Four Latino Groups: A Study of Intra- and Inter-Cultural Variation in Beliefs." *Medical Anthropology* 15 (1993): 109–136.

YOUNG, JAMES CLAY. *Medical Choice in a Mexican Village*. New Brunswick: Rutgers University Press, 1981.

ETHNOPHARMACOLOGY

Ethnopharmacology is the study of indigenous medicines that links the ethnography of health and illness to the chemical constituents of those medicines and their physiologic actions. Where the pharmacology of biomedicine is concerned with the sources, chemistry, and actions of drugs (pharmaceuticals), ethnopharmacology applies those principles in the cultural contexts of non-Western cultures that, until recently, have used primarily plant medicines. Researchers in ethnomedicine have traditionally been concerned with the cultural basis of therapeutics, the relationships between illness and supernatural forces, and the social relations of healing. The orientation of ethnopharmacology amplifies that inquiry to address plant chemistry (phytochemistry) as that informs

the criteria that people apply to select medicines and how they interpret the physiologic outcomes of using them. A variety of academic and applied disciplines contribute to the broader inquiry, each sufficiently different in method and objectives to create a constellation of study designs under an interdisciplinary umbrella.

Whereas all ethnopharmacology begins in the field, anthropologists who conduct such research typically engage more extensive in-field study. This provides the opportunity to develop an ethnography of sufficient depth to make sense of phytochemical action in a way that connects local and biomedical models of health in the same theoretical framework. Botany contributes proficiency in plant ecology and systematics, pharmacology and other medical sciences expertise in laboratory analysis, and the pharmaceutical industry interest in developing new products—all of which work out of a largely atheoretical and Western biomedical orientation. For its part, anthropology offers a biobehavioral (biocultural) perspective through which plant medicines are viewed simultaneously as cultural objects and biodynamic substances. The pharmacologic potential of these plants both transcends and contributes to their cultural meaning. This positions ethnopharmacology centrally among the contemporary dialogues in anthropology that endeavor to understand the dynamics of human-environment relations and how these affect health.

At the same time, however, because ethnopharmacology—by its very nature—uses methods developed from the paradigms of biomedicine and bioscience, some anthropologists have challenged the legitimacy of this and related research, in medical ecology and medical anthropology generally. More committed to interpretive studies of health and illness, some critical medical anthropologists have argued that these anthropological studies that abut the biomedical sciences diminish society, deprecate other-than-Western medical cultures, and depend on a reductionistic view of adaptation. This argument misses the point and ignores the fact that health-related phenomena—medicines, diseases, and treatment—have a physical reality that cannot be ignored, no matter how concerned one is with political economy and the social relations of healing. In this regard it is important to note that only the methods, but neither the methodology nor the theoretical underpinnings, of biomedicine shape anthropological inquiry in ethnopharmacology. Anthropologists are not concerned with phytochemistry to assess whether some local population "figured it out" (use pharmacologically active plants in a way that is consistent with the principles of biomedicine), but instead to exercise the techniques of bioscience as one element of a broad-based inquiry into indigenous plant use.

PRIMARY DATA IN ETHNOPHARMACOLOGY: CONTEXTS OF USE

The methods of ethnopharmacology combine established ethnographic techniques to explore the cultural basis of health and therapeutics, including how that is informed by the biological qualities of plants, and laboratory analysis and literature review to determine pharmacologic and other actions. What distinguishes anthropological ethnopharmacology very clearly from plant studies conducted by pharmacologists, botanists, and other related disciplines is that we understand the prefix "ethno-" to mark a topic for cross-cultural consideration or for analysis from the point of view of the indigenous perspective, both of these requiring extensive in-field interview and observation. Where others are content to simply carry lists of "Plants Used for X" out of the field, anthropologists advocate a long-standing ethnographic tradition that seeks considerably more detail. Anthropologists' studies accord the same rigor to gathering qualitative (and some quantitative) data that they do to the botanical and pharmacologic analysis of the medicinal plants to which interviews direct them. In this way, context of use is as significant for therapeutic outcome as is the chemical composition of the medicine.

The social relations of healing involve who treats whom, including self-treatment, and access to medicines and their social negotiation. In addition to self- and community-identified medical specialists, a representative sample of the adult population is interviewed as well so that the knowledge base recorded reflects the heterogeneity that invariably exists, even within small populations, regarding how people perceive illness and how familiar they are with the plants available to them.

The criteria applied in the selection of plants for medicinal use are complex and include such physical attributes as color, taste, smell, growing location, and physiologic action. Variations within each of these reflect the chemical composition of a plant. In many cultures medicinal plant selection overlaps cognitive principles based in binary oppositions, such as yin-yang, hot-cold, and other contrasts or continua. Ethnobiologists have recorded indigenous taxonomies of plant action, smell, and other attributes that reflect people's experiences with their physical environment and their interpretation of it. Some of this is reflected in the names assigned to plants; for example, deadly nightshade (*Atropa belladonna*, a powerful anticholinergic) and birthwort (*Aristolochia clematitis*, efficacious in assisting childbirth). Culturological interpretations of these classificatory schemes that focus only on what plants "mean" miss essential elements of the therapeutic exercise that is, at base, a studied conjunction of sign (color or taste, for example) with physiologic action. Thus, the red color of plants used in American Indian medicine to treat wounds may well be a signature that identifies plants by the color of blood (redwood *Sequoia sempervirens*, redbud *Cercis canadensis*), but it also signifies that the red quinones that impart color to some of these plants are hemostatic and antimicrobial—properties that users of those plants could identify through their own experiences. Indeed, those physiologic actions may be the primary criteria for selection, with red color simply the mnemonic tool for identification of wound-healing plants.

Because pharmacologic activity varies among individuals of a species and among plant parts, people can manipulate the pharmacologic activity of medicinal preparations by specification to plant part (leaf, root, stem, flower, fruit), developmental age of plant organ (new leaves, flower buds), and time of year and growing location (pharmacologic activity may vary with season, soil composition, rainfall, altitude, and other features of the local ecology). One observes, for example, that in northern Yemen prices for the psychotropic qat (*Catha edulis*) vary depending on source of harvest and time of day, reflecting that activity varies with growing location and diminishes over time, beginning when the leaves are cut early in the day for transport to market.

How plant medicines are prepared, including combination and administration, is important not only to expose the sacred or other "signed" elements of healing, but also because it can have profound effects on plant chemistry. A few examples illustrate this. Concurrent consumption of medicinal plants and minerals or soils (geophagy), especially clay, results in the adsorption of some constituents, reducing their availability. Similarly, plant fiber itself can interact with organic compounds, including some toxins. Softening plant materials by heating, addition of lye (sodium or potassium hydroxide) or sodium bicarbonate, and soaking in water increases the surface area on which digestive enzymes act and generally increases the availability of plant constituents. Potentially, this increases exposure to pharmacologically active substances, but it would be mediated by heat-inactivation of some chemicals, heat-denaturation of enzymes that would otherwise liberate active compounds, dilution of constituents with water, and the interaction of lye and bicarbonates with organic materials. Other preparatory techniques that can affect the chemical composition of plant medicines include crushing, pounding, and grating; drying; suspending, or decocting in alcohol, water, or oil; and changing acid-base status (pH). Clearly the pharmacologist's analysis of sterile extractions of single plants in acetone, methanol, and other solvents informs but is not an ethnopharmacologic study. That strictly pharmacologic studies do not illuminate the biologic relevance of culturally defined actions is illustrated as well in the case of composite plant medicines.

As every plant represents a bundle of constituents, the combination of plants in composite medicines presents a virtual chaos of pharmacologic potential. Interactions among these phytochemicals may be additive (when the combined action of two or more constituents is summed), potentiating (when the effect is greater than additive), synergistic (when the action of one constituent is conspicuously increased by others), or antagonistic (when one or more constituents diminish the activity of one or more others). Where pharmacologists often regard the emphasis on composite preparation a distraction, closer attention reveals interesting insights into the rationale of indigenous therapeutics. For example, while the three individual elements of the Ayurvedic *trikatu* demonstrate little activity against the various disorders for which this medicine is prescribed, *Zingiber officinale* (ginger), *Piper nigrum* (black pepper), and *P. longum* (long pepper) together significantly increase the bioavailability of constituents of the other plants to which they are added, for example, sparteine (anti-inflammatory, diuretic, oxytocic; in Spanish broom, *Spartium junceum*) and vasicine (expectorant, oxytocic, and abortifacient; in adhatoda, *Justicia adhatoda*).

The way in which a plant medicine is administered has pharmacologic implications as well. Biomedicine once dismissed the topical application of medicines for internal (nondermatologic) conditions as "theater" or "suggestive magic." Today, having "discovered" the principle of transdermal absorption of certain medicines, replaceable patches are used for drug administration, for example, nitroglycerin for heart conditions and nicotine as replacement therapy for individuals trying to stop smoking. Hausa in Nigeria characteristically include on-skin medicines as one element of complex treatments of measles, chicken pox, and other "spot diseases." Topical application of bitter and astringent medicines (e.g., neem, *Azadirachta indica*, *Nelsonia canescens*) treats the external phase of measles; medicines consumed by mouth are directed at the locus of the internal phase of the illness both to encourage egress of the internal sores through the skin with bitter and astringent medicines (e.g., *Entada africana*, *E. abyssinica*), and later to impart cold and aromatic attributes (e.g., *Citrus* spp., *Centaurea perrottetii*) because the illness responds to these qualities. Later, astringent and emollient medicines (cassava, *Manihot esculenta*) are applied to resolve the rash.

Perhaps the most significant and underexplored element of context is the intended outcome of therapy. Whereas one could generalize that the objective of all medicines is to "get better," especially outside of biomedicine this goal involves more than simply removing the agent of disease and resolving symptoms. Healing is not an event, but a process in which the ultimate objective is preceded by a number of proximate goals—diagnosing etiology, transforming the body or its parts to prepare for healing, seeking evidence of disease egress, and the like. The treatment of gastrointestinal disorders by Hausa is a case in point. Certain plants are taken to determine etiology. Discomfort as reaction to consuming *Agelanthus dodoneifolius*, for example, confirms spirit-caused illness; other reactions invoke witchcraft or elements of the natural environment (dirt, cold). Vomiting, purging, and discolored stools are signs that disease agents leave the body and are achieved with *Ficus capensis* (bush fig) and *Cassia occidentalis* (coffee senna). Later in the therapeutic process, emollient and costive plants relieve symptoms of intestinal disorder; for example, locust bean (*Parkia filicoidea*) and tamarind (*Tamarindus indica*). These examples illustrate again that interpretive studies tell only part of the story of healing, and that pharmacologic assessment devoid of cultural context—while informative on another level—is not *ethno*pharmacology.

BOTANICAL AND PHARMACOLOGICAL DATA

Plants collected in the field are represented by pressed voucher specimens for later taxonomic identification. Once the identifications have been established, literature review is conducted via computerized databases, such as NAPRALERT (Natural Products Alert Data Base), a distillation of the world literature on the pharmacology, ethnobotany, and chemical constituents of plant parts and extracts. This compilation includes extensive data on the chemistry and pharmacology of metabolites derived from natural products, including clinical studies with human subjects. Using the ethnographic data as guide to preparation and medical indication, any of a great variety of standardized laboratory protocols can be used to test plants for pharmacologic activities—antifungal, hypoglycemic, diuretic, anti-inflammatory, and so on.

MULTICONTEXTUAL PLANT USE

An increasingly productive area of inquiry examines the pharmacologic potential of plants used for more than one purpose, typically medicine and food. Multicontextual plant use has even more important implications for health than medicines only, or foods only, because it results in people experiencing greater exposure to pharmacologically active substances. Moreover, plants used as food tend to be consumed in larger quantities and often more regularly. Other contexts of use that have similar implications include circumstances in which some part of the body is in prolonged contact with plant materials, such as those used as cosmetics, items of personal hygiene (for washing, fragrance, tooth and gum care), and manufactured goods (e.g., dyes, plaited mats, basketry, wood carvings, seed ornaments, and jewelry). Figures summarizing Hausa plant use for just four categories illustrate the point: 374 medicinal plants include all but 5 of the 119 plants that this population identify as foods; the 20 cosmetic plants all have medicinal uses, 5 are food plants, and 3 are used also in hygiene; the 16 plants used in personal hygiene all have medicinal uses, 6 are used in diet, and 3 are also cosmetic. Building on the ethnography of Hausa plant use, we can make pharmacologic sense of this overlap by problematizing to an activity category, such as antimicrobial action: of the 8 plants that are used in 3 or more of the contexts considered, 7 contain antimicrobial principles. This type of problem focus not only links plant and activity to disorders that likely benefit from treatment with that plant, but also suggests how that value might be increased by additional exposure when that plant is used in other contexts.

ETHNOPHARMACOLOGY AND PHARMACEUTICALS

As biomedicines (pharmaceuticals) reach even the most remote populations, people begin to use these new products in conjunction with the local pharmacopoeia. This concurrent or serial use of pharmacologically active plants and drugs has generated interest in recording the tenacity of local traditions and their transformation following the introduction of new elements of medical culture. Conversely, one chronicles the "indigenization of pharmaceuticals" that are selected, prepared, and administered according to local therapeutic directions, which may contradict the intentions of the drugs' manufacturers. The physiologic implications of the concurrent use of plants and pharmaceuticals is perhaps even more compelling by its urgency, given the great likelihood of harmful interactions. For example, tannins, which are ubiquitous in plants, bind some classes of pharmaceuticals to form insoluble complexes. This antagonism is likely realized when high tannin plants, easily detected by their astringent taste, are selected for costive actions in the treatment of intestinal disorders in conjunction with pharmaceuticals directed at the same condition. Similarly, fruit juices—especially from *Citrus* and *Capsicum*, which are common among plant medicines—reduce the activity of some penicillins; and calcium, an important constituent of (especially leafy) plant medicines, has an antagonistic effect on tetracycline. In the other direction, several analgesic and antipyretic drugs are potentiated when consumed at the same time as plants of the Cruciferae family, suggesting that—with such knowledge—doses may need to be adjusted. These observations underscore further the value of embellishing medical ethnography with pharmacologic assessment.

NINA L. ETKIN

SEE ALSO: Adaptation; Belief Systems; Biocultural Anthropology; Cultural Ecology; Disease and Culture;

Ethnomedicine; Indigenous Peoples; Medical Anthropology; Nutritional Anthropology; Rural Health Care

ETKIN, NINA L., ed. *Plants in Indigenous Medicine and Diet: Biobehavioral Approaches.* New York: Gordon and Breach, 1986.

——— . "Ethnopharmacology: Biobehavioral Approaches in the Anthropological Study of Indigenous Medicines." *Annual Review of Anthropology,* 17 (1988): 23–42.

——— . "Ethnopharmacology." In *Medical Anthropology: A Handbook of Theory and Method,* edited by Thomas Johnson and Carolyn Sargeant. New York: Greenwood Press, 1990.

——— . *Eating on the Wild Side: The Pharmacologic, Ecologic, and Social Implications of Using Non-cultigens.* Tucson: University of Arizona Press, 1994.

JOHNS, TIMOTHY. *With Bitter Herbs They Shall Eat It: Chemical Ecology and the Origins of Human Diet and Medicine.* Tucson: University of Arizona Press, 1990.

ETHNOPSYCHIATRY

The study of mental illness and behavioral dis order in any particular culture, especially the ways in which that particular culture recognizes, evaluates, and responds to mental illness, is called ethnopsychiatry. Ethnographic evidence suggests that most cultures recognize forms of illness or inappropriate behavior that correspond to what Western observers term "psychiatric" disorders; as a special subfield of the broader discipline of ethnomedicine, ethno-psychiatry studies these conditions from the perspective of those cultures. Note that ethnopsychiatry is often distinguished from transcultural psychiatry, which is considered to be the application of Western psychiatric theory and practice to the evaluation and treatment of non-Western forms of mental illness.

HISTORY

Ethnopsychiatry first emerged as a distinct subfield in the writings of George Devereux, whose early work was influenced by the culture-and-personality school of anthropology. His studies of abnormal behavior among the Mohave Indians, first set out in the 1930s, culminated in the classic work *Mohave Ethnopsychiatry and Suicide* (1961). William Caudill's *The Psychiatric Hospital as a Small Society* (1958) may also be seen as a step in the development of contemporary ethnopsychiatry and, with Erving Goffman's classic work *Asylums* (1961), opened Western psychiatry and psychiatric institutions to the same kind of anthropological study that non-Western psychiatries were subject to in Devereux's work. Since the early 1970s the field of ethnopsychiatry has grown, generating its own set of conceptual and theoretical issues, methodologies, and debates.

By the mid-1990s, the major journals in which ethnopsychiatric research was being published included *Culture, Medicine, and Psychiatry; Transcultural Psychiatric Research Review;* and *Social Science and Medicine.* From time to time, ethnopsychiatric research also is presented in other anthropological journals, including *Medical Anthropological Quarterly, Medical Anthropology,* and *Ethos.*

SCOPE AND MAJOR ISSUES

The study of ethnopsychiatry builds upon the intersection of two conceptual issues. First, ethnopsychiatry is concerned with the ways in which cultures explicitly or implicitly demarcate "normal" from "abnormal" behavior. Although some research in cross-cultural psychiatric epidemiology has suggested that symptoms of severe psychosis are universally recognized as abnormal, the dividing line between the normal and the pathological is, in most cases, variable, context-dependent, and subject to local cultural interpretation. Trance, for example, is a sought-after, self-induced state in many cultures that opens subjects to contact with the supernatural; in the West these experiences may be considered pathological dissociative states or symptomatic of psychosis. Similarly, anthropologists working in Buddhist cultures have suggested that some of the stereotypic symptoms of depression in the West—dysphoric affect, feelings of hopelessness— may be valued by Buddhists as insight into the illusory nature of the world and the hopelessness of the human condition. Even within cultures behaviors may move over time from being considered abnormal to being considered normal—homosexuality in the United States, for example, has been essentially depathologized in formal psychiatric classifications. Other behaviors may become abnormal in a specifically medical sense. Premenstrual syndrome, for example, was proposed as a psychiatric disorder (late luteal phase dysphoria) by the American Psychiatric Association in 1992.

The second conceptual foundation of ethnopsychiatry is the cultural nature of personhood and its social construction. Ethnopsychiatry rests upon the widespread, but hardly universal, cultural assumption that persons are composed of minds as well as bodies, souls or spirits, and that some kinds of illnesses have their causes within (or their effects upon) this mind. The rather complex Western conception of mind is far from universal, and it has been debated whether cultures lacking such a conception can be said to recognize specifically mental illnesses. Studies of Japanese ethnomedicine, for example, suggest that Japanese cultural conceptions of personhood do not include the notion of a *mind* as a distinct component of persons that serves to drive the actions of the body. Consequently, there appears to be no distinct or elaborated category of mental illnesses in traditional Japanese culture. Even within the field of Western-style biomedicine in Japan psychiatry is poorly represented.

Much of ethnopsychiatric research may be thought of as relying upon exclusively cultural conceptions of behavioral disorders, or upon the extension of Western conceptions of behavioral disorders. The cultural approach taken by anthropologists, such as Lawrence Fisher (1985), declines to impose Western biomedical psychiatric constructions on indigenous illnesses and beliefs and focuses instead on indigenous or folk conceptions of locally recognized behavioral disorders. Thus, Fisher explicates Barbadian notions of "madness" and is reluctant to suggest that this is really a Western psychiatric condition. From this perspective the possibility that behavioral disorders may be identified with Western biomedical categories of illnes is irrelevant to the distinctly cultural, indigenous understandings of those disorders. Indeed, even Western psychiatric illness categories have been subjected to such a cultural analysis, and conditions such as schizophrenia, depression, anorexia nervosa, agoraphobia, and posttraumatic stress disorder have been examined as reflections of specifically Western cultural values and beliefs.

Alternatively, anthropologists have justified the ethnopsychiatic study of behavioral disorders on the assumption that Western psychiatric disease categories provide an adequate framework for the identification of non-Western disorders, whatever their particular construction within an indigenous culture. A common form of this essentialist approach treats Western psychiatric disease categories simply as convenient and useful, if not perfect organization labels, for studying illnesses in other cultures. Thus, Nancy Scheper-Hughes (1982), in her study of mental illness in rural Ireland, assumed that the behavioral disorders of her subjects were similar enough to the biomedical disease schizophrenia to justify using the formal psychiatric label. Some anthropologists and psychiatrists adopt a stronger form of this position, sometimes called "clinical universalism," that argues that the behavioral disorders found in other cultures are fundamentally identical to their Western psychiatric disease counterparts, with only a veneer of apparent difference imposed by local cultures or social practices. From this perspective, even the most exotic culture-bound syndromes have been termed "atypical psychoses," linking them to corresponding psychiatric disease categories.

Indeed, the clinical universalist perspective does not even require that the illnesses subject to ethnopsychiatric scrutiny be mental illnesses, at least from an indigenous point of view. Arthur Kleinman (1986), in his study of neurasthenia in China, identifies fundamental commonalities between depression—a Western mental illness—and neurasthenia, which in China is considered a physical illness. The special contribution of this perspective on ethnopsychiatric illness is to offer insights into the ways in which local cultural beliefs or social practices may shape psychiatric disorders, giving them potentially different expressions from culture to culture, even removing them, in some cases, from the realm of mental or behavioral illness altogether.

CULTURE-BOUND SYNDROMES

Culture-bound syndromes, specific behavioral disorders that are unique to one or only a few cultures, offer some of the most interesting and challenging disorders to ethnopsychiatric theory. Such disorders have been interpreted variously as providing evidence, on the one hand, that mental illnesses in general are highly culture-specific and less a function of universal human biophysiology than of unique cultural and social shaping and, on the other hand, that mental illnesses are, in fact, fundamentally similar across cultures, and are only "flavored" by local cultural and social conditions. Culture-bound syndromes include ethnographically familiar disorders such as *amok*, found primarily in Malaysia, and characterized by violent outbreaks followed by amnesia, and *susto*, a

Latin American disorder in which a wide variety of symptoms or ill-feelings is attributed to fright and temporary soul-loss. Culture-bound syndromes also include very culture-specific conditions, such as *heva*, a disorder found only on Easter Island, in which the victim violently runs around with a club in his hand and a rat in his mouth.

In many cases the cultural shaping of culture-bound syndromes appears fairly clear. The illness known as *koro*, for example, which involves an uncontrollable fear that the penis will retract into the abdomen with fatal results, is found in a number of southeast Asian cultures, including southern China. It appears to be associated with child-rearing practices that include threats of genital involution as a consequence of masturbation, and anxiety about competitiveness among men that focuses on loss of power or failure of performance, including sexual performance. Similarly, Japanese school children have in recent years developed a behavioral syndrome termed "school refusal syndrome," associated with strong cultural and social pressures for hard work and success in schools. Other culture-bound syndromes appear to lack such direct links to local cultural themes. The several syndromes that might be glossed as "hysterical running," which include *pibloktoq* or "arctic hysteria," and *grisi siknis* among Mískito Indians in Central America, are subject to indigenous interpretations, but appear to exhibit few characteristics that reflect unique shaping by the cultures in which they are found.

Ronald C. Simons and Charles C. Hughes (1985) have proposed a middle-ground view of culture-bound syndromes. They argue that some syndromes, such as "startle match" conditions (characterized by an exaggerated startle followed by other behaviors such as matching the words or actions of others) are largely neurophysiological with relatively little cultural shaping or modification, while other syndromes, such as *susto* ("fright illness") or *saladera* (a condition found in the Peruvian Amazon, diagnosed of someone who has experienced excessive misfortune) are defined less by essential features of the illnesses than by the context in which they are diagnosed and thus are extremely sensitive to cultural shaping. Simons and Hughes find that most of the ethnographically prominent culture-bound syndromes are most likely variations on several underlying conditions, such as extreme anxiety, dissociative states, or psychosis. From an anthropological perspective, however, culture-bound syndromes remain a particularly interesting example of the ways in which culture and social practices can shape the raw material of these underlying illnesses into radically different, even unique, overt expressions of behavioral disorder.

DEPRESSION AND SCHIZOPHRENIA

Some anthropologists have argued that even formal Western psychiatric diseases must be considered culture-bound syndromes, since they emerge within, and draw meaning from, specific forms of Western culture. Indeed, the fundamental division within Western psychiatric disease classifications between the affective disorders, of which major depression is the paradigm case, and the psychoses, of which schizophrenia is the paradigm case, may reflect a uniquely Western division of mind into two basic components: emotion or affect versus thought or cognition. Kleinman's (1986) research on depression and neurasthenia in China supports this possibility in the case of depression. Kleinman notes that the mentalistic or emotionalist understanding of the illness depression is relatively new, in historical terms, in Euro-American culture and is more or less restricted, in ethnographic terms, to this same culture. Kleinman identifies what he calls a "core depressive syndrome" that underlies both the emotional illness depression in contemporary Euro-American culture, as well as the somatic or physical illness neurasthenia (and similar conditions) in Euro-American culture up to the late nineteenth century and in other contemporary cultures around the world. Indeed, depression appears to be especially sensitive to cultural shaping and interpretation, as the collection of papers edited by Kleinman and Byron Good (1985) amply demonstrates; some cultures do not even possess terms that may be translated easily as "depression."

While depression is widely acknowledged to be either culture-specific or at least highly sensitive to the cultural shaping of its expression as an illness, the psychoses, especially schizophrenia, are more controversially considered culture-specific. Despite historical and ethnographic evidence that syndromes resembling schizophrenia did not clearly exist in Euro-American culture prior to the mid-nineteenth century, or in non-Western cultures prior to "modernization," many anthropologists and psychiatrists are reluctant to consider schizophrenia a culture-bound syndrome. Cross-cultural evidence for the incidence or prevalence of psychotic symptoms, derived primarily from the WHO-supported International Pilot Study of Schizophrenia (WHO 1973), in nine countries in the late 1960s and early 1970s, is ambiguous, methodologically questionable, and open to conflicting interpretations. It suggests rates of new cases of schizophrenia that vary from 1.5 per 10,000 in Aarhus, Denmark, to 4.2 per 10,000 in Chanighar, India, with wide variation in the incidence of different forms of schizophrenia. Psychiatrists generally take these data to indicate broad similarities in schizophrenia across cultures while anthropologists see in the same data evidence of striking differences among cultures.

Nonetheless, it has been argued that the specific Euro-American understanding of schizophrenia is saturated with Western cultural assumptions and values. This includes the belief that persons are "bounded" entities (and thus thought-projection or thought-control are symptomatic of psychosis because they represent a break in the boundaries of the self), the belief that selves and personalities are unique and unitary (and thus "splitting" or a divided personality is popularly associated with schizophrenia), and the belief that emotion and thought are essentially different mental processes (and thus schizophrenia is fundamentally different from manic-depression or other conditions that appear to be neither clearly psychosis nor clearly affective disorders).

Anthropological studies of behavioral disorders help to reveal how cultures identify and manage deviance or abnormality, especially those forms that are not appropriated to the moral category of sin or the juridical category of crime. In doing so, ethnopsychiatry also reveals much about the ways in which cultures promote and manage "normalcy." In more recent years, ethnopsychiatry has also offered a perspective from which to examine the professional psychiatry of Euro-American culture, a perspective in which psychiatry is considered a kind of folk practice that, in common with the ethnopsychiatries of other cultures, reflects and promotes a particular set of cultural values and beliefs. In addition, because Western professional psychiatry serves as an especially powerful social arbiter of normality and abnormality, the anthropological study of psychiatry joins other ethnographic examples to illustrate the ways in which formal medicine in any culture can perform implicit political functions as well. Last, ethnopsychiatry has

an applied cultural anthropological role. By providing culturally sensitive accounts of behavioral disorders in cross-cultural settings, ethnopsychiatry has contributed both to the practice of Western psychiatry in transcultural settings and to the practice of indigenous treatment of mental illness.

DONALD POLLOCK

SEE ALSO: Psychoanalysis; Psychological Anthropology

CRAPANZANO, VINCENT. *The Hamadsha: A Study of Moroccan Ethnopsychiatry.* Berkeley: University of California Press, 1973.

DEVEREUX, GEORGE. "Mohave Ethnopsychiatry and Suicide." *Bureau of American Ethnology Bulletin* 175, 1961.

DEVEREUX, GEORGE. *Basic Problems of Ethnopsychiatry.* Translated by Basia Miller Gulati and George Devereux. Chicago: University of Chicago Press, 1980.

FISHER, LAWRENCE. *Colonial Madness: Mental Health in the Barbadian Social Order.* New Brunswick, N.J.: Rutgers University Press, 1985.

GAINES, ATWOOD D., ed. *Ethnopsychiatry: The Cultural Construction of Professional and Folk Psychiatries.* Albany: State University of New York Press, 1992.

KLEINMAN, ARTHUR. *Social Origins of Distress and Disease: Depression, Neurasthenia and Pain in Modern China.* New Haven, Conn.: Yale University Press, 1986.

KLEINMAN, ARTHUR, and BYRON GOOD, eds. *Culture and Depression: Studies in the Anthropology and Cross-Cultural Psychiatry of Affect and Disorder.* Berkeley: University of California Press, 1985.

MARSELLA, ANTHONY J., and GEOFFREY M. WHITE, eds. *Cultural Conceptions of Mental Health and Therapy.* Dordrecht and Boston: D. Reidel Publishing Company, 1982 (reprint, 1984).

SCHEPER-HUGHES, NANCY. *Saints, Scholars, and Schizophrenics: Mental Illness in Rural Ireland.* Berkeley: University of California Press, 1982.

SIMONS, RONALD C., and CHARLES C. HUGHES, eds. *The Culture-Bound Syndromes: Folk Illnesses of Psychiatric and Anthropologic Interest.* Dordrecht and Boston: D. Reidel Publishing Company, 1985.

WORLD HEALTH ORGANIZATION. *The International Pilot Study of Schizophrenia.* Geneva: WHO, 1973.

ETHNOSCIENCE

See: Cognitive Anthropology

ETHNOZOOLOGY

The term "ethnozoology" was first employed by Junius Henderson and John Peabody Harrington (1914). "Ethnobotany" is an older term (1890s), and its usage is encountered much more frequently. Both terms are subsumed within ethnobiology, which may be defined as the cross-cultural study of systems of knowledge, belief, and practice with regard to plants and animals. Ethnozoological studies may be further refined by labels such as ethnoornithology, ethnoichthyology, ethnoentomology, and ethnomalacology, which focus respectively on birds, fish, insects, and mollusks. Ethnobiological studies may focus on cultural practice (i.e., how organisms are used), or on cultural knowledge and belief about plants and animals (i.e., how they are classified, named, and conceptualized). The related field of ethnoecology analyzes cultural knowledge and beliefs about the relationships among plants, animals, and people within an ecosystem (Hunn 1989).

Many traditional ethnographic accounts contain ethnozoological information. Most often this information is treated under such headings as "subsistence," "hunting," "fishing," "gathering," "material culture," and even "mythology." Explicitly ethnozoological studies are relatively rare and these—particularly before the late 1960s—consisted of little more than annotated lists of animal species known from the traditional territory of the society in question (e.g., Chamberlain 1908). Information reported in these lists included indigenous, English vernacular, and scientific Latin names with summaries of cultural beliefs and practices associated with each taxon. A considerably broader mandate for the study of ethnobiology is articulated by E. F. Castetter (1944).

During the 1960s ethnobiology gained sharper theoretical relevance for anthropology. Three theoretical trends were primarily responsible for this heightened profile for ethnobiology (and ethnozoology). First, ethnoscientists directed attention to the ethnobiological domains as fields for testing the Sapir-Whorf hypothesis, that is, to investigate systematically the mutual constraints of "language, thought, and reality" (Carroll 1956). Second, inspired by Claude Lévi-Strauss's (1963, 1966) analysis of totemism and Mary Douglas's (1957, 1966) consideration of the symbolic power of anomalous categories, symbolic anthropologists closely scrutinized the roles of animals as metaphors for social relations. Third, there was the new field of cultural ecology. Roy A. Rappaport's (1968) interpretation of the adaptive basis of Tsembaga pig sacrifice, Marvin Harris's (1966) provocative analysis of India's sacred cattle, and Richard B. Lee's (1968) studies of Kalahari hunting-gathering show the value of careful attention to the interaction between human societies and animals as economic resources. These three tracks have been pursued, by and large, in isolation one from the other. There has been some cross-fertilization, notably R. N. H. Bulmer's (1970) reflections on Lévi-Strauss's notion of "species" and Eugene S. Hunn's discussion (1979) of the naturalistic basis for the Bible's "abominations" in Leviticus. This latter had been the subject of an influential essay by Douglas (1966) in which she argues that these animals' powers of spiritual contamination stem from their anomalous structural position in the ancient Hebrew animal classification scheme. Also, ethnoscientific studies often reflect the ecological interests of their authors.

Ethnoscientific ethnozoology focuses on the ethnozoological domain as a whole rather than on selected exemplary species of animals, as is characteristic of symbolic and ecological studies of human-animal relationships. Such studies of the animal domain contribute to the larger theoretical program of understanding folk biological classification and nomenclature. Harold C. Conklin's 1954 study of Hanunóo ethnobotany established a basic conceptual frame and methodological standard for subsequent ethnoscientifically oriented ethnobiological research. Since the 1960s the field of ethnobiology has developed, in large measure, in response to Brent Berlin's hypothesized "general principles of ethnobiological classification and nomenclature" (Berlin et al. 1973; Berlin 1992). Berlin's ideas were grounded in his extensive experience with Tzeltal Mayan ethnobotanical systematics, but the equal relevance of zoological data for evaluating his hypotheses was established in the contemporary work by Bulmer on Kalam ethnozoology in the New Guinea Highlands (1974).

The Berlin-Bulmer synthesis stressed the basic "naturalness" of folk biological categorization of plants and animals and the pervasiveness of hierarchic or "taxonomic" relations among the taxa of ethnobiological classification systems. Berlin's scheme of universal taxonomic ranks, from "unique beginner" at the kingdom level down through taxa of "life-form," "intermediate," "generic," "specific," and "varietal," is still controversial, but most scientists now agree that there exists a basic level of folk biological classification—the "folk generic rank" in Berlin's scheme—that has particular psychological salience. The folk biological taxa at this level of classification are very strongly constrained by the existence of natural phenotypic discontinuities (Berlin et al. 1981). This explains the close correspondence between these basic folk biological categories and taxa recognized by Western biological systematics as phylogenetic units. For vertebrates this correspondence may approximate 90 percent (Hunn 1975). This had been remarked on previously by professional biologists impressed by the empirical knowledge of local native assistants (Diamond 1966; Irving 1958). This finding strongly qualifies the more radical versions of the so-called Sapir-Whorf linguistic relativity principle, which suggest that understanding of the world is determined by the grammatical and logical resources of our particular language, at least with respect to how humans conceptualize the basic biological entities they experience.

Most languages also distinguish subgeneric categories. Berlin, following Conklin, has shown that "folk species" are often named binomially, that is, the two or more subcategories of a polytypic folk genus may be named (A)X, BX, CX, and so forth, where "X" is the name of the inclusive folk genus, (A), B, and C being modifying expressions—optional in the case of "A"—as in English "rainbow trout" and "brook trout" or "honeybee" and "bumblebee." Scott Atran (1990) has shown in detail how modern biosystematic nomenclatural practice is grounded in European folk biological naming practices, which in turn are replicated independently in many of the world's languages.

The origins of binomial naming is thus shown to predate Linnaeus, the putative "father" of scientific biological classification. Cecil H. Brown (1985) points out, however, that binomial nomenclature is rare or absent in the reported ethnobiological systems of many hunting-gathering peoples. A variety of explanations have been proposed to account for this apparent lack

of binomial terminology among hunter-gatherers. Among these explanations are that it is an artifact of the fragmentary contemporary ethnographic record for hunting-gathering societies; that it reflects a greater intensity, and hence diversity, of environmental utilization by agricultural societies; or that the binomial principle was elaborated in response to the phenotypic diversification consequent to domestication (Berlin 1992).

Debates continue regarding the nature of suprageneric taxa as well. Robert A. Randall and Eugene S. Hunn (1984) argue, contra Brown (1984) and Berlin (1992), that life-forms only rarely conform to categories recognized as monophyletic by evolutionary biologists, and are thus not "natural" categories in the sense that folk generic taxa are. Rather, at the more abstract levels of folk biological classification, culturally diverse perspectives play an increasingly prominent role in defining the nature and scope of categories. Most life-form categories in folk biological systems are defined in part by nonphenotypic characteristics, most often considerations of habitat and/or usage (Hunn 1982).

These more abstract levels of life-form classification—where basic, biologically natural categories are arranged in accord with culturally specific purposes and perspectives—have commanded the attention of symbolic anthropologists. Douglas's theories of the symbolic power of categorically anomalous animals is representative. Pangolins, pigs, and otters are tabooed by virtue of the fact that they do not fit Lele, Ancient Hebrew, or Buddhist notions of natural order (Douglas 1957, 1966; Leach 1964; Tambiah 1969). Pangolins are mammals that have scales like reptiles, pigs "have cloven hooves but do not chew the cud," while otters are land mammals that are equally at home in the water. In these instances, cultural systems impose simple classificatory schemes upon complex patterns of natural variation.

By contrast, ethnoscientific studies emphasize the basic level of classification. They seek to understand how humans come to recognize the order *in* nature rather than to impose an artificial order upon it. Such studies have shown that folk biological classification systems are comparable to those of Western science in many respects, most notably that the basic taxa of each are directly comparable. Nevertheless, such systems vary both among themselves and in contrast to Western biosystematics in particulars worthy of careful comparative analysis. Such analysis requires systematic methodological procedures.

The model ethnozoological study documents the local knowledge of animals current within a specific community, or with respect to some defined subset of the local fauna. The essential first step in such a study is to record the local terms used to name categories of animals, and to record as well the "negative evidence" of animals present but either unnamed or classified under general categorical names. This inventory of local names must be systematically related to the Western scientific nomenclature applied to the local fauna. In the simplest case, there would be a perfect one-to-one correspondence between local vernacular names and scientific species names. This is rarely the case, although a close approximation may obtain for large terrestrial vertebrate species. It does not follow that there is no predictable relationship between the categories of Western scientific zoology and those recognized by the local people. Absent a one-to-one correspondence, scientific species names may be overdifferentiated or underdifferentiated in the local system.

Examples of overdifferentiation are typically encountered among domesticated species for which separate terms may apply to varieties or to various age and sex categories, as in the case of English terminology for cattle and dogs. Such terminological elaboration has also been noted for nondomesticated species of exceptional economic or symbolic value. Underdifferentiation is common with respect to smaller or less conspicuous vertebrates, such as mice, bats, and minnows, and is most often the case among insects and other invertebrates. Among insects, the basic folk categories may correspond to scientific families or even orders.

In most such cases, the groups recognized in the folk systems will correspond to some scientific taxon, though one of rank higher than the species. In the relatively rare case that animals of diverse appearance are classified together on the basis of shared habitat, use, or symbolic association, it can be shown that the category in question is a special-purpose category belonging to a taxonomy distinct from the general purpose classification based on morphological and behavioral similarities among the organisms classified.

Researchers need to be alert to the likelihood that more than one term may be used to name a given animal. This variation in naming practice need not indicate a lack of "sense" in the folk system. Rather, names of variable classificatory scope may be used in different contexts. Terms employed may represent the general-purpose classification or a variety of special-purpose classifications. Phonological and dialectal variants, synonyms, abbreviations, euphemisms, and nicknames must be sorted in order to characterize accurately the underlying conceptual order. If the target language has no literate tradition, a suitable phonemic alphabet must be used to render accurately the sounds of native names. Professional linguistic collaboration may be required for this aspect of the study.

Accurate scientific identifications of each individual organism named in the local vernacular is critically important and may require active collaboration with one or more professional zoologists. Voucher specimens provide a permanent record of the evidence on which one's nomenclatural correspondences are based. Experts must be found who can identify one's vouchers—and curators who will house them for the long term. Though vouchers may not be necessary for large, readily recognized vertebrates, some sort of voucher is essential for the majority of species. Birds and bats may be netted (with the appropriate permits) and photographed, or the vocalizations of birds and amphibians recorded as vouchers. A broad representative collection of local insects and small invertebrates requires little special equipment or expertise to gather and keep. Small mammals may be identified from skulls alone in most instances, and local hunters may be able to provide these without further preparation. Small fishes, amphibians, and reptiles may be preserved entire in alcohol. It is essential to record as much cultural information about each specimen as possible, including local names recorded from several individuals. This establishes a permanent record linking cultural information about the basic categories of animals recognized by local people to the database of Western zoology. This process of matching folk and scientific names provides a strong foundation for a variety of cross-cultural comparisons and generalizations, such as the nature and degree of correspondence among folk zoological classification systems and also between folk systems and the Western scientific worldview.

A number of comprehensive ethnozoological inventories have been published to date. These reports represent cultures occupying habitats as diverse as forests, coasts, islands, and deserts ranging from the tropics to the subarctic. Hunting-gathering, fishing, and farming economies are all represented. The number of folk genera of animals described in a series of such studies is presented in Table 1.

Table 1: Number of Taxa Reported for Certain Ethnozoological Studies (Adapted from Berlin 1992)

Group	Number of Generic Taxa
Aguaruna (Amazonian Peru)	606
Anindilyakwa (Northern Territory, Australia)	417
Hanunóo (Mindoro, Philippines)	461*
Kalam (highland Papua New Guinea)	345
Koyukon (north-central Alaska)	157*
Ndumba (highland Papua New Guinea)	186
Nuaulu (Seram Island, eastern Indonesia)	412*
Sahaptin (Columbia River Plateau, northwestern U.S.)	236 (290*)
Tobelo (Halmahera Island, Indonesia)	420 (596*)
Tzeltal (Mayan, highland Chiapas, Mexico)	335 (448*)
Wayampí (Amazonian Brazil)	589*

* Terminal taxa, that is, the most specific categories named, which may be basic level taxa or subdivisions of such taxa.

The number of categories recognized for each group varies in response to several factors, including the faunal diversity of the habitat occupied and the intensity of the research effort. Nearly all fall within the 200–600 range.

Bulmer and his colleagues published the first comprehensive modern ethnozoological analysis. It was for the Kalam people of highland Papua New Guinea (Bulmer and Menzies 1972–1973; Bulmer et al. 1975; Bulmer and Tyler 1968). Bulmer's work is based on nearly three decades of intensive field study. His essays titled, "Why Is the Cassowary Not a Bird?" (1967) and "Which Came First, the Chicken or the Egg-head?" (1970), are justly considered classics that address fundamental theoretical issues in light of Kalam ethnozoology. *Birds of My Kalam Country* (Majnep and Bulmer 1977), coauthored with his Kalam colleague Ian Majnep, dramatically juxtaposed Kalam and Western scientific knowledge and perspectives even before such collaborative ethnographic texts were considered experimental.

Hunn's Tzeltal ethnozoology (1977) complemented Berlin et al. Tzeltal ethnobotany (1974). The result

was the first comprehensive ethnobiological account for a single community, that of Tenejapa, a Mayan farming community of some 10,000 people in highland Chiapas, Mexico. While confirming the basic outlines of Berlin's taxonomic theories, Hunn identified certain inadequacies of the formal taxonomic model of folk classification, in particular noting the indeterminacy of the rank of certain taxa that exhibited properties of both generic and specific or of life-form and generic ranks. Hunn proposed a "perceptual model" (1976) to account for both the hierarchic properties of folk biological classification and the indeterminacy of taxonomic rank.

Well-documented analyses now have been published for the Koyukon of north-central Alaska (Nelson 1983), the Anindilyakwa of the Northern Territory of Australia (Waddy 1988), the Tobelo of Halmahera Island, Indonesia (Taylor 1990), and the Nuaulu of Seram Island, Indonesia (Ellen 1993). The results of other comprehensive ethnozoological studies remain available only in summary, thesis, or manuscript form, as, for example, Berlin's Aguaruna and Huambisa research (cf. Berlin 1992), Hunn's Sahaptin work (1990), John Kesby's Rangi study (1986), and Peter Dwyer on the Rofaifo (1976). All these authors address Berlin's theoretical proposals, often raising specific objections based on their particular experience.

Julie Anne Waddy's is the most detailed study extant of a hunting-gathering people. The scope of the Anindilyakwa ethnozoological lexicon suggests that Brown's characterization (1985) of hunting-gathering ethnobiological inventories as restricted relative to those of agriculturalists may be biased by the inadequacies of the ethnographic record. Paul Michael Taylor's work (1990) is characterized by exceptionally complete zoological documentation and by his close attention to the linguistic context of nomenclatural practice. Roy F. Ellen's (1993) analysis is informed by his emphasis on the social context of the practice of classification. While agreeing with Berlin that folk zoological classifications have a naturalistic basis, he stresses the flexibility and active nature of the process of classifying, which he distinguishes by the term "prehension."

Richard K. Nelson's (1983) account of Koyukon natural history incorporates an extensive description of the folk zoological classification system of this subarctic hunting people of northern Alaska. His work is distinguished by its lyrical prose style and emphasis on Athapaskan Indian understandings of natural species as moral agents. Nelson's work links generalizing and comparative ethnozoological studies with an extensive ethnographic literature focused on the ecological and economic roles of animals in human subsistence. Such studies are not ethnozoological in the strict sense of attempting to characterize systems of ethnozoological knowledge, but contain much data and valuable insights relevant to our understanding of the complex skein of connections that link people with their animal relations.

EUGENE S. HUNN

ATRAN, SCOTT. *Cognitive Foundations of Natural History*. London: Cambridge University Press, 1990.

BERLIN, BRENT. *Ethnobiological Classification: Principles of Categorization of Plants and Animals in Traditional Societies*. Princeton, N.J.: Princeton University Press, 1992.

BERLIN, BRENT, J. BOSTER, and J. P. O'NEILL. "The Perceptual Bases of Ethnobiological Classification: Evidence From Aguaruna Folk Ornithology." *Journal of Ethnobiology* 1 (1981): 95–108.

BERLIN, BRENT, DENNIS E. BREEDLOVE, and PETER H. RAVEN. "General Principles of Classification and Nomenclature in Folk Biology." *American Anthropologist* 75 (1973): 214–242.

———. *Principles of Tzeltal Plant Classification*. New York: Academic Press, 1974.

BROWN, CECIL H. *Language and Living Things*. New Brunswick, N.J.: Rutgers University Press, 1984.

———. "Mode of Subsistence and Folk Biological Taxonomy." *Current Anthropology* 26 (1985): 43–62.

BULMER, R. N. H. "Why Is the Cassowary Not a Bird?" *Man* 2 (1967): 5–25.

———. "Which Came First, the Chicken Or the Egg-head?" In *Échanges et Communications, Mélanges Offerts à Claude Lévi Strauss à l'Occasion de son 60ème Anniversaire*, edited by Jean Pouillon and Pierre Maranda. The Hague: Mouton, 1970.

———. "Folk Biology in the New Guinea Highlands." *Social Science Information* 13 (1974): 9–28.

———, and J. I. MENZIES. "Kalam Classification of Marsupials and Rodents." *Journal of the Polynesian Society* 81 (1972): 472–492; 82 (1972): 86–107.

———, J. I. MENZIES, and F. PARKER. "Kalam Classification of Reptiles and Fishes." *Journal of the Polynesian Society* 84 (1975): 267–307.

———, and M. J. TYLER. "Kalam Classification of Frogs." *Journal of the Polynesian Society* 77 (1968): 333–385.

CARROLL, JOHN B., ed. *Language, Thought and Reality: Selected Writings. Benjamin Lee Whorf 1897–1941*. Cambridge, Mass.: Technology Press of MIT, 1956.

CASTETTER, E. F. "The Domain of Ethnobiology." *American Naturalist* 78 (1944): 158–170.

CHAMBERLAIN, R. V. "Animal Names and Anatomical Terms of the Gosiute Indians." *Proceedings of the Academy of Natural Science of Philadelphia* 60 (1908): 74–103.

CONKLIN, HAROLD C. "The Relation of Hanunóo Culture to the Plant World." Ph.D. dissertation, Yale University, 1954.

DIAMOND, J. M. "Zoological Classification System of a Primitive People." *Science* 151 (1966): 1102–1104.

DOUGLAS, MARY. "Animals in Lele Religious Symbolism." *Africa* 27 (1957): 46–57.

———. *Purity and Danger*. London: Routledge Kegan Paul, 1966.

DWYER, P. "An Analysis of Rofaifo Mammal Taxonomy." *American Ethnologist* 3 (1976): 425–445.

ELLEN, ROY F. *The Cultural Relations of Classification*. New York: Cambridge University Press, 1993.

HARRIS, MARVIN. "The Cultural Ecology of India's Sacred Cattle." *Current Anthropology* 7 (1966): 51–59.

HENDERSON, JUNIUS, and JOHN PEABODY HARRINGTON. "Ethnozoology of the Tewa Indians." *Bulletins of the Bureau of American Ethnology* 56 (1914).

HUNN, EUGENE S. "Toward a Perceptual Model of Folk Biological Classification." *American Ethnologist* 3 (1976): 508–524.

———. *Tzeltal Folk Zoology*. New York: Academic Press, 1977.

———. "The Abominations of Leviticus Revisited: A Commentary on Anomaly in Symbolic Anthropology." In *Classifications in Their Social Context*, edited by Roy F. Ellen and David Reason. New York: Academic Press, 1979.

———. "The Utilitarian Factor in Folk Biological Classification." *American Anthropologist* 84 (1982): 830–847.

———. "Ethnoecology: The Relevance of Cognitive Anthropology for Human Ecology." In *The Relevance of Culture*, Morris E. Freilich, ed. South Hadley, Mass.: Bergin and Garvey, 1989.

———. *Nch'i-Wa'na "The Big River."* Seattle,

Washington: University of Washington Press, 1990.

———, and D. H. FRENCH. "Alternatives to Taxonomic Hierarchy: The Sahaptin Case." *Journal of Ethnobiology* 4 (1984): 73–92.

IRVING, L. "On the Naming of Birds in Eskimo." *Anthropological Papers of the University of Alaska* 6 (1958): 61–77.

KESBY, JOHN D. *Rangi Natural History: The Taxonomic Procedures of an African People.* New Haven, Conn.: Human Relations Area Files, 1986.

LEACH, E. "Anthropological Aspects of Language: Animal Categories and Verbal Abuse." In *New Directions in the Study of Language*, edited by Eric H. Lenneberg. Cambridge: Cambridge University Press, 1964.

LEE, RICHARD B. "What Hunters Do For a Living, Or, How To Make Out On Scarce Resources." In *Man the Hunter*, edited by Richard B. Lee and Irven DeVore. Chicago: Aldine Pub. Co., 1968.

LÉVI-STRAUSS, CLAUDE. *Totemism.* Boston: Beacon Press, 1963.

———. *The Savage Mind.* Chicago: University of Chicago Press, 1966.

MAJNEP, IAN S., and RALPH BULMER. *Birds of My Kalam Country.* Auckland: Auckland University Press, 1977.

NELSON, RICHARD K. *Make Prayers to the Raven.* Chicago: University of Chicago Press, 1983.

RANDALL, ROBERT A. and EUGENE S. HUNN. "Do Life-Forms Evolve or Do Uses for Life? Some Doubts about Brown's University Hypothese." *American Ethnologist* 11:329–349, 1984.

RAPPAPORT, ROY A. *Pigs for the Ancestors.* New Haven, Conn.: Yale University Press, 1968.

TAMBIAH, S. J. "Animals Are Good to Think and Good to Prohibit." *Ethnology* 7 (1969): 423–459.

TAYLOR, PAUL MICHAEL. *The Folk Biology of the Tobelo People.* Washington, D. C.: Smithsonian Institution Press, 1990.

WADDY, JULIE ANNE. *Classification of Plants and Animals from a Groote Eylandt Aboriginal Point of View.* Darwin, Australia: Australian National University, 1988.

EUROPE, EASTERN

The history of East Europe is characterized by the intermixing and competition of small nations and great empires. Consequently, to define East Europe as a cultural region is often a difficult and politically loaded process and therefore a topic of great anthropological concern. During the socialist years, cold war ideology influenced the region's definition and shaped the basic framework in which anthropological research was carried out. Most cold war regional definitions excluded the Soviet Union and its European territories which were considered by most social scientists a single political, economic, and social category in themselves, but included such disparate states as the German Democratic Republic (formerly East Germany) and Albania. North Atlantic Treaty Organization (NATO) members Greece and Turkey were excluded for political reasons, as were the Baltic countries of Estonia, Latvia, and Lithuania, then part of the Union of Soviet Socialist Republics (USSR).

With the cold war over, regional definitions are again geographically and culturally based, although still somewhat confused. For purposes of this essay's geographical coverage, East Europe is now considered as comprising the Baltic subregion (Estonia, Latvia, Lithuania), Central Europe (Poland, the Czech Republic, Slovakia, Hungary, Croatia, and Slovenia), Southeast Europe/the Balkans (Bulgaria, Romania, rump Yugoslavia, Bosnia, Macedonia, Albania, and to a lesser extent, Greece), and East Europe proper (Belarus, Ukraine, and western Russia). Because the Baltic countries—Belarus, Ukraine, and European Russia—were part of the Soviet Union, most regional anthropological effort was in the central and southeast zones.

Southeast Europe and the Balkans are largely Orthodox Christian (and, to a lesser extent, Moslem) and still are characterized by an extensive rural and peasant population. Culturally, this area shares many of the same features as identified for Mediterranean societies. Thus, there is a strong sense of family honor and shame by which individuals are evaluated. Furthermore, patriarchy, or at least the ideology of it, tends to dominate in family and household relations. Despite the presence of strong centralizing states, in some rural and mountainous areas of the region, notably Montenegro and Albania, blood feud is said to be resurgent in the postcommunist period.

Catholic and Calvinist Central Europe, in contrast, has a longer history of urbanism and industrial development and a more extensive market economy than the other subregions. Students of this region have tended to consider "central" or "middle" Europe as a cultural entity apart from the Baltic and the Balkans.

Even in the transition to democracy and market economies in the 1990s there were clear differences between the subregions. Poland, Hungary, and the Czech Republic made the greatest strides toward democracy and a market economy. Consequently, they received the greatest share of Western aid and are likely to be the first of the former socialist countries to be admitted to the European Union and possibly even NATO.

The role and significance of Eastern Europe in contemporary cultural anthropology are uncertain. Western anthropology's historical interest in preliterate, tribal, and non-Western peoples tended to marginalize East Europe as a region of intense anthropological scrutiny, but cold war suspicions and related restrictions on fieldwork during the socialist years limited activity there. Since the revolutions of 1989–1990, however, there has been a corresponding increase in the West's research effort with several publications reflecting this change. A special edition on European questions of the *American Ethnologist* (American Ethnological Society 1991) featured three of its nine articles on Eastern Europe. Also, the "Distinguished Lecture" to the 1991 annual meeting of the American Anthropological Association dealt with the significance of East Europe's transformation for anthropology (Harris 1992).

Anthropology as practiced by East Europeans also has an ambiguous history. Until the 1970s, what was called anthropology in East Europe consisted largely of physical or biological anthropology with a focus on anthropometry and the definition, description, and comparison of human physical types. To an extent, this was related to East European concerns for national self-definition. Archaeology, ethnography, folklore, and linguistics are also vibrant fields of East European scholarship, either with their own independent identities or subsumed under history or classical studies. For the most part, as with physical anthropology, these disciplines focus on national as opposed to more universal issues and concerns. Each East European nation can thus point to an ethnological mentor: Dimitri Gusti in Romania, Gyula Illyés in Hungary, Joszef Obrepski in Poland, Vuk Karadžić in Serbia, and the brothers Ante and Stejpan Radic in Croatia. These individuals and their students helped define their national cultures by their pioneering work among the rural peasantry who, throughout East Europe, popularly are said to reflect the essence of each people.

Under the tenure of socialist leadership, the anthropological sciences, when not attacked and limited outright, were placed in service to the ideological and organizational needs of the corporate state. Folklorists invented traditions and designed rituals to express state power and encourage the integration of diverse peoples. Cultural theorists discussed the meaning of life and labor in collectivist society. Meanwhile, other anthropologists performed contract work for state agencies, analyzing the adjustment of working populations to factory and farm, examining rural-urban migration, or researching changing village life. In some East European countries, contact with Western anthropologists became increasingly difficult.

The noted Hungarian ethnographer, Tamás Hofer, in a 1968 *Current Anthropology* article, defined what he considered key differences between American anthropologists and East European ethnographers working in central European villages. Among these were theoretical or problem orientations, as opposed to descriptive concerns, and, infrequent, but long-term fieldwork, as opposed to short frequent visitations. It is perhaps because of East Europe's developed ethnographic, historical, and literary traditions, then, that Western anthropologists were, until recently, reticent to enter this region with a large research effort of their own. However, Western anthropologists who do work in the area are invariably drawn to collaborative relationships with their East European colleagues.

East Europe's cultural characteristics make for especially important study in contemporary anthropology, with these characteristics consequently reflected in the overarching frameworks that anthropologists bring to the study of the region. Considerable concern has focused on explaining how and why East Europe became socially and culturally distinct from its Western counterpart. To answer this, anthropologists have often focused on the relations of dependency that characterized East Europe's relations with surrounding empires. Thus, conquest and manipulation by Russians, Hapsburgs, and Ottomans are considered a major influence on the region. Many scholars point to imperial use of East Europe for cheap agricultural produce, military conscripts, and corvée labor as partial explanations for its past highly differentiated class structure, extensive rural-urban variation, and antidemocratic politics. Those favoring dependency explanations even suggest that this history contributed to the region's use of draconian socialist policies to resolve its developmental predicament after World War II. The question remains whether regional distinctiveness will fade with the end of the cold war, or continue, under capitalist conditions.

Another effect of great-power rivalry in East Europe was the development of intense rivalries between the region's diverse ethnic groups for control of national states. Ethnic questions have dominated both Western and Eastern European anthropology of the region since it is the actualities and potentialities of ethnic conflict that especially provoke outside interest in East Europe. The region has been an ethnic pastiche for hundreds of years; it includes three main ethnic stocks and a wide array of other peoples.

Slavs predominate and include three subfamilies: Eastern (Russians, Ukrainians, and Byelorussians); Western (Poles, Czechs, and Slovaks); and Southern (Serbs, Croats, and Slovenes). The definition of other Slavic groups is more problematic. Bosnian Moslems are considered Slavic though they converted to Islam starting in the fifteenth century. Bulgars, who migrated to southeast Europe from central Asia, were also heavily influenced by Slavic language, culture, and religion and are now considered a Slav people. Macedonian identity, on the other hand, is more open to question, and ethnic affinity here is claimed by Slavs (Serbs and Bulgars), Greeks, and Albanians. The origins of the Slavs and their migration throughout the East European landmass are open to question. Contemporary notions place the original Slav habitat in the Pripet marshes of the Polish-Belarus borderlands. In this view their radiation through East Europe was a slow process occurring from the third through seventh centuries A.D.

Also prominent throughout the region were various Magyar-speaking groups including Hungarians, Szeklers, and Csangos. The latter two, however, are now essentially blended into the main Hungarian stock. The Finno-Ughric roots of their language suggests Magyar peoples arrived from central Asia in the ninth century A.D. Originally horse pastoralists, they quickly took up agriculture and settled village life as they spread through the Danubian Basin. Romanian ethnogenesis, meanwhile, dates to the first century A.D. and the intermixing of Roman colonists with the Thracian-Illyrian Geto-Dacian of the Danubian Basin and Carpathian foothills. Other ethnic groups include the diverse Romany (Gypsy) peoples, Jews, Turkic peoples (e.g., Bulgarian Pomaks and Gagauz Turkic Christians in Moldova), and Albanians, a people related to the ancient Illyrians. Many German-speaking peoples, including the Saxons and Swabians of Romania, the Volga Germans in Russia, and German-speaking Latvians, also settled in East Europe.

Mapping East European ethnic diversity is confused by the manipulation of national censuses and by a complicated distribution of peoples that rarely coincides with state borders. Thus, many nation-states dominated by one ethnic group often have other sizable populations within their borders—ethnic populations who may have a state of their own next door. Still other states are, or were, comprised of great numbers of different peoples of rough numeric equivalency. And, still other East European ethnic groups (e.g., Romany and Jews) were distributed throughout the region with no state to support their cause and interests.

Given the complex distribution and equivocal backgrounds of the East European peoples, the history of regional ethnic groups often serves as the context of international debate and territorial claim. This has been the case in Transylvania, contested by Hungarians and Romanians; Macedonia, contested by Yugoslavia, Bulgaria, Albania, and Greece, and now an independent country whose official name at its independence (1992) was a matter of international dispute; and elsewhere throughout the so-called Balkans. Much of the conflict in former Yugoslavia, for example, has been waged in the name of territorial rights based on alleged ancient settlement, with highly partisan evidence used to support such claims. The native anthropological sciences are used to provide evidence both for and against various sides in these territorial debates.

Further aiding territorial claims, East European leaders have, at times, averred undiluted biological heritage and encouraged ethnic exclusivist behavior and use of related symbols. Though linguistic and archaeological evidence suggest a long history of population intermixing, some East Europeans often infer basic cultural, and even biological, differences as the ultimate source of ethnic and nation-based conflicts. In contrast, anthropological analysis of East European ethnicity suggests that the development of exclusivist ethnic identities and related animosities are functions of both intergroup relations and/or political economic processes. Thus, the manipulation of popular sentiments by imperial rivalries often produced intense ethnic identification. Furthermore, the development of one ethnic movement will tend to spawn others in its wake. Several works illustrate these points (Beck and Cole 1981; Kideckel and Halpern 1993; Verdery 1983). Even the predominance of socialism failed to keep ethnic sentiments at bay. In fact, socialist political leaders often advocated ethnic policies to maintain support in the population at large (Verdery 1991).

Along with ethnicity, the anthropology of Eastern Europe has pointed out the importance of local level interpersonal relations and informal social and economic ties in regional culture. Anthropology's focus on such relationships, in part, was in conscious opposition to socialist state corporatism because such ties long characterized East European life. The quality of extended family and significance of network relations (e.g., godparenthood, kindred is commented on by a wide variety of anthropologists throughout Eastern Europe (Byrnes 1976; Fél and Hofer 1969; Hammel 1968; Thomas and Znaniecki 1958; Halpern 1967; Halpern and Kerewsky-Halpern 1983; Sanders 1975).

As in peasant societies generally, individual identity and access to resources depended first on household and kin ties. The extent to which individual behavior was controlled through such ties varied widely, however. Until the modern period, patriarchy was unchallenged in the South Slav extended family (*kuća* or *zadruga*) and Albanian *shtëpi*. Marriage was virilocal and generally arranged, and women, being considered similar to chattel, were enjoined from inheritance. In these societies larger agnatic kin groups (*bratsvo* in Serbia and *fis* in Albania) were also common and significant for organizing local and even national social relations. Further north in Hungary, Romania, Poland, and other countries, patriarchy-as-ideology prevailed in the rural areas, although in practice there was considerable variation.

Anthropological analyses of personal networks under socialist conditions, and a related literature devoted to analysis of state relations with the private sphere, form an essential framework of current anthropological interest. Such work challenges the idea of the determining force of totalitarian state, party, and infallible leaders by documenting how state rules and institutions, including those of the omnipresent

bureaucracy, were subverted and transformed by the actions of personal networks. One particularly fruitful research genre shows how, for example, the informal exchange relationships of the so-called "second economy" played havoc with the system of socialist planning and centralized production (Sampson 1984; Wedel 1986). Although the East European socialist states sought to remake society into a collectivist, classless construct via ideology and central planning, anthropological research suggests that the East European socialist states were not so much planned societies as societies with plans (Sampson 1984). Such plans were often confounded, neutralized, or otherwise transformed by local action, inaccurate information, or outright theft and deceit by officials and citizens alike, responding instead to the pressures and values of family and community. Similarly, workplace relationships such as those in collective farms and factories (Hann 1980; Kideckel 1993), the focus of socialist attempts to reorganize society along collectivist lines, were also shot through with the influence of personal relationships. The strength of family ties in the economy forced socialist societies like Poland (Hann 1985; Nagengast 1991) to dispense with collectivist organization in rural communities altogether.

Political anthropological approaches focused on the paradox of network-centered behavior in socialist society. Analyses showed how informal relations aided socialist state persistence even as they simultaneously eroded the state from within. That is, network connections enabled access to consumer goods in an economy of shortage, eased social and residential mobility, and helped secure political safety through favors from political decision-makers. However, such relations also produced extensive jealousy, competition, and mutual suspicion within and between social networks. In allegedly classless societies, then, the uses of personal ties combined to produce and maintain persisting class differentiation (Nagengast 1991; Kideckel 1993).

The persistence of the personal network in socialist East Europe also suggests that socialist practice was unable to transform totally the nature of community life from the presocialist era. The prominence of rich and vibrant folk traditions tempered the demands of socialism, mediated relations between state and populace, and occasionally even served to challenge, if only symbolically, the legitimacy of

Marxist-Leninist practice. For example, Kligman (1988) shows how the rites of passage in a Romanian Transylvanian community not only related community members to each other and to generations past, but also set up a symbolic barrier of poetry and ritual to the domination of socialism.

The economy of Eastern Europe can generally be classified as advanced industrial, though levels of development differ markedly throughout the region. Socialist labor and educational policies and concerns for class mobility produced universal literacy and a highly trained industrial work force. The deemphasis on agriculture, however, often left the rural labor force comprised largely of women and older men, emptying villages of their physically most capable and putting downward pressure on agricultural production and rural standards of living. In the aftermath of the revolutions of 1989, with decollectivization and the bankruptcy of many large state-supported industrial centers, there is some shift of population from urban to rural with some of the younger male population returning to the land. Unemployment, high inflation, environmental degradation, and technological backwardness continue to confound East Europe, however, exacerbating the confused political and ethnic situation.

Never allowed the West's luxury of development for development's sake, East Europe since the end of World War II has been a laboratory for planned social change. With the end of the cold war, the experiment continues. In the mid-1990s, however, the World Bank, the International Monetary Fund, and other lending agencies sought change through programs of privatization and democratization to support the growth of civil society. Such institutions seek nothing less than the reversal of five decades of socialist practice, but are confronted by influences from East European culture and history. For example, the socialist past (discussed as the "socialist unconscious" or the "phantom limb effect" by Gerald Creed and Katherine Verdery (in essays exploring the possible effects of socialism on the East European transition) conspires to limit the transition. Though market economies have quickly developed throughout East Europe, they have produced an intense culture of consumerism led by young entrepreneurs, the region's new people of property. Former Communist Party functionaries have also profited from the transformation to the market economy to such an extent that

many observers speak of East Europe as characterized by *nomenklatura capitalism*. Meanwhile, the workers and the collectivized peasantry who lived off state subsidy have largely balked at Western-inspired "shock therapy." By mid-1994 their votes had returned former socialists to power throughout the region.

Still, the regeneration of the East European centralized state seems unlikely. As could be predicted, external commercial interests and internal competing networks have rapidly delegitimized the state to the point that it has withdrawn from many sectors of public life. As could be predicted, competing networks have rapidly filled the vacuum left by this withdrawal, a development that leaves East European states subject to renewed dependence on outside powers. Unhappily, it was similar circumstances in the past that encouraged the growth of small-scale competitive nationalism, the importance of local community and personal networks, and the problematic nature of democratic government.

DAVID A. KIDECKEL

SEE ALSO: Europe, Southern; Honor; Soviet Union and Russian Cultural Anthropology

AMERICAN ETHNOLOGICAL SOCIETY. "Representations of Europe: Transforming State, Society and Identity." *American Ethnologist* (Special Issue), vol. 18(3), 1991.

BECK, SAM, and JOHN W. COLE, eds. *Ethnicity and Nationalism in Southeastern Europe*. Amsterdam: Anthropology-Sociology Research Center, 1981.

BYRNES, ROBERT F., ed. *Communal Families in the Balkans: The Zadruga*. Notre Dame, Ind.: University of Notre Dame Press, 1976.

FÉL, EDIT, and TAMÁS HOFER. *Proper Peasants: Traditional Life in an Hungarian Village*. N.Y.: Viking Fund Publications in Anthropology No. 46, 1969.

HALPERN, JOEL M. *A Serbian Village*. New York: Harper and Row, 1967.

———, and BARBARA KEREWSKY HALPERN. *A Serbian Village in Historical Perspective*. New York: Holt, Rinehart, and Winston, 1972.

———, and DAVID A. KIDECKEL. "Anthropology of East Europe." *Annual Review of Anthropology* 12 (1983): 377–402.

HAMMEL, EUGENE A. *Alternative Social Structures and Ritual Relations in the Balkans*. Englewood Cliffs, N.J.: Prentice Hall, 1968.

HANN, C. M. *Tázlár: A Village in Hungary*. Cambridge: Cambridge University Press, 1980.

———. *A Village Without Solidarity: Polish Peasants in Years of Crisis.* New Haven, Conn.: Yale University Press, 1985.

HARRIS, MARVIN. "Distinguished Lecture: Anthropology and the Theoretical and Paradigmatic Significance of the Collapse of Soviet and East European Communism." *American Anthropologist* 94 (1992): 295–305.

KIDECKEL, DAVID A. *The Solitude of Collectivism: Romanian Villagers to the Revolution and Beyond.* Ithaca, N.Y.: Cornell University Press, 1993.

KIDECKEL, DAVID A., ed. "Political Rituals and Symbolism in Socialist Eastern Europe." Special Issue of *Anthropological Quarterly* 56 (1982).

———, and JOEL M. HALPERN, eds. "War Among the Yugoslavs: Anthropological Perspectives." *Anthropology of East Europe Review,* Special Issue 11 (1993).

KLIGMAN, GAIL. *The Wedding of the Dead: Ritual, Poetics, and Popular Culture in Transylvania.* Berkeley: University of California Press, 1988.

NAGENGAST, CAROLE. *Reluctant Socialists, Rural Entrepreneurs: Class, Culture, and the Polish State.* Boulder, Colo.: Westview Press, 1991.

SAMPSON, STEVEN L. *National Integration Through Socialist Planning: An Anthropological Study of a Romanian New Town.* East European Monographs No. 148. New York: Columbia University Press, 1984.

SANDERS, IRWIN T. *Balkan Village.* Lexington: University of Kentucky Press, 1949.

THOMAS, WILLIAM ISSAC, and ZNANIECKI, FLORIAN. *The Polish Peasant in Europe and America.* New York: Dover Publications, 1958.

THOMAS, WILLIAM ISSAC. *The Polish Peasant in Europe and America.* Classroom edition. Urbana, Ill.: University of Illinois Press, 1995.

VERDERY, KATHERINE. *Transylvanian Villagers: Three Centuries of Political, Economic and Ethnic Change.* Berkeley: University of California Press, 1983.

———. *National Ideology Under Socialism: Identity and Cultural Politics in Ceauşescu's Romania.* Berkeley: University of California Press, 1991.

WEDEL, JANINE. *The Private Poland: An Anthropologist's Look At Everyday Life.* New York: Facts on File, 1986.

EUROPE, SOUTHERN

Southern Europe is defined as including Iberia (Spain and Portugal), Italy, Greece, Cyprus, Malta, and all offshore islands belonging to these sovereign national entities. In the past, southern Europe's anthropological interest often has been submerged in a more generalized Mediterranean culture area, but the rise of interest in Europe as a political entity, and, in the United States, the founding of the Society for the Anthropology of Europe, which publishes a regular information bulletin as well as a directory of its members (and systematically organizes the in-house publication of course materials and slide sets to accompany the teaching of ethnographies), appears to have recentered the areal focus to a significant degree. This is an epistemological as well as a practical and politically responsive realignment because contemporary research has moved beyond rural society to include urban communities (a necessary shift, given the long urban tradition in the region), historicized elites (McDonogh 1986), social bandits, anarchists, laborers, industrial workers, and categories between these last two (Holmes 1989). The research also examines the social and cultural context of political and bureaucratic practices and their effects at the local level and explores the effects of European unification and its relationship to regionalist and nationalist movements. Turning the discipline's analytic spotlight back onto the societies that originally engendered anthropology makes an empirical project out of the mid-1990s concern with reflexivity, investing Europeanist research with critical theoretical implications for the discipline as a whole. While these developments have occurred in research on the entire European continent, the view that southern Europe was the geographical and cultural center of the known world in classical times has provided a further impetus for regional ethnographic research and critical reflection on its implications.

Although the classical cultures of Greece and Rome and their modern successors figured largely in the writings of early anthropologists such as Sir James George Frazer and E. B. Tylor, and although a local tradition of folklore studies accompanied the emergence of nationalism in all southern European societies, it was not until after World War II that thorough ethnographic exploration of the region took hold. Whereas the southern littoral of the Mediterranean had provided Émile Durkheim and E. E. Evans-

Pritchard with material for their respective models of political segmentation, the European littoral and its hinterland long remained a region of folklore rather than ethnography. Indeed, local ethnological scholarship in the nineteenth century had strongly supported folklore research, usually in search of materials to buttress the emergent and sometimes fragile unity of the nation state, and it was only hesitantly in Italy and Iberia, and much more recently Greece, that social and cultural anthropologies came into their own (and then usually with a local rather than global or comparative ethnographic reach). In the strongholds of anthropological theory, on the other hand, only sporadic monographs on Greece and Italy initially attested to the ethnographic possibilities of the region, in contrast with the rich and rapidly developed literature on Africa and other regions colonized by the European powers.

When southern Europe began to interest anthropologists more widely, it did so largely through the energies of J. G. Peristiany. An Africanist in his original field research, Peristiany, through several conferences and published volumes (e.g., Peristiany 1966, 1976) encouraged the development of a specifically Mediterranean focus within social anthropology. Common themes included moral values, kinship, land tenure, and micropolitical relations. French scholarship in the region came later (e.g., Piault 1985) but has been richly informed by historical sensibilities often lacking in the more "exoticist" traditions of the Anglo-Saxon schools and by both psychoanalysis and Marxism.

The Mediterraneanist focus was developed around a central concern with predominant moral systems, a direction that, partly under the influence of feminism, led in the 1970s and 1980s to a greater emphasis on gender. Thus, aside from several volumes dealing with honor and related concepts, important collections increasingly focused on gender, including ones edited by Jill Dubisch (1986) and Peter Loizos and Evthymios Papataxiarchis (1991). In addition, ethnographies, such as those by Stanley H. Brandes (1980), David D. Gilmore (1980), and Michael Herzfeld (1985), all of which developed and enlarged the early insights of such work as that of John Kennedy Campbell (1964) into the role of male aggression in southern European rural society, may be read in conjunction with Constantina Nadia Seremetakis (1991), Sally Cooper Cole (1991), and Jane K. Cowan

(1990), the last an exploration of the ambiguities of gender and power through the social evaluation of bodily comportment.

John Davis (1977) points out that a key to understanding Mediterranean societies is a set of antinomies around which long-standing tensions are played out at many levels. These antinomies subsist between the state and the local community, coastal and mountain dwellers, and, above all, between town and country. State-local relations were an early focus for Jane and Peter Schneider in Sicily, while two prominent Dutch scholars—Anton Blok in Sicily and Jeremy Boissevain in Malta—were especially active in exploring questions of power and patronage. In Cyprus, Peter Loizos (1975) initiated the study of national electoral politics in a local ethnographic context, although F. G. Bailey (1971) and his students were also studying micropolitical processes in Italy and elsewhere in Europe; Loizos (1981) later extended his investigation as the community he studied was forced into refugee status by the Turkish invasion of Cypress in 1974.

Although the close but sometimes tense social relations between mountain and plain are apparent in several works, the development of urban anthropology in southern Europe was surprisingly slow in coming; its arrival, signaled in part by the volume edited by Michael Kenny and David I. Kertzer (1983), foreshadowed a number of important studies, notably those of Renée Hirschon (1989). If Campbell's (1964) work in Sarakatsan moved the Africanist models of Evans-Pritchard into Europe, Hirschon's book (and the several articles that preceded it), informed by a traditional social anthropological perspective and close acquaintance with the local scholarly tradition in urban and architectonic studies, moved rural ethnography into the city. By examining the shifting social and political alignments of a large Asia Minor refugee population that had been resettled in Piraeus in 1924, following a major war between Greece and Turkey, Hirschon explored internal tensions within the still-coalescing Greek national culture as well as the effects of deeply held religious sentiment on the practices of an ostensibly antiecclesiastical, left-wing, displaced community.

The city never had been totally absent. Studies of patron-client relations throughout the region (Campbell 1964; Boissevain 1974) emphasize the role of entrepreneurs, landowners, and politicians—in part at the urban centers—in creating the present distribution of power. Other studies have also sought to explore the emergence of cultural and political elites. While James Faubion (1993) and Charles Stewart (1991) investigated the creation of multiple modernities, others studied the rise of modern familial and larger social ideologies and practices. David Kertzer's (1980) exploration of communist-Catholic interaction in a Bologna ward is one of a few existing demonstrations that conventional ethnographic techniques can work well in an urban setting; it provides a solid ethnographic background to his more recent studies of the uses of political symbolism to regenerate discredited or outmoded ideologies.

Kertzer's work has importance also as an experiment in the interweaving of historical and anthropological theories and methods, and as a critique of the conventional wisdom about sexual morality. In the former respect, he shows how the intensive reading of archival materials in the light of present-day ethnographic data can help illuminate complex demographic trends. In the latter, his work highlights the problem that Italian towns faced in disposing of children born out of wedlock—a problem that contradicts earlier images of chastity enforced by the alleged honor and shame code, while confirming the role of the church and state in maintaining a version of it. Similar issues also are raised by the important works of Caroline Brettell (1986) and Juan Brian O'Neill (1987) in Portugal, where, however, the incidence of premarital sexual relations may long have been higher than elsewhere in southern Europe. In other historical research, some of it inspired by the anthropologically informed historiography of Carlo Ginsburg (1980), Douglas R. Holmes (1989) has traced the effects of bureaucratization in Friuli on economic organization and devotional practices from the Middle Ages to the present. Such work again undercuts older conceptualizations of southern Europeans as living only in isolated peasant communities, immune to skepticism.

Historical issues also lead to challenges to the meaning of history itself, especially in an area saturated with historical associations for the leaders of the powerful northern nations that have exercised varying degrees of domination over the region since the seventeenth century. One effect of the persistant jockeying for power is that the state and various local interests, sometimes intertwined, engage in ferocious battles over the meaning of the past, especially where that past entails bureaucratic attempts to control habitats in historic conservation regimes (as in Greece). Where bitter civil strife has taken place (e.g., Spain in the late 1930s); Jerome R. Mintz's (1994) ethnographically contextualized oral testimony permits a critical examination of the pronouncements of party or state officials. As Ruth Behar (1991) also notes, the present is saturated with the past; but, just as even in the most urbane circles the present is riven by contests over what Faubion (1993) calls "sovereignty," the question is always whose past. Because of southern Europe's rich history, such issues are relatively easy to trace. The silences are equally eloquent. Certain groups have always been underrepresented in ethnographic studies of the area—perhaps reproducing local official bias. Thus, with the exception of Faubion's study of Athens (1993), there is very little on alternative sexualities.

Minority studies are a particular problem in Greece, where they become entangled easily with national boundary disputes and provoke both official and unofficial ire. This notwithstanding, there have been studies on the Arvanites (Romanian-speakers), Koutsovlachs, Macedonians, and Pomaks. There also has been work on German-speakers in Italy, Gypsies in Spain, and "secret Jews" in Portugal. Generally speaking, however, there remain vast areas of research for exploration, including studies of religious minorities such as the Jehovah's Witnesses or comparative studies of Jewish communities throughout the region. (There is some interesting work on Italian Pentecostalists that has been initiated by Salvatore Cucchiari [1988] and George R. Saunders [1995]). There are also class exclusions: merchants and other professionals almost everywhere are better understood historically than ethnographically. Although one might be able to extrapolate from local ethnography to explain, for example, the notorious instability of small businesses, direct ethnographic observation is lacking.

On the other hand, certain themes are well represented, and make southern Europe a virtual showcase for comparative studies. In Iberia, Brandes (1980) and Brettell (1986) have conducted important work on migration—the former on kinship networks, the latter with an emphasis on migration's implications for gender values and relations. The matrifocality of many Portuguese rural communities is also a focus of interest for Sally Cooper Cole (1991), for example.

The several major studies of demographic change in Italy and Portugal owe their richness to the availability of historical records. In contrast, such records are relatively scarce and inaccessible in Greece except in areas long occupied by the Venetians. Also, some archival records from the Turkish period are now becoming more accessible. Religion, identified early as a key to the understanding of Greek rural society by Campbell (1964), and carried into unexpected areas by Hirschon (1989) on ritual lamenting (one of several ethnographies of death practices in the region), and by Loring M. Danforth (1989) on firewalking rituals—a comparative study that also encompasses New Age cults in the United States, has also been explored by Charles Stewart (1991) as a key locus for the hegemonic struggles over who defines modernity. In Stewart's analysis "superstition" becomes a weapon of upwardly mobile peasants at the very moment the elite discovers "tradition" in the same practices and beliefs (an example, as Stewart has pointed out, of what Ernestine Friedl [1968] described as "lagging emulation").

Although long characterized by their northern neighbors as heavily dependent on gesture, the "classical" southern European cultures geographically provide a focus on literacy and orality and are important for the study of the embodiment of social ideology. In fact, the tradition of semiotic analysis has a long history in Italy, which may help to explain the lively development of an anthropologically informed group of semiotic analysts in Palermo—the Circolo Semiologico Siciliano.

Italy is the site of the one relatively robust local anthropological tradition of some age. As Saunders (1993) has shown, the Italian ethnologist Ernesto De Martino developed an idiosyncratic but analytically useful synthesis of Gramscian hegemony theory and "Anglo-Saxon" anthropology; in a more international extension of such approaches, Mariella Pandolfi (1991) has recently explored female social experience. While some local scholars (e.g., João Cutileiro (1971) in Portugal and Carmelo Lison Tolosana in Spain) published early in English, they were products of the dominant Anglo-Saxon traditions. In Italy and Spain largely Marxist-inspired studies with a regional focus have made an impressive appearance. In Spain and Portugal, the discipline has now entered the curriculum, as, in 1986 it did in Greece (the University of the Aegean offers an ambitious program of publica-

tions in Greek, while a new department has been started at the Pandio University in Athens). In addition, the University of Malta is the seat of the strongly anthropological *Journal of Mediterranean Studies*, published primarily in English.

Of the few summative studies of southern Europe, John Davis's (1977), although controversial, is perhaps the most comprehensive; its call to take history seriously has generated a serious response by most ethnographers working in the region. Kenny and Kertzer's volume (1983) on urban life in Mediterranean Europe is a valuable comparative study. Local and "foreign" scholars have engaged in lively debates about priorities and about the politics of field research in the region, notably in a series of exchanges in the journal *Critique of Anthropology* (1987), while an influential article by João de Pina-Cabral, focuses on the political inequalities underlying Mediterraneanist stereotypes and their consequent epistemological inadequacies. On the whole, while the Mediterraneanist comparisons of north with south, and of predominantly Christian with predominantly Islamic areas, has proved valuable, differences among and within the various countries of this region now favor different kinds of comparison. Especially important are those that account for transnational patterns, for example work on various immigrant communities resulting from the political and economic upheavals in Eastern Europe and elsewhere, those on local-level political mobilization for a wide range of international causes such as environmentalism and the fight against racism, and those on the implications of bureaucratic and party-political realignments in the "new Europe" of Maastricht and beyond.

MICHAEL HERZFELD

SEE ALSO: Europe, Eastern; Gender Differences and Roles; Honor; Resettlement

BAILEY, F. G. *Gifts and Poison: The Politics of Reputation.* New York: Schocken, 1971.

BEHAR, RUTH. *Santa Maria del Monte: The Presence of the Past in a Spanish Village.* Princeton: Princeton University Press, 1991.

BLOK, ANTON. *The Mafia of a Sicilian Village, 1860-1960: A Study of Violent Peasant Entrepreneurs.* New York: Harper and Row, 1974.

BOISSEVAIN, JEREMY. *Saints and Fireworks: Religion and Politics in Rural Malta.* New York: Humanities Press, 1965.

——. *Friends of Friends: Networks, Manipulators, and Coalitions.* New York: St. Martin's Press, 1974.

BRANDES, STANLEY H. *Metaphors of Masculinity: Sex and Status in Andalusian Folklore.* Philadelphia: University of Pennsylvania Press, 1980.

BRETTELL, CAROLINE. *Men who Migrate, Women who Wait: Population and History in a Portuguese Parish.* Princeton: Princeton University Press, 1986.

CAMPBELL, JOHN KENNEDY. *Honour, Family, and Patronage: A Study of Institutions and Moral Values in a Greek Mountain Community.* Oxford: Clarendon Press, 1964.

COLE, SALLY COOPER. *Women of the Praia: Work and Lives in a Portuguese Coastal Community.* Princeton: Princeton University Press, 1991.

COWAN, JANE K. *Dance and the Body Politic in Northern Greece.* Princeton: Princeton University Press, 1990.

CUCCHIARI, SALVATORE. "Adapted for Heaven: Conversion and Culture in Western Sicily." *American Ethnologist* 15: 417–441, 1988.

CUTILEIRO, JOSE. *A Portuguese Rural Society.* Oxford: Clarendon Press, 1971.

DANFORTH, LORING M. *Firewalking and Religious Healing: The Anastenaria of Greece and the American Firewalking Movement.* Princeton: Princeton University Press, 1989.

DAVIS, JOHN. *The People of the Mediterranean: An Essay in Comparative Social Anthropology.* London: Routledge and Kegan Paul, 1977.

DUBISCH, JILL, ed. *Gender and Power in Rural Greece.* Princeton: Princeton University Press, 1986.

FAUBION, JAMES D. *Modern Greek Lessons: A Primer in Historical Constructivism.* Princeton: Princeton University Press, 1993.

FRIEDL, ERNESTINE. "Lagging Emulation in Post-Peasant Society: A Greek Case." In *Contributions to Mediterranean Sociology*, J.G. Peristiany, ed. (Paris and the Hague: Mouton), pp. 33–106, 1968.

GILMORE, DAVID D. *The People of the Plain: Class and Community in Lower Andalusia.* New York: Columbia University Press, 1987.

GINSBURG, CARLO. *The Cheese and the Worms: The Cosmos of a Sixteenth-Century Miller.* Baltimore: The Johns Hopkins University Press, 1980.

HERZFELD, MICHAEL. *The Poetics of Manhood: Contest and Identity in a Cretan Mountain Village.* Princeton: Princeton University Press, 1985.

——. *A Place in History: Social and Monumental Time in a Cretan Town.* Princeton: Princeton University Press, 1991.

HIRSCHON, RENÉE. *Heirs of the Greek Catastrophe: The Social Life of Asia Minor Refugees in Piraeus.* New York: Oxford University Press, 1989.

HOLMES, DOUGLAS R. *Cultural Disenchantments: Worker Peasantries in Northeast Italy.* Princeton: Princeton University Press, 1989.

KENNY, MICHAEL, and DAVID I. KERTZER, eds. *Urban Life in Mediterranean Europe: Anthropological Perspectives.* Urbana, Ill.: University of Illinois Press, 1983.

KERTZER, DAVID I. *Comrades and Christians: Religion and Political Struggle in Communist Italy.* New York: Cambridge University Press, 1980.

LOIZOS, PETER. *The Greek Gift: Politics in a Cypriot Village.* New York: St. Martin's, 1975.

——. *The Heart Grown Bitter: A Chronicle of Cypriot War Refugees.* New York: Cambridge University Press, 1981.

LOIZOS, PETER, AND EVTHYMIOS PAPATAXIARCHIS, eds. *Contested Identities: Gender and Kinship in Modern Greece.* Princeton: Princeton University Press, 1991.

McDONOGH, GARY W. *Good Families of Barcelona: A Social History of Power in the Industrial Era.* Princeton: Princeton University Press, 1986.

MINTZ, JEROME R. *The Anarchists of Casas Viejas.* Bloomington, Ind.: Indiana University Press, 1994.

O'NEILL, BRIAN JUAN. *Social Inequality in a Portuguese Hamlet: Land, Late Marriage, and Bastardy, 1870-1978.* New York: Cambridge University Press, 1987.

PANDOLFI, MARIELLA. *Itinerari delle emozioni: corpo e identita femminile nel Sannio campo.* Milano: Franco Angeli, 1991.

PERISTIANY, J. G. *Honour and Shame: The Values of Mediterranean Society.* Chicago: University of Chicago Press, 1966.

——. *Mediterranean Family Structures.* New York: Cambridge University Press, 1976.

PIAULT, P., ed. *Familles et biens en Grèce et à Chypre.* Paris: L'Harmattan, 1985.

PINA-CABRAL, JOAO DE. "The Mediterranean as a Category of Regional Comparison: A Critical View." *Current Anthropology* 30 (1989): 399–406.

SAUNDERS, GEORGE R. "Critical Ethnocentrism and the Ethnology of Ernesto De Martino." *American Anthropologist* 95: 875–893, 1993.

——. "The Crisis of Presence in Italian Pentecostal Conversion." *American Ethnologist* 22: 324–340, 1995.

SEREMETAKIS, CONSTANTINA NADIA. *The Last Word: Women, Death, and Divination in Inner Mani.* Chicago: The University of Chicago Press, 1991.

STEWART, CHARLES. *Demons and the Devil: Moral Imagination in Modern Greek Culture*. Princeton: Princeton University Press, 1991.

EUROPE, WESTERN

Anthropological study in western Europe has been beset with debates about what, exactly, anthropologists should be doing there. Questions have been asked about the kinds of locations in which anthropologists have worked; about what should be included and what excluded; about appropriate methods; and about what distinguishes anthropological research from that of other disciplines studying the region. It has even been asked, occasionally, whether western Europe is a proper site of study for anthropologists at all. The reasons for this debate are bound up with the self-definition of anthropology more generally.

Defining Western Europe is problematic. Geographically, its boundaries are uncertain and it is culturally far from homogenous. Western, eastern, southern, and northern Europe are overlapping rather than distinct areas, although as ideas they are often used contrastively (especially West versus East). It should be borne in mind that conceptual categories like western Europe often rely upon oversimplified contrasts and stereotypes that make their variation from other areas appear more clear-cut than might otherwise be the case. Such contrasts and stereotypes also have played their part in the anthropology of the region.

Although the eastern borders of western Europe can roughly be defined as stretching from Germany in the north to Greece in the south, this is not universally agreed and would be delineated otherwise in different historical periods. Some might argue, for example, that with the demise of communist regimes, western Europe has expanded eastward. Part of the reason for the disagreement is that, culturally, western Europe is closely associated with a particular type of society that is generally credited with having its origins there. This is so-called "modern" society, characterized by industrialism, capitalism, urbanization, democracy, and the nation-state. Western Europe today, however, cannot readily be distinguished from many other regions on these criteria, making the demarcation of its boundaries still more problematic.

What is more, not all areas within western Europe equally share these industrial, capitalist, urban features, as many anthropologists have shown.

The history of anthropological research in western Europe has been patchy, ethnographic studies in any number only beginning in the 1950s. Such studies were not really drawn together until the 1970s when a number of anthropologists began to question the scope and directions of that earlier research, and to set an agenda for future work in the region. Nevertheless, throughout the period some excellent studies were undertaken and there are a number of themes that can be identified.

DEVELOPING ANTHROPOLOGICAL INTEREST

Nineteenth-century armchair anthropologists, such as Sir James George Frazer and E. B. Tylor included descriptions of various western European cultural practices in their works, but the western Europe from which their examples came was not "modern," industrial, west European society, but the Europe of classical mythology along with segments of Europe that were considered "primitive" or "fossilized." As anthropology developed during the twentieth century, however, carrying out fieldwork in what, for the anthropologists concerned, were exotic locations, came to be seen as a hallmark of social and cultural anthropology. In Great Britain, a disciplinary division of labor emerged which seemed to allocate "modern" industrialized western Europe to the sociologists and the more rural regions to the folklorists or ethnologists. In other parts of western Europe, such as France and Germany, ethnology and folklore often were not distinguished from anthropology, which makes it difficult to identify and summarize anthropological work from these traditions here (but see Jackson 1987). Suffice it to say, various west European anthropological traditions did carry out research in western Europe during the periods that British and U.S. anthropologists mostly ignored the region, although the general avoidance of industrialized Europe was characteristic of many of these other anthropological traditions too.

The first published anglophone ethnographic study of western Europe was Conrad Maynadier Arensberg's *The Irish Countryman: An Anthropological Study*, published in 1937. It was one of the very few studies carried out before the 1950s. Arensberg, from Harvard

University, was an American, as were many of the other early ethnographers of the region, a pattern that has continued. Although Arensberg's study is unique in its detail, in some respects it can be seen as typical of many of the west European ethnographies that followed during the 1950s, 1960s, and 1970s. Arensberg chose to work in a remote rural location, the kind of place that the majority of later anthropologists also selected. Many of the themes that Arensberg discusses are to be found in the later ethnographies: the place of kinship and friendship networks; gender divisions and the organization of the household; local politics and social stratification; the local economy; and religion and belief systems. More specific themes also emerged, in particular, patronage, honor, and shame in the south of the region.

The scope in these ethnographies was generally wide and descriptive. A principal aim was to show different aspects of social life interrelated (e.g., how kinship and networks of indebtness played a part in local economic relations) and how practices that might initially not make sense to the outsider could be understood by reference to local cultural patterns. For the most part these studies concentrated upon the point in time when the studies were undertaken, making use of the rich material gathered through participant-observation fieldwork. Mention often was made of the historical background of the community and ethnographers sometimes gave accounts of the ways in which wider society was impinging upon the community and changing its way of life. On the whole, however, communities were depicted as naturally static. Change was usually assumed to come from the outside and to be disruptive of the carefully balanced internal workings of the community.

Even when during this period anthropologists did occasionally work in more urban locations, they still selected areas that they classified as communities. There were many reasons, some bound to the overwhelming historical concentration of research on remote rural locations and communities. In part, anthropologists' chosen method, detailed participant-observation of a year or more in one location, seemed more appropriate to the kinds of places where the majority of inhabitants were likely to know each other. Also, the holistic functional approach, which was the dominant paradigm at the time, sought to look at societies as integrated wholes and to look at the ways

in which different aspects of these wholes contributed to the overall balance. These, perhaps together with a sense that traditional communities should be described before they disappeared, prompted anthropologists to select relatively isolated and self-contained communities rather than modern western Europe.

COMMUNITY STUDIES CRITIQUES

During the 1970s and 1980s, earlier anthropological work in western Europe was criticized by a number of scholars. Their criticisms, some of which were part of a more general critique of functionalism, centered upon the rural community focus typical of earlier research. They argued that studying a small community in isolation from either its history or the wider political and economic processes of the state lent a spurious appearance of stability and untouchedness to such communities. Anthropologists were not simply studying marginal areas, they were actually contributing to the representation of those areas as marginal or backward. In the words of Jeremy Boissevain (Boissevain and Friedl 1975), Europe had been "tribalised."

Some of these critiques gained impetus from theories of underdevelopment that had been applied to so-called less developed countries (LDCs). Marginal areas of Europe, like LDCs, should not be regarded as simply left behind by economic development but as fulfilling particular roles in national and global patterns of dependency and power relations. A number of earlier studies were subject to reanalysis in historical perspective, the aim being to show that states of affairs presented in the ethnographies as timeless local cultural patterns might, in fact, be recently adopted, being part of wider social and economic developments. For example, crofting in the Scottish Hebrides could be shown to be not an outmoded way of life stretching back to time immemorial but a cultural pattern developed in response to the demands of capitalism.

A number of ways in which west European research could move "beyond the community" (Boissevain and Friedl 1975) were identified. At a practical level anthropologists could work beyond the community by carrying out fieldwork in less isolated locations. At a conceptual level they could move beyond it by expanding their studies both in time and in context— by focusing on state-community mediators such as bureaucrats, for example. It was also argued that researchers in western Europe had restricted their studies overly much to the kinds of issues which anthropologists looked at in non-European cultures, such as kinship and household. Further, critics also argued that they had paid insufficient attention to matters potentially equally significant in the west European context, such as literacy and the role of texts, media, racism, and immigration. Anthropologists had also "tribalised" western Europe, it was claimed, by failing to engage in comparative research.

DEVELOPMENTS SINCE THE 1970s

The amount of anthropological research carried out in western Europe has expanded greatly since the 1970s. The Society for the Anthropology of Europe, established in 1986, has one of the largest memberships of any society within the American Anthropological Association. The European Association of Social Anthropologists, founded in 1989, although not specifically an organization dedicated to the study of Europe, lists more members in its registers studying west European locations than any other. The reasons for this expansion include the interest in the region generated by previous research and also the wider political developments in which anthropology is always, at least partially, implicated. With the demise of colonialism and growth of independence movements in formerly colonized countries, anthropologists often have found it more difficult both to gain research access from these countries' governments and to obtain research funding for study of such areas from research councils and foundations in their own countries. What is more, social and cultural developments in western Europe, such as the growth of ethnonationalism and moves toward greater pan-European political and economic union, have raised questions about the extent of west European homogeneity, or heterogeneity, and about what kinds of allegiances west European peoples have. These kinds of questions are ones that anthropologists, with their in-depth studies, are particularly well placed to tackle.

Recent research in Europe has built upon the community studies critiques and drawn upon other theoretical developments in anthropology such as reflexivity and postmodernism, making some of the insights from the earlier critiques more sophisticated. For example, rather than simply highlighting the analytical problems of the concept of community and then trying to avoid them, some anthropologists have looked at the ways in which the idea of community has entered into the lives of the people studied, perhaps

being reshaped in the process. Regarding history, too, anthropologists have built upon the idea that cultures should not be represented as diachronically sealed, but looked at the different kinds of history that are produced. Contrasts made between western Europe and other parts of the world, and between the margins and centers of Europe, have been analyzed to show how certain images and assumptions (e.g., of "otherness" or cultural difference) have informed both anthropology and representations of western European cultures.

Contemporary west European anthropological research is not easily summarized, partly because one feature of it is an increased diversification of focus both in terms of location and subject matter. Rather than attempting a rounded portrait of a whole community, many anthropologists have focused on specific dimensions of life, such as dance, sexuality, architecture, or new technologies. Increasingly, such anthropologists have turned to urban locations and particular institutions, especially those which might be of importance in producing representations of European traditions or cultural knowledge (e.g., the European Economic Commission, political parties, museums, tourist sites.) In an increasing proportion of this work anthropologists have attempted to bring together detailed ethnography and wider perspectives, and in so doing have made contributions to the development of anthropological theory more generally, especially in areas such as nationalism and ethnonationalism, identity, history, gender, and personhood.

Western Europe is one of the most important birthplaces of anthropology itself. As such, some of the assumptions deeply embedded in anthropological thought are bound up with ideas about the region and can even be encountered in ethnographic fieldwork there. The many years that anthropologists avoided western Europe, particularly its modern dimensions, suggest that the region acted as an implicit "self" against which "the other" was defined. By turning to western Europe, and subjecting this implicit "self" to the same critical scrutiny that other parts of the world have been subjected to, anthropologists of western Europe can make a particular contribution to one of cultural anthropology's aims, that of uncovering ethnocentrism, especially that which may lurk within anthropological theory itself.

SHARON MACDONALD

SEE ALSO: *Ethnocentrism; Europe, Southern; Functionalism; History of Anthropology; Honor; Nationalism; Patronage; Political Economy; Postmodernism; Reflexive Anthropology; World System Theory*

ARENSBERG, CONRAD MAYNADIER. *The Irish Countryman: An Anthropological Study.* Garden City, N.Y.: Natural History Press, 1968.

BOISSEVAIN, JEREMY, ed. *Revitalizing European Rituals.* New York: Routledge, 1992.

———, and J. FRIEDL, eds. *Beyond the Community: Social Process in Europe.* The Hague: Department of Educational Science of the Netherlands, 1975.

COHEN, ANTHONY PAUL, ed. *Symbolizing Boundaries: Identity and Diversity in British Cultures.* Wolfeboro, N.H.: Manchester University Press, 1988.

GODDARD, V., J. LLOBERA and C. SHORE, eds. *The Anthropology of Europe.* Oxford and Providence: Berg, 1994.

GRILLO, RALPH D., ed. *"Nation" and "State" in Europe. Anthropological Perspectives.* New York: Academic Press, 1980.

HASTRUP, KIRSTEN, ed. *Other Histories.* New York: Routledge, 1992.

HERZFELD, MICHAEL. *Anthropology Through the Looking-Glass: Critical Ethnography in the Margins of Europe.* New York: Cambridge University Press, 1987.

JACKSON, ANTHONY, ed. *Anthropology at Home.* New York: Tavistock, 1987.

MACDONALD, SHARON, ed. *Inside European Identities: Ethnography in Western Europe.* Providence, R.I.: Berg, 1993.

WILSON, THOMAS M., and M. ESTELLIE SMITH, eds. *Cultural Change and the New Europe: Perspectives on the European Community.* Boulder, Colo.: Westview Press, 1993.

EVOLUTION

SEE: *Cultural Evolution; Human Evolution; Primate Evolution*

EXCHANGE

Exchange is a ubiquitous and meaningful activity, present in all societies, by which valuables are transferred between persons, between groups, and, in religious contexts, between persons and spiritual entities. As such, exchange includes such varied forms as gift giving, resource pooling, barter, sacrifice, potlatch, bride-wealth payments, ceremonial and competitive distributions, credit, stock trading, the purchase and sale of commodities, and even the everyday exchange of courtesies and favors. Some theorists would include in this list such negative exchanges as theft, exploitation, and enclaving of wealth. Exchange can be viewed as both reflecting and constituting social relations and as expressive of the emotional states of partners and their ambitions. With its universal and richly elaborated character, exchange also serves as a widespread idiom for expressing ideas about social relations, fairness and morality, value, and cosmological order.

Models of money, value, and exchange typical in sociology and economics explain the interactions of everyday life in terms of assumed universal motives of rational benefit maximization on the part of individuals. Whereas such marketistic transaction analyses are not unknown in anthropology, values and motives are generally assumed to be socially embedded and politically laden, with symbolic associations that are not predictable from rational market models. In the course of exchanges, wider fields of power relations and cultural meanings may be manifested, expressed, subverted, or negotiated. Actual exchange encounters, although offering the concerned parties a range of possibilities, take place in specific social settings, in which the forms and meanings of recognized types of transactions have been culturally and historically constituted, so that they form part of the common-sense practical knowledge of the concerned persons.

INTELLECTUAL FOUNDATIONS

Early anthropological thought on exchange took shape around two central formulations received from nineteenth-century philosophy. One of these is an analytical dichotomy between gifts and commodities, associated with a corresponding classification of societies as having either moral economies organized by gift exchange or rational economies organized by commercial-market exchange. The second idea that shaped early exchange theory is that a norm of reciprocity can be assumed as axiomatic in noncommercial societies. This assumption means not only that the process of gift exchange was conceived in terms of simple obligatory units of gift and balanced countergift, but also that reciprocity was seen as the logically prior basis of all social relations. These initial formulations have been elaborated, supplemented, and challenged in subsequent theoretical and ethnographic work.

Before the mid-1970s anthropologists focused on exchange mainly as an organizing concept for understanding patterns of social life in the societies that they saw as noncommercial and relatively simple. Bronislaw Malinowski was among the first to contribute significant ethnographically based writings on exchange, using data from his fieldwork in the Trobriand Islands of Melanesia, in which he maintained the analytic opposition of economies organized by gift versus those based on market exchange. He argued that reciprocity, enforced by normative social pressure, is the basis of all social relationships in "primitive" societies. Malinowski's famous work *Argonauts of the Western Pacific* (1922) is primarily an analysis of *kula*, a complex system of delayed exchange along chains of partners on neighboring islands, whereby highly valued treasure items in the form of necklaces and armshells are circulated, and successful traders make and broadcast their fame. Emphasizing the symbolic and ceremonial aspects of *kula*, Malinowski illustrates the nonutilitarian, although by no means irrational, character of gift exchange. His work also provided an ethnographic basis for the idea that, by establishing relationships between givers and receivers, prestation is central to the social construction of the person.

In his seminal essay *The Gift* (1925), Marcel Mauss presented a theoretical perspective on exchange that was largely congruent with Malinowski's account. Mauss used comparative and historical data to characterize the prevalent forms of prestation in noncommercial societies as total social phenomena, involving all aspects of collective life. He also posited a universal reciprocal structure by which gifts must be given, received, and returned with equal or greater value, in order to maintain social relationships. Mauss suggested that gifts retain something of the identity of their donors and that they are thus "inalienable" to a greater degree than are the objects of commodity exchange. Lack of precise equivalence and temporal delays between gift and countergift promote ongoing cycles of prestations and differentiate gifting from other forms of exchange, such as barter or purchase. Gift cycles are characterized as permanent contracts between groups that articulate the principal institutions of the society. To explain the obligatory character of reciprocity, Mauss generalized from the Maori concept of *hau*, which he understood to be the "spirit of the gift" that demands a return gift in order to return to its place of origin.

Gift-exchange economies are contrasted with the amoral, individualistic, and alienated practices of modern market economies, and Mauss praises redistributions of wealth in the form of social security and health-insurance benefits for workers. He saw in them a recognition that all exchange, including the sale of labor, entails a giving of the self that demands a return beyond a simple wage. For Mauss, such reforms meant a reappearance of precapitalist values, signaling both the collective basis for moral action and a positive restoration of unalienated human social relations.

FORM, FUNCTION, AND MEANING

Generations of anthropologists have written in response to Mauss's work. It inspired some of the basic argumentation used by Claude Lévi-Strauss in developing French structuralism. Although accepting Mauss's general formulation of reciprocity in terms of a gift-countergift unit, Lévi-Strauss rejected his universalization of the *hau* concept as a motivational explanation. Instead, he employed a linguistic model to localize the universal structure of exchange in the binary operations of the human mind. The primary function of gift exchange, according to the analysis of Lévi-Strauss adapted from Mauss, is not simply to promote solidarity within social groups but to forge alliances between groups, thus widening the network of sociality to include those who had been potential enemies. The classic case for him was the intergroup exchange of women in marriage, made imperative by incest prohibitions. This, he argued, was the basis of all kinship systems and, ultimately, the basis of all human society.

Influential anthropological studies of exchange by Lévi-Strauss (1949) and Marshall D. Sahlins (1972) accept reciprocity as a given principle underlying and giving shape to social relations in noncommercial societies. Both men were also concerned with distinguishing among types of exchange. Lévi-Strauss distinguished between restricted exchange taking place directly between two partners, which can produce links between pairs of social groups, and generalized exchange, whereby valuables move through indirect links, such as through centralized collection and subsequent redistribution. Generalized exchange is capable of linking larger numbers of groups. Sahlins also notes this distinction and posits a reciprocity continuum along which particular cases can be analytically located. This continuum includes generalized reciprocity on the one extreme, referring to continual and varied gifting without thought of return, such as might occur among close family members. At the other extreme is self-interested, negative reciprocity, such as outright theft. In the middle lies mutual balanced reciprocity, in which exchange partners view gift and return gift as connected and of roughly equivalent value over time.

A large, ethnographically informed literature on exchange has developed in which particular attention has been paid to identity and social relations and documented the widespread practices of ceremonial and competitive (agonistic) exchanges, by which relations between social groups are managed, wealth is redistributed, and hierarchy, leadership, and power are produced. An important example of such studies are those of Annette Weiner (1976, 1992), who worked in the Trobriand Islands. Through detailed studies of gift exchange in relation to gender, descent groups, and political hierarchy, she clarified the significant functions of exchange as a mechanism for generating, maintaining, and communicating social identity and relations. Weiner's recording of the gendered symbolic associations of different kinds of valuables and the significance of women's exchange institutions signaled a feminist corrective in a literature in which exchange had typically been depicted as an exclusively male activity.

Weiner (1992) also turned inside out Lévi-Strauss's argument about incest prohibitions and the exchange of women, recasting the way anthropologists have conceptualized exchange in normative units of gift and countergift, arguing instead that it is by holding back from exchange certain possessions imbued with authenticating tradition and ancestral authority that persons maintain, display, and are enabled to exercise powerful identities. Arguing from her Pacific data, Weiner claims that the essential feature of social reproduction is not the exchange of women between groups of men in these societies but rather the productive character of brother-sister bonds that continue after marriage. Such analysis privileges cultural meaning over structural forms. A growing literature on the semiotics of exchange also explores the symbolic-meaning systems that generate particular logics of exchange.

The relationship of vertical and competitive exchange to political process and status hierarchy has also been an area of ethnological focus. Of special interest have been studies of New Guinea big men and of potlatch, as exemplified by the practices of tribes on the Northwest Coast of the United States. In the case of both big men and potlatch, conspicuous generosity is employed to enhance the honor and prestige of the givers while placing burdens of indebtedness on the receivers. For big men, this is a primary means of building a political following. The distinctive features of potlatch include a pattern whereby political rank among rival groups is settled through competitive and antagonistic ceremonial distributions of goods to guests in a series of reciprocally sponsored events of escalating scale. Potlatching also entails the ceremonial destruction of valuables, both as a display of superfluous wealth and as sacrificial gifts to the gods and spirits. Vertical exchange between humans and spiritual entities are common in many parts of the world. They are well documented in Latin American folk religion, for example, in which the faithful request favors of the saints in exchange for performing devotional acts.

Anthropologists have also focused on questions of value, highlighting African and Pacific cases in accounts of primitive money and spheres of exchange. The latter are cases in which a transactional order includes divisions into multiple economic domains within which different types of valuables are exchanged against each other. Typically, such spheres of exchange are symbolically ranked in terms of an order of morality or prestige, and the convertibility of currencies from one sphere to another varies cross-culturally.

SOCIAL ACTION, CHANGE, AND MIXED EXCHANGE SYSTEMS

Anthropologists with a theoretical orientation that emphasizes social action and practice have questioned the assumption that reciprocity is a behavioral norm to which individuals are generally obliged to conform. In action-oriented analyses, exchange of all types is construed as being risky business, the outcome of which is not predetermined by a norm of reciprocity or by one of profit maximization. A focus on the culturally conditioned motivations, strategies, resources, goals, and choices of actors participating in exchange helps to illuminate its apparently contradictory dynamics. After all, despite efforts to determine an essential character, source, and function for exchange, the ethnographic record shows that, in practice, people creatively manipulate the meanings, values, and norms associated with various kinds of exchange recognized in their society. They also can use them to whatever ends they wish, with the social effect of producing endlessly nuanced versions of division or integration, conflict or alliance, and hierarchy, as well as leveling.

This perspective on exchange is built on the work of Georg Simmel (1990), a contemporary of Mauss, who emphasized power, resistance, and the risk of loss in analyzing the creation of value through exchange. Simmel's approach assumed social actors staking claims and taking risks, gaining and losing, as well as producing personhood and social identity through exchange.

Anthropologists also continue to rework the basic concept of gift-commodity opposition that has shaped so much of the exchange literature. Summing up what has been learned through the Maussian framework, Chris Gregory argues convincingly in *Gifts and Commodities* (1982) for the continued usefulness of an analytical distinction between the two. As an ideal type, gifts are inalienable objects of similar kind, exchanged by persons who already have social ties— a practice that promotes the reproduction of social relationships. Commodities, at the other extreme, are alienable objects of different kinds, exchanged among strangers, which promotes the reproduction of things and relations among them. Other anthropologists have sought to demolish both the explanatory primacy of this distinction and its linkage to an opposition between traditional and modern societies. For example, Caroline Humphrey and Stephen Hugh-Jones (1992) point out that exclusive concentration on this binary pair has encouraged theorists and ethnographers to ignore other, equally ubiquitous and significant forms of exchange, such as barter, whereby qualitatively different objects are exchanged simultaneously and without ceremonial elaboration or reference to prices. They and many others have demonstrated the coexistence of gift, market, and other forms of exchange in all societies today, sets of options that cannot be reduced to a dominant type.

In the introduction to *The Social Life of Things* (1986), Arjun Appadurai further blurs the gift-commodity distinction in favor of a focus on the objects that are circulating, in terms of their passage through a succession of phases in which they may be used and recontextualized in a variety of ways. Cultural classifications of things in terms of their exchangeability and social arenas that encourage one or another kind of exchange are additional factors in what he calls exchange situations. When objects move across boundaries between culturally defined regimes of value, conflicts may arise over their exchangeability. As Jonathan Parry and Maurice Bloch point out in the introduction to *Money and the Morality of Exchange* (1989), shifting the analytical focus away from one or another form of exchange to the meanings of entire transactional orders clarifies the dynamic relations among forms of exchange (i.e., how one may historically change to another), as well as the relations between different transactional orders.

Much of the exchange literature on problems of social change concerns the consequences of introducing money into previously nonmonetized economies. Such accounts conventionally have assumed a view of money, received from nineteenth-century European thought, as a social corrosive capable of dissolving traditional exchange systems based on qualitative differences among things exchanged by indexing them all to a single quantitative standard. In the process, it was further assumed, money works as an agent replacing moral communities based on relations of reciprocity with the individualistic market relations envisioned in liberal philosophy. A more complex picture is emerging from ethnographic work on the so-called mixed-exchange systems that are typical of contemporary world societies, documenting a wide variety of outcomes.

Such critiques of conventional exchange theory tend to come from perspectives emphasizing historical, political, and intersocietal specificities. Contemporary ethnographic studies of colonial encounters, of industrialized societies, and of the transnational dimensions of exchange emphasize such problems as asymmetrical transactions, entanglement of gift and market spheres, consumer practices of identity construction, and the multiple meanings of money and commodities. They represent a revision of classical characterizations both of capitalist culture as market determined and of its relation to the indigenous economies on the colonial periphery.

CAROLINE S. TAUXE

SEE ALSO: *Economic Anthropology; Money; Sacrifice*

APPADURAI, ARJUN, ed. *The Social Life of Things: Commodities in Cultural Perspective.* New York: Cambridge University Press, 1986.

GREGORY, CHRIS. *Gifts and Commodities.* London: Academic Press, 1982.

HUMPHREY, CAROLINE, and STEPHEN HUGH-JONES, eds. *Barter, Exchange, and Value: An Anthropological Approach.* Cambridge: Cambridge University Press, 1992.

LÉVI-STRAUSS, CLAUDE. "The Principle of Reciprocity." In *The Elementary Structures of Kinship,* 1949. Rev. ed., translated by James H. Bell, John R. von Sturmen, and Rodney Needham; edited by Rodney Needham. Boston: Beacon Press, 1969.

MALINOWSKI, BRONISLAW. *Argonauts of the Western Pacific.* 1922. Reprint. New York: E. P. Dutton, 1966.

MAUSS, MARCEL. *The Gift: Forms and Functions of Exchange in Archaic Societies.* 1925. Reprint. New York and London: W. W. Norton, 1967.

PARRY, JONATHAN, and MAURICE BLOCH, eds. *Money and the Morality of Exchange.* Cambridge: Cambridge University Press, 1989.

SAHLINS, MARSHALL D. *Stone-Age Economics.* New York: Aldine de Gruyter, 1972.

SIMMEL, GEORG. *The Philosophy of Money,* 2nd ed., translated by Tom Bottomore and David Frisby; edited by David Frisby. London: Routledge, 1990.

WEINER, ANNETTE. *Women of Value, Men of Renown: New Perspectives in Trobriand Exchange.* Austin: University of Texas, 1976.

———. *Inalienable Possessions: The Paradox of Keeping-While-Giving.* Berkeley: University of California, 1992.

EXPRESSIVE CULTURE

Cultural expression is the realization of emotions and ideas in cultural activities and forms, such as oral and written literature, the plastic and graphic arts, music, dance, games, religion, ritual, and drama. Instrumental activities are primarily goal-oriented or bear on either physical or social survival, while expressive activities tend to not be goal-oriented except insofar as the expression of human identity is a goal in itself. Because most if not all human activities have some expressive coloration, however, it is often more profitable to consider mental, behavioral, and material aspects of culture along an instrumental-expressive continuum than to attempt to itemize things as expressive or instrumental. Clay pots are primarily utilitarian in that they are used to carry or store something, but they are also often decorated with designs or coloration that may be unique to individual potters or cultures, and this aspect of the pots is expressive. If the range of human cultural activities is viewed in this way, even some kinds of warfare—where chivalry or similar codes of conduct are in force—have an expressive side.

Like other components of culture, expressive activities are learned and shared, but while some of them (e.g., music and games) seem to be cultural universals, others are not. Further, even among universals, forms and styles differ both cross-culturally and intraculturally. While all cultures have games, for example, games of strategy are more common in complex societies. Body decoration appears to be universal, but the prevalence of earrings, body tattooing, or lip plugs as forms of decoration differs widely among societies. Within general expressive categories, such as games or body decoration, intracultural differences commonly occur along common social cleavages—age, gender, and/or social class.

EXPRESSIVE CULTURE AS AN ANTHROPOLOGICAL CONCERN

Expressive culture is surely one of the first aspects of a society noticed by outsiders. Thus, early travelers and chroniclers often described the religion, arts, and games of those people they encountered. In his 1881 text *Anthropology*, Edward B. Tylor included a chapter titled "Arts of Pleasure," and his discussion of art, music, games, play, and other entertainments is one of the earliest systematic expositions of expressive culture.

During the 1930s and 1940s, anthropologists relied heavily on Freudian or neo-Freudian theory in their analyses of expressive culture. In the late 1930s, the psychoanalyst Abram Kardiner, along with anthropologists Cora Dubois and Ralph Linton, developed a psychoanalytically oriented view of culture and personality. Kardiner and Linton (1939) asserted that cultures are integrated because members share a number of early experiences that lead to the formulation of a specifiable "basic personality structure" (BPS). The BPS then is a causal agent in the development and maintenance of other aspects of the culture. Thus, in their view, culture can be divided into primary institutions, those aspects of culture that bring about the BPS, such as type of subsistence, household form, and child training methods, and secondary institutions, those aspects of a culture that result from the local BPS, including religion, ritual, and mythology. The primary institutions, especially those dealing with child training, were delineated largely on the basis of Freudian theory. Secondary institutions, which served to satisfy the basic personality needs created by the primary institutions, were termed "projective systems." The children of nurturant and benevolent parents, for example, would develop personality types that would find satisfaction in supernaturals of similar character. Thus, the character of the supernaturals are "projections" of early childhood experiences.

A more recent approach to culture and personality is that of John W. M. Whiting and his colleagues. With Kardiner's system it was not obvious why things such as subsistence methods and household types were primary while other cultural subsystems were secondary. Whiting and his colleagues (Whiting and Child 1953) made maintenance systems causally prior to child training practices. Maintenance systems include the economic, political, and social institutions that provide for the survival and well-being of members of a society. In turn, child training practices influence the formation of personality variables and personality variables lead to the projective systems of a culture. Harsh or benign environments, for example, result in differences in the amount and kind of care given to children. These differences lead to different personality types that are manifested in varied projective systems. Whiting and his coworkers also put the model to rigorous testing through the use of cross-cultural statistical methods and in the Six Cultures Project, an effort to apply the scheme in field research (Whiting and Whiting 1974).

Projection is a central concept in both the Kardiner and the Whiting models. For Sigmund Freud, projection meant the attribution of unacceptable impulses to external persons or things. Thus, an individual's unconscious hostility toward another is converted to "she hates me." Similarly, for Kardiner and Whiting, projective systems are the expressed symptoms of intrapsychic conflict. In the Six Cultures study, religion, magic, ritual and ceremony, art, recreation, games, and even crime and suicide rates were considered parts of projective/expressive systems. The change in terminology from "projective" to "projec-tive/expressive" reflected a growing disenchantment with Freudian theory in anthropology.

The psychological functionalism of Bronislaw Malinowski was also a major influence in the study of expressive culture. Malinowski (1939) believed that there were seven basic human "needs," some social and others individual. As a functionalist, he sought to show how the various parts of culture contributed to the integration and systematic operation of cultures as wholes. His emphasis on individual, psychological, and biological factors clearly distinguished his approach from that of the British structural-functionalists, such as A. R. Radcliffe-Brown, who pursued "social facts," in a Durkheimian sense. Malinowski's brand of functionalism permitted the study of the individual and psychological functions of expressive systems.

In summary, at least three lines of thought helped launch the study of expressive culture. First, anthropologists have always been concerned with describing other cultures, and expressive forms such as art and music are often first to catch the eye of a visitor. This descriptive tradition is exemplified by the work of Franz Boas (1929) on "primitive" art. Second, the culture and personality models proposed by Kardiner and Whiting, with their incorporation of the Freudian notion of projection, held that people express their psychological characteristics in cultural activities such as religion, art, games, and music. Third, Malinowski's psychological functionalism provided a theory of culture wherein expressive activities hold a rightful place in the integration of culture as "secondary needs," contributing as such to the integration and harmonious operation of societies.

CONTEMPORARY APPROACHES TO EXPRESSIVE CULTURE

A culture's expressive array may be thought of as the sum of the outlets for cultural expression available to members of a society. Although the situation is complicated by the fact that virtually all aspects of culture have expressive qualities, all cultures have an ensemble of activities that are primarily expressive. Not surprisingly, large and complex cultures typically have larger expressive arrays than smaller and simpler cultures, although many small-scale societies are amazingly rich in folklore, ritual, and other expressive traditions.

EXPRESSIVE MODELS

Elements of the expressive array usually model or represent important real-world cultural activities. Models are devices used for the storage and dissemination of information. Maps, for example, are models and come in a variety of types. Road maps and topographic maps emphasize different features and provide different information to users. Some maps, such as a visitor's guide to Disney World, have a larger expressive component than road or topographic maps, while a child's hand-drawn treasure map is almost completely expressive. Models also differ along several other dimensions. They may differ in terms of scale—a model of an atom is much larger than a real atom while a toy bow and arrow is smaller than the real thing. Models can differ in terms of complexity. Some models of ships or trains constructed by hobbyists are exceedingly intricate, with many pseudo-working parts, while toy ships or trains may be extremely simple. Models may also differ in terms of true-to-lifeness. Plastic scale-models of airplanes may accurately depict the originals, but are static. Powered models may be less accurate portrayals but actually fly like the original. An individual or couple who want but lack a child may substitute an expressive model. A dog may be initially similar to a child in terms of scale, complexity, and even verisimilitude when compared with other potential models, such as a goldfish or a petunia.

Models have a variety of purposes. They often serve as information-reduction devices by eliminating useless or irrelevant detail. For example, information about topography is usually not important in a road map. Models also function as information-storage devices. Bow-and-arrow or black-powder-arms hunters maintain knowledge of the use of obsolete weaponry while paintings or photographs preserve scenes, clothing styles, and behavior patterns. Models such as toy bows and arrows or flight simulators are also used in teaching and learning. Further, models act as buffered learning devices. One could learn to fly a jet fighter by strapping in and taking off, but the potential for disaster in such a real-world situation far exceeds that possible in a flight simulator. Models also often have information-generation functions, that is, they are used to simulate situations that have never actually occurred before, so that solutions or strategies may be discovered or evaluated. Model airplanes

are tested in wind tunnels (themselves models) for aerodynamic characteristics, and model battlefields are constructed to appraise strategies.

Expressive models or systems, including religion, also have palliative effects, helping people adjust to existing states or to frustration. There are few veteran drivers who have never wished that they could ram an incompetent driver on the highway. The bumper cars at amusement parks—expressive models of real-world automobiles—permit frustrated commuters to do just that. Gambling, an expressive activity that is enjoying prodigious growth in the United States, provides a "chance" at riches. A lottery ticket symbolizes the possibility of wealth and models the capitalist system of speculative investment with the hope of a high return.

Expressive models often exhibit extreme resistance to change. This expressive persistence is characteristic of myths, folktales, legends, games (e.g., chess, go), and many "folk" items (e.g., dance, art, music, clothing). Sometimes the "folk" themselves persist in the face of outside pressure to change, partly by maintaining expressive reminders, such as dress style, language, rituals, and behavior patterns, denoting their distinctiveness from others. The Amish in the United States are an example. Because of expressive persistence, outmoded, obsolete, or historical aspects of cultures are often preserved in the expressive realm. Items or activities that were once almost purely instrumental, such as tilling with a horse-drawn plow, preparing maple syrup over an outdoor fire, or flying World War II fighter planes, are now frequently made the focus of festivals. In the process, the character of these items or activities has been changed from primarily instrumental to primarily expressive.

Expressive things and activities are often the object of expressive intolerance, that is, people who are involved in one expressive area may be intolerant of the expressive activities of others, or, even within the same expressive realm, individuals may enjoy some styles but disfavor others. Individuals who express themselves primarily through religious participation may be intolerant of pornography, for example, while artists who enjoy painting landscapes may dislike abstract art. In the United States, adults are often intolerant of the preferred music of adolescents and vice versa. Parents not only seem to dislike what they regard as the cacophonous sound of their children's music but also the seditious themes it may express. While expressive intolerance often results in conflict (religious wars are an extreme example), it may also help to maintain a large expressive array in cultures, especially within populous societies.

Cultural Expression in Art

Although expressive culture, including art, seemingly should have great latitude to vary, numerous researchers have observed that art models or symbolizes other aspects of the culture in which it is found. Expressive culture thus represents themes that are important to those who create it while unimportant or nonexistent themes are unlikely to be addressed. In turn, this suggests the integration of cultures and the psychological characteristics of their members.

In an important study of art and culture, John L. Fischer (1961) suggests that social fantasy is an important determinant of art form and style. He means that artists express fantasies in their work about social situations that may provide security, comfort, or pleasure. He hypothesizes that designs that repeat a number of relatively simple elements should characterize egalitarian societies, while designs that integrate multiple unlike elements should occur in hierarchical societies. He further hypothesizes that security in egalitarian societies rests on multiple comrades of equal status, while security in hierarchical societies depends on relationships with individuals of greater or lesser rank. Similarly, egalitarian societies should be characterized by figures without enclosures, symmetrical designs, and designs with substantial empty or irrelevant space. Hierarchical societies should be marked by figures with enclosures, asymmetrical designs, and designs with little or no empty or irrelevant space. All of these hypotheses are supported using cross-cultural data (although the sample that Fischer uses is open to criticism by today's standards).

In an intracultural replication of Fischer's study, William W. Dressler and Michael C. Robbins (1975) studied social stratification as expressed in painted pottery from three different historical periods of Greece. The first, 1000–750 B.C., was a period of low social stratification. The second, 750–600 B.C., was characterized by the development of land-owning social classes and tenant farmers who might be claimed as slaves if they could not pay their debts. During the third period, 600–450 B.C., the debts by which the debtor's person could be claimed were annulled and slaves were set free. Dressler and Robbins had two judges evaluate pottery from these periods in terms of whether designs were simple or complex, empty or crowded, and open or closed. They found that the designs from the first period were simple, empty, and open, while those from the second period were complex, crowded, and enclosed. The designs from the third period were intermediate, although more similar to the first period than the second.

Elizabeth B. Merrill (1987) also reexamined Fischer's hypotheses using two samples of designs from the Shoshone, one from an early reservation period (1870–1901) and the second from a contemporary period (1973–1983). She codes the art in terms of the same four variables used by Fischer and compares the results based on measures of Shoshone sociopolitical complexity during the two periods. While her results for the enclosed figures variable were not statistically significant, those for each of the other three variables, plus a summary score, support Fischer's conclusions. Sociopolitical change seems to be followed by adjustments in art style.

Cultural Expression in Music

Music, like art, exhibits wide cross-cultural variation in style and may be regarded as a form of expressive communication or a model of human speech. The verisimilitude of music to human speech varies substantially, with folk songs being quite similar to speech (although more repetitive), while jazz instrumentals are quite dissimilar. In the former, meaning, values, and worldview are expressed in the lyrics, as well as in the music, while in the latter, they are expressed abstractly through tone, rhythm, tempo, melody, and so on.

In a large cross-cultural study, Alan Lomax and his colleagues (1968) found that a number of song and instrumental performance features vary with cultural complexity. In addition, certain features of song style mirror themes characteristic of the sociocultural system of both musician and listener. Although the first of these conclusions has been challenged on the basis that differences in styles can be explained by regional variation, suggesting diffusion, the second, much as the case with art, points to the integration of culture.

Other research suggests that child-rearing practices are related to some variations in music. Barbara C. Ayres (1973) found that the nature of musical rhythm correlates with how children are carried. When children are carried more or less constantly by their mother or an older sibling, experiencing rhythmic motion when their bearer walks, then the music produced in their society tends to have a regular rhythm. Where children are cradled or carried in a cradleboard, the music tends to have either an irregular or a free rhythm. Other work by Ayres suggests that early stressing of children, through circumcision, clitoridectomy, tooth evulsion, scarification, or other methods, is related to songs with a regular rhythm, a wide vocal range, and forceful accenting.

Cultural Expression in Games

The idea that real-world cultural activities or themes are modeled expressively is probably best developed in the study of games. John M. Roberts, who was influenced by Malinowski's psychological functionalism and was a colleague of Beatrice and John Whiting at Harvard University in the early 1950s, spent much of his career in the study of expressive culture, especially games. In 1962 Roberts and psychologist Brian Sutton-Smith proposed the "conflict-enculturation hypothesis of game involvement." Later broadened to include other expressive activities, it was renamed the "conflict-enculturation theory of model involvement." The theory is based on several assumptions. First, cultural maintenance requirements lead to particular socialization practices. Second, psychological conflicts are engendered in children through the processes of child training. Third, these conflicts are noxious, and individuals seek to reduce or eliminate them. Fourth, individuals are curious about the sources of their conflict. Finally, individuals seek to gain mastery over the sources of conflict. In games, cultures provide playful models of real-world activities. Roberts and Sutton-Smith (1962) hold that involvement in such models provides a buffered learning context in which mastery can be developed and the conflicts themselves can be assuaged.

Game outcomes can be determined by physical skill, strategy, and/or chance. Moreover, many games clearly model real-world activities. Among games of physical skill, American football is a transparent model of warfare while trap shooting models hunting. Chess, a game of strategy, models war, but also represents a stratified social system. Games of chance, including dice or guessing games, appear to model fate, divination, or interactions with the supernatural. Indeed, fate is often enjoined by little "prayers" ("Come on, seven!" or "Baby needs a new pair of shoes!") before the toss of the dice in craps. In several cross-cultural studies, Roberts, Sutton-Smith, and their colleagues found that games of physical skill seem to be associated with conflict over achievement, games of strategy with conflict over obedience, and games of chance with conflict over responsibility. Thus, societies that stress achievement training in children have many games of physical skill, those that stress obedience have games of strategy, and where responsibility is stressed games of chance occur. In addition, while all cultures have games of physical skill, those of intermediate complexity tend to include games of chance, while games of strategy most often occur in cultures of high complexity.

Cultural Expression in Other Forms

Expressive culture includes numerous forms other than art, music, or games and many of them, such as folktales, riddles, sexual behaviors, drug use, food preferences, humor, and dance have been studied by anthropologists. Findings are varied, of course, but a common thread seems to be that forms and/or styles of expressive behavior relate, statistically speaking, to cultural complexity. This makes perfect sense if elements of expressive culture are regarded as either models of real-world activities or expressions of important themes in societies. Where the real-world activities or themes do not exist, models or representations of them are unnecessary and may be literally inconceivable.

Culture permits humans to interface with nature and with each other. The part of culture devoted to the needs of survival and reproduction has received the most attention from anthropologists, although a significant portion of culture is devoted to the expression of what it means to be human, part of a particular group, or an individual. Although theory regarding this area is not yet well developed, there are several questions that seemingly must be addressed by any general consideration of expressive culture. First, with respect to different cultures, why do some expressive forms, but not others, exist? Second, within particular cultures, why do individuals participate in some expressive forms and not others? Third, how do the expressive and the instrumental aspects of culture interrelate, given that the two cannot be neatly dichotomized? Last, how do the instrumental and expressive aspects of culture coevolve?

GARRY E. CHICK

SEE ALSO: Adornment; Art; Games; Music

AYRES, BARBARA C. "Effects of Infant Carrying Practices on Rhythm in Music." *Ethos* 1 (1973): 387–404.

BOAS, FRANZ. *Primitive Art.* New York: Dover, 1955 (originally published 1929).

DISSANAYAKE, ELLEN *What Is Art For?* Seattle: University of Washington Press, 1988.

DRESSLER, WILLIAM W., and MICHAEL C. ROBBINS. "Art Styles, Social Stratification, and Cognition: An Analysis of Greek Vase Painting." *American Ethnologist* 2 (1975): 427–434.

FISCHER, JOHN L. "Art Styles as Cultural Cognitive Maps." *American Anthropologist* 63 (1961): 79–93.

KAEMMER, JOHN E. *Music in Human Life: Anthropological Perspectives on Music.* Austin: University of Texas Press, 1993.

KARDINER, ABRAM, and RALPH LINTON. *The Individual and His Society.* New York: Columbia University Press, 1939.

LOMAX, ALAN, ed. *Folk Song Style and Culture.* Washington, D.C.: American Association for the Advancement of Science, 1968.

MALINOWSKI, BRONISLAW. "The Group and the Individual in Functional Analysis." *American Journal of Sociology* 44 (1939): 938–964.

MERRILL, ELIZABETH B. "Art Styles as Reflections of Sociopolitical Complexity." *Ethnology* 26 (1987): 221–230.

ROBERTS, JOHN M., and BRIAN SUTTON-SMITH. "Child Training and Game Involvement." *Ethnology* 1 (1962): 166–185.

TYLOR, EDWARD B. *Anthropology.* New York: Appleton and Company, 1881.

WHITING, BEATRICE, and JOHN W. M. WHITING. *Children of Six Cultures.* New York: Wiley, 1974.

WHITING, JOHN W. M., and IRVIN L. CHILD. *Child Training and Personality: A Cross-Cultural Study.* New Haven, Conn.: Yale University Press, 1953.

F

FAMILY AND HOUSEHOLD STRUCTURE

The fundamental relationships of human family organization are marriage, parenthood, and shared descent, which are based on the social identities of spouse, parent, child, and sibling. These social identities are defined differently from society to society and have associated with them characteristic sets of rights and duties which also differ. The most variable relationship underlying family organization is marriage. Sometimes a delimited part of a larger society (e.g., a subcaste or a utopian community) does not utilize this relationship or has marriage arrangements so tenuous that they play no role in family organization. These instances, however, are exceedingly rare.

In animal species, the counterpart of human marriage is the formation of stable pair bonds between males and females. However, our closest phylogenetic relatives, the great apes, do not form such bonds. Hence, it is likely that pair bonding in the human species developed after our separation from the apes several million years ago. This development is plausibly associated with expansion of brain size, increase in symbolic capacity, and elaboration of systems of linguistic communication, which also occurred during this period. Larger adult brain size led to births in which the infant was less mature, thus increasing the degree and length of dependence of human offspring.

In addition, increasingly elaborate language systems and a greater emphasis on learning and symbol manipulation, as a means of adapting to the environment, also contributed to an extended period of childhood dependence. It takes a long time, indeed, for a human infant to become a fully enculturated adult. An almost incalculable amount of cultural and linguistic knowledge has to be individually acquired by each human newborn. This longer period of childhood dependence greatly increases the burden of human child rearing and may have contributed to the development of pair bonding in the human species.

Bonding between human males and females, while it may have a biological base, is primarily cultural, in contrast to the pair bonding of other animal species. Human marriage is always defined culturally and is always hedged around with prescriptions and proscriptions. Some animal species form stronger pair bonds than humans do. The widespread existence of divorce is evidence of the brittleness of human marriage. Only a few societies prohibit divorce entirely, while most have regular, culturally institutionalized procedures for securing and implementing it.

FAMILY ORGANIZATION

The ubiquity of marriage across human cultures brings into existence various forms of the conjugal, or marriage-based, family. The minimal conjugal family unit is the nuclear family, consisting of a spousal pair and their offspring. The major alternative to conjugal family organization is a group consisting of a woman and her offspring, or the nonconjugal family. This unit differs from the conjugal family in that the husband/father role is largely or entirely nonexistent. Nonconjugal family organization is never the sole form of family organization in a society and is usually infrequent where it does occur. However, in a few large-scale industrial societies, including our own, this family form has become relatively common.

Behavioral bonding or "attachment" between a mother and her offspring underlies both conjugal and nonconjugal family organization. Human females, like those of many other animal species, typically shelter and care for the offspring they bear. Infant and child care could be arranged differently in cultures: adult females could primarily rear unrelated children; adult males could primarily rear children; aged males or females could primarily rear children; impersonal social institutions could primarily rear children; older children could primarily rear infants and young children, and so forth. In fact, all of the above do sometimes rear children or participate in child care cross-culturally, but it remains the case that human females strongly tend to play a primary role in caring for the infants they bear.

While the bonding that typically occurs between a mother and her infant may have an innate biological component, it also has important environmental and cultural inputs, and these can vary greatly. The degree to which these latter components are influential is evidenced by the strong bonds that often form between adoptive mothers and other maternal surrogates and their children. Males in pair-bonding species also tend to play an important role in rearing offspring.

Incest prohibitions, which forbid sexual intercourse between parents and children, and brothers and sisters, are part of human family organization. These restrictions are always extended outwardly to more distant kin. While no society lacks incest restrictions, sometimes a delimited segment of a larger society abrogates one or more of these prohibitions. Ruling elites, for example, have in rare instances allowed and even encouraged brother-sister marriage. Incest restrictions ensure that young adults look for mates beyond the confines of their immediate family.

Prescribed behavioral norms that obtain within dyadic relationships are another feature of family organization. For instance, the degree of formality of the brother-sister relationship within a society varies greatly across cultures. Formal behavior ranges from respectful interaction to various forms of avoidance (e.g., restrictions on speaking, physical contact, and being alone together). Informal behavior ranges from casual interaction to light joking (e.g., teasing, mild insults, and discussion of sexual matters). Formality characterizes brother-sister interaction in 70 percent of cultures worldwide and informality makes up the remainder. Variation in degree of formality of this relationship, in turn, is associated with certain residence and descent patterns cross-culturally.

FAMILY FUNCTIONS

The most important function of family organization is the production of new adult members of a society. Enculturation of children involves publicly acknowl-edged nurturing and caretaking obligations, such as feeding, clothing, housing, and educating children. Mating in conjugal families involves publicly acknowledged rights of sexual access between members of a marital pair which may lead to procreation. Rights of sexual access within societies, however, are seldom limited to those obtained between marital partners, and even attempts at such limitation occur in only about 5 percent of the cultures of the world.

The importance of procreation across cultures is shown in a study of societal responses to childlessness. The approximately forty societies in the study showed a concern with childlessness and a range of cultural responses to this condition. Supernatural appeals and ethnomedical procedures were most frequent. These remedies were typically tried first by a couple, since they were generally inexpensive and involved no disruption of social relationships. Another remedy, adoption or fosterage, was an option in 85 percent of the societies studied. Additional responses were divorce and taking a second wife, each being options in about two-thirds of the societies.

Another function of the conjugal family is economic cooperation and provisioning. Economic cooperation can range from various conventions involving division of labor between the sexes to contemporary arrangements involving the pooling and allocation of income when both spouses work outside the home. Tasks commonly allotted to females cross-culturally tend to be those compatible with the care of infants and young children. Some evidence exists that provisioning difficulties faced by lone females in feeding young offspring is a primary determinant in the development of pair bonding in many animal species. Tying a male willing to help in feeding and other caretaking tasks to a female and her offspring might select for strengthened pair-bonding tendencies within a species by allowing more offspring to survive.

Mating in nonconjugal families usually involves a series of consensual relationships with little or no involvement by the procreating males in child care or economic provisioning. It may be that placing the entire burden of childrearing and economic provisioning on a lone human female accounts for the very low frequency of this family form in most cultures. In addition, social welfare policies in some large-scale societies, including our own, may encourage this form of family organization by allowing subsistence payments only to households which do not include a cohabiting adult male.

Family organization may also involve the development of common structures of symbolic meaning and significance. These shared cognitive structures may, in turn, facilitate the formation of strong companionship and emotional intimacy bonds. Another function of the family is the social placement of individuals. This can range from the assignment of kinship statuses of various sorts, to the ascription of ethnic or caste status. Even statuses that can be altered as an individual matures, such as class status, are first determined by family membership.

A final function involves the organization of decision-making processes within families. In conjugal families, adult males tend to control instrumental decisions, while adult females play a major role in organization and control of expressive processes involving emotions and feelings. In matrilineal societies, husbands often share instrumental power within the family with the brothers of their wives. In this situation, women often achieve considerable informal power by playing these two off against each other.

In addition to marriage-based families of the nuclear type, other forms of conjugal family organization exist based on plural marriage. One type of plural marriage is the concurrent marital union of one man with two or more women forming a polygynous family. Polygyny is extremely common cross-culturally, occurring in more than three-fourths of the world's cultures. In most of these cultures, polygynously married men are a minority of all married men. Since the pool of adult males in societies may be approximately equal to the pool of adult females, special arrangements may be necessary if most men expect to be polygynously married. One common mechanism is to allow females to become married adults at a much earlier age than males are allowed to achieve this status.

It might be expected that only a few men in any society would be able to command the economic resources necessary to provision more than one woman and her offspring. Polygyny, however, is not always economically costly. In societies where women make a large contribution to subsistence, polygyny often contributes to a man's economic well-being. Not surprisingly, polygyny is especially common and frequent in these societies.

The polygynous family shares to some extent the central characteristic of nonconjugal families (i.e., a great diminution in the importance of the husband/father role), since the attention of a man is divided among several women and several sets of offspring. Still, the husband/father role does exist in polygynous families and the position is regularly occupied, even if it is somewhat attenuated functionally.

Another form of plural marriage is polyandry, the concurrent marital union of one woman with several men, typically a group of brothers. Polyandrous families are rare cross-culturally, occurring in only about one of every 100 cultures, and are seldom statistically frequent even where they do occur. At least some instances of polyandry appear to occur as a response to economic scarcity, suggesting that the provisioning of several males is considered necessary to maintain a desired standard of living for a family. This seems similar to the practice, common in large-scale societies, of limiting the number of children in a family to maintain a desired standard of living.

A final family form is the group family which results from the rare practice of "group marriage" in which two or more men are united with two or more women. Among the Kaingang, a people of the Amazonian region of South America, 8 percent of all marital unions observed over a period of 100 years were group marriages. A study of twenty group marriages in the United States included sixteen composed of two women and two men, and four composed of five to six adults. Most of these groups broke up in less than a year, with only a few staying together for two years or more. Thus, group families are highly unstable, at least in societies such as our own which do not encourage such arrangements.

HOUSEHOLD ORGANIZATION

Households are composed of one or more people, typically a family or several families, who reside together and form a functioning domestic group. Coresidence occurs when a domestic unit occupies a common dwelling or a portion of a dwelling or an aggregation of dwellings in a delimited space or territory. For societies with impermanent dwellings, the bounded space or territory may be more salient than the physical dwelling. A functioning household may entail sharing economic resources, sleeping quarters, a cooking pot, or other domestic functions. Since households are often composed of one or more family units, their functions tend to include those associated with families (i.e., mating, socialization of children, economic cooperation and provisioning, social placement, instrumental and expressive decision-making, and provision of emotional intimacy, companionship, and shared structures of meaning).

Conjugal families are not always residentially aggregated. For example, among the traditional Ashanti of Ghana, West Africa, it was common for a male to sleep in the household of his maternal kin, while his wife and children occupied the household of her maternal kin. Special arrangements were necessary when spouses wished to sleep together. In addition, food was regularly carried from the mother's cooking shed to the father's house. In short, Ashanti husbands did not regularly reside with their wives and children (i.e., their family of procreation). Instead, they remained members of the household in which they grew up (i.e., they continued to live with their family of orientation).

Another example of noncongruence between family and household occurs among the Kipsigi in East Africa. The Kipsigi have polygynous families but these families are not residentially aggregated. Each co-wife has a separate dwelling located at a considerable distance from that of other co-wives. A Kipsigi husband alternates his residence from wife to wife. Much of the time, a Kipsigi co-wife and her children form an independent household. Mother-child households in which the husband-father lives elsewhere much of the time are relatively common cross-culturally, occurring in about 25 percent of the world's societies.

Another type of exception involves men's houses in which males regularly reside apart from their families. In these instances, too, households and conjugal families are not fully congruent. Among the Mundurucu, who live in the Amazonian region of South America, communities are composed of two separate residential units, one including all the men and the other all the women and children. In cultures which institutionalize noncongruence between households and conjugal families, the functions of the conjugal family may be greatly reduced.

While institutionalized noncongruence of household and family occurs in many societies, there are also many instances in which congruence is the norm but an assortment of "leftover" individuals or part-families of various sorts, such as an elderly widowed mother, an unmarried adult sibling, or a set of orphaned children, are regularly attached on the basis of kin ties to family-based households. In addition, congruence may be the norm but separations of various sorts may occur on a contingent basis. For instance, there may be long separations of adult males from their households due to labor migration or military service. An interesting alternation between congruence and noncongruence of family and household is institutionalized in societies which isolate individual women or groups of women in separate dwellings during their menstrual periods.

EXTENDED HOUSEHOLDS

Most humans are members of two families during their lifetimes: they occupy the role of children in their family of orientation and the role of parents in their family of procreation. In about half of the world's cultures, these two families occupy a single extended household, forming a residentially aggregated three-generation kin group. Extended households are sometimes composed of a male and his family and the families of his married sons, forming a unit whose core consists of a group of solidary males. Similarly, an extended household may consist of a female and her family and the families of her married daughters, forming a group of solidary females.

Sharing of tasks such as child care is facilitated between the constituent families comprising extended households. In terms of economic cooperation, extended households often function as a single unit. The ability of these households to marshall a greatly expanded labor force is almost certainly one reason for their existence, since they are better able to optimally juggle labor demands, especially when these activities involve otherwise incompatible scheduling requirements. Extended households are also more effective in utilizing and allocating their labor force when this factor of production is in scarce supply as compared to other factors of production such as land and capital.

Stem households consist of the residential aggregation of a parental family and the family of one child, usually the eldest son. Nonconjugal families may also be residentially aggregated into a larger kin group including a mother, her children, and the children of her daughters. Again such residential aggregation may serve to promote economic cooperation and sharing domestic chores.

The residential aggregation of several related families into a larger kinship group almost certainly lessens the separate functional importance of each constituent family. For instance, the importance of a single family in fulfilling the emotional intimacy and companionship needs of its members may be reduced, since other individuals in the extended household can fulfill these needs. Similarly, sharing domestic tasks and cooperating economically may reduce the salience and importance of the separate constituent families.

Extended households sometimes pose problems for their members. In marrying, spouses in particular may have a difficult time as they are required to leave their natal household, while their mates continue to reside with their family of orientation. This creates a great disparity between the spouses, one of whom is living with close kin while the other is not. Another common problem in extended households involves allocation of authority within the household, generally to senior adults versus junior adults. This may lead to quarreling and fission of the household into its constituent families.

When an extended household fissions, each new domestic group may attempt to recreate an extended household. These new extended households, in turn, may fission over time, creating additional independent households to begin the cycle anew. Independent nuclear family households also proceed through a developmental cycle. A newly married couple establishes a household to which children may be added. As the children mature and, in turn, marry and establish separate households, the original household shrinks in size. Finally, the household disappears with the death of the founding couple. Nonconjugal family households may also develop over time into conjugal family households or alternatively into extended nonconjugal households. Polygynous households also have a typical developmental cycle. A young adult male would be unlikely to have more than one wife. As he matures, he may add additional wives as circumstances allow. Thus, a nuclear family household may expand over time into a polygynous family household.

Family types and household types tend to vary in regular ways with overall societal complexity. In large-scale societies, families organized on the basis of plural marriage are rare; thus monogamy is the rule. The highest proportion of families based on plural marriage tends to occur in medium-scale societies. Small-scale societies fall in between these two. The same pattern holds for extended households, which are most common in medium-scale societies, next most common in small-scale societies, and least common in large-scale ones.

A phenomenon relatively common in large-scale societies, in addition to occurrence of nonconjugal families and households, are nonkinship-based households. These include households composed of a single individual, those composed of same-sex individuals, and those composed of other combinations of nonkin related individuals. The strong tendency toward establishment of independent nuclear family households in large-scale societies may be a result of the mobility requirements of urban industrial life. However, recent historical research suggests that this family and household type developed prior to the industrial revolution in England and Western Europe rather than after it.

The present survey has concentrated on what has been learned about family and household organization through systematic comparative research. Important uniformities exist in these structures cross-culturally which speak to the common biological heritage of humans and to common problems of group living and societal continuity. In addition, immense diversity also occurs in family and household organization cross-societally and much remains to be learned concerning the detailed causes and consequences of this great variation.

STANLEY R. WITKOWSKI

BOHANNAN, PAUL, and JOHN MIDDLETON, eds. *Marriage, Family, and Residence.* Garden City, N.Y.: Natural History Press, 1968.

EMBER, MELVIN, and CAROL EMBER. *Marriage, Family, and Kinship: Comparative Studies of Social Organization.* New Haven, Conn.: HRAF Press, 1983.

GOLDSCHMIDT, WALTER. *Comparative Functionalism: An Essay in Anthropological Theory.* Los Angeles: University of California Press, 1966.

GOODENOUGH, WARD H. *Description and Comparison in Cultural Anthropology.* Chicago: Aldine Publishing, 1970.

LEVINSON, DAVID, and MARTIN J. MALONE. *Toward Explaining Human Culture.* New Haven, Conn.: HRAF Press, 1980.

MARSH, ROBERT M. *Comparative Sociology.* New York: Harcourt, Brace and World, 1967.

MURDOCK, GEORGE P. *Social Structure.* New York: Free Press, 1965.

PASTERNAK, BURTON. *Introduction to Kinship and Social Organization.* Englewood Cliffs, N.J.: Prentice-Hall, 1976.

ROBERTSON, A.F. *Beyond the Family: The Social Organization of Human Reproduction.* Los Angeles: University of California Press, 1991.

SCHLEGEL, ALICE. *Male Dominance and Female Autonomy.* New Haven, Conn.: HRAF Press, 1972.

STEPHENS, WILLIAM N. *The Family in Cross-Cultural Perspective.* New York: Holt, Rinehart and Winston, 1963.

VAN DEN BERGHE, PIERRE L. *Human Family Systems.* New York: Elsevier, 1979.

FEASTS AND FESTIVALS

The word "festival" is derived from the Latin *festus* (of a holiday) and from the Indo-European *dhes* or *dhesto,* the root of several words linked with religion. Through *festus* it is related to the Latin *feralis* (concerning the dead) and *feriae* (holidays, fairs). *Dhes* is possibly related via *dheso* to the Greek *theos* (god). Feasts and festivals are major events created by an entire community in symbolic and active form to show the essential life of that community—at once the distillation and typification of its corporate existence. At a festival the culture of a group is brought to its fullest expression and is consciously deployed in the public view. Thus, festivals constitute a prime act of reflexivity, whereby a society extrudes an arm out of itself, as it were, with an eye at its end and looks at itself. The concept of festival embraces two modes—play and ritual. Play inverts the social order and leans toward license, whereas ritual is real, a matter of the seriousness of life. It is the tension between ritual and play that gives festival much of its piquancy and power. Everyone may participate in festival because of its play element.

Anthropological theories of festival developed primarily in the 1970s and 1980s. Victor Turner (1982) wrote widely on the topic of celebration, and his concept of liminality is part of the current theory of festival. Frank Manning (1983) edited a book on celebration, using anthropology to show the flux, duality, and ambiguity in festival. Alessandro Falassi (1987) compiled essays on festivals that unpack their inner workings. Elihu Katz and Daniel Dyan (1985) put all major world happenings, including festivals, in a class of media events. They emphasize television, which creates a class of viewers situated in a very different position from that of festival participants. Here one's viewpoint when watching a festival, whether in the street, from a balcony, or at home on television, becomes significant. John J. MacAloon (1984), Roger Abrahams (1982), and others have richly contributed to festival studies.

One of the two main anthropological views of festivals regards them as rites of intensification, whereby the values and solidarity of the society are enhanced. A second view points to a class of festivals, often in the form of carnivals, that makes statements of antistructure, which is more or less subversive of the social order. Especially during carnivals, once the holiday opens, the social structures and social negotiations that prevail in the outside world rank low in value. A festival may be seen primarily as a performance and its purpose is to entertain, and as entertainment, festival is prolific of humor (Cox 1969).

Classifying festivals tends to be problematic. They may be religious, political and national, economic, or sporting. Most festivals take place regularly on specific calendar dates. In traditional societies many festivals celebrate arrival of the seasons, important in an agricultural economy. The seasons and major anniversaries also have effects on the human body itself, giving a subtler dimension to the festival. Certain rites of passage may also be classified as festivals, such as the Apache sunrise ceremony (Farrer 1991), Asian weddings, and major African puberty rites, because these rites and ceremonies empower the whole community. Some healing rituals may also be classified as festivals (Kapferer 1983).

CARNIVAL

Modern anthropological theory of carnival has roots in Mikhail M. Bakhtin's *Rabelais and His World* (1968), which inverts the value system that gives high rank to the culture of the elite. Historians trace carnival to the Saturnalia celebrations of ancient Rome and to the Celtic and later Catholic seasonal festivals. Quintessential carnival is seen in the *carnaval* of Rio de Janeiro, which celebrates Mardi Gras, the day before Lent, and in similar carnivals held in New Orleans, Trinidad, and wherever Catholic syncretisms flourish, that is, in the African populations of Latin America and also in Catholic Africa, for example,

Angola. The German equivalent of Mardi Gras is Fastnacht. In Rio de Janeiro, as described by Roberto DaMatta (1991), the poor take over the streets, homes are opened, and reversals of the daily order are common. The city's space is commandeered and transformed. *Communitas*, that is, universal fellow feeling, reigns for those who are willing to stay in town. Sound in the form of percussion and song bears the carnival parade along and, by means of music's access to the nonspeech centers of the brain, reaches levels beyond verbal description. Dancing, swaying, and forms of acrobatics produce delight and near trance by means of the dissociation produced by vertigo. The display of a beautiful, near-naked body asserts a certain democratic power, because the body is a resource possessed by all. Extraordinary costumes, called *fantasias,* represent the person one would like to be, and emphasize the world of fantasy, a world in the subjunctive mood. Society looks at itself transformed.

MUMMING AND CHARIVARI

Other carnivalesque customs have included mumming, exemplified by the Philadelphia Mummers' parade and play, and by a variety of celebrations consisting of home visits by groups of maskers, as in Newfoundland. One class of these, charivaris, took the form of feigned attacks on offenders against local norms, as described by Natalie Zemon Davis (1971). They were commonly carried out by young unmarried men, and were often of a licentious character. The young men represented a group in a transitional phase of life—they were liminal. They were not children and they were not yet integrated into the structured adult community. In similar events held among Germans in Pennsylvania, called belsnickling, the performances of maskers frightened the children, who had been told, "The belsnicklers will get you if you are not good." If they had been good, the children were given candies. In this way the young men steered children toward the values of the community, themselves receiving food and thus the approval of the adult world. This performance was typical of a class of festivals that contain an element of anti-structure while yet remaining the unity of the society.

NEW YEAR FESTIVALS

Calendrical festivals celebrating the new year are held in many cultures. They punctuate and emphasize the cycling of time. Judaism reckons the new year from September (Rosh Hashanah); the Iroquois celebrate

winter with the False Face Ceremony, in which participants dance while blinded by masks and fall into a dream state in which they see life-guiding scenes. As with the other examples cited, there are large numbers of festivals in this category, as well as many varieties.

RELIGIOUS FESTIVALS

Religious festivals regularly celebrate the anniversaries of the religion's gods or founders, holy figures, or great events. There are many examples in which the spirit beings or animals concerned call their people to gather together. Religious festivals illustrate the importance of the social factor in religious experience. Religious festivals include enormous gatherings. The largest festival in the world, the Maha Kumbha Mela of India, is held every twelve years, timed to take place at an auspicious position of the planet Jupiter. The Maha Kumbha Mela draws 15 million participants to the banks of the Ganges River. Ascetic holy men abound, seeking the opportunity to cleanse themselves from sin by bathing at the auspicious moment, thereby obtaining merit. Before the twentieth century, bloody battles were fought for the right to bathe at this moment.

The major world pilgrimages also include massive festival occasions, such as Guadalupe Day (December 12), near Mexico City, where the Virgin Mary appeared to Juan Diego in 1531; this festival is the most heavily attended Christian pilgrimage in the world, attracting more than 5 million pilgrims a year. Lourdes, a town in southwestern France, celebrates Saint Bernadette's visions of Mary in 1858 and attracts about 5 million people a year. Rome, Chartres, and Cologne are also major pilgrimage centers in greater Christendom, each with its own festival. Varanasi (Benares) celebrates many Hindu gods. Mecca, a city in Saudi Arabia, draws Muslim pilgrims every eleven months for an intense few days to celebrate the life of Muhammad, their founding prophet, and that of the ancient prophet Ishmael. Buddh Gaya in Bihar, India, the site of Buddha's bo tree; Adam's Peak in Sri Lanka, where a large depression is believed to be the footprint of Adam (Christians and Muslims), Buddha, or the god Shiva (Hindus); Jerusalem (Judaism, Christianity, and Islam); and Kyoto, Japan, are also sites for religious festivals. Each of these occasions provides opportunities for market sellers to make money on the sale of religious goods. At the pilgrimage centers of most religions, fun fairs and other carnivalesque entertainments are available but are often condemned by clerics.

Other religious festivals take the form of passion plays, such as the one performed during Muharram, the Shiite Muslim celebration in Iran of the martyrdom in 680 of Husein (Hasan, Husayn), the grandson of Muhammad. Hindus perform the *Ramlila* (play of the god Rama) described by Richard Schechner (1985), which depicts the adventures of Rama and Sita his consort and is staged beside the Ganges River in India. Productions feature elephants, boats, an actual maharaja, and child actors who play the gods themselves and are said by the audience to become the gods. The attendance for this thirty-one-day play is enormous. In Israeli and other Jewish communities, *Purimspiel,* the play depicting the story of Esther and the deliverance of the Jews from the Persians, is performed at the feast of Purim in February or March. The crucifixion of Jesus Christ is reenacted at Oberammergau, Austria, where the main role-taker is said to feel Christ within him. The Native American-Catholic syncretisms of Easter in the U.S. Southwest (the Black Hills Passion Play) and in Mexico also enact the Christian Passion story; within these plays time is telescoped and participants feel a sense of their founding events as taking place in the present.

Another type of religious festival primarily takes the form of a public procession, such as St. Patrick's Day parades in the United States; the Whit Walks of Manchester, England; the Holi festival at Kishangarh, India, celebrating Krishna and with many lampooning aspects as during carnivals; and the Hindu festival at Puri in Orissa, India, known as the Jagannatha or Juggernaut procession, during which an enormous mobile tower bearing the image of Jagannath is drawn through the streets. Processions inevitably make a political statement and may cause communal strife, such as that between Muslims and Hindus in some parts of India. It appears that humans are encoded for religious action, an endowment that may provide forces toward peaceful intercommunication or may be an impetus toward war.

The Western versions of Christmas and Easter and the Seder meal of Passover (Pesach) are classified as domestic religious festivals but are by no means minor in their importance and symbolism. For Christmas and Easter, the public aspect is transmuted into commercialism; therefore they lack the wide provenance of carnival. Their link with Christianity plus the small scale of the core celebration—in the home and churches—keys in with Western individualism. Semana Sagrada, the Latin American Easter, however, is public. The universal gift exchanges at Christmas emphasize *communitas*, and the gift in some way is the giver, and at this level the gift-giving renders the giver and the receiver one. The focus of the Seder, the quintessential feast held on the first night of Passover, is on the sacred family meal and subtly draws in long generations of the past, the ancient Hebrews and the revered Jewish story of the exodus from Egypt.

POLITICAL AND NATIONAL FESTIVALS

Two subclasses of political and national festivals can be distinguished. The first subclass celebrates the triumph of state power, from British coronations to the rallies of Adolf Hitler in Nazi Germany and the Apo ceremony of Ghana, which latter includes a "swearing at the chief" episode; such festivals may also be classified as rites of intensification. The other subclass includes celebrations of national independence. Each has a special date for rejoicing in the liberation of its people. Many of these parades express the military power of newly independent states. Thus, nationalism follows on the heels of liberation movements—structure after *communitas*. Festivals in opposition to straight society have also taken place, including the 1968 demonstrations by French students, noted for their *communitas* as well as their violence, and the hippie Woodstock festival of 1969 in New York State, where the rock band the Grateful Dead—players who create a festival wherever they play—has a place, as do the celebrations during the pilgrimage to Graceland, the home and gravesite of Elvis Presley.

FESTIVALS OF THE ECONOMY

Among festivals of the economy can be counted trade exhibitions, Macy's Thanksgiving Day parade in New York City, and chamber of commerce parades. Also included are fruits-of-the-earth celebrations, usually ritualized, such as Thanksgiving, the whaling festival among the Alaskan Inupiat, related to the Inuit, the potlatch of the northwest coast Native Americans, and the dragon-boat festival of China. In the "big man" feasts in Melanesia, Oceania, and many preindustrial cultures one feasts one's fellows to enhance one's own symbolic capital and position in the group, for example the Indonesian *slametan* feast and the Oceanian *kava* (herbal drink) gathering.

FESTIVALS OF SPORT

Sport is based on strength and skill, which is essentially a democratic concept, as in carnival. In sport, therefore, nature is celebrated, as well as the sense of flowing, when action and awareness coalesce into moments of great skill and perfection, as symbolized by such athletes as Magic Johnson. The major festivals of sport include the Olympic Games, the Super Bowl (football), the Indianapolis 500 (car racing), the Kentucky Derby (horse racing), the World Series (baseball), and the World Cup (soccer). A great deal of symbolism and ritual is included in these sports festivals.

FOLK AND GENRE FESTIVALS

A much newer type of festival is the folk festival, dating from the 1930s. Some folk festivals are conducted by indigenous and minority groups for themselves to assert their cultural importance. Another type of indigenous folk festival, performed by minorities and folk groups that are closer to assimilation into the mainstream society, attracts outside spectators and tends to become less participatory. Such a festival, once it has been commercialized, may become part of popular culture, as distinct from folk culture, while still maintaining folk support. Another variation is the monocultural festival, such as music festivals, film festivals, or the African-American celebration of Kwanzaa, introduced in 1977, which are organized to celebrate one art or one culture. Multicultural festivals include world fairs and craft fairs.

COMMON ELEMENTS IN FESTIVAL

A number of elements can be seen in festivals throughout the world, but no one festival shows them all. Generally, festivals occupy a niche in and out of time, and they are liminal, constituting a break in everyday life. They are also ephemeral, using temporary decorations and fireworks that are instantaneous. The mood is one of *communitas*, also an ephemeral characteristic, that is in contrast to the mode of everyday structured life. Ritual inversion is common (Babcock 1978), as shown in the absurdities of carnival and its surplus of signifiers (dizzying and multiplex confrontations rather than logical thought), lampooning (the poor critiquing the powerful), transvestism (sex reversals), and the reversal of city style from a rapid business manner to that of leisurely enjoyment. Bakhtin (1968), for example, described these two poles as the official world and the people's second life.

Homes that usually remain private and with doors closed are opened. That which is counterstructural can have its say.

Play and games and their many elements are emphasized during festivals. Using Roger Caillois's (1979) categories of play, we see competition (sport), mimesis (the reenactment of founding events), chance (gambling at the fairgrounds), and giddiness (dance and fairground rides). There is also the inordinacy of festival—overeating, the display of gigantic objects that are distended and caricatured (the huge cartoon character balloons of the Macy's parade), extravagant costumes and the outlandishness of masking, the weird (also often masked) figures that weave in and out, the devil, or a licentious clown figure. Loud music and drums, along with the dancing, transport participants into a different world, and pyrotechnics, such as bonfires, fireworks, and the burning of huge demonic figures. Play and ritual in many genres flows on, often in different milieus at the same time, as in a three-ring circus. Market stalls are crowded and money is exchanged freely. Festival, therefore, like true ritual, is a second-level performing of heightened life (also an alternative version of it), and thus provides the necessary echo for the human mind, life recreated, beside itself.

EDITH TURNER

SEE ALSO: *Games; Humor; Music; Play; Reflexive Anthropology; Ritual; Sports; Symbolic Anthropology*

ABRAHAMS, ROGER. "The Language of Festivals: Celebrating the Economy." In *Celebrations: Studies in Festivity and Ritual,"* edited by Victor Turner. Washington: Smithsonian Institution Press, 1982.

BABCOCK, BARBARA A., ed. *The Reversible World: Symbolic Inversion in Art and Society.* Ithaca, N.Y.: Cornell University Press, 1978.

BAKHTIN, MIKHAIL M. *Rabelais and His World,* translated by Helene Iswolsky. Cambridge, Mass.: MIT Press, 1968.

CAILLOIS, ROGER. *Man, Play and Games.* New York: Schocken, 1979.

COX, HARVEY G. *The Feast of Fools: A Theological Essay on Festivity and Fantasy.* Cambridge, Mass.: Harvard University Press, 1969.

DAMATTA, ROBERTO. *Carnival, Rogues, and Heroes.* South Bend, Ind.: University of Notre Dame Press, 1991.

DAVIS, NATALIE ZEMON. "Charivari, Honor and Community in Seventeenth-Century Lyon and

Geneva." In *Rite, Drama, Festival, Spectacle: Rehearsals Toward a Theory of Cultural Performance.* edited by John J. MacAloon. Philadelphia: Institute for the Study of Human Issues, 1971.

FALASSI, ALESSANDRO, ed. *Time Out of Time: Essays on the Festival.* Albuquerque: University of New Mexico Press, 1987.

FARRER, CLAIRE R. *Living Life's Circle.* Albuquerque: University of New Mexico Press, 1991.

KAPFERER, BRUCE. *A Celebration of Demons: Exorcism and the Aesthetics of Healing in Sri Lanka.* Bloomington: Indiana University Press, 1983.

KATZ, ELIHU, and DANIEL DYAN. "Media Events: On the Experience of Not Being There." *Religion* 15 (1985):305-314.

MACALOON, JOHN J., ed. *Rite, Drama, Festival, Spectacle: Rehearsals Toward a Theory of Cultural Performance.* Philadelphia: Institute for the Study of Human Issues, 1984.

MANNING, FRANK, ed. *The Celebrations of Society: Perspectives on Contemporary Cultural Performance.* Bowling Green, Ohio: Bowling Green University Press, 1983.

SCHECHNER, RICHARD. *Between Theater and Anthropology.* Philadelphia: University of Pennsylvania Press, 1985.

TURNER, VICTOR, ed. *Celebration: Studies in Festivity and Ritual.* Washington: Smithsonian Institution Press, 1982.

FEMINIST ANTHROPOLOGY

Anthropology has long been known as a discipline with a substantial number of women practitioners (Margaret Mead and Ruth Benedict among the most famous). Some, particularly Elsie Clews Parsons, considered themselves to be feminists and many (including Phyllis Kaberry, Ruth Landes, Ruth Underhill, Sylvia Leith-Ross, and Denise Paulme in addition to Mead, Benedict, and Parsons) wrote about the lives of women in non-Western societies. Feminist anthropology, however, as a topic within cultural anthropology that embodies a coherent point of view and a growing literature, emerged in the mid-1970s with the publication of *Woman, Culture, and Society* (Rosaldo and Lamphere 1974) and *Toward an Anthropology of Women* (Reiter 1975).

During the next twenty years this new "subfield" has seen growth and change as feminist anthropologists have turned their attention from rediscovering women and critiquing the androcentric bias of anthropology to more particularistic and historically grounded studies that place gender at the center of analysis. They are more clear about the positionality of the anthropologist as researcher and ethnographer. Taking to heart many of the criticisms by women of color, lesbians, and Third World peoples, as well as the insights of postmodern theorists concerning the nature of objectivity, science, and truth, feminist anthropologists are less apt to make broad generalizations and are more careful to engage in research that is in dialogue with the women they study. At the same time, feminists retain a critical stance with regard to the impact of hierarchy and power on the lives of women in our own and other cultures.

These transformations within feminist anthropology are neither lineal nor totalizing; instead, they represent the interweaving of different issues and themes, creating a diversity among feminist anthropologists in terms of both their research interests and their theoretical bents.

REDISCOVERING WOMEN/ UNIVERSALIZING ASYMMETRY

The essays in *Woman, Culture, and Society* emerged from a course at Stanford University in the spring of 1971, as well as papers delivered at the 1971 American Anthropological Association meetings, and from the network of colleagues of both editors. The collection *Toward an Anthropology of Women*, edited by Rayna Reiter, grew out of her participation in a student-organized course and included a number of graduate students and faculty connected to the University of Michigan. Both reflect the training of women anthropologists in departments with differing theoretical orientations (social structuralists at Harvard, symbolic anthropologists at Chicago, and materialists at Michigan) and the impact of the feminist movement of the 1970s.

In writing the introduction and first chapter to *Woman, Culture, and Society*, Rosaldo and Lamphere were faced with building a framework where none existed. They gravitated toward the work of Margaret Mead and Simone de Beauvoir and found in both an analysis of pervasive sexual asymmetry that fit their own reading of the ethnographic literature. The introductory essays by Rosaldo, Ortner, and Chodorow offered an integrated set of explanations, each at a different level, for the universal subordination of women: that is, in terms of social structure, culture, and socialization. All three argued that in every society, women bear and raise children and that women's socially and culturally defined role as mother provided the basis for subordination.

Both Rosaldo's and Ortner's analyses used theoretical dichotomies as a lens through which to examine subordination. Whereas Rosaldo argued that motherhood and the "domestic orientation of women" confined women to a domestic sphere, leaving men able to dominate the political sphere, Ortner used a Lévi-Straussian dichotomy to propose that men are associated with culture and women, being closer to nature, are viewed as ambiguous, dangerous, polluting, and to be devalued.

The argument for universal sexual asymmetry followed a long tradition of seeking human universals across cultures, although the authors were careful to make clear that there were important variations in women's roles in different cultures. Variation was the theme that was taken up in many of the remaining articles in *Woman, Culture, and Society* and those in *Toward an Anthropology of Women.*

RETHINKING/BUILDING A CRITIQUE

Soon after the publication of *Woman, Culture, and Society,* a number of feminist anthropologists began to challenge the thesis that women were universally subordinate and the usefulness of dichotomies like public/private and nature/culture.

Alice Schlegel and Jean Briggs argued that women and men in many foraging and tribal societies held roles that were "complementary but equal." Karen Sacks used a modes-of-production analysis to show that hunter-gatherers possessed a communal political economy in which sisters, wives, brothers, and husbands all had the same relation to productive means and resources and therefore equal power in relation to the whole. Eleanor Leacock and others presented material to demonstrate that contact between Europeans and native peoples transformed and undercut many native economies, in turn creating inequality between the sexes where autonomy had been the norm.

Others suggested that the dichotomy between public and private did not fit the realities of other cultures. For example, it failed to characterize Yoruba lineages, in which kin relations seemed to be both political and domestic at the same time. In Egypt, where there was a clear separation of private and public, women's activities (e.g., marriage arrangements) had clear political implications for the status of men, and men were important actors in the domestic sphere.

A second line of argument has been to show how these dichotomies are really Western categories that have a specific historical development within Western culture. For example, the nature/culture dichotomy has historic roots in the Enlightenment. As L. J. Jordanova and Maurice and Jean Bloch have shown, notions of nature had a complex development during this period, and the association of women and the female body with either nature or civilization was often blurred or contradictory (MacCormack and Strathern 1980).

Anthropologists in Britain were also involved in developing feminist anthropology in the 1970s. Shirley Ardner edited two collections focusing on the perception of women and their status as a "muted group," and Pat Caplan, Janet Bujra, and others in the London Women's Anthropology group analyzed various aspects of female solidarity. The growing interest in Marxist theory in Britain led to theoretical analyses of women, production, and reproduction in both capitalist and noncapitalist societies.

THE TURN TO HISTORY AND GENDER

Feminist anthropology of the 1970s was handicapped by a lack of data; many were painfully aware that their field notes and dissertations did not contain much material on women's lives. In the late 1970s and early 1980s, feminist anthropologists began to formulate research projects that centered on women and trained graduate students whose own dissertation fieldwork examined women's experience. Some turned their attention to the United States, but others continued to focus on women in the Pacific, Southeast Asia, Africa, the Middle East, and Latin America. As they became more absorbed in new particularist projects, it seemed more difficult and less necessary to synthesize and generalize.

Jane Collier, Sylvia Yanagisako, and others who built on the legacy left by Michelle Zimbalist Rosaldo urged feminists to turn their attention to the relations between men and women and analyze gender as it was socially constructed through hierarchy. At the same time, partly owing to the influence of Marxist approaches and labor historians like E. P. Thompson, more attention was given to historical analysis, not just as a preliminary chapter in a contemporary ethnography but as a central part of understanding how women's lives had developed.

The outpouring of research by feminist anthropologists continued into the 1980s and early 1990s, much of it focused on three areas: production and work, reproduction and sexuality, and gender and the state.

In examining women's work in the United States, feminist anthropologists have joined social historians and sociologists in analyzing women's industrial work (in textile mills, canneries, apparel factories, and electronics plants) as well as women's jobs in hospitals, nursing homes, and clerical settings. Much of this research has uncovered women's resistance on the job, examining the creation of women's work culture as it provides mechanisms for crossing ethnic boundaries, coping with piece-rate systems or participative management schemes, engaging in subtle acts of opposition, or organizing unions.

Anthropologists have also contributed to the expanding literature on women and development, which, on the whole, has stressed the exploitation of women as capitalism has penetrated developing economies. In Third World countries, women have been incorporated into the informal sector as vendors, domestics, and casual workers and also hired by multinational corporations as electronics or apparel workers. Despite the fact that factory employment in new export-processing firms has brought young, unmarried women's bodies and subjectivities into submission, Malaysian women have employed tactics of resistance that range from crying to damaging components to spirit possession, whereas South Korean women have joined unions and participated in militant labor activities (Ong 1991).

An increasing interest in "the body," both historically and in contemporary U.S. culture, has led feminist anthropologists to examine women's reproductive activities, particularly as defined and acted upon by the biomedical establishment. Several researchers have explored the impact of the religious right in defining the discourse surrounding sexuality, abortion, and pornography (Ginsburg and Tsing 1990), and others have investigated the impact of the new reproductive technologies on women (surrogacy, in vitro fertilization, ultrasound, and amniocentesis). Ginsburg and Rapp's collection (1995) takes a global perspective and looks at the role of the state and new reproductive technologies in countries as disparate as the United States, India, China, Romania, Egypt, and Brazil. The editors argue that "women actively use their cultural logics and social relations to incorporate, revise or resist the influence of seemingly distant economic and social forces."

Finally, the most coherent body of theorizing in feminist anthropology has been the research on women and the state. Work in the 1970s by Leacock, Reiter, and Sacks showed the ways in which the rise of the state circumscribed women's activities. During the 1980s, feminists examined colonial contexts and their impact on gender relations as well. In Tonga, a society with ranked estates, missionary activity and capitalist penetration during the nineteenth century brought a class-based state, the erosion of kin-group autonomy, and the subordination of women (Gailey 1987). Irene Silverblatt (1988), argues that state formation did not lead to the subordination of women in equivalent ways; it is important to analyze the differences between the various paths to state formation, contrasting Europe, the Middle East, Africa, and her own work on the Inca. Her study of the Spanish conquest in Peru shows how Andean women resisted their definition as witches, becoming "the defenders of pre-Columbian ways of living in the face of onslaught by an illegitimate regime."

REDISCOVERING OUR ROOTS

At the same time, feminist scholars began researching the lives of early female anthropologists. Spurred on by the biography of Margaret Mead by her daughter, Mary Catherine Bateson (1984), and by Peter Hare's book about his great aunt Elsie Clews Parsons (1985), feminist scholars looked deeper into the lives of the women around Franz Boas. One impetus for this was a Wenner-Gren Conference and Exhibit called "Daughters of the Desert," which examined the research of women anthropologists who studied the Native American Southwest. The conference brought together many women in their 70s and 80s who reminisced about their training and fieldwork experiences, and the resulting videotape and books (Babcock and Parezo 1988; Parezo 1993) gave a sense of the context in which women archaeologists, ethnologists, applied anthropologists, and museum specialists made important contributions but were institutionally marginalized.

The contributions of early anthropologists like Alice Fletcher and Matilda Coxe Stevenson, and the feminist roots of both Ruth Benedict's and Elsie Clews Parsons's writing have become clear. More important, African-American women like Caroline Bond Day, Katherine Dunham, Ellen Irene Diggs, and Vera Green, as well as Dakota scholar Ella Cara Deloria, have been resurrected and made visible (Gacs et al. 1988).

DIVERSIFYING OUR VOICES

Although the initial resurgence of feminism was primarily fueled by white, U.S. middle-class women, with the increasing number of women of color being trained in the United States, and Third World women anthropologists publishing about women in their own countries, feminist anthropology has become more diversified. In the late 1970s, women of color began critiquing the white women's movement for assuming all women had similar situations and for ignoring the impact of race, class, and sexual orientation in creating different structural and cultural constraints on women's lives as well as differing experiences for women.

There has been increasing research on the lives of women of color in the United States, much of it conducted by sociologists and historians as well as anthropologists, many of them from the same ethnic or racial background as their subjects (Romero and Higgenbotham 1995). New research on lesbian families and communities, including Elizabeth Lapovsky Kennedy and Madeline D. Davis's study of the Buffalo bar community of the 1950s, Ester Newton's portrait of Cherry Grove, Fire Island, and Kath Weston's analysis of lesbian and gay families of choice and Ellen Lewin's study of *Lesbian Motherhood,* has provided new insights into sexuality, the cultural construction of gender, and family and household forms. Feminist anthropologists of mixed national ancestry ("halfies") have become more conscious of the complexity of their connection to field sites in the countries of their parents or grandparents. By the 1990s, feminist anthropology had become more diverse, not only in terms of theoretical perspectives but also in terms of the voices and experiences represented in print.

THE IMPACT OF POSTMODERNISM

Much of the critique and change in feminist anthropology during the late 1980s occurred because of the dialogue among and between feminists and post-modernists. Postmodern writers, primarily in the field of literary criticism, have followed the theories of Lyotard, Lacan, Derrida, and Foucault, which critique "modernism" and its commitment to science, objectivity, and truth. In anthropology, postmodernism has inspired an interest in examining ethnographies as texts and in interrogating the relationship between the anthropologist and the "objects of study," the native Other.

Feminists, including feminist anthropologists, have been wary of a postmodernist stance that dissolves the speaking subject and focuses primarily on writing and discourse rather than on material reality (Mascia-Lees et al. 1989).

On the other hand, the debate regarding postmodernism has made feminists conscious of the colonial heritage of their discipline, of their positionality as Western, often white, and almost always middle-class observers, and of the problematics of treating those one studies as objects rather than as subjects and collaborators. Thus, feminist ethnographers have become engaged in examining their different textual strategies, clarifying their own positionality, and producing multivocal texts.

CONCLUSION

In the late 1980s, through the Gender and Anthropology project, a teaching guide summarizing sources on women and gender within the four subfields of anthropology and across world areas as well as work with textbook authors to include more research on gender in introductory textbooks was published (Morgen 1989). Several other new textbooks and collections appeared (Moore 1988; di Leonardo 1991; Brettell and Sargeant 1992), and the Association for Feminist Anthropology, a unit of the American Anthropological Association, was founded. As of 1993 it had a membership of over 700, sponsored sessions at the annual meetings, and had initiated a publication series and newsletter.

By the early 1990s, feminist anthropology, unlike the feminism of the 1910s and 1920s, was well incorporated into the curriculum of traditional departments and continues to have an impact on women's studies programs. Feminists argue that they have created new theoretical frameworks—ones that may owe their initial impetus to men like Marx, Durkheim, Weber, Foucault, Geertz, and Wolf. These frameworks, however, by incorporating gender and women, have something new to say about society, whether it be about state formation, the role of power and resistance in the work place, the cultural construction of reproduction, or the crafting of identities. Most feminists feel that the outpouring of feminist research and theory will continue to bring feminism to the center of anthropology and reclaim the feminist heritage that Elsie Clews Parsons first brought to the discipline.

LOUISE LAMPHERE

ARDNER, SHIRLEY, ed. *Perceiving Women.* New York Halsted Press, 1975

———. *Defining Females.* New York: Halsted Press, 1978.

BABCOCK, BARBARA, and NANCY PAREZO. *Daughters of the Desert: Women Anthropologists and the Native American Southwest, 1880-1980.* Albuquerque: University of New Mexico Press, 1988.

BATESON, MARY CATHERINE. *With a Daughter's Eye: A Memoir of Margaret Mead and Gregory Bateson.* New York: Morrow, 1984.

BRETTELL, CAROLINE, and CAROLYN SARGEANT. *Gender in Cross-Cultural Perspective.* Englewood Cliffs, N.J.: Prentice-Hall, 1992.

BRIGGS, JEAN. *Never in Anger: Portrait of an Eskimo Family.* Cambridge, Mass.: Harvard University Press, 1970.

CAPLAN, PATRICIA and JANET M. BUJRA, eds. *Women United, Women Divided: Comparative Studies of Ten Contemporary Cultures.* Bloomington: Indiana University Press, 1979.

DI LEONARDO, MICAELA. *Gender at the Crossroads of Knowledge: Feminist Anthropology in the Postmodern Era.* Berkeley and Los Angeles: University of California Press, 1991.

GACS, UTE, AISHA KAHN, JERRIE McINTYRE, and RUTH WIENBERG, eds. *Women Anthropologists: A Biographical Dictionary.* Westport, Conn.: Greenwood Press, 1988.

GAILEY, CHRISTINE. *Kinship to Kingship: Gender Hierarchy and State Formation in the Tongan Islands.* Austin: University of Texas Press, 1987.

GINSBURG, FAYE, and RAYNA RAPP, eds. *Conceiving the New World Order: The Global Stratification of Reproduction.* Berkeley and Los Angeles: University of California Press, 1995.

GINSBURG, FAYE, and ANNA LOWENHAUPT TSING. *Uncertain Terms: Negotiating Gender in American Culture.* Boston: Beacon Press, 1990.

HARE, PETER. *A Woman's Quest for Science: A Portrait of Elsie Clews Parsons.* Buffalo, N.Y.: Prometheus Books, 1985.

KENNEDY, ELIZABETH LAPOVSKY, and MADELINE D. DAVIS. *Boots of Silver, Slippers of Gold: The History of a Lesbian Community.* New York: Routlege, 1993.

LEACOCK, ELEANOR B. *Myths of Male Dominance.* New York: Monthly Review Press,1981.

LEWIN, ELLEN. *Lesbian Mothers: Accounts of Gender in American Culture.* Ithaca, N.Y.: Cornell University Press, 1993.

MacCORMACK, CAROL, and MARILYN STRATHERN. *Nature, Culture, and Gender.* Cambridge: Cambridge University Press, 1980.

MASCIA-LEES, FRANCES, PATRICIA SHARPE, and COLLEEN BALLERINO COHEN. "The Postmodernist Turn in Anthropology: Cautions from a Postmodernist Perspective." *Signs: Journal of Woman, Culture and Society* 15(1) 1989: 7-33.

MOORE, HENRIETTA L. *Feminism and Anthropology.* Minneapolis: University of Minnesota Press, 1988.

MORGEN, SANDRA. *Gender and Anthropology: Critical Reviews for Research and Teaching.* Washington, D.C.: American Anthropological Association, 1989.

NEWTON, ESTHER. *Cherry Grove, Fire Island: Sixty Years in America's First Gay and Lesbian Town.* Boston: Beacon Press, 1993.

ONG, AIWHA. "The Gender and Labor Politics of Postmodernity." In *Annual Review of Anthropology.* edited by Bernard Siegel. 20 (1991): 279 -310.

PAREZO, NANCY, ed. *Hidden Scholars: Women Anthropologists and the Native American Southwest.* Albuquerque: University of New Mexico Press, 1993.

REITER, RAYNA (RAPP). "Men and Women in the South of France: Public and Private Domains." In *Toward and Anthropology of Women, edited by* Rayna Reiter (Rapp). New York: Monthly Review Press, 1975.

———. *Toward an Anthropology of Women.* New York: Monthly Review Press, 1975.

ROMERO, MARY, and ELIZABETH HIGGENBOTHAM. *Women and Work: Race, Ethnicity and Class.* Newberry Park, Calif.: Sage Press, 1995.

ROSALDO, MICHELLE ZIMBALIST, and LOUISE LAMPHERE. *Woman, Culture, and Society.* Stanford: Stanford University Press, 1974.

SACKS, KAREN. *Sisters and Wives: The Past and Future of Sexual Equality.* Westport, Conn.: Greenwood Press, 1979.

SILVERBLATT, IRENE. "Women in States." In *Annual*

Review of Anthropology, edited by Bernard Siegel. Palo Alto, Calif.: Annual Reviews, 1988.

SCHEGEL, ALICE. "Male and Female in Hopi Thought and Action." In *Sexual Stratification: A Cross-Cultural View,* edited by Alice Schlegel. New York: Columbia University Press, 1977.

WESTON, KATH. *Families We Choose: Lesbians Gays Kinship.* New York: Columbia University Press, 1991.

FEUDING

Definitions of feuding abound. Keith F. Otterbein and Charlotte Swanson Otterbein, in a cross-cultural study of feuding (1965), define it as "blood revenge following a homicide," and distinguished it from warfare, an armed contest between two independent political units. In later publications (1986, 1994) Otterbein explicitly defines feuding as occurring within a political community and being revenge for an injustice, again differentiating feuding from warfare, which is now defined precisely as armed combat between political communities. Leopold Pospisil identified three salient features of feuding: a series of three or more acts of violence, usually involving killings; occurrence within an overall political authority; and a common duty to avenge with common liability.

Christopher Boehm (1984), who conducted a case study in Montgomery, defines feud as "deliberately limited and carefully counted killing in revenge for a previous homicide, which takes place between two groups on the basis of specific rules for killing, pacification, and compensation." For Boehm, there are two key elements to feuding: retaliatory homicide is a righteous act, and some means is available for stopping the conflict, which usually involves third-party intervention, truces, and material compensation. Ten other distinctive features are identified: rules, scorekeeping, turn taking, need for honor, notions of dominance, notion of controlled retaliation, cross-cutting social ties that retard feuding, a means to avoid warfare, difficulty of resolution, and impossibility of avoidance when population density is high. Rolf Kuschel (1988), who studied blood feuds and homicides on Bellona Island, states that feuding covers "at least three alternating killings or homicide attempts," "autonomous groups . . . parts of a shared ethno-linguistic entity," and "can be brought to an end." Martin

Daly and Margo Wilson (1988) discuss "retaliatory killings" and treat the concept so broadly that blood feud, capital punishment, and any "expressions of the desire for blood revenge" in a society are considered to be "evidence for the idea of taking a life for a life." Karen Paige Ericksen and Heather Horton (1992) consider feuds as being present in a society when the "kin group was recognized as the appropriate unit to avenge transgressions against its members."

Analysis of these definitions reveals two essential elements of feuding. First, kin groups are involved, homicides occur, and the killings occur as revenge for injustice (the terms duty, honor, righteous, and legitimate appear in discussions of motivation for the homicides). Second, three or more killings or acts of violence occur. The element that is in dispute is whether the unit within which feuding occurs is political or ethnolinguistic. It appears that in politically developed societies the unit is the political community, and that in acephalous societies without any formal overall political authority the unit is the ethnolinguistic group. Nevertheless, it is difficult to identify the political community in only a small number of societies.

The possibility of payment of compensation (i.e., blood money) or other means of ending the feud is sometimes built into the definition. This is not necessary, and whether compensation can be paid is subject to investigation on a case-by-case basis. Its absence or presence can be used to distinguish types of feuding, as was done by Otterbein and Otterbein (1965). Thus, societies with feuding can be classified as either type A, in which there is no institutionalized means by which compensation can be paid, or type B, where payment of compensation can either prevent a counter killing or stop a feud. Early evolutionists believed that as sociopolitical complexity developed type A evolved into type B. Although these types are not related to the level of sociopolitical integration (Otterbein and Otterbein 1965), ethnographic examples do sort themselves into these types. Type A societies appear to have much higher homicide rates than type B societies. Boehm's fieldwork with the Montenegrins, a type B society, led him to develop the hypothesis that feuding controls violence.

Three scales or variables pertaining to feuding have been used in cross-cultural research. A three-point scale was developed by Otterbein and Otterbein (1965), and used with a sample of fifty societies drawn by the authors: kin of the deceased are expected to kill the offender or any member of the offender's kin group (8 cases); compensation is sometimes accepted (14 cases); and feuding is absent if a formal judicial procedure always leads to settlement through compensation or if homicides are rare (28 cases). Two additional scales were developed by Ericksen and Horton (1992) and applied by them to the Standard Cross-Cultural Sample, a sample of 186 cultures developed at the University of Pittsburgh in the 1960s. Their first scale used six points to describe the legitimacy of kin group vengeance: moral imperative (38 cases); most appropriate (14 cases); circumstantial (18 cases); last resort (20 cases); formal adjudication only (63 cases); individual self-redress (15 cases). Their second scale used three points to describe the target of vengeance: anyone in the malefactor's kin group (35 cases); the malefactor if possible, otherwise selected members of his kin group (23 cases); and malefactor only (23 cases). (This scale is not applicable to cases where there is only formal adjudication or individual self-redress.)

Three primary issues have concerned researchers of feuding. First, can feuding be distinguished from warfare in small-scale societies? Otterbein believes that they can be distinguished if a political community can be identified. He looks for a political leader who announces group decisions (1977). The group is often small. Some researchers have despaired of distinguishing feuding from warfare and include feuding under the rubric of internal war (war within the same culture or ethnolinguistic unit). To most researchers, however, feuding and warfare appear to be qualitatively different. Application of the concept of political community to a specific case leads to reclassification of feuding on Bellona Island, a Polynesian outlier, as warfare. Bellona clans were politically autonomous fraternal interest groups, and the feuding between these clans can thus be classified as warfare. Further support for this interpretation arises from Kuschel's contention that the intent of a raid was not to even the score but to reduce enemy manpower (1988). Once a pattern of mutual raiding was set in motion, it was likely to continue until one group was nearly annihilated, which is uncharacteristic of classic feuding societies, such as Montenegro.

The second issue is whether feuding is a legitimate course of action for a kin group that believes itself to be wronged or whether feuding is an illegal act. For some researchers feud occupies an intermediate position between law and crime, and thus has been designated quasi-law or self-help. Although feuding may be carried out following a large body of culturally defined roles, the political leaders and kinship groups not involved in the feud are usually highly desirous of seeing the feud end or settled. Political leaders in such a status-role almost always attempt to arrogate to themselves the exclusive right to judge whether a crime has been committed and to do the punishing. For these reasons Otterbein views feuding not as legal action but as a highly disruptive sequence of antisocial acts. Actions taken by political leaders to prevent feuding are viewed as legal but not the revenge killings of kinship groups (Otterbein 1985).

The third issue is whether feuding is uncommon, common, or nearly universal. Cross-cultural studies have provided different answers. Otterbein and Otterbein found that 44 percent of their sample societies had feuding; Ericksen and Horton found that 54 percent of the Standard Cross-Cultural Sample societies viewed violent action as legitimate; Daly and Wilson, using the Human Relations Area File sixty-society probability sample found evidence that 57 societies (95 percent) harbored "the idea of taking a life for a life" (1988). To achieve near universality, the researchers needed to include capital punishment as evidence of the desire for blood revenge, a result that is not surprising because Otterbein (1986) found, using the same sample, that 51 of the 53 societies (96 percent), for which there was information, had the death penalty (1986). The results of these three studies lead to the conclusion that approximately 50 percent of the world's societies practice feuding, although the concept of revenge—a life for a life—may be nearly universal.

Numerous theories have been offered to explain feuding. Five theories have achieved tentative acceptance and two have not. Several are single-factor theories; the remaining have been used in conjunction with other theories. One of the accepted theories is that of Daly and Wilson, whose research is anchored in sociobiology. They argue that blood revenge serves inclusive fitness (1988); that is, the use of retaliation to deter homicidal attacks upon one's kin group protects the gene pool of that group while diminishing the fitness of the other kin group. From a fitness perspective, killing is rational. It has been noted by several researchers that a major reason for homicidal retaliation is to preserve honor (Boehm 1984), particularly when premarital chastity has been violated (Ericksen and Horton 1992). This concern is so strong in some societies that if the woman is believed to have initiated the liaison, she may be executed by her own kinship group (Otterbein 1986). On the other hand, if she is seduced or raped, a feud is almost inevitable. In a cross-cultural study of rape, Otterbein (1979) found a high correlation between the frequency of rape and the frequency of feuding. Ericksen and Horton (1992) found their strongest correlation to be between the violation of premarital chastity and classic blood feuds. These findings are highly consistent with inclusive fitness theory.

A series of cross-cultural studies have shown a strong relationship between fraternal interest groups and feuding. In a cross-cultural study using five measures of peacefulness and nonpeacefulness, including the presence or absence of blood feuds, H. U. E. Thoden Van Velzen and W. Van Wetering (1960) demonstrated that the presence of fraternal interest groups is responsible for the conflicts that occur within local groups. Fraternal interest groups—power groups of related males—arise through following a rule of patrilocal residence and/or practicing polygyny (Otterbein and Otterbein 1965). Otterbein and Otterbein showed that fraternal interest groups, using either patrilocal residence or polygyny as an index of the presence of fraternal interest groups, predict feuding. Two other theories were also tested by Otterbein and Otterbein: a political evolution theory (societies with a high level of political integration lack feuding) and a conflict-cohesion hypothesis (political communities at war are likely to be internally cohesive in that they lack feuding). Neither level of political integration nor warfare considered alone had any influence upon feuding. The results obtained, however, show that if a political community is centralized and if it engages in warfare, it is unlikely to have feuding even if fraternal interest groups are present. The explanation is offered that officials in centralized political systems have the authority and power to prevent feuding only when their political communities are faced with warfare (Otterbein and Otterbein 1965). Studies by Boehm, Kuschel, and others show clearly that societies with fraternal interest groups are concerned with honor and the chastity of their female members and engage in feuding. Furthermore, fraternal interest groups are kinship groups and for

those groups that keep their casualties low, feuding contributes to their inclusive fitness. Thus, all five accepted theories of feuding combine to form a single general theory.

One of the theories of feuding that has not gained acceptance emerged during the florescence of ecological theories in the 1970s. It was argued by some that resource competition resulted in feuding, but more recent writers have rejected this contention. Boehm (1984) points out that the scarce-resource competition model assumes that feuds are interminable, an attribute that is not characteristic of feuds. Kuschel (1988) also rejects the notion that scarce resources are the cause of feuding on Bellona, because the carrying capacity of the island was calculated at about 1,000 persons and the population of the island probably seldom exceeded 500. Furthermore, Kuschel noted, "according to the Bellonese, the population pressure under normal conditions was never so high it resulted in killing." Usher Fleishing and Sheldon Goldenberg (1987) undertook a cross-cultural study, with the intention of using ecological variables to show that the relationship between fraternal interest groups and feuding was spurious. The results of the study, however, supported the relationship between fraternal interest groups and feuding and found that the ecological variables dropped out or, at best, played a conditional role. Thus, both case studies, as well as a cross-cultural study, lead to the conclusion that ecological theories of feuding cannot be accepted.

The second theory of feuding that has not gained acceptance is Boehm's hypothesis that feuding is an alternative to warfare. Feuding arises, Boehm suggests, because the potential combatants realize that all-out warfare at close quarters would be disastrous. Therefore, tribesmen all over the world have developed similar sets of rules to control their conflicts by feuding—social order is maintained through the cultural practice of settling feuds through payment of compensation. Boehm recognized that his "assumption about the avoidance of warfare is inferential," but he believes "it is susceptible of testing where ethnographic materials are very rich."

KEITH F. OTTERBEIN

BOEHM, CHRISTOPHER. *Blood Revenge: The Anthropology of Feuding in Montenegro and Other Tribal Societies.* Lawrence: University Press of Kansas, 1984.

DALY, MARTIN, and MARGO WILSON. *Homicide.* New York: Aldine de Gruyter, 1988.

ERICKSEN, KAREN PAIGE, and HEATHER HORTON. "Blood Feuds: Cross-Cultural Variations in Kin Group Vengeance." *Behavior Science Research* 26 (1992): 57–85.

FLEISHING, USHER, and SHELDON GOLDENBERG. "Ecology, Social Structure, and Blood Feud." *Behavior Science Research* 21 (1987): 160–181.

KUSCHEL, ROLF. *Vengeance Is Their Reply: Blood Feuds and Homicides on Bellona Island,* part 1. Copenhagen: Dansk Psykologisk Forlag, 1988.

OTTERBEIN, KEITH F. *Comparative Cultural Analysis: An Introduction to Anthropology,* 2nd ed. New York: Holt, Rinehart & Winston, 1977.

———. "A Cross-Cultural Study of Rape." *Aggressive Behavior* 5 (1979): 425–435.

———. "Feuding: Dispute Resolution or Dispute Continuation." *Reviews in Anthropology* 12 (1985): 73–83.

———. *The Ultimate Coercive Sanction: A Cross-Cultural Study of Capital Punishment.* New Haven: Human Relations Area Files, 1986.

———. *Feuding and Warfare: Selected Works of Keith F. Otterbein.* New York: Gordon and Breach, 1994.

OTTERBEIN, KEITH F., and CHARLOTTE SWANSON OTTERBEIN. "An Eye for an Eye, a Tooth for a Tooth: A Cross-Cultural Study of Feuding." *American Anthropologist* 67 (1965): 1470–1482.

THODEN VAN VELZEN, H. U. E., and W. VAN WETERING. "Residence, Power Groups, and Intra-Societal Aggression." *International Archives of Ethnography* 49 (1960): 169–200.

FIELDWORK

Cultural anthropologists use fieldwork as a basis for describing different cultures. Fieldwork means living with, talking with, and observing the people one is trying to understand, whether they be inhabitants of small islands in the Pacific Ocean, peasants in large nations, patients in hospitals, or executives in large bureaucracies. It seems easy to describe the culture of these people. In Bronislaw Malinowski's (1922) words, "Imagine yourself suddenly set down surrounded by all your gear, alone on a tropical beach" as the boat that brought you disappears. Imagine yourself in a boardroom surrounded by lawyers, bankers, or government bureaucrats getting ready to discuss fisheries policy, investment instruments, or political and economic developments; in a ward of a hospital surrounded by patients, doctors, and nurses; in a high-tech factory surrounded by managers, workers, and machines; in an airport surrounded by puzzled European, Japanese, Australian, and U.S. tourists as they deplane in northwestern Thailand; on a farm surrounded by cows, hogs, tractors, and heavy equipment; or at any of the other sites where anthropologists study. Further, imagine, as Malinowski asked his readers in 1922 to do, that you have nothing to guide you and your task is to describe the culture of the people, whether they are bureaucrats, bankers, tourists, farmers, or others.

Anthropologists discuss methodology because it is not obvious what to do next—how to do fieldwork. In 1933 American anthropologist Paul Radin pointed out, in despair, that since 1923 the increasing discussions of methodology in the anthropological literature were not a sign of approaching maturity or a sign that anthropologists were devising methods to keep them from error, but were a substitute for real work, a sign of an impasse or that anthropologists had exhausted their methods. In the mid- 1990s, more than sixty years later, the discussion became even more animated than in Radin's day and the prognosis is not encouraging.

Nothing about culture or cultures is obvious. If something seems to be obvious, we probably misunderstand it. The "obvious" is defined by cultural assumptions about the world, unexamined preconceptions about our society, tacit presumptions about our place in the social order, and unconscious ideas about how society operates. The "obvious" is an artifact of our own culture, whether it be American, Chinese, or Zuñi. Chinese anthropologist Li An-Che made this very clear in his comparison of his understandings of Zuñi life with those of American anthropologists in a 1937 paper about his experiences of learning the field techniques of U.S. anthropology by doing fieldwork among Zuñi (Manners and Kaplin 1968). What he found interesting, problematic, and obvious was quite different from what American anthropologists had seen from the vantage point of their culture.

If different anthropologists from different cultures, genders, class backgrounds, social positions, or ethnic groups see things differently, what are the chances of any objective description at all? This question is more striking when ethnographers of similar backgrounds render different visions of the same people, as Robert Redfield (1930) and Oscar Lewis (1951) did for peasants and rural townspeople in Mexico. A more recent debate is about whether Margaret Mead's (1928) or Derek Freeman's (1983) accounts of life in Samoa are more adequate. Contemporaries of Mead also questioned her methodology. From a humanistic perspective, Radin chastised Mead in 1933 for creating generalized individuals and situations rather than describing the culture so that readers could feel they were dealing with specific and actual men and women, situations, and traditions. He doubted whether any outsider could gain the kind of information imparted by Mead, even after a lifetime of study, much less a period of less than a year. Twelve years later, in 1945, Jesse Bernard (Manners and Kaplan 1968) criticized Mead for impressionistic rather than systematic observations and because she used them to serve predetermined stereotypes. Bernard likened Mead to a novelist who tells rather than shows what the characters are like and suggested that her descriptions of peoples' characters often contradicted her reports of their behavior. He analyzed her rhetorical forms and suggested that her conclusions were not reliable, that is, others would not describe the same things in the same way. Bernard argued not for more complete humanistic understanding but for reliable and valid instruments for measurement.

Such issues and discussions pose the questions of methodology in ethnographic fieldwork. Whether we agree with the more humanistic or more scientific outlook, we must keep two dimensions in mind—reliability and validity. How can we be sure that what we see, understand, and describe is the same as what someone else would see, understand, and describe? All scientific and humanistic knowledge is built on verifiable reliable information that is accessible to everyone who learns the techniques of observation. In the old English system of measurements, a yard was the distance from the end of your nose to the tips of your fingers; a fathom was the distance between the tips of your outstretched fingers. Obviously, the length of a yard or a fathom depended on whose arms or fingers were stretched for the measure. Such measures are not reliable. For this reason, people who depend on measures to make their livings develop bureaus of standards to define universal measures to resolve the problem of reliability. Everyone uses the same yard and fathom. People only do this when it becomes important, however, and that seems to be

when it affects them economically. It may be the same in anthropology, that such issues become important when they involve anthropologists' access to funding sources. If anthropologists can make a living and find an audience writing as novelists, there is no particular need to attend to methodological issues, and one person's fathom is as good as another's.

As for validity, how do we know we are observing what we think we are observing? Suppose we want to measure the length of objects. We can convert freely from the English to the metric system if we know the conversion ratios. The metric system, based on universals shared by all people, such as the circumference of the planet Earth and the temperature at which water boils at sea level, was designed to be even more reliable and universal than the English system, which depended on some individual's body measurements. If, there are no standardized relationships, as between meters and feet, we have to check our measures again and again to be sure that they really do measure what we think they do. Are we measuring length or temperature? Are people's reports of their behavior valid descriptions of what they do? To check, we have to ask for the reports and then check the reports against observations of what people do. If Scholastic Aptitude Test scores are valid measures of students' ability to make grades, they should correspond to students' grades. Are grades a valid measure of anything? These are the types of questions methodologists discuss.

Anthropologists usually want to check things for themselves. They are unwilling to substitute one cultural construct for another. Is an economist's model a better way to predict the future than reading the entrails of birds for omens? The only way to know is to check, and the results are pretty disappointing for economists, according to Burton Gordon Malkiel (1990). Many disciplines, from economics to marine biology, have faith in the deductive power of their models. Such experts have replaced the priests who used to read omens. Given the problems of validity and reliability, wouldn't it be just as simple for anthropologists to stay home and make up models as economists and marine biologists do? Because we always have to consider the problems of validity and reliability, seeing for ourselves is never easy. Are we seeing or measuring what we think we are seeing or measuring? Would anyone else see the same thing or get the same measurement?

In a 1920 paper, (reprinted in Bohannan and Glazer 1988), Franz Boas characterized European anthropology as dominated by either evolutionism, the idea that all peoples followed uniform laws of development, or diffusionism, which suggested that uniformities among cultures are results of migration or cultural borrowing. American anthropologists, on the other hand, he argued, were less willing to take on such grand questions without any concrete data on which to base their answers. They were therefore interested in understanding processes they could observe among living people. Rather than answering questions by proposing various formulas for them, he argued that American anthropologists were involved in detailed investigations that would bear on the answers to such great questions. Anthropologists should, he continued, know how things are and how they came to be by comparing ethnographic details among neighboring cultures and across the range of cultures. All cultural forms are in flux, Boas argued, and nothing is as stable as it appears in the short run, the limited period of time of fieldwork. Anthropologists should not simply enumerate standardized beliefs and customs but also understand how individuals react to their social environments, analyze differences of opinion, and comprehend the range of points of view because these are the loci of change. Boas also repeatedly made analogies to the study of language. Just as anthropologists cannot expect speakers of a language to outline their grammar, they cannot expect such accounts for the rest of culture. Rather than relying on models of European theorists, Franz Boas advocated seeing for ourselves by doing fieldwork. The question of how to do this remained somewhat unclear.

In *Argonauts of the Western Pacific* (1922), Malinowski outlined a detailed method for doing fieldwork. He argued that such methodological details were necessary for others to be able to assess the accuracy and adequacy—the validity and reliability—of any such ethnographic account. There is no shortcut without effort or trouble, he says, but by following certain procedures one can produce reliable and valid ethnographic information.

Malinowski outlined three approaches that would lead to the final goal of grasping the point of view of the people we are trying to understand: describing the social constitution, adding examples from daily life, and illustrating people's views by recording and presenting what they say. An ethnographer cannot wait passively for revelations but must actively seek information about the people by living with them and speaking their language. This quest is guided by theoretical questions, quite a different thing from preconceived ideas, because a scientific attitude is always questioning, revising, and seeking new ideas and facts.

The first task of fieldwork is to discover the regularities of the society and separate them from the irrelevant things to ascertain the skeleton of the peoples' lives, the constitution of the society. The anthropologist should survey all social phenomena, each aspect of the culture, then join all of the parts into a coherent whole. People do not necessarily formulate constitutions, as explicitly as the U.S. Consitution, but if they do, their formulations may serve other interests than description. Therefore, it is up to the anthropologist to discover and formulate the constitution of the people. To do so, anthropologists observe events and talk to people about them, elicit stories about similar events, and thus develop a catalogue of kinds of events and how people respond to them. Anthropologists will discover the missing pieces of the puzzle when they try to put the accounts together into a coherent pattern. These questions then guide further work. Ethnographers should, Malinowski argued, collect, tabulate, and chart a wide range of data, using maps, genealogies, plans, censuses, patterns of ownership, and other resources. Malinowski called this approach the method of statistic documentation by concrete evidence.

Such skeletal accounts may portray the constitution of a society but not life in it. Because real life does not follow rules closely, Malinowski argued, such skeletal accounts should be filled out by examples from daily life. Because we cannot elicit these events (what Malinowski called "the imponderabilia of actual life,") by questioning people, anthropologists have to record recurrent behavior as well as less usual behavior. In addition to recording the social constitution and the daily life and behavior of the people they are studying, ethnographers should ascertain their views and opinions about what they do and their society. The best procedure for discovering and presenting peoples' ways of thinking and feeling is to quote important statements verbatim.

This tradition of fieldwork came to be called "participant observation" because anthropologists both observe and participate in the society they try to understand. As anthropologists began to write about their experiences, a literature about fieldwork grew and with it perhaps a simplified view of participant observation. Some came to think of it as living among a people and keeping track of their own responses rather than the active quest for information Malinowski outlined. An aura of mysteriousness and romanticism grew up around the commonplace activities of ethnographic description, a notion that ethnographers tried to "get into the minds" of the people under study, rather than to see life from their points of view by systematic observation and recording.

In a 1974 paper Clifford Geertz wrote that the trick is not to get into the minds of others but to figure out what they think they are up to. Geertz wrote that, instead of imagining himself to be someone else and then see what he thought, he searched out and analyzed the words, images, institutions, and behaviors by which people understood themselves. To do so, he described the regular patterns of life by moving back and forth between asking about the general form of the people's lives and the precise practices and material forms in which their lives take place. Our sense of what people are comes from our ability to analyze the ways they express themselves. There is no mystery to it, simply attention to local detail connected to larger and larger frameworks of questions to formulate patterns of regularity that describe how people see their own lives, in the way recommended by Malinowski. Geertz argued that these forms are public, because everyone learns them from confronting them in their own society, so they are equally accessible to anthropologists.

Geertz and Malinowski did similar things—observe, record, talk to people, elicit their views and opinions, compare what they say with what others say and with what one observes, and from this develop a description of daily life, unusual events, and the assumptions that people use in dealing with both. Geertz compares his approach to interpreting literature or poetry or a game such as baseball. You have to know the system before any part of it makes sense, and you have to know each part before you can know the system. Geertz does get mysterious when he shifts from his down-to-earth discussion of ethnography to hermeneutics or interpretation. For some, he leaves the impression that he meant to substitute his opinion (interpretation) for the ethnographic reality. Interpretation is like getting a joke or understanding

a poem, but Geertz's readers are left to wonder whether anyone could get the joke, or whether only Geertz really understands the punch line. Can this be the basis for reliable and valid reporting?

How does one judge an adequate or appropriate interpretation from an inadequate or inappropriate one except by the authority of the person who presents it? If all interpretations are equally good, whom do we believe? The loudest? The most powerful? How can we guarantee validity and reliability? One solution is to say that it does not matter and give up on the idea of anthropology as a science or humanity— a path that some have taken. Another solution is to try to specify methods that anyone can learn and do that will guarantee validity and reliability.

Thus, Charles O. Frake in a 1977 paper (Dil 1980) says that he does not want to join the hermeneutic circle and bury data under repetitive personal interpretations. He wants to reveal reality rather than create a fantasy. In a 1962 paper (Dil 1980) Frake argues that discovering words and terms people assign to things is more than an exercise in translation but a way to find out what kinds of things are in that cultural world. In describing systems of kinship terms, he suggests that ethnographers do not try to find the local words for "uncle" or "nephew," but attempt to articulate the system of kinship relations. The meaning of each kinship category has to be determined empirically in each case, and the meaning of each depends on its place in the system. He discusses ways to analyze systems of terms to reveal the conceptual principles associated with them. Because kinship categories form systems that can be formally analyzed, kinship is methodologically more rigorous than other systems of terms or categories. Frake suggests that the same approach be applied in other areas. The goal is to develop public, nonintuitive (i.e., reliable and valid) procedures to elicit and present information on principles of classification. He discusses methods for eliciting taxonomies and discovering the defining attributes of things in different cultures.

Frake observed that when people talk, they negotiate interpretations of what is happening, and that is just what anthropologists want to understand, but interpretations have to be connected to what an ethnographer can observe, to provide the context of the speech, to know what the interpretation is interpretating. Ethnographers look for cultural constants not in the content of the talk but in the principles people use to formulate interpretations, principles for making sense of life. In 1969 Stephen A. Tyler collected some of Frake's papers with the work of others who began to call what they were doing "the new ethnography" or "ethnoscience" to outline their operations of acquiring data and discovering underlying semantic features, how they are arranged, and how they relate to everyday life. Taylor emphasizes that this approach focuses on discovering how people organize their cultures, and the works in his collection specify explicit methods for doing so.

In 1978 Pertti J. Pelto and Gretel H. Pelto noted that their teachers in the 1950s had assured them that only personal immersion in the complexities of doing fieldwork would enlighten them as to the mysteries of the procedures by which anthropologists gain knowledge of the people they want to understand. They pointed, as Radin had some forty years earlier, to an increasing discussion of methodological issues, but they found a shortage of explanation of the logical steps and requirements for converting raw observations into anthropological knowledge. They discuss the elements of developing evidence from which we can derive statements about the human condition. While they emphasize quantifiable and statistical methods, they do not slight qualitative methods. They emphasize the importance of operationalizing concepts and of testing hypotheses by judiciously mixing quantitative and qualitative materials.

The Peltos and Tyler offered explicit answers to the question of how anthropologists can describe other cultures. The most complete contribution to this discussion is by H. Russell Bernard (1988), in which he discusses many details of the procedures for doing research in anthropology—from formulating problems, sampling, selecting research sites, searching the literature, and ways of collecting data from observation to questionnaires and taking field notes to various methods of analyzing data.

Such explicit discussions have not banished the debates about methodology to the history of anthropology but seem to have created even more discussion, much of it familiar from the 1920s and 1930s, when the same issues were the hot topics of the day: Is anthropology humanistic? Does a humanistic discipline require validity and reliability? Can anthropology be a science? Can we compare different cultures? Can we really know about other cultures? Can different people agree about what they observe?

Can we be sure we are observing the same things? Can we believe any of the reports that anthropologists publish? The answers are the same today as they have always been, and to all of the above the answers are "yes" if you want and "no" if you do not. The central question returns to the central reasons for doing anthropology. If the reason is to gain an understanding of the human condition and of other people as well as ourselves, then we do anthropology scientifically and humanistically and as well as we can. That is why anthropologists pay attention to methodology. If people do anthropology for some other reason, it doesn't really matter and no amount of talking about methods makes any difference.

E. PAUL DURRENBERGER

SEE ALSO: Ethnography; Mead-Freeman Controversy

BERNARD, H. RUSSELL. *Research Methods in Cultural Anthropology.* Newbury Park, Calif.: Sage Publications, 1988.

BOHANNAN, PAUL, and MARK GLAZER, eds. *High Points in Anthropology,* 2nd ed. New York: McGraw-Hill, 1988.

DIL, ANWAR S., ed. *Language and Cultural Description: Essays by Charles O. Frake.* Stanford, Calif.: Stanford University Press, 1980.

FREEMAN, DEREK. *Margaret Mead and Samoa: The Making and Unmaking of an Anthropological Myth.* Cambridge, Mass.: Harvard University Press, 1983.

GEERTZ, CLIFFORD. *Local Knowledge: Further Essays in Interpretive Anthropology.* 1974. Reprint. New York: Basic Books, 1983.

LEWIS, OSCAR. *Life in a Mexican Village: Tepoztlán Restudied.* Urbana: University of Illinois Press, 1951.

MALINOWSKI, BRONISLAW. *Argonauts of the Western Pacific: An Account of Native Enterprise and Adventure in the Archipelagoes of Melanesian New Guinea.* New York: Dutton, 1922.

MALKIEL, BURTON GORDON. *A Random Walk Down Wall Street,* 5th ed. New York: Norton, 1990.

MANNERS, ROBERT A., and DAVID KAPLAN, eds. *Theory in Anthropology: A Sourcebook.* Chicago: Aldine, 1968.

MEAD, MARGARET. *Coming of Age in Samoa: A Psychological Study of Primitive Youth for Western Civilization.* New York: Morrow, 1928.

PELTO, PERTTI J., and GRETEL H. PELTO. *Anthropological Research: The Structure of Inquiry,* 2nd ed. New York: Cambridge University Press, 1978.

REDFIELD, ROBERT. *Tepoztlán, A Mexican Village: A Study of Folk Life.* Chicago: University of Chicago Press, 1930.

TYLER, STEPHEN A., ed. *Cognitive Anthropology.* Chicago: Holt, Rinehart, 1969.

FOLKLORE

The term "folklore" was coined in 1846 by British antiquarian William John Thoms who defined it as "the manners, customs, observances, superstitions, ballads, proverbs, etc., of the olden time" (quoted in Bauman 1992). This definition, which developed out of mid-nineteenth century notions about romanticism and nationalism, appealed to individuals who went about their inquiries of folklore out of a "nostalgia for the past and/or the necessity of documenting the existence of national consciousness or identity" (Dundes 1980). Today, the notion of tradition remains central to folklore, and scholarship in the field remains for the most part devoted to the collection and study of particular genres of folklore, for example, folktales, legends, myths, jokes, superstition, and so on. These genres, however, have never been adequately defined, leaving the field itself inadequately defined (Dundes 1980, 1989). More important, the concept of tradition and the definition of the term "folk" have changed considerably. While tradition was once simply indicative of "relics" from the past, the term has now come to signify a "temporal continuity, rooted in the past but persisting into the present in the manner of a natural object" (Bauman 1992). With this perspective it is now assumed that folklore is not simply a product of the past that survives in the present but is emergent, the result of a complex interaction of communication, social goals, individual creativity, and performance (Bauman 1992), that is, the forces that produced folklore in the past are present today and folklore is being shaped and created constantly (Dundes 1980).

The term "folk" has experienced a similar change in its definition. Originally, the term was used in reference to "a relatively homogeneous group of peasants," but today it may be used to refer to any group of people who share a common feature (Dundes 1980). Therefore, many different folk groups can be found in modern societies, e.g., members of particular corporations or industries, users of a particular brand of computers, participants in a vast array of self-help groups, residents of a particular neighborhood, or devotees of a certain rock and roll band. From these examples it should be obvious that most individuals in modern societies belong to not one but several folk groups.

Prose narrative is probably the most studied form of folklore and what most people associate with the term. There are three types of prose narratives: myths, legends, and folktales. William R. Bascom (1984) defines them as follows. Myths are considered, by the people who relate them, to be truthful events of the primeval past. The characters in myth are usually deities. The stories in the myths most often offer explanations of the natural world or the origins of cultural groups as well as their beliefs and practices. Examples of mythological motifs include the creation of the earth and stars, the origins of plants, animals, and humans, and the establishment of the natural order (Thompson 1977). Legends are also considered to be true but from a past that is not as ancient. The subject matter of legends is mostly secular, often concerning the heroic exploits of great human characters. Examples of legends include the stories about King Arthur and the Knights of the Round Table or the Old English story of Beowulf. Folktales, unlike myths and legends, are considered to be fictional by the people who relate them. The characters found in folktales are varied—human, animal, or divine. Children's stories, fairy tales, stories with morals, tales of monsters and ogres, romances, and even many religious stories are all types of folktales.

While folklore is universal and anthropologists agree that it constitutes an important feature of cultures everywhere, there is no consensus about either the meaning of folklore or its function in the lives of humans. Franz Boas, who compiled extensive collections of folklore from the Tsimshian and Kwakiutl of North America, rejected the idea that folklore represented an attempt to explain the natural world (Boas 1940). Rather, he believed that prose narratives creatively depicted the social worlds in which people lived. Indeed, he went so far as to offer reconstructions of traditional Tsimshian and Kwakiutl life from evidence he gleaned from their folklore. The view that folklore serves as a mirror of the real world and as a historical document is also offered by Robert Darnton (1984) to account for the presence of evil stepmothers, orphans, hunger, and the drudgery of daily life as depicted in fairy tales from France in the time of the Old Regime.

Bronislaw Malinowski believed that folklore, especially mythology, served a specific function in so-called "primitive" cultures: "It expresses, enhances, and codifies belief; it safeguards and enforces morality; it vouches for the efficiency of ritual and contains practical rules for the guidance of man" (Strenski 1992). That is, myth serves as a "charter" for how a culture expects its members to think and behave. A variation of this theme can be found in the work of Bascom (1965b), who claims that all of the functions of folklore—escape from the frustrations of social life, validation of culture, education, maintaining conformity—can be categorized "under the single function of maintaining the stability of culture."

A third perspective on the meaning and function of folklore is that of psychoanalytic theory, which posits that much of the content and meaning of folklore comes from the unconscious and represents projections of "anxiety-producing topics" (Dundes 1980). Bruno Bettelheim (1976) offers the image of the evil stepmother as an example. This figure from European folklore, according to Bettelheim, reflects a child's mixed emotions about feeling anger toward his mother. Sigmund Freud believed that fantasy life often represented the attempt of the ego to gain "psychic mastery" over traumatic events and anxiety.

A fourth perspective on the meaning and function of folklore can be found in the so-called psychocultural model (Kardiner 1939, 1945). In brief, this model combines psychoanalytic theory with evidence from anthropology. Thus, the fantasy content of a culture's projective systems (folklore, religion, art) is the result not only of unconscious processes but of shared experiences. For example, individuals in a given culture are likely to have had common childhood experiences that produce common anxieties. These anxieties would then become the basis for the fantasy content of the projective systems.

Alan Dundes (1989) believes that folklore scholarship has failed "to employ a broader, more comprehensive form of the comparative method," with the result that folklorists have generally have not tried to discover laws about the meaning and function of folklore. Most folklore scholarship has been narrowly concerned with the distribution and variation of particular motifs or interpretive analysis of one or a small number of texts. Systematic, cross-cultural research has been extremely rare, although there are examples in the work of Alex Cohen (1990) and George O. Wright (1954).

ALEX COHEN

BASCOM, WILLIAM R. "Folklore and Anthropology." In *The Study of Folklore*, edited by Alan Dundes. Englewood Cliffs, N.J.: Prentice Hall, 1965a.

———. "Four Functions of Folklore." In *The Study of Folklore*, edited by Alan Dundes. Englewood Cliffs, N.J.: Prentice Hall, 1965b.

———. "The Forms of Folklore: Prose Narratives." In *Sacred Narrative: Readings in the Theory of Myth*, edited by Alan Dundes. Berkeley: University of California Press, 1984.

BAUMAN, RICHARD. "Folklore." In *Folklore, Cultural Performances, and Popular Entertainments: A Communications-Centered Handbook*, edited by Richard Bauman. New York: Oxford University Press, 1992.

BETTELHEIM, BRUNO. *The Uses of Enchantment: The Meaning and Importance of Fairy Tales*. New York: Alfred A. Knopf, 1976.

BOAS, FRANZ. *Tsimshian mythology*. Washington, D.C.: Bureau of American Ethnology, 1909–1910.

———. *Race, Language, and Culture*. New York: Macmillan, 1940.

———. *Kwakiutl Culture as Reflected in Mythology*. New York: Kraus Reprint, 1969.

BRUNVAND, JAN H. *The Vanishing Hitchhiker: American Urban Legends and Their Meanings*. New York: W. W. Norton, 1981.

———. *The Choking Doberman and Other "New" Urban Legends*. New York: W. W. Norton, 1984.

———. *Curses! Broiled Again!: The Hottest Urban Legends Going*. New York: W. W. Norton, 1989.

———. *The Baby Train and Other Lusty Urban Legends*. New York: W. W. Norton, 1993.

COHEN, ALEX. "A Cross-Cultural Study of the Effects of Environmental Unpredictability on Aggression in Folktales." *American Anthropologist* 92 (1990): 474–479.

DARNTON, ROBERT. *The Great Cat Massacre and Other Episodes in French Cultural History*. New York: Basic Books. 1984.

DUNDES, ALAN. *Interpreting Folklore*. Bloomington: Indiana University Press, 1980.

———. *Folklore Matters*. Knoxville: University of Tennessee Press, 1989.

KARDINER, ABRAM. *The Individual and His Society: The Psychodynamics of Primitive Social Organization*.

New York: Columbia University Press, 1939.

———. *The Psychological Frontiers of Society.* New York: Columbia University Press, 1945.

STRENSKI, IVAN, ed. *Malinowski and the Work of Myth.* Princeton, N.J.: Princeton University Press, 1992.

THOMPSON, STITH. *The Folktale.* Berkeley: University of California Press, 1977.

WRIGHT, GEORGE O. "Projection and Displacement: A Cross-Cultural Study of Folktale Aggression." *Journal of Abnormal and Social Psychology* 49 (1954): 523–528.

FOOD AND DIET

It is food not sex that makes the world go round. This point is often overlooked, particularly in highly affluent, industrialized nations. In such nations as the United States, where a large percentage of the population is overweight, thoughts pertaining to food generally concern resolutions to cut down on fattening foods or to avoid many foods entirely. Where food comes from, how it is produced, or even an understanding of why food is essential are not topics of immediate concern to the average American. Thus, the overwhelming role of food on human evolution and its considerable influence on present-day human biology and behavior remains largely underappreciated and unexplored.

Contrast this situation with that of the rest of the world, both human and non human, where for most individuals obtaining sufficient food each day is an omnipresent pressure generally requiring a considerable expenditure of time, energy, and, frequently, strong competition. As pointed out by Thomas Malthus well over a century ago, the amount of high-quality food at any particular moment is finite and can only slowly increase while the number of mouths seeking to devour it often increases exponentially. This tension between the potential for increase in living organisms and the finite nature of their food supply stimulated Charles Darwin's formulation of the evolution of species by the action of natural selection. The human species, like any other, has evolved over millions of years in response to particular selective pressures. In my view, the first members of our genus, *Homo*, made their initial breakthrough into the adaptive zone of culture primarily in response to dietary challenges.

THE NICHE OF THE CULTURAL OMNIVORE

The distinguishing characteristic of the human genus has been its unusually large brain, far bigger than would be predicted for a mammal of our size (Jerison 1973). Because brain tissue is fueled by a steady supply of glucose, it is energetically very expensive to maintain. Unusually large brain size in the earliest humans seems clear evidence that the first humans made some radical breakthrough in securing a dependable source of high-quality, energy-rich foods.

Katharine Milton views the pivotal step in human evolution as a breakthrough into a new type of dietary niche; she calls it the niche of the cultural omnivore. We know that altering climatic conditions during the Plio-Pleistocene affected the food supply of many animal species; competition for food may have greatly intensified at this time. The African savanna, from where humans are believed to have evolved, is currently occupied by a number of highly specialized herbivores and carnivores. In contrast, members of the primate order—to which humans belong—are regarded as relatively generalized animals (Le Gros 1959). During the Plio-Pleistocene era, less specialized savanna dwellers, such as australopithecines, may have faced new dietary pressures, perhaps placing a strong premium on adaptation to new dietary behaviors in order to survive.

Milton views these new dietary behaviors as falling into two basic, strongly interrelated categories involving both technological and social innovations (Isaac 1978; Milton 1987). Technological innovations, such as digging sticks, grinding stones, and rudimentary weapons to capture prey, could have enhanced dietary quality and/or food availability. In terms of dietary breakthroughs, however, early humans also appear to have depended very much on social adaptations, particularly cooperative social interactions to procure food items, most particularly the development of a division of labor (Lancaster 1975; Isaac 1978; Milton 1987). The radical nature of this cooperative dietary strategy remains underappreciated (Milton 1987, 1993). It is an almost totally novel food-acquisition tactic among mammals and yet it provides dietary benefits that can be overwhelming for, in effect, it enables different members of the social unit to become specialists at different aspects of food procurement and on totally different types of foods. Further, these acquisition skills are achieved largely through cultural, therefore, easily modifiable means—rather than genetic adaptations—which are very slowly acquired and take many generations to modify. Foods procured by this new foraging strategy can then be shared—in effect providing a nutritious dietary mix for all members of the social unit. Furthermore, this is an ideal dietary strategy in terms of the expansion of a species' geographical range. As new groups bud off from the parent population and colonize new areas, they adjust their foraging behavior to deal with the new dietary opportunities at each locale—precisely the pattern that our genus and species appear to have followed.

Human beings take this type of food acquisition behavior as the norm because we are used to it. But it cannot be overstressed that this means of food acquisition is, in effect, the key to the origins of the genus *Homo*. The pressures related to food acquisition were the driving force in human evolution, as they have been for all animal species. The remarkable spread and proliferation of the human species over a very short period of time evolutionarily speaking clearly shows the great advantage provided by entrance into the dietary niche of the cultural omnivore—a niche marked by use of foods from two tropical levels (i.e., plants and animal foods) by a division of labor and food sharing and by a dependence on brain power—mental constructs and behavioral plasticity—for its successful enactment. Edward O. Wilson of Harvard University has estimated that for more than 2 million years (until around 250,000 years ago), the human brain grew by about a tablespoon every 100,000 years. Apparently, each new tablespoon of brain matter added in the genus Homo brought rewards that favored intensification of the trend toward technological and social complexity (Wilson 1978).

Entrance into the dietary niche of the cultural omnivore has provided the human species with benefits heretofore unprecedented on the planet, for the more mastery one gains over one's food supply and the more dependable the food supply becomes, the more time individuals have to turn their attention to other areas. Today, this capacity for innovation is a mixed blessing for as humans' control over their food supply has intensified, particularly since the advent of agriculture, so has human population size and human technology.

The Early Human Diet

Until around 10,000 years ago, there was no evidence of agriculture or animal domestication. All humans lived exclusively as hunter-gatherers, adapting their food acquisition strategies to the particular range of plant and animal species found in particular environments. The notion that the hunter-gatherers led a life of affluence and ease is not borne out by data on the activities of present-day hunter-gatherers who, since they lack methods of food preservation, generally hunt and gather almost every day. Both men and women in present-day hunter-gatherer societies probably devote between five and eight hours per day to activities specifically related to food procurement and its preparation (Milton 1991).

Animal protein and fat were probably extremely important components of the early human diet. These may initially have been obtained largely through scavenging (Blumenschine and Cavallo 1992), but evidence from stone tools and caches of animal bones suggests that early humans turned increasingly to hunting, in some cases to cooperative big-game hunting, to secure animal foods. As discussed by Leslie Sue Lieberman (1987), despite the broad alimentary flexibility of the human omnivore, there appears to be a panhuman preference for meat and other animal products, such as milk, eggs, and blood. Animal protein supplies essential amino acids and complements for human nutritional needs and serves as a good source of certain essential vitamins and minerals (Bryant et al. 1985; Lieberman 1987). Meat is also a volumetrically concentrated and almost totally digestible food for humans. Although most extant monkeys and apes take by far the greatest percentage of their diet from plants Milton (1987), believes that hunting and a reliance on meat protein were extremely important characteristics of most human populations until only a few hundred years ago.

This idea may be distressing to those who believe that human ancestors did not include meat in the diet. Such individuals tend to forget that until the advent of agriculture and the development of reliable plant-based cuisines it would have been difficult if not impossible for most—or perhaps all—hunter-gatherer populations to secure or even to ingest sufficient high-quality plant foods each day to meet all of their nutritional requirements. Examination of human burials shows that, as a rule, hunter-gatherer populations were better nourished than early agriculturalists (Cassidy 1980). Thus, Milton views the vegetarian lifestyle, as one generally dependent on a settled existence and the continuous availability of staple plant foods, as relatively recent for our species.

Pure vegetarianism is very rare and probably not more than 1,000 years old. In societies where vegetarianism predominates, trial-and-error learning over many generations has resulted in plant-based diets suitable for human nutritional needs. However, as many a novice vegetarian in the United States knows, to eat properly in the absence of such time-honored dietary traditions requires considerable nutritional knowledge about plant foods, knowledge that has only very recently become available.

The necessary nutrients for humans have been fairly well established since the 1930s and 1940s, although the quantities needed are constantly under revision as new facts become available (e.g., Lieberman 1987). There do not appear to be many population-wide genetic differences between people in terms of either their nutrient requirements or their ability to process foods. For example, the circumpolar people's diet of mostly raw meat and blubber seems very extreme. One might postulate that any human population eating such a diet must have many unique genetic adaptations to it. In fact, no real evidence of genetic adaptations for this specialized diet have been discovered yet (Draper 1977). Humans, as cultural omnivores, depend largely on nonsomatic, (i.e., cultural or learned adaptations) to solve their dietary problems. For example, Eskimos have traditionally eaten their meat raw and obtained their required vitamin C, which would have been lost if their meat had been cooked. Thus, for the human species, selective pressures for genetic adaptations to cope with problems posed by new foods or dietary change, tend to be low. For this reason, it is not surprising that most humans are basically the same in terms of their nutritional needs and digestive physiology.

However, there are examples of genetic differences between human populations in terms of the prevalence or absence of certain digestive enzymes. In such cases, however, it is not that humans have acquired something new via natural selection but rather that the genetic machinery already in place has been altered via simple point mutations. For example, members of some Eskimo populations lack the enzyme sucrase, needed to digest sucrose. As their cold environment generally lacks ripe fruits or other sucrose-rich foods, selection apparently has favored the loss of manufacture of this unnecessary enzyme. A similar case concerns the enzyme lactase, needed to digest the milk sugar lactose. Prior to the domestication of animals, humans had access to milk only when they were very young. At the age of weaning—three to four years—a regulatory gene then turned off the production of lactase as, once the infant was weaned, there would be no further need for it. After the domestication of cattle, sheep, and other milk-producing animals, however, milk and milk products became generally available as foods throughout the human life cycle. In many such pastoral populations, we find that a simple point mutation has resulted in supression of the action of the regulatory gene which puts an end to lactase production. In such populations, lactase continues to be secreted throughout the life cycle, permitting milk drinking and the utilization of lactose as an energy source by adults as well as childresn (Simoons 1982).

MODERN CONCERNS

Nutrition, a relatively new field, has only developed over the past few decades. Yet for thousands of years, humans in dozens of different societies worldwide have worked out acceptable diets totally in ignorance of the existence of protein, essential fatty acids, or vitamins. How is this accomplished? We need to bear in mind that our present-day condition, a condition in which most of us are totally cut off from any involvement in food production, is a very recent phenomenon. Until fifty to a hundred years ago, most individuals spent their entire lives in the same geographical locale, producing and eating local diets created after many generations of experimentation.

CUISINES

"Cuisine" refers to the manner in which cultures manipulate and transform potential foodstuffs into proper human foods (Rozin 1982). Lévi-Strauss (1979) focused attention on the mental constructs that humans bring to food and eating. He views food in its natural state as raw—that is, of nature, untransformed. Humans take this raw material, and through the medium of culture transform it into non-nature, figuratively cooked items suitable for human consumption. Cuisines can be simple, such as the custom of many Amazonian Indians of cooking an entire game animal on a wood fire, or they can be elaborate, as in the case of French haute cuisine. Most cultures possess a mix of both simple and elaborate culinary practices. For example, the Hagahai, a fringe-Highland group in Papua New Guinea, make a rich fermented sauce out of the nuts of a wild forest tree. The preparation of this sauce is extremely elaborate, involving the collection of the nuts in the forests, roasting them in a pit filled with hot rocks, cracking and extracting the cooked kernels, then tying them tightly into large banana leaf packets which are then immersed in the river for a month or more while fermentation occurs. The ensuing oily sauce is then stored in bamboo tubes stoppered with leaves and used as a garnish for sweet potatoes or cooked bananas. The preparation of this sauce is as elaborate as is the preparation for many dishes in haute cuisine.

Many societies have developed methods of preparing foods which enhance their nutritional value. For example, in Latin America, a number of cultures mix corn and beans together as a dietary staple. Chemical analysis has shown that each of these plant foods is deficient in a different essential amino acid. An essential amino acid is one which is required by the body but which the body cannot provide; therefore, it must be obtained from foods (Bryant et al. 1985). Corn is low in the essential amino acid lysine, while beans are low in methionine. Mixing corn and beans together in the same meal provides the human eater with a sufficiency of both essential amino acids, a practice called protein complementation (Bryant et al. 1985). Often it is not sufficient simply to pass a new crop from region to region—the cuisine must come with the crop for its most efficient utilization (Katz 1987).

Because until recently many activities in human cultures revolved around food acquisition, it is not surprising that every human culture attaches enormous symbolic weight to foods. Even in highly technological nations such as the United States, it is human tradition to celebrate important occasions with the preparation and eating of special ceremonial foods. In many cultures, what is celebrated is the acknowledged importance of the food itself—to wit the yam festival in the Trobriand Islands; the banana festival of the Yanamamo Indians in Brazil; or the German may wine festival. Key animal foods are also the object of special ceremonies in many cultures—for example, pig festivals in Papua New Guinea or turtle festivals in the Amazonian rain forest. In other cases, special ceremonial foods mark an event in the life cycle, such as foods used for puberty rituals, marriages, and funerals. All human cultures have particular foods which are viewed as the proper foods for particular special events and whose preparation and presentation follow time-honored ritual patterns.

Food is an ideal symbolic medium not only because it is essential to life but also because there is generally recognition, either conscious or unconscious, that food is potentially both dangerous and powerful in that it is taken into the body via the mouth—a very vulnerable region—and then in essence is incorporated into and becomes part of the body. Food can be used to mark ethnic and social boundaries, as well as to symbolize important occasions or emotional states. Many Amazonian Indians have tabooed (prohibited) prey foods. On examination, these tabooed foods often turn out to be the foods most favored by their traditional enemies (Milton 1991). Thus, food can be used not only to define one's cultural identity but also to make pejorative inferences about the origins of others. Tabooed or prohibited foods are a cultural universal; they are found in highly technological societies as well as in those of hunter-gatherers. For example, most people in the United States do not eat dogs, insects, or horses. Yet many other cultures find these items delicious. Each particular culture or ethnic group teaches its members what is and is not proper food and often these mental constructs are so powerful that perfectly nutritious foods—such as dog, horse, or deer meat—are regarded with horror or revulsion simply because they lie outside of one's own culturally transmitted dietary traditions. This is what Lévi-Strauss meant when he said that for humans, foods are often not so much good to eat as they are good to think (Lévi-Strauss 1963).

Foods also figure strongly in religious rituals, perhaps most dramatically in the Christian tradition in which the act of communion may be viewed as symbolic cannibalism with the congregation consuming the body and blood of the diety (bread and wine) to purify the body of sin. Cannibalism is regarded as a strong almost panhuman taboo and yet in this Christian ritual, the ultimate taboo is symbolically transformed into a sanctified and highly acceptable act. Foods are also used as class markers, as in the differentiation of castes in India, as symbols of prestige and status (wine drinkers versus beer drinkers), as definers or markers of gender, (e.g., "real men don't eat quiche"), to differentiate age classes, and for a huge range of other social and ethnic differentiations.

Though modern technological nations believe that they have tremendous nutritional knowledge and sophistication, almost all of the major diseases affecting people in countries such as the United States are related to diet; this is most emphatically not the case of present day hunter-gatherers who do not tend to suffer from heart disease, high blood pressure, cancer, or obesity. Modern health problems strongly suggest that in such nations present-day dietary habits have gotten out of line with human biology. It seems that recent scientific knowledge of the chemical constituents of foods and the presumed knowledge of human nutritional needs do not compensate for past generations of traditional nutritional wisdom. Are domesticated and genetically modified plants and animals as nutritious as we are led to believe? Some evidence suggests that they are not.

The very high fat content of domesticated beef is quite different from the lean meat of wild animals such as deer, whose bodies also lack the hormones, antibiotics, and other additives used by animal breeders. Domesticated plants, too, have been genetically manipulated and such differences may be of considerable importance in terms of human health. Studies of the chemical constituents of wild plant foods eaten by monkeys show that the plant foods they routinely eat are extremely high in vitamin C and differ in other important respects from many domesticated plant foods routinely consumed in highly industrialized societies (Milton and Jenness 1987). These differences warrant careful study, as do effects of the continued modification of traditional healthful cuisines throughout the world by the introduction, often the forced introduction, of new seed crops and new staple foods, such as white bread or foods high in sugar and fat. Many such foods can be regarded as "junk food," low in nutritional value. A few domesticated species and some convenience foods cannot compensate humanity for its loss of traditional dietary knowledge nor for the genetic diversity of the still existing myriad plant and animal species which are rapidly being exterminated. Now is the time to pause and reevaluate our situation as the human species fast becomes a global village of nomadic travelers whose dietary heritage in terms of thousands of generations of regional cultural wisdom along with the plants and animals that have sustained it fade rapidly and eternally from this earth.

KATHARINE MILTON

BLUMENSCHINE, R. J., and J. A. CAVALLO. "Scavenging and Human Evolution." *Scientific American* 276 (1992): 90–96.

BRYANT, CAROL A., ANITA COURTNEY, BARBARA A. MARKESBERY, and KATHLEEN M. DEWALT. *The Cultural Feast: An Introduction to Food and Society.* New York: West Publishing, 1985.

CASSIDY, CLAIRE M. "Nutrition and Health in Agriculturalists and Hunters and Gatherers." In *Nutritional Anthropology,* edited by Norge Jerome, Randy Kandel, and Gretel Pelto. New York: Redgrave Publishing, 1980.

DRAPER, H. H. "The Aboriginal Eskimo Diet in Modern Perspective." *American Anthropologist* 79 (1977): 309–316.

ISAAC, GLYNN. "Food Sharing and Human Evolution: Archaeological Evidence from the Plio-Pleistocene of East Africa." *Journal of Anthropological Research* 34 (1978): 311–325.

JERISON, HARRY J. *Evolution of the Brain and Intelligence.* New York: Academic Press, 1973.

KATZ, SOLOMON H. "Fava Bean Consumption: A Case for the Coevolution of Genes and Culture." In *Food and Evolution,* edited by Marvin Harris and Eric Barry Ross. Philadelphia: Temple University Press, 1987.

LANCASTER, JANE B. *Primate Behavior and the Emergence of Human Culture.* New York: Holt, Rinehart, and Winston, 1975.

LE GROS, CLARK W.E. *The Antecedents of Man.* Edinburgh: Edinburgh University Press, 1959.

LÉVI-STRAUSS, CLAUDE. *Totemism.* Boston: Beacon Press, 1963.

———. *The Raw and the Cooked.* New York: Octagon Books, 1979.

LIEBERMAN, LESLIE SUE. "Biocultural Consequences of Animals versus Plants as Sources of Fats, Proteins and Other Nutrients." In *Food and Evolution,* edited by Marvin Harris, and Eric Barry Ross. Philadelphia: Temple University Press, 1987.

MILTON, KATHARINE. "Primate Diets and Gut Morphology." *Food and Evolution: Toward a Theory of Human Food Habits,* edited by Marvin Harris and Eric Barry Ross. Philadelphia: Temple University Press, 1987.

———. "Comparative Aspects of Diet in Amazonian Forest Dwellers." *Philosophical Transactions of the Royal Society (Series B).* 334 (1991): 253–263.

———. "Diet and Primate Evolution." *Scientific American* 269 (2) (1993): 86–93.

MILTON, KATHARINE, and ROBERT JENNESS. "Ascorbic Acid Content of Neotropical Plant Parts Available to Wild Monkeys and Bats." *Experientia* 43 (1987): 339–342.

RICHARDS, AUDREY. *Hunger, Work and Sex in a Savage Society.* Westport, Conn.: Greenwood Press, 1985.

ROZIN, ELIZABETH. "The Structure of Cuisine." *The Psychobiology of Human Food Selection,* edited by L.

M. Barker. Westport, Conn.: Avi Press, 1982.

SIMONNS, FREDERICK J. "Geography and Genetics as Factors in the Psychobiology of Human Food Selection." In *The Psychobiology of Human Food Selection*, edited by L. M. Barker. Westport, Conn.: Avi Press, 1982.

WILSON, EDWARD O. *On Human Nature.* Cambridge: Harvard University Press, 1978.

FORAGING

SEE: Optimal Foraging Theory; Hunting and Gathering Societies

FORENSIC ANTHROPOLOGY

SEE: Human Osteology

FOUR-FIELD APPROACH

The term "four-field approach" has been given to the distinctive form of anthropology that is practiced primarily in North American anthropology. It applies to the use of the traditional four main areas of study (subfields) within anthropology: biological anthropology, archaeology, linguistic anthropology, and cultural anthropology. The four-field approach generally refers to the integration of these areas with the goal of obtaining a more holistic and overall global understanding of being human in the past and present. The four fields are often partitioned into two categories: one biological (including biological anthropology) and the other cultural (including archaeology, linguistic anthropology, and cultural anthropology). This division highlights the uniqueness of anthropology as compared with other academic disciplines in that it incorporates both a biological and a cultural perspective on humans throughout time and space. In this sense, anthropology is a biocultural endeavor.

HISTORY OF THE FOUR-FIELD APPROACH

Most current introductory texts in anthropology stress the importance of the four-field approach for a comprehensive study of humans. The approach to understanding ourselves gained prominence during the Age of Enlightenment in the eighteenth century as the systematic and scientific study of people was emphasized. At that time scholars attempted to categorize individuals and populations according to biological and cultural classificatory systems. During the late eighteenth and throughout the nineteenth centuries, North American scholars recorded information on Native Americans from perspectives that, in retrospect, could be said to have included many dimensions of the four-field approach. As the sciences and humanities began to separate into specialized disciplines, the origins of the four fields of anthropology and their integration took root in both areas. As Eric R. Wolf (1974) wrote, anthropology became "the most scientific of the humanities, the most humanist of the sciences."

From the mid-nineteenth century to the early twentieth century, a number of anthropological periodicals and organizations were formed for the explicit purpose of conveying the diversity of studying the multiple dimensions of being human. Groups such as the American Ethnological Society (AES), organized in 1842; the American Association for the Advancement of Science (AAAS); Section H-Anthropology, formed in 1882, and its offshoot, the American Anthropological Association (AAA), set up in 1902, were all designed to bring together specialists within the four fields. This diversity is well illustrated in the first volume of the *American Anthropologist,* published in 1888, which included articles representing the four fields.

When the AAA was founded, its bylaws did not even specify the four fields, which were assumed to be an integral part of doing anthropology. Since then numerous organizations and journals have developed to accommodate various specializations within one field of anthropology. Through it all, the AAA has remained a unifying force for the continuance of a four-field orientation to anthropology. During periodic reorganizations, the AAA has consistently specified in its bylaws the importance of keeping the four-field breadth and approach. This has occurred even as more specialist groups are gaining representation at the annual meetings.

In 1892 Daniel Brinton became one of the first to call for university resources to be organized for the teaching of anthropology, which would include the four fields. This differed from the organization of

European academic departments, in which each of the four fields became separate departments unto themselves. As academic departments of anthropology in North America were established, they incorporated course work in each of the four fields in their plan of study. Some anthropologists, such as Franz Boas, carried out research in all four fields. In 1899 Boas also organized the first teaching department of anthropology in the United States at Columbia University. Boas and his students were important in maintaining the four-field approach within North American anthropology. With mounting specialization during the twentieth century, it has become more and more difficult, if not impossible, for any one anthropologist to master the growing body of literature and theory in all four fields. Still, the importance of cross-field communication and collaborative, intradisciplinary field research, along with receiving a basic training in the four fields, have remained the foundation of an education in North American anthropology.

Alfred L. Kroeber, a student of Boas, produced the first general textbook for anthropology in 1923, entitled *Anthropology*, which outlined the four fields, although not as explicitly as they are defined today. Many texts have followed that devote their introduction or first chapter to explicit discussions on the merits of the integrative approach to anthropology drawing from the traditional four fields.

CONTEMPORARY TRENDS IN THE FOUR-FIELD APPROACH

Given the increasing specialization within anthropology in the latter half of the twentieth century, some North American departments began separating into distinct departments representing each of the four fields or some other specialities. For example, at some institutions biological anthropologists have joined departments of biology. Ironically, certain European institutions, such as Oxford University, have moved in the opposite direction, bringing the formerly separated departments into one, embracing the four-field approach.

In an interview by Richard Handler (1991) with Clifford Geertz, Geertz suggested that many departments of anthropology "don't do much more than give lip service to the four-field notion," and even when they do, "there are just four little departments within the larger one." For North American anthropologists,

Geertz's observations bring up the question of whether the four fields as a unifying concept is myth or reality. His comments would suggest the former. Fewer and fewer anthropologists receive in-depth training in all of the four fields, in part because of the increasing specialization within anthropology and the subsequent need to focus not only on one of the fields but to specialize further within a subdivision of a field. The reality, however, is most anthropologists would agree that, in theory, the four-field approach is the most constructive framework within which a holistic perspective on humans can be obtained. Therefore, as an approach, it is still maintained as an integral part of one's education as an anthropologist.

Another reality for all anthropologists in the late twentieth century is the recognition of a fifth field of anthropology, applied anthropology, which generally refers to research and service being completed by anthropologists outside of academic contexts and applied to contemporary concerns and issues. Each of the traditional four fields has many applied dimensions. In order to fully recognize this fifth field, it might be necessary in the future to refer to the five-field approach to anthropology.

Most anthropologists today agree that the four-field approach is critical for maintaining a holistic perspective on the study of humans. As a means of counteracting the possible fragmentation from growing specialization, there is a need for continuing the communication between the four fields and their subdivisions. Such a dialogue is essential to the viability of anthropology. This commitment is necessary for the survival of anthropology as both an academic discipline and a humanistic endeavor that seeks a comprehensive understanding of our own biological and cultural diversity.

For a sample of discussions going on in North American anthropology today concerning the four-field approach the reader is directed to several issues of the AAA's *Anthropology Newsletter*, published between October 1992 and May 1993, which included relevant articles by David B. Givens and Susan N. Skomal (1992) and by Nathalie F. S. Woodbury (1992).

BARRETT P. BRENTON

SEE ALSO: American Anthropological Association; American Association for the Advancement of Science; Applied

Anthropology; Archaeology; Biocultural Anthropology; Biological Anthropology; Linguistic Anthropology; Periodical Appendix

DARNELL, REGNA *Readings in the History of Anthropology.* New York: Harper and Row, 1974.

DE WAAL MALEFIJT, ANNEMARIE. *Images of Man: A History of Anthropological Thought.* New York: Alfred A. Knopf, 1974.

GIVENS, DAVID B., and SUSAN N. SKOMAL. "The Four Fields: Myth or Reality?" *Anthropology Newsletter* (October 1992): 1, 17.

HANDLER, RICHARD. "An Interview with Clifford Geertz." *Current Anthropology* 32 (1991): 603–613.

KROEBER, ALFRED L. *Anthropology: Culture Patterns and Processes.* New York: Harcourt Brace, 1923.

WOLF, ERIC R. *Anthropology.* New York: W. W. Norton, 1974.

WOODBURY, NATHALIE F. S. "In My Father's House: Subfields in Anthropology." *Anthropology Newsletter* (October 1992): 5, 17.

FUNCTIONALISM

Functionalism is the theory that the institutions of society perform functions to meet the needs of its personnel or to maintain the social system. The recognition of function is long-standing in both biology and sociology, but as a school of thought in anthropology it emerged early in the twentieth century, promulgated by the two most prominent anthropologists in Great Britain at the time: Bronislaw Malinowski and A. R. Radcliffe-Brown. Developed between 1910 and 1930, the two versions were most fully expressed in two volumes: one that appeared posthumously (Malinowski 1960) and one that appeared late in career (Radcliffe-Brown 1948). Functionalism served as a corrective to the empty evolutionary theories that dominated nineteenth-century anthropology and the historicism of the early twentieth century. Beyond the thesis that institutions and customs were to be seen as instrumentalities in the service of society, the two formulations were different in construction.

Malinowski's functionalism begins with the idea of needs—the physiological needs of man as an animal—and has a table of "impulses" (e.g., hunger, thirst) for which "acts" (eating, drinking) lead to "satisfactions" (satiation). To meet these needs, humans create social institutions, which are "the real isolate of cultural analysis." Each institution has personnel, a charter, a set of norms or rules, activities, material apparatus (technology), and a function. There are also culturally derived needs and, finally, four basic "instrumental needs" (economics, social control, education, and political organization), for which institutional devices are necessary. Malinowski's influence on anthropology rests on his insightful examination of Trobriand culture rather than on his functional theory, but the latter did influence the sociologists Talcott Parsons and Robert Merton.

Radcliffe-Brown's functionalism was more austere and parsimonious and had greater impact on anthropology. Following Auguste Comte, it was based on the perception that the social constituted a separate "level" of reality distinct from those of biological and inert matter, with the further tenet that explanations of social phenomena had to be constructed within the social level. He took from Èmile Durkheim the tenet that the explanation of social life lies in the nature of society itself, that society is not merely the sum of individuals but a system, and that human nature provides the conditions for, but not the explanation of, social forms. Radcliffe-Brown rejected all biological considerations as being reductionist; individuals were replaceable, transient occupants of social roles and therefore irrelevant. He also denied the relevance of history and called for synchronic rather than diachronic research and for nomothetic rather than idiographic analyses. Society, he argued, had concrete reality whereas culture was but an abstraction. He sought the formulation of social laws comparable to those of physics, through a comparative sociology (Radcliffe-Brown 1948, 1952).

The focus of Radcliffe-Brown's attention was on social structure. A society is a system of relationships maintaining itself through cybernetic feedback. Institutions are orderly sets of relationships whose function is to maintain the society as a system. Structural concerns led Radcliffe-Brown to the examination of kinship and one of his early essays showed that the mother's-brother relationship had sociological function and was not merely an evolutionary survival from matrilineal times. His second major area of concern was with kin-based social groups, such as clans, which he saw as jural entities ("corporate groups") that served as political systems with rights and obligations.

Both Malinowski and Radcliffe-Brown were charismatic and challenging teachers, and the students entering anthropology during the interwar years in Great Britain were attracted to their ideas, particularly to those of Radcliffe-Brown. The rich fieldwork inspired by him focused on the structuring of social life and constitutes a permanent monument to his influence on anthropology. The list of scholars who identified themselves as functionalist, with varying degrees of conviction, reads like a who's who of anthropology in Great Britain and includes Mary Douglas, E. E. Evans-Pritchard, Raymond Firth, Daryll Ford, Meyer Fortes, Max Gluckman, Hilda Kuper, Edmund Leach, Lucy Mair, Clyde Mitchell, S. F. Nadel, Audrey Richards, and I. Schapera. Radcliffe-Brown taught at the University of Chicago (1931-1937) and influenced many American scholars, notably Fred Eggan, Kalervo Oberg, Edward Spicer, Alexander Spoehr, and Sol Tax.

Functional theory has been criticized for its disregard of the historical process, for its presupposition that societies are in a state of equilibrium, and for its inherent conservatism, although many individual functionalist studies do not merit such criticism. More trenchant are the logical problems that have been pointed out by philosophers: namely, that functional explanations are teleological and tautological. Nagel (1961) has shown that the presence of an institution cannot be explained by its function, because the use cannot precede the institution's existence, unless one presents the teleological argument that its development anticipated its function. This criticism can be met by recognizing either an evolutionary or a historical process at work, but functionalism specifically rejected such ideas. Nagel also indicated that the argument is circular, that needs are postulated on the basis of existing institutions, which are then used to explain their existence. This criticism can be met by establishing a set of universal requisite needs, or functional prerequisites. Although Malinowski set forth a list of needs, Radcliffe-Brown apparently did not recognize the need for one.

He thought that functional theory could lead to social laws, but none were ever formulated nor did anyone ever set forth propositions amenable to empirical testing. The rich ethnographies inspired by functionalism are just so many "case studies." Neither of the two volumes of essays designed to showcase functionalism (Radcliffe-Brown and Forde 1950;

Fortes and Evans-Pritchard 1940) emerged with any generalizations, much less laws. For instance, in the latter, two classes of political system, state organized and acephalous, were recognized, but there is no explanation as to why a society should have one system rather than the other.

The doctrinaire rejection of all alternate theories was a weakness of functionalism: antihistoricism made it impossible to examine social processes, rejection of psychology made it impossible to understand attitudes and sentiments, and the rejection of culture led to a lack of recognition of the ecological context or the subtlety that is captured in the word "ethos," although students in the field did not disregard these aspects of human social life.

Anthropological functionalism influenced the sociology of Talcott Parsons and others, especially in collaboration with anthropologists and psychologists in the Department of Social Relations at Harvard. They came to acknowledge that functional theory demanded the recognition of (the failure potential, extinction, or dissolution of) a society and hence the need to postulate a set of elements necessary to prevent such demise. A group of them formulated a set of "social prerequisites" (Aberle et al. 1950) including provision for adequate utilization of the environment and for sexual recruitment, the definition of social roles and their assignment, systems of communication, shared cognitive and goal orientations, the normative regulation of the means for goal attainment and for expression of affect, and processes of socialization. Clyde Kluckhohn, the senior anthropologist among them, attempted a functional explanation of Navaho witchcraft ([1944] n.d.). As Cancian (1968) pointed out, to avoid tautology Kluckhohn's explanation had to postulate a social need (to manage hostility), bringing a psychological assumption into the analysis, and it showed that more overt means of managing hostility had not been available because of governmental controls, bringing in historical and ecological factors. This leaves the functional "explanation" embedded in other parameters of explanation.

Goldschmidt (1966) sought to rescue the value in functionalism by "turning Malinowski on his head," as Turner and Maryanski (1979) put it in their summary study of functionalism. Recognizing the "Malinowskian dilemma" (if each culture is unique, institutional comparison is impossible) and the salience of functional prerequisites and Malinowski's "needs," Goldschmidt argued for a "comparative functionalism" that starts with what is problematical and seeks to discover how institutional devices solve what is problematic; that is, problems are consistent from culture to culture, but institutional solutions vary. He assumes a biological "affect hunger," which is transformed into a prestige drive that leads to potential antagonism and self/other conflict, and sees institutions as preventing society from being rent by the centrifugal force of individual self-interest. Using Kathleen Gough's classic examination of the Nayar "marriage," Goldschmidt notes the inherent falsification in cross-cultural definitions and points to the manner in which functions usually performed by marriage are met by other institutions and to the social and psychological consequences when they are not. Goldschmidt's functionalism is not a universal theory but is embedded in a broader theoretical frame.

By the late 1970s functional studies had gone out of style, but the legacy of the research undertaken under functionalism's inspiration is a rich one, functionalism injecting much of value into anthropological discourse through attention to institutions and social interrelationships. Its primary contribution was the recognition of society itself. U.S. ethnologists had treated social institutions as mere customs rather than as organizations for action—understandably, because they had mostly studied reservation Indians, where social interaction had been set by the circumstances of their subjection. Their studies also reflected a lack of interest in sociology and interpersonal conflict. The eminent U.S. anthropologist Alfred Kroeber (1952) had said that "Terms of relationship...are determined primarily by language"—a cultural happenstance. No one today would make such a statement or question the assumption that institutions are instrumentalities. Nor would anyone today say that such functions explain their existence.

WALTER GOLDSCHMIDT

ABERLE, D. F., A. K. COHEN, A. K. DAVIS, M. L. LEVY, JR., and F. K. SUTTON. "The Functional Prerequisites of Society." *Ethics* 60 (1950): 100-111.

CANCIAN, FRANCESCA. "Varieties of Functional Analysis." In *International Encyclopedia of the Social Sciences*, edited by David Sills, vol 6. New York: Macmillan and Free Press, 1968.

FORTES, M., and E. E. EVANS-PRITCHARD, eds. *African Political Systems*. London: Oxford University Press, 1940.

GOLDSCHMIDT, WALTER. *Comparative Functionalism: An Essay in Anthropological Theory*. Berkeley and Los Angeles: University of California Press, 1966.

KLUCKHOHN, CLYDE. n.d. *Navaho Witchcraft*. 2nd ed. Boston: Beacon Press. (Originally published in 1944.)

KROEBER, A. L. "Clarificatory Systems of Relationships." In *The Nature of Culture*. Chicago: University of Chicago Press, 1952.

MALINOWSKI, BRONISLAW. *A Scientific Theory of Culture and Other Essays*. New York: Oxford University Press, 1960.

NAGEL, ERNEST. *The Structure of Science: Problems in the Logic of Scientific Explanation*. New York: Harcourt, Brace & World, 1961.

RADCLIFFE-BROWN, A. R. *A Natural Science of Society*. Glencoe, Ill.: Free Press, 1948.

———. *Structure and Function in Primitive Society*. Glencoe, Ill.: Free Press, 1952.

RADCLIFFE-BROWN, A. R., and DARYLL FORDE, eds. *African Systems of Kinship and Marriage*. London: Oxford University Press, 1950.

TURNER, JONATHAN, and ALEXANDRA MARYANSKI. *Functionalism*. Menlo Park, Calif: Benjamin/Cummings, 1979.

G

GAMES

Games are defined as competitive activities with agreed-upon rules that organize play and provide criteria for determining winners and losers (Roberts et al. 1959). Games are usually played for diversion, although some activities, such as duels, meet most of these criteria but are rarely recreational. Similarly, combats between gladiators in ancient Rome, for example, were apparently recreational for spectators but probably not for participants. The same may be true of many professional game players today. Games have also been played in many cultures as part of religious rites in which any recreational component was secondary to other features, such as propitiation, supplication, or divination.

Systematic anthropological scholarship on games began during the second half of the nineteenth century, led by pioneers such as Edward B. Tylor and Stuart Culin. Because of apparent similarities in games found in different parts of the world, Tylor felt that games might provide clues to early culture contacts. In his text *Anthropology* (1881), he also indicated that some children's games model adult activities and suggested that toys and game implements may function both for play and for education. Culin sought to show that games are an integral and important part of human culture. He published at least seventeen important articles and books on games (Avedon and Sutton-Smith 1971), including the encyclopedic *Games of the North American Indians* (1907), still the most comprehensive work on the topic.

In the early twentieth century, diffusionist approaches such as those of Tylor and Culin lost favor in anthropology and interest in games themselves declined sharply. From 1888 to 1928 seventeen articles dealing with games were published in *American Anthropologist,* the flagship journal of the American Anthropological Association. From 1929 to 1958, however, only one article was published that dealt with games. Anthropological interest in games was revitalized somewhat in 1959, when John M. Roberts, Malcolm J. Arth, and Robert R. Bush published their seminal article, "Games in Culture," which provided both a concise definition (given above) and a system for classifying games, both of which remain the most commonly used in anthropology. For classification, Roberts, Arth, and Bush chose the primary outcome-determining attribute of a game as their criterion. Thus, their typology includes games of physical skill (e.g., foot races, basketball), strategy (e.g., chess, checkers), and chance (e.g., dice games, guessing games). The majority of games, however, involve two of these outcome determinants; most athletic games entail physical skill and strategy, whereas many board games and most card games involve strategy and chance. Games that include all three are rare, as are games that combine only physical skill and chance.

GAMES IN CROSS-CULTURAL PERSPECTIVE

Roberts, Arth, and Bush held that games are expressive models of real-world activities. Cross culturally, games of physical skill, such as boxing or trapshooting, simulate warfare or hunting. Games of strategy, such as chess or backgammon, may simulate war or the hunt but also seem to model social interaction, particularly as it occurs in stratified social systems. Games of chance appear to simulate interaction with the supernatural, especially where a higher power is sought to influence or to provide knowledge of the future, as in supplication or divination. In addition, Roberts, Arth, and Bush suggested that games appear culturally in a developmental sequence. All or nearly all cultures seem to have games of physical skill, but games of strategy tend to occur only in cultures with complex sociopolitical organization. Games of chance appear to be less closely related to cultural complexity but tend to occur in the presence of environmental uncertainty (e.g., where the weather is harsh or unpredictable).

Roberts and Herbert Barry III (1976) developed a three-element game-combination scale with which to examine relationships between games and child-socialization variables. This scale consisted of three levels: games of physical skill; games of physical skill and games of chance; and games of physical skill, games of chance, and games of strategy. The scale was based on two premises. First, physical skill, chance, and strategy were purported to represent a developmental sequence for games in culture, and, second, it was hypothesized that game types in combination have mutually interactive effects. For example, games of physical skill may differ qualitatively, depending on whether or not they coexist with games of strategy or chance or both. Using a sample of ninety-six cultures from the Standard Cross-Cultural Sample (Murdock and White 1969), Roberts and Barry correlated their game-combination scale with measures of cultural complexity and with thirteen indexes of child training. The game scale correlated positively with each of ten indicators of cultural complexity and several of the child-training scales. Three game-type cultures (i.e., those cultures that have games of physical skill, of strategy, and of chance) tend to be low in the inculcation of self-reliance and achievement during the early-childhood period, but both obedience and self-restraint are strongly emphasized. Industriousness is stressed for both boys and girls during late childhood, but boys are inculcated to be responsible during both early and late childhood. Trust and honesty are not strongly inculcated at any time. One game-type culture has the opposite profile, and two game-type cultures fall in between.

Based on these findings, Roberts and Barry observed that contemporary Western sports mirror the profile associated with the three game-type cultures. Coaches relieve baseball, football, and basketball players, for example, of the need to be self-reliant but they value industry, responsibility, obedience, and self-restraint. Further, players for the most part never report fouls that they have committed to officials, suggesting that honesty is not a virtue developed in sport participation despite the folk wisdom that sport builds character. Brian Sutton-Smith and Roberts (1981) suggested that the relationships found between cultural complexity and game-type combinations imply that individuals in complex societies must be skilled in the assessment of the motives of others. In less complex societies, survival often depends on individual physical skills and on trust and honesty in collaboration with others. Personal physical skill is frequently irrelevant in modern societies, but skills in the deception of others and distrust of their motives often have great survival value in business, politics, and other social relationships.

GAMES IN INTRACULTURAL PERSPECTIVE

Numerous descriptions of games or of the games of particular cultures exist in the literature (see Avedon and Sutton-Smith 1971 and Chick 1984 for bibliographies), but studies of the internal organization of games are less common. The game preferences of individuals and aspects of games that relate to individual players require more attention, although several studies suggest that many games are viewed, interpreted, and participated in differently by children, adolescents, and adults, as well as by males and females.

Roberts and his colleagues have studied the internal organization of several games, including eight-ball pool, tennis, trapshooting, and soccer, using observational and free-listing techniques (i.e., asking knowledgeable informants to list as many items as they can) to obtain inventories of behaviors that were then examined for patterning of cultural knowledge (Chick 1984). Multidimensional scaling and cluster analyses revealed numerous similarities in the internal structure of different games. Game-behavior domains have always had two general categories, one of which was termed "seemly play" and the other "unseemly play." The former includes behaviors that are appropriate and may eventually lead to winning the game. Unseemly play, on the other hand, includes errors and other inept play that may lead to losing a point, missing a shot, or losing the game. Expert and nonexpert players were found to differ in the ways in which they viewed, used, and experienced physical skill, strategy, and chance. Other studies indicate that the very nature of games changes for players as they develop expertise. Skilled pool players found the strategic aspects of the game to be much more interesting, absorbing, and important than did less expert players, who found the physical skills in shot-making to be paramount.

Games are universal or nearly universal in human cultures. They appear to model culturally salient activities and beliefs and often provide an important mechanism for socialization and enculturation. Games commonly furnish a cultural medium for the acquisition of important but physically or socially perilous skills—such as those required for the hunt, warfare, or social interaction—in a buffered learning environment. At the individual level, the degrees of involvement, choices of games, and meanings attached to them may differ, depending on the ages, gender roles, levels of expertise, and personal idiosyncrasies of the participants. Last, games are functionally related to and reflect the values of the cultures of which they are a part. As such, they are neither trivial nor random in design or distribution.

GARRY E. CHICK

SEE ALSO: Leisure; Play; Sports

AVEDON, ELLIOT M., and BRIAN SUTTON-SMITH. *The Study of Games.* New York: Wiley, 1971.

CHICK, GARRY E. "The Cross-Cultural Study of Games." In *Exercise and Sport Sciences Reviews,* edited by Ronald L. Terjung, vol. 12. Lexington, Mass: Collamore Press, 1984.

CULIN, STEWART. *Games of the North American Indians.* Twenty-Fourth Annual Report of the Bureau of American Ethnology. Washington, D.C.: U. S. Government Printing Office, 1907.

MURDOCK, GEORGE P., and DOUGLAS R. WHITE. "Standard Cross-Cultural Sample," *Ethnology* 8 (1969): 329-369.

ROBERTS, JOHN M., MALCOLM J. ARTH, and ROBERT R. BUSH. "Games in Culture." *American Anthropologist* 61 (1959): 597-605.

ROBERTS, JOHN M., and HERBERT BARRY III. "Inculcated Traits and Game-Type Combinations: A Cross-Cultural View." In *The Humanistic and Mental Health Aspects of Sports, Exercise, and Recreation,* edited by T. T. Craig. Chicago: American Medical Association, 1976.

SUTTON-SMITH, BRIAN, and JOHN M. ROBERTS. "Play, Toys, Games, and Sports." In *Handbook of Cross-Cultural Psychology,* edited by Harry C. Triandis and Alastair Heron, vol. 4. Boston: Allyn & Bacon, 1981.

TYLOR, EDWARD B. *Anthropology.* New York: Appleton, 1881.

GANGS

Gangs are typically viewed as groups of inner-city, low-income adolescent males who congregate for antisocial and criminal endeavors. Although gangs fulfill many other functions—male socializing and counseling, courting, dating, sports and recreation, cruising in cars, and so on—it is the mayhem, violence, and other destructive and illicit activities that have captured attention, especially that of the media and law-enforcement authorities. Drug use, shootouts, and drive-by shootings have especially attracted public notice.

Explanations of the origins of gangs tend to focus on such features and forces as economic barriers and limited opportunities; breakdowns of family, schools, and other community institutions; subcultural developments and street socialization; and varied personal and psychological motivations. It has been suggested that, in the absence of other prosocial influences, gangs have become the parenting, schooling, and policing force of the streets. Because clusters of variables act and react to one another in an integrated holistic way in creating gangs and shaping gang members, no one factor can totally illuminate an understanding of gangs. Several theoretical constructs have been used to analyze gang formation and behavior, and most of these frameworks were generated in the 1950s and 1960s or earlier.

Some of the conceptual constructs that have been devised to explain gangs variously emphasize ecological, economic, social, cultural, and psychological issues and factors. The contribution of anthropologists to these formulations have been minimal, with the exception of the Chicago School researchers earlier in the twentieth century, when anthropology and sociology were typically housed in the same university department. These scholars utilized ethnographic approaches to urban issues and problems, including crime and gangs. The classic and seminal work by Frederic Thrasher, *The Gang* (1927), was a product of this effort, and even though the notion of social reform lies just below the surface of this social survey, current investigators still find it resonant.

The theories that have been advanced for understanding gangs and gang behavior can be subsumed generally under the labels of strain, control, subculture, and psychosocial. Strain explanations stress the discrepancies between present economic means and higher-status goals that especially handicap lower-income populations. Control theory focuses on the weakened social bonds of youths when family, schooling, police, and other socialization forces become problematic. "Birds of a feather flock together" is a short summary of the learning that takes place when a subcultural reference group, such as those found on the streets, begins to shape and dominate one's thoughts and actions. Last, to account for "becoming a man" during the psychosocial moratorium of adolescent passage, acting out of hypermasculine behavior directs some youngsters through conflicts of identification.

In the past ten years, ethnographic investigations, in combination with other methods, have contributed new information about contemporary gangs, thus adding to the broader understanding of how basic elements of the gang are deeply embedded within the fabric of society. When anthropologists began to turn their focus onto the cities, they found what social reformers had noted during the large-scale immigration to the United States in the latter half of the nineteenth century. Culture contact, conflicts, and a breakdown of social control had produced such changes in the lives of the children of immigrants that an errant street population had emerged. At that time these youths were known as pavement children and boy gangs. Where those earlier gangs were mostly white ethnics of southern and eastern European backgrounds, the gangs of the 1990s (note that labeling them as children is now eschewed) are mostly Mexicans and Latinos, African Americans, some Asian Americans, and a few skinheads and neo-Nazis of the disaffected white working and lower-middle classes.

In all that has been written about gangs, it has become increasingly evident that no one single factor can explain gangs and gang members. Working on integrated models that approximate the working notion and point of view of holism, it is commonly suggested that several factors, or clusters of variables, dynamically act and react with one another in the making and shaping of gangs and gang members.

First, what makes a gang and where might one be found? As noted, it is the inner-city area, commonly an ethnic or racial ghetto or barrio (neighborhood), where gangs are forged (since the 1980s aspects of the gang lifestyle have spread to suburban environments, affecting white working and lower-middle class youths). It is fairly clear that, both in the present and the past, certain neighborhoods have spawned gangs and that these neighborhoods were spatially separate and visually distinct from those occupied by the dominant social groups, whose housing developments and neighborhoods were better tended. The gangs originated in sections of the city in which incomes were low, poverty rates were high, and unemployed, untrained, and unhirable youths abounded. Unsupervised by conventional authority, such youths would congregate to while the time away. In time, a street gang subculture emerged. Being born into a neighborhood at such a socioeconomic level subjects one to many social, cultural, and psychological reverberations and ripple effects, such as strains and breakdowns in family life. Educational problems often develop early in the lives of children who are at risk to become gang members. This downturn then contributes to associations at school with similarly troubled youths in special classes or programs, and bonds are formed that make for a more solid pregang foundation. Similarly, on the streets or in the schools there may be older brothers or other relatives who have already charted a path toward gang involvement and who, by their presence, function as role models. Without a meaningful education and the acquisition of adequate skills and knowledge, these at-risk youths are poorly positioned for employment or even training opportunities. Street socialization to a street subculture takes over the reins of their lives.

Anthropology has amassed insights into a number of fields that can help to illuminate gang dynamics. Age-graded cohorts, initiation, and rites of passage, as documented worldwide, provide a context for considering the habits and customs of many contemporary gangs. Similarly, cross-cultural studies of adolescence and human development, early childbearing practices and later adult-character formation, and especially the marginal crisis status in the passage from adolescence to adulthood, where age-sex clarification is expected and required, provide frameworks for the consideration of gang phenomena. The burgeoning debate on gender roles and socialization is testimony to this fact; interest and research in the 1990s on female gang members has enhanced knowledge of them, but there are still major gaps to be filled. Females apparently comprise a little more than one in twenty gang members, and an even smaller proportion of gang research has focused on them.

Gangs exhibit age-grading and initiation features in some ways similar to patterns found in kinship-based non-Western societies. Each gang, to a degree and intensity determined by the neighborhood and ethnic group, follows a clique-formation pattern that incorporates early, middle, and late teens as well as seasoned veterans (*veteranos* in the case of Mexicans and Latinos and O.G.'s, or Original Gangsters, in the African-American instance) in the hierarchy based on age, experience, reputation, and prestige. These *klikas,* or sets, differ from age sets in that the larger culture affords them no legitimacy, and they are not lifelong entities. The group formed by youngsters aged fourteen to sixteen is the largest in membership and the most dedicated and active in gang involvement and commitment. In most instances, to bring the younger, lower cliques into this more active segment, there must be an initiation ordeal. Generally, this rite of passage involves a beating by a group of older fellow-gang members, and in the aftermath the novitiates wear the bruises and abrasions of the pummelings as badges of honor—each now belongs and is accepted as a "man."

All adolescents face major role and behavior shifts and adjustments, and the ease or difficulty with which they are met stems in part from early-childhood experiences. The early life and family experiences of gang members, especially the core members, are very strained and often involve a single-parent household. Economic and other social household hardships (e.g. crowding), often result in very little guidance and supervision for the child, who thus is likely to spend more time out on the streets. In the early childhood of many gang members, family ties are loosened and schooling influences are minimal; thus street socialization is the process in which the learning and acting out occurs. Children who grow up and develop in the streets must learn a street culture for survival. To do so, a street identity is fashioned.

At this point—the nexus of age grading, adolescence, and human development—gender roles and socialization become paramount. This process is especially difficult when the household is headed by a single parent, typically the mother, or when the mother regularly must handle all affairs because the father, although present, participates in the family only in an attenuated way. The gender influence of a female-centered household becomes all the more difficult for a boy who must contend with the streets, which are largely dominated by males. Many anthropologists have noted that cultures in which boys are largely raised in the absence of adult-male participation often require an initiation ordeal for pubescent males, in order to break the female influence and quickly infuse a sense of masculinity in the young male. Street socialization makes its imprint in the period of early childhood and is further intensified during adolescence, when body and chemical changes accelerate a person's maturation and encounter with destiny, that is, when he or she must choose how to fashion, manufacture, create, or adopt an age- and sex-role persona.

In many poor, distressed neighborhoods, a proportion of the youth (depending on the community, anywhere from about 4 percent to 15 percent) are street socialized to the point that for them the gang has become a substitute for family, school, and police. This street life and culture leads to violent and destructive activities, which have always been a part of gang behavior. The increased access to firearms and drugs that has occurred since the 1970s has escalated the former fist fights and rumbles with knives and sticks into drive-by shootings, in which homicides and serious injuries are far more common, and increasingly involve innocent bystanders, including children.

Gang members have also instituted certain norms and values that set them apart. The protection and friendship that gangs provide to members solidify the bonds that may have developed earlier—bonds that certainly harden by the early teens, when street socialization reaffirms these ties. Objectives and goals of the group are established to defend the turf or neighborhood territory and to keep outsiders from threatening or harming its members. Individuals come to think of themselves as subsumed in a group entity, and they protect, serve, counsel, and offer nurturance to one another. To effect this end, older, experienced gang members—sometimes relatives—tutor the younger gang members in what to do, how and when to do it, and so on. Learning the gang's values in this fashion brings a person status and prestige within the group, as does joining in the protection and demonstration of friendship by fighting the intrusions of rival gang members.

As adolescence proceeds, gang youths typically have increasing amounts of time to engage in gang activities. Most of them quit or are expelled from school, and their limited skills preclude most employment opportunities. They thus fill their time with such activities as drug and alcohol use and abuse, gang-banging (i.e., responding to other gangs' threats or acts), and other criminal pursuits. These activities become a central part of the day's agenda—things to do when all else fails. Last, a belief and value system becomes internalized. Blueprints for action include showing that one can act "crazy" in situations that call for daring and unpredictability, often for fending off real or imagined threats. Mexican-American gangs refer to such behavior as *locura* (quasi-controlled insanity), and doing "loco" things operates as an outlet for those youths, who act out their aggressions and frustrations from a traumatized childhood. Younger gang members are expected to learn how to do loco acts, if not become loco actors.

Many signs and symbols involving dress, manners of walking and talking, gestures, and other habits and customs have become a part of the gang subculture. Many of these patterns overlap with the behavior patterns of nongang youth. Rap music of African-American entertainers, for example, has disseminated nationwide many of the baggy-pants, baseball-cap, and earring costumes of the street-gang subculture, to the extent that even upscale suburban populations have attempted to mimic this posture. Dress varies, however, among the distinct street groups; that of blacks contrasts with that of Mexicans and Latinos, and so on. Gang members also often sport nicknames acquired through gang membership, which they scrawl on all types of public and private surfaces. Usually such a monicker is written with the name of one's clique or set (age cohort within the gang) and neighborhood gang name. Thus, "Wino" (monicker), "Termites" (clique), and "White Fence" (barrio and gang) might be written in a vertical arrangement to draw attention to oneself as well as to mark turf boundaries or intrusions into rival territories. Often, gang fights between different neighborhoods are initiated or fanned when *placas* (Chicano gang term for graffiti markings) are either placed on enemy grounds or written over an enemy's *placa*. Tattoos are personalized graffiti—*placas* on the body. Drawings and designs are placed on the arms, shoulders, and even face (for example, below the outer edge of the eye in the form of a teardrop). With incarceration, especially with long-term "revolving door" gang members-prisoners, tattooing often becomes intensified.

Since the 1970s, changes in U.S. society have also led to increased street-gang membership and intensified street-gang activities. Immigration from Mexico, Central America, and Southeast Asia has brought new types of immigrant gangs; Chinese, Vietnamese, and Cambodian gangs in southern California in the 1980s caught the attention of public authorities. Mexican and other Latino immigrant youths have often either joined existing Chicano gangs or, in response to threats from these gangs, formed their own street groups that borrow extensively from the prevailing street-gang subculture. In addition, the economic restructuring in the United States since about 1970 has further eroded the lives of residents in entrenched African-American and Chicano communities. Greater unemployment and underemployment, coupled with the competition of a reservoir of immigrant labor in some cities, has led to a descending deterioration of opportunities and options. The persistence and concentration of poverty in neighborhoods already rife with gangs results in many youths turning to the illicit economy of drug sales and criminal-opportunity structures. Thus, gangs not only persist in U.S. cities but have multiplied, becoming more pervasively violent, and turned more systematically to crime for economic gain. As long as the urban conditions that foster gang formation and growth persist, these trends are likely to continue.

DIEGO VIGIL

CAMPBELL, ANNE. *The Girls in the Gang: A Report from New York City.* Oxford: Basil Blackwell, 1984.

CUMMINGS, SCOTT, AND DANIEL J. MONTI, eds. *Gangs: The Origins and Impact of Contemporary Youth Gangs in the United States.* Albany: State University of New York Press, 1993.

DAWLEY, DAVID. *A Nation of Lords: The Autobiography of the Vice Lords.* Prospect Heights, Ill: Waveland Press, 1992.

HAGEDORN, JOHN. *People and Folks: Gangs, Crime, and the Underclass in a Rustbelt City.* Chicago: Lake View Press, 1988.

HUFF, RONALD, ed. *Gangs in America.* Newbury Park, Calif.; Sage Publications, 1990.

MOORE, JOAN W. *Going Down to the Barrio: Homeboys and Homegirls in Change.* Philadelphia: Temple University Press, 1991.

PADILLA, FELIX M. *The Gang as an American Enterprise.* New Brunswick, N.J.: Rutgers University Press, 1992.

SPERGEL, IRVING A., and DAVID CURRY. *Gangs, Schools, and Communities.* Chicago: University of Chicago School of Social Service Administration, 1987.

TAYLOR, CARL S. *Dangerous Society.* East Lansing: Michigan State University Press, 1990.

THRASHER, FREDERIC. *The Gang.* 1927. Reprint.

Chicago: Univertisy of Chicago Press, 1963.

VIGIL, JAMES DIEGO. *Barrio Gangs: Street Life and Identity in Southern California.* Austin: University of Texas Press, 1988.

GENDER DIFFERENCES AND ROLES

Everyone knows that humans, like most animals, come in two varieties—female and male. After all, two sexes are required for reproduction. It is not so clear, however, why human males and females differ beyond their reproductive anatomies. In many animals the sexes are barely distinguishable in appearance or behavior. Human females and males, however, not only have obvious physical differences by sex (sexual dimorphism), they also typically display differences in behavior and other aspects of personality. This is not to say that these behavioral and personality differences are universal or inevitable but rather that there are some consistent differences between the sexes cross-culturally.

Currently differences between females and males tend to be referred to as "gender differences" rather than as "sex differences." This change in terminology reflects the idea that male-female differences stem ultimately from cultural experiences (including role assignments) and cultural expectations (including future role assignments) rather than from biological differences. Similarly "gender roles" is now the preferred term instead of "sex roles." The term "sex differences" often is used to refer to differences that are clearly biological in nature. However, most differences cannot clearly be attributed to biology or to culture, so the decision to use one term or another may be based more on assumption than on evidence.

Because many believe that differences in gender roles in part cause gender differences in behavior and personality, we turn to what is known about the cross-cultural patterns of gender roles and how those patterns may be explained.

GENDER ROLES
Economic Activities

In theory, every society could assign the same economic activities to women and men. In fact, they generally assign men and women different work, and cross-cultural evidence suggests that there are consistent patterns in the division of labor by gender (Murdock and Provost 1973). Women usually gather wild plants, prepare plants for eating (e.g., grind grain), prepare tea, beer, and other beverages, make cheese and butter, cook, fetch water, obtain fuel for heating and cooking, launder, and spin yarn. Men almost always hunt and fish, catch birds, trap animals, lumber wood, mine and quarry minerals, and make products out of wood, metal, stone, shell, and bone; they also tend large animals, clear land and prepare the soil for planting, collect wild honey, butcher animals, build houses, and make net and rope. There is no clear gender pattern for other economic activities such as planting, tending, and harvesting crops or making leather products, baskets and mats, clothing, and pottery.

Four major explanations have been suggested for these division-of-labor patterns. These include physical capacity (men typically have greater muscular strength and higher aerobic work capacity and thus are assigned work requiring such capacity—Murdock and Provost 1973); compatibility with child care (women need to breast-feed infants and therefore often are assigned activities that are interruptible and not dangerous—Brown 1970); economy of effort (it is advantageous for the gender that starts an activity to continue it through the production sequence—White et al. 1977); and expendability (because the number of women, not men, limits reproduction potential, it is advantageous to assign men to the more dangerous activities—Mukhopadhyay and Higgins 1988).

Although these theories are plausible, it is important to note that work assignments generally are made on the basis of assumed differences between genders rather than on actual measurement of the amount of physical strength required for a particular task or of the degree of incompatibility with child care. More research is needed to untangle the many possible explanations of how economic activities are assigned by gender.

Child Care

In few societies are mothers exclusive caretakers for infants, but in most they are the principal ones. Cross-culturally, fathers rarely care for infants. In looking after young children the situation changes, with mothers usually providing less than half the care and the remainder largely taken over by girls (often older siblings) and other women (Weisner and Gallimore 1977). Infants the world over are usually nursed, so the economy-of-effort theory suggests it is more efficient to leave other aspects of infant care to women as well. Because infant care is probably safer at or near home, this theory also might explain why most household chores are done by women.

War and Political Activities

Relatively few societies allow women to take part in active combat (Whyte 1978); waging war usually is a male activity and steps often are taken to ensure that women are excluded from gaining knowledge about military matters (for example, they may be forbidden to own or use weapons and excluded from war discussions). Similarly men usually dominate the political arena, even in matrilineal societies. In one cross-cultural survey (Whyte 1978) of mostly preindustrial societies, 88 percent have only male political leaders. Because war is preeminently dangerous the incompatibility-with-child-care and expendability theories may explain why women usually do not participate as combatants.

Control of Resources, Autonomy, and Deference

Most societies favor one sex or the other in structuring social groups and access to resources. The rule of residence determines other structured inequalities. For example, whether a couple lives matrilocally (with or near the wife's kin) or patrilocally (with or near the husband's kin) seems largely to determine whether a rule of descent will be traced through women or men. Rules of descent, in turn, may determine how resources are allocated. Since patrilocality is more common than matrilocality, in most societies males are somewhat more likely to control vital resources, have more autonomy, and command deference from their wives. However, such patterns are far from universal. Where societies are matrilocal and matrilineal women are likely to control property, be more valued, have more equal rights regarding their sexuality, and have more domestic authority (Whyte 1978). However, matrilineal societies do not inevitably have high female autonomy. In many matrilineal societies males (husbands and/or brothers) have considerable authority over women; where husbands and brothers are equally dominant, women tend to have the most control over their own lives (Schlegel 1972).

In general, among societies that are not highly industrialized it is the more complex ones (those with political hierarchy, intensive agriculture, social stratification, private property, and craft specialization) that

are likely to have more gender inequality (Whyte 1978). Women in more complex societies tend to have more domestic work and more children, which may keep them in or around the house, but whether these factors are solely responsible for more inequality is unclear (Ember 1995).

Although we do not yet fully understand the causes of gender inequality, we do know what does *not* predict it. Contrary to traditional theory, cross-cultural research (Whyte 1978; see also Sanday 1973) has shown that high contribution to primary subsistence by males does not appear to predict male dominance, nor does heavy involvement in hunting or war.

GENDER DIFFERENCES

When Margaret Mead studied the Arapesh, Mundugumor, and Tchambuli tribes in New Guinea she reported no consistent differences across the three cultures in the personality of females and males, concluding that "many, if not all, of the personality traits we have called masculine or feminine are as lightly linked to sex as are the clothing, the manners, and the form of head-dress that a society at a given period assigns to either sex" (Mead 1935). Mead's research implied that cultures lack consistency in role assignment and that personality differences between the genders are a function of the particular assignments and expectations of each culture. As we have seen, despite Mead's three New Guinea cases there are many consistencies across cultures in role assignment. But do these assignments completely explain personality differences?

When females and males are assigned different roles by their cultures it hardly needs explaining why they behave somewhat differently in performing these roles. So if men usually are the warriors we are not surprised that they, but not women, engage in killing the enemy. If we ask whether females and males generally differ in aggressive interpersonal behavior, however, the answer is not so clear. Here the realm is personality differences, for which we need a different type of comparison—systematic comparisons of individuals interacting with others.

To date, most research on female-male differences has been conducted in the United States, but we can draw upon some systematic comparisons conducted in other cultures such as those of the Six Cultures project (Whiting and Whiting, 1975). Systematic behavior observations of children were made in

Orchard Town, New England; Juxtlahuaca, Mexico; Taira, Okinawa; Khalapur, India; Nyansongo, Kenya and Tarong, Philippines. Much of the Six Cultures' research does not support Mead's view that there are no consistent differences in temperament between males and females. (This does not imply that Mead's descriptions of the three groups she studied were incorrect; they could be unusual cases.)

What are the consistent differences? Unless noted otherwise the findings summarized below draw on research conducted outside as well as inside the United States and are based on systematic comparisons of individual data (see research summarized in Ember 1981, 1995).

Social Behavior

In the realm of aggression (attempts to hurt or injure others) most studies show that among children aged three and older boys are more aggressive than girls. Research in the United States suggests that this difference continues into adulthood but we have few studies of adults in other cultures. If we consider homicides, males are responsible for most of the lethal violence cross-culturally. Aggression is the most consistent arena of difference but there is also considerable evidence that girls are more nurturing in settings where younger children are present, more responsible, and more cooperative with and compliant to adult requests. Boys are more apt to exert dominance over others for egoistic reasons. In play both boys and girls show preferences for their own sex, a trend that increases with age. Also, infants and children look more often at those of their own sex.

Some stereotyped beliefs about girl-boy differences are not supported. Girls are not more dependent—if anything, boys score slightly higher on dependency. If there are any differences in dependency it is in style: girls are more apt to seek physical proximity to mothers and boys are more apt to seek attention. In addition, the evidence does not support the view that girls are more sociable or more passive than boys (Whiting and Edwards 1973).

Are these differences due to biological differences and/or social learning? Some may assume that if a sex difference appears early and is a universal or near-universal difference there must be a biological reason. That logic is not compelling. Humans begin treating the sexes differently from the moment they are born. Moreover, human societies universally have the cus-

tom of marriage, the incest taboo, and kinship terminologies—but that doesn't mean that these cultural traits are biologically determined. Considerable evidence suggests that the hormone androgen is implicated in producing more aggression. Experimental evidence on nonhuman animals suggests that androgen, particularly if introduced during the critical time of sexual differentiation (prenatally in guinea pigs and primates, early in the postnatal period in rats), may predispose genetic females to exhibit more aggression. Early castration of male rodents (which reduces androgen) seems to lower aggression. In humans, some studies suggest that sex-hormone abnormalities (e.g., those caused to the fetus by drugs during pregnancy) show parallel effects. While the evidence is consistent with the view that prenatal androgen may be implicated in causing more aggression in males, there are other possibilities that cannot yet be ruled out. First, androgen generally causes genetic females to look like males (they acquire male genitalia) and they may smell like males in those species that depend on olfactory cues, which means that others may treat them like males (e.g., they may be attacked more). Second, in the case of humans, the affected individuals (and the parents) usually know they have an abnormality, which may alter their behavior. Thus the possible effects of social learning cannot be discounted.

What evidence is there for social learning? Because experiments placing children randomly into different social environments are unethical we do not have direct evidence linking social treatment differences to ultimate behavior differences. What we have are documented natural differences in the ways boys and girls are treated. Cross-culturally, in cases in which there are reported gender differences in socialization (and there often are no reported differences), boys are pressured by parents to be more aggressive, whereas girls are pressured to be more responsible, obedient, and nurturing. While these different socialization pressures do correspond to observed behavior differences, the socialization differences are far from universal—in fact, most cultures show no obvious differences in socialization of boys and girls, at least as reported by ethnographers. Learning, however, may take place through much more subtle mechanisms such as the assignment of chores, the encouragement of certain kinds of games, the rough or gentle handling of a child, the kind of attention a parent gives to a child, or the amount of time a child spends in different settings requiring different behaviors. Social learning also comes from the child. As mentioned above, research suggests that a child looks more at her or his own sex. As long as there are gender role differences, children may observe and perceive how they are expected to behave. Indeed, by the age of four or five in the United States, girls and boys generally have very clear and different gender stereotypes.

Some evidence links differential task assignment to behavior. In cultures where children are assigned more chores, children tend to be more nurturing and responsible. In a study conducted in Kenya (Ember 1973, cited in Ember 1981) I found that boys who were assigned "girls' work" (e.g., baby-sitting, household chores) were significantly less aggressive and more responsible than other boys even when they were not doing chores. These boys, who did not do as much girls' work as girls, were intermediate in their social behavior between other boys and girls, suggesting that task assignment had something to do with the behaviors they developed. If girls generally do more work than boys and most of the work assigned to children is women's work then differential task assignment may generally explain girl-boy behavior differences to some extent. A major influence on children may also be the company they keep. Findings from the Six Cultures project suggest that being around peers (which boys have more time to do) generally increases aggressive behavior; being around younger siblings (which girls are more apt to be) generally increases nurturant behavior.

Cognitive and Perceptual Differences

Research mainly in the United States has suggested that females excel in verbal ability and males in mathematical ability. However, we may have to revise that conclusion in light of subsequent analyses (Hyde and Linn 1988). With regard to verbal ability females still do somewhat better on verbal tests, but the differences have narrowed over time and there is now so little difference as to make the distinction meaningless. Similarly, in the United States, if the SAT is excluded from consideration there is very little gender difference in mathematical ability (Hyde et al. 1990). In fact, in tests taken by the general population (i.e., not restricted to more able or academically more interested samples) females do slightly better and they generally obtain higher grades than do males in mathematics. However, males do substantially better on the math SAT (which is a more

select sample of college-bound students) as well as in other more selected samples (e.g., gifted students). Why the SAT favors males particularly is still a puzzle. In any case the data from other countries (Lummis and Stevenson 1990) suggest there are few gender differences in mathematics.

Overall there are more consistent gender differences in visual-spatial abilities. Males generally perform better across a variety of ages in the United States. In some other cultures where this research has been done, and where there is a difference, it usually favors males, but the differences are not completely consistent by type of test or age (Linn and Peterson 1986).

Some perception tests are designed to see if a person has a field-dependent perceptual and cognitive style (parts are fused with the field or seen as global) or a field-independent style (parts are viewed as discrete from the field as a whole). Data from the United States are fairly consistent in showing that males are generally more field-independent; data from other societies generally show the same patterns, but there are some exceptions, most notably in societies where subsistence is traditionally based on food collection (hunting, gathering, fishing—Berry 1976). Some researchers (Hall 1984) have suggested that field independence-field dependence mainly is based on visual-spatial ability. If so then these results are consistent with the results on visual-spatial tests.

In the United States women tend to be better than men at rapidly identifying matching items, which is referred to as perceptual speed. They also remember better whether an item has been displaced and they recall landmarks better on a route. Whether these differences turn out to be replicable cross-culturally remains to be seen.

Most of the biological explanations that have been offered to explain visual-spatial differences (brain lateralization, prenatal hormones, hormones at puberty) suffer from inconsistent evidence, notably that the gender differences have narrowed over time and that training helps females considerably. However, there are a few intriguing findings. One is that visual-spatial abilities are somewhat related to handedness, with different effects for females and males. Some studies (Silverman and Phillips 1993) show varying visual-spatial test scores for women in different phases of the menstrual cycle. If these findings hold up it would be difficult entirely to rule out the role of biological factors.

So far relatively few studies have investigated directly the socialization factors that may increase visual-spatial skill. Some evidence (Munroe et al. 1985) suggests that object manipulation as well as time spent away from the household may enhance such skills. In the related area of field independence/dependence the socialization style of "tight" parental control appears to predict more field dependence. In societies where school is not universal, education also predicts more visual-spatial skill and more field independence (Berry 1976). It is possible, then, that girls often score more field dependent or lower in visual-spatial skills if they are assigned more work as children (the discrepancy between boys and girls is probably greater for agriculturalists who have more work to assign children), if they are kept out of school to do work more often than boys, and if the attempt to control them is greater than the attempt to control boys.

Hunting and gathering societies may show little or no sex difference because both males and females need to spend time away from the household to learn to negotiate their way through space; parents in such societies therefore emphasize individual assertiveness over compliance.

Emotion and Concern for Others

Some theorists (e.g., Gilligan 1982) have suggested that women are more apt to be concerned with interpersonal relationships and have more empathy for the feelings of others. To date, studies outside the United States (e.g., Stimpson et al. 1992) suggest a fairly consistent pattern in the predicted direction, based largely on self-report. Perhaps consistent with these findings are those related to the realm of nonverbal communication. Across a large number of studies (Hall 1984) females are shown to be better than males at understanding nonverbal cues and express more emotions nonverbally (e.g., they have more expressive faces). Even in dreams women describe more emotion than men do (Munroe et al. 1985).

SUMMARY

Taken together, gender roles, behaviors, and personality traits are quite consistent with one another. Adult females are assigned tasks that are less dangerous and closer to home and are claimed to be more compat-

ible with child care. Girls generally are more nurturant and responsible in their behavior and conform more to the wishes of adults. In their perceptual or cognitive style girls consider their surroundings more (they are more field dependent), perhaps reflecting their concern for others. Women and girls also are concerned more with emotions and read nonverbal cues better than men and boys. Indeed, some researchers have suggested that the sense of themselves that females develop is more connected to others than is males' sense of themselves. In general both females and males seem to develop traits consistent with what societies expect them to be. Males are expected to grow up to engage in riskier activities that take them further from home. As children they do less work and are freer to play with their peers. They behave in ways that are less acceptable to adults (i.e., they tend to be more aggressive, more interested in egoistic dominance). Cognitively and perceptually boys display more field independence and visual-spatial skill. Even the dreams of males and females differ in consistent ways: women dream more of indoor settings and express more emotion; males dream more of outdoor settings and express less emotion. Males consider it less important to be connected to others and are less attentive to the feelings of others.

Because roles, expectations, behavior, self-concept, values, and other factors are fairly consistent across cultures, the task of uncovering causality is difficult. Biological difference is hardly separable from different social experience. If we wish to understand whether biological factors and/or social factors account for gender differences we need to search harder for variation in cultures and among families where biology and culture are not so confounded. We need to design research to find out if variation in role, expectation, experience, and/or some aspect of biology is responsible for later variation in gender difference. When more of this work is done we might better understand why gender differences occur.

Carol R. Ember

See also: Breastfeeding; Child Development; Cross-Cultural Research; Dreams; Feminist Anthropology; Sexual Division of Labor

Berry, John W. *Human Ecology and Cognitive Style.* New York: John Wiley and Sons, 1976.

Brown, Judith K. "A Note on the Division of Labor by Sex." *American Anthropologist* 72(1970): 1073-1078.

EMBER, CAROL R. "A Cross-Cultural Perspective on Sex Differences." In *Handbook of Cross-Cultural Human Development,* edited by Ruth H. Munroe, Robert L. Munroe, and Beatrice B. Whiting. New York: Garland STPM Press, 1981.

———. "Universal and Variable Patterns of Gender Difference." In *Cross-Cultural Research for Social Science,* edited by Carol R. Ember and Melvin Ember. Englewood Cliffs, N.J.: Prentice Hall, 1995.

GILLIGAN, CAROL. *In a Different Voice: Psychological Theory and Women's Development.* Cambridge, MA: Harvard University Press, 1982.

HALPERN, DIANE F. *Sex Differences in Cognitive Abilities.* Hillsdale, N.J.: Lawrence Erlbaum Associates, 1986.

HALL, JUDITH A. *Nonverbal Sex Differences: Communication Accuracy and Expressive Style.* Baltimore: Johns Hopkins University Press, 1984.

HYDE, JANET SHIBLEY, and MARCIA C. LINN. "Gender Differences in Verbal Ability: A Meta-Analysis." *Psychological Bulletin* 104 (1988): 53–69.

HYDE, JANET SHIBLEY, ELIZABETH FENNEMA, and SUSAN J. LAMON. "Gender Differences in Mathematics Performance: A Meta-Analysis." *Psychological Bulletin* 107 (1990): 139–155.

LINN, MARCIA C., and ANNE C. PETERSEN. "A Meta-Analysis of Gender Differences in Spatial Ability: Implications for Mathematics and Science Achievement." In *The Psychology of Gender: Advances Through Meta-Analysis,* edited by Janet Shibley Hyde and Marcia C. Linn. Baltimore: Johns Hopkins University Press, 1986.

LUMMIS, MAX and HAROLD W. STEVENSON. "Gender Differences in Beliefs and Achievement: a Cross-Cultural Study." *Developmental Psychology* 26 (1990):254-263.

MARKUS, HAZEL, and DAPHNA OYSERMAN. "Gender and Thought: The Role of the Self Concept." In *Gender and Thought: Psychological Perspectives,* edited by Mary Crawford and Margaret Gentry. New York: Springer-Verlag, 1989.

MEAD, MARGARET. *Sex and Temperament in Three Primitive Societies.* New York: Morrow, 1935.

MUKHOPADHYAY, CAROL C., and PATRICIA J. HIGGINS. "Anthropological Studies of Women's Status Revisited: 1977-1987." *Annual Review of Anthropology,* 17(1988): 461-95.

MUNROE, ROBERT L., et al. "Sex Differences in East African Dreams." *Journal of Social Psychology* 125 (1985): 405–406.

MUNROE, RUTH H., ROBERT L. MUNROE, and ANNE BRASHER. "Precursors of Spatial Ability: A Longitudinal Study Among the Logoli of Kenya." *Journal of Social Psychology* 125 (1985): 23–33.

MURDOCK, GEORGE P., and CATERINA PROVOST. "Factors in the Division of Labor by Sex: A Cross-Cultural Analysis." *Ethnology* 12 (1973): 203–225.

SANDAY, PEGGY R. "Toward a Theory of the Status of Women." *American Anthropologist,* 75(1973): 1682-1700.

SCHLEGEL, ALICE. *Male Dominance and Female Autonomy: Domestic Authority in Matrilineal Societies.* New Haven, Conn.: HRAF Press, 1972.

SILVERMAN, IRWIN, and KRISTA PHILLIPS. "Effects of Estrogen Changes During the Menstrual Cycle on Spatial Performance." *Ethnology and Sociobiology* 14 (1993): 257–269.

STIMPSON, DAVID, LARRY JENSEN, and WAYNE NEFF. "Cross-Cultural Gender Differences in Preference for a Caring Morality." *Journal of Social Psychology* 132 (1992): 317–322.

WEISNER, THOMAS S., and RONALD GALLIMORE. "My Brother's Keeper; Child and Sibling Caretaking." *Current Anthropology,* 18(1977): 169-190.

WHITE, DOUGLAS R., MICHAEL L. BURTON, and LILYAN A. BRUDNER. "Entailment Theory and Method: A Cross-Cultural Analysis of the Secual Division of Labor." *Behavior Science Research* 12(1977): 1-24.

WHITING, BEATRICE B., and CAROLYN P. EDWARDS. "A Cross-Cultural Analysis of Sex Differences in the Behavior of Children aged 3–11." *Journal of Social Psychology* 91 (1973): 171–188.

———. *Children of Different Worlds: The Formation of Social Behavior.* Cambridge, Mass.: Harvard University Press, 1988.

WHITING, BEATRICE B., and JOHN W. M. WHITING. *Children of Six Cultures: A Psycho-Cultural Analysis.* Cambridge, Mass.: Harvard University Press, 1975.

WHYTE, MARTIN K. *The Status of Women in Preindustrial Societies.* Princeton: Princeton University Press, 1978.

GENETICS

In order to document the application of genetics to cultural anthropology clearly, a brief summary is needed of the development of genetic research during the twentieth century. Mendelian genetics and the rules governing the inheritance of so-called simple, monogenic traits was the first field of inquiry that specified genes as the units of transmission. Following the rediscovery of Gregor Mendel's laws at the beginning of the century, research was initiated along the lines of human or medical genetics, which sought to ascertain gene causation of human diseases, and population genetics, which investigated evolutionary processes and population relationships. In the 1960s, behavior genetics was formulated to study not only animals but humans as well. Most recently, the fields of anthropological genetics and molecular evolution have extended genetic inquiry into the basic gene or DNA level of variation as observed within extant human populations and between humans and their close evolutionary relatives, that is, other primates.

While it is true that none of these areas of genetic research has had a major impact upon the development of cultural anthropology, some have stimulated considerable interest and even controversy. Before considering the implications of this research, however, it is useful to introduce a number of terms that bear close relationship to genetics, because only rarely does that term as such appear in anthropological discussions. More often, particularly in the early literature, one finds a plethora of such terms as "hereditary," "inherited," "inbred," "organic," "innate," "instinctual," "biological," "natural," "constitutional," and "racial," all denoting characteristics (mostly physical but some mental) and their form of transmission that was deemed to be separate and distinct from human conditions and learned behaviors that are transmitted through social or cultural means. The incorporation of genetics into evolutionary theory was a major feature in the development of another subfield of anthropological inquiry—biological anthropology. A possibly more genetic/biological flavor was introduced into cultural anthropology by Franz Boas (1940) and other founders of the American school, as compared with the European schools, where anthropology, as the biologically oriented subfield, remained academically more distinct from the development of ethnology/ethnography and prehistory.

The principal categories relating cultural anthropology to genetics are race classification and racism, cultural universals and antecedents to culture, personality and culture, sociobiology and coevolution, medical anthropology and biocultural interaction, kinship analysis and incest taboo, and sexual dimorphism and gender role differences. Perhaps the overarching theme of all of these is the time-honored quest to discover who we are, what makes us human, and how we got to where we are. An appropriate, if somewhat stormy, beginning might be that involving human races.

RACE CLASSIFICATION AND RACISM

In 1885 races were defined as "hereditary types" (Stocking 1982), but this declaration was disputed on the grounds that "hereditary" did not mean immutable and stable and that "types" were not sets of homogeneous individuals. Leading the attack was Boas, who through his extensive empirical studies attempted to resolve an issue within racial biology that arose following the rediscovery of Mendel's laws of inheritance. What was the mechanism for inheriting morphological traits, such as human head form? Head form, expressed as the ratio of head breadth to length in the cephalic index, was considered by many early race biologists to be the standard for determining racial assignment, and also by those inclined toward racist doctrines for evaluating mental ability.

Boas looked into a Mendelian model as well as applying a version of Lamarckian inheritance, which assigned an important role to environmental factors in the transmission process. In fact, Boas's research that showed a changed head form in offspring of European immigrants to the United States helped dismiss the notion of stability of race traits based on genetic determinism. He worked diligently in pursuit of a clearer understanding of the respective roles of nature and nurture in the expression of anthropometric measurements.

Even though Boas could not resolve the heredity/environment equation (it still is being worked on), his research clearly established that morphological traits, such as head form, were not so stable as claimed by the race classifiers. But what about human behavior? Could the laws of heredity shed any light there? Boas tackled that issue with methodical rigor, opposing the view that race determined a person's character by showing that correlation does not mean causation and concluding that populational differences in character were not caused by race (which presumably signify genetic differences). Obviously, Boas's writings did not stem the tide of racism that swept the world at that time, but his research successfully incorporated an understanding of the principles of heredity known at the beginning of the twentieth century.

The Boasian tradition of the general anthropologist was carried on by one of his students, Alfred L. Kroeber, who also addressed the racism issue and entered into important considerations of genetic principles. In his effort to explain the dual meanings of heredity—social/cultural versus biological/organic—he argued that the leaders of the eugenics movement, notably Francis Galton and Karl Pearson, had wrongly confounded these meanings. Kroeber seemed to be saying that the Lamarckian notion of "use inheritance," or the hereditary transmission of acquired traits, only applied to the organic (or genetic) realm, and that cultural inheritance specifically related to social progress, which was restricted to social transmission. Lamarckian inheritance has been dismissed but the value of maintaining and investigating distinctive cultural and genetic modes of inheritance continues.

Kroeber further developed the distinction between cultural and organic inheritance in his widely known article that appeared in 1917, "The Superorganic," (1952) which arose from what he perceived as a trend toward biological reductionism, wherein culture and biology merged into the question of racial variation. The article presented several examples to show how social inheritance differed from organic heredity. One example was that while whales had evolved anatomically to a boat-like shape, humans moved on water by inventing boats (through cultural technology). Kroeber further clarified what he considered to be the distinction between language (nonhereditary) and race (in which the features of the eyes, nose, and hair were all hereditary). Although he acknowledged that humans have a partial animal basis for their speech expressions of laughing and crying, he argued that animals are governed by instinct and humans by learning. This position would now be recognized as creating an extreme dichotomy, but Kroeber was voicing a commonly held notion of his day.

Even more pointedly than Boas, Kroeber argued that there was no hereditary basis for racial differences in mental ability and that they were due only to social differences. Furthermore, he posited the notion, also found in Boas, that the rediscovered laws of heredity only applied to the individual and that a race was simply a collection of individuals. He felt that the success of the Mendelian methods of studying heredity rested in isolating traits and individuals. The thrust of his argument in "The Superorganic" was to proclaim that social evolution was not a con-founding or simply a continuation of organic evolution, but that it represented "a leap to another plane." Kroeber then used the analogy that the inception of civilization was qualitatively distinct, much like the point at which water begins to boil. The organic plane was left behind as humans established their "civilization gap" from all other creatures.

In Boas and Kroeber, anthropology could be defined as a much broader field than that of today, when North American anthropologists generally fall within one of the four major divisions of anthropology: archaeology, cultural and social anthropology, biological anthropology, and anthropological linguistics. It is a tribute to these early founders of American anthropology that they were able to synthesize so much of what later became grounds for separation between cultural and biological anthropology. They are to be recognized for their attempts at making sense of the newly rediscovered laws of heredity, and for the most part, of accurately portraying the relationship between genetics and races. For example, Boas and Kroeber were instrumental in establishing two major propositions of cultural anthropology: that behavioral variation between human groups was due to culture and that genetically influenced capacities are equivalent for all populations or races. Unsuccessful challenges to these propositions came later, particularly in the 1970s when unscientific claims were made regarding racial differences in mental ability and intelligence.

CULTURAL UNIVERSALS AND ANTECEDENTS TO CULTURE

While racial determinism focused primarily on accounting for cultural differences, another generalizing concept, derived from the nineteenth-century evolutionists Edward B. Tylor, Herbert Spencer, and Lewis Henry Morgan, was that of the "psychic unity of man," which purported to explain cultural similarities. That these similarities could have a common genetic basis was certainly advanced. For example, in his text *Anthropology* (1898), Tylor asserted that human temperament and mental capacity were inbred. Later anthropologists, including Clark Wissler, Bronislaw Malinowski, and George P. Murdock, extended the notion of psychic unity by offering their own versions of universal patterns of culture. The obvious question to address was what would account for these apparent similarities across cultures in several categories, including speech, religion, art, and government. Murdock understood cultural behavior to follow two basic mechanisms, either instinct or habit formation. Instinct referred to well-organized behavior transmitted through heredity and acted upon by natural selection. Habit formation dealt with behavior that developed to satisfy basic needs. Wissler perhaps most closely leaned toward a biological basis of cultural universals when he considered that whatever behavior all humans shared in common might be genetically inherited. Melville J. Herskovits (1966) opposed this view on the grounds that no genetic mechanism had been found that would provide a genetic basis for culture. Instinct was generally rejected as a mechanism by many cultural anthropologists, in particular by Ruth Benedict in her widely read *Patterns of Culture* (1934). She argued repeatedly that culture was not biologically transmitted and that there was no evidence for instinctive behavior in humans.

Within biological anthropology, culture was viewed by James N. Spuhler as a biological adaptation, the origins of which could have been founded on a set of several somatic paths, including brain evolution and anatomical changes leading to precision hand manipulation and erect bipedalism. Clifford Geertz (1973) continued the discussion by reconciling a degree of genetic influence within an evolutionary process that established the antecedents to culture in our hominid or prehuman ancestors. For example, Geertz surmised that during an early stage of human evolution, tight genetic control over behavior gave way to a higher degree of flexibility and adaptability, but he felt that determining the boundary between what is innately controlled and what is culturally controlled in human behavior is not always so straightforward. Geertz sums up his position by noting that cultural expressions, such as ideas, values, and emotions are derived from innate tendencies, capacities, and dispositions.

PERSONALITY AND CULTURE

Genetics enters the discussion of personality and culture in a manner parallel to the areas of racial variation and cultural universals, and, thus, the focus is again on the respective roles of heredity and environment, in this case, how a person's personality is formed, a topic discussed by Ralph Linton in his *The Study of Man* (1936). Although he spent considerable time in promoting the notion that culture provides the predominant sources of influences on personality makeup, or in his terminology, "psychological types," Linton also postulated the existence of two other kinds

of influence: constitutional qualities of the individual and the individual's personal-social relationships. Constitution is implicated in what Linton refers to as the "physiological theory of psychological type," which allows a prediction of a particular genetic outcome. This theory assumed that psychological types were inherited according to Mendelian rules of dominance and recessiveness, from which Linton surmised that inbred groups would tend to have a hereditary predisposition to share a common type. While considering this theory attractive, he nonetheless dismisses it in favor of a three-fold interaction that incorporates cultural, constitutional, and personal-social factors, all as sources of influence.

Margaret Mead (1935) briefly considered the extreme environment and genetic models before opting for cultural conditioning and social production of personality types. Later studies within culture and personality and the subspecialty area of psychological anthropology tended to ascribe a diminished role for genetic heredity but retained recognition of biological background for psychological development, for example, through stages proposed by psychoanalysts Jean Piaget and Sigmund Freud.

A direct application of genetics to cultural studies, however, appeared in *Culture and Biological Man* (1970) by Eliot D. Chapple. This book seemed to expand on earlier notions of the biological foundations of culture but was more explicit in utilizing the state of development of the newly formed field of behavioral genetics. Chapple explored the model of heredity/environment interaction that led to the development of personality and temperament characteristics of the individual. He strongly cautioned, however, that even though genes established limits within which environment could have an influence, that did not mean that humans were governed as genetic "automatons." Chapple served as a forerunner to a slightly later development that applied genetic/evolutionary theory to human social behavior, that is, sociobiology.

SOCIOBIOLOGY AND COEVOLUTION

The areas of sociobiology and coevolution represent attempts at synthesizing aspects of biology and behavior, and, as might be expected, also involved genetics, which was not always warmly received. Within cultural anthropology, much has been written concerning the limited value and potential harm that sociobiology brought to the understanding of human cultural commonalities and differences (Sahlins 1976). There could have been some misunderstanding of the aims of sociobiological research, but probably Marvin Harris (1989) represented the concern of many cultural anthropologists when he noted that sociobiologists were misdirecting their research and diverting resources in attempting to identify genetic control of cultural traits when in fact the great majority of cultural traits are not under genetic control.

Sociobiology, according to its practitioners, synthesized evolutionary biology and behavior, but to cultural anthropology it meant a reemergence of some long-standing, problematic issues related to cultural universals and fundamentals of human nature, all of which seemed to foster biological reductionism underscored by genetic determinism.

Another long-standing issue in anthropology centered on the dual inheritance involving genetic and cultural mechanisms, which were generally considered to involve independent evolutionary processes, best kept distinct. Quickly following on the heels of sociobiology, however, there was a surge of activity in an area termed "coevolution," which specified the linkage between biological evolution and culture history (Chagnon and Irons 1979). (This is not to be confused with "coevolution" as used in evolutionary biology that specified a mutually beneficial evolutionary connection of two unrelated species). Several major publications appeared in rapid succession, offering models and extended discussions of why it was necessary to consider simultaneously both biology and social behavior in order to understand fully the adaptiveness of culture.

The use of genetics in coevolution was not quite the same as that for sociobiology. What the two subjects had in common was the continuation of the argument that genes were responsible for capacities for cultural expression but not for the expression itself. In addition, however, many of the models devised within coevolution attempted to define units of cultural transmission comparable to the gene. Thus, terms such as "meme," "sociogene," "idene," and "culturgen" were devised and could be quantified, to a degree, and subjected to statistical analysis. The analogy between biological and cultural evolution has been pointed out by many researchers. For example, Alexander Alland and William Durham are two anthropologists who have proposed that biological evolutionary processes, particularly selection and adaptation, could be applied to cultural evolution.

MEDICAL ANTHROPOLOGY AND BIOCULTURAL INTERACTION

Medical anthropology deals primarily with health and disease in relation to biological and cultural responses, often considered in an adaptive process. Genetics becomes involved in both the diagnosis of certain diseases known or suspected to have a gene or chromosomal basis, and in tracing epidemiological patterns of disease occurrence. A related subspecialty area is that of biomedical anthropology, which considers genetic differences as one of the many categories to account for ethnic and racial differences in diseases, along with environmental factors, demography, and socioeconomic and other conditions (Polednak 1989). More recent development in the area of genetic epidemiology has moved biomedical research closer to biological anthropology, but it remains clear that proper study of human health and welfare necessitates the conjoining of biology and culture, although different emphases might well characterize certain approaches.

A widely cited example of biocultural interaction involves populations of agriculturalists in sub-Saharan Africa who evolved a genetic resistance to malarial infection. Slash-and-burn agriculture inadvertently provided favored breeding grounds for a mosquito that carried the malarial parasite, which then placed the people at greater risk for malaria, but persons who carry a single gene of a hemoglobin variant, so-called sickle-cell carriers, are protected from infestation of the malarial parasite. In this case, a genetic adaptation interacted with cultural practices to bring about successful population growth and expansion.

In general, human adaptability research has documented the value of a biocultural approach. An important concept employed in some of this work is that of developmental plasticity or genetic potential for modifying the phenotype, especially during the growth of a young child (Moran 1979). This concept nicely illustrates the role of heredity in setting forth potentials and the role of environment (including cultural aspects), which influences the expression of that ability. It is an area where genetics and culture have not only been reconciled but proven to be equally necessary in order fully to comprehend human adaptability and adaptation. In addition, the earlier notion that pitted nature versus nurture is thereby replaced with biocultural interaction of genes and culture.

KINSHIP ANALYSIS AND INCEST TABOO

The topics of kinship analysis and incest taboo are included under a single heading because genetically they both deal with degrees of relatedness. In his discussion of kinship analysis, Murdock (1960) refers to the science of genetics in citing exact probabilities of common heredity between consanguineal or blood relatives. These probabilities are determined by degrees. For example, primary relatives (consisting of parent-offspring and sibling sets) on average share one-half of their genes in common. Of interest is Murdock's use of genetic probability of relatedness, which closely resembles the coefficient of relationship as used by geneticists. Of additional interest, contemporary cultural anthropologists who study kinship have shown that some cultures do not construct classifications solely on genealogical or genetic relatedness but rather on socially defined relationships.

Murdock covered the widely discussed notion that biological harm might come to offspring whose parents are close relatives. This observation is based on the expectation that close relatives could be carrying in their genotype a recessive gene that, if inherited from both father and mother, could be deleterious to the child—physically, mentally, or in overall development. Murdock also claims, interestingly but not very testably, that it is equally probable for so-called recessive traits to be either harmful or desirable.

Murdock's discussion of inbreeding, or mating between relatives, was in the context of accounting for incest taboos, which essentially defined marriages and matings between close relatives as unacceptable. In addition to the theory of harmfulness due to deleterious recessives to explain the widespread (possibly universal?) occurrence of incest taboos, instinct avoidance of incest (advanced by Robert Lowie), familiarity avoidance of incest (Edward Westermarck), and the Oedipal complex (Sigmund Freud) were all considered over the years. Whichever theory he favored, Murdock noted that the avoidance of close inbreeding was not always followed, because many societies had preferential marriages among first cousins. He also questioned how the non-Western cultures that lacked a genetic awareness of heredity or even a biological understanding of paternity could have

based their incest taboo on a conscious desire to avoid deleterious consequences that might appear in their children.

An earlier and different perspective was offered by Linton (1936). For those groups he defined as "uncivilized," there was a severe restriction in opportunity for mate selection, because the groups were so small in size, generally territorial, and hostile toward each other. To Linton, this meant that there would be a high level of inbreeding, even if there were some rules that did not allow marriage between close relatives. As a consequence of long-term inbreeding, Linton surmised that all of the persons in the small tribe would share a great deal of their genes in common. Furthermore, as new variation arose through mutation, such as a change in a physical trait, this trait would tend to become fixed so that members of the tribe would show a distinct family resemblance. This discussion requires some revision in light of current population genetics thinking, but it does consider genetics with respect to the origins of racial variation, this at a time when race classification based on genetic information was still in its infancy. In addition, Linton provided extensive reference to the process of natural selection (acting on genetic traits) and social selection (acting on cultural factors). Interestingly, Linton viewed mutations as selectively advantageous even when fixed under close inbreeding. In contrast, somewhat later, others, such as Murdock, were trying to account for the universality of incest taboos and included outbreeding along with the possibly of avoiding having children with deleterious recessives as one of the prevailing theories. More recently, sociobiology (Shepher 1983) has been invoked as yet another theory for incest, while on the cultural side of the argument, Harris (1989) voiced a widely held opinion that incest taboos can be accounted for on economic grounds and social values, within the framework of alliance theory.

SEXUAL DIMORPHISM AND GENDER ROLE DIFFERENCES

Differences between the sexes have been studied by anthropologists, in terms of both physical/biological and cultural variation. While little question arose with regard to assigning an underlying genetic foundation to account for male and female biological characteristics (as studied by biological anthropologists in terms of growth patterns or skeletal traits), that was not the case when genetics was presumed to underlie gender role differences. Here again, the issue was initially contested on the grounds of a strict nature/nurture dichotomy. On one side were the proponents of biological determinants and instincts, those who presumed to know what was "natural" behavior for men and women. Others, including Mead (1935), while recognizing certain biologically given sex differences, nonetheless attempted to break down what she saw as American standards and stereotypes of sexuality. She offered a cross-cultural analysis in which New Guinea societies apparently did not conform to traditional American gender role distinctions. Although she has been accused of making overextending and highly impressionistic generalizations, her resistance to biological reductionism based on sex was basically accepted. A noteworthy anthropological contribution to the topic was written by M. Kay Martin and Barbara Voorhies (1975) and was a comprehensive treatment covering all aspects of sex and gender differences. Principles of heredity are carefully explained under sex as a biological process, which has evolutionary implications. There is also a discussion of what was then known about sex-linked traits, including human aggression and other aspects of personality. The authors essentially applied a genetic/learning interaction model in explaining different levels of aggressivity in men and women, but they ascribed a much larger component of social learning in the case of aggression and other traits. That assertion can be tested using a form of genetic analysis referred to as "heritability" and more recently developed quantitative genetic methods. It should be noted, however, that the question of which is more important, heredity or environment, is not scientifically proper at the individual level but can only be applied to the study of variation among individuals of a given group.

CURRENT USE OF GENETICS IN CULTURAL ANTHROPOLOGY

In reviewing the current literature of cultural anthropology and its use of genetics and application of principles of heredity, it is apparent that much of the earlier historical use continues, along with a carryover of particularly vexing issues. Accordingly, some introductory texts spend a chapter or so covering genetics and evolution, but others offer only brief discussions of the role of genes in establishing potentials or predispositions that are more or less fulfilled as the individual experiences life within social and cultural contexts. Importantly, the influence of genes and biology on such aspects as personality development and sexuality continues to generate debates. That this remains a controversial topic is understandable in light of current research that attempts completely to map or record the genetic makeup (genome) of human chromosomes. As the Human Genome Project proceeds, fairly regular announcements are made concerning the discovery of yet another human trait apparently having a genetic determination. Unfortunately, news media do not always caution the public that discoveries of this sort can be very tentative and usually only indirectly identify the actual genes involved. Furthermore, genes never act in a vacuum, and thus they should not be viewed as totally deterministic but rather as chemical instructions for possible courses of development, depending upon environmental circumstances.

Most recent developments in genetic research, such as the Human Genome Project, should have no direct impact on cultural anthropology. Cultural behavior and variation are by definition what humans have learned and what they socially transmit. That there exists a genetic and biological foundation of the capacities for cultural behavior, especially with regard to human brain function, was appreciated by the early American anthropologists Boas and Kroeber. New research might help clarify how these human capacities developed during the course of the human species's evolution and, indeed, how they developed within each of us as individuals. Cultural anthropologists over the years, however, have generally not felt compelled to incorporate genetic theory into their models for understanding cultural variation. To a limited degree, genetics has been employed for understanding cultural similarity, mostly on the basis of certain species-specific aspects of human nature.

There is a development within genetic research that does raise concerns for cultural anthropology, because it has the potential for infringing human rights of indigenous peoples around the world. A plan of the Human Genome Diversity Project, an offshoot of the Human Genome Project, is to collect and preserve cell samples from native groups for studies of evolutionary and medical significance. It is likely that some cell lines will be genetically altered and become the basis for patent applications. Such a patent application was withdrawn in 1994 after being strongly objected to by the native group involved, the Guaymi of Panama. In contrast, a patent case was recently approved with the support of the Hagahai People from Papua New Guinea. In a related area, there are ongoing efforts by "bioprospecting" companies to solicit from Third World shamans and traditional healers their knowledge of herbal medicine and other intellectual property rights, again from which patent applications might be derived. It is certainly expected that consent for such studies should be gained and that anthropologists may well be called upon to facilitate obtaining consent from the indigenous peoples involved. In initial response, organizations of native groups have begun to speak out on the issue, raising ethical questions, fearful that their human rights could be overlooked and they will once more be subjected to exploitation by outside interests.

ROBERT J. MEIER

SEE ALSO:: Adaption; Biological Anthropology; Biological Diversity and Race; Cultural Evolution; Disease and Culture; Ethics; Group Selection; Human Evolution; Human Rights and Advocacy Anthropology; Incest; Inheritance; Medical Anthropology; Racism; Sexual Orientation; Sociobiology

ALLAND, ALEXANDER. *Adaptation in Cultural Evolution: An Approach to Medical Anthropology.* New York: Columbia University Press, 1970.

BENEDICT, RUTH. *Patterns of Culture.* Boston: Houghton Mifflin, 1934.

BOAS, FRANZ. *Race, Language, and Culture.* New York: Macmillan, 1940.

CHAGNON, NAPOLEON A., and WILLIAM IRONS. *Evolutionary Biology and Human Social Behavior: An Anthropological Perspective.* North Scituate, Mass.: Duxbury Press, 1979.

CHAPPLE, ELIOT D. *Culture and Biological Man.* New York: Holt, Rinehart and Winston, 1970.

GEERTZ, CLIFFORD. *The Interpretation of Cultures.* New York: Basic Books, 1973.

HARRIS, MARVIN. *Our Kind.* New York: Harper and Row, 1989.

HERSKOVITS, MELVILLE J. *Cultural Anthropology.* New York: Alfred A. Knopf, 1966.

KROEBER, ALFRED L. "The Superorganic." In *The Nature of Culture.* Chicago: University of Chicago Press, pp. 22-51, 1952.

LINTON, RALPH. *The Study of Man.* New York: D. Appleton Century, 1936.

MARTIN, M. KAY, and BARBARA VOORHIES. *Female of the Species.* New York: Columbia University Press, 1975.

MEAD, MARGARET. *Sex and Temperament in Three Primitive Societies.* New York: Morrow, 1935.

MORAN, EMILIO. *Human Adaptability.* North Scituate, Mass.: Duxbury Press, 1979.

MURDOCK, GEORGE P. *Social Structure in Southeast Asia.* New York: Macmillan, 1960.

POLEDNAK, ANTHONY P. *Racial and Ethnic Differences in Disease.* New York: Oxford University Press, 1989.

SAHLINS, MARSHALL D. *The Use and Abuse of Biology: An Anthropological Critique of Sociobiology.* Ann Arbor: University of Michigan Press, 1976.

SHEPHER, J. *Incest: A Biosocial View.* New York: Academic Press, 1983.

STOCKING, GEORGE W., JR. *Race, Culture, and Evolution.* New York: Free Press, 1968.

TYLOR, EDWARD B. *Anthropology.* New York: D. Appleton, 1898.

GENITAL MUTILATION

Genital mutilations are essentially Old World customs, virtually absent in all of aboriginal North and South America, but surgical alterations of sex organs continue to occur regularly in many societies around the world. Since World War II male circumcision has spread to many traditionally noncircumcising groups because of its alleged hygienic benefits. Various forms of female mutilation, however, seem to be retreating because of campaigns by feminists and others. Plastic surgery—ranging from attempts to increase the length of a penis to complete sex change operations—is another twentieth-century development.

Theorizing about the origin of such mutilations goes back at least to Herodotus in the fifth century B.C.; he speculated about who first developed male circumcision, the Egyptians or the Ethiopians. At least some genital mutilations are probably prehistoric in origin, but no clear-cut archaeological evidence supports this theory. Today's hunters and gatherers normally do not practice such mutilations, although the practice exists among some Australian groups. The genitals of ancient Egyptian mummies are usually ambiguous, although it is known that at least some Egyptian males were circumcised; reliefs from Old Kingdom tombs depict the operation on youths. The biblical account of the institution of infant male circumcision as a covenant between God and Abraham (Genesis 17:10-14) apparently refers to customs in the second millennium B.C. The suggestion that female mutilations may be even earlier—possibly even the impetus for the male ones (believed by some nineteenth-century evolutionists to have occurred when patriarchy triumphed over matriarchy)—is not yet supported by any evidence.

The most common mutilation is male circumcision, in which the foreskin is totally removed. The Nandi of East Africa seem to be the only group in the world who burn the foreskin off with a hot coal (circumbustion). Circumcision is religiously enjoined on Jews, Samaritans, and Muslims, although it is not specified in the Koran, and is observed by Copts but not usually other Christians, even though January 1 is celebrated as the feast of the circumcision of Jesus. It is practiced by a great many other groups, including certain Australian aborigines and various East and West African cultures. Attempts by Reformed Jews in Germany to abandon the custom in the 1840s spread to the United States but ultimately proved unsuccessful. The original grounds for abandoning it included the fact that circumcision is not exclusively a Jewish custom and that Moses was not given a commandment to circumcise and did not even circumcise his own son.

Superincision (or supracision) involves making a slit in the top of the foreskin. It is most commonly found in Polynesian societies although not universally (e.g., not Hawaiians or the Maori). At least one African group, the Kikuyu, also seems to practice it. Genital flaying involves removing not only the foreskin but also the skin of the shaft of the penis. Only two societies in the world have been reported as practicing genital flaying—the Dowayo of Cameroon and groups in Saudi Arabia, who are said to remove even the skin of the scrotum and adjacent areas (a custom that has been outlawed by the Saudi government). Subincision, or ariltha, involves cutting the ventral side of the penis from one end to the other. This custom occurs almost exclusively among certain aboriginal Australian groups, such as the Aranda, and the Samburu of East Africa are the most notable exception. Hemicastration, or semicastration or monorchy, requires removing a single testicle. The Janjero of Ethiopia and the Ponapeans of Micronesia are two of the very few groups reported as having

practiced this in modern times. Total castration has been carried out for a number of different reasons: as a punishment; to produce a certain vocal range in male singers (the *castrati*) in Roman Catholic countries until 1878; among the Skopsy, a nineteenth-century Russian Christian group, as a sign of special dedication to God; in ancient Rome as a requirement for certain priests of the goddess Cybele; and in Imperial China by various grades of civil servants.

Holes are sometimes made in the genitals, such as penis perforation among certain Mayan groups, and various objects are inserted. Women on the island of Truk in the Pacific formerly inserted objects in their genitals that tinkled when they walked. Rings, rods, pellets, bells, and other objects have been inserted into the genitalia in different groups, such as a penis bar or *ampalang*. Genital piercing to accommodate rings and other jewelry developed a certain vogue among Westerners in the late twentieth century but hardly promised to become a fashion.

The two most common female genital mutilations are clitoridectomy and infibulation. Clitoridectomy, or female circumcision, refers to a variety of procedures ranging from excision of the prepuce of the clitoris (the Sunna circumcision practiced by many Muslim groups) to the removal of the entire clitoris and the labia minora. Among the Nandi the clitoris is burnt off with a hot coal. It is estimated that in 1995 there were some 20 to 80 million women in the world who had undergone some form of clitoridectomy. The practice is less common than male circumcision but occurs only in societies where male circumcision also occurs. Apart from Islamic groups, the major areas where the practice takes place are East and West Africa. Infibulation is almost entirely restricted to Muslim groups in the Horn of Africa, notably the Somali and Galla and a few other neighboring East African groups. It is sometimes called pharaonic circumcision, suggesting that the ancient Egyptians practiced it (there is no evidence that this was the case). Infibulation requires blocking access to the vagina, generally by sewing the labia majora together leaving only a small opening to accommodate urination and menstruation.

A third form of female genital mutilation, introcision—cutting of the perineum to enlarge the vaginal opening—is practiced by a few Australian groups but only those who also practice subincision. In Western gynecological practice a somewhat less extensive operation, episiotomy, is performed to prevent uncontrolled tearing during childbirth, and the subsequent suturing is referred to as "husband stitching," presumably because the resulting tightening of the vaginal opening is aimed at a husband's sexual pleasure.

Female mutilations are almost always assumed to exist to ensure a higher degree of paternity certainty, the sociobiological notion that males need as much assurance as possible that the offspring of their mates are their own. Like male genital mutilations, female mutilations are usually prerequisites for achieving full adult status, particularly marriage. Occasional counterexamples include the Konso of Ethiopia, who circumcise men at about the age of sixty to mark the end of conventional adult male roles (the circumcised men sometimes become transvestites). The Bambara of West Africa and some Jews perform circumcision even on the dead.

Ritualized mutilations, however, occur around or shortly before puberty. In George Peter Murdock's *Ethnographic Atlas,* for the 176 societies cited as practicing male circumcision or superincision, 126 did so between the ages of six to fifteen (of these 78 did so from eleven to fifteen). Roger T. Burton and John W.M. Whiting (1961) suggest that the mutilations at about puberty symbolically cut boys away from their mothers and counter cross-sex identity problems. The Dogon of West Africa have a somewhat similar belief, that the foreskin contains the feminine soul of a male, the clitoris the male soul of a woman; excision resolves identity problems. Frank Young (1965) theorizes that circumcision merely helps the bonding process between males.

Sigmund Freud believed that male circumcision was a symbolic castration. Bruno Bettelheim interpreted subincision and other male mutilations as an attempt to mimic female sexuality on some level; with regard to subincision he speaks of "menstruation envy" because the wounds are reopened on ritual occasions and allowed to bleed. Yehudi Cohen (1964) agrees with Bettelheim about subincision but not circumcision. Australian aborigines who subincise reportedly suggest it is done to play up ties with a totemic animal ancestor, such as the kangaroo, which has a two-headed penis that vaguely resembles a subincised human penis. This theory, proposed by two different sets of anthropologists, has been labeled "kangaroo bifid penis envy."

Native Polynesian explanations of superincision play up the importance of cleanliness and, in particular, the avoidance of stench from accumulated smegma. Justification for male circumcision in terms of hygiene is of relatively recent origin. Modern procircumcision advocates have asserted it helps prevent cancer of the penis and, in the partners of circumcised men, of the cervix, various infections of the urinary tract, and even AIDS. Whatever its merits, circumcision occasionally still has some unambiguous drawbacks, ranging from a deformed penis because of botched surgery to death from hemorrhaging. Even the Talmud exempts a parent with two sons who have died from circumcision from having a third circumcised (Yevamot 64b). Physical problems stemming from female mutilations are considerably more frequent, ranging from cysts and tetanus to septicemia and death. Infibulation often produces special complications, such as the inability to urinate or pass menstrual blood freely, infertility, pain during copulation, and various problems in childbirth, including brain damage to the child.

Presumably most if not all genital mutilations have an impact on sexual response. The twelfth-century Jewish philosopher Maimonides noted approvingly that circumcision reduced the intensity of a man's sex drive. William H. Masters and Virginia Johnson, based on research conducted in the 1960s, deny that circumcision has any impact on response but none of the men they observed had been circumcised as adults. Masters and Johnson's sample also failed to include women who had been genitally altered. The modern feminist condemnation of such practices plays up the charge that any damage to the clitoris virtually robs women of their sexuality, which is apparently the goal of the operations. A great deal of anecdotal evidence supports this charge, as do clinical investigations of the clitoris itself. Curiously enough, this was apparently not true in the one case of a declitorized woman investigated scientifically, a French girl treated for "excessive" masturbation, subsequently examined by the psychoanalyst Marie Bonaparte.

Unlike male circumcision, the various female mutilations have been routinely attacked by various Western groups. A well-known example of this was recorded by Jomo Kenyatta in *Facing Mount Kenya* (1938), in which he describes events among his own people, the Kikuyu. From the first contacts, missionary groups had unsuccessfully opposed mutilation. In

1929 the Church of Scotland Mission barred its schools to the children of persons who did not renounce the practice. Kikuyu reaction was intense and led to the creation of independent schools shortly thereafter and, some say, the Mau Mau uprising in the 1950s. Kenyatta, a student of Bronislaw Malinowski, presents the Kikuyu justification for the mutilations as the *conditio sine qua non* of the whole teaching of tribal law, religion, and morality. Thus, the Kikuyu were convinced that attempts to abolish clitoridectomy were nothing short of an attempt to destabilize the social order.

Anthropological theorizing has upheld in part the essence of Kenyatta's thesis by suggesting that a woman's mutilation is taken to be a reaffirmation of her family's honor and the political solidarity of her male kin—for a woman not to be declitorized would therefore be disruptive of the social structure. Seen in this light, it is understandable that African feminists in an international women's conference in Copenhagen in 1980 rejected anti-clitoridectomy proposals. In 1984, however, a small group of African women founded a movement in Senegal to combat these customs. A few years earlier, in 1979, the World Health Organization meeting in Khartoum condemned female genital mutilations, and the Sudan government outlawed them later that year. In 1982 the Sixth World Congress of Sexology meeting in Washington, D.C., also condemned the mutilations. Great Britain, Sweden, Switzerland, and France have passed laws against such mutilations, and France has prosecuted parents—generally immigrants from West Africa—for subjecting their daughters to them. Interestingly, anthropologists often testify on behalf of the defendants in such cases.

Some feminists have berated anthropologists for defending native customs while glossing over the real dangers to individual women. The anthropologist, trying to avoid the Scylla of cultural insensitivity or cultural imperialism, is seen as succumbing to the Charybdis of sexism and downright immorality. One thing is certain: cultural relativity is being tested with a vengeance.

EDGAR A. GREGERSEN

BRYK, FELIX. *Circumcision in Man and Woman: Its History, Psychology, and Ethnology.* New York: American Ethnological Press, 1934.

BETTELHEIM, BRUNO. *Symbolic Wounds: Puberty Rites and the Envious Male,* rev. ed. New York: Collier Books, 1952.

BURTON, ROGER V., and JOHN W. M. WHITING. "The Absent Father and Cross-Sex Identity." *Merrill-Palmer Quarterly of Behavior and Development* 7(1961): 85-95.

CAWTE, J. E., N. DJAGAMARA, and M. J. BARRETT. "The Meaning of Subincision of the Urethra to Aboriginal Australians." *British Journal of Medical Psychology* 39 (1966): 245-253.

COHEN, YEHUDI. *Transition from Childhood to Adolescence.* Chicago: Aldine, 1964.

DAREER, ASMA EL. *Woman, Why Do You Weep? Circumcision and Its Consequence.* London: Zed Press, 1982.

HUELSMAN, BEN R. "An Anthropological View of Clitoral and Other Female Genital Mutilations." In *The Clitoris,* edited by Thomas P. Lowry and Thea Snyder Lowry. St. Louis: Warren H. Green, 1976.

KENYATTA, JOMO. *Facing Mount Kenya.* 1938. Reprint. New York: Vintage Press, 1965.

MASTERS, WILLIAM H. and Virginia JOHNSON. *Human Sexual Response.* Boston: Little, Brown, 1966.

MURDOCK, GEORGE PETER. *Ethnographic Atlas.* Pittsburgh: Pittsburgh University Press, 1967.

PAIGE, KAREN ERICKSEN, and JEFFREY M. PAGE. *The Politics of Reproductive Ritual.* Berkeley: University of California Press, 1981.

YOUNG, FRANK. *Initiation Ceremonies.* Indianapolis: Bobbs-Merrill, 1965.

GENOCIDE

Genocide is the destruction of one people by another, more powerful people. The term is derived from the Latin *caedere* (to kill) and the Greek *genos* (race) and was first published in 1944 by Polish lawyer Raphael Lemkin. He used the word to describe the Holocaust, the attempt by German Nazis and their collaborators to eradicate the Jews and the Roma (Gypsies) in Europe from 1938 to 1945. The Nazis killed between 5 million and 6 million Jews, more than half the total number in Europe, and more than 500,000 Roma, in an attempt to eliminate the Jewish and Roma peoples, as well as other sectors of the population, such as mental patients and homosexuals. The Nazis practiced a level of cruelty that has often been equaled but rarely exceeded. In the final phase of the

Holocaust, they constructed extermination camps to kill as many people as possible. Special rooms were built at the camps where cyanide gas killed hundreds of people at one time. These gas chambers were attached to crematoriums, where thousands of bodies could be burned each day. Nazi brutality went beyond mass killing. Children were used in medical experiments, often operated on without anesthetic, and repeatedly beaten unconscious to observe behavior patterns. The Nazis who planned the killings and experiments were educated men. Medical doctors were employed in the camps, and at one key planning meeting, on 20 January 1942, more than half the Nazis present had university doctorates. Under the leadership of Adolf Hitler, the Nazis blamed the Jews for the social and political ills that had beset Germany. They believed they were saving a world threatened by an inferior race and identified themselves with the Aryan race of tall, fair, healthy people. Spurious anthropological theories were used to lend credence to this fabrication, and such theories still crop up to support racist ideologies in such places as South Africa and the southern United States.

In response to the Holocaust, the United Nations passed a Resolution in 1946 that defined genocide as "a denial of the right of existence of entire human groups." On 9 December 1948 the UN adopted the Convention on the Prevention and Punishment of the Crime of Genocide, which defined genocide as "any of the following acts committed with intent to destroy, in whole or in part, national, ethnical, racial or religious groups, as such: (a) killing members of the group; (b) causing serious bodily or mental harm to members of the group; (c) deliberately inflicting on the group conditions of life calculated to bring about its physical destruction in whole or in part; (d) imposing measures intended to prevent births within the group; (e) forcibly transferring children of the group to another group." In addition to genocide, other punishable acts mentioned in the covenant are conspiracy, incitement, the attempt to commit genocide, and complicity in genocide.

There are several problems with the UN definition of genocide. One is that it excludes social and political sectors of a population. For example, between the Russian Revolution of 1917 and the end of the cold war in 1989, the Soviet government killed millions of people (60 million according to some estimates) because they were thought to threaten the state. Although many were from separate nations (such as the Ukraine), many others were Russians. Similarly, during the 1970s Cambodian communists, known as the Khmer Rouge, killed about one-third (1.5 million) of Cambodia's population. The question is whether genocide should include mass killings whether or not the victims are from particular national, ethnical, racial, or religious groups. Many scholars believe that the UN definition is too restrictive. For example, Irving Louis Horowitz (1982) defines genocide as "a special form of murder; state-sanctioned liquidation against a collective group, without regard to whether an individual has committed any specific and punishable transgression." Israel W. Charny also proposes a wider definition: "mass killing of substantial numbers of human beings, when not in the course of military action against the military forces of an avowed enemy, under conditions of the essential defenselessness and helplessness of the victims" (Lemkin Symposium, Yale University, 1991).

These wider definitions omit the complex issue of whether the intent to destroy the victim group as such is vital to the crime. Experts have observed that in many examples of genocide the primary intention is not in fact the destruction of the victims as a group. For example, in practically all genocides of colonization the intention is simply to take over the victims' lands, and in cases where the colonized accept this invasion, no genocide results. In other genocides the primary intention might be to remove a perceived threat to those in power. It has even been argued that the primary intention of the Nazis was the supposed protection of Germany and not the destruction of the Jews.

Some scholars feel that certain conditions are necessary for genocide, such as a brutal dictatorship, hatred of victims, war, a compliant bureaucracy, and modern technology. Many understand genocide to be a modern phenomenon, possible only in highly differentiated societies, but some hunter-gatherer cultures, with little or no hierarchy, bureaucracy, or modern technology, have annihilated weaker neighbors, and some believe this should be classed as genocide.

Although genocide has been called the greatest crime of all and millions have died through genocidal acts in the twentieth century, more people have died through starvation and war. Some radical thinkers believe that the way the developed world maintains other nations in a state of poverty—the violence inherent in the market structures regulating the production and distribution of wealth—is responsible for the premature deaths of many millions and should be viewed as genocide.

Other twentieth-century reports of genocide include the killing of the Herero in Southwest Africa by Germans (1904); of Armenians by the Turks and Kurds (1915-1922); of Africans in southern Sudan (1955-1972) and the Nubas (since 1989) by the northern Arab population; of the Aché and other Indians by Paraguayans (1950s to 1970s); the atrocities committed during the Chinese colonization of Tibet (particularly during the 1960s); the killing of those who resisted Indonesia's colonization of nearby islands, particularly the people of East Timor and West Papua (Irian Jaya) (1965 to the present); of the Ibos by Nigerians (1966-1970); of the Tutsis by the Hutus, and vice versa, in Burundi (1960s to early 1970s); of the Bengalis in what was to become Bangladesh by Pakistanis (1971); of the Jumma by Bangladeshis (1970s to the present); mass killings by the Ugandan army (1976-1978); the killing of Kurds and Marsh Arabs by Iraqis (1987 to the present); and the killing of Moslems in Bosnia-Herzegovina (beginning in 1992).

Most, if not all, recorded genocides, including those that are thoroughly documented, have elicited denials. Those sympathetic to the perpetrators of genocide, as well as others who prefer a narrow definition of the crime, often reject the evidence of mass killing or assert that there was no intention to destroy the victims. An extreme example is the apologists who maintain that the Nazi elite was unaware of the destruction of the Jews or even deny that the Holocaust killings took place.

STEPHEN CORRY

SEE ALSO: Nationalism; Racism

CHALK, FRANK, and KURT JONASSOHN. *The History and Sociology of Genocide.* New Haven, Conn.: Yale University Press, 1990.

CHARNY, ISRAEL W. *Genocide: A Critical Bibliographic Review,* vol. 1. New York: Facts on File, 1988-1992.

DOBKOWSKI, MICHAEL N., and ISIDOR WALLIMANN. *Genocide in Our Time.* Ann Arbor, Mich.: Pierian Press, 1992.

HOROWITZ, IRVING LOUIS. *Taking Lives: Genocide and State Power.* New Brunswick, N.J.: Transaction Books, 1982.

KUPER, LEO. *Genocide: Its Political Use in the Twentieth Century.* New Haven: Yale University Press, 1981.

———. *The Prevention of Genocide.* New Haven: Yale University Press, 1985.

LEMKIN, RAPHAEL. *Axis Rule in Occupied Europe.* New York: Columbia University Press, 1944.

GESTURE AND MOVEMENT

Human beings everywhere engage in complex structured systems of bodily actions that are socially acquired and laden with cultural significance. Some structured movement systems, such as the martial arts, sporting activities, idioms of dancing, dramatic arts, ceremonials, and ritual events, involve highly deliberate choreographed movement. Other uses of body movement remain out of the focal awareness of their actors due to habit and skill. Examples include ways of eating, dressing, walking, and sitting as well as modes of physical labor such as digging, planting, bricklaying and fishing, all of which vary according to cultural and subcultural conventions. Also out of focal awareness most of the time are the hand gestures, postures, facial expressions, and spatial orientations that accompany speech in social interaction. There are also signed languages as well as gestures of the mouth, lips, and tongue that produce speech. All these manifestations of human actions in their cultural context comprise the anthropology of human movement.

Despite the obvious fact that this kind of handling of space and the handling of one's body are an intimate part of one's being, one's language, and one's ability to exist in a complex world of social action, the detailed study of human movement constitutes a relatively minor tradition in sociocultural anthropology, albeit a long-standing one. The reasons for this relative neglect are cultural and stem from a long-standing bias against the body in the Western philosophical and religious traditions, which, in turn, has led few social theorists to include physical being and bodily actions in their definitions of social action. The Platonic legacy, together with Descartes's radical separation of mind and body during the rise of science in the seventeenth century, provided a set of unexamined assumptions that has permeated all the social sciences. Generally the Western model of "person" provides a conception of mind as the non-material locus of rationality, thought, language, and knowledge. In opposition to this the body is regarded as the mechanical, sensate, material locus for the physical expression of irrationality, feeling, and emotion. After Darwin such physicality has been most often understood as "natural" rather than "cultural," a survival of our animal past. In the Western Christian tradition, the body as flesh has been viewed as the location of sinful desire, corrupting appetites, and irrational passions, frequently subjected to disciplinary and ascetic practices with the goal of achieving transcendence.

In light of this legacy it is not surprising to find that expressions of curiosity and disgust over alien bodily practices, unfamiliar domestic activities, "excesses" of gesticulation, "exotic" rituals, and "wild" dancing frequent the accounts of early explorers, missionaries, and nineteenth-century amateur ethnologists. Such accounts provided a rationale for labeling non-Western peoples "primitive" and distancing them as "other." On the whole, the greater the variation from acceptable European norms of physical behavior the more primitive a society was judged to be. This line of reasoning provided justification for widespread colonial efforts to "civilize the savages" through the radical control of bodily practices (clothing, hairstyles, eating habits, sexual liaisons, social manners, work ethic, and ritual activities). For example, in North America the U.S. Office of Indian Affairs book of regulations for 1904 listed participation in Native American religious rituals and dancing as a punishable offense because they stirred the passions of the blood and hindered progress toward "civilization" (that is, assimilation).

Although this radical separation of mind and body in Western culture remained constant at a meta-theoretical level until poststructuralist and postmodern challenges in the late twentieth century, theoretical perspectives arose in U.S. cultural anthropology and British social anthropology that viewed human movement and gesture in contrasting ways. In the mid-nineteenth century, for example, the work of British anthropologist Edward B. Tylor (1878) on gesture and sign languages reflected upper-class Victorian English attitudes toward gesticulation as "natural" and therefore "rude," meaning raw and unformed. Tylor regarded sign languages and gesture

as "a natural language" and therefore as more primitive than speech or writing, and he expected the elements of gesture to be universally recognizable. This was the source of his interest in what he called "the gesture language." Tylor collected data from the sign systems of German and English deaf communities and compared them with data from North American sources. He believed he was close to discovering the original sign-making faculty in humans that once led to the emergence of spoken language. He did not, however, go as far as to suggest that "the gesture language" represented a separate stage of evolution through which humankind had passed before speech had developed. These interests in gesture and language origins were shared by the nineteenth-century German psychologist Wilhelm Wundt, who thought that human language could have originated in innate expressive actions characteristic of emotional states.

In the United States, Tylor's work provided theoretical support for Garrick A. Mallery's extensive collection of data on signing and gesture. Mallery (1981) compared Native North American signing systems with deaf sign languages, accounts of the use of gesture in classical times, in Naples, and among contemporary actors.

In contrast to the universalist theories of gesture espoused by these evolutionists, American anthropologist Franz Boas stressed the learned, culture-specific nature of body movement. He recognized that artistic form and cultural patterning were present not only in Native American dances but also in the complex hand gestures and other body movements that accompanied song, oratory, and the performance of oral literature. He nevertheless chose to exclude "gesture-language" from his influential writings (Boas 1911), limiting his consideration to "communication by groups of sounds produced by the articulating organs [of mouth and tongue]." Boas thus nadvertently set the pattern for the exclusion of body movement from future research in U.S. linguistic anthropology. Subsequent research became focused on a rather narrow conception of spoken language structure.

Boas's student Edward Sapir also recognized that manual gestures interplay constantly with speech in communicative situations, but the communicative and social significance of what he referred to as an "elaborate and secret code" were left unexplored. Although Sapir, like other Boasians, regarded culture as symbolic patterns of behavior, investigation of the symbolic patterning of human body movement in space as constitutive of that behavior remained absent from investigations. Consistent with the high status of U.S. psychology, interest in the psychological (mental) took precedence over the body, as witnessed by the rise of interest in culture and personality. Alfred L. Kroeber (1958) did write on Plains Indian sign language and supported La Mont West's pioneering descriptive linguistic research on that sign system (1960), but this was a departure from Kroeber's major works, and West's dissertation had little impact on anthropological linguistics.

Other students of Boas contributed to a functionalist view of human movement systems. According to this theoretical framework a culture was a functioning, integrated, patterned whole, and ritual events, dances, and gestures were to be understood insofar as they fulfilled some kind of social need or function. For example, Margaret Mead (1928) regarded the dances of Samoan adolescents as a vehicle for psychological adjustment; for Ruth Benedict (1934) the function of the entire Kwakiutl Winter Ceremonial (a series of religious rites) was to rehabilitate the individual back into secular society. Actual body movement is epiphenomenal in such descriptions, as ritual actions and dancing are described in terms of adaptive responses to either the social or the physical environment. Similar descriptions appear in the work of many British functionalist anthropologists such as Bronislaw Malinowski, Raymond Firth, and A. R. Radcliffe-Brown.

French anthropologist Marcel Mauss (1935) prefigured the interests of Benedict, Mead, and others in noting how each society imposes a rigorously determined use of the body upon the individual in the training of a child's bodily needs and activities. Mauss's essay clearly illustrated how seemingly "natural" bodily activities were (Durkheimian) social facts, simultaneously sociological, historical, and physiopsychological.

In the 1940s and 1950s the potential importance to anthropologists of recording and analyzing body movements was demonstrated by Gregory Bateson and Margaret Mead's photographic analysis of Balinese character (1942), David Efron's contrastive analysis of the gestures of Italian and Southeastern European Jewish immigrants in New York (1942), Weston La Barre's essay on the cultural basis of emotions and gestures, and Gordon Hewes's cross-cultural comparison of postural habits. However, the outstanding early pioneer in anthropological research on bodily communication was Ray Birdwhistell (1970), who coined the term "kinesics" to describe his approach. Inspired by what he viewed as Sapir's anticipation of the interdependence of linguistic and kinesic research and by H.L. Smith and G.L. Trager's attempts to apply the methods of structural linguistics to other aspects of vocalization ("paralinguistics"), Birdwhistell suggested a discipline that would parallel linguistics but deal with the analysis of visible bodily motion. Influenced also by the work of Bateson and of the sociologist Erving Goffman, Birdwhistell's research centered on body movements in social interaction, usually in clinical settings. Using filmed data Birdwhistell applied a linguistic model, identifying movement units based on contrastive analysis in a manner similar to that established by structural linguists for establishing the phonemes and morphemes of a spoken language. His descriptions frequently lapse into functional anatomical language, however, and the status of movements as meaningful actions becomes lost in the endeavor to divide up the "kinesic stream."

Birdwhistell limited kinesics to interaction contexts. Indeed, he stressed that writings about formalized systems of gesture such as those found in dancing, drama, mime, and religious ritual were beyond the interests of kinesics. This was unfortunate as it narrowed the scope of the potential field and separated kinesics from much that was of interest to mainstream anthropology. A truly inclusive anthropology of human movement systems as a subfield similar in scope to linguistic anthropology had to await the work of Drid Williams and Adrienne Kaeppler.

Adam Kendon has suggested that the program of work Birdwhistell proposed might have gotten underway had the interest of many people in linguistics and related disciplines not been redirected in the 1960s by the work of Noam Chomsky. Chomsky's generative linguistics was exclusively concerned with the formal analysis of linguistic competence and proposed "structures of the mind" that generate language per se. Actual acts of speaking were consigned to what Kendon called the "wastebasket of 'performance'" (1982). Only when linguistic anthropology embraced an "ethnography of speaking" in explicit contrast to the Chomskian agenda did attention return to pragmatics, ethnopoetics, and verbal art as performance. This provided a theoretical climate for the 1980s and

1990s in which gesture, spatial orientation deixis (the spoken and gestural organization of space/time), and indexicality (connections to the communicative context) became of interest to some linguistic anthropologists (Farnell 1995).

Birdwhistell (1970) also recognized the need for a notation system for recording and analyzing body movement. He devised a system specific to his particular communication analysis even though by his own admission the results were crude and static with relatively little capacity for recording movement. The development of an adequate writing system already had emerged as a formidable problem for the study of movement, earlier attempts having been made by French dancing masters Pierre Beauchamps, Raoul Feuillet, and others, as well as the Englishman Gilbert Austin in his research into gesture and rhetoric (1806).

Anthropologists Williams, Kaeppler, Farnell and others use a movement script called Labanotation to create ethnographic records of movement events. Although originally used in the United States and Europe in choreographic contexts, Labanotation (invented by Rudolph Laban circa 1928) was designed from the outset as a generalized system that could notate any kind of human movement. Two other generalized systems also exist: Benesh notation (1956) and Eshkol-Wachman notation (1958). The idea of movement literacy is a central component of Williams's semasiology, not simply as a method of recording for specialists but as a means by which any anthropologist can arrive at post-Cartesian ontological and epistemological insights on embodiment and social action (Farnell 1994).

While Birdwhistell's "kinesics" focused on body motion, Edward T. Hall's "proxemics" drew attention to the role that space plays in human relations. Hall (1959) postulated that there are socially or culturally established zones of space surrounding individuals that are generally out of awareness but that influence and may even determine daily interactions. Hall's writings include many excellent ethnographic observations about spatial usages in different contexts as well as in situations of culture contact. He has been criticized, however, for failing to clarify his theoretical position on the relationship between proxemics and ethological notions of territoriality in other animals. His own data would suggest that the rich diversity of culturally defined human spaces make trivial any comparison with notions of programmed responses to critical distancing and territoriality in animals. However, many ethologists as well as psychologists who specialize in nonverbal communication continue this behaviorist, Darwinian universalist agenda. Objectivist views of movement as "behavior"—as raw physical data of some kind, the result of biologically triggered impulses or survivals of an animal past—have been of little interest to sociocultural anthropologists because cultural and symbolic dimensions are excluded.

Birdwhistell's kinesics and Hall's proxemics provided important sensitizing constructs in the 1960s and 1970s. They raised important questions and provided a framework that could be advanced by later investigators such as Kaeppler, Williams, and Kendon. Moving in an interdisciplinary sphere between anthropology, linguistics, nonverbal communication, and semiotics, Kendon has been a most active researcher of gesture and signed languages. While his earliest work on face-to-face interaction was behaviorist, he shifted his orientation to a view more compatible with that of semiotics and symbolic anthropology, which sees human actions as connected to sociolinguistic contexts, intentions, and belief systems. Kendon has produced a definitive work on Australian Aboriginal sign languages (1988) and written extensively on gesture and its connections to speech, insisting that "the gestural modality is as fundamental as the verbal modality as an instrument for the representation of meaning" (1983).

Kaeppler and Williams, like Birdwhistell, turned to structural linguistics for conceptions on which to base rigorous analyses of structured movement. Kaeppler (1972) took an ethnoscientific approach, applying Kenneth Pike's emic/etic distinction to an analysis of the structure of Tongan dance and Hawaiian dance and song texts. Williams's semasiology is grounded in British poststructural semantic anthropology and Saussurian semiology (Williams 1991). Neither Kaeppler nor Williams fell into the trap of applying a linguistic *model* to the medium of movement as Birdwhistell had done in his attempt to match "kinemorphs" directly with spoken language morphemes. Instead they used linguistic *analogies*, that is, they took insights from linguistics insofar as such insights facilitated theory building specific to understanding human movement systems. Part of their post-Cartesian thrust is not to separate theories of the body and human action from spoken language meanings because, as their work clearly illustrates, semiotic systems integrate: the mind that uses spoken language does not somehow switch off when it comes to moving.

Central to Williams's semasiology are fundamental post-Cartesian shifts that replace the body-mind split (and old notions of "objectivity") with a conception of persons as embodied meaning-making agents. She advocates use of the term "action" instead of "behavior" in order to emphasize this theoretical commitment. Her work on entirely different action sign systems—the Post-Tridentine Catholic Mass, the ballet *Checkmate* (choreographed by Dame Ninette de Valois of the Royal Ballet, England), the exercise technique t'ai chi ch'uan, and Cape York (Australian Aboriginal) dances—demonstrates the comprehensive power of her approach.

A generation of students trained in semasiology have produced work on systems as varied as the classical Indian dance form Bharata Natyam (Rajika Puri); Plains Indian sign language and Assiniboine storytelling performance (Brenda Farnell); Martha Graham dance technique and American Sign Language (Diana Hart-Johnson); classical ballet (Dixie Durr); the liturgical use of space and action in the United Church of Australia (Jennifer Farrell); and Dalcroze Eurythmics (Gillian Fisher);(see Jashim; Williams 1982; Farnell 1995).

The possibility of a new paradigm of embodiment in socio-cultural anthropology in the 1990s may provide further post-Cartesian metatheoretical shifts that will enable the anthropology of human movement systems to flourish.

BRENDA FARNELL

SEE ALSO: Dance; Emic/Etic Distinctions; Linguistic Anthropology; Psychological Anthropology; Ritual; Semiotics; Sports

AUSTIN, GILBERT. *Chironomia: Or a Treatise on Rhetorical Delivery; Comprehending Many Percepts, Both Ancient and Modern, for the Proper Regulation of The Voice, The Countenance, and Gesture. Together with an Investigation of the Elements of Gesture, and a New Method for the Notation Thereof; Illustrated by Many Figures.* 1806. Reprint. London: Southern Illinois University Press, 1966.

BENEDICT, RUTH. *Patterns of Culture.* Boston: Houghton Miflin, 1934.

BIRDWHISTELL, RAY L. *Kinesics and Context: Essays on Body Motion Communication.* Philadelphia: University of Pennsylvania, 1970.

BOAS, FRANZ, ed. Introduction to *The Handbook of American Indian Languages.* Bulletin 40 (1911): 1-83.

EFON, DAVID. *Gesture and Environment.* New York: Kings Crown Press, 1942.

FARNELL, BRENDA. "Ethnographics and the Moving Body." *Man* 29, 4(1994):929-974.

FARNELL, BRENDA, ed. *Action Sign Systems in Cultural Context: The Visible and the Invisible.* Metuchen, N.J.: Scarecrow Press, 1995.

HALL, EDWARD T. *The Silent Language.* New York: Doubleday, 1959.

JOURNAL FOR THE ANTHROPOLOGICAL STUDY OF HUMAN MOVEMENT (JASHM). Anthropology Dept., University of Iowa. Volumes 1–8, 1979-.

KENDON, ADAM. "The Study of Gesture: Some Observations on Its History." *Semiotic Inquiry* 2 (1982):45–62.

———. "Gesture and Speech: How They Interact." In *Nonverbal Interaction*, edited by J.M. Wiemann and R.P. Harrison. Beverly Hills, Calif.: Sage Publications, 1983.

———. *Sign Languages of Aboriginal Australia: Cultural, Semiotic and Communicative Perspectives.* Cambridge: Cambridge University Press, 1988.

KROEBER, ALFRED. "Sign Language Enquiry." In *International Journal of American Linguistics.* 24 (1958): 1-19.

MALLERY, GARRICK A. *Sign Language Among North American Indians Compared with that Among Other Peoples and Deaf-Mutes.* The Hague: Mouton, 1972. [Photomechanic reprint of pp. 263–552 of Bureau of American Ethnology First Annual Report, Volume 1, 1879–1880. Washington, D.C. Government Printing Office, 1881.]

MAUSS, MARCEL. "Body Techniques." In *Sociology and Psychology*, translated by Ben Brewster. 1935. Reprint. London: Routledge and Kegan Paul, 1979.

MEAD, MARGARET. *Coming of Age in Samoa.* 1928. Reprint. New York: Mentor Books, 1959.

———, and GREGORY BATESON. *Balinese Character: A Photographic Analysis.* New York: New York Academy of Sciences, 1942.

UMIKER-SEBEOK, DONNA JEAN, and THOMAS A. SEBEOK, eds. "Aboriginal Sign Languages of the Americas and Australia." Vol. 1 of *North America:*

Classic Comparative Perspectives. New York: Plenum Press, 1978.

TYLOR, EDWARD B. *Researches into the Early History of Mankind and the Development of Civilization.* Boston: Estes and Lauriat, 1878.

WEST, LAMONT, JR. *The Sign Language: An Analysis.* PhD dissertation: Indiana Universty, 1960.

WILLIAMS, DRID. "Semasiology: A Semantic Anthropologist's View of Human Movements and Actions." In *Semantic Anthropology,* ASA Monograph 22. London: Academic Press, 1982.

——— . *Ten Lectures on Theories of the Dance.* Metuchen, N.J.: Scarecrow Press, 1991.

GODPARENTHOOD

Godparenthood, and the interrelated coparenthood, are the English terms for two sets of social relationships that derive from but are not limited to the act of sponsorship in Christian religious practice. The relationships pattern the behavioral expectations of three social roles and form the core complex that is best known in the anthropological literature by the Spanish term *compadrazgo* (or *compadrinazgo*), although the languages of the many cultures where the complex is found have their own terms for it. The three roles are parent, child, and godparent. The separate but interrelated relationships are between godparent and godchild (godparenthood); and parent(s) and godparent(s) (coparenthood).

Historically, the complex had its origins in the rituals of Christian initiation. The early church is believed to have adopted the Jewish practice of immersing converts in water to symbolize cleansing and rebirth. In the Jewish practice two men read from the Torah during the conversion ceremony. During the early Christian period, when most of those being baptized were adults, readers were transformed into sponsors who vouched for, almost in the legal sense, the worthiness of the candidate. Later, when those being baptized were mostly children, the act of sponsorship changed. During the baptism the child was asked if it would be religiously devout. The sponsor responded affirmatively on the child's behalf, thereby accepting responsibility for its future behavior. This committed the sponsor to educating the child in the holy life, establishing a long-term bond between the two that was to last at least until the child became an adult. Because anyone who instructed another in religious knowledge was considered to be his or her "spiritual father" (or mother), sponsors came to be called "god" parents, and because the godparents shared with the biological parents responsibility for educating the child, a de facto relationship (coparenthood) existed between them.

By the middle of the third century Adam's disobedience to God, referred to as "original sin," was interpreted in such a way as to have disastrous consequences for his descendants. It was believed that after the fall humans ceased to be immortal, necessitating sexual reproduction. Placed in opposition to the purity of the spiritual world, sex and its consequences of physical birth were considered dirty and impure. By coming into the world as the result of sexual intercourse, children were believed to be born in original sin. Baptism undid the damage a child inherited as the result of Adam's transgression. It was a second birth, literally a rebirth, that was purifying and cleansing. In church theory the parents in this spiritual rebirth were God the Father and Mother Church. In social practice, however, the sponsors came to be accepted as spiritual parents. When they took the child from the baptismal font they were considered to have given birth to it. This second birth, however, unlike the tainted carnality in which the biological parents had given life to it the first time, was considered to be spiritually pure and to have eternal grace.

By being baptized every Christian had two sets of parents, one biological and the other spiritual. Since sponsor, child, and the child's parents were considered to be related, the incest taboo was extended to include them all. First in customary practice and then by church decree, godparents were prohibited from marrying and/or engaging in sexual relations with either their godchildren or their coparents, which was to be an important feature of social life in Western Europe from the ninth to the sixteenth centuries and in other parts of the world thereafter.

As Christianity in both its Roman and Orthodox forms spread from its Mediterranean birthplace to Western and Northern Europe and then to Eastern Europe and Asia, the baptismal ritual and spiritual kinship, including godparenthood and coparenthood, went with it. The complex quickly became integrated into the ongoing social systems of the many diverse peoples who accepted the new religion. Sponsorship was and continues to be voluntary, at least for the parents and sponsors. An expecting couple may invite whomever they choose to stand for their child. In most Christian communities such a request, even today, is difficult to refuse.

Sponsorship was used in medieval Europe, as it is in many parts of the world today, both to reinforce existing alliances and/or build new ones. In egalitarian communities, composed mostly of peasants that are not marked by social and economic stratification, kinsmen and neighbors tended to be selected as sponsors, reinforcing weak kin links. In stratified societies, however, parents often chose sponsors from socially superior groups. Sidney W. Mintz and Eric R. Wolf (1950) have shown how the alliance-building potential, primarily of the coparenthood relationship, was used in medieval Europe to enable some enterprising individuals to bridge the feudal land tenure system and its rigid class structure.

Recognition of the advantages to be gained from relationships based on sponsorship led to the creation of further opportunities for sponsorship—to establish relationships with new individuals or to reinforce those with previous sponsors—both within and outside the church. Confirmation, which at first was a part of the baptism ritual, was separated as an independent event. First communion, marriage, and at times even death became occasions at which sponsors were needed. Secular rituals, such as bonfires built on Saint John's eve (June 24), were used in Italy, and today in Brazil, as opportunities to establish relationships of godparenthood and coparenthood. Moreover, especially after the complex spread to other parts of the world, pre-Christian religious practices and nonreligious events, such as wedding anniversaries and the blessing of a new house or motor vehicle, also became occasions for establishing relationships of god-parenthood and coparenthood.

Of special importance to the worldwide diffusion of the complex was the introduction of Christianity into the Iberian Peninsula and its retention there despite more than six centuries of Moslem domination. It was from Iberia that *compadrazgo* was carried, along with Christianity, to the Western Hemisphere, Africa, East and Southeast Asia, and the Pacific during the period of exploration and expansion of the fifteenth and sixteenth centuries and later. By then the church had integrated the diverse experiences peoples in different parts of Europe and Asia had with sponsorship, and a unified Christian view of the complex crystallized at the Council of Trent (1545-1563). The church had provided moral legitimacy for the Spanish and Portuguese conquests, the subsequent subjugation and/or enslavement of indigenous peoples, and the appropriation of lands and other resources. In return the conquistadors actively participated in missionizing and in the conversion of conquered peoples.

The first step in the often forced conversion process was baptism. Thus, sponsorship, godparent-hood, and coparenthood were introduced into the lives of otherwise culturally diverse peoples around the globe. Because Christianity was often mixed with aspects of their various precontact traditions, and because of different courses of social and political change over the past five centuries, the specifics of role expectations, content of relationships, and relative importance of extensions have come to differ in detail throughout the contemporary Christian world.

While the complex was being integrated into the lives of more and more peoples in distant parts of the world, however, the coparenthood relationship fell into disuse in Northwest Europe, especially in Great Britain. This has been associated by many scholars with the rise of Protestantism, which downplayed extensions of the role of baptismal sponsorship, and with the industrial revolution and the institutionalization of capitalist social forms that downplayed all interpersonal ties other than those of the market. One consequence of this was that early anthropologists, many of whom were products of Anglo-American culture, were surprised to encounter vital and dynamic relationships of coparenthood when they began to do research.

Many of the early field studies of the 1920s and 1930s were in Central and then South America. In these mostly Spanish Catholic societies the coparent relationship was found not only to be present, but, in contrast with the Anglo-American experience, more important than godparenthood. A large literature developed on the subject. Unfortunately, however, since the Spanish term *compadrazgo*, which refers only to the coparent relationship, was used to refer to the entire complex, much of the reporting and analysis was limited in scope and overly associated with Latin

America. Present-day research has shown that godparenthood and coparenthood are present and important, with variation in details, in the social systems of peoples throughout the Christian world. Despite this, much anthropological writing on the subject still focuses on Latin America.

Mintz and Wolf (1950) provided the first systematic examination of the historical background and contemporary functioning of the complex. After summarizing its development and transfer to the Western Hemisphere, they present historical data from medieval Europe demonstrating how the relationship was used both to solidify social relationships horizontally among members of the same neighborhood and social class and to integrate the class structure by means of vertical ties between individuals in different socioeconomic positions. They emphasize the importance of the complex in face-to-face societies, arguing its incompatibility with the impersonal institutions of the modern urban-industrial world. This accounts for its continuing importance in the primarily rural areas of Latin America and Mediterranean Europe and its absence in the urbanized, industrialized cultures of Northwest Europe and the United States. They also examine some of the community studies of the period, establishing a tentative typology based primarily on social and economic factors, to account for the extension specifically of coparenthood bonds either horizontally or vertically.

Historian Joseph H. Lynch (1986) criticized Mintz and Wolf's use of the historical sources and what he considered their overdependence on the Marxist vocabulary of class struggle. Despite this the Mintz-Wolf paper remains the most widely cited source on the subject by anthropologists. Stephen Gudeman (1972), after reviewing fifty-one works published between 1936 and 1970, 80 percent of which were on Latin America, criticized the overly materialist, utilitarian approach to the subject taken by most anthropologists. Gudeman was interested in the meaning of the complex and he analyzed it in structural terms.

The most comprehensive anthropological treatment of the topic is to be found in the two-volume work by Hugo G. Nuitini and Betty Bell (1980, 1984). They exhaustively analyze the workings of both godparenthood and coparenthood in the small Mexican municipality of Belen and trace its introduction into Central America back to the Spanish Conquest. They analyze the acculturation process and the syncretic mixing of aspects of the European baptismal sponsorship complex and pre-Conquest institutions. What appears to have received insufficient attention in the literature is the overlap between godparenthood and coparenthood and patterns of patronage and clientage that also are important in many of the same parts of the world.

The societies of Latin America and other parts of the world established by the Spanish and Portuguese were highly stratified. Large extended family households, composed mostly of Europeans and, at times, their mixed offspring, owned and controlled land and other productive resources that were worked by dependent local peasants and slaves. With the abolition of slavery and political independence in the nineteenth century, the sociopolitical foundation of the earlier class-based relationships changed. For the elites to be able to maintain their control over the economy and society of new independent nations, most of which adopted modified versions of the system of political representation based on elections developed in the United States, they needed the votes of the poor and the landless dependents. What developed from Mexico south to Tierra del Fuego, in southeast Asia, and elsewhere were systems in which access to the resources controlled by the elites were given to the poor in exchange for their loyalty and support (including their votes). In return for their patronage, the elites were able to retain control over the machinery of government, and with it, the resources they dominated from the time of the conquest.

The alliance-building potential of godparent-hood and coparenthood were used by dependents to add the moral authority of the church to their personal relations with their patrons. In brief, the poor would ask those on whom they were dependent to sponsor their children, thereby becoming their coparents. While this did not necessarily improve their situation, it did provide them with a greater hope of receiving affirmative responses to specific requests for help. Moreover, the prohibition of sexual relations between ritual kin provided some protection for poor and dependent women who have always been preyed upon by elite males. It was not unusual for elites in Latin America, for example, to have dozens if not hundreds of godchildren and coparents.

Bonds of godparenthood and coparenthood between unequals are commonplace today in the many national societies characterized by social inequality and stratification, especially those that are Latin and Catholic. In contrast with the predictions of modernization theorists, it appears that as these new nations have urbanized and industrialized, relations based on sponsorship have not declined in importance. Opportunities for establishing these valued relationships and the number of them have increased.

Although the subject of godparenthood no longer holds the place it once held in anthropological discourse, the institutional complex derived from church sponsorship that has been syncretized with so many of the diverse pre-Christian traditions of peoples throughout the world continues to be of considerable importance in the lives of many new and developing Third World societies.

SIDNEY M. GREENFIELD

See Also: Patronage; Structuralism and Poststructuralism

FOSTER, GEORGE M. "Godparents and Social Networks in Tzintzuntzan." *Southwestern Journal of Anthropology* 25 (1969): 261-278.

GUDEMAN, STEPHEN. "The Compadrazgo as a Reflection of the Natural and Spiritual Person." *Proceedings of the Royal Anthropological Institute for 1971.* London, 1972.

HART, DONN V. *Compadrinazgo: Ritual Kinship in the Philippines.* De Kalb, Ill.: Northern Illinois University Press, 1977.

LYNCH, JOSEPH H. *Godparents and Kinship in Early Medieval Europe.* Princeton, N.J.: Princeton University Press, 1986.

MINTZ, SIDNEY W., and ERIC R. WOLF. "An Analysis of Ritual Co-Parenthood (Compadrazgo)." *Southwestern Journal of Anthropology* 6 (1950): 341-368.

NUITINI, HUGO G., and BETTY BELL. *Ritual Kinship,* 2 vols. Princeton, N.J.: Princeton University Press, 1980, 1984.

PITT-RIVERS, JULIAN A. "Ritual Kinship in Spain." *Transactions of the New York Academy of Sciences.* Second series 20 (1957-1958): 424-431.

RAVICZ, ROBERT S. "Compadrinazgo." In *Handbook of Middle American Indians,* vol. 6, edited by Robert Wauchope. Austin: University of Texas Press, 1967.

GOSSIP

Gossip is commonly defined as a negatively evaluative and morally laden verbal exchange concerning the conduct of absent third parties that takes place within a bounded group of persons in a private setting. In many societies, gossip is regarded as devoid of value and consequence, or as a reprehensible activity to be avoided or even feared; yet gossip is so pervasive that it is probably a universal phenomenon in one form or another. It is closely related to "scandal," defined as gossip that has become public knowledge, and "rumor," defined as the unconstrained propagation of information about an event of importance to the group.

These general characterizations raise a number of problems. First, they leave open the question of what constitutes a private setting and when a situation can be considered private enough for gossip to take place. Even though the private and its contrasting category, the public, are highly elaborated cultural categories in some societies (e.g., middle-class North America), these notions are generally of a dynamic nature, in that the events that take place in a setting are what define it as private, a situation that leads to circularity for the social-scientific definition of "public" and "private." Second, the issue of when a third party is considered to be absent is more problematic than may be apparent at first glance. For example, interactors can make innuendos and veiled remarks about a person who is within hearing range, and these activities bear close resemblance to gossip. Similarly, conversationalists can make morally damaging statements about their own behavior, and whether this type of activity should be considered gossip is open to question. Third, characterizing gossip as a form of criticism raises the issue of whether any form of talk is ever devoid of moral evaluation, and therefore brings up the question of from which forms of talk gossip should be differentiated. Furthermore, the evaluative character of gossip is often skillfully disguised under the appearance of a straightforward narrative, in which case what constitutes gossip and what does not may require careful analytic scrutiny.

Whether a particular conversation is to be considered an instance of gossip depends in part on the perspective of the participants themselves. Here again, however, analytic difficulties arise. Members of a society may lack a label for the range of activities roughly comparable to what English speakers term "gossip," or may fail to recognize gossip as a significant interactional category. Such is the case for the Zinacantan of southern Mexico, who engage in verbal exchanges that ethnographer John B. Haviland clearly identified as gossip, even though Tzotzil, the language spoken by the Zinacantan community, offers no specific descriptive term for such exchanges (Haviland 1977). In other societies, gossip is defined as an activity in which only certain types of individuals engage. For example, on Nukulaelae Atoll in the Central Pacific, the word that most closely resembles "gossip" is *fatufatu*, literally, "to make up [stories]." This term, however, is most clearly associated with women's interactional activities. When men engage in what an outsider would recognize as gossip, they are said to *sauttala*, "chat"; labeling their chatting as fatufatu would implicitly question their masculinity, even though men's sauttala resembles women's fatufatu in many respects. The characterization of women's communicative activities as reprehensible and unwholesome gossip and of men's as morally neutral talk, a phenomenon observed in numerous societies, enables men to denigrate women's social activities and thus justify gender hegemony.

In short, an airtight and universal definition of what constitutes gossip is probably not possible because the category itself is subject to context-dependent interpretations, and possibly contestation, by members of the same society. Indeed, an adequate definition of gossip must take into account the dynamic and shifting nature of the category. To date, our theoretical and comparative understanding of gossip has been hampered by the lack of detailed ethnographic descriptions of gossip in specific societies. This dearth of documentation results from the fact that gossip is a difficult topic to investigate, for a number of reasons. First, gossip typically takes place in small, intimate groups, from which the ethnographer, as an outsider, is typically excluded. Although it has been claimed that the information ethnographers gather in the field consists mainly of gossip, there are fundamental differences between gossip that is addressed to an ethnographer during an ethnographic interview and gossip among members of the same society. Second, a careful investigation of gossip as a communicative and social practice necessitates a sophisticated understanding of language, norms, and presuppositions, as well as an intimate familiarity with the personal biographies of the persons who are gossiping and are being gossiped

about. For example, gossips on Nukulaelae Atoll often do not even mention the name of the person about whom they are talking, to the extent that autochthonous interlocutors themselves sometimes have difficulties guessing the identity of the target of the gossip (Besnier 1989). Understanding gossip thus presupposes a degree of intimacy with persons and events that is rarely attained by anthropologists; as Haviland (1977) points out, understanding gossip amounts to understanding a culture.

Gossip as a legitimate object of inquiry first came into focus in the work of structural-functionalist Max Gluckman (1963). Gluckman was particularly concerned with the function of gossip in society, arguing that its principal role is to maintain the unity of social groups: gossip provides a way of asserting the boundary between morally acceptable action and deviant behavior, and thus helps to solidify consensus and to control dissent without recourse to direct confrontation. It was Gluckman who first recognized that gossip is an effective political tool. Political anthropologists had traditionally focused on social contexts and events in which political dominance in its various guises is displayed, enacted, and contested; yet probably in all societies of the world, much political action takes place behind the scenes, in highly informal, domestic, or private settings. Gossip is exemplary of such informal forms of political action: focusing on anything from the actions of the most insignificant members of society to the doings of the most prominent, gossip emerges as a powerful tool through which the social and moral order can be manipulated.

Gluckman's interpretation of the functions of gossip has been subjected to intense critical scrutiny, particularly by scholars such as Robert Paine (1967), who maintains that gossip, rather than being a harmony-maintaining mechanism, is a tool that individuals use to foster their own agendas and to undermine the interests of others. This thesis has come to be known as the "transactionalist" stance. The debate between supporters of the structural-functionalist and transactionalist views, of which Sally Engle Merry (1984) provides an excellent summary, dominated the anthropological study of gossip until the mid-1970s, diverting scholarly attention from aspects of gossip that later researchers would show to be of great importance, such as the aesthetic and micro-organizational aspects of gossip as verbal performance and communicative practice. Subsequent work demonstrated that the hypotheses that Gluckman and Paine put forth are not mutually exclusive: gossip can have both cohesion-building and self-serving purposes or consequences. Furthermore, by focusing on the needs of speakers in contrast to the needs of the group, scholars involved in this early controversy ignored an important aspect of gossip—namely, the role of the audience. In certain societies, such as that of Bhatgaon, a Fiji Indian village, speakers and audiences cannot even be easily differentiated because gossip is created jointly by all participants, and the authorship of particular gossip stories is fundamentally blurred (Brenneis 1984). Even in social settings in which speakers are rarely interrupted in the course of storytelling, gossip depends crucially for its effectiveness on the cooperation and active participation of the audience. For example, successful Nukulaelae gossips often pause dramatically at strategic moments in their narratives and wait for an interlocutor to issue an interjection or comment on the scandalous nature of what has been narrated (Besnier 1989). More than any other form of interaction, gossip is jointly created by interactors, a fact that an anthropological investigation of gossip must be able to reflect.

Even though gossip is commonly thought of in many societies as an insignificant activity, it can have dramatic consequences for its victims. Indeed, the potency of gossip as a political tool often derives from the contrast between its social evaluation as trivial talk and the seriousness of its potential repercussions. Thus, the question of the consequences gossip may have for the individuals who are targeted is an important concern in the anthropological study of gossip. A focus on consequences differs from the focus on functions that characterized early investigations in that consequence, unlike function, is not an intrinsic characteristic of gossip; it is, rather, what derives from gossip. Understanding the consequences of gossip thus helps explain how gossip is embedded in a broader social and political context. According to Merry (1984), gossip can have economic consequences, in that it can restrict its target's access to resources, particularly those obtained from cooperative efforts. Gossip may have political consequences: it can help to mobilize support for particular individuals, to level structures of inequality, and to delimit factionalism in disputes. Social consequences of gossip may include ridicule, ostracism, or even death. Finally, gossip sometimes has no consequences; individuals who are already socially marginalized (e.g., the rich, the poor, and the

different) may be immune to gossip and may even turn it to their advantage. Why some forms or instances of gossip are consequential whereas others are not is a question that merits further scrutiny.

A closely related issue is the question of whom gossip benefits or harms. Because gossip is particularly difficult to repress or contain, it frequently emerges as an instrument of protest and resistance in the hands of those with restricted access to more overt forms of political action. It thus can provide a political voice to individuals and groups (e.g., women, younger people, underdogs) that are excluded from more overt political processes. The extent to which the powerless can bring about a change in the status quo through gossip alone is open to question; it depends on the political dynamics of the particular context.

In contrast, gossip can also be used by those in power to control people, as well as material and symbolic resources, and thus to ensure the continuity of preexisting structures of inequality. For example, among the Kwanga of Papua New Guinea, leaders commonly encourage rumors about their ability to perform maleficent sorcery to enhance their own prestige and intimidate potential rivals and dissidents (Brison 1992). In short, who benefits or suffers from gossip is contingent on the sociopolitical makeup of particular groups.

The position of gossip among other forms of social and political action, particularly various forms of conflict and aggression, is a crucial question. Specifically, what alternatives to gossip are available to members of particular societies in dealing with particular situations? Anthropologists to date have been concerned mostly with the escalating consequences of gossip (i.e., with the role of gossip in fomenting conflict, dissent, and hegemony), but gossip can also deflect conflict: people sometimes gossip in order to avoid aggressive confrontations. For example, Goodwin (1990) describes how African American children in a Philadelphia working-class neighborhood tattle on one another about each other's gossip, using complex narrative structures consisting of multiply embedded reported speech constructions. Because these narratives implicate many individuals, they provide a way for the children to engage in forms of aggressive behavior that deflect responsibility and thus avert more serious physical confrontation, while allowing the protagonists to save face. Here again, whether gossip aggravates conflictual situations or soothes strained relations hinges on the dynamics at play in the broader social setting.

The articulation of gossip within the broader sociocultural context in which the gossip takes place is most fruitfully investigated through an approach that takes as its object of inquiry both the microscopic aspects of gossip and the sociocultural context in which the gossip is embedded. Research conducted in this vein recognizes that the meaning of gossip (and, for that matter, of talk in general) cannot be derived by simply analyzing words. The structural and organizational aspects of the interaction, such as turn taking, reported speech constructions, and ways of interweaving evaluative elements with the narrative representation of events all carry great import. The richness of gossip as communicative and social action can be understood only through an investigation of minute aspects of actual samples of naturally occurring gossip, even though these details may appear at first glance familiar and unworthy of analytic scrutiny (Bergmann 1993). The importance of basing analyses of gossip on original-language data, rather than on translations and paraphrases, has also been amply demonstrated.

A significant finding of microscopic approaches is that gossip aside from being a form of political action, frequently constitutes a form of artistic performance for those who partake in it. The contexts in which gossip takes place often provide narrators the opportunity to display their aesthetic creativity for their own enjoyment and that of their audience. Particularly notable analyses of the aesthetic dimensions of gossip include Roger Abrahams's research on gossip in a St. Vincent village in the Caribbean (1970) and Donald Brenneis's research on gossip among rural Fiji Indians (1987). Brenneis, for example, demonstrates that Fiji Indian gossip is characterized by sustained rhythmic structures, repetitions, strategically timed overlaps, and word-play sequences. These features provide a coordinated harmony to the interaction that is both aesthetically pleasing and socially rewarding to members of a society that places much value on the maintenance of an egalitarian ideology. In many societies, gossip is thus the meeting ground for politics and aesthetics, and the dual nature of gossip as aesthetic performance and political action enhances the efficacy of gossip as a form of social action.

At the root of the various questions that anthropologists have addressed on the issue of gossip is the basic recognition that gossip occupies a pivotal position between the sociopolitical structure of the group and the agency of particular members of the group. Thus, gossip can enhance social structure and perpetuate the status quo, but it can also be used by individuals to bring about more or less fundamental and lasting changes. Studying gossip is thus tantamount to investigating the relationship between individual action and the structure of society in which the individual is embedded.

NIKO BESNIER

ABRAHAMS, ROGER D. "A Performance-Centered Approach to Gossip." *Man*, n.s., 5(1970):290-301.

BERGMANN, JÖRG R. *Discreet Indiscretions: The Social Organization of Gossip.* Translated by John Bednarz Jr. Communication and Social Order Series. New York: Aldine de Gruyter, 1993. (Originally published as *Klatsch: Zur Sozialform der diskreten Indiscretion.* Berlin: Walter de Gruyter, 1987.)

BESNIER, NIKO. "Information Withholding as a Manipulative and Collusive Strategy in Nukulaelae Gossip." *Language in Society* 18(1989):315-341.

BRENNEIS, DONALD. "Grog and Gossip in Bhatgaon: Style and Substance in Fiji Indian Conversation." *American Ethnologist* 11(1984):487-506.

————. "Performing Passions: Aesthetics and Politics in an Occasionally Egalitarian Community." *American Ethnologist* 14(1987):236-250.

BRISON, KAREN J. "Just Talk: Gossip, Meetings, and Power in a Papua New Guinea Village." *Studies in Melanesian Anthropology*, 11. Berkeley and Los Angeles: University of California Press, 1992.

GLUCKMAN, MAX. "Gossip and Scandal." *Current Anthropology* 4(1963):307-15.

GOODWIN, MARJORIE HARNESS. *He-Said-She-Said: Talk as Social Organization in a Black Peer Group.* Bloomington: Indiana University Press, 1990.

HAVILAND, JOHN B. *Gossip, Reputation, and Knowledge in Zinacantan.* Chicago: University of Chicago Press, 1977.

MERRY, SALLY ENGLE. "Rethinking Gossip and Scandal." *In Toward a General Theory of Social Control*, edited by Donald J. Black. vol. 1, 271-302. New York: Academic Press, 1984.

PAINE, ROBERT. "What is Gossip About? An Alternative Hypothesis." *Man*, n.s., 2(1967):278-285.

GRIEF AND MOURNING

Grief can be defined as the emotional and cognitive reactions of the individual to loss. Mourning can be defined as the behaviors, including participation in rituals, that a culture defines and often seems to prescribe for people who grieve or who are expected to grieve for a specific loss. The distinction between grief and mourning suggests that what looks like grief may be culturally prescribed behavior that does not accurately represent the person's underlying feelings. The distinction between grief and mourning is fragile, however, because it is often impossible for an observer (or even for a bereaved person) to know when feelings following a loss are expressed in culturally appropriate ways and whether there would be grief feelings independent of the required mourning.

Grief can be understood as a basic human psychological response to loss and as a human expression that differs from culture to culture and is linked to many different aspects of a culture—including religion, social structure, meaning systems, matters of gender, and the economy. When one assumes that humans are biosocial organisms, with an enormous amount in common, it is easy to find evidence in the area of grief and mourning that seems to support that assumption. Some bereaved people in many different cultures cry, self-mutilate, are depressed, express anger, experience changed appetite and sleeping patterns, feel physically ill, and say words that express emotional pain and feelings of loss. Although considerable anthropological research questions the assertion of universals, it is difficult if not impossible to find a culture in which people do not grieve for the death of persons who are important in their lives. This common pattern can be taken to mean that it is basically human to be linked to others. Grieving can be understood both as part of what maintains those links (i.e., people try to prevent grief, grief pulls some people toward others) and as a basically human consequence of those links.

Seemingly in contrast to a biosocial perspective, a major achievement of anthropology has been to escape the assumptions and defined realities of Euro-American cultures, to move toward documenting human diversity and toward understanding people and their cultures in their own terms. From that perspective, it is obvious that there is considerable variation across cultures (and even within many cultures) in what is defined as a loss, in how losses are understood, in

the appropriate ways of responding to loss, in the meanings imparted to losses, and in the expression of grief feelings. With that in mind, one must be skeptical of terms ("grief," "mourning," "loss") that have meaning within a specific culture. To understand reactions to deaths and other losses in a specific culture, it might be best to put aside all concepts from the culture of Euro-American social science and to work toward understanding the concepts, experiences, and emotional expressions of a people as they themselves understand them.

The catalog of what factors prompt grief may also show something like universals across cultures, with death, forced migration, torture, culture loss, and prolonged separation from people important to one being among the circumstances that may be universal in producing grief. It will also show that what triggers grief in some societies does not in others—for example, loss of owned land is not a loss issue where there is no concept of owned land, and soul loss will not be grieved where there is no such concept.

There is growing evidence that grief for major losses goes on for quite a long time, perhaps a lifetime. It does not go on constantly, but comes and goes, being aroused by reminders, among which other losses are prominent. Thus, people who have experienced major losses may recurrently grieve, and in a society in which many have had major losses (for example, where violation of human rights is a common experience, or where there have been many losses as a result of warfare), there may be a pervasive atmosphere of grief. It is also true, however, that cultures vary enormously in how expressive people are in their grief and in what they express. There are cultures in which the expectation and the general practice is that the expression of grief is quite constrained or even looks (to an outsider) as though grief is being denied. There are also cultures in which grief for some losses is expressed intensely for many years.

Grief often seems to make people less available to others and more needy of social support. Mourning rituals sometimes seem to be adapted to such reactions—for example, they may isolate the bereaved from others during a defined mourning period and at the same time see to it that others are charged with being available to support the bereaved in important ways. Isolation of the bereaved, however, may be understood quite differently among the cultures in which it is part of mourning.

Mourning rituals for deaths are diverse, but among the common elements are efforts to define the loss itself, as well as the person who has died and the bereaved, both spiritually and socially. There are typically elements of "passage" that move the lost person from the world of the living to the world of the dead and the bereaved into a mourning state and eventually out of mourning. A death may be defined as a single event or as a series of events, and it may be understood to have occurred even before the cessation of breathing.

In the majority of societies, mourning rituals do not occur at one point in time but are spread out, with a funeral ritual, held months or years after the death, marking a formal end to mourning. The long time span of mourning rituals may be due to the necessity of getting resources together for a ceremony, or a result of the necessity of having a body decay completely before funeral rituals can be completed, or a result of any of a wide number of other factors. Although a long time span for mourning rituals may be a great inconvenience for some of the people who observe it, in some societies it provides an opportunity for bereaved individuals to engage in grief work in a socially and spiritually supported environment. The long time span also provides a period of time for dealing with a loss at many other levels, including the level of roles (determining who, if anybody, will take over roles the deceased had performed), property, and allocation of blame (mourning may often include processes of deciding who caused a death, even a death that might seem by Euro-American standards to be a result of natural causes).

In virtually all societies, there is a belief in something like ghosts. The ghosts that people experience are usually those of people who were closest to them. Thus, in virtually all cultures, death does not end a relationship. It may, however, transform a relationship, perhaps making the deceased more dangerous or more powerful, and usually, in the long run, making the deceased more distant from the world of the living.

Cultures are by no means unitary or unchanging. Indeed, the most challenging and significant aspects of the anthropological study of grief and mourning are the documentation and accounting for social-construction processes, blending cultural ideas and prac-

tices that may not always fit together, and working out conflicting cultural standards, rules, and interpretations in coming to terms with a loss. Grief and mourning involve, among many things, processes of problem solving, negotiation, and conflict resolution.

PAUL C. ROSENBLATT

SEE ALSO: Death and Dying

COUNTS, DAVID R., and DOROTHY A. COUNTS, eds. *Coping with the Final Tragedy.* Amityville, N.Y.: Baywood Publishing Company, 1991.

HERTZ, ROBERT. *Death and the Right Hand.* Translated by Rodney Needham and Claudia Needham. Glencoe, Ill.: Free Press, 1960.

IRISH, DONALD P., KATHLEEN F. LUNDQUIST, and VIVIAN JENKINS NELSEN, eds. *Ethnic Variations in Dying, Death, and Grief: Diversity in Universality.* Washington, D.C.: Taylor & Francis, 1993.

PALGI, PHYLLIS, and HENRY ABRAMOVITCH. "Death: A Cross-Cultural Perspective." *Annual Review of Anthropology,* vol. 13, 385-417, Bernard Siegel, ed. Palo Alto, Calif.: Annual Reviews, 1984.

ROSENBLATT, PAUL C. "Grief: The Social Context of Private Feelings." *Handbook of Bereavement,* Margaret S. Stroebe, Wolfgang Stroebe, and Robert O. Hansson, eds. New York: Cambridge University Press, 1993.

ROSENBLATT, PAUL C., R. PATRICIA WALSH, and DOUGLAS A. JACKSON. *Grief and Mourning in Cross-Cultural Perspective.* New Haven: Human Relations Area Files Press (HRAF), 1976.

WELLENKAMP, JANE C. "Notions of Grief and Catharsis among the Toraja." *American Ethnologist* 15(1988):486-500.

WIKAN, UNNI. "Bereavement and Loss in Two Muslim Communities: Egypt and Bali Compared." *Social Science and Medicine* 27(1988):451-460.

WIKAN, UNNI. *Managing Turbulent Hearts.* Chicago: University of Chicago Press, 1990.

GROUP SELECTION

The problem of the levels of natural selection has a long history among scientists interested in evolutionary biology. It concerns whether the well-adapted properties of organisms evolve because they benefit themselves or their groups. Because natural selection is the main direction-giving and adaptation-producing factor in evolution, this concern over the mechanism of selection addresses the foundation of evolutionary thinking and has important implications for human behavior, mind, and culture.

DARWIN'S CONTRIBUTION

Although Charles Darwin thought that most natural selection occurs at the level of individual organisms, he allowed for group selection as well. Aware that altruistic and self-sacrificial behavior pervades the insect world, Darwin wrote that such behavior was "a special difficulty which at first appeared to me insuperable, and actually fatal to the whole theory." To account for these phenomena, he expanded his theory of evolution by natural selection to include selection between individuals, kin groups, or populations.

For example, consider why deer run fast rather than slowly and compare this with why bees leave their stinger in their victim. Deer who ran faster were better able to escape predators than deer who ran more slowly, and thus were more successful in surviving and reproducing. In this case, the individual organism is the unit of selection. The individual, by definition, is a unit of selection in the evolution of a trait when the trait evolved because it conferred a benefit on the individual possessing it. Bees who sting intruders to the nest leave their barbed stinger in the intruder at the price of disemboweling themselves and dying. The barb did not evolve because it helped the bee who had the barb; it evolved because it aided the protection of the hive. In this case, the group is the unit of selection. The group, by definition, is a unit of selection in the evolution of a trait when the trait evolved because it conferred a benefit on that group.

When traits evolve because of their individual- and group-level effects, the trait's design is a product of the relative effects of individual and group selection. In the 1870s Darwin explained the evolution of moral virtue using both individual and group selection. Bravery is selected against within tribes because brave individuals are more likely to be killed in battle. Bravery is selected for between tribes because tribes with brave members have an advantage in battle. The nature of bravery reflects the balance of opposing selective forces.

Darwin succeeded in converting nineteenth-century biologists to evolutionism but not to belief in the efficacy of natural selection, and so group selection was not an issue for them. Mendelian genetics was reconciled with Darwinian ecology during the evo-lutionary synthesis of the 1930s, but the synthesis was incomplete. Population genetics theory, the mathematical heart of the synthesis, focused on selection for organismic benefits. Ecological studies proposed adaptive benefits for an individual's group, population, community, ecosystem, or even the world.

SELECTION BETWEEN BREEDING GROUPS

Vero C. Wynne-Edwards (1962) called attention to this tension between evolutionary theory, which gave individual selection exclusivity, and ecology, which invoked either group or individual selection as a matter of preference. He proposed that "good-of-the-group" explanations must be backed up by an appeal to evolutionary mechanism in order to be legitimate. Arguing that group selection is a major force controlling population size, he interpreted daily chorusing of birds as a way of censusing population density to avoid overpopulation. Birds acting on those cues voluntarily restrict their breeding in high-density situations, because groups that did not do so went extinct more often than those that did.

The form of this explanation applies Darwin's theory to groups, as attested to by the following set of assumptions and inferences. Assumption 1: All species are capable of overproducing offspring. Assumption 2: The size of populations of individuals tends to remain relatively stable over time. Assumption 3: Resources for supporting groups are limited. Inference 1: A struggle for existence among groups ensues. Assumption 4: Groups differ in their ability to go extinct. Assumption 5: Some variation between groups in this ability is heritable. Inference 2: Differential contribution of offspring to the next generation by groups of different proportions of genotypes (group selection) occurs. Inference 3: Through many generations, traits more and more adaptive for the group in their local environments evolve.

In response, George C. Williams (1966) criticized all well-known group selection explanations. His "weak force" argument is that selection between groups occurs far more slowly than selection between individuals, and thus, group selection is a weak evolutionary force, almost always producing adaptations for the genetic survival of individuals rather than groups. His "parsimony" argument is that virtually all cases of purported group selection can be understood at the level of the individual, and so Ockham's razor (the principle that entities are not to be multiplied beyond necessity) counsels that there is no need to invoke group selection in such cases. For example, Wynne-Edwards (1962) interpreted the fact that some birds lay fewer eggs than physiologically possible as a reproductive restraint favoring the group. David Lack's (1940) empirical work showed that egg mortality increases with clutch size, and that the actual number of eggs laid maximizes the individual bird's total reproduction. What appeared to be group selection was explained more parsimoniously as individual selection.

The early 1960s also witnessed William D. Hamilton's (1964) mathematical "inclusive fitness" models, which provided a way to expand individual selection to include kinship effects and thus additional resources to explain cases of altruism that reduce personal reproduction. Inclusive fitness takes into account not only the effect of an allele on its bearer but also on the bearer's relatives. Altruism among unrelated individuals could be explained as favored via individual selection maximizing personal fitness, and altruism among related individuals could be explained via individual selection maximizing inclusive fitness.

Together, Williams's ecological critique and Hamilton's mathematical genetic models gave "good-of-the-group" explanations a near fatal blow. Ever since then, group selectionism has been viewed with suspicion, likened to Lamarckism as an obsolete viewpoint, and ridiculed derisively. A new group selection school emerged in the 1970s, owing to the construction of a new class of genetic models having ecologically valid applications. The wider community of scholars remains largely unaware that the new models were designed to escape criticisms.

SELECTION BETWEEN TRAIT GROUPS

The difference between Wynne-Edwards's "old group selection" and David S. Wilson's (1980) "new group selection" is easily visualized. On the old model, imagine three distinct breeding populations, each containing a mixture of altruistic and selfish individuals. Population 3, containing the highest proportion of selfish individuals who destroy their resources by overbreeding, goes extinct. The area vacated by population 3 is recolonized by dispersers from population 2. Here, we have selection between breeding populations, known as "demes," that results in the increase of the frequency of altruists in each deme.

On the new model, imagine a metapopulation divided into trait groups—populations within which every individual feels the effect of every other individual. Trait groups need not be spatially or temporally isolated. Trait groups may or may not be demes. Group selection need not be restricted to extinction of entire trait groups. Imagine three trait groups, such as mosquitoes hatching in three different pools of water, each with a different mixture of altruistic and selfish individuals. After reproduction in trait groups, there is a mixing phase in which each trait group sends dispersers into the breeding population as a whole. Suppose trait group 3 has the highest frequency of altruists, which enables it to send more dispersers than the other trait groups. Even though individual selection against altruism decreases the frequency within each trait group, in many conditions the frequency of altruists within the metapopulation as a whole increases by selection between trait groups. Wilson and Elliott Sober (1994) argue that trait group selection is implicit in the logic of individual selection.

It had been assumed that game theory and kin selection must be understood in terms of individual selection. In reply, the two theories can be redescribed in trait group selection terms: an n-person game is a game among groups of size n and kin selection is selection operating between family groups. An obvious objection is that heritability applies to individuals and not to groups. In rebuttal, since two-person game theory is mathematically identical to a diploid single-locus model, with individuals in groups instead of genes in individuals, the associated concepts of average effects, breeding values, parent-offspring correlations, and narrow-sense heritability can be shifted upward to the group level.

Another objection is that genes are replicators and individuals are their vehicles (interactors), but groups are not like individuals. Group selectionists reply that groups are vehicles (interactors) in the sense required for selection to apply to them and that the evolution of group-level adaptation and organization can turn groups into organisms (superorganisms). Genic selectionists view groups as nothing but environments of genes. In response, just as the fact that individuals are environments of genes does not prevent individuals from being units of selection, the fact that groups are environments of genes does not prevent groups from being units of selection.

A common charge is that there is no empirical evidence for group selection. Group selectionists regard female-biased sex ratios as a case in which the relative intensity of individual selection within trait groups and group selection between trait groups can be measured. Deviation from a 50-50 sex ratio toward a female-biased sex ratio shows that group selection is measurable.

Model-theoretic studies have shown that the genic selection, individual selection, and group selection are mathematically equivalent ways of looking at adaptations. Group selectionists reply that although the evolutionary effects of selection can be represented at the levels of genes or individuals or groups, the causes differ. Answers to questions about causes (e.g., why a sex ratio is female-biased) are either right or wrong. Individual selectionists have rebuttals (e.g., female-biased sex ratios are due to individual selection and mate choice).

Lee A. Dugatkin and Hudson K. Reeve (1994) have noticed that by "individual selection" trait group selectionists mean selection between individuals within their trait group, whereas individual selectionists mean selection between individuals within the whole deme. Trait group selectionists have partitioned the individual selectionist's concept of individual selection into two components, only one of which is called individual selection. The issue dissolves or becomes: what counts as group selection?

HUMAN APPLICATIONS

The group selection controversy contains implications for the issue between (methodological) individualists and holists. Can social groups be fruitfully treated as adaptive units whose organization is irreducible to individual interactions? Biologists answer that group-level adaptations can evolve only by a process of natural selection at the group level. Controversy centers on just how effective group selection has been in designing adaptations.

Because individual selection is known to effectively produce adaptations, we are justified in studying human eyes on the assumption that they adapt organisms for survival and reproduction. Because species selection and ecosystem selection are not known to effectively produce adaptations, we are not justified (without special argument) in studying spider-fighting behavior on the assumption that it evolved to ensure the survival of the species or in studying earthworm-feeding behavior on the assumption that it evolved to aid the efficacy of the ecosystem. Holistic accounts of group-level functional organization in humans go against the grain of the dominant mode of theorizing about human and nonhuman organisms and are thus held to higher standards in justifying their assumptions to gain plausibility.

In the 1960s such neofunctionalist ecological anthropologists as Marvin Harris, Andre P. Vayda, and Roy Rappaport explained a variety of human social behaviors and social institutions in terms of their functions for the group. To evolutionists, such holistic explanations fall prey to the "naive group selectionism" of ecology prior to Wynne-Edwards.

For human behaviors to be legitimately interpreted as group-benefiting adaptations, the following desiderata must be met: there must be heritable variation in fitness among groups; the account must specify an evolutionary mechanism and the mechanism must clearly differentiate whether selection is between trait groups, demes, species, ecosystems, and so on; the evolutionary mechanism must be theoretically possible according to population genetics models; the mechanism must be competent to have produced the adaptation once all the relevant costs, benefits, genetic relations, and constraints are considered; the adaptation must exhibit not a fortuitous effect that benefits the group but design for group benefit; there must be evidence that the evolution of group-beneficial design is not subverted by counteracting individual selection against it; and additional evidence must support design in the environment of evolutionary adaptedness of the species relevant to the trait.

Evolutionary psychologists regard the human mind as adapted to Pleistocene, not present, environments. Past group selection bears on whether humans by nature are selfish or altruistic, or both. Have our species-typical psychological propensities been designed to serve the fitness interests of ourselves or of our groups or of both? Individual selectionists hold that our psychological propensities are designed mainly or exclusively by individual selection. Group selectionists take it to be an open empirical question of what may be the relative effects of the two selection processes on our psychology.

A key component of group-beneficial design in humans involves psychological altruism. An objection against old group-selection accounts—that group selection can effectively counteract individual selection only in rare conditions—fails to see that some conditions permitting effective group selection are common in humans. Within-group competition can be suppressed by religious norms, by morality, and by custom. Examples of such group-level functional organizations may be found in military units, corporations, and some traditional societies, such as the egalitarian Mae Enga in Highland New Guinea.

European Hutterites supply an extreme example, in which their ideology and social organization punish selfish cheaters more severely the worse the offense is to the group. It is now objected that there is nothing altruistic about going along with a system that gives one a higher probability of reproductive success than one could get outside the system. Trait group models view Hutterites as altruistic because they achieve their success by benefiting a collective of which they are members. Whereas this objection compares fitness differences of someone choosing to be in or out of a group (a comparison of the group with n versus $n + 1$ members), trait-group models compare fitness differences of individuals within each trait group and between trait groups. The relation between psychological (motive-related) and evolutionary (fitness-related) conceptions of altruism and selfishness remains an unsolved problem.

Trait group selection is controversial but is gaining ground in the 1990s and should no longer be rejected out of hand. Instead, the best chance of progress on the issues may be to use both individual and group selection to examine the way population structure affects evolution.

HARMON R. HOLCOMB III

SEE ALSO: Adaptation; Altruism

ALEXANDER, RICHARD D. *Darwinism and Human Affairs.* Seattle: University of Washington Press, 1979.

BRANDON, ROBERT, and RICHARD BURIAN, eds. *Genes, Organisms, and Populations.* Cambridge, Mass.: Massachusetts Institute of Technology, 1984.

DAWKINS, R. *The Selfish Gene.* Oxford: Oxford University Press, 1976.

HAMILTON, WILLIAM D. "The Genetical Evolution of Social Behavior" *Journal of Theoretical Biology* 7(1964):1-52.

DUGATKIN, LEE A. and HUDSON K. REEVE. "Behavioral Ecology and Levels-of-Selection: Dissolving the Group Selection Controversy." *Advances in the Study of Behavior* 23(1994):101-133.

LACK, DAVID. "Pair Formation in Birds." *Condor* 42(1940):269-286.

SOBER, ELLIOTT. *The Nature of Selection: Evolutionary Theory in Philosophical Focus.* Cambridge, Mass.: Bradford/Massachusetts Institute of Technology Press, 1984.

WILLIAMS, GEORGE C. *Adaptation and Natural Selection.* Princeton: Princeton University Press, 1966.
——— . *Natural Selection: Domains, Levels, and Challenges.* Oxford: Oxford University Press, 1992.

WILSON, DAVID S. *The Natural Selection of Populations and Communities.* Menlo Park, Calif.: Benjamin Cummings, 1980.

WILSON, DAVID S., and ELLIOTT SOBER. "Re-Introducing Group Selection to the Human Sciences." *Behavioral and Brain Sciences* 17(1994):585-654.

WYNNE-EDWARDS, VERO C. *Animal Dispersion in Relation to Social Behavior.* New York: Hafner Publishing, 1962.

H

HEALTH

See: Food and Diet; Medical Anthropology; Pluralistic Medical Systems; Psychological Anthropology; Rural Health Care

HERMENEUTICS

The term "hermeneutics" has been used since at least the time of the Christian church father and philosopher Augustine of Hippo (354–430 A. D.) to refer to the scholastic exegesis of sacred texts. Modern hermeneutics is a German interpretive tradition emphasizing the combination of detailed empirical investigation and subsequent subjective understanding of human phenomena. It is understood by its practitioners—including literary critics, art historians, historians of religion, sociologists, and theologians as well as anthropologists—as an alternative to textual literalism, positivism, and materialism. It played a major role in the critique of nineteenth-century theories of cultural evolution and contributed to the development of ethnography as the detailed investigation of cultural systems. In the past twenty years it has shaped the development of interpretive and critical anthropologies.

ORIGINS

Modern hermeneutics dates to the late eighteenth-century German theologian and philosopher Friedrich Ernst Schleiermacher, who devised hermeneutics to salvage Christianity from the intellectual insolvency of Protestant biblical literalism. It originated as a mode of textual exegesis focusing on a subjective understanding rather than literal reading of scripture. He articulated two ways of knowing or encountering textual materials—a grammatical mode, which examines the literal meaning of a text, and a subjective psychological feeling *(fühl)* of its ultimate significance. For Schleiermacher, the purpose of grammatical under-standing is to resolve the ambiguities inherent in texts and to explore the semantics of the words and phrases of which they consist. Psychological understanding allows the interpreter to appreciate the transcultural, transhistorical, and transcendental essence of the narrative. Schleiermacher's hermeneutics is theological, and its ultimate purpose is to ascertain the ways in which God is manifest in the world and in human experience. Although theological hermeneutics remains central to contemporary Christian thought, it has had little direct influence on anthropology.

Anthropological hermeneutics has been more directly influenced by the works of mid-nineteenth-century German philosopher Wilhelm Dilthey and early twentieth-century German sociologist Max Weber. Dilthey's philosophy of the human sciences can be understood as a secularized version of Schleiermacher's theology. Dilthey proposed a clear distinction between the human and natural sciences, arguing that because the human sciences involve the study of minds by minds, objective observation of the inner life of the mind is impossible. Minds are the subject as well as the object of the human sciences. Dilthey justified this distinction and called for the unity of the human sciences by referring to the depth and fullness of human self-consciousness, the sovereignty of will, and the human capacity for subordinating the external world to thought. Put in more contemporary terms, Dilthey's point is that because human systems are self-created and self-regulating they are not subject to the same types of laws as those of the natural environment. He proposes an inter-subjective *Verstehen* (understanding) rather than causal explanation as the final goal of interpretation in the human sciences.

The critical difference between Dilthey and Schleiermacher is that for Schleiermacher, like German philosopher Georg Hegel, works of art, literature, and human action unfold from a manifestation of the divine planted in the mind at birth. For Dilthey the mind and self-knowledge are constructed from the totality of lived experience, which is in turned applied to the interpretation of the external world. He argues that humans understand the natural and social environments through worldviews *(Weltanschauung)* that are in turn based on abstraction from lived experiences. The study and understanding of relationships between world views and lived experience are therefore among the most important components of the human sciences.

For Dilthey, as for Weber, understanding is an attempt to reconstruct the mental worlds of other individuals and to discover the subjective concepts motivating action in the world. Dilthey's prose is exceedingly dense and includes numerous phrases such as "a rediscovery of the I in Thou." Herbert Hodges (1952) characterizes Dilthey's understanding as follows: "By virtue of my grasp of the other person's experience as a self-differentiating unitary process, I become able to let the whole course of it unroll itself in my consciousness in the order that it actually took place, and so not merely understand, but even share or relive, the life of another person." There is an almost mystical quality to this notion of understanding. Realization of an immanent self is Dilthey's equivalent of Schleiermacher's realization of the divine. Dilthey was not, however, as prone to mystical flights of the soul as Hodges's passage might suggest. He was as opposed to idealism as he was to strict empiricism. It is critical to observe that for Dilthey the process of understanding was the capstone and not the basis of the historical and social sciences. He clearly recognized that it is a goal that, in most instances, cannot be fully attained. Dilthey was aware that understanding must be based on rendering the historical narrative, and even that of a theatrical performance, in an abstract, condensed form. The investigation of these condensed forms, which Weber terms "ideal types," are the means through which understanding of human thought and action is obtained.

Whereas Dilthey was concerned primarily with European philosophical traditions and the origins of science, Weber used the hermeneutic method in the analysis of sociological and historical materials. He was particularly concerned with relationships between culture, social change, and economic action. Weber is best known for his studies of Calvinism and its role in the development of modern capitalism, and of

ancient Judaism, India, and China. Weber's hermeneutics differs from that of Dilthey in that Weber argued that although understanding is essential even for the description of sociological and historical materials, their analysis also requires causal explanation.

THE PROBLEM OF UNDERSTANDING

Hermeneutics presumes careful attention to philological and ethnographic detail, or what Schleiermacher called "grammatical knowledge." There is less unanimity concerning the ultimate aim of the interpretive process. Theological hermeneutics attempts to locate transcendental, transhistorical meanings of texts and symbols and to convey these meanings in terms that can be understood by historically and culturally located individuals. For Dilthey, the goal of understanding was to reconstruct the mental world of the author. More recently, Paul Ricouer (1979) has argued that for understanding the importance of texts in any particular context, it is necessary to abandon the notion of authorial intent and focus instead on the way a text is used and interpreted. For Clifford Geertz (1973) the goal of hermeneutics is to arrive at an understanding of the complex interrelations of the symbolic forms employed in social discourse by moving back and forth between ethnographic detail and high-level generalization. In his later works, Victor Turner (1982) drew directly on Dilthey's hermeneutics in an attempt to explore the unconscious purposes of ritual and other modes of expressive culture.

Differential understandings of the hermeneutic endeavor and differential emphasis on the subject and object of interpretation have led to a distinction between interpretive anthropology, which seeks to understand cultural phenomena from what Geertz calls "the native point of view," and critical anthropology, which reflects on the nature of the ethnographic encounter to develop critical understandings of Western and other cultures.

HERMENEUTICS AND
THE RISE OF U.S. ANTHROPOLOGY

Hermeneutics played a significant role in the development of anthropology in the United States in the late nineteenth and early twentieth centuries. Franz Boas, who is considered by many one of the founders of anthropology as an academic discipline in the United States, was greatly influenced by German neo-Kantian philosophy and particularly by Dilthey's conception of the human sciences. Boas emphasized the descriptive arch of the hermeneutic circle. His emphasis on what Geertz would subsequently term "thick description" played a major role in the development of participant observation as the central method of cultural anthropology. It contributed equally to the demise of the speculative evolutionary, diffusionist, and racist theories characteristic of nineteenth-century anthropology.

Critics of Boas have pointed to the fact that his historical particularism excludes the possibility of the scientific explanation or comparative study of cultures. This view is strongly articulated by Marvin Harris (1968) and contributed to the emergence of British structural functionalism and French structuralism as dominant paradigms. The basic question at issue in the debate between Boas and other proponents of hermeneutic anthropology, and others, who understand the discipline as a search for explanatory theories, is the intellectual location of the discipline. Hermeneutic anthropologists would locate it in the humanities, or what Dilthey terms the "human sciences." Their opponents speak from diverse perspectives but agree that a scientific method employing concepts of causality and working with empirically testable hypotheses can be employed in the study of human culture and social organization.

The debate between humanistic and scientific anthropologies is metatheoretical and enduring. Because proponents of these positions operate within different paradigms, it is unlikely that either can prevail. Even during the period during which positivist theories were in ascendancy—roughly from the 1930s to the 1960s—humanistically oriented anthropologists, among them E. E. Evans-Pritchard, continued to employ hermeneutic perspectives in creative and insightful ways. The differences between the two approaches can be understood either as a dichotomy in which scholars seek to establish a single paradigm as hegemonic or, more productively, as a creative tension fostering clearer understanding of cultural differences and regularities.

HERMENEUTICS IN CONTEMPORARY ANTHROPOLOGY

The revival of the hermeneutic tradition in cultural anthropology can be attributed largely to Geertz. Taken as a whole, his work can be understood as an attempt to employ Weber's sociological hermeneutic in the analysis of ethnographic materials. Like Weber, Geertz is concerned with how cultural concepts motivate social and economic action. Geertz's method involves the detailed study of symbol systems, especially those of personhood, in an attempt to come to an understanding of the means through which people understand and act in social, religious, and economic contexts. Also like Weber, Geertz focuses on how religious ideas and symbols influence the historical development of social institutions. He moves beyond Weber in his analysis of the ways in which world religions are interpreted in varying cultural contexts. Geertz's use of hermeneutics is explicitly comparative and empirical. Unlike Dilthey, he maintains that it is not possible to reconstruct the mental worlds and experiences of others but only to come to an understanding of the symbols and concepts they employ in the construction and interpretation of reality.

Turner's use of hermeneutics more closely resembles that of Dilthey. Turner did not employ the hermeneutic method until late in his career but came to understand it as a means through which the meanings of cultural performances such as ritual, social drama, and theater and the emotional, as opposed to cognitive, content of what Dilthey termed "lived experience" can be understood. Unlike Geertz, Turner emphasizes the intersubjective character of the ethnographic encounter. For Turner, ethnography was not simply an attempt to understand a cultural other. He came to see it as intersubjective communication of meaning through cultural performance and as an alternative to the deliberate misunderstanding of the other in a highly politicized and dangerous world.

Turner's moral tone is an example of the ways in which hermeneutics has contributed to the development of critical anthropology. Whereas the tradition of critical anthropology can be traced to Boas and his students, contemporary critical anthropologists have focused more closely on the epistemological foundations of ethnography and the ways in which the lived experience of the ethnographer shapes the ways in which data are collected and ethnographic texts are constructed. Recognition of the inherent subjectivity of the ethnographic enterprise has led to a self-conscious subjectivism in which Marxist, feminist, and other critical theories are employed to highlight the oppressive hegemonic discourse these scholars find to be characteristic of Western and other cultures. As George Marcus and Michael M. J. Fischer (1986) observe, the polemical nature of critical anthropology is highly controversial. Activist scholars understand it as the liberation of anthropology from the shackles of a Euro-U.S. hegemonic discourse. Those who consider anthropology to be a science rather than an interpretive enterprise consider the value-laden character of critical anthropology a symptom of intellectual chaos or, alternatively, as simply another form of hegemonic essentialism that masks the voices and concerns of indigenous peoples.

MARK R. WOODWARD

COMBS-SCHILLING, ELIZABETH. *Sacred Performances: Islam, Sexuality, and Sacrifice.* New York: Columbia University Press, 1989.

EVANS-PRITCHARD, E. E. *Nuer Religion.* Oxford: Clarendon Press, 1956.

GEERTZ, CLIFFORD. *The Interpretation of Cultures.* New York: Basic Books, 1973.

HARRIS, MARVIN. *The Rise of Anthropological Theory.* New York: Thomas Y. Crowell, 1968.

HODGES, HERBERT. *The Philosophy of Wilhelm Dilthey.* 1952. Reprint. Westport, Conn.: Greenwood, 1974.

MARCUS, GEORGE, and MICHAEL M. J. FISCHER. *Anthropology as Cultural Critique: An Experimental Moment in the Human Sciences.* Chicago: University of Chicago Press, 1986.

RABINOW, PAUL, and WILLIAM SULLIVAN, eds. *Interpretive Social Science: A Reader.* Berkeley: University of California Press, 1979.

RICOUER, PAUL. "The Model of the Text: Meaningful Action Considered as Text." *In Interpretive Social Science: A Reader.* Rabinow, Paul and William Sullivan, eds. Berkeley: University of California Press, 1979.

TAUSSIG, MICHAEL. *The Devil and Commodity Fetishism in South America.* Chapel Hill: University of North Carolina Press, 1980.

TURNER, VICTOR. *From Ritual to Theatre: The Human Seriousness of Play.* New York: Performing Arts Journal Publications, 1982.

WEBER, MAX. *The Protestant Ethic and the Spirit of Capitalism.* N.Y.: Charles Scribner's Sons, 1958.

WELCH, CHARLES. *Protestant Thought in the Nineteenth Century,* vol. 1. New Haven, Conn.: Yale University Press, 1972.

HISTORICAL ECOLOGY

In the context of global ecology, historical ecology explores complex chains of mutual causation in human-environment relations and draws on concepts from the natural sciences—biology, geology, climatology—and from ecology, archaeology, history, and sociocultural anthropology. To frame effective environmental policies for the future, the past and present human use of the earth must be understood, which necessitates deft integration of both environmental and cultural information at a variety of temporal and spatial scales. Historical ecology employs an explicitly cultural perspective; its practice stands in contrast to econometric characterizations, which offer no cultural or historical context for assessing the impacts on and the effects of human activities.

It is just these contexts, however, that shape human interaction with the environment, if only indirectly, through a cognized nature. Thus, perceptions, attitudes, and behaviors must be considered within the broad frames of intercultural relations and transgenerational communication, or loss, of values and institutions. Cultural understandings undergird decisions about which practices are maintained or modified and which ideas are given substance; landscapes, the spatial manifestation of the relation between humans and the evironment, retain the physical evidence of these understandings. In landscapes, both intentional and unintentional acts are recorded, and through them the role of humans in the modification of the global ecosystem can be assessed.

Beginning with the International Geophysical Year in 1958, there has been dramatic improvement in the quality and quantity of data that document change in the global ecosystem; this has enabled researchers to ask new questions about how humans affect and are affected by their environment. Contemporary studies of human-environment relations, in contrast to those of the early twentieth century, do not assume a deterministic role for the environment; instead, it is assumed that humans can both instigate and respond to fluctuations in resources or climate. Studies by anthropologists and historians question earlier deterministic, mechanistic, and dualistic characterizations; they call for an integrated framework that would admit spatially and temporally specific natural and social-scientific information and would also include evidence of changing values, perceptions, and awareness.

Construction of such an integrated framework has proven to be a difficult task. One issue has been the incompatibility of human activity with planetary-scale atmospheric phenomena. Patterns of settlement and land use, emissions, and extractive procedures must be investigated at both regional and local levels. On the other hand, collective response to global-scale changes (e.g., climate) must be verified through analysis of parallel changes events in widely dispersed regions. An increased scientific understanding of the interconnectedness of the atmosphere, hydrosphere, biosphere, and geosphere in the global system has provided a reasonable background of cause-and-effect linkages and cyclicity, but wide-ranging social-science theories and methods are needed to monitor and evaluate human activity at all temporal and spatial scales. Without environmental and cultural information at local and regional levels, there is no opportunity to test and refine global models; without planetary-scale confirmation of the long-term effects of human activity, arguments over values (embedded, among other things, in environmental policy) will continue without generating any action. Inaction is potentially lethal to our species.

A theoretical rapprochement between science and the humanities is critical. Geography and history, classic arbiters of space and time in the human sciences, have, drawing on the French historical tradition of the *Annales,* joined forces to introduce a multiscalar, humanistic, dialectical approach. Especially useful is the concept of different processes operating among temporal scales of varying duration. These broad divisions are termed *événement* (event), *conjoncture* (cultural and historical context), and *longue durée* (long-term history). Broad temporal frameworks, such as those that characterize an *Annales* approach, also guide the historical sciences. Interpretation, both in history and the sciences, relies on all three—events, whether they are described in a cleric's account of famine or in stratigraphic evidence of flood, must be set in both immediate and far-ranging contexts. Geographic information systems (GIS) integrate data at a variety of levels and support both qualitative and quantitative analysis, so that "what if" scenarios with different cultural parameters can be examined.

In the past twenty years, American researchers have reinterpreted and refined the central *Annales* concept of landscape to include both human and nonhuman agency, offering a means by which the social and natural sciences may be combined in the analysis of regional biocultural change. This advance offers the practical support for integration across the natural and social sciences and humanities. Landscape, defined as the spatial manifestation of the relations between humans and their environment, offers a common unit of analysis that admits all varieties of evidence and for which changes can be traced through time.

Historically informed environmental analysis provides an important opportunity for anthropologists, archaeologists, historians, and geographers to demonstrate the relevance of the work in which they have been engaged for a century. Such a multidisciplinary approach is traditional for archaeologists, who employ both natural and physical sciences (biology, geology, physics, chemistry) and the humanities (history, classics, philosophy, linguistics) and who routinely consult science and humanities colleagues or have training themselves in these disciplines. Most important, archaeology offers the temporal and spatial breadth required for long-term ecological analysis. Environmental historians critically examine documents for evidence of human actions, relations, and attitudes. Historical evidence about past ecosystems may be divided into written (diaries, government documents), oral (stories about storms or pest invasions), and visual (dated drawings of Alpine glaciers documenting advances and retreats). Such information provides important cross-checks among environmental, social, and instrumental data. Based on observations and understandings, ethnographers study the customs that guide adaptive strategies. The memories and opinions that living peoples have about their regions are a rich and relatively untapped resource. Such information is transferred—whether in complex ritual behavior or in casual conversation—between and across generations; in addition to patterns of material relations with the environment, cognitive patterns are also transmitted.

Established natural-scientific approaches document environmental changes, and an integrated social-science approach can document changes in human activity through time. The computer-assisted manipulation of GIS both supports visual display and enables researchers to engage in quantitative and qualitative analyses, including the interactive cause-and-effect scenarios that occur when key parameters change, at levels from global to local. A lively critical tradition guides the integration of these broad scholarly endeavors, informs studies of changing cognition, and maintains ethical principles. This array of conceptual and practical tools permits the systematic investigation of inclusive ecosystemic change at global, regional, and local levels. Inasmuch as the meanings that are attributed to the past and to nature give periods and cultures their character, the record of changing human-environment relations can be read in the empirical record of changes in landscapes (broadly defined) and cultural traditions.

Advances in the 1990s have refined the practice of historical ecology, Don Stephen Rice (1976) attributes the first use of the term to ecologist Edward S. Deevey, who directed the Historical Ecology Project at the University of Florida in the early 1970s. The historian J. Donald Hughes uses the term "environmental history" (1975) but joins anthropologists, a human ecologist, an economist, and other historians in contributing to *Historical Ecology*, a journal edited by fellow historian Lester J. Bilsky (1980). Anthropologist Alice E. Ingerson organized a session on historical ecology at the 1984 annual meeting of the American Anthropological Association to address the chasm between cultural (e.g., nature as metaphor) and environmental (energy-cycles) studies in anthropology and to explore political-economy and social-history approaches. Whereas environmental history has a distinguished and somewhat parallel development among historians, the more inclusive term "historical ecology" facilitates intra- and interdisciplinary collaboration in the study of changing human-environment relations. The role of anthropology and its subdisciplines, especially sociocultural anthropology and archaeology, is to cement those connections.

CAROLE L. CRUMLEY

BILSKY, LESTER J. *Historical Ecology: Essays on Environment and Social Change.* Port Washington, N.Y.: Kennikat Press, 1980.

BLOCH, MARC. *The Historian's Craft,* translated by Peter Putnam. New York: Knopf, 1953.

BRAUDEL, FERNAND. *The Mediterranean and the Mediterranean World in the Age of Philip II.* New York: Harper & Row, 1972.

BURKE, PETER. *The French Historical Revolution: The Annales School, 1929–1989.* Stanford: Stanford University Press, 1990.

CRONON, WILLIAM. *Changes in the Land: Indians, Colonists, and the Ecology of New England.* New York: Hill & Wang, 1983.

CROSBY, ALFRED W. *Ecological Imperialism: The Biological Expansion of Europe 900–1900.* New York: Cambridge University Press, 1986.

CRUMLEY, CAROLE L., ed. *Historical Ecology: Cultural Knowledge and Changing Landscapes.* Santa Fe, N.Mex.: School of American Research Press, 1994.

CRUMLEY, CAROLE L., and WILLIAM H. MARQUARDT, eds. *Regional Dynamics: Burgundian Landscapes in Historical Perspective.* San Diego: Academic Press, 1987.

HUGHES, J. DONALD. *Ecology in Ancient Civilizations.* Albuquerque: University of New Mexico Press, 1975.

INGERSON, ALICE E. "Tracking and Testing the Nature/Culture Dichotomy in Practice." In *Historical Ecology: Cultural Knowledge and Changing Landscapes,* edited by Carole L. Crumley. Santa Fe, N.Mex.: School of American Research Press, 1994.

LEROY LADURIE, EMMANUEL. *Times of Feast, Times of Famine: A History of Climate Since the Year 1000.* New York: Doubleday, 1971.

RICE, DON STEPHEN. "The Historical Ecology of Lakes Yaxha and Sacnab, El Petén, Guatemala," Ph.D. diss. Pennsylvania State University, 1976.

WORSTER, DONALD. *Nature's Economy: A History of Ecological Ideas.* New York: Cambridge University Press, 1977.

HISTORICAL LINGUISTICS

Diversification processes covering thousands of years of human history have resulted in approximately 6,000 different languages spoken worldwide. As innovations occur in a language spoken by numerous speakers over a wide geographic area, these new practices seldom diffuse to the entire speech community. Since each region tends to innovate in different ways, new speech customs accumulate in each area until distinctly different dialects appear. As this process continues, dialects become so different that their speakers are no longer able to understand each other without special training. By this point, these divergent dialects have become separate languages, albeit highly similar ones.

The regional varieties of English spoken in Great Britain differ from those spoken in the U.S. Since speakers of English have been residing in Great Britain and have been differentiating from each other for more than 1,000 years, dialects of British-English differ greatly from each other. Although the U.S. is vastly larger in territory, fewer differences have accumulated within American speech due to a shorter period of occupation and diversification. Similarly, fewer differences have developed between regional varieties spoken in the recently settled western U.S., as compared to those spoken in the longer-occupied east.

In time, British and American English may become so different that speakers of each may no longer be able to understand each other. When the Angles, Saxons, and Jutes invaded and occupied England about 1,500 years ago, they spoke language varieties which were mutually intelligible with those spoken by ancestors of contemporary Dutch and German speakers. Although English is still very similar to Dutch and German, mutual understanding no longer exists between these two groups and they are continuing to differentiate. The very strong tendency of languages to diverge over time into regional dialects and then into separate languages tends to produce families of genetically related languages that share descent from a common ancestor. These divergence processes are the dominant form of language change and shared common ancestry is the major form of historical relatedness between languages.

BORROWING

Another type of language change is borrowing, or convergence, which increases similarity between languages. Borrowing is most common in the lexicon, less common in phonology and syntax, and least common in morphology. The more closely two languages are related genetically, the more similar they will tend to be. This similarity can lead to high rates of bilingualism, which in turn will tend to promote borrowing. In short, similarity due to borrowing tends to be strong where similarity due to close genetic relationship is also strong, assuming that the languages are contiguous and can borrow readily from each other. Indeed, languages that are closely related genetically do tend to be contiguously located since they typically develop through dialect differentiation processes.

Although borrowing is an important force in language change, these convergence tendencies are almost always weaker than concomitant diversification tendencies. There are, however, occasional exceptions to this general principle. For instance, ancient Greek

languages had developed very different regional dialects prior to Alexander the Great. During this time and after, Greeks who spoke these divergent dialects communicated with each other frequently due to extensive movement and mixing of their local populations. As a consequence, the differences in Greek were leveled out and a uniform variety, the Koine, arose. Leveling processes were such that the idiosyncratic features of individual dialects were dropped in favor of more widespread features. Borrowing of widely shared features was so extensive that dialect divergence disappeared and Greek became homogeneous again.

Another instance of dialect leveling may have occurred when speakers of the divergent dialects of England came to America and settled near each other and began communicating regularly. Following this leveling process, divergence would have begun anew based on the geographic dispersion of American English speakers in their new land. As speakers of the newly divergent varieties of American English in the east moved west, convergence processes would have been operative again due to mixing of populations, contributing along with shallow time depth of occupation to the relative lack of differentiation in the language varieties spoken in the large central and western zones of the U.S.

Although languages are historically related primarily through shared common ancestry, they also show evidence of historical contact through borrowing. Languages that are closely related genetically tend to be contiguous and to borrow heavily from each other. Thus, similarity due to close genetic relationship tends to be strong where similarity due to borrowing is also especially strong. Language divergence processes in the past have almost always been stronger than convergence processes, thus the overwhelming tendency of language change has been diversification, which has produced the thousands of languages spoken today.

LANGUAGE DIVERGENCE

The length of time two languages have been diversifying can be estimated by noting that the similarity between them continually decreases. Differences will accumulate in the phonological, grammatical, and lexical components of the two languages. For the lexicon, a "basic" vocabulary of 100 words has been identified that is likely to be lexically encoded in all languages and is unlikely or less likely to be borrowed.

Included are terms for body parts, such as hand, foot, head, eye, nose, and mouth; for natural phenomena, such as tree, fish, water, sun, and moon; and so forth.

Languages with long histories of written records have been examined to determine the average rate at which names for these common semantic categories are replaced. This rate is 14 percent per 1,000 years. Nonbasic vocabulary is replaced at a somewhat faster rate. If a language is spoken in two regions and these speech communities change independently (i.e., if there is no borrowing between them), they will share approximately 74 percent of their basic vocabulary after 1,000 years, 55 percent after 2,000 years, 40 percent after 3,000 years, and so forth. When the rate of vocabulary sharing drops below about 5 percent (roughly 10,000 years time depth), lexical sharing due to genetic relationship becomes very difficult to assess. So many sound changes have occurred in each of the two languages that it becomes difficult to judge whether words have descended from a common ancestral word, and thus are cognate, or whether they merely show chance phonological similarities.

The basic vocabularies of languages unrelated genetically and too distantly located to have borrowed from each other, such as Russian and Navajo or English and Vietnamese, have been examined to determine the rate of similarity in basic vocabulary that will be produced by chance factors alone. This rate ranges from about 1 to 3 percent. Thus, lexical similarity due to genetic relationship between languages is little greater than the lexical similarity that would be expected by chance alone after about 10,000 years of diversification.

DISTANT GENETIC RELATIONSHIP

The grammatical component of languages, however, may still be similar enough after 10,000 years of divergence to determine that a genetic relationship exists. Although a few instances of extensive and highly detailed grammatical borrowing are known, such cases are exceedingly rare and occur only in highly unusual sociolinguistic situations. Thus, extensive and detailed similarities between grammatical systems and subsystems are almost always indicative of genetic relationship even when lexical similarity is no greater than chance.

For example, the Tlingit language spoken in coastal regions of southern Alaska and northwestern Canada shares an overwhelmingly similar and very distinctive morphological system with the Athapascan-Eyak languages spoken in parts of Alaska, Canada, and the western U.S. However, except for a few recent loanwords almost no lexical similarities exist between these two languages. Another example involves the Catawba-Woccon languages spoken in the eastern United States and the Siouan languages spoken widely in eastern, midwestern, and plains states. The grammatical similarities between these two are substantial and very distinctive, yet there is almost no lexical sharing.

AREAL LINGUISTICS

Languages without lexical sharing sometimes display striking and very detailed phonological similarities. This is true for the Tlingit and Athapascan-Eyak languages. Unfortunately, phonological features, even very distinctive ones, are more readily borrowed between genetically unrelated languages than are highly distinctive grammatical structures. Although Tlingit and the Athapascan-Eyak languages share numerous distinctive phonological features, so do all the other language groups located in the northwest coast region of North America. The distinctive phonological features characteristic of this "linguistic area" are more likely due to diffusion than to distant genetic relationship.

Another example of widespread sharing of distinctive phonological features involves languages spoken in southern and central Africa. These languages have "click" consonants that are not found in any other language in the world. At least six groups of languages share this feature but do not display lexical similarities strongly indicative of genetic relationship. There are three San (Bushman) language families (Southern, Central, and Northern San); a Khoi (Hottentot) language family; and two language isolates, Sandawe and Hadza. Language isolates are single languages that have been differentiating from their genetic relatives for well over 10,000 years; thus their phylogeny is not easily recoverable.

Lexical borrowing has occurred between these languages but is largely superficial. An exception involves Central San languages, which have borrowed very heavily from Khoi languages. One language, Nharo, has borrowed at least one third of its total lexicon, including basic vocabulary. This language often has lexical doublets, an indigenous term for a semantic category and a borrowed Khoi term. Other Central San languages show lexical borrowing from

Khoi languages but at lower rates. The Nharo rate of borrowing is extraordinary, especially for basic vocabulary. However, a similar instance of massive lexical borrowing, including basic vocabulary, has occurred between two of the aboriginal languages of Australia. These two instances of astoundingly high borrowing of basic vocabulary (more than 30 percent) should caution scholars when they are assessing distant genetic relationship based on lexical evidence alone.

The San families contain languages which have the largest phonemic inventories of any languages in the world. !Kung, a Northern San language, has an inventory of about 120 phonemes and Southern San inventories are equally large. The Central San languages have inventories smaller than Northern and Southern San but very large from a worldwide perspective. Sandawe, Hadza, and the Khoi languages have phonemic inventories only slightly larger than average. The largest phonological inventories known from outside this area range from 60 to 80 phonemes. The average cross-language inventory is approximately 30 phonemes.

Most San languages have a series of glottalized stop consonants. !Kung, however, has two contrasting series of glottalized stop consonants, a phonological feature that seems to be unique. Even a single series of glottalized stop consonants is infrequent in Old World languages, occurring in fewer than 3 percent of them. However, glottalized stops are common in New World languages, occurring in about 15 percent of South American languages and in about 40 percent of those in North America; thus, glottalized stop consonants are an areal feature of New World languages. Another unusual phonological feature possessed by San languages are pharyngealized vowels. These vowels have a worldwide distribution but are very infrequent in languages, occurring in fewer than 2 percent of them.

In short, these six groups of languages share click consonants. In addition, the San languages have very large phonemic inventories, extraordinarily so for Northern and Southern San. The San languages also display several other distinctive phonological features. Whether these phonological similarities are due to genetic relationship or to borrowing is unclear. Click consonants have been borrowed, but not extensively, by several Southern Bantu languages. In addition, a Cushitic language spoken in northeast Africa has a small vocabulary component which displays click consonants, indicating that these lexical items have been borrowed from a non-Cushitic language. In short, these languages comprise a "linguistic area" in terms of sharing click consonants, and these consonants have been borrowed by several Bantu languages and a Cushitic language. In addition, the San languages, at least, share several additional distinctive phonological characteristics.

There has been a tendency in historical linguistics to expect languages worldwide to be assignable to large language families. However, huge genetic language groups seem the exception rather than the rule for the languages of the world. That much of the world is populated by language isolates and very small language families is not a problem that needs to be fixed by lumping them into unjustified large groupings. Instead, it suggests that languages have been diversifying for a very long time, for several tens of thousands of years at least.

LANGUAGE RECONSTRUCTION

The traditional comparative method in historical linguistics is the primary tool for demonstrating the detailed genetic relatedness of a group of contemporary languages and for recovering their common ancestor. Comparison of the daughter languages reveals sound correspondences and these, in turn, allow reconstruction of the sound system, lexicon, and ultimately the grammar of the parent language. The reconstructed lexicon can be very helpful in elucidating the cultural history of speakers of the protolanguage. If a full panoply of terms for domesticated plant and animal species and for associated products and tasks is recovered, it is reasonable to infer that speakers of the protolanguage practiced agriculture and animal husbandry. In contrast, if such terms do not reconstruct, then speakers of the protolanguage were probably hunter-gatherers.

Once the protolanguage is recovered, the changes that took place in the developmental history of each daughter language can be traced. The types of changes observed can give information valuable to formulation of general principles of language change. Linguistic constraints on types of change and on processes of change could then be compared with general principles of cultural change to determine if there are common principles and mechanisms.

THE REGULARITY PRINCIPLE

The comparative method in historical linguistics is based on the principle of the "regularity" of sound change, which is a powerful empirical generalization that allows recovery of language history to a time depth of about 10,000 years. This principle states that if a particular phoneme in a language changes in one word (e.g., if /p/ changes to /f/), the same change will occur in all other words in which this phoneme occurs. Sometimes the sound change has a conditioning environment (e.g., /p/ may change to /f/ only when it occurs in initial position of a word). In another genetically related language, /p/ in initial position might change instead to /b/. When these two languages are compared, /b/ and /f/ will regularly correspond in initial word position, while in other positions /p/ will regularly equal /p/. The exact sound correspondences that obtain between these two languages will contribute greatly to demonstrating their genetic relatedness. These correspondences will also help in separating relatively recent loanwords from cognate lexical items, since recent loans will tend to violate the sound correspondences.

The regularity principle holds for a sound change that is complete or finished, but it does not describe an ongoing sound shift. While a change is in progress, individual speakers will gradually change /p/ to /f/ in initial position. In this way, sound changes diffuse through the mental lexicon of individual speakers. These changes follow an ogival or S-shaped pattern characteristic of a typical learning curve, indicating that sound changes are learned behavior. In the slow early period of change for an individual speaker, only a few /p/'s in word initial position change to /f/'s, then a rapid middle period occurs in which most of the remaining words with /p/ in initial position change, followed by a final period in which the few remaining words with initial /p/ gradually replace their /p/'s with /f/'s. There is a tendency for frequently used words to change before those which are less frequently used.

In addition to diffusion through the mental lexicon of an individual speaker, sound changes diffuse from speaker to speaker within a speech community, and from speech community to speech community within a language. A sound change may have diffused through the vocabularies of all speakers in one speech community, while in a more distant community speaking the same language it has not yet begun. In an intervening community, some speakers may have changed completely, while others have not yet started to change, with the remaining speakers occupying positions of partial change. Sometimes sound changes

occur relatively rapidly, sometimes they take hundreds of years to accomplish.

Sound changes also tend to expand from one phonological environment to another until the change becomes a general or unconditioned one, occurring in all environments. For example, in Chorti, a Mayan language spoken in Guatemala and Honduras, /l/ is changing to /r/. This language has a basic morpheme shape of C_1VC_2 (C = any Chorti consonant, V = any Chorti vowel). The change started in C_2 position and has spread to almost all /l/'s in this position (i.e., most /l/'s in this position have changed to /r/). In addition, this change has recently spread to C_1 position and a few morphemes show /r/ instead of /l/ in this position. Indeed, the language name Chorti shows the sound change, as the former neighboring and closely related Cholti language did not undergo this shift.

RATES OF CHANGE

Language change is usually relatively slow. Although records of the sign languages of the deaf are not extensive, slow change seems to be the usual condition for these languages, too. Rates of change, however, vary between languages and may fluctuate within a language over long time periods. In addition, rates can vary independently for the major components of language. For example, phonological change can be relatively rapid while grammar and lexicon are changing very slowly. For instance, Siouan languages, although closely related grammatically and lexically, show immense phonological variation, much more than would be expected given their very close genetic relationship. Alternatively, the Mixe-Zoque languages spoken in southern Mexico are lexically more diverse than the Siouan languages are, yet they show very little phonological diversity.

Language change is based on innovation by individuals and on the subsequent spread of these new practices to other speakers who either accept or reject them. Individual speakers can innovate deliberately or nondeliberately. Nondeliberate innovation is basically divergence from speech norms due to slips of the tongue or other speech errors, drunken speech, child language, and so forth. Although this sort of unintentional innovation is huge, the vast majority of it is rejected by the speech community. Even if attractive accidental innovations are few, however, this source of novelty is so great that it almost certainly exercises an effect. A language with numerous speakers is subject to many more "happy accidents" than those with few speakers. However, acceptance of an innovation is more difficult when speakers are many than when they are few. Therefore, rates of change tend to be roughly equivalent between languages with many speakers and those with few speakers.

LANGUAGE VARIATION

Successful innovation always establishes a new variant practice (i.e., a new pronunciation, grammatical construction, lexical name, or semantic categorization) in a language. Over time this new practice either ousts the old variant or itself is lost. For "slang" lexical innovations, the new speech variant is usually lost. Variation within a speech community, then, is often evidence of a change in progress since change always begins as language variation. Several factors have been identified that may favor or disfavor the acceptance of new variant practices. Prestige considerations are one such factor. However, prestige comes in two varieties: overt prestige associated with high social status or with features associated with such status and covert prestige associated with medium or even low social status. Both sorts of prestige seem operative, but in very complex ways, in favoring or disfavoring innovations.

Phonological variation has been investigated more thoroughly than grammatical or lexical variation due to the relative ease of data collection. One theory of phonological change proposes that elite speakers innovate phonologically and that over time nonelite speakers adopt these innovations due to the high prestige associated with them. In this way ordinary speakers try to narrow the differences between themselves and prestige speakers, forcing elite speakers to keep innovating to maintain their distinctiveness in speech. Such a process would serve to drive language change and would fit the empirical observation that change is constant in language.

Sociolinguistic research, however, has not been kind to this theory. Innumerable studies show that the phonological innovations that gain currency in a language seldom arise in elite speech, but instead in nonelite speech. Elite speakers resist adopting these innovations partly due to conservatism and partly as a means of marking themselves off as a distinct group with a special form of speech. Thus, elite speakers tend strongly to resist innovations which bubble up from popular vernacular speech. The overwhelming ten-

dency of elite speakers to condemn language change as a falling away from an ideal, pure language state may trace to the fact that these changes typically originate in nonelite speech. Sometimes elite speakers are successful in stemming the tide of language change and sometimes they are not.

MARKEDNESS THEORY

Markedness is another factor that strongly influences language change. This theory applies to all components of language: phonology, grammar, and lexicon. Markedness is based on linguistic relatedness and linguistic salience. For instance, the lexical items "typical/atypical" are linguistically related, as are "probable/improbable" and "happy/unhappy." For these examples, the first member is unmarked, while the second is "overtly" marked by a negative prefix. Related items typically differ in relative salience, such that unmarked items are high in salience while marked items are low. Several linguistic features correlate strongly with relative salience. For instance, the unmarked member of a pair tends to be simpler than the marked one. For the lexical pairs above, the unmarked member lacks the overt mark (i.e., the negative prefix), thus is simpler than the marked member. There is a strong tendency for linguistic relatedness and relative salience to be shared across languages. (i.e., linguistic elements related within individual languages are almost always similarly related in other languages). In addition, the relative salience of related linguistic elements tends to be similar across languages. Thus, markedness phenomena comprise a powerful set of intralanguage and cross-language regularities.

Several features characterize the relative salience of linguistic elements related through markedness. They follow:

1. As already mentioned, the unmarked member of a pair is generally simpler (i.e., shorter, fewer articulatory movements) than the marked member. The marked member is sometimes overtly marked.

2. The unmarked member of a pair generally has a higher frequency of use within a language as compared to the marked member.

3. The unmarked member is generally acquired earlier than the marked member by a child who is learning language.

4. If the contrast between the unmarked and the marked member is linguistically neutralized, the unmarked member will generally appear in this context. For example, in a neutral question context one usually asks how "typical" something is, not how "atypical" it is.

5. The unmarked and marked members of a pair are related such that both may be present in a language or both may be absent, but if only one is present it is always the unmarked. Thus, the unmarked member is more frequent in occurrence across languages, since if only one of the two is present, it is always the unmarked member. In addition, there are several implications for language change. For example, if both members of a pair are present and one is lost, it is always the marked member that is lost. Similarly, if both are absent and one is added, it is always the unmarked member. Finally, there is an overall tendency in language change for marked language features to become less marked or even to be lost entirely. Given this powerful tendency we might expect languages to become maximally unmarked and ultimately to stop changing. This never happens, however, because each language is a complex interlocking set of systems and subsystems and a change in one area typically causes an unintended change in another area.

In French, for example, nasal consonants in final word position were lost but the vowel preceding the nasal consonant was nasalized. Thus, all lexical items with final nasals were shortened (i.e., became simpler or less marked) as compared to those without a final nasal consonant. But the phonological system of French became more complex due to the addition of a set of nasalized vowel phonemes to the language. These new vowel phonemes are less frequent in occurrence in words, and thus in their frequency of use. As a consequence they are marked, as compared to their oral vowel (or nonnasalized) counterparts. Several of these nasalized vowel phonemes have since been lost due to merger. These vowel mergers, in turn, have produced many homonyms, (i.e., names or labels with two or more unrelated meanings). Homonyms, in turn, are more complex, and thus marked, in language as compared to nonhomonyms. Consequently, these homonyms are starting to be lost. In short, a whole cascade of changes has occurred over about a 1,000-year period in French, such that a simplification in one area has produced a corresponding complication in another area. This, in turn, has tended to trigger another round of changes and a relatively continuous state of language change has resulted. In this way, changes in one part of language tend to spill over into other areas, producing new marked features which in their turn often lead to further changes.

CONCLUSION

Constant change is the normal condition of language and this change is usually differentiation rather than convergence. Thus, languages are historically related primarily through shared common ancestry rather than borrowing. Except for a few language isolates, the thousands of languages spoken in the world today belong to language families. Most of these families are relatively small, suggesting that languages have been diversifying for a very long time. Reconstruction of the common ancestor of a group of genetically related languages can provide knowledge of the past way of life of speakers of the protolanguage. Study of language change can also provide evidence that can favor or disfavor a proposed linguistic theory or explanatory framework and, thus, can contribute to general knowledge of the human capacity for language.

STANLEY R. WITKOWSKI

BATISTELLA, EDWIN L. *Markedness: The Evaluative Superstructure of Language.* Albany, N.Y.: State University of New York Press, 1990.

BYBEE, JOAN, REVERE PERKINS, and WILLIAM PAGLIUCA. *The Evolution of Grammar.* Chicago: University of Chicago Press, 1994.

CHAMBERS, J. K., and PETER TRUDGILL. *Dialectology.* London: Cambridge University Press, 1980.

CROFT, WILLIAM. *Typology and Universals.* New York: Cambridge University Press, 1991.

CROFT, WILLIAM, KEITH DENNING, and SUZANNE KEMMER, eds. *Studies in Typology and Diachrony.* Philadelphia: John Benjamins, 1990.

EMENEAU, MURRAY B. *Language and Linguistic Area: Collected Essays.* Stanford, Calif.: Stanford University Press, 1980.

GREENBERG, JOSEPH, CHARLES A. FERGUSON, and EDITH A. MORAVCSIK. eds. *Universals of Human Language.* Stanford, Calif.: Stanford University Press, 1978.

HAAS, MARY R. *Language, Culture, and History.*

Stanford, Calif.: Stanford University Press, 1978.

LABOV, WILLIAM. *Sociolinguistic Patterns.* Philadelphia: University of Pennsylvania Press, 1973.

———. *Principles of Linguistic Change: Internal Factors.* Cambridge, Mass.: Blackwell, 1994.

MADDIESON, IAN. *Patterns of Sounds.* London: Cambridge University Press, 1984.

MILROY, JAMES. *Linguistic Variation and Change.* Cambridge, Mass.: Blackwell, 1991.

SHERZER, JOEL. *An Areal-Typological Study of American Indian Languages North of Mexico.* North-Holland Linguistic Series 20. Amsterdam: North-Holland, 1976.

THOMASON, SARAH G., and TERRENCE KAUFMAN. *Language Contact, Creolization, and Genetic Linguistics.* Los Angeles: University of California Press, 1988.

WANG, WILLIAM, ed. *The Lexicon in Phonological Change.* The Hague: Mouton, 1977.

HISTORY OF ANTHROPOLOGY

The history of anthropology, as with any discipline, discloses a continuous search for identity. Realization of this identity involves six core elements: 1) exponents of a discipline have a strong sense that they are investigating a subject matter to which no others have a claim; 2) the subject matter has an order or quality that requires causal explanations not commonly used by other disciplines; 3) factual materials that describe the order and explain the subject matter are distinctive; 4) special attitudes, training, methods, and conceptual vocabularies are essential to the collection, classification, analysis, and generalization of factual materials; 5) associations, conventions, and publications develop to allow professionals to share subject matter, clarify changes in objectives, and introduce new methods; and 6) members of a discipline gain respect as collectors and dispensers of knowledge within centers of research and of public education. The history of anthropology discloses shifting perceptions and accomplishment along each of these major axes.

Anthropology got its start when cumulative effects of intellectual, economic, social, political, and philosophical developments initiated during the Renaissance converged during the eighteenth century to produce the simultaneous rise of the natural and social sciences in Europe. The appearance of the natural and social sciences at this moment revealed the dynamic relationship linking them to the intellectual, social, and cultural developments of the eighteenth century and forecast that their continuities and futures would reflect European trends.

The image of an exact science has pervaded the development of anthropology along with a strong humanistic orientation. Critical changes in theoretical orientations, aims, and methods reveal correspondence with the shifting perceptions of physical scientists with regard to the structured character of the "reality" studied and their capabilities to predict events in an absolute or probabalistic key.

The description and analysis of prehistoric and historic cultures of preindustrial peoples has been a primary objective of anthropologists as they sought to portray the human experience. The expansion of European settlements provided the opportunity for the description of world cultures. The research dialogue has not been wholly one-sided as anthropologists through their philosophy of cultural relativism have defended the validity of native cultures and challenged prejudicial misunderstandings often manifest in public attitudes. Applied anthropologists also have contributed positive influences to the administration of "native affairs."

In their study of man and his works anthropologists in large part have depended on the theoretical orientations and methods developed in other disciplines that could be accommodated to their purposes. Anthropologists have made their major contributions to research methods with the participant-observer method and fieldwork techniques.

Anthropology early became a loose federation of four "fields," physical or biological anthropology, linguistics, prehistory, and ethnology or cultural anthropology. From its beginnings in the eighteenth century, the history of anthropology can be ordered in three stages: 1) developmentalism (ca. 1725 to 1890); 2) structuralism (ca. 1890 to 1950); and 3) differentiative specialization (ca. 1950 to present).

DEVELOPMENTALISM (CA. 1725–1890)

The idea that human experience and destiny consisted of a civilizing process that led to the moral and intellectual perfection of human beings and of society dominated the social thought of Europeans during the eighteenth and nineteenth centuries. A humanistic philosophy of human progress prevailed during the initial phase (ca. 1725 to 1840) while an evolutionary philosophy of biological conflict, adaptation, and survival or extinction prevailed during the second phase (ca. 1840 to 1890), with anthropology emerging as a distinct discipline around 1860 to 1870.

Progress and the Science of Mankind

Historians of progress in the eighteenth century were convinced that they were on the threshold of a revolution in human knowledge which, if applied according to natural law, would enable mankind to take charge of their destinies. They set out confidently to describe the gradual refinement of mankind's intellectual, artistic, and language achievements from their simplest forms to their most "polished" expressions. The task was achievable because common psychological capabilities drew the varieties of mankind into a single species, despite physical differences, and made progress inevitable and attainable for all. The reports of navigators, explorers, traders, clerics, and settlers provided descriptions of the beliefs and customs of peoples throughout the world, which, by logical classification, would reveal the unilinear path all peoples would follow to civilization.

The "human faculty" lifted man above the brutal realities of animal life and committed him to a destiny that could only be realized in the company of other men. Society therefore provided the superorganic environment for cultivation of the human faculty, and reason in turn made possible the inevitable march to civilization by adding progressive improvements to the social experience. In the continuing march into the future, Europeans would lead, for Europe was leaving behind the outmoded monarchial agrarian system and was forging ahead to a new industrial economy and civil society where knowledge, law, equality, individual liberty and opportunity, and democratic government would reign.

The history progressivists intended to write would be a scientific history, certified by laws operating in nature; and would not deal with the "accidental" in human life as ordinary historians. "Natural history" would bring purposive achievement to the human drama in place of the wars, assassinations, crimes, and follies Edward Gibbon described in his monumental review of Rome's decline. Men in a savage state would no longer represent the degenerate endproducts of scriptural history but the ancestral beginnings of those who had attained a civilized state. Instilled with a desire for property, these original collectors and hunters would compete for wealth, and in the process diversify their intellectual and craft skills to meet the demands of new needs and wants. They would establish new functional interrelations and this would increase the institutional complexity of their societies and lead to establishment of a political state. Property not only was the key to the march from savagery to barbarism, and civilization, but also of rule of law and the guaranty of individuality and of individual rights. Human needs and wants supplied the energy and direction of change, but a balanced resource base and a temperate climate, as the Greeks observed, energized people with moderate stimuli and gave them an edge over peoples challenged by extremes of cold and heat.

By the 1830s "natural historians" had established a solid base for a social science discipline with the progressive development of mankind as its subject matter. Their histories of law, religion and other institutions introduced a new social and cultural fact. They invented the "comparative method" by classifying ideas, customs, and institutions on a scale from simplicity to complexity and converting the classification into an evolutionary history. They also joined theologians, philosophers, literary figures, and artists with a claim to act as primary interpreters of the ultimate meaning of life. Humanistic in orientation but scientific in self-image, historians of progress introduced the identity ambivalence that has followed anthropology throughout its career; that is, whether anthropology is a science aligned with the physical sciences in method, or is a humanistic study (*Geisteswissenschaft*) in alliance with history, sociology, political science, and economics.

Progressivists like W. Robertson and A. Ferguson built the new social science largely on Newton's laws governing the universe and Locke's views on the refinement of ideas from sensory perceptions. They paid no attention to the implications of Linnaeus's assignment of man and ape to the order Anthropomorpha or to racial classifications. Forces were at work, however, that focused on human evolution, racial history, and the correspondences of physical types with differences in language, intellect, moral qualities, and cultural achievement. J. Herder observed that the bonding of "folk" and land shaped national character. Nationalism inspired the formation of academies dedicated to Germanic, Celtic, and British prehistory and by 1837, as in the Danish National Museum, national achievements were sequenced in the Stone, Bronze, and Iron Ages. Lamarck in 1809 raised the possibility that family lines and nationalities could be improved by the inheritance of acquired characteristics.

Evolutionary Developmentalism

Ethnological societies formed in Paris (1839), London (1841), and New York (1842) signaled a determination to put man back in nature and to investigate the biological background of human behavior and achievement. During the 1830s paleontologists and geologists were not ready to support the idea that plants, animals, and men could change their original forms through the action of natural forces; but by 1858 they were prepared to accept organic evolution as proposed by Wallace and Darwin because their experiences pointed to the same conclusion. The association of extinct animals with stone tools in England (Brixham Cave), hand axes found by Boucher de Perthes in Somme River glacial gravels, and the Neanderthal skeleton unearthed in a cave in Germany in 1856 all suggested that more primitive types ancestral to modern humans were yet to be found. Geologist Charles Lyell's use of life forms to construct a relative chronology of strata to sequence the Cenozoic Era also implied organic changes.

Charles Darwin's detailed research described in *The Origin of Species by Natural Selection* (1859) opened the floodgates to acceptance of the theory of evolution and intensified the search for man's ancestors and the study of native peoples as representatives of prehistoric life and thought. A dynamic developmental perspective once again catalyzed efforts to found a science of mankind with new societies formed to investigate the early history of mankind. In selecting this subject matter, members of the new societies in Paris (1859), London (1863), Berlin (1869), Vienna (1870), London (1871), Stockholm (1873), and Washington (1879) formally launched anthropology as a separate discipline. They realized that anthropology must be a federation of scientists drawn from geology, zoology, anatomy, physiology, paleontology, prehistory, psychology, and philology; but it would be the most noble of sciences because it dealt with mankind as a whole. The first international congress of anthropology met in Switzerland in 1866, and when, in 1869, Adolph Bastian, ethnologist, and Rudolf Virchow, pathologist and anthropometrist, teamed to found the Berlin society, they designated it the Society for Anthropology, Ethnology, and Prehistory. The American Anthropological Society was formed in 1902. It was declared as a federation of physical anthropology, prehistory, cultural anthropology, and linguistics.

The evolutional phase of Developmentalism occurred when Euro-Americans were completing a rapid industrialization, nationalities were struggling to fulfill political and state aspirations, and the great powers were carrying out final imperialistic expansions. In applying natural selection to society, J. A. Gobineau merged the fate of individuals with the adaptive survival of their races as cultural creators and leaders, H. S. Chamberlain with racial-national populations, and K. Marx and R. Engels with social classes. A. Retzius in 1842 provided the procedure for categorizing races metrically by head shape (dolichocephals, mesocephals, brachycephals) and spurred the development of anthropometry and attempts to correlate Europeans with the largest cranial capacity and civilization.

Before Darwin, Spencer projected a biological-psychological evolution based on Lamarck's acquired characteristics and the transformation of energy into organic-physical, mental, and social power vital to nature's competitions and "survival of the fittest." "Savages" were destined for extinction because they lacked adaptive capabilities for civilized life. Natural forces were inexorable and amoral, and the weaker and less adaptive always succumbed to the stronger. Spencer also made use of the second law of thermodynamics to construct a dynamic model of evolutionary change regulated by the input of energy and its gradual loss. Social systems achieved a high degree of functional equilibrium, but the gradual dissipation of energy led to disorganization and disintegration. Individual instances of advance and retrogression were possible, but in the general advance to civilization, differentiation and convergence ensured an ever-increasing sophistication and complexity of ideas and institutions.

As with progressivists, evolutionists considered mental development the central civilizing process and conceptualized the stages of savagery, barbarism, and civilization as gradients of rational thought. When in 1871 E. B. Tylor claimed "culture or civilization" as the proper subject matter for anthropology, he defined ethnography's task as the discovery of the uniform operations of the mind by which mankind had advanced from savagery to civilization. Culture included customs, ideas, morality, laws, habits, skills—whatever one acquired as a member of society. Tylor expected the mythology, religious beliefs, and customs of primitive culture to reveal the psychological foundations of "survivals" found in the behavior of civilized men, especially peasants. Survivals were not only customs but emotional residues of disturbing social experiences of the distant past that now were a part of the unconscious psychological inheritance of races or of human beings generally, according to E. Crawley.

The adaptive forces of natural selection that would release the human mind from the unconscious processes holding primitive men captive in his social and cultural state were twofold and equally positive. The bitter competition not only eliminated the physically unfit but also eradicated maladaptive ideas and customs (social Darwinism). But natural selection also instilled the emotional foundations for the development of social practices that preserved a population from the decay of inbreeding and made certain that the original human family was monogamous (E. Westermarck). Brothers and sisters and fathers and mothers in their daily intimate contacts experienced a sense of sexual aversion that inhibited incest and generated exogamic rules. The progressive adaptations of natural selection in conjunction with Lamarck's acquired characteristics led evolutionist develop-mentalists to conclude, as did the progressivists, that man must transcend his biological limitations and that society provides the superorganic environment for attainment. Individuals might acquire social instincts, but it was society that aroused the moral consciousness.

Origins

Tylor's cultural anthropology appeared in England while a potpourri of classicists, historians, and lawyers were exploring the origins, descent, and forms of social groups. Their interest in status and jural rights and the relation between community and individual rights sustained a sociological tradition set by A. Comte and H. Spencer. In J. F. McLennan's view individuals would be inclined to gather around women, and in time formed a maternal descent group by tracing origins to a female ancestor represented by an animal or plant. United by a blood feud obligation and reverence for a totemic ancestor, the totemic clan constituted the first cult group. Food scarcities induced female infanticide with a consequent disproportion of males to females, and clan men were forced to capture brides from another group; and in time exogamic marriage became a moral obligation. Fatherhood emerged from polyandrous households not unlike that of Tibetans as a putative father gave gifts to establish his rights to a child of his own.

Henry Maine countered McLennan's matrilineal theory with a patrilineal group of agnates united under a patriarch as the original social unit. As in ancient India the patriarch acted as trustee for the agnatic corporation, whose members reconsecrated their consanguine relations and common rights in ritual sacrifices. Personal freedom and rights arose only as individuals obtained ownership of land and the communal group gradually broke down, especially as land was redistributed and feudalized following conquest. Law began with custom, and law as a codification of divine dictates followed.

The view that the "natural" bonding of mother and child produced the first families and social groups provoked interest in how the "artifical" bonding of males came to dominate the social order and produce the state. Lewis H. Morgan held that property in land, flocks, and herds transformed the ancient female society into a patriarchal monogamous system similar to the Hebrew and Roman. Historian Bachofen dramatized the change as a victory of male energy and reason over passive and emotional female principles that organized an ancient matriarchy associated with the earth and female deities. Heinrich Schurtz argued that male interest groups based on age and sex were more adaptive to a variety of associations, including the state, than the maternal family and clan.

Morgan viewed the family as the product of unconscious moral reform stretching from promiscuous group marriage to monogamy. His attempt to demonstrate the evolutionary course of moral reform by correlating the grouping of individuals in different kinship terminologies with increasingly restrictive marriage rules laid the foundations for a correlation of terminologies with different kin-based units and social practices.

Developmentalists generally sought the origins of religion in primal experiences from which the "savage mind" could derive an awareness of an inner double. In Tylor's view, reflections on death gave rise to the idea of a soul, and dreams then revealed the image of a ghost soul, which "primitive philosophers" projected into the outerworld as a spirit. An animistic belief suffused all religions from ancient spiritism to polytheistic nature gods and monotheism. Spencer also relied on dreams to induce the idea of a second self, and a natural fear of awe-inspiring personalities to contribute the emotional foundations for propitiation of the dead and their worship as deities. In J. G. Frazer's view, primitive men arrogantly attempted to coerce threatening natural forces with magical spells before subordinating themselves to a superior intelligence or spirit. R. R. Marett stressed the awsome feelings aroused by the mysterious appearance of supernatural power, such as found in the Melanesian concept of mana. Such sacred power associated with idols gradually was transformed into a personification, and at that point prayer and religion began (animatism or preanimism). In A. Lang's opinion there had never been a unilinear progression from spirits to ethical deities, since some Australian natives had the belief of a powerful sky god, Daramalun, who had always existed.

Developmentalist Legacy

Evolutionist developmentalists bequeathed their successors a loose federation of specializations consisting of prehistory, human paleontology, physical anthropology (anthropometry), linguistics, and cultural and social anthropology united by a common interest in the early history of mankind. Culture and society provided the basic subject matter, but the psychological processes by which people perceived and organized their relations to nature and others constituted a major objective. Each of the specializations had developed conceptual vocabularies distinctive from other disciplines. They had instituted field collection of basic materials (Bastian, A.C. Haddon, Morgan) in all specializations and compiled for comparison a vast amount of social and cultural facts of peoples around the world.

Evolutionists had generated a variety of theories on the origins and evolutionary histories of beliefs, customs, technology, social organization, religion, law, and the state. They had extended the anthropological horizon by including biological processes in the psychological development of mankind but unfortunately this holistic effort became implicated in the nationalistic and racial ideology that gripped Europe and the New World and with the idea of an unconscious heritage of ancestral social and psychological experiences.

In method they relied on the subjective comparative method to determine developmental stages and on symbolic behaviors as the probable source for custom ("doctrine of survivals"). Tylor introduced statistical procedures to uncover the tendencies of different social practices to cluster, and L. T. Hobhouse, G. D. Wheeler, and M. Ginsberg surveyed some 643 societies without finding a direct relationship between economies and ideas for justice, morality, or the status of women. Anthropological societies and publications were in place during the 1860s and in England Tylor's appointment as Reader in Anthropology at Oxford introduced the discipline to higher education. The complement of features essential to establishment of anthropology as a discipline now were in place.

STRUCTURALISM (CA. 1890–1950)

Developmentalists had investigated the dynamics of culture growth within an evolutionary framework and anthropologists now considered the positive forces that integrated cultures and societies and kept them operating systemically. As a theoretical orientation structuralism arose at a time when industry attempted to increase productivity by improving the efficiency of functional interrelations between management, machines, and workers. Governments also manifested a similar concern for the integration of individuals within the social system.

Three variants of structural theory developed within national boundaries: 1) French and British, 2) biocultural functionalism (Bronislaw Malinowski in Britain), and 3) culture historicism formulated by American culture historians, German-Austrian *Kulturkreislehrer*, and British migrationists. Structuralists had little interest in grand evolutionary stages or ultimate origins, and mistrusted psychological explanations developmentalists derived from analogical reasoning. They claimed the social and cultural as the exclusive subject matter of social and cultural anthropology and denied reductionist explanations of social and cultural facts with biological or other facts derived from a common human psychology. The social and cultural constituted a superorganic domain where social and cultural facts could be explained only by other social and cultural facts, that is, by a sociocultural psychology. Structuralists generally agreed that anthropologists should research preindustrial peoples, but they were not restricted from studying the cultures of industrialized peoples. There was also the expectation that the mythology, ceremonies, and folklore of preindustrial peoples would yield universal psychological processes and social units fundamental to social organization generally.

Structuralists were staunch empiricists. They developed field work to collect valid and reliable facts for analysis and strove to raise anthropology to the status of a science. The scientific orientation encouraged the description and analysis of cultures and societies by the functional interrelations of their parts without regard for individuals. Structuralists shared a common interest in the sociopsychological processes that integrated the individual into the community and ensured social and cultural continuity. Individuals were viewed as programmed by their social and cultural environments psychologically, emotionally, and with regard to ends and means. The conditioning was two-tiered, unconscious and conscious.

French Structuralism

Émile Durkheim, founder of French structuralism, and Marcel Mauss, his nephew and collaborator, wished to establish a comparative sociology that derived its social laws from universal social structures found in an evolutionary sequence. Every social order rested on a social sentiment aroused by the interrelations of two constrastive organizational categories, such as age and sex, or winter and summer. Durkheim was convinced that any explanation of social phenomena by individual psychology would be patently false. He was equally convinced that the suggestibility of individuals in crowd situations was sufficient to generate a collective feeling which people could conceptualize as an idea, and then could give form to in a symbol, such as a flag.

Durkheim selected native Australians to illustrate his theory because they were the simplest people known technologically and represented the original evolutionary stage of mankind. Their lives were divided between two constrastive seasons: a time when they simply hunted for food and another when they gathered to renew in ceremony the sense of the sacred. In coming together at some time in the past, a sense of good feeling was transformed by suggestion into a feeling that carried individuals beyond themselves. Without the stimulus of others an individual could not generate this feeling, and on reflection concluded that each shared a portion of a transcendent sacred power, a god, whom the group represented in a totemic bird, animal, or plant ancestor. When local groups gathered for totemic ceremonies, they renewed this collective feeling of solidarity.

Mauss continued Durkheim's procedure of deriving primal facts from a detailed analysis of a type situation. In a comparative analysis of gift exchange, Mauss traced the origin of reciprocal exchanges to a sacralized social sentiment. In its evolution, exchange began with a generalized form involving families or clans and ended with private contract. His search for "total facts" that would give him a broad framework for analysis led Mauss to introduce fieldwork into French sociology.

Claude Lévi-Strauss also pursued the goal of comparative and evolutionary sociology, but determined that the human brain was programmed to classify things by contrastive features. The arousal of collective ideas, feelings, and representations thus did not require the generation of an unconscious social sentiment. Reintroduction of the biological factor accorded primitive man a positive role in organizing his world of beliefs, practices, and social unions, but he still was subject to unconscious biopsychological processes. Anthropologists interpreted these unconscious processes; historians dealt with the conscious.

The biological orientation led Lévi-Strauss to view exchange processes between social units as serving survival functions. In social life reciprocal exchange was a most fundamental principle because it assured access to scarce resources through a network of alliances comprised of givers and receivers. The binary contrast of matrilateral and patrilateral cousin marriage established a fundamental survival reciprocity and accounted for incest and exogamic regulations in preindustrial societies. In marriage alliances Lévi-Strauss also observed that the "generalized" and "restricted" exchanges characteristic of early societies united religious, magical, utilitarian, jural, moral, and sentimental features, besides the economic, in a functional network. Either exchanges were governed by rules, a "mechanical type," or various factors influenced choices, a "statistical" type. Lévi-Strauss also applied a binary analysis to mythology in order to reconstruct the unconscious development and modifications of generalized myths among local and more distant groups.

British Social Anthropology

A. R. Radcliffe-Brown, founder of British Social Anthropology, drew upon Spencer's analogy of society as an organism, the British jural tradition, and Durkheim's theory of social solidarity for his structural-functional interpretation of the positive forces influencing the harmony, growth, and persistence of social systems. Any society was greater than the sum of its parts, and structure organized the systemic whole which a functional correlation of activities sustained ideally in equilibrium. Individuals during socialization identified unconsciously with the group and in the representational symbolism of rituals and customs, reexperienced basic social sentiments.

The correlation of systemic activities established a natural ranking of parts and functions, and the "social function" of any institution was to instill and transmit the basic sentiments which unified and gave continuity to the society. Values and principles conveyed a logical consistency to the social structure while rights and duties enforced with legal, religious, and moral sanctions defined the place of individuals in the functional hierarchy.

The ultimate design or purposive function of a social system was the key to its understanding. In this regard, totemism illustrated the way hunters ritualized their relations with animal and plant species to form a social collective that reflected the moral and social order of the universe. In more complex societies ultimate design was concentrated in a political institution that exercised legal power to maintain the normative order and to dramatize with ritual and symbols the solidarity sentiments. The "sacred symbols" and "mystical values" of kingship that guaranteed a moral and just order, as well as prosperity and health, were far more important in stabilizing African societies than economic considerations.

Radcliffe-Brown hoped to define the laws or conditions by which societies were integrated, structured, and rendered harmonious and flexible for survival. Functional consistency, differentiation of jural and moral rights, and obligations regulating social relationships and corporate continuity were first-order principles. Second-order principles organized operations with dyadic relationships, sex, generation, and the unity of siblings. A differential application of these principles introduced stylistic distinctions in social integration and morphology, and Radcliffe-Brown tested the validity of his "laws" with covariant associations. If the lineage principle was present, an extension of sororal polygyny along lineage lines was expectable.

Radcliffe-Brown's students implemented his general theory in African colonial societies and produced excellent sociological descriptions of the corporate nature of descent groups, the jural nature of status, and the ritualization of communal sentiments, symbols, and values that transcended individual needs and stabilized the social order. They illustrated the flow of social privilege and obligations along descent lines and argued that the anxiety individuals experienced on breaching a social rule was not a natural psychological response but an anxiety implanted by social conditioning.

Biocultural Functionalism

Malinowski programmed cultures around seven basic physiological needs. Satisfaction of the need transformed the cultural instrumental activity into an acquired drive through psychological reinforcement. His model of an institution organized by a charter of beliefs, personnel, norms, technology, and a purpose or function steered him toward a theory of culture.

Malinowski used the institution as the focus for fieldwork and produced excellent descriptions of Trobriand life and participation in the interisland Kula trade. His descriptive analysis of the Kula drew attention to the way individuals learned and exploited social attitudes, techniques, and rules essential to the use of cultural tradition for personal advantage. He noted differences between normative expectations and actual behaviors.

Uniform psychological responses were correlates of physiological needs and Malinowski traced magic and religion to common human efforts to reduce anxieties aroused by hostile environments and situations. He challenged the social and psychological context of the Freudian Oedipus complex by citing the Trobriand matrilineal order as encouraging a male to focus incestuous desires on a sister and to direct his hostility at the authoritarian mother's brother, rather than at the father.

Malinowski's institutional method and common human psychological orientation did not approach the integration of culture directly, and most of the students he trained deserted his functionalism for Radcliffe-Brown's focused investigation of the social order his students R. Firth, H. I. Hogbin, and A. I. Richards revealed in their research. Harmony, balance, equilibrium, and solidarity were as important to Malinowski's theory of culture as to Radcliffe-Brown's theory of society.

Culture and Culture History

Formulation of the culture concept and its association with ethnology, or cultural anthropology, was the work of culture historicists intent on substituting culture processes for the psychological processes of developmentalist explanations. Culture was conceptualized as a superorganic and supraindividual domain that operated according to its own processes and accounted for changes in the structural-functional interrelations of cultures. Culture historicists were to study each culture and its history without imposing personal or absolute value judgements (cultural relativity).

Definitions of culture were many, but cultures were like fabrics, interwoven with the patterning of ideas and meanings that individuals lived out and expressed in values, attitudes, goals, beliefs, customs, ceremonies, material objectives, and social rankings. Such a configuration of ideas, feelings, and activities depended for its continuity on conditioning individuals to adhere unconsciously to ideal patterns regulating behavior. In the superorganic stream of patterned events, the individual was visible only when behavior illustrated or contradicted normative expectations.

The mapping of cultural features worldwide and the delineation of cultural boundaries by geographers such as F. Ratzel kindled interest in the recovery of culture histories by developing a relative chronology of culture elements according to spatial location. The conversion of distributions in space into a time sequence required assumptions about the uniformity of diffusion rates as well as a spread in all directions. Relative age was determined from a point of origin, with the oldest at the margins of a culture area of continents. Continuous distributions were reliable evidences of historic contact, and where discontinuities occurred, a clustering of forms that were functionally or stylistically related could be taken as evidence of historic contact.

American culture historicists, with the exception of C. Wissler, generally rejected global reconstructions, traced the diffusion of trait complexes within geographic regions, and used the clustering of similar complexes among neighboring tribes to define culture areas and culture types. Alfred Kroeber explored the relationship between a surplus of local resources and culture growth and concluded that an abundant environment favored the emergence of innovative centers and more diversified cultures ("culture climax"). Ralph Linton and Homer Barnett added meaning, use, and principle to form and function comparisons to trace reasons for the acceptance and rejection of traits. Leaving aside earliest migrants, American culture historians generally rejected attempts to prove that accidental contacts from Africa or Asia had added measurably to the cultural inventory of American Indian cultures and their cultural development. Thor Heyerdahl's raft (1953) and balsa (1969) flotations with oceanic currents provided no new information regarding transoceanic contacts.

German and Austrian Kulturkreis exponents (L. Frobenius, F. Gaebner, W. Schmidt) viewed world history as an evolutionary series of culture strata, some global, continental, or inter-continental. Ancient cultures had spread from Eurasian or African centers like great circular waves and remnants of these cultures could be found in refuge areas or at the extremes of continents. Migrants spread these ancient cultures, and Schmidt's evolutionary strata stretched from simple food gatherers through cultivators and pastoralists to the ancient civilizations of America, Asia, and Europe. Adolf Jensen continued the culture morphology tradition, stressing the integration of culture types by ideas rooted in emotion-laden perceptions of the order and processes of life, such as death and fertility.

British migrationists G. Elliot Smith and W. J. Perry linked the rise of all civilized centers to the spread of a funeral complex associated with the Egyptian pharaohs (sun worship, mummification, pyramids). Search for the elixir of life associated with precious metals, gold, and jewels provided the incentive for migration, colonization, and trade. In their Oceanic culture histories, ethnologists W. R. Rivers and C. Fox concluded that megalithic monuments and mummification were introduced by migrants influenced by the Egyptian complex.

Integration of Culture

The historical orientation Franz Boas brought to American cultural anthropology did not encourage the view that cultures were tightly integrated functional systems. From mythology and folklore, he was convinced that culture elements easily slipped their functional bonds and became attached to other complexes. However, Boas in his analyses sought to uncover the sociopsychological structures that accounted for the acceptance, modification, and rejection of forms introduced by historic contact. The growth of cultures through diffusion was a problem in process and not of structure.

Concentration on the diffusion and analysis of trait complexes (e.g., maize, guardian spirit, Sun Dance) afforded but limited appreciation of design in cultures and structural-functional interrelations. As a consequence, American historicists explored a number of approaches to cultural integration that generally emphasized an inner configuration of unconscious sociopsychological processes and values that contributed style, pattern, and continuity to cultures. Kroeber noted that a progressive integration of ideas, "styles, standards, and values " accompanied development of a culture climax. Ecologically oriented Steward considered that culture types varied according to differences in their economies and levels of sociocultural integration. In Yucatan, R. Redfield described the erosion of peasant life integrated by moral values embedded in a sacred world order as the heterogeneous and secular urban order penetrated the rural countryside. In the American Southwest, F. Kluckhohn and F. Strodtbeck found that rural Navaho, Zuni, Mormons, Spanish-Americans, and Texas homesteaders held firmly to their seperate "value orientations" despite close contacts on a daily basis.

Ruth Benedict penetrated the "unconscious canons of choice" (ethos) regulating behavior by viewing cultures as historic elaborations of temperament, contrasting the sober Apollonian Zuñi with the aggressive and egotistical Kwakiutl. Mead used three New Guinea cultures to illustrate the plasticity of male and female temperments. Men and women exhibited stereotypic masculine behaviors among the Mundu-gumor, a female personality among the Arapesh, and among the Tschambuli, women were masculine-dominant and men feminine-subordinate.

By the midthirties interest in personality and culture led American anthropologists to explore with Abram Kardiner the contributions of psychoanalytic theory to culture and personality. Psychoanalytic reaction formations drew a picture of cultural institutions as largely repressive and a source for projective correlates of aggression and Oedipal yearnings commonly expressed in dreams, folklore, and some religious beliefs and practices. Rorschach protocols of Alorese obtained by C. DuBois were not comparable to European ones.

Application of psychoanalytic theory to ethnographic research revealed unconscious aggressions, anxieties, and fears lurking behind an overt facade of harmonious social relations, laughter, and self-control. Psychoanalytic theory found application in personal narratives, national character analyses produced for war purposes, and in acculturation studies. Psychoanalytic theory also kindled interest in man as an emergent self-conscious being and strengthened relations with primatology. G. P. Murdock used an ethnographic sample of world societies to test statistically various theories of avoidance and license behaviors and concluded that a full explanation of incest required contributions, theoretical and factual, from psychoanalysis as well as sociology, cultural anthropology, and behavioristic psychology. His detailed classification of kinship terminologies and testing of correlations of descent, cousin terminologies, residence, family types, and exogamic rules established a framework for future work in kinship and social organization.

American anthropologists, in contrast with British social anthropologists, did not consider that any single institutionalized pattern integrated cultures. Cultures developed largely by incorporating new elements offered by chance contacts. Linton conceded that a dominant interest could provide the focus for a number of related activities, but cultures were not driven by an ultimate design. There was an interplay between the "ideal" patterns to which individuals were enculturated and "real" patterns. Ideal patterns defined normative expectations while real patterns included the variations of actual responses. The most popular responses or mode provided a basis for describing the patterned structure and could be used to predict behavior.

DIFFERENTIATIVE SPECIALIZATION (CA. 1950 TO PRESENT)
Postwar Transition

"Cargo" cults, "revitalization" movements, and political resistance movements signaled that the Third World was astir with change and a search for "national" identities that challenged the superorganic view of culture anchored to unconscious sociopsychological processes. Anthropologists were again faced with a redefinition of their perceptions of culture and research objectives, and a confrontation with the timeless problems of structure and variation and the relations of individuals to society and culture.

The signs of change were evident in the thirties when anthropologists began to study acculturation and governments, recognizing that their colonial subjects had reached a new threshold of development, prompted the emergence of applied anthropology and ethnohistory with requests for anthropological research. Anthropologists also had begun to question the cultural reality reflected in their ethnographies as critics decried the focus on culture elements rather than people. A structuralist position still prevailed as Alfred Kroeber and Clyde Kluckhohn admitted that the use of patterns, averages, and modes produced descriptions that were logical constructs; but in portraying basic structure, ideal patterns were more precise than the behavior patterns of individuals. Kroeber advised anthropologists to shift their interests in part to the great cultural traditions that led to civilization, and he tested the reality of the culture pattern by the clustering of genius in Greco-Roman culture history. Culture in essence was a stream of ideas that changed configurations without reference to humans. Edward Sapir and Benjamin Whorf emphasized the unconscious patterning of thought by language.

Leslie White challenged the view that culture was an abstraction of reality. He pointed out that any science must define a subject matter of objective things and events. Culture was just that, a communication system of symbols that could be researched historically, as a structural-functional system, or as an evolutionary process. In White's view, every science in seeking a precise and comprehensive perspective had opted for an evolutionary approach, and he urged anthropologists to do the same.

Reintroduction of the evolutionary perspective generated interest in the rise of civilization and of the state with a consequent specialization in political anthropology. A combination of social, economic, religious, military, and political factors provided the dynamics for the rise of urban centers at points where different ecological zones were in contact and stimulated trade. The research of archeologists R. Braidwood, G. Willey, V. G. Childe, and J. H. Steward accented the role of trade in contributing a material and ideological base that accelerated culture growth and interregional networks which eventually would be consolidated by conquest states. E. R. Service distinguished band, tribe, chiefdom, state, and empire as evolutionary levels of political development.

Julian Steward expanded cultural-ecological investigation by focusing on the way groups organized to exploit different environments and defined patrilineal and composite bands as social types adapted to variant ecologies. Variable ecological conditions induced variable social adaptations and for that reason multilineal rather than unilineal evolution prevailed. Parallel evolution occurred where ecological conditions and adaptations were alike, whether in tropical or temperate regions. Ecological adaptation raised anew the issue as to whether environment selected adaptive cultural variations or whether groups took the initiative and exploited ecological niches according to their technologies. Roy A. Rappaport described the Tsembaga of New Guinea as ideally adapted to their environment and regional neighbors by a homeostatic scheduling of rituals that allowed a steady carrying capacity for the land, population growth, trade, and pig surpluses for nutritious protein, interregional feasting, and peacemaking. Marvin Harris challenged the view that the "sacred cow" complex of India contradicted rational economics. From his analysis, the relationship between cattle and peasant was functionally symbiotic rather than competitive.

Major theoretical orientations, field work, and personal interests often combined to develop specializations. American cultural anthropologists were leaders in ethnomusicology, folklore, psychological anthropology, cultural psychiatry, and clinical anthropology while British social anthropologists pioneered in political and legal anthropology.

Malinowski's detailed investigation of Trobriand economics and the stimulus he brought to his students (Firth, Richards) provided an initial base for the development of economic anthropology. However, the standard view that exchange in preindustrial societies was so involved in kinship obligations that profit never was a serious consideration inhibited contact with economists. Karl Polanyi incorporated this "noneconomic" view in an evolutionary sequence that ended with the unique market system of the West. He determined that archaic societies of the Old and New World were redistributive societies that regulated market prices and collected taxes in kind and with archaic currencies. Field studies confirmed that some kinship societies (Ashanti, Zulu) controlled careers by merging private interest with the corporate welfare. On the other hand, Kapauku "big men" (tonowi) manipulated kin and resources to increase wealth, status, and political influence. Kapauku tonowi resembled industrial tycoons whose careers rose and fell according to shrewd investments, key friendships, and luck. Edward Leach found that Sinhalese at marriage made a choice of virilocal or matrilocal residence according to land inheritance. The formalist-substantivist debate brought exponents of redistributive economic theory and of end-means maximizing strategy into confrontation; and while the issue was never resolved, it became apparent that optimization strategies were not unknown in kinship societies. The lure of the city proved just as strong for African countrymen in search of wealth, independence, and a more comfortable life as for Europeans.

The image of an economic man allocating scarce resource and maximizing ends added support to a view of man as actively organizing his world. The perception of man-as-actor promoted the rise of cognitive anthropology and the beginnings of a "new ethnography." Anthropological interests began to cluster around the classification and processing of materials, and communication as process. With componential analysis (ethnosemantics), H. Conklin reduced the logic of Hanunoo color classification to four basic criteria: lightness, darkness, wetness, and dryness; and the procedure found ready application to folk taxonomies. The intent of cognitivists, as in transformational grammar, was to plot the rules governing performance. Sociolinguistics (anthropological linguistics, language, and culture) addressed performance variation in speech in accordance with social and cultural situations, or by individual action. Semiotics concentrated on the patterned behavior of individuals during communication, including body cues and meanings (kinesics) and proxemics (unconscious control of space and interpersonal distance). Norbert Wiener's cybernetic model and information theory with its control of noise, redundancy, and entropy in feedback received wide application. Game theory introduced competitive strategies and optimization of goal outcomes, while "cognitive maps" and "mazeways" charted the personal organization of cultural rules and correspondence between the models and inner reality. Kenneth Pike raised the issue of an insider's versus an outsider's view with his emic-etic distinction.

The cognitive orientation introduced a view of culture as a configured "code" or "text" that defined the organization and primary relations within the world and concentrated attention on signs and symbols as expressive messengers of meanings and their logical connections. Hermeneutics described the critical method of interpreting the cryptic code or text. Grand rituals centered in fertility, rites of passage, and accession to office commonly revealed opposition within the social system, cosmogonic themes, stages of development, and a mixing of symbolic categories to frighten or demonstrate power. Arnold van Gennep's concept of liminality provided a useful model for the ritual progression of the initiate from one boundary to the next. Performance theory has been applied to theater, folklore, art, and language to reveal the correspondence between cognitive conditioning and the expression of traditional values and themes symbolically, and often metonymy and metaphor. Michel Foucault's discourse on institutionalized disciplinary practice to produce and symbolize subordination in relation to authority gave new significance to the body as a conveyor of social meaning and prompted an anthropology of the body.

Gender

Gender studies accompanying the civil rights movement raised again the age-old problems of the original state of nature, its egalitarian or authoritarian character, and whether present-day societies could be used as models for that early time. Foraging and hunting societies focused debate on the economic, ecological, reproductive, and power factors that influenced relations between the sexes. In evolutionary perspective, hunting models stressed the bonding of males, their food contribution, and protection of females and children. Baboon colonies served as the primate model for a hypothesized male dominance in early hunting societies. Some recent interpretations of foraging and hunting societies accord women economic contributions equal to or greater than men. The autonomous nature of chimpanzee foraging and the "matrilocal" character of their social bonds has served as a model for women as primary foodgatherers and family figures in hominid societies. As long as individuals could provide for themselves, cooperative action and sharing depended on consensus, and equality prevailed. Eleanor Leacock and Linda Fedigan concluded that a concentration of power over resources in the hands of men brought inequality to women as society evolved.

The recent discovery of a possible "stone age" people in the Philippines has focused attention on the Tasaday as an egalitarian society. The Kalahari San have become a center of controversy with regard to stone age egalitarian characteristics because of differing views of their relative isolation and place in a network of trade and regional political history.

Problem Networks

The multiplicity of specializations encouraged development of research networks to resolve complex problems. The distant origins of language and the boundary for the transformation of thought patterns has combined research in prehistory, human paleontology, paleodemography, ecological anthropology, paleoclimatology, primatology, neurobiology, comparative anatomy, and cognitive anthropology. The evolutionary base has been extended to include primate and human calls, gestures, and signals (iconic and deictic), paleolithic cave paintings, and tool making. Sociobiology heightened debate with claims that a biogenetic process (inclusive fitness) operated to the exclusion of social and cultural processes in the production of social and other behavioral qualities essential to community life and language potential. In its extensions medical anthropology developed links with folk medicine, biomedicine, and urban and industrial anthropology. Network analysis drew attention to the interconnections of formal and informal structures through quasi groups, personal networks, and "cultural brokers" with consequent linkages to social, urban, political, legal, economic, and demographic anthropology. The concept of "schema" in cognitive science has linked cognitive anthropology, cognitive linguistics, cognitive psychology, and computer science in search of "schemata," the elemental structures of cognition.

The infusion of new methods has accompanied the differentiative process and research networking.

Mathematical models have supplied the precision desired as anthropologists have incorporated statistical techniques, stochastic models, and matrix analyses along with Boolean algebra, scalograms, Venn diagrams, and computers for simulation of models.

Revision and Reflexivity

Revision of the data base, interpretation, analysis, and theory has been indispensable to the development of anthropology. The description, analysis, and interpretation of another culture demands a sympathetic interest and a determination to be as accurate and free of bias as possible. During the thirties, anthropologists considered a personal psychoanalysis as a way to become aware of unconscious bias. Applied anthropologists developed an ethical guide governing relations with native communities undergoing development programs and the American Anthropological Association has adopted a similar ethic.

The fifties were critical in that anthropologists began to question the authenticity of their ethnographic research. In 1954 linguist Pike raised a methodological issue when he observed that the "emic" descriptions of informants were subject to distortion by the alien "etic" categories of the researcher. The problem brought up the omnipresent issue of variation in relation to structure; but without etic classification there could be no cross-cultural or hologeistic comparisons and generalizations. By the midsixties anthropologists echoed physical scientists and abandoned prediction for probabilities. The British social anthropologist Evans-Pritchard counseled his colleagues to abandon the search for laws in the image of natural science and become historians. They should search for "design" and interpret rather than explain. In 1968 C. Castaneda challenged the capability of anthropologists to cross cultural thresholds and to interpret the worldview of others.

Civil-rights and gender studies drew attention to the consciousness-raising process and intensified the perception that the experiencing of culture rather than cultural roles should be the focus of anthropology. In 1987 reflexivists James Clifford and George Marcus proposed to make the cultural experience come alive through dialogue and a record of the "polyphonic" character of the plural socket. The anthropologist was part of the problem, and they envisioned the researcher drawn into the dialogue of cultural experience as a morally responsible person. The language of "ethnopoetics", drawn from literary criticism and

Marxism was designed to "demystify" and "deconstruct" the biased constructs of "traditional" anthropologists.

A restudy of a community is an excellent device to correlate the authenticity of ethnographic descriptions, provided the restudy collects data that are comparable. Twenty years after Redfield, Oscar Lewis revisited Tepoztlan, Mexico, but, unlike Redfield, he made extensive use of Rorschach protocols. Lewis's description of Tepoztlañeros was filled with suspicion, anxiety, conflict; and repressed feelings masked by the formalities of custom cast doubt on Redfield's "idyllic" portrait. Thirty-seven years after Mead, Derek Freeman revisited Samoa and determined that her description of Samoa as a paradise for adolescent lovers was a myth. Mead, it would appear, was aware of Samoan adolescent conflict but underplayed that aspect to accent conflicts experienced by American adolescents because of cultural restrictions. The anti-science posture of reflexivists, in conjunction with the social and political struggles of native populations and social reform objectives, has added a political dimension to fieldwork. Marxists faulted British social anthropologists for overlooking the contradictions in production that energized African lineage and clan performance in support of the social structure, and Andean anthropologists are urged to take steps toward a "politically constructive anthropology."

SUMMARY

From its inception anthropology has made the psychological processes by which mankind organized their social and cultural environments a primary focus of research. Evolutionary considerations extended the problem in depth and united prehistory, biological anthropology, linguistics, and cultural anthropology in a common task. In a succession of paradigms anthropologists explored the determining and reciprocal influences of human nature, culture, and ecology on the construction of a cultural heritage and its transmission.

Each of these paradigms advanced anthropological capabilities to describe, analyze, and generalize the cultural contexts of human experience. The differentiative process has been integral for enlarging perspectives, producing new data, incorporating new methods, and initiating responses to changes in Western Civilization and those researched. The differentiative process continues as anthropologists discover specialized niches (e.g. ethnologic, cyber-

culture) that articulate with new dimensions of problems. Research networking with related disciplines has strengthened the capacity to cope with a broad range of complex problems, but syntheses may be restricted to rather limited domains. Networking also has weakened the unity of the four fields.

Present ethnographic differentiation explores the dialectic of power and subordination in cultural contexts, and is reflected in part by the organization of societies and councils within the American Anthropological Association. There are associations for feminist anthropology, political and legal anthropology, black anthropologists, Latina and Latino anthropologists, senior anthropologists, museum anthropology, anthropology and education, nutritional anthropology, culture and agriculture, practice of anthropology, anthropology of consciousness, anthropology of Europe, cultural anthropology, humanistic anthropology, urban anthropology, and visual anthropology.

Fred W. Voget

See Also: Postmodernism

Bloch, Maurice. *Marxism and Anthropology: The History of a Relationship.* Oxford: Clarendon Press, 1985.

Bryson, Gladys. *Man and Society: The Scottish Inquiry of the Eighteenth Century.* Princeton, NJ: Princeton University Press, 1945.

Clifford, James A., and George E. Marcus, editors. *Writing Culture: The Poetics and Politics of Ethnography.* Berkeley: University of California Press, 1986.

Geertz, Clifford. *Works and Lives: The Anthropologist as Author.* (Lévi-Strauss Malinowski, Benedict, Evans-Pritchard). Stanford: Stanford University Press, 1988.

Honigmann, John J., editor. *Handbook of Social and Cultural Anthropology.* Chicago: Rand McNally and Company, 1973.

Kuper, Adam. *Anthropology and Anthropologists: The Modern British School.* London: Routledge & Kegan Paul, 1983.

HOMELESSNESS

Homelessness can be broadly defined as the condition either of having no access to shelter or of having access to shelter that is so precarious that life itself is threatened. The opposite of being homeless is having adequate shelter, which includes having protection from the elements, access to potable water, provision for removal of human wastes, protection from intruders, and freedom from sudden removal. Homelessness is one of the most tangible forms of extreme poverty.

Homelessness includes the condition both of the visibly homeless—such as the pavement dwellers of India, the homeless men of the Skid Rows of the United States, and the street children of Latin America—and also of the less visibly homeless, such as individuals and families in shelters and hostels throughout the industrialized world, institutionalized children in parts of Latin American and eastern Europe, and families sharing accommodations wherever there is a shortage of affordable housing. Moving from place to place, as in the case of nomadic people, such as the Inuit or Gypsies, is not construed as homelessness, if the culture of the group includes such movement.

Cultures of the world view homelessness from different perspectives, which are often revealed by the words that are used for the homeless. These words reflect the dichotomy between the "lack-of-housing" and the "personal-pathology/detachment" understandings of homelessness. Terms that stress a lack of shelter include roofless/houseless (India), *sin techo* (Latin America), and *sans-abri* (France and Canada). On the other hand, terms that suggest the personal failings of the individuals and their lack of connection with others include *clochard* (tramp-France), *desamparado* (abandoned-Latin America), *furosha* (floating person-Japan), and *puliukko* (male alcoholic-Finland). The term "homeless," including its direct translation into other languages, often conjures up an image of the single, unconnected individual, perhaps sleeping in the streets over a heating grate in a large industrialized city.

Historically, homelessness was a term reserved for single men (the classic work on that topic is Anderson 1923). The homeless man has variously been viewed as a saintly mendicant, a fiercely independent traveling man, a sick and lonely creature, or a drug-addicted or psychotic threat. By the 1960s, the term "homelessness" came to include families living in squatter settlements of the developing world and families in shelters and shared accommodations in the industrialized world.

Squatter settlements are made up of informal housing units constructed out of found material by the residents themselves. Often the land (public or private) upon which these structures are built has been "invaded" by a group of families. Examples of squatter settlements are the *bidonvilles* (tin cities) of Africa, the *favelas* of Brazil, the *pueblos jóvenes* (young towns) of Peru, and the *kampungs* (villages) of Indonesia. There are also increasing numbers of squatter settlements in North America and Europe.

Homeless children, especially the visible street children of the developing world, have received a lot of attention recently. Examples of these children include the *gaminos* of Colombia, the *khate* (rag pickers) of Nepal, the *pixote* of Brazil (named after the film *Pixote*, directed by Babenco in 1981), and the parking boys (referring to their association with parking cars, a common job in the informal economy) of Kenya. The children are vulnerable both to the dangers of the street and to officially sanctioned violence in campaigns to "clean up the streets." Homeless children in the industrialized world are usually discussed within the context of homeless shelters and institutions.

Knowledge about homelessness comes from scholarly research, agency reports, censuses, journalistic inquiries, and a small number of firsthand accounts (for example, de Jesus 1963). Anthropology has made a major contribution to our knowledge of homelessness, because of its ability to engage in in-depth studies requiring participant observation. For example, Baxter and Hopper (1981) explored the streets and subway tunnels of New York City and found that homeless people were interested in leaving the streets but were deterred from entering shelters because of the violence and degrading conditions there. Their research became the basis for a major overhaul of the city's shelter system.

Anthropologists tend to be critical of categorizations of people that do not coincide with how the people themselves see the world. For example, Goode (1987), in discussing the state of knowledge about *gaminismo* (the street-child phenomenon) in Colombia, observes that the categories "pregamin" and "gamin," as used by social-service agencies, do not reflect the fluidity of the street child's continual cycling through home, streets, and institutions.

Anthropology has also been able to document systems of mutual aid and friendship within various cultures of the homeless (on the streets, in soup kitchens, in shelters), through the charting of social networks. Where previous research has characterized the homeless as "disaffiliated," anthropology has highlighted their complex web of interrelationships. Finally, anthropological research on homelessness has introduced a global perspective (Glasser 1994). The cultural relativism of anthropologists allows them to study homelessness as a human adaptation to a set of conditions, rather than merely as a social problem.

Causes of homelessness may be conceptualized as belonging to either the "personal-pathology/detachment" or the "lack-of-housing" school of thought. Until very recently, homelessness in the industrialized nations was viewed as an outgrowth of alcoholism, mental illness (exacerbated by the deinstitutionalizing of the hospitalized mentally ill), drug addiction, and family disintegration. In the countries of the developing world, the existence of people on the street has been conceived in terms of burgeoning populations whose needs for housing cannot be met by either government agencies or the private market. This population increase occurred because of the lowering of mortality rates and the increase in rural-to-urban migration, with a subsequent rise in pavement dwellers, street children, and squatter settlements. More recently, there has been a recognition in the industrialized world that the deterioration and demolition of older housing in cities, the "gentrification" of existing housing (i.e., the upgrading of housing to such an extent that the former poor occupants can no longer afford it), and the withdrawal of government sponsorship for new housing, have all contributed to the lack of adequate and affordable housing.

An unresolved issue within the research on homelessness is the question of numbers—how many homeless people are there? The answers depend on the definitions used, the rigor and sophistication of the enumeration techniques, and the cooperation of service providers and the homeless themselves. The number of homeless estimated by the United Nations Centre for Human Settlement (1990), based on the contributions of 144 countries, was one billion people living in conditions of inadequate shelter or literal homelessness. In the United States, the 1990 Bureau of the Census counted 178,638 persons in emergency shelters and 49,734 persons visible at preidentified street locations, for a total of 228,372. These numbers (especially the street count) are widely disputed as missing significant numbers of people (see Wright and Devine 1992). India includes the houseless population in its decennial census and gives enumerators three weeks to locate the pavement dwellers whom they will count on the night of the census.

Efforts to ameliorate homelessness include the preventative measures that help people keep their housing during times of economic hardship through efforts such as Canada's social-housing programs or through mediation efforts to prevent eviction. Once on the street, homeless people may have access to food and shelter from traveling vans, respite day centers, or temporary shelters. Another level of help involves transitional housing, which includes the kind of longer-term temporary accommodations that enable a person to leave the streets and eventually enter permanent housing. In developing countries, there are numerous projects to upgrade squatter settlements, often with material provided by governmental or nongovernmental organizations and labor provided by the people themselves (see Turner 1976). Advocates for the homeless in the industrialized world are now recommending similar self-help and political empowerment as strategies to address homelessness.

IRENE GLASSER

SEE ALSO: *Adaptation; Alcohol and Drugs; Cities; Cultural Relativism; Emic/Etic Distinctions; Fieldwork; Network Analysis; Poverty; Refugees; Urban Anthropology*

ANDERSON, NELS. *The Hobo*. Chicago: University of Chicago Press, 1923.

BABENCO, HECTOR, dir. *Pixote*. Burbank, Calif.: Embrafilms; RCA/Columbia Picture Home Video, 1981.

BAXTER, ELLEN, and KIM HOPPER. *Private Lives/Public Spaces: Homeless Adults on the Streets of New York City*. New York: Community Service Society, 1981.

DE JESUS, CAROLINA MARIA. *Child of the Dark: The Diary of Carolina Maria De Jesus*. New York: New American Library, 1963.

GLASSER, IRENE. *Homelessness in Global Perspective*. New York: G. K. Hall, 1994.

GOODE, JUDITH. "Gaminismo: The Changing Nature of the Street Child Phenomenon in Colombia." Indianapolis, Ind.: Universities Field Staff International, no. 28 (reprint), 1987.

HARDOY, JORGE E., and DAVID SATTERTHWAITE.

Squatter Citizen: Life in the Urban Third World. London: Earthscan Publications, 1989.

TURNER, JOHN. *Housing by People.* London: Marion Boyars, 1976.

UNITED NATIONS CENTRE FOR HUMAN SETTLEMENTS. *Shelter: From Projects to National Strategies.* Nairobi: United Nations Centre for Human Settlements, 1990.

WRIGHT, JAMES D., and JOEL A. DEVINE. "Counting the Homeless: The Census Bureau's 'S-Night' in Five U.S. Cities." *Evaluation Review* 16 (4): 355-64, 1992.

HONOR

With the advent of ethnography in the Mediterranean region in the late 1950s, a focus on value systems—largely derived from the Oxford focus on moral communities—began to crystallize around the subjects of honor and shame. This polarity, which carried strong implications of gender opposition and a powerful association with sexuality and aggression, was identified in virtually all circum-Mediterranean cultures, whether predominantly Christian or Muslim. While there was some recognition that honor codes existed elsewhere, such occurrences were usually viewed as either anachronistic (American South) or extensions of the influence of Islam (Indian subcontinent) or Christianity (Latin America, where they could also be attributed directly to Iberian cultural domination).

Several ethnographies contributed to the effect of creating a coincidence of Mediterranean culture and an honor-shame code. Prominent among these ethnographies is the nuanced account of the Sarakatsani, a transhumant northern Greek population, by J. K. Campbell (1964), who argues that the horizontal values of mutual obligation, crucial in a society where otherwise all sociability will be overwhelmed by the tensely agonistic quality of relationships among unrelated households and individuals, intersect with the vertical patron-client relationships based on the similar regard for the morality of obligation. This nexus of ideas was embedded in a local reading of Orthodox Christian doctrine, in which social tension was attributed to the fallen condition of humankind (original sin) and the solidarity of the household—and, to a lesser extent, of the larger cognatic kindred—modeled on the ideal model of the holy family. This early ethnographic treatment is the first to reveal the significance of grace as a mediating concept, although it was not to reemerge as a key issue until nearly two decades later.

A collection of essays edited by John E. Peristiany, revealingly entitled *Honour and Shame: The Values of Mediterranean Society* (1965), includes a chapter from Campbell's book, on the role of the devil in corrupting honor, plus essays on Spain, Greek Cypriot society, the Kabyle of Algiers, and the Egyptian Bedouin. Peristiany's introduction lays out the close association of the honor-shame moral code with the Mediterranean region and emphasizes the agonistic quality of honor. He points to the extreme fragility of honor, given that an excess of honor-motivated actions (such as hospitality) can collapse into shame. Julian Pitt-Rivers's essay on Spain addresses issues of class, showing that plebeian families are more constrained by this code than middle-class families and have to demonstrate their honor as virtue, while the top stratum possesses honor by social ascription (honor as precedence) and is thus free from all pragmatic controls. Pitt-Rivers's later works, notably *The Fate of Shechem* (1977), contributed to the closer examinations of a Mediterranean economy of sexuality by showing, as Campbell had for the Sarakatsani, how the control of women's virtue could serve as the measure of an entire kin group's reputation.

In an advance on the original formulation of honor and shame as key concepts for understanding Mediterranean societies, Jane Schneider (1971) argues that in order to understand the predominance of these values one should examine the history of subsistence and social organization in the region, and suggests that men's tight control of female sexuality was, in effect, an ideological and political means for men to contest the control of resources. Her work also marks the beginning of serious research on the effects of the state's intervention in local morality, while Campbell's ethnography focuses more on a local population's engagement of the state's representatives in a nexus of existing, notionally shared, moral values.

John H. R. Davis (1977), still within the compass of a cross-Mediterranean culture-area concept, suggests that the entire basis of the honor code was material, thereby similarly departing from the idealist Pitt-Rivers model. Three years later, Michael Herzfeld criticized both models on the grounds that the uniformity with which honor and shame were represented throughout the region actually glossed over significant and often highly localized divergences; he suggested that closer attention to semantic aspects would reveal neither a uniform code nor, necessarily, an agonistic one. He also proposed that comparative research on differences within common linguistic and national traditions would, paradoxically, better serve a global context of analysis.

This critique was not initially representative of a widespread position. Indeed, Anton Blok (1981) sought instead to establish the sexual dimensions of a uniform Mediterranean morality as expressed through animal metaphors rooted in direct observation of nature. Blok persuasively argues that industrialized nation-states have appropriated the values of honor to the national entity, but his Mediterraneanist focus, as well as similar work by Anthony H. Galt (1982) on the evil eye, led Herzfeld to expand his response; his *Anthropology Through the Looking-Glass* (1987) is a critique of Mediterraneanism in general, one that recognizes the local use of a Mediterranean stereotype throughout the region but situates it within the larger symbolic economy.

Herzfeld also contributed the one dissenting essay to a collection edited by David D. Gilmore. Herzfeld argues that relations such as hospitality, in which the inversion of global power through localized social relationships can be examined with relative ease, provide a more useful comparativist framework. Gilmore's own ethnographic contribution revived the centrality of honesty, which Pitt-Rivers had already accorded a central place. Mariko Asano-Tamanoi's essay in the same volume, by comparing Spain with Japan, somewhat breaks the exclusive focus on the Mediterranean, but the remaining essays are largely within the framework of recognizing honor and shame in countries of a broadly defined Mediterranean region.

A major contributor to the study of honor is Pierre Bourdieu. He originally considered honor (in the Peristiany volume) the basis of a structural opposition (i.e., as against shame) and as radically engaged with the respective sexual attributes of women and men. Honor later became a key demonstration of Bourdieu's theory (1977) about the relationship between hexis, habitus, and social practice. In this work, the term "honor" remains internally undifferentiated, and the variety of its realizations is viewed as a consequence of the elasticity to be found in social contest.

Other writers, however, have become considerably more critical of the honor-shame moral code. Unni Wikan (1984), on the basis of Cairene and Omani data, suggests that the balance of the relationship between honor and shame is highly labile, that it is often affected by the relatively unreflexive character of shame as opposed to honor, and that it could only be understood in the broader context of gender relations. In an even sharper vein, Alison Lever (1986) questions whether the concept is more than a distraction, and points up its failure to articulate the factors of gender and class. Meanwhile, a shift to urban ethnography has led many writers on the Mediterranean region to focus on significantly different issues. *Embourgeoisement* and the growth of national youth cultures, for example, may have produced engendered ambiguities, making it even more difficult to sustain a view that accords absolute centrality to honor and shame in social life.

MICHAEL HERZFELD

BLOK, ANTON. "Rams and Billy-Goats: A Key to the Mediterranean Code of Honour." *Man* (n.s.) 16 (1981): 427–440.

BOURDIEU, PIERRE. *Outline of a Theory of Practice.* Translated by Richard Nice. Cambridge: Cambridge University Press, 1977.

CAMPBELL, J. K. *Honour, Family, and Patronage: A Study of Institutions and Moral Values in a Greek Mountain Community.* Oxford: Clarendon Press, 1964.

DAVIS, JOHN H. R. *The People of the Mediterranean: An Essay in Comparative Social Anthropology.* London: Routledge & Kegan Paul, 1977.

GALT, ANTHONY H. "The Evil Eye as Synthetic Image and Its Meanings on the Island of Pantelleria." *American Ethnologist* 9 (1982): 664– 681.

GILMORE, DAVID D., ed. *Honor and Shame and the Unity of the Mediterranean.* Washington, D.C.: American Anthropological Association Special Publications, No. 22.

HERZFELD, MICHAEL. "Honour and Shame: Some Problems in the Comparative Analysis of Moral Systems." *Man* (n.s.) 15 (1980): 335–351.

———. "The Horns of the Mediterraneanist Dilemma." *American Ethnologist* 11 (1984): 439–454.

———. *Anthropology Through the Looking-Glass: Critical Ethnography in the Margins of Europe.* Cambridge: Cambridge University Press, 1987.

LEVER, ALISON. "Honour as a Red Herring." *Critique of Anthropology* 6 (1986): 83–106.

PERISTIANY, JOHN E., ed. *Honour and Shame: The Values of Mediterranean Society.* London: Weidenfeld & Nicolson, 1965.

PERISTIANY, JOHN E., and JULIAN PITT-RIVERS, eds. *Honor and Grace in Anthropology.* Cambridge: Cambridge University Press, 1992.

PITT-RIVERS, JULIAN. *The Fate of Shechem: Or, the Politics of Sex.* Cambridge: Cambridge University Press, 1977.

SCHNEIDER, JANE. "Of Vigilance and Virgins: Honor, Shame, and Access to Resources in Mediterranean Societies." *Ethnology* 10 (1971): 1– 24.

WIKAN, UNNI. "Shame and Honour: A Contestable Pair." *Man* (n.s.) 19 (1984): 635–652.

HORTICULTURE

SEE: Agriculture and Farming Systems

HUMAN EVOLUTION

Evolutionary theory is enthroned at the center of biology, but it is doubtful that knowledge of human evolution has had a significant effect on cultural anthropology. It has been said in the past that humanity has been so embedded in culture as a milieu that the natural world is irrelevant. That view is extremist; our biological nature and genetic variation are increasingly obtruding on our scientific attention. Our understanding of human evolution, in particular, has expanded rapidly in the most recent years.

COMPARATIVE ANATOMY

Carolus Linneaus, no evolutionist himself, gave evolutionary thinking a logical frame with his eighteenth-century classification of living things. Among the mammals, he created the order of primates to include humans, monkeys and lemurs, and bats. Traits now recognized as essential include grasping limbs and a rotation of the eyes to the front of the head, giving binocular, stereoscopic vision. Lower primates (e.g., lemurs) manifest such trends, but in fully developed higher primates (monkeys, apes, and humans), these features provide hand-eye coordination, essential to the eventual development of culture.

Charles Darwin's friend Thomas Huxley, in a famous essay, presented in detail our anatomical closeness to the anthropoid apes. Thus, the tone was set for such studies, repeated and refined by many. Tabulations of traits were used to assess which ape was closest to ourselves physically and, by implication, in phylogeny. Studies of teeth demonstrated the gradual development of the molar crowns from those of lower primates, giving rise to the "Dryopithecus pattern" of cusps and fissures seen in ourselves and apes. This is evidently parental to the more specialized pattern in "Old World" monkeys rather than the reverse. It is named from the fossil ape *Dryopithecus*, found in 1856 in Spain, and is of critical importance because variations on the pattern allow fine-grained study of the numerous species of extinct apes of the Miocene era, from whom teeth form the bulk of fossil evidence. The same kind of evidence emphasizes the close kinship of apes and human beings, which is recognized in taxonomy by grouping them in a superfamily Hominoidea distinct from the superfamily Cercopithecoidea, which comprises the monkeys of Africa and Asia.

Later work, including that on behavior and function and not simply relying on uncritical counting of separate traits, began to stress the special closeness of African chimpanzees and gorillas to humans and to each other, and the relative separation of all of them from the orangutan (and from the smaller Asiatic ape, the gibbon).

MOLECULAR BIOLOGY

This view was powerfully reinforced by the entrance of molecular studies, first involving proteins like hemoglobin as the medium of comparison between species, but recently going on to DNA, the controlling basis of protein formation. As the substance of the chromosomes, the total length of the DNA includes, but is not limited to, the genes, and is far from being fully understood: studies have been carried out on limited sections of the whole.

Work has resoundingly demonstrated the closeness of human beings and apes, relative to other primates, with more than 98 percent of the known DNA being identical in chimpanzees and humans. Further, the orangutan is clearly separated from the humans and the two African apes as a group. Traditionally, two families have been recognized: Hominidae for ourselves and our known ancestors, and Pongidae for the three large apes. This is a commonsense classification when viewing the four-handed, tree-using, smaller-brained anthropoids: an ape is an ape. But the phylogeny suggested by molecular evidence would place the division elsewhere, making Hominidae (hominids) of humans and the two African apes and consigning the orangutan alone to the family Pongidae, and this is getting increasing usage. Furthermore, debate continues on whether the three hominids, thus recognized, are mutually equally distant or whether in fact chimpanzees and humans are more closely related than either is to the gorilla. In other words, it is suggested that chimps and humans share an ancestor already distinct from that of gorillas.

In either case, the implications for human nature are considerable, not the least of which is the time of human origins. It is assumed that mutations occur in DNA at a fairly regular rate, with differences thus accumulating between species after their evolutionary separation; this allows a "molecular clock" to give rough estimates of time. Instead of 15 to 20 million years once assumed from fossil evidence, the favored reckoning from molecular work is 6 to 8 million years.

TERTIARY FORERUNNERS

Such a date agrees with what is known from fossil primates in the Tertiary era, beginning some 65 million years ago. The record is expanding rapidly, but is always limited to the places where fossils are found by natural exposure, not all the places where the animals in fact lived. The chapters of progress accord with the geological epochs, or divisions, of the Tertiary, as follows:

Paleocene, 65–53 million years ago. The actual origin of primates, as simple animals retaining much of the original mammalian body pattern, is not known. The Paleocene saw a proliferation of primate-like forms, to none of which primates can be traced.

Eocene, 53–36 million years ago. An abundance of lemur-like, and probably tarsius-like, species is known from North America, Europe, and China. Paradoxically, though very few such fossils are known from Africa, because of paucity of Eocene exposures, it appears likely that this continent was the real source of this expansion, partly because the living lower primates are found here and in southern Asia.

Oligocene, 36–23 million years ago. This period saw the appearance of primitive higher primates (i.e., "simian primates," covering all monkeys, apes, and humans), known particularly from the Fayum depression in Egypt near Cairo. Here, the oldest clear

ancestor, *Catopithecus*, is of late Eocene age, and another species, *Algeripithecus*, apparently a good deal older, is known by three teeth from Algeria. So it seems that ancestral higher primates were already off and running in the heyday of their lemur-like cousins. It is still not agreed, from the evidence, whether simian primates derive from, or are closer to, the lemur-like or the tarsius-like branch of prosimians.

The numerous Fayum fossils comprise at least nineteen species falling into six 2or more families. The best known is *Aegyptopithecus*, which was the size of a cat and had a tail. But, because of features of teeth and skull formation, it is classed, along with *Catopithecus*, as a hominoid and thus as standing near the beginning of the line leading to apes and men, At the least this shows that such a conformation of traits was already in being, although a viewer of the living animal would certainly not see anything like a small ape. The relationships of many of the other Fayum species, i.e. possibly to monkeys, are not now clear.

Miocene, 23–5 million years ago. This period saw a flourishing of actual hominoids, or true apes, extending from southern Africa to Europe and southern Asia. Many are identified as "dental apes," because much of their material consists of jaws and skulls with teeth, with few bones of the skeleton. Nevertheless, enough bones are available to establish important conclusions for this stage. Two early forms show clear relations to Aegyptopithecus. One of these, *Proconsul* of East Africa, is well known; though tailless it was conservative in skeletal form. Being an arboreal quadruped like a monkey, it does not have the long-armed suspension and swinging locomotion of later and extant apes.

In another finding, east Asiatic species typified by *Sivapithecus* exhibit the uptilted face characteristic of orangs. This suggests that phylogenetic separation of that branch had already taken place, which would agree with molecular evidence that would separate the orangs from the chimp-gorilla-Homo clade at some 14 million years ago. Ancestors of this latter group are not currently recognized among known fossils, although a Greek form, *Ouranopithecus*, is seen by some to suggest a chimp-human ancestor. A third finding is a reminder that not all such evolution has the same result: the somewhat mysterious *Oreopithecus* of Italy had an orangutan-like body form and lacked a tail, but had teeth so divergent from those of all hominoids that it cannot be related satisfactorily among the higher primates.

A principal suggestion is that this period saw the appearance of a suspensory tree-going gait, in these forest hominoids, that fostered upright or semiupright positioning of the trunk, with effects on spine and pelvis that facilitated bipedal walking in the eventual hominids (i.e., Hominidae proper). Chimpanzees and gorillas, and even orangutans, can readily walk erect and will do so in the wild when it is convenient. While the suspensory gait allows large size in tree-using animals, in fact the apes declined dramatically during the later Miocene, perhaps from competition with the emerging monkeys of the Old World, who were more agile both in trees and on the ground.

Pliocene, 5–1.7 million years ago. This time saw the appearance of the first recognizable human ancestors (i.e., bipedal hominids as distinct from other hominids). The actual transition is obscured, however, by the virtual absence at present of fossils from the latest Miocene and 4.5 million years ago, following which the first hominids appear.

THE AUSTRALOPITHECINES

In 1925, Raymond Dart in Johannesburg described a juvenile fossil skull having its first permanent molars, as an intermediate form between apes and humans, pointing to features of teeth, eye sockets, forehead, and profile that suggested an approach to hominids. He named it *Australopithecus africanus* and placed it in a new family signifying its intermediate position. British and American anthropologists at that time rejected his view, seeing it as a new ape with only possible suggestions of humanlike traits. It was not until the late 1940s, after further finds including other skulls and pelvic and spinal parts, that the fossils were firmly placed in the family Hominidae, as a subfamily, Australopithecinae. There are now major collections from many cities in South and East Africa.

The earliest is named *Australopithecus ramidus*, deservedly called a "missing link", since it currently represents a first divergence from a chimp-human ancestor, much more primitive than later australopithecines although clearly hominid. Known at present from fragments found in the Awash region of Ethiopia, dated to almost 4.5 million years, the teeth are more hominid than chimplike, but barely so, with reduced canines and incisors. Chimpanzee-like traits are missing from arm bones, and the skull base has

a hominid marker; it is unknown whether these characteristics signify bipedalism, but there is nothing to disprove it. From Kanapoi in Kenya, a single fragment of similar age—the elbow end of a humerus—is identifiable as hominid and may belong to this or another species. *A. ramidus* appears to have been living in a still wooded area, judging from the presence of numerous monkeys (but no apes) among the accompanying fossils.

The picture appears as one of early ground-going hominids, in unforested country, behaviorally facing new opportunities and constraints and exhibiting a degree of accelerated branching evolution, giving rise to somewhat diverging species which do not form a single line of development to later hominids and which differ in apparent anatomical commitment to bipedal walking. The two earliest speies, not yet well known, illustrate the distinction. The first is named *Ardipithecus ramidus*, deservedly called a "missing link", since it currently represents an early divergence from a chimp-human ancestor, clearly hominid but clearly more primitive than later species (White et al., 1994.) As known from fragments found in the Awash region of Ethiopia, dated to 4.4 million years, the teeth are more hominid than chimp-like, but barely so, with reduced canines and incisors. Chimpanzee-like traits do not appear in limb bones, as so far described. Accompanying fossils include numerous monkeys, but no apes, which suggests that *A. ramidus* living in a wooded but not forested region.

Australopithecus anamensis, known from sites in northern Kenya and dated from 4.1 to 3.9 million years, is distinguishable from *Ardipithecus* cranially and dentally and with limb parts that give good indications of well-established bipedalism. There is no reason to think the species is descended from *Ardipithecus*. Somewhat later (3.9–3.1 mya), is the well known *Australopithecus afarensis* of Ethiopia and Laetoli (Tanzania), which is recognized popularly as the family of "Lucy", a diminutive female skeleton. This is somewhat less primitive than *A. anamensis* in the teeth, as is shown by less robust canines and other details of molars and premolars, while apparently having a more sloping face. As to gait, there is an uncertainty. Lucy and her ilk, while evidently upright walkers, as shown by pelvis, leg and foot skeletons, nevertheless had toe proportions different from our own, and had arms and hands suggesting a surviving capability for climbing in trees. This has been a puzzle, because of the famous footprints preserved in volcanic ash at Laetoli, contemporary with *A. afarensis* (Lucy.) These prints were made by individuals with feet and foot action more similar to our own, with great toes and other toes as close together as in ourselves. Accordingly, the suggestion arises that the prints were in fact made by *A. anamensis*, and that the two species coexisted. This remains a current problem. Although perhaps on an intellectual level with chimpanzees, *Australopithecus afarensis* was not simply a stage to humanhood, being entirely successful in its own right, since it seems to have endured from 3.9 for about a million years. (The environment can be judged partly from the fact that it included no apes of the tree-living kind.) This species was followed, after 3 million years ago, by *Australopithecus africanus*, known mainly or entirely from South Africa. (Dart's original specimen is too immature to reveal if it should actually be referred to this species.) Whether or not it derived directly from *afarensis*, it exhibited a skull less primitive or ape-like than before, and a brain volume slightly larger (420 cc vs 385 cc; modern volume is 1400-1500 cc), while the skeleton, as known, showed no significant advance; one early foot skeleton was definitely more ape-like than that of the feet which made the still older Laetoli prints.

A further example of evolutionary experimentation in the new hominids, from about 2.5 mya, was another group, the "robust" australopithecines. Although only roughly of the body size of the others, they are referred to as robust because of their massive jaws and cheek teeth, expressed also in flaring cheek arches and large faces, with crests like a gorilla's on the top of the skull to accommodate the heavy chewing muscles. The anterior teeth (incisors and canines) were actually quite small, contrasting with molars and premolars, which were very large and of which the chewing surfaces ground down flat in wear.

Consigned by many writers to a separate genus *Paranthropus*, as many as three species are recognized: *robustus* (South Africa), *aethiopicus*, and *boisei* (East Africa), according to time, place, and some differences in form. There has been much discussion of their relations to one another, and to other australopithecines and later hominids—one school finds them actually closer to Homo in ancestry—but the essential matter is the presence, by this special further adaptation, of such heavy-jawed australopithecines.

They existed in parallel with *A. africanus*, surviving the latter and enduring contemporaneously with Homo until after 1 million years ago. The cause of their eventual extinction is unknown—perhaps a climate change affecting special dietary sources, perhaps too great source competition with *Homo* after a common existence of some 1.5 million years. One lesson may be drawn: The hominid pattern of bipedalism did not necessitate brain expansion and other human progress.

THE RISE OF *HOMO*

Such progress, which included brain expansion, appeared in a species and place unknown, except that it was certainly African. Unlike the evolutionary stasis enjoyed by *A. afarensis*, the period after 3 million years ago was evidently one of change and some diversification. The period also saw an extinction of many African mammals and a climatic cooling and drying, things which may have been implicated in the development of the robust australopithecine species and their success in eating coarse savanna foods.

At 2.5 million years ago, *Australopithecus africanus* was present in South Africa, with a brain hardly larger than *afarensis* and with arms similarly reflecting a definite tree-climbing ability. Between about 2.3 and 1.6 million years ago, there existed in East Africa a species distinguishable in cranial traits, with larger brain and higher braincase, and with smaller jaws to such a degree that Leakey, Tobias, and Napier felt obliged, in 1964, to include it in *Homo*, as the species *Homo habilis*. This was based on specimens found at Olduvai Gorge. Continued discoveries there have indicated that this was correct but that the arms (not the legs) were still close in proportions to those of a chimpanzee, implying continuation of some tree use.

Koobi Fora, a site on the east shore of Lake Turkana in Kenya, has yielded numerous fragments and some good skulls for this period. The picture has been slowly coming into focus, but from a full review of the materials, Bernard Wood (1991) has proposed that no fewer than three *Homo* species are present: *habilis*, *rudolfensis*, and another one more advanced. *Rudolfensis* is recognized because, from close examination, the apparent variation among *habilis*-like skulls seems too great for a single species. In this second species, the skull was slightly more primitive in character but lacked bony brows, which are present in *habilis*, and contained a slightly larger brain (750 cc versus 600 cc). From this little information, the hind limb was more like later hominids. Finally, a single fragment of skull base from a Kenyan site appears to be *rudolfensis*, is dated to 2.4 million years ago or more, and so may signal a minimum age for already existing diversity in *Homo*.

The third species, *Homo ergaster*, is actually probably a member or an immediate forerunner of *Homo erectus*, below. It is not clear whether *habilis* or *rudolfensis*, or either, gave rise to this next level. Thus, it can be seen that this time period was not one of simple stage-by-stage progress but again one of branching and evolutionary experimentation. Furthermore, little can be assessed from physique as to behavior in any of these, but the date of 2.5 million years ago is also that of the appearance, in several places in East Africa, of the first recognizable manufactured stone tools. Thus, the beginning of the cultural record is associated in time with that of *Homo*.

THE REIGN OF *HOMO ERECTUS*

Now began another long period of apparent stability in human evolution, from about 1.8 million to a million years ago or more. Except for surviving robust *australopithecines*, all human fossils are placed in a single species, *Homo erectus*, now expanded to out of Africa. There has been much discussion of differences over time and space, but this has not led to any agreement as to classificatory subdivision of a significant kind. It is only the variations that lead to further questions, including arguments that this should be considered a stage rather than a species. General opinion is to the contrary.

In *H. erectus*, the braincase now dominates the face and the skeleton is essentially fully human, though tending to be heavier than in moderns. The skull is thicker than in the other hominids described. Brain volume has risen to about 1000 cubic centimers. The face is surmounted by a thick continuous bony brow, and a flat shelf joins the frontal bone. There is apt to be a keeling of the vault in the midline, and the profile of the back of the skull is sharply angled. There are various special traits of the ear region.

In Africa, two good early skulls found at Koobi Fora were immediately seen to be very similar to later crania from China, giving brain volumes of 800 to 850 cc. A splendidly complete skeleton of an adolescent male was found at the Lake Turkana site of Kariokotome, who was surprisingly tall and showed a modernity of form contrasting with *Homo habilis* and australopithecine remains, differing from moderns mainly in delicacy of the lumbar spine. These early finds are the ones that have been classed as a species *Homo ergaster*, a view which, however justified, does not alter their close resemblance to later *erectus*. Meager remains from Olduvai Gorge, 500,000 years younger, consist of a thick partial cranial vault, and parts of pelvis and femur, robust but generally modern in form, though in one detail, a thick reinforcing pillar in the ilium, less refined in structure than in ourselves.

Escape from Africa was evidently prompt. A partial lower jaw with a full set of well preserved teeth, from Dmanisi, in Georgia, has an age of at least 1.8 million years, and can be assigned only to *Homo erectus*. Otherwise, remains are Far Eastern. Thick and robust skulls and jaws have constantly recovered in Java, the scene of the first discovery of an early hominid in 1891 which, as *Pithecanthropus erectus*, was the source of the species's name. The earlier Javanese skulls, unlike the earliest African *erecti*, are particularly heavy, and were followed later by less robust examples. Still later, possibly 300,000 years ago or less, there is an important set of skull vaults recovered at Ngandong in Java, which are again very robust and larger (brain volume about 1050 cc) but assignable to *H. erectus*. Thus, the time span for the species in this quarter is a long one.

A similar span is known for China, beginning later and lasting until perhaps less than 200,000 years ago. The bulk of the material came from the Peking Man cave at Zhoukoudian and was known in detail, though lost during World War II. This presents a more gracile form than the Javanese specimens, and earlier and later specimens from other sites display a possible degree of forward evolution, though in no case falling outside *erectus* limits.

THE CHANGE TO MODERNS

The species's unity of *Homo erectus* has frequently been disputed but is generally accepted. The unity of the living species, *Homo sapiens*, is unquestioned, as demonstrated by the universal interfertility of its populations. Despite the racial diversity in outer appearance the common cranial characters, as contrasted with *H. erectus*, are evident. The skull is thin-walled and high, with vertical sides, a rounded occipital profile in the rear, and a brain volume of 1400–1500 cc. The face is short and retracted, with a hollow in the cheekbone under the eyes, and a protruding chin on the lower jaw; it is surmounted by bony brows that no longer form a torus or bar but have disintegrated into central and lateral parts so that there is a discernible notch over the middle of each eye socket.

Evidence for the evolution from one to the other, over the period from perhaps 500,000 BP (Before the Present) to a few thousand years ago, is far from complete. Specimens from any level above *Homo erectus* are accepted as *Homo sapiens*, and many have been assigned to various subspecies of sapiens (with ourselves as *Homo sapiens sapiens*). More generally, most are referred to as "archaic *Homo sapiens*" a desgination with the possible advantage of being non-committal. Very early finds, ambiguous as to assignment, have been made in Europe, where it was once thought that *Homo erectus* never arrived. In the Gran Dolina cave, near Burgos in Spain, were found skull and jaw fragments, teeth, and simple flaked tools, well dated at 780,000 years or older. The parts are primitive for *Homo* but appear to differ from Asian *H. erectus*, being if anything more advanced, at least in the frontal region. Likewise a tibia or shinbone, from Boxgrove in southern England, is large and heavy, and there is no proper background for assigning it either to *Homo erectus* or to a later species. The site itself is significant: with a date approximating 500,000 years ago it yielded not only the tibia but some good bifacial Acheulean handaxes. This is the tool tradition known abundantly then and earlier in Africa (not Asia.)

More complete early finds from Africa and Europe, with probable dates of 400,00 BP, are indeed only slightly more progressive than *erectus* but have clear differences is some structures such as a less angled occiput as well as a somewhat larger brain. Well known examples are the Broken Hill skull from Kabwe, Zambia and the Petralona skull from Greece. Much later, preceding moderns at about 130,000 to 80,000 BP, are archaics of almost modern character, in North, East and South Africa and in the Levant. In Asia, with the apparent long survival of *H. erectus*, critical evidence is meager. In Europe, by contrast, there is good evidence of a continuing evolution toward the Neanderthal population from perhaps 300,000 BP, especially with good skulls of about that date from the Sima de Los Huesos, again in northern Spain. Whether this ancestry could extend back to the Gran Dolina people, signifying a very early divide of

Neanderthals from other *Homo*, is an interesting question.

MULTIREGIONAL EVOLUTION

The pattern of the transition from *erectus* to *sapiens* has for some time been the subject of the most heated and adversarial controversy in the whole matter of our evolution. Two opposing hypotheses exist. The older one, termed multiregional evolution (MRE), holds that following the early dispersal of *Homo erectus* from Africa, regional populations in Africa, Europe, China, and Australasia underwent separate progressive evolution, with distinctions that can be traced locally from *erectus* to *sapiens*. At the same time, migration and gene exchange passed new traits among all these groups, maintaining species unity across the Old World and across any grade line; thus, no speciation event occurred. Adherents argue for local continuity from this no-speciation model and from detailed specification of likenesses between earlier and modern populations, demonstrating local continuity. In particular, these workers see an evolution of Neanderthals into Europeans from evidence in a few East European sites, and argue that apparently distinct Neanderthal and archaic modern communities in the Levant are actually no more varied than may be expected in modern major populations. In China, traits specific for Zhoukoudian *Homo erectus* are traced in modern skulls, and Australian Aboriginals, with their heavy-browed, rather low skulls, and large teeth, are seen as a logical local derivation from the Java *erectus* population via the later Ngandong people.

Writers of the opposing camp see things quite differently. They contend that the Australians, being somewhat archaic among moderns, share cranial traits with the Ngandong people that are simply archaic, rather than being specific to the region and not seen elsewhere. They are not convinced that the alleged Chinese connecting traits are exclusive to China. In Europe, the Neanderthals, after a long local evolution (Neanderthals occurred nowhere else except the Near East), were clearly displaced rather abruptly at about 35,000 BP over most of Europe; whether by their own descendants or by European-like Caucasoid immigrants of probable descent from the Skhul-Qafzeh people of Israel, almost-moderns that are dated to over 80,000 BP. These critics also observe that, despite their worldview, the MRE adherents argue largely from local histories rather than from systematic analyses over the whole Old World.

As for the Neanderthals, they are special because of numerous finds and because of their particular character. At the end, they had skeletons of great robustness together with special traits not seen in moderns. Also, they had a cranium with a brain size equivalent to moderns but distinct in form: low, with bulging sides, a continuous double-arched bow with large internal sinuses, large rounded eye sockets and nose, and a very projecting face with flattish sides. This pattern seems to have been developing steadily from about 400,000 BP, a trend evidenced by important new finds in Spain and Italy, until their displacement about 35,000 BP. The argument is that this represents a separate regional evolution, over several 100,000 years, which was not exchanging genes with other lines (as held by the MRE model), and which was indeed replaced by immigrants from nearer Africa. Here the question may arise of whether the extremely early Gran Dolina people represent a first regional seedling from *Homo erectus* leading, through Neanderthals, to the Europeans, or whether they simply became extinct early or late, as suggested below.

OUT OF AFRICA

The opposing camp argues from the fossil material taken more broadly, and from inferences from various studies using not only cranial but also molecular and other evidence from the living, studies which generally speak to falsify the general MRE model. Their view is one of Recent African Origin (RAO) of a population, or more than one, which was already essentially modern (at some date like 100,000 BP), migrants who replaced descendants, in the other quadrants, of *Homo erectus* without absorbing significant genetic contributions from those replaced.

Because of important molecular studies, this Out-of-Africa hypothesis has also become known popularly, if unfortunately, as the African "Eve" hypothesis. This is based on analysis of mitochondrial DNA (mtDNA). Mitochondria are small, energy-producing bodies in a cell, outside the nucleus which carries the DNA of the chromosomes; there are many in a cell but all carry the same small segment of DNA. This bit is only 1/200,000th as long as the DNA in the nucleus and is thus easier to study; furthermore, since at conception the sperm brings only the male chromosomes of the father, with the egg providing the fertilized cell body, mtDNA is determined by the mother alone. Mutations occur in the mtDNA, giving rise to new patterns or types according to the analysis performed.

The greatest variety of types is found in Africans. The argument is that all humans include one single woman in their ancestry (not that she was the only ancestress), hence "Eve." From her unspecified type, mutations have continuously given rise to new types in all regions, suggesting a time of dispersal (from Africa) which is much less than the age of *Homo erectus*, and which is thus the period of later migrations of more modern people. In the present-day regional assemblages of mtDNA, there are no signs of perturbations due to hybridizing with preexisting local populations, so that replacement is implied. In addition, modern humans overall exhibit less variation than the living apes. Finally, possible family trees are computed among the regional groups from their mtDNA types. Many objections have been made to the estimated dispersal time (allowing the differentiation to be pushed back to the time of *Homo erectus*, i.e., the MRE model), and to family trees, on the basis of methods of computation. But the research is still new, and the fact remains that the greatest diversity exists in Africa.

The discussion has moved on to cranial analyses of some complexity. One such, treating China in great detail, favors regional evolution but is restricted to this region which limits the force of the argument. Other studies, hemisphere-wide in scope, in general find some evidence of local continuity but more evidence favoring refutation of the main MRE hypothesis without actually rejecting it. These analyses emphasize modern cranial homogeneity and also a diversity in Africa as compared with other regions, a finding in parallel with the mtDNA data. Further inferences from cranial data, not direct but derived from a mathematical model, allow estimates of past population sizes and rates of migration. This study emphasizes longer times of diversification within Africa, as well as suggesting more than one emigration from Africa followed by further intraregional diversifications. Probabilities from all this do not disprove the MRE thesis, but render much more likely a version of the RAO hypothesis in which populations diversify significantly in Africa and later migrate outward, continuing to diversify and to replace previous populations.

MODERNS ARRIVE

The debate continues. The known arrival, in different regions, of fully modern people is late and not satisfactorily documented. For Africa, fragments from a South African cave (Klasies River Mouth) indicate such presence at 100,000 BP. For China, the slender evidence of a single skull (Liuijiang) gives a questioned date of 67,000 BP or more; the skull is a possible Mongoloid forerunner. It is in Europe and Australia that the evidence is better, for different reasons.

In Europe and the Near East, true moderns probably make an appearance at about 45,000 BP. While MRE advocates see signs of evolution of moderns from Neanderthals in Eastern Europe, there is clear evidence of replacement in the West and the Levant. Also, while near-moderns and Neanderthals differed little in the stone tools they made—although there are small signs of distinctions in the nature of their living-sites—the new Upper Paleolithic folk arriving in Europe (referred to as Cro-Magnons) had a much more varied and refined tool kit and, significantly, made a rich variety of personal ornaments and art objects using bone and ivory, supplemented later by cave art. Archaeologists are so impressed by this development as to call it the "sapiens explosion," inferring an actual biological development occurring at some time after 100,000 BP in our species.

This reflects on arrivals in Australia. Despite considerable water barriers, the first Aboriginals arrived there at 55,000 BP or before. Although lacking the complex stone tools of the Europeans (perhaps not called for in that region), and although slightly archaic in skull form, these Aboriginals, as known from somewhat later skeletal remains, are clearly of our modern species and were practicing art as well. The inferences are double; that before leaving an original home, they had partaken in whatever evolutionary shift is signalled by the "sapiens explosion," and that they may represent a definable, early exit of moderns from Africa through southern Asia.

A closer solution of such problems is for the future, as well as other questions of biological bases for culture. Current estimates for the point of appearance of human language range from *Homo habilis* to shortly before the "sapiens explosion"; some writers even suspect the Neanderthals of being limited in language production. That range may suggest how wide remains the field for investigating questions of human evolution and cultural development.

W. W. HOWELLS

HOWELLS, WILLIAM. *Getting Here: The Story of Human Evolution.* Washington, DC: Compass Press, 1993.

JONES, STEVE, ROBERT MARTIN, and DAVID PILBEAM, eds. The Cambridge Encyclopedia of Human Evolution. Cambridge University Press, 1992.

KLEIN, RICHARD G. "The Archaeology of Modern Human Origins." *Evolutionary Anthropology* 1 (1992): 5 -14.

LEAKEY, MAEVE G., CRAIG S. FEIBEL, IAN MC-DOUGALL, and ALAN WALKER. "New four-million-year-old hominid species from Kanapoi and Allia Bay, Kenya." In *Nature,* 376 (1995): 565-571.

POPE, GEOFFREY G. "Craniofacial Evidence for the Origin of Modern Humans in China." *Yearbook of Physical Anthropology* 35 (1992): 243–298.

RICE, PATRICIA C. "Paleoanthropology 1994." *General Anthropology* 1 (1994): 5–8.

RIGHTMIRE, G. PHILIP. *The Evolution of Homo erectus.* New York: Cambridge University Press, 1990.

SHERRY, STEPHEN T., ALAN R. ROGERS, HENRY HARPENDING, HIMLA SOODYALL, TREFOR JENKINS, and MARK STONEKING. "Mismatch Distributions of mtDNA Reveal Recent Human Population Expansions." *Human Biology* 66(5)(1994): 761–775.

STONEKING, MARK. "DNA and Recent Human Evolution." *Evolutionary Anthropology* 2 (2) (1993): 60–73.

SUSSMAN, ROBERT W., ed. "A Current Controversy in Human Evolution." *American Anthropologist* 95 (1993): 9–96.

TATTERSALL, IAN. *The Human Odyssey: Four Million Years of Human Behavior.* New York: Prentice Hall, 1993.

WHITE, TIM D., GEN SUWA, and BERHANE ASFAW. "*Australopithecus ramidus,* a New Species of Early Hominid from Aramis, Ethiopia." *Nature* 371 (1994): 306–312.

WOOD, BERNARD. "The Problems of Our Origins." *Journal of Human Evolution.* 27 (1994): 519–529.

HUMAN OSTEOLOGY

Since its inception the majority of research in biological anthropology has depended on the study and analysis of human skeletal or osteological remains—bones and teeth. The scope of biological anthropology has expanded, new techniques have been developed, and questions have changed, but the key data and inferences from biological anthropology are still most often derived from detailed observation, comparison, and analysis of bones and teeth. Because so much information about individuals is reflected in their skeletons, human osteological analyses can provide insights into a wide variety of questions, ranging from the genetic relationships of a fossil hominid from France to the diet of a slave in eighteenth-century Virginia to the identity of individuals in a mass grave in El Salvador.

HISTORY

The roots of human osteological studies begin with studies of natural history and medicine in Europe and the United States in the late eighteenth and early nineteenth centuries. In many regards the early work in biological anthropology was based entirely on osteological studies; until the twentieth century biological anthropology and human osteology were nearly synonymous.

Historically, research in human osteology focused on two overarching problems: to understand evolutionary changes in the human skeleton and thus the evolution of our species and to understand patterns of variation in contemporary and nearly contemporary humans. Particularly in France and the United States, a great deal of research was done to establish skeletal traits that would reflect intelligence and thus make it possible to compare intelligence in individuals and groups (usually defined in terms of the now-outmoded idea of race). Leading candidates included cranial capacity and the angle of the face. This idea—that intelligence however defined is well reflected in a simple osteological measurement—has been discredited. This research was motivated by predetermined biases regarding the innate superiority or inferiority of certain groups.

From early concerns with human evolution and contemporary variation, work on skeletal remains branched out. Detailed fundamental studies involved the comparative skeletal anatomy of humans and other primate species. Methods were developed to estimate an individual's sex and age at death from the remaining skeletal material. During the first half of the twentieth century Earnest A. Hooton, a Harvard professor who trained many of the next generation of physical anthropologists, used osteological methods to determine the health of past Native American populations. Hooton developed an ecological and populational approach, still common today in bioarchaeology.

THE SCOPE OF HUMAN OSTEOLOGY TODAY

The main subdisciplines of biological anthropology that are based on osteological analyses include human paleontology and functional anatomy, forensic anthropology, and bioarchaeology. Human paleontology is a subfield of physical anthropology that focuses on the evolution of humans via the discovery, reconstruction, and interpretation of human and human-like fossils. While this research once focused on gross differences in the morphology of bones and teeth, new methods and instrumentation have led to more detailed studies. Now, as often as they might measure and compare tooth sizes, human paleontologists analyze past diets by employing scanning electron microscopes to study the pattern of microscopic scratches on teeth and analyze the evolution and development of vein directions via the use of computer imaging techniques.

A key concept of human osteology is that osteological forms reflect function. Thus, studies of bone and tooth morphology can provide insights into use and habitual activities. For example, the development of a midsagittal crest, a large area of muscle attachment at the top of the skull, is imposed by long and powerful chewing masseter muscles, which suggests function, such as habitual chewing on a coarse, nutty, and fibrous vegetarian diet.

Forensic anthropology is an applied field of human osteology in which techniques of human identification are applied to medical legal problems, mostly having to do with the identification of humans from skeletal remains or the detection of evidence of foul play. Identification is based on a number of techniques that typically include estimation of sex (in adults), age at death, stature, and "race." Determination of sex, age at death, and stature is never perfect, but with relatively complete remains these biological characteristics can be determined with high accuracy. Determination of race, still a common practice of forensic anthropologists, is more problematical. The technical problem is that human variation is much greater within than between so-called races; thus accuracy of determination is limited. More important, race is not a true biological characteristic, rather, in this as in most contexts, it is a social identifier. To alleviate this problem some forensic anthropologists are working on more precise methods of identification of ancestry that do not rely on the outmoded nineteenth-century idea of race. Interest in forensic anthropology, also an applied branch of biological anthropology, has been growing, with the creation of the physical anthropology section of the American Academy of Forensic Sciences and the offering of advanced degrees in forensic anthropology at several universities.

Bioarchaeology, the study of human skeletal remains in archaeological contexts, may be the area of human osteological research that is of greatest interest to cultural anthropology. Bioarchaeological studies require individual identification, using the same techniques as those employed in forensic anthropology. Bioarchaeology, however, differs in its goals of understanding the diet, nutrition, health, activity patterns, and other aspects of lifestyle of past populations. These studies fall into categories with such names as paleopathology or paleoepidemiology, paleonutrition, and paleodemography, respectively, studies of the patterns of disease, nutrition, and demography (life expectancy, survivorship) in past populations. Because these lifestyle aspects result from the interaction of culture and environment with biology, they provide insights into past cultures.

Interests in bioarchaeology began to flourish in the late 1960s and 1970s. At that time ecological and processual studies were developing in archaeology and other disciplines. Bioarchaeology developed as a means for studying the interaction between environment, culture, and biology. A test case for bioarchaeology revolves around whether the transition from hunting and gathering to agriculture involved improvements or decrements in nutrition and health. Methods include comparison of life expectancies, frequencies of various diseases, and growth patterns. The results of more than twenty case studies (Cohen and Armelagos 1984) suggest that health and nutrition tend to decline, but this pattern is not invariable. The type of agriculture seems to be important, and it is apparent that sociopolitical factors having to do with the control of resources also affect health.

More recently bioarchaeological methods have been employed to understand other economic and cultural changes. Since the mid-1980s a number of volumes (Verano and Ubelaker 1992) have reported on changes in health, nutrition, and demography of indigenous Americans in the wake of European contact and colonization. Skeletal analyses are being used to supplement archaeological and historical techniques to understand lifestyles of historic groups, such as free blacks and poorhouse whites. These studies provide direct testament to the pattern of health and disease in recent groups.

The human skeleton is far from static. Bone and teeth are dynamic and complex systems that provide a number of clues and insights into evolution and development. Because humans biologies reside within cultural systems, it is not surprising that the skeleton mirrors culture.

ALAN H. GOODMAN

See Also: Biocultural Anthropology; Biological Anthropology; Biocultural Diversity and Race; Disease and Culture; Medical Anthropology

BASS, WILLIAM M. *Human Osteology: A Laboratory and Field Manual,* 3rd ed. Special Publication No. 2. Columbus: Missouri Archaeological Society, 1987.
COHEN, MARK N., and GEORGE J. ARMELAGOS, eds. *Paleopathology at the Origins of Agriculture.* New York: Academic Press, 1984.
SAUNDERS, SHELLEY R., and M. ANNE KATZENBERG, eds. *Skeletal Biology of Past Peoples: Research Methods.* New York: Wiley-Liss, 1992.
VERANO, JOHN W., and DOUGLAS H. UBELAKER, eds. *Disease and Demography in the Americas.* Washington, D.C.: Smithsonian Institution Press, 1992.
WHITE, TIM D. *Human Osteology.* Orlando, Fla.: Academic Press, 1991.

HUMAN POPULATION BIOLOGY

The coalescence of several different research areas within or closely associated with biological anthropology, human population biology emerged in the early 1980s as a distinct field of inquiry crossing the boundaries of many existing scientific disciplines. It involves the scientific study of physiology, body morphology and composition, genetics, demography, growth and senescence (the life cycle), biochemistry, nutrition, physical activity, and health and disease; it focuses broadly on explaining patterns of biological variation in human populations over time and across space. Central to human population biology are considerations of the natural environment, patterns of sociocultural (including technological) and behavioral variation, and evolution (in particular, adaptation). Within biological anthropology, human population biology, including its component fields, is the most popular subject of scientific focus, when compared with paleoanthropology and primatology.

A major catalyzing factor in the emergence of human population biology was the work of Paul T. Baker in the late 1960s and early to middle 1970s. Baker studied a variety of biological phenomena within the context of the adaptability of Quechua natives to living at high altitude in the Peruvian Andes. Other scientific disciplines, however, have also been important in the historical development of the field, which traces its early roots to the 1950s. The Human Adaptability Section of the International Biological Programme (IBP) contributed to Baker's success. Some recent support for these projects has come from the Man and the Biosphere Programme, which began in the mid 1970s after the completion of the IBP. The multidisciplinary study of the high-altitude Quechua spawned many similar efforts that focussed on such human populations as the Yanomamo, Samoans, Eskimos, Solomon Islanders, and Turkana pastoralists of East Africa, among others, since 1974.

THE UNIQUENESS OF HUMAN POPULATION BIOLOGY

The most fundamental concepts associated with human population biology are variation and population. Biological anthropologists, largely to the exclusion of other scientists who study the biological aspects of living *Homo sapiens*, focus on human populations that are real, natural, socioculturally delineated units (rather than clinically derived subjects) and that tend toward marriage within the unit. Moreover, biological anthropologists typically focus on biological variation within a population, or between or among human populations. They seek to explain such variation in terms of its causes, evolutionary explanation, biological significance, and its relationship to environmental and sociocultural phenomena.

In the latter regard, human population biology is a biocultural science, which is another way in which it differs from its allied sciences. Typically, only anthropologists take the holistic biocultural view of humanity and try to understand and explain the complexity of the human condition in terms of its

biological and cultural correlates and their relationships to the natural environment.

SCOPE AND SOURCES OF HUMAN POPULATION BIOLOGY VARIATION

Homo sapiens is an extraordinarily diverse species in terms of biological variation within any specific population and also in the patterns of variation among the many populations worldwide. People are biologically variable in almost every externally visible way; body morphology and the pigmentation of eyes, hair, and skin are among the most obvious differences. In addition to that phenotypic variation, there is biological variation in physiological, genetic, and biochemical ways, which are not readily observable to the naked eye. Individuals and populations also vary with regard to rates and patterns of growth and aging, fertility and mortality, physical activity and energy expenditure, the pathological conditions, and in the types and levels of nutrients they ingest. Indeed, genetic variation alone manifests itself at several levels, from the population to the individual, to the cell (e.g., blood group antigens), and to the configuration of the DNA itself within cells.

The ultimate objective of human population biology is thoroughly to understand and explain patterns of variation biology within single populations and between and among different populations, including similarities and differences in patterns of variation over time and across space. Another objective is to understand and explain why a population's patterns of biological variation change or remain static over time and why different populations at the same time may have similar or different patterns of biological variation. Ideally, explanations ought to be as specific as possible with regard to the factors, processes, and mechanisms responsible for these patterns of variation. That is an exceptional challenge for human population biologists because population histories, the environment, and patterns of sociocultural variation are extremely complex and often interrelated. Indeed, many such explanations are particularly challenging because they may ultimately lie in physiological, biochemical, or metabolic pathways at the cellular level within individuals—a level at which human population biologists have not, as of yet, been heavily involved.

A finite set of fundamental causes and explanations for patterns of biological variation in human populations exists. It includes the operation of the evolutionary forces of mutation, selection, admixture or gene flow, and genetic drift. Central to understanding this variation is a specific explanation for it, such as the mechanism by which the genetically determined hemoglobinopathy variant Hb^s has come to be so relatively frequent in human populations inhabiting much of tropical Africa, despite one of its genetic configurations causing the almost always lethal disease sickle-cell anemia.

This explanation involves malaria, the life cycle of its infectious agent, the malaria plasmodium, and its vector, the anopheles mosquito, as well as the presence of slash-and-burn horticulture. The ultimate explanation is that the malaria plasmodium is unable to successfully reproduce in the presence of red blood cells having a certain genetically determined hemoglobin configuration, thus conveying an immunity to malaria in such individuals.

Population history and the natural environment are contributing factors to patterns of biological variation within and among human populations. Episodes of famine such as those afflicting parts of Africa; such conquests as the European invasion of the Americas about 500 years ago; epidemics such as the plague which swept Europe in the Middle Ages; and the availability of resources, demographic structure, and other such important phenomena inherent to a population's history may greatly influence the evolution and the ongoing survival and well-being of human groups. The prevailing natural environment (e.g., humidity, temperature, altitude, available energy for consumption, sunlight, and human-made pollution) influences patterns of intra- and interpopulation biological variation.

Sociocultural configurations are extremely powerful contributors to patterns of biological variation within and among human populations. For example, variations in culturally prescribed marriage rules, religious taboos influencing diet, economic options, differential access to resources, health care practices, treatment of illness, and methods of contraception differ considerably worldwide and thus contribute to these patterns of variation.

THEORETICAL AND METHODOLOGICAL UNITY

Despite that scientists from other disciplines focus on human population biology, its research has common theoretical and methodological bases. The theoretical foundation of evolution, especially that component involving adaptation and adaptability, is at the heart of all human population biological research. Much, but not all, variation in human population biology is ascribable to mutation, selection, gene flow (admixture), and genetic drift.

Humans respond biologically to the environment, especially to such extreme circumstances as high altitude or temperature, in three basic ways. Long-term change in gene pools is known as genetic adaptation and occurs via the interactive mechanisms of mutation and selection. In cold climates, long, narrow noses (nasal shape is generally under genetic control) offer an adaptive advantage; they warm inhaled air to a temperature similar to that of the internal environment within the lungs. A second mechanism of adjustment to environmental circumstance is through the growth process itself. The enlarged vital capacity of the lungs, which aids highland Peruvians in survival of oxygen deprivation, occurs during the growth process. The juvenile stage of growth permits the human adult phenotypes to develop more slowly. For an animal inhabiting a range of environments, this ultimately allows an adult organism to conform better to its environment. The third response is known as biological plasticity. Perhaps more than any other species, humans have the individual flexibility to modify their biological patterns on a short-term basis, in reaction to specific environmental stimuli. For example, when one moves from sea level to high altitude (exceeding 2,500 meters or 8,200 feet), rates of respiration and pulse, and the production of red blood cells increase concomitantly in order to maximize the transportation of oxygen to the body cells.

Although the data relevant to human population biology are collected using different techniques the methodological bases of such study are generally a finite few. Geneticists, physiologists, and demographers use different techniques to describe the patterns of biological configuration and variation within and among human populations. However, the methods by which they analyze the descriptive data on which human population biology is built are a common few. Three prevail: the comparative analysis of variation within single populations; the comparison of patterns of variation between and among more than one population; and the generation of models that accounts for differences and similarities in patterns of biological variation within and among human populations.

Less frequent, but valuable in understanding patterns of biological variation is the experimental method. Using it, subjects carefully controlled in many ways experience some laboratory-based intervention (treadmill activity at different levels of temperature or humidity, for example) and biological responses before, during, and after the interventions are monitored.

The "natural laboratory" approach is a common feature of much research in human population biology. Such research attempts to focus on natural situations in which as many potential variables that might confound scientific explanation are controlled. For example, studying samples of the same population having the same sociocultural configuration and living in two different ecological contexts would most likely allow an environmental explanation for patterns of biological variation, because the genetic and sociocultural backgrounds of the samples would be constant factors.

HUMAN POPULATION BIOLOGY SYNERGISMS

Two sets of synergistic relationships relate to human population biology. One involves the fact that different biological phenomena within individuals and populations, and among populations, can influence one another to various degrees. The other synergistic relationship is the interaction among the three realms of variation involved with human population biology: patterns of sociocultural and behavioral variation, environmental variation, and the biological variation itself. The latter set of synergistic relationships is described below.

BIOLOGY, CULTURE, AND ENVIRONMENT

Culture directly influences the environment by pollution and contamination of such natural resources as the water, and land itself. Human population biologists study the biological impact of this unfortunate phenomenon on childhood growth and development. Indeed, the environment that constitutes urbanization is itself virtually entirely a product of cultural factors; the urban environment is a relatively new one to confront and impact the biological patterns of human populations.

On the other hand, the environment often limits the kinds of energy available for human dietary consumption. Nutrition influences health, growth, and susceptibility to disease and, therefore, patterns of biological variation within and among human populations. Biological patterns influence the environment, and disease and health variation among populations, in conjunction with patterns of fertility and age-specific mortality; and may burden and change the environment as population size and density increase. As the environment is so burdened its propensity to yield healthy energy resources for dietary consumption changes and may correspondingly alter patterns of biological variation related to disease susceptibility, physiology, reproduction, and biochemistry in human populations.

Sociocultural and behavioral variations influence human population biology. Culturally prescribed marriage rules influence the delineation of human breeding populations themselves. Socioeconomic stratification and its sequelae, access to dietary resources and health care, impact childhood growth. Rules of polygamy impact differential fertility and, therefore, the operation of selection. Westernization significantly changes patterns of diet and disease in traditional societies, especially in adiposity and the prevalence of cardiovascular disease, for which fatness is a documented risk factor. Certain aspects of human population biology influence cultural practices and institutions and human behavior as well. In Western societies, such cultural institutions as genetic screening programs respond to such genetically determined consequences of evolution as thalassemia, sickle-cell anemia, and Tay-Sachs disease.

CULTURAL ANTHROPOLOGY AND HUMAN POPULATION BIOLOGY

Cultural anthropology is fundamental to understanding the patterns of current biological variation in human populations. Indeed, cultural factors and variations in cultural patterns impact on virtually every kind of biological variation in *Homo sapiens*. Our cultural capability and our technology give us the flexibility, unique among all animals, to inhabit the gamut of terrestrial environments on earth, and therefore to respond biologically to such different ecological circumstances as the Peruvian Andes, the Sahara Desert, the Arctic, and the tropical rain forests of Africa and South America.

Cultural variations associated with economic choices and religious proscriptions influence the different energy resources (diets) of different human populations. This impacts on growth rates, disease susceptibility, adult body size, shape, and composition, and fertility. In another realm, mating patterns, including a variety of culturally prescribed practices, impact on patterns of biological variation in human populations. These include endogamy, polygamy, preferred cousin-marriage, culturally based ideal mate phenotypes, and preferential assortative mating on phenotypic bases.

Slavery, conquest, colonization, historical patterns of population fission and fusion, and cultural ideals, attitudes, and practices regarding fertility and family size also have clear impact on the patterns of biological variation within and among human populations. The biological variables impacted by patterns of sociocultural variation range from genetically based serological and physiological factors to all manner of phenotypically manifested morphological differences.

CURTIS W. WIENKER

See Also: Adaptation; Biocultural Anthropology; Biological Anthropology; Biological Diversity and Race; Demography; Food and Diet; Genetics; Natural Selection; Nutritional Anthropology

BAKER, PAUL T. "Human Population Biology: A Viable Transdisciplinary Science." *Human Biology* 54 (1982): 203–220.

BAKER, PAUL T., JOEL M. HANNA, and THELMA S. BAKER, eds. *The Changing Samoans: Health and Behavior in Transition.* New York: Oxford University Press, 1986.

BAKER, PAUL T., and MICHAEL L. LITTLE, eds. *Man in the Andes: A Multidisciplinary Study of High-Altitude Quechua.* Stroudsburg, Pa.: Dowden, Hutchinson, and Ross, 1976.

FRISANCHO, A. ROBERTO. *Human Adaptation and Accommodation.* Ann Arbor: University of Michigan Press, 1993.

HARRISON, G. A., J. M. TANNER, D. R. PILBEAM, and P. T. BAKER, eds. *Human Biology,* 3rd ed. New York: Oxford University Press, 1988.

LITTLE, MICHAEL A., and JERE D. HAAS, eds. *Human Population Biology.* New York: Oxford University Press, 1989.

OVERFIELD, THERESA. *Biologic Variation in Health and Illness,* 2nd ed. Baco Ranton, Fl.: CRC Press, 1995.

SHEPHARD, ROY J. "Factors Associated with Population Variation in Physiological Working Capacity."

Yearbook of Physical Anthropology 28 (1985): 97–122.

UNDERWOOD, JANE H. *Human Variation and Human Microevolution.* Englewood Cliffs, N.J.: Prentice-Hall, 1979.

HUMAN RELATIONS AREA FILES

The Human Relations Area Files (HRAF) is a private, nonprofit educational and research institution located in New Haven, Connecticut, and affiliated with Yale University. The primary mission of HRAF is to encourage and facilitate the cross-cultural study of human culture, society, and behavior. This mission has mainly involved the continuous expansion, updating, refinement, and distribution of the HRAF archives, called the Human Relations Area Files Cultural Information Database (HRAF Database), which in 1995 contained nearly 1 million pages of text. At the same time the database contained both historic and contemporary descriptive information on the ways of life of people in 358 different cultural, ethnic, religious, and national groups around the world.

HRAF is the result of the work of George P. Murdock, Clelland S. Ford, and their colleagues, who created the Cross-Cultural Survey at Yale's Institute of Human Relations in the 1930s and 1940s. The intellectual roots of HRAF can be traced back much further—to sociologist Herbert Spencer's efforts in the late nineteenth century to collect and organize information on the cultures of the world and sociologist William Graham Sumner's more systematic efforts along the same lines in the first two decades of the twentieth century. HRAF was incorporated as an interuniversity consortium in 1949. At that time the five original sponsoring members—Yale, Harvard University, and the Universities of Pennsylvania, Oklahoma, and Washington—had carbon copies of the database. During the next few years, the number of sponsors increased to twenty, and in 1995 there were twenty-two. Beginning in 1958, in order to make the database more widely available, HRAF began to reproduce documents on microfiche. At this time the category of associate membership was established. From 1990 to 1995 portions of the database were made available on CD-ROM (known as the Cross-Cultural CD). By 1994 the database had been distributed in microfiche or electronic format to more than 400 institutions of higher education in the United States and thirty other nations, with nearly 300 of those institutions adding HRAF's annual updates to their databases. Beginning in 1995 the annual installments of the HRAF database were distributed only in electronic form on CD-ROM (the Electronic HRAF).

HRAF membership is open to nonprofit educational, research, and cultural organizations and government agencies. Sponsoring members are institutions that have complete sets of the database, pay dues of $5,000 per year, and are entitled to one seat and one vote on the HRAF Board of Directors. The board sets organizational policy, approves the annual budget, and elects the officers. Associate members are institutions that hold all or a portion of the database and pay annual dues ranging from $2,900 to $3,900 in order to receive the annual updates of the Electronic HRAF.

The material in the database comes from nearly 8,000 source documents, including books, dissertations, government reports, journal articles, and unpublished works. About 10 percent of these documents have been translated from fifteen different languages into English. The database is updated and expanded by about 20,000 pages from about 250 documents each year, through the addition of new sources both on cultures already covered and on cultures new to the database.

In the early years of HRAF, decisions about what cultures to include were made largely on the basis of the needs of the financial supporters of HRAF, especially the Department of Defense and the Ford Foundation. Since the mid-1960s, however, decisions about what to include have been made largely on the basis of recommendations from the scholarly community, as represented by the members of the HRAF Board of Directors. Because one purpose of the database is to document the full range of human cultural diversity, information is provided on a broad range of cultural types that fall into six general categories: nonindustrialized cultures, native North American cultures, national cultures, cities and urban cultures, North American ethnic cultures, and preindustrial civilizations. For each culture, information is usually included for two or more points in time, in order to make the database useful for longitudinal studies of single cultures as well as comparisons across cultures.

As a research resource, the information in the database has served as an important source for hundreds of scholarly books, doctoral dissertations, journal articles, and conference papers. Although originally intended as a reference resource mainly for researchers interested in conducting worldwide cross-cultural studies of human culture and behavior, the database has also become popular as a teaching resource. Many educators believe that the database is valuable because it serves as a "laboratory" in which students can experience the cross-cultural diversity of human behavior and can actually conduct their own cross-cultural research. Thus, the database is used by instructors as a resource for correcting biased views of human culture, clarifying materials introduced in the classroom, encouraging a deeper appreciation of other viewpoints, and studying the effects of contemporary social forces such as modernization and urbanization.

In addition to the database, HRAF provides other services to the anthropology and social science communities, including workshops and training institutes, grant and contract research, topical and cultural bibliographies, and sponsorship of multivolume academic encyclopedias and the journal *Cross-Cultural Research*. HRAF also publishes on-demand series of ethnographic monographs, quantitative data, and bibliographies.

DAVID LEVINSON

SEE ALSO: Archives; Cross-Cultural Research

BARRY, HERBERT. "Description and Uses of the Human Relations Area Files." In *Handbook of Cross-Cultural Psychology*, edited by Harry C. Triandis and John W. Berry. Boston: Allyn and Bacon, 1980.

BERNARD, RUSSELL H. *Research Methods in Cultural Anthropology*. Newbury Park, Calif.: Sage Publications, 1994.

EMBER, CAROL R., and MELVIN EMBER. *Guide to Cross-Cultural Research Using the HRAF Archive*. New Haven, Conn.: HRAF Press, 1988.

LEVINSON, DAVID. *Instructor's and Librarian's Guide to the HRAF Archive*. New Haven: HRAF Press, 1988.

MURDOCK, GEORGE P., et al. *Outline of Cultural Materials*. 5th rev. edition. New Haven: HRAF Press, 1987.

———. *Outline of World Cultures*. 6th edition. New Haven: HRAF Press, 1983.

HUMAN REPRODUCTION

Human reproduction is defined as the process by which human beings reproduce themselves to create the next generation. Broadly speaking, it includes such topics as sexual behavior, sexual selection, marriage, and demographic anthropology. In order to reproduce, humans have to establish conditions for ovum and spermatozoa to meet in order to produce a pregnancy, the pregnancy must proceed without interruption, and parturition (birth) must take place under conditions that favor survival of the offspring. A classic article by K. Davis and J. Blake (1956) outlines the means by which human behavior affects reproduction, including factors relating to whether or not sexual intercourse takes place, variables relating to whether or not conception takes place, and variables relating to the growth and survival of the fetus (spontaneous or induced abortion). To these can be added variables surrounding parturition and survival of the offspring after parturition (Ford 1964; Scrimshaw 1978, 1984). Clellan S. Ford's classic works on human reproduction (1945, 1964) also include infant care, nursing, and weaning. There is a real question of when to stop. Technically speaking, true reproductive success would mean that offspring are produced, live to reproductive age, and themselves reproduce. Because the first year of life contains more risk than subsequent years until adulthood, the cutoff of the first twelve months is used here to define reproductive success.

The individual behavioral factors affecting human reproduction can be divided into five categories. The first, exposure to intercourse, concerns the age at first heterosexual union; the proportion of the population that never enters into any sexual union or any heterosexual union; time spent in between or after unions; simultaneous multiple unions; frequency of coitus; and abstinence, which can be either voluntary (e.g., postpartum, during menstruation, for religious or ritual reasons) or involuntary (e.g., absence of a sexual partner). The second category is likelihood of conception, including the timing of coitus in the menstrual cycle; use or nonuse of conception enhancers, such as artificial insemination and fertility drugs; and the use or nonuse of contraception. Third is the growth and survival of the fetus and includes such factors as spontaneous or induced abortion and the care and behavior during pregnancy. Parturition makes up the fourth category and is concerned with delivery techniques, postnatal care of the infant, infanticide, and postnatal care of the mother. Last is survival of the offspring, including such behavioral factors as breastfeeding, other infant-feeding patterns, and care of the infant through the first year.

The term "union" is used in human reproduction research rather than "marriage," because many heterosexual encounters take place outside the formal rituals to create what is called "marriage" in some cultures. For purposes of reproduction, heterosexual coitus is the key predisposing factor, although artificial insemination is also a possibility. Earlier lists such as the one developed by Davis and Blake (1956) do not use the modifier "heterosexual" before terms like "union" and "marriage." Again, it is heterosexual coitus that is the key behavior to consider in looking at reproduction.

Many of the factors listed above are straightforward and are discussed in detail throughout the literature. The factors surrounding care during pregnancy and parturition may be less obvious, as may those surrounding infant feeding. Care during pregnancy can range from protective behaviors, such as special and appropriate diets, more rest, and more social support to no change in hard physical labor and dietary restrictions and no support. Care during parturition can range from being expected to give birth alone (as in parts of Benin) to overindulgence in technological support (parts of the United States). There is still debate about what constitutes optimum care. Infant feeding may include forbidding of colostrum (a premilk substance in human lactation that is rich in antibodies), introducing foods besides human milk early in the first hours, days, or weeks (thus introducing a source of infection), and inadequate and inappropriate weaning foods. Whether or not lactation takes place is also important. In addition to Ford (1964), Margaret Mead and Niles Newton (1967) provide a detailed review of cross-cultural behavior during pregnancy, childbirth, and the immediate postpartum. A more recent, comprehensive review is contained in a work by Margarita A. Kay (1982).

The Davis and Blake variables and their subsequent expansions or modifications (e.g., Nag 1968) all reflect individual behavior. Individual behavior is, of course, influenced by the social and cultural context. In looking at this context, several macro or overarching ways of looking at human reproduction emerge (Levine and Scrimshaw 1983), including such topics as population homeostasis, culture and reproductive success, social structure and fertility, cultural evolution and population growth, environment and reproduction, and interface between biology and behavior as they influence reproduction.

Population homeostasis (Wynne-Edwards 1962) is the concept that population size represents an adaptation to a specific environment, including the way the environment is used and the way food, energy, and other resources are extracted from it. In proper homeostasis, the population growth is regulated or stabilized so that the population does not exceed the capacity of the environment to support it. Alexander Alland (1970), Steven Polgar (1972), A. C. Swedland (1978), and others note that human populations are not and have not been at the mercy of high mortality rates, which require high fertility to maintain a stable population. Instead, there has always been individual and culturally induced regulation of fertility and mortality. This very important concept stands in contrast to some of the conventional wisdom in demography, where many early humans are seen as reproducing as rapidly as possible to keep up with high mortality rates.

Culture and reproductive success is the concept that culturally patterned behaviors help ensure the maximum likelihood of successful reproduction of the next generation. Examples include the Orthodox Jewish rules about timing of coitus in the menstrual cycle, which ensure that it will take place during the optimum period for fertilization. In a contrasting example, N. B. Blurton Jones and R. M. Sibley (1978) argue that postpartum sexual taboos among the !Kung protect offspring by spacing children to optimize their survival in a difficult environment.

Social structure and fertility refer to the idea that social and behavioral factors may provide varied ways to succeed, even in similar environments. The classic example is provided by Charles Wagley (1969) in an analysis of two lowland South American Indian groups, the Tapirapé and the Tenetehara. The environment and hunting and planting systems were identical for both groups and could not support communities much larger than 200 people. The Tapirapé had a harmonious culture with strict limi-

tations on family size. Families could have three children, and both sexes had to be represented among the children. Any excess newborns were left in the jungle to die. The Tenetehara had no restrictions on family size but had a contentious social and political system that ensured the breaking apart into two or more new communities every time the population got uncomfortably large. Thus, cultural norms provided two different ways of dealing with reproduction in a restrictive environment. Another model is to vary the way in which the environment is used. For example, Native Americans in the American Southwest and immigrants from other continents make very different use of the same land. In theory, these different uses will support different population densities. Social structure and fertility also encompass social and economic groupings, such as the family, which may support (or inhibit) reproduction. There is a vast literature on the family, and there have been recent attempts to take interdisciplinary looks at the family, combining anthropology, demography and economics (Robertson 1991).

Cultural evolution and population growth concern the concept that cultures become more efficient at extracting energy (food and other resources) from the environment. As this happens the environment can support larger populations, and cultural norms change to reflect this (Netting 1974). There is general agreement that people do not usually hold town meetings and say, "With these new crop yields we can afford to let marriage age go down," but, for example, marriage age went up after the famines in nineteenth-century Ireland. We need to go further in our understanding of the relationship between culture change, cultural norms, and reproduction.

Environment and reproduction refer to the effects of environmental factors, such as high altitude (Baker 1978) on fertility. The evidence suggests that there are more spontaneous abortions and higher perinatal mortality (related to low birth weight) at altitudes over 10,000 feet (Clegg 1978). A great deal of work remains to be done on other environmental factors, such as extreme heat and cold and lack of such dietary necessities as iron and iodine.

The interface between biology and behavior as they influence reproduction is emerging as a strong area as anthropologists, physicians, and biologists increasingly work together. This includes such obvious areas as postponement of childbearing and reproductive success (Ellison 1994), as well as subtler areas such as the relationship between stress and pregnancy outcome (Lobel et al. 1992). Other questions include behavioral factors affecting the probability of conception, other behavioral factors affecting pregnancy outcome, and behavioral factors (including medical practices) surrounding childbirth. A major area of debate involves the precise interface between cultural norms and individual behaviors, cultural norms and environment, and between biology and behavior. Much is said about cultural influences on individual behavior, but it remains clear that individuals do not always follow cultural ideals and often "push the envelope" to create new cultural norms. It is important to keep up with where individuals are now instead of where cultural norms say they ought to be.

One example of arguments that can develop from a failure to deal with this interface is the concept of natural fertility (Henry 1961; Wood 1994), which is defined as the absence of parity-specific behaviors to control fertility. In other words, no deliberate attempts to avoid a particular pregnancy are observed. From the anthropological perspective, this theory fails to acknowledge such factors as age at heterosexual union formation, culturally influenced time spent between unions (e.g., norms that forbid immediate widow remarriage), and lactation-induced birth spacing, to name a few. The theory takes a narrow view of contraception rather than a wider view of social and cultural influences on reproductive behavior.

In the area of cultural norms and the environment, concepts such as population homeostasis and cultural evolution and population growth are based on the ideal that there is some kind of interaction between culture and environment that, ideally, results in a balance favoring optimum conditions for people without degrading the environment. In small, relatively isolated environments evidence for this can be found. What about our current, complex, interactive multinational cultures? Have we gone beyond homeostasis? Is human reproduction "out of control"? Finally, what about biology and behavior? We are currently asking such questions as: Is there a biological basis for a certain proportion of the population to prefer same-sex sexual partners, thus reducing (for women) and eliminating (for men) the likelihood of producing biological offspring? Is there a biological basis for differences in birthweight and, thus, in perinatal mortality in people of different ethnicities? Instead, is there a biological basis for these differences that is culturally induced, such as stress?

SUSAN C. M. SCRIMSHAW

SEE ALSO: Birth; Breastfeeding; Demography; Infanticide; Marriage; Sexual Behavior; Sexual Selection

ALLAND, ALEXANDER. *Adaptation in Cultural Evolution: An Approach to Medical Anthropology.* Columbia University Press, New York, 1970.

BAKER, PAUL T., ed. *The Biology of High Altitude Peoples.* London: Cambridge University Press, 1978.

BLURTON JONES, N., and R. M. SIBLEY. "Testing Adaptiveness of Culturally Determined Behavior: Do Busmen Women Maximize Reproductive Success by Spacing Births Widely and Foraging Seldom?" In *Human Behavior and Adaptation.* Edited by N. B. Blurton Jones and Vernon Reynolds. Symposium Number 18 of the Society of the Study of Human Biology. London: Taylor-Francis, 1978.

CLEGG, E. J. "Fertility and Early Growth." In *The Biology of High Altitude Peoples.* Edited by Paul T. Baker. London: Cambridge University Press, 1978.

DAVIS, K., and J. BLAKE. "Social Structure and Fertility: An Analytical Framework." *Economic Development and Cultural Change* 4 (1956): 211–235.

ELLISON, P. T. "Advances in Human Reproductive Ecology." *Annual Review of Anthropology.* Palo Alto, Calif.: Annual Reviews, Inc., 1994.

FORD, CLELLAN S. *A Comparative Study of Human Reproduction.* New Haven, Conn.: Yale University Press, 1945.

———. *Field Guide to the Study of Human Reproduction.* New Haven, Conn.: HRAF Press, 1964.

HENRY, L. "Some Data on Natural Fertility." *Eugenics Quarterly* 8 (1961): 81–91.

KAY, MARGARITA A. *Anthropology of Human Birth.* Philadelphia: F. A. Davis, 1982.

LEVINE, R. A., and SUSAN C. M. SCRIMSHAW. "Effects of Culture on Fertility: Anthropological Contributions." In *Determinants of Fertility in Developing Countries.* Edited by R. Lee and R. Bulatao. Washington, D.C.: National Academy of Sciences Press, 1983.

LOBEL, M., C. DUNKEL-SCHETTER, and SUSAN C. M. SCRIMSHAW. "Prenatal Maternal Stress and Prematurity: A Prospective Study of Socioeconomically Disadvantaged Women." *Health Psychology* 11 (1992): 32–40.

MEAD, MARGARET, and NILES NEWTON. "Cultural Patterning of Perinatal Behavior." In *Childbearing: Its Social and Psychological Aspects.* Edited by S. A. Richardson and Alan F. Guttmacher. Baltimore: Williams and Wilkins, 1967.

NAG, MONI. *Factors Affecting Human Fertility in Nonindustrial Societies: A Crosscultural Study.* New Haven, Conn.: HRAF Press, 1968.

NETTING, R. M. "Agricultural Ecology." *Annual Review of Anthropology.* Palo Alto, Calif.: Annual Reviews, Inc., 1974.

POLGAR, STEVEN. "Population History and Population Policies from an Anthropological Perspective." *Current Anthropology* 13 (1972): 203–211.

ROBERSTON, A. F. *Beyond the Family: The Social Organization of Human Reproduction.* Berkeley: University of California Press, 1991.

SCRIMSHAW, SUSAN C. M. "Infant Mortality and Behavior in the Regulation of Family Size." *Population and Development Review* 4 (1978): 383–403.

———. "Infanticide in Human Populations: Societal and Individual Concerns." In *Infanticide: Comparative and Evolutionary Perspectives.* Edited by G. Hausfater and S. B. Hrdy. New York: Aldine, 1984.

SWEDLAND, A. C. "Historical Demography as Population Ecology." *Annual Review of Anthropology.* Palo Alto, Calif.: Annual Reviews, Inc., 1978.

WAGLEY, CHARLES. "Cultural Influences on Population: A Comparison of Two Tupi Tribes." In *Environment and Cultural Behavior.* Edited by A. P. Vayda. New York: Natural History Press, 1969.

WOOD, J. W. *Dynamics of Human Reproduction: Biology, Biometry, Demography.* Hawthorne, N.Y.: Aldine, 1994.

WYNNE-EDWARDS, V. C. *Animal Dispersion in Relation to Social Behavior.* Edinburgh: Oliver and Boyd, 1962.

HUMAN RIGHTS AND ADVOCACY ANTHROPOLOGY

It could be argued that anthropology as the description and explanation of "the other" (non-Europeans) and anthropological interest in human rights both began with the European colonization of the Americas. This relationship is embodied in the life of Bartolome de las Casas, a missionary, historian, and anthropologist of sorts, who, as a witness to the early decades of this colonization, was also a defender of the rights of indigenes. The Europeans encountered a whole new world of biological and cultural diversity that they attempted to describe and explain in various ways, but, with colonization, questions of morality and justice inevitably arose. Indeed, colonization is predicated on the violation of human rights, although it was rationalized in the name of Christian missionization, civilization, progress, and, more recently, in terms of economic development and national security in the world's remaining frontier zones such as the Amazon and New Guinea.

Anthropology is not only a child of colonialism; it has yet to be fully decolonized. Part of this separation of anthropology must come from recognition of human rights as one vital arena for research, publication, teaching, and action. The Columbian Quincentennial (1992) and the United Nations International Year of the World's Indigenous Peoples (1993) have stimulated some renewed consideration of these and related issues in anthropology and beyond (Morris 1993), although the surprisingly limited amount of such attention has been disappointing.

HUMAN RIGHTS

The concept of rights carries a double meaning: that which is universal and inalienable, and that which is morally appropriate or just. "Human rights" refers to those elemental rights which any human deserves to have honored in order to survive, enjoy well-being, and flourish or fulfill him- or herself, simply by virtue of being human. They include the right to life and freedom from physical and psychological abuse, including torture; freedom from arbitrary arrest and imprisonment and, accordingly, the right to a fair trial; freedom from slavery and genocide; the right to nationality; freedom of movement, including departure and return to one's own country, as well as the right to seek asylum in other countries from persecution in one's homeland; rights to privacy and the ownership of property; freedom of speech, religion, and assembly; the rights of peoples to self-determination, culture, religion, and language; and the right to adequate food, shelter, health care, and education (Donnelly 1989; Lawson 1991).

The roots of human rights extend back through the history of Western civilization to the ancient Greeks; however, only since the atrocities of World War II have human rights become widely recognized, codified, and agreed to in principle by most of the countries of the world. The United Nations established the Genocide Convention (1946). Subsequently, the U.N. developed other conventions like the Universal Declaration of Human Rights (1948), the International Covenant on Civil and Political Rights (1966), and the International Covenant on Economic, Social, and Cultural Rights (1966). Together these three conventions are referred to as the International Bill of Human Rights.

There have also been regional agreements such as the European Convention for the Protection of Human Rights and Fundamental Freedoms (1950); the American Declaration of the Rights and Duties of Man (1948) and the American Convention on Human Rights (1969) of the Organization of American States; the African Charter on Human and People's Rights of the Organization of African Unity (1981); and the Cairo Declaration on Human Rights in Islam (1990) (Blaustein et al. 1987; Lawson 1991). Equally noteworthy is the International Labour Organization Convention Concerning Indigenous and Tribal Peoples in Independent Countries (1989).

Such agreements help promote human rights, but their implementation and enforcement are very difficult (Donnelly 1989). Human rights are usually framed as the rights of the individual in relation to the state; ironically, the political authority charged with protecting and promoting human rights, as well as bringing to justice those who violate them, is also the entity that is most often the violator of human rights. This ambiguous position of the state is one of the most fundamental dilemmas for human rights.

Because modern countries are recognized as sovereign political entities, the international community is hesitant to intervene in their internal affairs when violations of human rights are alleged or proven. Often, little can be done other than to embarrass a country by publicizing its violations of human rights, although sometimes political and economic sanctions are imposed by individual nations, regional alliances, and/or the U.N. (Donnelly 1989).

The Human Rights Caucus of the Congress of the United States, the United Nations Educational, Scientific, and Cultural Organization (UNESCO), and other agencies issue annual reports surveying the human-rights records of countries and other publications on human rights (e.g., UNESCO 1987).

Nongovernmental advocacy organizations such as Amnesty International, Human Rights Internet, and Human Rights Watch monitor human rights on a regular basis, provide annual reports surveying each country, occasional case reports, and other publications to expose violations. They also initiate letter-writing campaigns to protest infringements and to pressure governmental authorities by holding them to their own international agreements. Amnesty International, the Human Rights Centre of the United Nations, the Inter-American Commission on Human Rights of the Organization of American States, and other organizations have adopted standard procedures for documenting and pursuing human rights complaints (e.g., Indian Law Resource Center [ILRC] 1984).

ANTHROPOLOGY AND HUMAN RIGHTS

Although many aspects of anthropology are relevant to human rights, and individual anthropologists have occasionally gotten involved with human rights, the profession as a whole has tended to avoid the subject until the last few years for at least five reasons: (1) universal human rights did not reach the consciousness of the world community until after World War II; (2) human rights tend to be treated in legalistic and nation-state frameworks that have left anthropologists on the periphery (Messer 1993); (3) in part, anthropology developed in connection with colonialism, which inherently involves violations of human rights; (4) many anthropologists were rather apathetic on the assumption that indigenous cultures would inevitably become extinct or be assimilated; and (5) science supposedly requires detachment and neutrality to maintain objectivity (Bodley 1990).

Nevertheless, anthropology is in a unique strategic position to deal with human rights for at least four reasons. Human rights is predicated on a theory of human nature. Anthropology is the humanistic science of humankind that documents and celebrates the biological and cultural aspects of the unity and diversity of the human species. There has been substantial research that bears theoretically on human nature and therefore on human rights. For example, all societies proscribe murder—the unjustified taking of human life—although they may justify killing in some contexts such as warfare.

Violations of human rights occur when individuals or groups are targeted, often, at least in part if not in whole, simply because they are different in some way. Thus, the Commission for Human Rights of the American Anthropological Association has formulated the following statement:

Anthropology as an academic discipline studies the bases and the forms of human diversity and unity; anthropology as a practice seeks to apply this knowledge to the solution of human problems. As a professional organization of anthropologists, the AAA has long been, and should continue to be, concerned whenever human difference is made the basis for a denial of rights—where "human" is understood in its full range of cultural, social, linguistic and biological senses. (Commission for Human Rights of the American Anthropological Association 1993)

Countries often respond defensively to accusations of human-rights violations by claiming that they are an interference in their internal affairs; they are developing countries and thus need more time to cultivate their own formulation and mechanisms for the promotion and defense of human rights; and/or human rights are an ethnocentric and racist Western concept that is incompatible with cultural relativism and represents a form of moral colonialism or imperialism. Anthropology is the profession that has traditionally studied culture, cultures, cultural diversity, and cultural relativism, as well as human nature, cultural universals, and related phenomena. Accordingly, anthropology is the most appropriate profession to grapple with these matters both in theory and practice; however, the issue of the universality of human rights versus cultural diversity and relativism has yet to be adequately explored and resolved by anthropologists. It remains one of the greatest challenges for human rights and anthropology (An-Na'im 1992; Benting et al. 1990; Donnelly 1989; Dwyer 1991; Messer 1993; Renteln 1990; Washburn 1987).

"Human rights" refers to what is elemental and essential to any human being, notions that in principle transcend cultural diversity and relativism. Furthermore, most countries, which reflect most of the cultures of the world, have agreed in principle to the U.N. and regional conventions on human rights. Thus, it is blatantly hypocritical for a country to agree to universal human rights and then hide behind cultural relativism when violations are exposed within its borders. Individuals who have their rights abused may not take any comfort in rationalizations about cultural relativism.

At the same time, culture may conflict with individual rights, as in the case of the practice of female circumcision, which is widespread in many societies of Africa and the Middle East (Downing and Kushner 1988). Ideally, cultural diversity and relativism deserve to be respected and promoted, but many would assert that this should not be at the expense of the violation of human rights that are even more fundamental. Reconciling rights at the individual, group (collective), national, and international levels remains problematic (Messer 1993).

Traditionally, anthropologists conduct fieldwork in communities of indigenous societies and ethnic minorities that are among the least powerful segments of society economically and politically as well as among the least vocal, although this situation has been improving since the 1970s (Bodley 1990; Moody 1988; Wright 1988). Thus, anthropologists in the field have a privileged position for studying and monitoring human rights, but they are also vulnerable. For example, an anthropologist in a foreign country operates at the liberty of the host government with a visa and research permit that can be readily revoked. The anthropologist has the option of continuing research elsewhere, but the local people whose rights are violated often cannot leave their country. Involvement with human rights can be dangerous, even deadly, for the anthropologist, informants, and/or host community. In the field, the anthropologist must proceed with extreme caution, sensitivity, and pragmatism. At the same time, one can not be apathetic and still remain ethical professionally. According to the American Anthropological Association (AAA 1990) "Statement on Professional Responsibility":

Anthropologists' first responsibility is to those whose lives and cultures they study. Anthropologists must do everything in their power to protect the dignity and privacy of the people with whom they work. Their physical, social, and emotional safety and welfare are the professional concerns of the anthropologists who have worked among them. The rights, interests, and sensitivities of those who entrust information to anthropologists must be safeguarded.

If interpreted in the broadest sense, this statement clearly embraces human rights.

ADVOCACY ANTHROPOLOGY

Advocacy anthropology rejects the supposed neutrality of science, adopts a stand on some problem or issue on behalf of a host or client group, and tries to effect change for the better. Although anthropologists have often served as advocates for one cause or another, this was mostly on an individual basis until the 1960s (e.g., Stocking 1979). Just as the world was beginning to be decolonized after World War II, so was anthropology. The controversial Vietnam War stimulated many anthropologists to examine more explicitly, systematically, and deeply the politics, ethics, and practical relevance of their profession (Hymes 1972). There was also increased alarm over accumulating reports of genocide and ethnocide in the Amazon and elsewhere. An important but inadequately recognized conference of mostly Latin American anthropologists issued the Declaration of Barbados, which criticized orthodox anthropology for its scientism, hypocrisy, opportunism, and apathy in the face of forced acculturation (cultural change) and even ethnocide and genocide. The document became a manifesto for some anthropologists to join the struggles for liberation and self-determination of indigenous peoples and ethnic minorities (Bodley 1990; Wright 1988). These and other factors contributed to the emergence of advocacy anthropology, which subsumed human rights but encompassed a much broader agenda for social and political activism, promoting the cultural survival, identity, economic opportunities, quality of life, and political self-determination of indigenous peoples and ethnic minorities throughout the world (Solo 1992).

In the 1960s anthropologists were seminal in the establishment and growth of several advocacy organizations, most notably: Cultural Survival in Cambridge, Massachusetts; the International Work Group for Indigenous Affairs in Copenhagen, Denmark; and the Minority Rights Group and Survival International in London, England. These and similar organizations not only deal with cases of the violation of the rights of indigenous societies and ethnic minorities but also collaborate with them in applied research (Bodley 1990; Miller et al. 1993; Paine 1985; Sponsel 1992; Wright 1988; see also *Cultural Survival Quarterly* and the publications catalog of Cultural Survival).

AMERICAN ANTHROPOLOGICAL ASSOCIATION

The American Anthropological Association contributed to the development of the U.N. Declaration of Human Rights through preparing the "Statement on Human Rights" (AAA 1947). This initiative seems to have triggered the first major debate within the profession on human rights, centering on two issues: (1) the objectivity through neutrality of anthropology as a science that is supposedly apolitical and amoral and (2) the principle of cultural relativism as being incompatible with the idea of human rights as moral universals (see comments in *American Anthropologist* 1947).

Nevertheless, human rights have been a recurrent concern within the AAA. For example, some 65 percent of the more than ninety resolutions that have been proposed, discussed, and passed by vote in annual business meetings of the AAA since World War II have, to some degree, dealt with human rights. They have encompassed a wide breadth and diversity of subjects, including land claims of Alaskan natives, apartheid in South Africa, Asian Americans, Brazilian government treatment of indigenes, coca use in the Andes, civil rights in the United States, congressional actions linking human rights and foreign aid, discrimination (ethnic, political, racial, religious, sexual), ethnocide, genocide, homosexuality, imprisonment of indigenous persons in the United States, Navajo-Hopi land disputes, and political refugees. Clearly, in these resolutions the AAA, even though a scientific organization, has repeatedly voted in favor of taking a moral and/or political stand on numerous controversial and vital social issues that were considered relevant to anthropology.

Since the late 1980s, there has been growing concern with establishing a formal entity within the AAA to focus on human rights. After various initiatives, a three-year Commission for Human Rights was finally established, which first met at the annual convention of the AAA in San Francisco in 1992. This commission is charged with planning the operation of the eventual standing Committee on Human Rights through working out conceptual issues, strategies for networking and education, and mechanisms for action and advocacy that will complement rather than compete with or duplicate activities of other human-rights organizations. Beyond this planning function, the commission has also taken action on selected cases, including the brutal massacre by illegal Brazilian gold miners of sixteen Yanomami in Venezuela during the summer of 1993 (Berwick 1990). Members of the commission are George N. Appell, Robert K. Hitchcock, Ellen Messer, Victor Montejo, C. Patrick Morris, Carole Nagengast, Mary Margaret Overbey, James Peacock (as AAA president-elect and later president), Leslie E. Sponsel (chair), and Terence Turner.

Additional initiatives within the AAA that involve human rights include various task forces and committees on hunger and famine, AIDS, homelessness, involuntary resettlement, and refugees.

Other anthropological organizations have also become involved with human rights. The Society for Applied Anthropology issued a special report on the relationship between human rights and environmental problems (Johnston 1993). The European Association of Social Anthropologists recently established a Human Rights Network.

CONCLUSION

Although the human-rights movement represents one of the greatest sociopolitical transformations of the twentieth century (Messer 1993), nevertheless, numerous difficulties remain and many desperate situations of human-rights abuses continue to be reported (Amnesty International 1992; Bodley 1990; Burger 1987; Miller et al. 1993). Unfortunately, the human-rights situation is likely to become worse rather than better in the near future, given the continued growth of population and consumerism, which put more and more pressure on the land, resources, and labor of indigenous peoples and ethnic minorities, and given the interrelated growth in political organization of these oppressed and exploited societies. A further factor is that other human-rights issues, such as "ethnic cleansing" in the former Yugoslavia, have emerged with the end of the cold war. Such instances are likely to develop elsewhere as historic racial, ethnic, and religious prejudices and conflicts are wedded with new politics and nationalism, generating various forms of violence (Nordstrom and Martin 1992). One of the greatest challenges for the human-rights movement is to help create conditions that prevent abuses rather than just react to them after it is too late.

Anthropologists will inevitably be drawn into these struggles for sheer survival as well as for the recognition, protection, and promotion of basic human rights by the peoples with whom they live and work. These peoples increasingly perceive anthropologists as either part of the solution or part of the problem. More and more host communities no longer allow free license for basic research and demand better than the usual token reciprocity of anthropologists. Increasingly, the consciences of anthropologists also demand

more. Human rights can be like quicksand or a minefield politically and morally, but desperate circumstances require greater responsibility and response, including from anthropologists. Fortunately, the conventions, organizations, and literature, including AAA initiatives, offer substantial resources for constructive action and advocacy (e.g., Human Rights Internet 1992). This can also have a positive, if not even revolutionary, impact on the profession of anthropology, contributing direction, purpose, and priorities for teaching, research, and publications and thereby counterbalancing many postmodern fashions and fantasies. A genuine concern for human rights could help anthropology regain its Enlightenment promise of becoming the humanistic science of humankind (Downing and Kushner 1988; Pandian 1985).

LESLIE E. SPONSEL

SEE ALSO: Indigenous Peoples

AMERICAN ANTHROPOLOGICAL ASSOCIATION. "Statement on Human Rights." *American Anthropologist* 49 (1947): 539-43.

———. "Statement on Professional Responsibility." Washington, D.C.: American Anthropological Association, 1990.

AMNESTY INTERNATIONAL. *Human Rights Violations Against Indigenous Peoples of the Americas.* New York: Amnesty International, 1992.

AN-NA'IM, ABDULLAHI AHMED, ed. *Human Rights in Cross-Cultural Perspective: A Quest for Consensus.* Philadelphia: University of Pennsylvania Press, 1992.

BENTING, JAN, et al., eds. *Human Rights in a Pluralistic World: Individuals and Collectivities.* Westport, Conn.: Meckler, 1990.

BERWICK, DENNISON. *Savages: The Life and Killing of the Yanomami.* London: Hodder & Stoughton, 1990.

BLAUSTEIN, ALBERT P., et al., eds. *Human Rights Sourcebook.* New York: Paragon House, 1987.

BODLEY, JOHN H. *Victims of Progress.* Mountain View, Calif.: Mayfield Publishing, 1990.

BURGER, JULIAN. *Report from the Frontier: The State of the World's Indigenous Peoples.* Atlantic Highlands, N.J.: Zed Books, 1987.

COMMISSION FOR HUMAN RIGHTS OF THE AMERICAN ANTHROPOLOGICAL ASSOCIATION. "Report of the AAA Commission for Human Rights." *Anthropology Newsletter* 34 (March): 1, 5, 1993.

DONNELLY, JACK. *Universal Human Rights in Theory and Practice.* Ithaca, N.Y.: Cornell University Press, 1989.

DOWNING, THEODORE E., and GILBERT KUSHNER, eds. *Human Rights and Anthropology.* Cambridge: Cultural Survival, 1988.

DWYER, KEVIN. *Arab Voices: The Human Rights Debate in the Middle East.* Berkeley and Los Angeles: University of California Press, 1991.

HUMAN RIGHTS INTERNET. *Master List of Human Rights Organizations and Serial Publications.* Ottawa: Human Rights Internet Reporter, 1992.

HYMES, DELL, ed. *Reinventing Anthropology.* New York: Random House, 1972.

INDIAN LAW RESOURCE CENTER. *Indian Rights, Human Rights: Handbook for Indians on International Human Rights Complaints.* Washington, D.C.: Indian Law Resource Center, 1984.

JOHNSTON, BARBARA R., ed. "Who Pays the Price? Examining the Sociocultural Context of Environmental Crisis." *Report on Human Rights and the Environment.* Norman, Okla.: Society for Applied Anthropology, 1993.

LAWSON, EDWARD, ed. *Encyclopedia of Human Rights.* Bristol, England: Taylor & Francis, 1991.

MESSER, ELLEN. "Anthropology and Human Rights." *Annual Review of Anthropology* 22 (1993): 221-49.

MILLER, MARC, et al., eds. *State of the Nations: A Global Human Rights Report on Societies in Danger.* Boston: Beacon Press, 1993.

MOODY, ROGER, ed. *The Indigenous Voice: Visions and Realities,* vols. 1-2. Atlantic Highlands, N.J.: Zed Books, 1988.

MORRIS, C. PATRICK, guest editor. "Special Edition: International Year of Indigenous Peoples: Discovery and Human Rights." *American Indian Culture and Research Journal* 17 (1993): 1-240.

NORDSTROM, CAROLYN, and JOANN MARTIN, eds. *The Paths to Domination, Resistance, and Terror.* Berkeley and Los Angeles: University of California Press, 1992.

PAINE, ROBERT, ed. *Advocacy Anthropology.* St. John's: University of Newfoundland Press, 1985.

PANDIAN, JACOB. *Anthropology and the Western Tradition: Toward an Authentic Anthropology.* Prospect Heights, Ill.: Waveland Press, 1985.

RENTELN, A.D. *International Human Rights: Universalism versus Relativism.* Newbury Park, Calif.: Sage, 1990.

SOLO, PAM, ed. "At the Threshold: An Action Guide for Cultural Survival." *Cultural Survival Quarterly* 16 (1992): 1-80.

SPONSEL, LESLIE E. "Information Asymmetry and the Democratization of Anthropology." *Human Organization* 51 (1992): 299-301.

STOCKING, GEORGE W., JR. "Anthropology as Kulturkampf: Science and Politics in the Career of Franz Boas." In *The Uses of Anthropology,* edited by Walter Goldschmidt. Special Publication no. 11. Washington, D.C.: American Anthropological Association, 1979.

UNESCO. "Anthropology and Human Rights." *Human Rights Teaching,* no. 6, 1987.

WASHBURN, WILCOMB E. "Cultural Relativism, Human Rights, and the AAA." *American Anthropologist* 89 (1987): 939-43.

WRIGHT, ROBIN. "Anthropological Presuppositions of Indigenous Advocacy." *Annual Review of Anthropology* 17 (1988): 365-90.

HUMAN UNIVERSALS

Throughout the world, humans communicate with languages composed of basic units of sound (phonemes) that form basic units of meaning (morphemes) that are employed in accordance with rules of grammar (syntax) to produce meaningful utterances. Everywhere in the world, humans supplement these basic linguistic features with gestures and tones of voice. Moreover, the content of what all peoples say and do exhibits numerous similarities.

People everywhere classify each other by status and roles, but they recognize individuals. There is kinship and a division of labor by sex and age. People display recognizable emotions and empathize with others. They have aesthetic standards and they adorn their bodies. They reckon time, make binary distinctions, think causally, and are concerned with right and wrong. They understand basic logical operations, and they envisage times and places outside their present conditions. They know that people may mislead or cheat and they guard against it. They form and recognize coalitions and collective identities.

One can go on to list hundreds of universals—some readily available to consciousness, many not (Brown 1991). Universals are more than just numerous; they are crucial to our ability to distinguish human from inhuman, and fundamental to the entire enterprise of anthropology. Without some of these universals, anthropologists could not communicate with or understand the peoples they study.

THE TYPES OF UNIVERSALS

There are several types of universals. For example, because "gesture" is a broad rubric covering many specific kinds, gesturing is called a universal of classification. Because pointing with the finger is a specific gesture, it is called a universal of content. Defining and conceptualizing universals may begin with a survey of some important ways in which they are classified; that is, according to the medium in which they occur, the degree and mode of their universality, and the processes that produce them.

Although it is true that humans are universally bipedal, have skin, ingest nutrients, and excrete waste, sociocultural anthropologists normally omit traits of anatomy and physiology from lists of universals, even though such traits may figure in the explanation of universals. Thus the traits that sociocultural anthropologists do list as universals may usually be classified as cultural, social, linguistic, behavioral, or psychological (and often some combination of these conventional categories).

Generally, when anthropologists think about universals, they have in mind what are called absolute universals (also called nonconditional or unrestricted universals), defined by their presence among all peoples. But there are both practical and theoretical reasons for designating lesser degrees of universality. Thus there are near universals as well as absolute universals, because in some cases near and absolute universals are closely related. For example, the domestic dog was unknown to a small number of relatively isolated populations until recently. We would not understand the basic process by which the awareness of the dog became widespread any differently if it had in fact become absolutely universal.

Even further removed from absolute universals are statistical universals: traits that have a worldwide distribution exceeding what chance alone would determine—and that thereby require transcultural explanations. Examples are words for the pupil of the eye and for muscles. Terms meaning "little person" are widespread for the former and terms meaning "small animal" are widespread for the latter, presumably because one sees a little person in pupils (one's own reflection), and because muscles move under the skin like little animals (Brown and Witkowski 1981).

An alternative mode of universality is found in the conditional (or implicational) universal: it has a limited manifest distribution, but seems to rest on one or more latent but absolute universals. For example, if a language has three or more color terms, one will be red (if it has only two color terms, neither will be red). Note also the distinction between latent and manifest universals.

Another mode of universality is found in the universal pool. This consists of a set of possibilities from which a selection is made in any particular case. The International Phonetic Alphabet, for example, is a finite set of possible speech sounds; each language comprises a lesser set drawn from that pool. Early in the twentieth century, it was discovered that a small set of semantic distinctions (distinguishing male from female, one generation from another, lineal from collateral kin, etc.) were drawn upon to inform the otherwise diverse kinship terminologies from peoples all over the world.

Among the theoretically most significant aspects of universals are the three or four basic causal processes that produce them. Fire and cooking are examples of cultural traits and complexes that became absolute universals by the process of diffusion, facilitated by two combined conditions: great antiquity and great utility. A possible variant is what have been called *archoses*, traits that have great antiquity (so that they spread with humanity as it spread around the globe) but apparent utility. A possible example of that is a statistical universal and perhaps a near universal is the belief that brain, bone marrow, and semen are a common substance. This belief underlies or rationalizes both the widespread belief that masturbation weakens the mind and body and the widespread practice of taking heads to ensure fertility (La Barre 1984).

Another process that produces universals may be called cultural reflection or recognition. For example, because all peoples experience changes in weather, and are seriously influenced by the weather, cultural responses in the form of terms for weather or even means of trying to influence the weather are universal. Similarly, the universality of kinterms presumably reflects, at their base, the relationships that are created by the universal processes of biological reproduction. Resulting from common human experiences, universals of this sort are also called experiential universals.

Last but surely not least is the set of processes that result more or less directly from features of human nature, especially the human mind, which leaves some of its traces in a uniform manner among all peoples. Thus the binary distinctions (such as night and day, good and bad) that everywhere inform human thought and symbolic expression appear to be part of the way in which the human mind works. All peoples acquire language—even two at a time—with great ease and perfection during childhood, but only with difficulty and mixed success in later years. This strongly indicates, as the linguist Noam Chomsky cogently argues (see below), that the human mind is wired by nature to acquire language in childhood. As the case of language acquisition indicates, universals of human nature are sometimes delimited by age; they may also be delimited by sex.

THE PLACE OF UNIVERSALS IN ANTHROPOLOGICAL THOUGHT

Although it is often said that the task of anthropology is to document and explain the similarities and differences among the peoples of the world, both past and present, sociocultural anthropologists have given most attention to differences. Thus, however much anthropologists may and must implicitly rely upon universals in order to do their work, the literature in anthropology that explicitly deals with universals is relatively slight.

Nevertheless, universals were clearly a part of anthropology's early foundations. For example, Edward B. Tylor (1870), generally regarded as the founder of cultural anthropology, cited the similarity of gestures throughout the world as evidence for the psychic unity of humanity, an important conceptual tool in the development of an anthropology that could explain population differences in nonracial terms. Franz Boas, perhaps the single most important figure in the development of cultural anthropology in the United States, wrote about the "traits common to all cultures" in his *The Mind of Primitive Man* (1911), a powerful defense of the psychic unity of humanity in the face of still pervasive racist claims.

This early anthropological attention to universals culminated in a chapter entitled "The Universal Pattern" in Clark Wissler's *Man and Culture* (1923). Wissler presented an outline of universals that consisted of such items as "speech," "material traits," "art," "mythology and scientific knowledge," and so on, along with subheadings. He considered these to be universals of "classification," but he also noted the existence of universals—such as the drill, string, and certain beliefs—that were highly specific. Wissler's argument (1923) that universals were rooted in a common human biology became an orthodox view.

Perhaps for this very reason, anthropologists showed little interest in universals, or appeared to be ambivalent about them, during much of the remainder of this century. Most anthropologists, particularly in the United States, devoted their attention to the culture concept and to versions of it that were as free as possible from attempts to explain culture in what were seen as psychobiologically "reductionist" terms. In the debate between proponents of nature or nurture as determinants of human behavior, anthropologists generally came down hard on the nurture side, and they were gravely suspicious that the nature side fostered such overlapping evils as social Darwinism, eugenics, and racism.

By the 1930s an extreme culturological or culture-determinist form of anthropology was taking shape in the United States. Its earmarks were cultural particularism and relativism; unconcern with or opposition to the study of origins and evolution; a rigid dichotomy between nature and nurture, biology and culture, the instinctual and the learned; the reification of culture as an autonomous, "superorganic" level of phenomena that cannot be reduced to psychobiological causes; an emphasis on the arbitrariness of culture; and a conception of culture as the primary shaper of human behavior and affairs, because the human mind is a blank slate (*tabula rasa*) until culture gives it content (Brown 1991).

These developments were not confined to anthropology; they were part of a groundswell that swept much of American social science. The dictum that social facts should be explained only with social facts was a sociological counterpart of the culture-determinist view that culture cannot be reduced to lower levels of phenomena. In psychology the rise of behaviorism reinforced the notion that the human mind is a largely blank slate.

These ideas were and are uncongenial to the study of universals, for if culture is arbitrary, and if the mind is a blank slate, universals are unlikely to occur. Even drawing attention to universals risked aligning oneself with the "wrong" side of the nature-nurture debate.

However, the years around World War II saw renewed interest in universals, perhaps due to realization that extreme forms of cultural relativism provided no basis for criticism of Nazi culture. A few examples of the renewed interest in universals will have to suffice. In 1939 and 1940, the anthropologists Alexander Lesser (1952) and A. V. Kidder (1940) delivered or published papers attacking cultural particularism and defending universalistic perspectives, especially with reference to sociocultural evolution. In 1945, George Peter Murdock published "The Common Denominator of Cultures," which contained an influential list of universals and supporting arguments for universalistic perspectives. And in 1948, Burt and Ethel Aginsky published a brief essay on linguistic universals, mentioning various nonlinguistic universals as well. Concluding this trend, Clyde Kluckhohn published his "Universal Categories of Culture" (1953). It provided no new listing of universals, but focused more on their causes and implications. Murdock's (1945) and Kluckhohn's (1953) papers remained the standard works on universals for decades.

Developments outside of anthropology have decisively shaped the present theoretical conceptions of universals. The study of linguistics has been particularly important. In a lengthy book review, Chomsky (1959) criticized behavioristic explanations of language, and he showed the necessity of positing "deeper processes" of language acquisition that are complex, innate, and universal. Chomsky's work led to a search for the "deep structure" of language that he explicitly linked to human biology. He likened a child's acquisition of speech to the instinctive behaviors that ethologists found to be acquired by "imprinting" during "sensitive periods" of maturation. Chomsky's work was seminal in eroding the notion of the human mind as a blank slate.

In 1966, Joseph H. Greenberg published *Language Universals*, which listed a number of universals and launched a broad search for more. Of particular concern to Greenberg was the process of "marking," which occurs at phonemic, semantic, and grammatic levels of all languages. Marking results in many implicational universals, as well as some unrestricted universals. The English consonants "p" and "b" and words such as "man" and "woman" or "author" and "authoress" provide familiar examples. In each set, the latter is the marked form, which is generally indicated by being more complex ("b" and "p" are identical ex-

cept that "b" is voiced). It is the frequency of use of each term, and the selective pressure to conserve speech effort, that apparently determines which is more complex and, hence is the marked form.

Some of the universals that result from marking are as follows. In any language, if or when one form can stand for the other, it is the unmarked form that does so (as when "man" means both male humans and humans in general). Further examples are terms with the meanings "long" and "short," "big" and "small," "wide" and "narrow," and "deep" and "shallow." In any language in which terms with these meanings occur, it is the term with the former meaning in each set that is unmarked. In any language that distinguishes singular and plural, it is the plural that is marked.

Note that statements like "in any language that has x, then y will occur" are examples of implicational or conditional universals. Anthropology is indebted to Greenberg for clarifying and standardizing some of the basic terms for universals.

Perhaps the most important direct influence of linguistics on the anthropological study of universals came with the methodological developments that are associated with componential analysis. Anthropologists who employed this method may not have searched for universals, but their studies have produced them. Drawing an important lesson from universals documented in this manner, Maurice Bloch (1977) pointed out that practical interactions with nature (as in production and reproduction) provide the context that tends to produce the universals constituting knowledge; by contrast, social structure, especially instituted hierarchy, tends to be the matrix of cultural particulars that partake more of ideology than knowledge.

Parallel to, and reinforcing Chomsky's work (1959), have been developments in the study of animal behavior and of psychology. Analogues between animal and human behaviors have been increasingly suggestive in making sense of universals, and close observation of animal behavior showed that the distinction between "learned" behavior and "instincts" was simplistic and misleading. Experiments conducted by the psychologist John Garcia in the 1960s were particularly crucial in showing the inadequacy of behavior-ism's assumptions (Garcia and Koelling 1966). He and others showed that it was easier for animals to make some associations than others, indicating that the animals did not have blank-slate minds. Rather, animals come to learning experiences with minds already adapted to acquire some behaviors, not others.

Two further developments were also of crucial importance in eliminating the possibility that the human mind is a blank slate: studies of brain anatomy and function—especially studies of the results of accidental brain lesions—and the implications of attempts to produce artificial intelligence with computers. It is now clear that a blank-slate, general-purpose mind is no more likely to have evolved than is any other general-purpose organ. Rather than the human mind being a blank slate, neuroanatomical evidence indicates that it is wired in very great detail. The findings from artificial intelligence indicate that even seemingly simple tasks are, in fact, complex, and that a large amount of innate information is required in order to perform them. It is the complexity of the human mind, not merely its capacity to absorb culture, that makes us what we are.

The anthropologists Lionel Tiger and Robin Fox brought a number of these trends together with an extensive discussion of the links between universals and human biology. More comprehensive treatments of these trends in relation to universals and human nature may be found in essays by Brown (1991) and by Tooby and Cosmides (1992).

EMPIRICAL ISSUES

In recent decades, empirical issues have focussed on particular universals, such as the incest taboo. Early in this century a debate centered around whether the incest taboo was the very prototype of a cultural rule, severing humanity from its animal past and launching its cultural career, or whether incest was avoided spontaneously by persons who had been reared in familial intimacy. In the heyday of culturological views, the latter argument, set forth by the Finnish anthropologist Edward Westermarck (1922), was given little credence. However, when it was discovered that children who were not siblings, but who were reared in family-like settings in Israeli communes, spontaneously avoided marriages with each other, Westermarck's views looked more credible. Similar phenomena were soon noted among Chinese who adopted little girls and raised them alongside their intended future husbands, and later among Near Eastern Muslims who raised first cousins in sibling-like conditions and then married them to each other.

The idea that incest may be avoided spontaneously, not only among humans but among many nondomesticated animals, is now well established, but considerable debate still surrounds some aspects of the universal (see Brown 1991 for a summary).

Another important finding concerns color terms. Whereas anthropologists and linguists had found color classification a particularly apt illustration of cultural and linguistic relativity (divisions of the color spectrum appeared to be arbitrary), Brent Berlin and Paul Kay (1969) provide evidence for a patterned order in which "basic" color terms develop in any language. They show both the nonconditional universal that all languages have terms for black and white (or "dark" and "light") and such conditional universals as the one cited earlier: if a language has three color terms, one will be red. The extensive research that was set in motion by these findings quickly expanded to such other domains of classification as plants and animals.

At about the same time, the psychologists Paul Ekman and his associates and Carroll Izard (1971) presented evidence that certain facial expressions of emotion are universal—happiness, sadness, disgust, fear, anger, and surprise are well documented. A particularly telling confirmation of the universality of facial expression of emotions came from the comparison of just two unrelated populations: one sample of Americans and another of New Guineans who were relatively unacquainted with the outside world (Ekman et al. 1969). The complexity of the expressions and of what they convey makes an accidental convergence between the American and New Guinean patterns highly unlikely. Anthropologists had not previously said much about facial expressions, but there is reason to think that expressions would have been treated like gestures and hence assumed to be fundamentally arbitrary in form.

Whereas Margaret Mead's classics, *Coming of Age in Samoa* (1928) and *Sex and Temperament in Three Primitive Societies* (1935), purported to show, respectively, that adolescent stress and male dominance were not universals, restudies opened the issues again. Deborah Gewertz (1981) restudied the society in which, according to Mead, sex roles were reversed from what is considered normal. Gewertz found that Mead had misunderstood what she observed and, in fact, had provided no evidence of women successfully challenging male dominance. Derek Freeman (1983) restudied the Samoans and found that the conditions of Mead's fieldwork allowed her informants to mislead her, while conditions in American cultural anthropology bred a ready acceptance for her findings. These restudies do not establish universals, but they do set aside otherwise compelling evidence against the universality of adolescent stress and male dominance.

In 1982 Melford Spiro reopened the issue of the universality of the Oedipus complex by reanalyzing Bronislaw Malinowski's (1927) data and his argument against such a complex among Trobriand Islanders. A year later, one of the most famous arguments for cultural relativism, Benjamin Whorf's thesis that the Hopi lacked a concept of time as we understand it, was empirically refuted by Ekkehart Malotki (1983).

A THEORETICAL FRAMEWORK FOR UNIVERSALS

At present, universals lack a single orderly framework for further study. If there is a place to anchor such a framework, it may lie in the rapidly developing understanding of the human mind. Consider the following: It is now clear that the human mind is not a blank slate. It is a complex collection of problem solving mechanisms, "mental organs," each of which is an adaptation to a particular problem that was regularly faced by our ancestors over evolutionary time. Moreover, the very complexity of the mind necessitates its basic universality: given that each mental organ is almost certainly genetically complex, the shuffling of genes that takes place during sexual reproduction requires that the genes that direct the development of each organ must be identical or equivalent in all normal humans (Tooby and Cosmides 1990).

It is equally clear that the human mind is not culture's putty. Each individual receives vastly more culture than he or she creates, but individual human minds are nonetheless the ultimate source of culture. And universal mental organs impart uniformities to all peoples' thoughts, feelings, behaviors, and artifacts—despite the variety and emergent properties those entities exhibit.

It follows, then, that human universals provide vital clues to the nature of the human mind. And since cross-cultural studies are crucial to identifying universals, this reasoning suggests that an alliance of anthropology's comparative and evolutionary concerns with the various sciences concerned with the human mind could provide an orderly framework for the study of universals—and deeper insight into the generation of culture.

Donald E. Brown

SEE ALSO: *Adaptation; Adornment; Age Grades, Age Sets, and Age-Generation Systems; Aging; Animal Domestication; Biocultural Anthropology; Child Development; Cognitive Anthropology; Color Terminology; Componential Analysis; Cross-Cultural Research; Culture; Diffusion; Ethnozoology; Gender Differences and Roles; Genetics; Gesture and Movement; History of Anthropology; Human Evolution; Human Reproduction; Incest; Kinship Terminology; Language; Linguistic Anthropology; Mead-Freeman Controversy; Natural Selection; Person and Self; Primate Behavior; Primate Evolution; Psychological Anthropology; Race Relations; Racism; Sexual Division of Labor; Sexual Selection; Social Control; Sociobiology; Taboo*

AGINSKY, BURT W., and ETHEL G. AGINSKY. "The Importance of Language Universals." *Word,* 4(1948):168-172.

BELMONTE, THOMAS. "Alexander Lesser (1902-1982)." *American Anthropologist,* 87 (1985):637-644.

BERLIN, BRENT, and PAUL KAY. *Basic Color Terms: Their Universality and Evolution.* Berkeley and Los Angeles: University of California Press, 1969.

BLOCH, MAURICE. "The Past and the Present in the Present." *Man* 12 (1977):278-292.

BOAS, FRANZ. *The Mind of Primitive Man.* New York: Macmillan, 1911.

BROWN, CECIL H., and STANLEY R. WITKOWSKI. "Figurative Language in a Universalist Perspective." *American Ethnologist,* 8(1981): 596-615.

BROWN, DONALD E. *Human Universals.* Philadelphia: Temple University Press, 1991.

CARROLL, JOHN B., ed. *Language, Thought, and Reality: Selected Writings of Benjamin Lee Whorf.* Boston: Technology Press of MIT, 1956.

CHOMSKY, NOAM. "Review of B. F. Skinner's Verbal Behavior." *Language* 35 (1959): 26-58.

EKMAN, PAUL, E. R. SORENSON, and WALLACE V. FRIESEN. "Pan-Cultural Elements in Facial Displays of Emotion." *Science* 164(1969):86-88.

FREEMAN, DEREK. *Margaret Mead and Samoa.* Cambridge: Harvard University Press, 1983.

GARCIA, JOHN, and ROBERT A. KOELLING. "Relation of Cue to Consequence in Avoidance Learning." *Psychonomic Science,* 4 (1966): 123-124.

GEWERTZ, DEBORAH. "A Historical Reconsideration of Female Dominance among the Chambri of Papua New Guinea." *American Ethnologist*, 8 (1981): 94-106.

GREENBERG, JOSEPH H. *Language Universals*. The Hague: Mouton, 1966.

IZARD, CARROLL E. *The Face of Emotion*. New York: Appleton-Century-Crofts, 1971.

KIDDER, A. V. "Looking Backward." *Proceedings of the American Philosophical Society*, 83 (1940): 527-537.

KLUCKHOHN, CLYDE. "Universal Categories of Culture." *Anthropology Today*. Chicago: University of Chicago Press, 1953.

LA BARRE, WESTON. *Muelos: A Stone Age Superstition about Sexuality*. New York: Columbia University Press, 1984.

LESSER, ALEXANDER. "Evolution in Social Anthropology." *SW Journal of Anthropology*, 8 (1952): 134–146.

MALINOWSKI, BRANISLAW. *Sex and Repression in Savage Society*. N.Y.: Harcourt, Brace and Co., 1927.

MALOTKI, EKKEHART. *Hopi Time*. Berlin: Mouton, 1983.

MEAD, MARGARET. *Coming of Age in Samoa*. New York: Morrow, 1928.

____. *Sex and Temperament in Three Primitive Societies*. New York: Morrow, 1935.

MURDOCK, GEORGE PETER. "The Common Denominator of Cultures." R. Linton, ed. *The Science of Man in the World Crisis*. N.Y.: Columbia Univ. Press, 1945.

SPIRO, MELFORD. *Oedipus in the Trobriands*. Chicago: University of Chicago Press, 1982.

TIGER, LIONEL, and ROBIN FOX. *The Imperial Animal*. New York: Holt, Rinehart & Winston, 1971.

TOOBY, JOHN, and LEDA COSMIDES. "On the Universality of Human Nature and the Uniqueness of the Individual: The Role of Genetics and Adaptation." *Journal of Personality*, 58(1990): 17-67.

——. "The Psychological Foundations of Culture." Jerome H. Barkow, et al., *The Adapted Mind: Evolutionary Psychology and the Generation of Culture*. New York: Oxford University Press, 1992.

TYLOR, EDWARD B. *Researches into the Early History of Mankind*. 2nd ed. London: Murray, 1870.

WESTERMARCK, EDWARD. *The History of Human Marriage*. 5th ed. vol. II. New York: Allerton, 1922.

WISSLER, CLARK. *Man and Culture*. New York: Thomas Y. Crowell, 1923.

HUMANISTIC ANTHROPOLOGY

What is humanistic anthropology? To obtain a quick answer is not only unwise but runs counter to the humanistic spirit. As we would be mistaken to attempt a comprehensive, smoothly ironed definition of human, likewise, we must not rush to a elegantly formal but conceptually empty definition of humanistic anthropology. Like the species, the field necessarily remains messy. Thus, we best begin by reviewing how the terms "humanism" and "humanistic" are used. We may find a common core and can suggest that humanistic anthropology is the application of that common core to the field of anthropology. This field has its own unique character, which will be modified.

Our task is made much easier by an issue of the journal *Anthropology and Humanism* titled "Special Issue: Humanism and Anthropology" (Brady and Turner 1994). Since the founding of the Society for Humanistic Anthropology, its journal has provided a forum for the diverse views of its members. This issue is especially wide-ranging in its discussion of renaissance humanism, naturalistic humanism, and literary humanism.

Renaissance humanism emerged as part of the revival of learning in Western Europe and the rediscovery of the literature of classical Greece and Rome. While not necessarily antireligious, it emphasized scholarly reading, as opposed to divine revelation, as the path to knowledge. It professed a skeptical attitude toward authority and dogma. Naturalistic humanism appeared much later in the nineteenth and twentieth centuries. It stressed the capacity of reason and science to solve human problems. It was (and is) even more antithetical to religion and still speaks out against the blindness of religious beliefs. Literary humanism is even more recent and has been a response to the literary critiques of poststructuralism, which minimize the tie between text and life. In the poststructuralist's view, texts address other texts more than they do our lives. In contrast, the humanistic critic argues that characterization in fiction of good fiction allows us to understand the complexities of social life through the actions of specific, fictive characters.

This brief review suggests that humanism is synonymous with a concern for the human enterprise.

It is frankly anthropocentric, meaning not only that it rejects supernatural, or divine, causation but it also places the human experience at the center of its purview. It values what humans do above all other actions. Its faith resides in the human condition. The application of anthropocentric faith to the field of anthropology suggests a foundation for the building of a humanistic anthropology. Yet, because of anthropology's own built-in desire to seek a balanced view, the application of humanism to anthropology tempers the anthropocentrism and results in more cautious statements of purpose.

In considering the field, the reader will note how often humanistic anthropology looks to adjacent undertakings in anthropology and beyond to other disciplines. This outward searching is diagnostic of humanism. Humanism in any of its permutations is never narrow. Thus, it is appropriate to recognize Peter L. Berger's *An Invitation to Sociology: A Humanistic Perspective* (1963) as the classic exposition of humanism in social science. Humanism in social science, Berger argues, is a form of intellectual liberation that permits us to stand at some distance from the most institutionalized truths of society and ask: Why?

Humanism has a long tradition in anthropology. Major figures in the discipline, such as Ruth Benedict and Robert Redfield, have argued that as a study of humanity, anthropology must look not only to the physical and natural sciences but also to the humanities to achieve a comprehensive view of humans and their preoccupations. Developing out of this history, the current humanistic movement achieved a particular stance in anthropology with the establishment of the Society for Humanistic Anthropology in 1974. By sponsoring annual meetings and publications, the society promotes a lively exchange of humanistic ideas.

Some characteristics and aspirations of contemporary humanistic anthropology include as following.

1. Humanistic anthropology, like other forms of humanism, remains anthropocentric. Consequently, it stands skeptical of the theocentric claims of religion and of supernatural causation. It is likewise critical of the coercive practices of state religions and of religious fundamentalism. It opposes the effort to require public schools to provide equal time in biology classes for the teaching of "scientific creationism."

   At the same time, an anthropocentric view fosters an appreciation of the species's unique qualities, for example, religion. As anthropology, humanistic anthropology is committed to understanding religion on its own terms. A response to this apparent dilemma is a scholarship that is objective and critical, but also imaginative and empathetic. Such scholarship, with more than a passing nod to the qualities associated with renaissance humanism, withholds judgment as to the empirical validity of the belief claims of religions. It strives to recognize the role of beliefs in constituting the lived-in world of practitioners and so attempts to disclose belief claims as pronouncements, often eloquent, sometimes cruel, but always significant, about human yearning. The writings of Victor Turner (1975) and Eric R. Wolf (1974) exemplify the humanist as scholar and interpreter of religion.

2. In its interpretation of religion and any other human activity, humanistic anthropology seeks to grasp the whole of human experience. This means that the ambiguities, the nuances, the individual idiosyncrasies that inevitably intertwine human action and aspiration attract the humanistic eye as much as, if not more than, the commonalities and conventionalities that also characterize the human effort. To do justice to the complexities of human living is a fundamental intent of humanistic scholarship.

   In this intent, humanistic anthropology looks to recent developments in linguistic anthropology. In the latter field, the earlier prevailing focus on language led to the analysis of linguistic systems as relatively self-contained, disembodied structures, independent of speakers—not unlike the type of criticism that literary humanism has found wanting. Today, linguists see language as a system of communication in which people inform each another about what is going on, as well as to persuade each other of the legitimacy of what they are up to. This discourse approach to language resonates with the humanistic emphasis on real people engaging in real tasks, in which outcomes are critical to people's sense of themselves as agents acting in the world.

   One purpose of the discourse approach is to understand the manner in which people accomplish a conversation—and in the process how they often violate some of the treasured rules of language analysis. Understanding a conversation begins with the recognition that the conversationalists are not simply self-contained units sending out and taking in messages in the manner of a radio transmitter-receiver. As the conversation proceeds, the participants become co-speakers and listeners, whose mutual presence reciprocally affects what is said and what is interpreted. As a result, the conversation emerges as its own social reality, however brief may be its existence.

Humanistic anthropologists may apply this model to ritual, the Catholic mass, or the evangelical service. Some questions that an anthropologist might ask include: How does the material setting, the church structure itself, relate to the understanding of what is going on? What is the contrasting role of touching religious icons, as compared to reciting religious text? How do the participants incorporate icon or text into their actions and experience? In this pursuit, the purpose is to disclose how the participants accomplish the ritual to achieve a reality of its own—if they are successful. Rituals, like conversations, may fall flat on their faces, and that failure, no less than the success, requires accounting.

3. As "the most scientific of the humanities and the most humanistic of the sciences" (Wolf 1974), anthropology has always looked to the humanities for models to employ in its quest for understanding the species. These models promote a research agenda whose goal is not so much a prediction based on why we do the things we do, as it is an explication of how we explain to one another what it is we are up to. While humanistic anthropology has some concern for the causes that operate upon us and the constraints that distort our finest intentions, it remains focused on the lived-in world that people bring about, in the manner that they bring about a conversation or a ritual. One model with wide appeal is human action as text. While this model sounds overly bookish, correctly applied, it opens to a vista in which we see humans authoring—through word, deed, and artifact—their own lived-in world. The text that people write is far from a Hollywood, R-rated hyper-real extravaganza of lust and mayhem, but an authentic document of small defeats and tenuous victories. The plot of the truly popular text (i.e., the text of the people) is never resolved and is under constant revision. The book of the people remains open; consequently, the anthropologist's reading of this book is never complete.

4. The language that people use in composing the text of their lives is as metaphoric as it is representational. This holds true for the language of belief, such as the use of the birth experience as a description of religious conversion among Christian evangelicals, to wit, "born again in Christ." It also applies to the material things we produce, which brings us to archaeology, the study of such things.

In archaeology, humanistic anthropology naturally finds a space for itself in the field's documentation and explanation of humanity's route from the earliest pebble tool to the lunar landing. Such a record provides a text for the anthropocentric reading of the species's achievements. In addition, among the intellectual positions being debated in contemporary archaeology, humanistic anthropology finds a close affinity with interpretive archaeology. Departing from the more common ecological explanation, interpretive archaeology argues that artifacts are more than devices employed to extract foodstuffs from the environment or to keep the body dry. Shaped by both hand and mind, artifacts, from burial mounds to war memorials, communicate social information on the claims that people assert about themselves and on how they want future generations to remember them.

The humanistic anthropologist turns to geography for a fuller understanding of how people inscribe their life's text upon the landscape. Works such as *Humanistic Geography* and *Space and Place* argue that wherever we humans are, we are always somewhere in that we relate to one another in the context of particular places. The evangelical's plain meeting hall, or the Catholic's elaborate cathedral, informs the understanding that each has as to the appropriate way to worship, with shouts of enthusiasm or on one's knees in quiet meditation, and contributes to the manner in which the participants experience their lived-in world.

5. To grasp the whole of human experience means to grasp the sweaty body as well as the deodorized thought, to rejoice in the creature that we feel as well as in the symbols that we speak, and to recognize our kinship with other animals as

well as to celebrate our uniqueness. In this effort, although often thought antithetical to humanistic pursuits because of its grounding in biochemical causation, biological anthropology may be humanistic anthropology's most congenial intellectual partner. When a biological anthropologist such as Theodosius Dobzhansky contrasts the highly precise, clock like, and closed Newtonian world that contemporary creationists seek to resurrect with the adventurous, open-ended Darwinian world—the latter a world on the move, where existence is to be struggled for and consciousness is to be gained—he points to an evolutionary narrative of great appeal. The emergence of upright stature; the first shaping of tools; the movement from African origins to Europe and Asia; the emergence of self-reflexivity conjointly with the development of language; the crossing over into the New World; and, eventually, the navigation of the distant Pacific are the events of an epic story whose plot is still unfolding. In their recitation we gain a sense of unique accomplishment and perhaps of destiny.

Clearly, as embedded in cultural anthropology and given its affinity to the humanities, humanistic anthropology recognizes the constituent role of symbols in human living. We humans live in a world of symbols, and the interpretation of those symbols requires us to understand how symbols achieve their definition in the context of other symbols. Words address other words as much as, if not more than, they represent nature. Yet, while symbols may speak to other symbols, they go from mouth to ear, from one mammalian body to another.

Consequently, although appreciative of the ethereal symbol, humanism dwells in the body. The body is the two-legged, hand-holding, breast-feeding, mouth-sustaining, nurturing body of mammalian energetics. In it, the genetic code does not condemn us to unthinking and unthinkable acts that a darker sociobiology might suggest, but instead, speaks of potentiality. "Anatomy is not destiny, but, rather, a set of possibilities…" (Murphy 1990). This statement grips us further when we realize the man who wrote it, Robert Murphy, wrote it from a wheelchair.

Alfred L. Kroeber, the most literate of Boasians, considered anthropology a natural science, more related to field biology than to sociology. In his view of a naturalist, anthropology attempts a description that integrates the rich particularity of human experience (Kroeber 1952). It is not accidental that anthropologist's greatest lyricist was Loren Eiseley, a man of words and a biological anthropologist (Eiseley 1975).

6. To speak and to celebrate the accomplishment of species is to articulate humanism's prevailing anthropocentrism. The celebration of the species notwithstanding, humanistic anthropology voices an equal concern for the individual. The liberation of the individual through knowledge has always characterized the humanistic pursuit. In such a pursuit, humanistic anthropology often finds itself pitted against scientific anthropology in a manner that suggests a divide between the two. Indeed, humanists welcome the chance to speak against the dehumanization of a narrow scientism that fragments our quest for a better world into so many dependent variables. Yet, at a fundamental level, science liberates far more than it negates, and it is appropriate to speak, as does Stan Wilk, of a "scientific humanism." Scientific humanism, Wilk argues, is science practiced for the benefit of the individual, a "moral practice of science" that constitutes a way of life in which it "reasonable to love" (Wilk 1991). This view of humanism, again with more than a nod to the renaissance revival of knowledge, is a pursuit of truth that will set us free of the chains of degradation. This is humanism as enlightenment.

The celebration of the species and the liberation of the individual proclaim the optimistic anthropocentrism of humanistic anthropology. Alongside this lighter side of humanistic anthropology dwells a darker side that wonders at our brashness and at our eagerness to proclaim our achievements, a side that Leslie White—not usually placed among the humanists—articulated, when he observed, "The cosmos does little know nor will it long remember what [humans have] done here on this tiny planet. The eventual extinction of the human race—for it will come sometime—will not be the first time that a species has died out" (White 1949).

Language, the hallmark of the species, allows us to communicate information through symbols and thereby permits us to achieve what no other terrestrial life form has done: leave footprints in the lunar dust. This astonishing feat derives from the awareness that life is finite, that the cosmos has plans other than ours, and that our proud anthropocentrism may fade into infantile, narcissistic indulgence. Yet, Ernest Becker (1973) observes that we are not simply blobs of vegetative protoplasm but creatures with names engaged in the defiant creation of lives that signify and consequently, "our central calling, our main task on this planet, is the heroic."

Trafficking in symbols allows us to construct a future; it also contributes the awareness, the knowledge, that in that future, death awaits. The anticipation of death, as Dobzhansky argues, sharpens the intensity of self-awareness of our own individual uniqueness and separation both from other animals and from each other. In that Becker inhabits the South, we might refer to this image as Southern Gothic, a genre of interpretation in which we find a crazed lover locked in the attic of the self, a schizophrenic lover, who, when we open the door, shows the persona of "Death" and then, on our next visit, that of the beguiling pronoun "I."

7. In articulating either the lighter or the darker side of human experience, humanistic anthropology searches for writing that not only depicts those qualities but also evokes them. To encourage the search, the Society for Humanistic Anthropology sponsors an annual competition in anthropological poetry and fiction and publishes the winners in *Anthropology and Humanism*. The Society also offers the Victor Turner Prize for innovative ethnographies, and a book-length poem, Dennis Tedlock's "Days from a Dream Almanac" (1990) won in 1991. In this chronicling of the "poetics of fieldwork," Tedlock joins field experiences and nightly dreams to the cycle of day names the Quiché Maya of highland Guatemala employ to figure out time's meaning. Experience, dream, and the day's portent—the Lord of that day—intertwine so that

> On the holy and cherished day
> Lord Thirteen Marksman
> dawn is written in the sky
> as a great flower.
> The morning star is written
> as the living heart of the flower.
> The Great Star is born for the fortieth time

since it first came to light on One Marksman. Marksman, brother of Little Jaguar Sun escapes the Lords of Death once again (p. 81).

In the developing genre of narrative anthropology, humanists use the fiction techniques of dialogue and characterization to advance an expository account of the conflicts within a culture, as in the case of Gregory C. Reck's *In the Shadow of Tlaloc* (1986), based on his research in the village of Jonotla in Puebla, Mexico.

Narrative anthropology also embraces the more purely fictional exploration of the human enterprise, and among such explorations are John O. Stewart's *Drinkers, Drummers, and Decent Folk* (1989), placed in Stewart's own Caribbean, and Miles Richardson's *Cry Lonesome* (1990), located principally in the author's American South. Both authors are committed to research and to "getting the facts straight" with the same intensity as are writers of more conventional anthropology. The goal of anthropological fiction is not to impose an overly dramatic, made-for-TV-movie model upon anthropological data but to disclose the fictive, story quality of everyday life. The distance between fact and fiction is intentionally blurred not to trivialize fact but to suggest the lives people lead resemble stories more than they do the mechanistic, cause-and-effect models of conventional science. This is not to say humanistic anthropologists have no regard for cause, but rather to propose that humanists are more focused on the lived-world of you and me, concerned more with the surface, how we live, rather than with the assumed deeper why.

Given the prominence of narrative in the way we explain ourselves to one another, the matter may not simply be that everyday life, the life we lead when we meet on street, resembles a story, but that human life is, a story. Thus, for an anthropologist to write stories about humans may place the anthropologist closer to human reality than might be the case were the anthropologist to employ a more abstract model of independent and dependent variables.

Having considered both aspects of being human, experience and symbol, body and word, as we conclude this piece, let me note again their relationship.

Committed to the explication of the trafficking in symbols and wary of claims of empathetic experience, the semiotic anthropologist asks, "Do we know the outward world of words or do we know the inner and seclusive, secret self?" In reply, the humanist agrees that we, first and foremost, know words, but as Miguel de Unamuno (1974), the Spanish man of letters, wondered that beneath the public, noisy world of chatter, the world of the word, is there a mystery? Have you ever noticed, he asks us, the spectacle of two friends talking about everything except what matters most? The reason for their avoidance is that they are joined by the mystery. The mystery, the secret of you and me, the secret of life, only speaks in silence.

We ask again: What is humanistic anthropology? We can list attributes. It is anthropocentric, but its anthropocentrism is tempered by the knowledge that just as natural processes brought us about, so too those same processes will end our story. It rejects supernatural causation but is committed to understanding religion as a fundamental attribute of the species. It seeks to grasp the whole of human experience, and it finds in the discourse, text model of culture a possible procedure for achieving that aspiration. While not rejecting causation, it recognizes that people inscribe their own stories, and it sees how people author their accounts not only in words and actions but also in artifacts and places. It is appreciative of the symbol's constituent role in our being, but it dwells in the body. It believes in knowledge as a means to liberate the individual, yet suggests a darker side to our lives that knowledge cannot remove. Finally, it searches for ways of acclaiming human qualities in poetry and story.

Humanistic anthropology is not simply an abstract curiosity about people as subjects of research, but it is a commitment to the enterprise of being human. The enterprise continues, for humans are not yet finished; we remain incomplete. We are a questing species. Driven by an evolutionary adaptation, we are condemned to dream; it is, to repeat Becker, our central calling. In this calling we must realize in our anthropocentrism that the hand, the molder of nature, the world inscriber, is also the hand that embraces, the hand that caresses, the hand of a mammal who cares. So let us stop here, you and I, and let the secret speak.

Miles Richardson

Becker, Ernest. *The Denial of Death.* New York: The Free Press, 1985.

Berger, Peter L. *An Invitation to Sociology: A Humanistic Perspective.* Garden City, N.Y.: Doubleday, 1963.

Brady, Ivan, and Edith Turner, eds. "Special Issue: Humanism and Anthropology." *Anthropology and Humanism* 19 (1994): 1–103.

Dobzhansky, Theodosius. "Religion, Death, and Evolutionary Adaptation." In Melford Spiro, ed., *Context and Meaning in Cultural Anthropology.* New York: Free Press, 1965.

Eiseley, Loren. *All the Strange Hours.* New York: Charles Scribner's Sons, 1975.

Kroeber, Alfred L. *The Nature of Culture.* Chicago: University of Chicago Press, 1952.

Lamont, Corliss. *The Philosophy of Humanism.* 7th edition. New York: Continuum, 1990.

Ley, David, and Marwyn S. Samuels, eds. *Humanistic Geography.* Chicago: Maaroufa Press, 1978.

Murphy, Robert F. "The Dialectics of Deeds and Words: Or Anti the Antis (and the Anti-Antis)." *Cultural Anthropology* 5 (1990): 331–337.

Reck, Gregory C. *In the Shadow of Tlaloc.* Prospect Heights, Ill.: Waveland Press, 1986.

Richardson, Miles. *Cry Lonesome and Other Accounts of the Anthropologist's Project.* Albany: State University of New York Press, 1990.

Stewart, John O. *Drinkers, Drummers, and Decent Folk.* Albany: State University of New York Press, 1989.

Tedlock, Dennis. *Days from a Dream Almanac.* Urbana: University of Illinois Press, 1990.

Tuan, Yi-Fu. *Space and Place.* Minneapolis: University of Minnesota Press, 1977.

Turner, Victor. *Drama, Fields, and Metaphors.* Ithaca, N.Y.: Cornell University Press, 1975.

Unamuno, Miguel De. "The Secret of Life." *The Agony of Christianity and Essays on Faith,* translated by Anthony Kerrigan. Volume 5, Selected Works of Miguel de Unamuno. Princeton, N.J.: Princeton University Press, 1974.

White, Leslie. *The Science of Culture.* New York: Farrar, Straus, and Cudahy, 1949.

Wilk, Stan. *Humanistic Anthropology.* Knoxville: University of Tennessee Press, 1991.

Wolf, Eric R. *Anthropology.* New York: W.W. Norton, 1974.

HUMOR

One of the many definitions of humans is that they are laughing animals. For many scholars laughter and humor are synonymous and are panhuman traits. Humor is defined here as a mirthful state of mind often manifested by a smile or laughter in response to external stimuli. No human society exists without humor and laughter, which are an integral part of human communication involving biological, sociocultural, and psychological aspects. Of intense interest and inquiry since antiquity, humor has been studied in many fields of knowledge from the natural sciences to the humanities.

Humor research by cultural anthropologists often involves related disciplines such as linguistics, psychology, sociology, and folklore. Unlike psychologists, however, cultural anthropologists have not given the study of humor the same kind of priority as marriage, kinship, descent, role and status, religion, ecology, and political and economic systems, for example. Nor have they have attempted to develop broad, cross-cultural theories of humor. Rather, their interest in humor has been topically oriented, as reflected in their description and analysis of specific types of humor in individual societies.

Descriptions of humorous episodes, attitudes towards joking and humor, inappropriateness of certain types of humor in specific social situations, and children's play, games, and humorous activities exist in many ethnographies. However, cultural anthropologists have focused on few examples, which have come about as the epiphenomena of other studies considered to be more important. Cultural anthropologists have provided, however, extensive ethnographic data and analyses of the specific topics of humor they have studied, especially their socioculturally constituted nature and dimensions. Such data are essential in providing a universal base for developing global theories of humor.

JOKING RELATIONSHIP

The term "joking relationship" refers to institutionalized humor based on social relationship, especially kinship. Its nature appears broad and varied, and typically entails verbal and nonverbal exchanges including teasing, banter, repartee, sexual innuendo, wordplay, name-calling, snatching and stealing personal effects, grabbing sexual organs, lewd and obscene gestures, horseplay, and other similar activities exchanged between two individuals related by kinship. Neither is supposed to take offense at the other's verbal and nonverbal acts. The frequent occurrence of such kin-based joking in sub-Saharan African

societies first alerted cultural anthropologists to this phenomenon and numerous studies have been carried out since the 1920s (Apte 1985).

The major variables considered crucial for analyzing kin-based joking relationships are participants' sex, age, generation, nature of kin relation (blood or marriage) and of privileges, mutual obligations, and reciprocity. The fact that such joking was initially noticed in preliterate societies added to the perspective that it was typically kin-based. A major weakness in studies of joking relationships is that, but for a few exceptions, the actual instances of such activities have been rarely described and analyzed in detail. The focus has been more on the structural aspects of joking relationships and their many presumed sociocultural functions. The explanatory theories of joking relationships have been primarily structural-functional.

In the 1950s, anthropologists and other social scientists began to identify similar phenomena occurring outside the domain of kinship relationships in complex, large-scale, industrial societies. Among the factors considered crucial for developing a nonkin joking relationship were friendship and intimacy, and routine close proximity in the workplace over a period of time. This broadened the research to include nonkin joking relationships in such societies. The resulting descriptive and analytical studies helped highlight the differences between kin-based and nonkin joking relationships.

It appears that, in general, kin-based joking relationships are obligatory, kin-category based, and can be either reciprocal or nonreciprocal depending on the nature of kinship. For example, in many African societies, a nephew is allowed to take all kinds of liberties with his maternal uncle who is obligated not to take offense, and cannot and normally does not reciprocate such behavior. Kin-based joking relationships between individuals of different sexes suggest potential and/or anticipated sexual and marital union. On the other hand, joking relationships in industrial societies are optional, voluntary, mutually agreed upon, person-oriented, and generally reciprocal. Such joking is also creative in contrast to kin-based joking which appears to be ritualized or stylized.

Joking relationships in both preliterate and industrial societies have been analyzed within the theoretical framework of structural-functionalism following A. R. Radcliffe-Brown (1965). Since then, anthropologists have generally followed this theoretical approach. Anthropologists have suggested various functions of joking relationships including seeking enjoyment and pleasure; reduction of tension and/or boredom; maintaining and reinforcing amicable social relationships; resolution of ambivalence because of conflict of interest; and potential development of sexual relations. These functions have been imputed by researchers and are not necessarily articulated by those engaged in joking. Equally important is the fact that not all types of joking relationships serve all putative functions.

HUMOR IN RELIGION

Humor in religion has its origin in anthropologists' investigation of religion among non-Western, preliterate societies, especially Native Americans. Western anthropologists found it incongruous that joking and humorous activities occured simultaneously with rituals and ceremonies and often parodied and mocked them. Another dimension of this research focused on unique personalities and their exploits in cosmic-order-origin myths. Humor in religion, therefore, falls into two major categories: a) clowns and clowning; and b) tricksters.

Clowns and Clowning

Humorous behavior in religious ceremonies involved exaggerated imitation of the sacred rituals themselves and exaggerated simulated acts of defecation, urination, copulation, bestiality, displays of false sexual organs, pretense of eating feces and drinking urine, imitating the opposite sex, walking backward, riding animals backward, saying the opposite of what is meant, and so on. Such conduct was usually engaged in by a few select individuals, either specially trained or marked by some special status, who were labeled "ritual clowns" by anthropologists.

Many studies of ritual clowning have been carried out among Native Americans and cultures of Africa, Asia, and the South Pacific (Apte 1985; Mitchell 1992). Anthropological research on ritual clowning focuses on two types of ceremonies: calendrical festivals and birth and death anniversaries of saints and other religious figures; and rites of passage commemorating important transitions in the life cycle of individuals such as birth, initiation, onset of puberty, marriage, and death.

The theoretical thrust of these studies has been toward explaining the perceived incongruities in terms of mixing the sacred and the profane and its symbolic significance in the hidden meanings of humorous activities. Such activities are also explained in functional terms such as their entertainment value, the social critique functions of ritual clowns, the reinforcement of existing social order by focusing on its reversal, freedom from norms of approriateness in behavior, especially in life cycle rituals, emphasizing the transition period from one life stage to another, and warding off of evil spirits through outrageous behavior. Clowning has also been interpreted as hegemonic humor and a reflection of postmodern imagination (Mitchell 1992). Secular clowning has not been studied by anthropologists, perhaps because of its absence in preliterate societies.

Tricksters

Tricksters have been studied by anthropologists, folklorists, and scholars of religion in the process of gathering and analyzing Native American myths. Tricksters and their behavior constitute etiological explanations of the cosmic-order-origin myths. There are very few studies of tricksters from other parts of the world except Africa, where they figure prominently in the animal tales of numerous tribes.

Analytical studies of the trickster figures have focused on the oppositional and contradictory nature of the trickster. In general, tricksters appear to be immortal male personages of unknown origin. Either human or animal, they can transform themselves from one to the other. Among the Native Americans, Old Man, Bluejay, Coyote, Hare, Mink, and Raven have been recognized as tricksters, while in African cultures Jackal, Spider, Squirrel, Tortoise, and Weasel are portrayed as tricksters.

Trickster tales are generally about the various adventures they engage in to satisfy their primordial desires. Comparisons from many cultures suggest that tricksters typically have the following characteristics: ability to transform into any shape and/or object, animal, or human; grotesque forms such as eyes both inside and outside sockets, intestines outside the body, and long penis wrapped around the body; insatiable appetite for food and sex; lack of control over the excretory body processes; strong urge to satisfy basic desires and willingness to do anything for such an objective; inability to discriminate between right and wrong, good and evil; tendency to behave in ways that are taboo, deviant, outrageous, and antisocial; overall proclivity for blunders; and lack of restraint and social responsibilities.

Despite the specific personality traits of tricksters in different cultures, some common traits can be extrapolated—egotism, cleverness, selfishness, cruelty, cunning, and deceit. Tricksters are also portrayed as boastful, inordinate, foolish, lazy, and ineffective. Thus they represent incongruities at the biological, psychological, cognitive, and sociocultural levels, and manifest overall inappropriateness of human existential realities. According to the religious belief systems of Native American cultures their significance lies in their being unintentionally responsible for the shape of the metaphysical world, e. g., existence of water, sky, mountains, rivers, rocks, trees, and other natural phenomena. Among some of these cultures, ritual clowns are either identified with tricksters or are considered their descendants.

VERBAL JOKING

Studies by sociolinguists, folklorists, and anthropologists have focused on the nature of joking and its functions in social interaction as manifested in natural, everyday discourse and conversations. The studies found that, while narrative jokes constitute a major aspect of humor manifested in everyday talk, other forms of humor such as puns, funny stories, irony, satire, personal anecdotes, tall tales, mocking, and deliberately outrageous comments also appear extensively in conversations. From the 1970s onward the development of systematic transcription techniques of tape-recorded conversations including laughter enabled anthropologists and sociolinguists to systematically analyze naturally occurring conversations in social interaction (Norrick 1993). Such analyses have paid particular attention to the natural flow of conversations and the strategies used by participants such as switching from one language, dialect, or style to another, interruption, increasing tempo and loudness in speaking, snatching a conversational turn, and introducing and picking up on contextualization cues.

These strategies are used for various purposes such as projecting a positive self-image in social interaction, and securing approval by the participant listeners. Humor and joking play a major role in achieving these objectives. The more adept an individual is at using the types of humor mentioned above, the better is his or her approval and popularity. In short, humor is used as a major technique in performance. There is often an explicit or implicit competition among several participants in demonstrating their conversational skills.

Many studies (Norrick 1993; Oring 1992; Wilson 1979) have analyzed how jokes are told, what kinds of responses occur to indicate they have been understood and appreciated, how deliberate or unintentional puns occur in conversation and what purpose they serve, how ambiguity helps in offering opportunities for participants to be witty or to introduce puns, wordplay, and funny episodes. They have also analyzed how joking, once introduced, gains momentum and is manifested in numerous ways through personal narratives, jokes, irony, ludicrous comments, puns, repartee, teasing, and so on. Such use of humor stimulates laughter, provides entertainment and enjoyment, smooths the course of interaction, develops a sense of solidarity, draws attention to the structural aspects of the language used, allows individuals by use of self-mockery to demonstrate that they have a sense of humor, and permits criticism without being overtly aggressive.

While the topics discussed above have been the focus of anthropological research on humor, increasing attention is also being given to ethnic humor, speech play and games, political use of humor, and form and function of jokes and riddles.

MAHADEV L. APTE

APTE, MAHADEV L. *Humor and Laughter: An Anthropological Approach.* Ithaca: Cornell University Press, 1985.

DAVIES, CHRISTIE. *Ethnic Humor Around the World.* Bloomington: Indiana University Press, 1990.

MCGHEE, PAUL E., and JEFFREY H. GOLDSTEIN eds. *Handbook of Humor Research.* New York: Springer-Verlag, 1983.

MITCHELL, WILLIAM E., ed. *Clowning as Critical Practice.* Pittsburgh: University of Pittsburgh Press, 1992.

MULKAY, MICHAEL. *On Humor.* Cambridge: Polity Press, 1988.

NORRICK, NEAL R. *Conversational Joking.* Bloomington: Indiana University Press, 1993.

ORING, ELLIOTT. *Jokes and Their Relations.* Lexington: The University Press of Kentucky, 1992.

PELTON, ROBERT D. *The Trickster in West Africa.* Berkeley: University of California Press, 1980.

RADCLIFFE-BROWN, A. R. *Structure and Function in Primitive Society.* 1952. Reprint. New York: The Free Press, 1965.

RADIN, P. *The Trickster*. New York: Greenwood Press, 1969 (1956).

RASKIN, VICTOR. *Semantic Mechanisms of Humor*. Boston: D. Reidel Publishing Co., 1985.

WILSON, C. P. *Jokes: Form, Content, Use and Function*. London: Academic Press, 1979.

HUNTER-GATHERER REVISIONISM

The notion of contemporary hunter-gatherers as a separate, identifiable people and culture, with a distinct mode of subsistence and societal type, is an area of study that has been challenged and subjected to revision. Questions have also been raised about the premise that such societies are of great antiquity, with evolutionary roots reaching back to the Paleolithic period, and thus suitable as an analogy for the understanding of prehistoric society. This was the predominant view held by anthropologists about hunter-gatherers in the 1960s and 1970s, and it had special appeal for ethnoarchaeologists and paleoanthropologists of the day, who searched for parallels among extant societies for early human and hominid behavior. In its more extreme expression, revisionists, such as Edwin N. Wilmsen (1989), in the context of the Kalahari Bushmen, question the very existence of contemporary hunter-gatherers and the anthropological enterprise of hunter-gatherer studies. They see such peoples not as culturally autonomous, pristine "aboriginals"—the position ascribed, somewhat gratuitously, perhaps (Lee 1992), to the other view they label "isolationist"—but as social and economic "marginals," who are tied economically and politically, through trade or dependency relations, to regional agricultural societies.

Hunting-gathering is carried out not for subsistence but for commercial reasons, to provide commodities to be traded with the agriculturalists. The study of contemporary foragers would thus fall within the confines of a study of those larger more complex food-producing societies that encapsulate or incorporate such hunter-gatherer groups as live within or outside their bounds. It is argued that this interactionist forager-agriculturalist relationship is of long standing—centuries or millennia—and through it the social organization of hunter-gatherers has come to contain the same elements of property, class, and domination found in the wider society. Such a view

challenges the egalitarianism and sharing ethos attributed to such societies by the opponents of the revisionists, such as Lee (1992), as entailed by his concept of "communal mode of production."

The revisionist challenge to hunter-gatherer studies was raised in the early 1980s, specifically and most urgently at the 1983 International Conference on Hunting and Gathering Societies in Bad Homberg, Germany. The conference aired the revisionist view, from the perspective largely (although not exclusively) of the Khoisan peoples of southern Africa (Schrire 1984). Throughout the decade the issues raised at the conference were explored by researchers among foragers in other regions of the world (Headland and Reid 1989, Shott 1992), as well as at other, earlier times, as its implications for archaeology and its applicability for the study of prehistoric hunter-gatherers were examined. (Solway and Lee 1990; Shott 1992; Barnard 1992; Headland and Reid 1989; Wilmsen and Denbow 1990).

In its proliferation over the geographic and conceptual landscape of anthropology throughout the 1980s and early 1990s, the new approach to hunter-gatherer studies gained theoretical momentum and was soon hailed as the "new paradigm" of the field. Its attainment of this epistemological status is due largely to the work of Edwin N. Wilmsen, especially his controversial book *Land Filled with Flies: A Political Economy of the Kalahari* (1989). Instead of being rooted in evolutionary ecology and based on detailed ethnography, the revisionist theoretical base is political economy (specifically world systems and dependency theory) and its methodological thrust historiography. Another theoretical element is postmodernism and poststructuralism. In an effort to expose the relativism and fragility of truth claims, the argument is presented that the category of the egalitarian, pristine hunter-gatherer—or any of his ethnographic manifestation, such as Bushman/San or Tasaday—is a figment of romanticism and evolutionism. It is reified by being projected onto certain socially and economically marginal, trading or client folk whose ethnic, social, economic, and cultural identity is thereby distorted.

In the process of its dissemination and theoretical elaboration, the revisionist paradigm was met with determined resistance from those working with the previous model of hunter-gatherer society. Along with Lee, one of the model's key architects, they continued to see the egalitarian, foraging and/or communal band society as "an eminently sensible category of humanity with a firm anchor in empirical reality" (Lee 1992). The ensuing debate unleashed what was to become one of the most heated and protracted scholarly disputes in the history of the field. While fought in all of the various geographic hunter-gatherer constituencies (Headland and Reid 1989; Shott 1992), it was especially intense amongst the Kalahari researchers, whose strident, "reprimanding," at times vitriolic rebuttals and counterrebuttals filled the pages of several volumes of *Current Anthropology*, as well as other journals. The reason the Kalahari assumed theoretical and geographical center stage in the debate was the exemplary and paradigmatic position the !Kung Bushmen had come to hold in hunter-gatherer studies and in anthropology generally, thanks to the prolific writings of Lee and the many members of the "Harvard Group" who worked with the !Kung at and around Dobe (and, prior to them, Lorna Marshall, as well as Elizabeth Marshall-Thomas and, through the medium of film, John Marshall).

Apart from criticisms about methodology and accuracy of data voiced by the revisionists about the work of the Harvard Group, their paradigm questioned all of the fundamental assumptions of the work of the latter researchers, bringing about a sea change in the views they had held about the !Kung for about two decades and a "crisis" in their field of study (Lee 1992). The counterarguments they marshaled against the revisionists were in part conceptual (such as misunderstanding of the nature and meaning of such processes as contact, domination, dependence, and autonomy), in part ideological (denial of history, agency, and cultural autonomy to the Bushmen), and in part methodological (careless use of historical and linguistic sources) (Solway and Lee 1990; Wilmsen and Denbow 1990; Lee and Guenther 1993).

While not over, the debate by the mid-1990s was abating, in part because of the realization that, despite its au courant postmodern and world systems guise, the issues raised are, in fact, not new, having been debated in various ethnographic arenas by earlier generations of anthropologists (Headland and Reid 1986; Wilmsen and Denbow 1990). The recognition by researchers (such as Alan Barnard, Susan Kent, and Mathias Guenther) of the extensive regional diversity of hunting-gathering societies also suggests that instead of only one or the other of the two models having explanatory and theoretical merit for hunter-gatherer studies, both do, depending on the specific case at hand. Carol R. Ember (1978) presents another point of view on the controversy. The diversity may be one of relative isolation and social fluidity or, on the other end of the spectrum, of relative interdependence and social complexity; thus, either model becomes theoretically appropriate.

Thus, the conciliatory message of some researchers on the debate is that there is not just the one correct position about hunter-gatherers. The two paradigms should be synthesized, rather than remain polarized (Kent 1992). Such a double-barreled conceptual approach would expand the temporal and structural parameters of hunting-gathering societies and take their study to a new theoretical plateau. Complex, lateral thinking about hunter-gatherers could replace what has in essence been simplistic, linear thinking.

MATHIAS GUENTHER

SEE ALSO: Hunting and Gathering Societies; Tasaday Controversy

BARNARD, ALAN. *The Kalahari Debate: A Bibliographical Essay.* Occasional Papers No. 35. Edinburgh: Centre for African Studies, 1992.

EMBER, CAROL R. "Myths About Hunter-Gatherers." *Ethnology* 17 (1978): 439–448.

HEADLAND, THOMAS N., and LAWRENCE A. REID. "Hunter-Gatherers and Their Neighbours from Prehistory to the Present." *Current Anthropology* 30 (1989): 43–66.

KENT, SUSAN. "The Current Forager Controversy: Real Versus Ideal Views of Hunter-Gatherers." *Man* (n.s.) 27 (1992): 45–70.

LEE, RICHARD B. "Art, Science, or Politics? The Crisis in Hunter-Gatherer Studies." *American Anthropologist* 94 (1992): 31–54.

LEE, RICHARD B., and MATHIAS GUENTHER. "Problems in Kalahari Historical Ethnography and the Tolerance of Error." *History in Africa* 20 (1993): 185–235.

SCHRIRE, CARMEL, ed. *Past and Present in Hunter-Gatherer Studies.* Orlando, Fla.: Academic Press, 1984.

SHOTT, MICHAEL J. "On Recent Trends in the Anthropology of Foragers: Kalahari Revisionism and Its Archaeological Implications." *Man* 27 (1992): 843–871.

SOLWAY, JACQUELINE S., and RICHARD LEE. "Foragers, Genuine or Spurious? Situating the Kalahari San in History." *Current Anthropology* 31 (1990): 109–146.

WILMSEN, EDWIN N. *Land Filled with Flies: A Political Economy of the Kalahari.* Chicago: University of Chicago Press, 1989.

WILMSEN, EDWIN N., and JAMES R. DENBOW. "Paradigmatic History of San-Speaking Peoples and Current Attempts at Revision." *Current Anthropology* 31 (1990): 489–524.

HUNTING AND GATHERING SOCIETIES

Hunting and gathering societies are groups of people who derive all or most of their subsistence from wild foods, with little contribution from agriculture or domesticated livestock. Although hunting-gathering is an economic categorization, the term is also associated with a host of cultural traits among a wide variety of groups ranging from Australian Aborigines, African Pygmies, and Greenland Inuit to the Kwakiutl of the northwest coast of North America.

STEREOTYPES

Long-held stereotypes about hunters and gatherers have colored the opinions of government officials and anthropologists working among them. On the one hand, hunter-gatherers were thought to be living in a state of nature, with none of the amenities of modern Western culture, and by implication, none of the intelligence or drive that produced these amenities. This attitude served the interests of colonial powers and missionaries, whose aims included the extinction, eviction, or at least the religious conversion of hunter-gatherer subjects. In a milder form, this stereotype resulted in a strong paternalism by governmental officials, who saw the need to protect the "helpless" hunter-gatherers from the outside world while guiding them to the "enlightenment" of settled life and Western goods.

Quite opposite in tone is the overly positive view of hunter-gatherers as earth's original custodians, living in harmony with both nature and each other, with none of the evils of modern society such as pollution, theft, and violence. This view has been embraced by certain environmentalists who see hunter-gatherers as both worthy of emulation for their

environmental wisdom and needing protection from commercial and governmental exploitation.

Such extreme views contain elements of truth, but both are, ultimately, wrong and dangerous, because they ignore the extreme variations within and among hunting and gathering societies, and because they dehumanize and disempower the people themselves. By rendering hunter-gatherers in such extremes, these stereotypes make them truly "the other," set apart from the rest of humanity.

Variability in Subsistence, Settlement, and Sociopolitical Organization

Anthropology has created new stereotypes by codifying and classifying the variations among hunting and gathering groups. Proposed classification schemes emphasize different criteria, the most frequent of which are elements of sociopolitical organization. "Simple" groups, such as the Mbuti Pygmies of central Africa, are distinguished from "complex" groups such as the Chumash, the Tolowa, and other Californian societies. The former are characterized by a differentiation of roles made largely on the basis of age, sex, and a strong ethic of egalitarianism, while the latter are ranked with considerable differentiation among individuals in activities, status, and authority. Although virtually all anthropologists recognize that such characteristics vary along a continuum, it has become commonplace in general anthropological texts to contrast simple versus complex groups, as though they were discrete subgroups of hunter-gatherers.

A remarkable feature of the differences in sociopolitical complexity is that they covary with a number of other differences among these societies. So, for example, simple groups tend to live in environments that are poorer, more homogeneous, or more unpredictable than those of more complex groups. The subsistence economies of simple foragers tend to emphasize year-round food procurement and immediate consumption, widespread sharing, and an emphasis on resources, such as many big game animals and wild roots, the production of which is not easily intensified. By contrast, more complex foragers, living in richer, more predictable environments, have economies based largely on stored foods obtained during particular seasons, placing less emphasis on food sharing, and concentrating on the intensified procurement of resources such as salmon, nuts, and grass seeds. Patterns of demography, land use, and settlement also show correlations. Simple groups tend to have low population densities (<5/100 sq. km; 12.5/100 sq. mi.), are highly mobile, and recognize somewhat vaguely bounded communal territories, while more complex groups have higher densities (up to 500 or more/100 sq. km; 1250+/100 sq. mi.), are more sedentary, maintain clearer territorial boundaries, and recognize individual or family property as well.

As a result of these patterns of co-variation, anthropologists have categorized hunter-gatherers as "immediate-" vs. "delayed-return" economies, "storers" vs. "nonstorers," "mobile" vs. "sedentary" groups, and "sharers" vs. "aggrandizers." Although each classification emphasizes a different aspect of behavior, all such schemes tend to group the same hunter-gatherer societies together into subgroups, on the basis of the strong patterns of correlation among environment, subsistence, settlement patterns, and sociopolitical organization.

EXCHANGE

Variation among groups is also evident in other areas of behavior and is only loosely related to the characteristics mentioned above. Exchange, for example, is practiced in some form by all groups, but its nature varies widely, as do its benefits. One type of exchange, seen among the !Kung of the Kalahari and many of the desert Aborigines of Australia, takes the form of the circulation of gifts, usually craft items, which may ultimately change hands numerous times. They are given on a one-to-one basis between partners and reciprocation is usually delayed. Partnerships link individuals across the landscape, with the social relations, rather than the gifts themselves, having the greatest importance in these transactions. One benefit of these exchanges is subsistence security: individuals can call upon their partners for support in times of need, such as drought. Variable and unpredictable environments encourage this form of exchange.

Another widespread type of exchange entails the exchange of foods, raw materials, and manufactured goods between individuals and groups and is more clearly economic in motive. Along the North Slope of Alaska, for example, coastal and interior groups regularly exchanged inland products such as furs and deer hides for marine goods such as waterproof sealskin. Reciprocity is usually immediate in such transactions, and the exchange appears to be simply an efficient way to obtain goods not easily available locally.

Environments that show considerable spatial variations in resources would be most conducive to this form of exchange.

A third type of exchange, intimately associated with sociopolitical complexity, appears to involve prestige rather than economic security or efficiency. Important, high-status, individuals obtain exotic materials or crafts through individual partnerships and food from within their local groups, only to give these away lavishly and publicly to members of other groups. The very act of generosity, coupled with the value of the gifts, builds debts among the recipients and gains status for the giver. Reciprocity is often quite delayed.

CONFLICT

As with other aspects of behavior, there is considerable variation among hunter-gatherers in how they deal with disputes and conflict. Disagreements arise most frequently over perceived inequities in food sharing, failure to reciprocate gifts, and suspicions of adultery. Commonly, the aggrieved parties voice their complaints loudly, perhaps at night across the camp, seeking public support. If a group consensus develops, the offender usually conforms to their expectations. If not, he or she may face ridicule, avoidance, and even ostracism. Long-standing disputes with no easy resolution frequently lead to a break-up of the group, with the disputants moving apart. In this respect, mobility and flexibility of residence—hallmarks of the simpler hunter-gatherer societies—serve as much to redistribute people to avoid conflict as to provide easy access to food resources.

Disagreements may also lead to violence, with men suddenly attacking others in the heat of argument. Although sometimes fatal, these attacks are more often interrupted by other group members seeking to prevent injuries. It is not uncommon among many groups for men to attack their wives and severely beat them. In these cases, others rarely interfere, but if the beatings occur frequently with little justification, the wife's close relatives may intervene and the marriage may even be ended by her moving back with her kin. When fatalities do occur, they can lead to new disputes, giving rise to another major cause of conflict: revenge. In such cases, relatives of the victim may seek redress by ambushing the murderer and killing him, and long-standing feuds can result.

A number of groups have developed means to resolve such conflicts and avoid or end violent reprisals. Among the Tiwi of northern Australia, for example, ritualized "duels" are held, in which the aggrieved, often an older man with a young wife, throws spears at the younger man suspected of adultery. The latter is compelled by public opinion to face this ordeal, dodge the spears for a time, but ultimately to accept a wound. Fatalities are rare. More complex groups, such as the Tlingit of southeastern Alaska, for whom wealth is an important measure of status, allow the payment of fines for various infractions.

Disputes also develop between members of different groups. Many hunter-gatherers have long-standing hostile relations with certain neighbors, particularly those differing in language, culture, and ethnicity. Throughout northern Alaska and Canada, for example, relations between Inuit and Athapaskans were marked by suspicion, which frequently prompted raids with high incidences of fatality. The causes of such ongoing enmity, found also among groups in California and the Northwest Coast, often lie in past cycles of feuding and vengeance, but may also be a result of trespassing into a group's territory. Additionally, motivation may be provided by some of the results of such raids: looted items of wealth, women captives as wives or slaves, and prestige for bravery and killing. It is no accident that the most highly developed warfare appears among the most sociopolitically complex groups, for whom territories and social groups are most clearly defined and bounded, among whom wealth and prestige are most emphasized, and for whom slaves are just one of the many recognized social categories.

LEADERSHIP

It has become a truism that hunter-gatherers have little formal leadership and government, but here, too, there is considerable variability. Leaders of some sort exist in every group, and almost everywhere they exhibit certain qualities: good social skills, speaking ability, and generosity. Leaders are commonly adept hunters, they possess a large group of close kin who can provide support in decisions and disputes, and, in some cases, they supply labor to produce abundant food for feasting.

Among the simpler groups, leaders have no real authority; they are just individuals whose opinion is respected and who therefore may have slightly more influence in decisions than others. Such leadership may be ephemeral and shift among individuals. The strong egalitarian ethic of people like the !Kung and the Mbuti precludes anything else.

By contrast, more complex groups are in part defined by their greater differentiation and centralization of authority. "Big Men" among the Tiwi are older heads of large households, containing their numerous (up to twenty or so) wives, children, and other relatives. These men do little of their own food gathering, but are instead supported by their households. This frees them to plan and coordinate the household activities, participate in exchange and ceremonies, and serve as advisers on ritual and as arbiters of disputes. They attain their position through shrewd marriages and manipulation of the betrothal of their mothers and daughters. Social mobility is not as common among the Tanaina and other Northwest Coast groups. Leaders come from the small class of noble families and often inherit their position as the heads of the larger households of the larger clans. These leaders protect and coordinate the use of clan territories and organize the elaborate give-aways in potlatches and other feasts.

IDEOLOGY

Concepts of ideology and religion vary widely, but most share some essential features, one of which is animism, the belief that animals and even nonliving entities have spirits that are active in the world. Many groups have an elaborate mythology about these spirits that gives meaning to their lives and explains natural phenomena. For example, a common theme appearing in both the Australian concept of the Dreamtime and the Athapaskan Distant Time, is that these spirits once walked the earth, performing both wondrous and mundane acts, and thereby established the landscape and the relations between humans and the environment. To maintain this natural order, people must follow various rules, such as treating the remains of animal prey with respect, following taboos about women's menstrual seclusion, and holding rites of renewal for certain resources.

Another common feature is the idea of spiritual power that can be acquired and used by people. Because the spirits are still active, they can be induced to share their power. The most common means by which power is acquired is by dreaming, often enhanced by fasting, isolation, sweat baths, and other physical ordeals. In many Athapaskan societies, boys undergo vision quests in order to obtain a personal guardian spirit, who will assist them in hunting and other endeavors. Some groups, like the Ojibwa of Ontario, and many of the Australian Aborigines, trace their descent to particular spirits and seek their aid throughout their lives.

Among many groups, particular individuals are perceived as uniquely receptive to, or adept at, acquiring spiritual power. These individuals become shamans and may use their abilities in various ways. Because illness is usually attributed to spiritual forces, healing is a major activity of the shaman, who may also use his or her power to perform divination using special tents, animal shoulder blade bones, blood mixtures, or other devices in order to advise on decisions about hunting or camp moves. Some shamans can also direct their power against other people and, as a result, may become feared and powerful individuals within the group. Australian Aborigines, for example, attribute virtually any misfortune to sorcery performed by others, and enlist their shaman to perform spiritual revenge. Among many of the Northwest Coast groups, the shaman participates in warfare, accompanying the raiding party and directing his power against the enemy.

THEORETICAL IMPORTANCE

Despite the considerable variations among groups, anthropologists and others commonly lump these people together as "hunter-gatherers," due largely to the theoretical importance of this category of societies. In the evolutionary history of humankind, hunting and gathering played a prominent role, representing the only economic form until roughly ten thousand years ago. In order to understand the formative context of human cultural development, many feel that it is essential to understand the modern representatives of this way of life. Prehistorians constantly use analogies with living hunter-gatherers to help understand and interpret the archaeological record of the Palaeolithic, Mesolithic, Palaeoindian, and Archaic periods in both the Old and the New Worlds. Most archaeological reconstructions of the role of hunting, the division of labor, and the form of social organization, for example, draw heavily upon such analogies. The practice of "ethnoarchaeology," in which archaeologists such as John Yellen (1977) live with contemporary groups like the San, has been used to study the relationship between observable behavior and the material remains created. Important insights have been gained about the archaeological visibility of food-

sharing and sedentism and about the cultural and natural processes that create patterns in archaeological sites.

Research into the cognitive development of humans also turns to living hunter-gatherers, since this way of life predominated during much of our evolutionary past. Debates about universal human psychological characteristics and innate gender differences in abilities frequently cite modern hunter-gatherers, under the assumption that widespread social forms and patterns of the division of labor may have deep evolutionary roots and comprise the selective context for our cognitive development.

Another related research area in which hunter-gatherers occupy a prominent position is evolutionary ecology, which posits that much of human behavior has been shaped by natural selection. Perhaps the best known work in this area involves the application of Optimal Foraging Theory, first developed in biological ecology, to examine human patterns of food-getting, land use, and group size. The fundamental assumption of such studies is that these behaviors evolved so as to maximize net energetic efficiency, a proximate measure of fitness in these models. They have proven useful to anthropologists in accounting for at least the broad trends of subsistence patterns in terms of resources exploited and alterations in diet with environmental or technological change.

OUTSIDE RELATIONS

Many of the reasons for the theoretical importance of hunter-gatherers derive ultimately from the assumptions that there are some universal qualities of the hunting and gathering way of life and that modern representatives are suitable models for our prehistoric past. This latter assumption might be questioned on several grounds. First, most contemporary groups inhabit rather marginal environments such as the high Arctic, the deserts of Africa and Australia, and the dense tropical forests of Africa, South America, and southeast Asia. Adaptations to these environments may not necessarily be typical of past hunter-gatherers in richer environments. In fact, most of the simpler societies exist in precisely these marginal environments; the more complex groups exist in such areas as the Northwest Coast of North America.

Second, these groups are not "pristine" representatives of a Palaeolithic past. They are modern people who have survived, and presumably evolved culturally, into the modern world, just as every other modern society has. Moreover, it is now clear that virtually all modern hunting and gathering groups have had significant contacts with other, non-hunter-gatherer societies. The !Kung have been in contact with Bantu peoples for over 1000 years and were involved in cattle-tending and exchange relationships. Aborigines of north Australia interacted with Chinese and southeast Asian traders for centuries. Most Athapaskan and Algonkian groups of Canada and Alaska became participants in the fur trade beginning in the 1600s. It has even been suggested by Bailey et al. (1989) that all tropical forest groups, like the Mbuti, required trade contact with agriculturalists in order to survive in these environments. The extent to which these outside relationships affected hunter-gatherer societies is not known, but they cannot be ignored in using modern groups as models of a very different past.

The most obvious impacts of outside contacts are visible beginning with the massive Western colonial expansion. Even though each local situation was different, common themes run through the histories of many groups of hunter-gatherers. Exposure to foreign diseases caused the rapid decimation of large numbers of people and led to the disruption of old social groupings and the amalgamation of unrelated people. Introduction of foreign technology—axes, machetes, and other metal implements, decorative beads, cloth, guns, and new kinds of food—led to the loss of former manufacturing skills, changes in diet and mobility, and the development of a dependence on trade ties for continued access to goods and ammunition. Often, this dependence required subsistence changes to produce marketable goods such as furs or ivory. Trading posts and mission stations became magnets for settlement, drawing people, at least seasonally, into more sedentary camps in their proximity.

During the twentieth century, colonial and national governments became more directly intrusive into hunter-gatherers' lives, forcing them to move to larger settlements, where many were pushed or drawn into working on farms, on ranches, or in mines. Their former lands were used by new settlers or commercial logging and mining interests and the once dispersed and mobile hunter-gatherers were consolidated for administrative ease, facilitating the distribution of medical care, welfare, and education. Either cultural or physical extinction was the final fate of many of the original groups.

Beginning in the 1960s, however, many of the remaining groups became increasingly politically active. By developing new forms of organization into larger units that could speak in one clear voice, they found that they could be much more successful in their dealings with outside governments. Assisted by a small, international community of sympathetic supporters, many groups are pressing claims to their original lands, are fighting for rights to maintain their original language through education of their children, and are teaching children about their original subsistence activities. Although many of these endeavors have not been very successful, they demonstrate the growing political sophistication and visibility of the hunter-gatherer groups.

There have been some notable successes. An Inuit homeland of Nunavut has been established in northern Canada, providing these people with substantial local autonomy. In the Canadian Northwest Territories, a number of Aboriginal languages have been granted official status, requiring that education and government services be available in these languages. In 1992, an Australian court decision recognized, for the first time in that country's history, the principle of Aboriginal land rights. Many native Americans, including former hunter-gatherers, have won control over the skeletal remains of their ancestors as well as of many artifacts that constitute their cultural patrimony. Today, there are few, if any, groups who live wholly by hunting and gathering. "Hunter-gatherers" in any pure sense are extinct, but as culturally distinct and politically aware entities, many live on.

MICHAEL JOCHIM

BAILEY, ROBERT, GENEVIEVE HEAD, MARK JENIKE, BRUCE OWEN, ROBERT RECHTMAN, and ELZBIETA ZECHENTER. "Hunting and Gathering in the Tropical Rain Forest: Is It Possible?" *American Anthropologist* (1989) 91:59-82.

BETTINGER, ROBERT. *Hunter-Gatherers: Archaeological and Evolutionary Theory.* New York: Plenum Press, 1991.

CAVALLI-SFORZA, LUIGI LUCA, ed. *African Pygmies.* Orlando: Academic Press, 1986.

DAMAS, DAVID, ed. *Arctic. Handbook of North American Indians*, Vol. 5. Washington, D.C.: Smithsonian Institution, 1984.

D'AZEVEDO, WARREN, ed. *Great Basin. Handbook of North American Indians*, Vol. 11. Washington, D.C.: Smithsonian Institution, 1986.

HEIZER, ROBERT, ed. *California. Handbook of North American Indians*, Vol. 8. Washington, D.C.: Smithsonian Institution, 1978.

HELM, JUNE, ed. *Subarctic. Handbook of North American Indians*, Vol. 6. Washington, D.C.: Smithsonian Institution, 1978.

LEE, RICHARD. *The !Kung San: Men, Women, and Work in a Foraging Society*. Cambridge: Cambridge University Press, 1979.

SUTTLES, WAYNE, ed. *Northwest Coast. Handbook of North American Indians*, Vol. 7. Washington, D.C.: Smithsonian Institution, 1990.

TINDALE, NORMAN. *Aboriginal Tribes of Australia*. Berkeley: University of California Press, 1974.

YELLEN, JOHN. *Archaeological Approaches to the Present*. New York: Academic Press, 1977.

I

INCEST

Incest, its avoidance, and its taboo constitute one of the most enduring of anthropological puzzles. Though its recognition and avoidance are among the most ubiquitous of human phenomena and have accumulated a rich ethnographic record, there is still no consensus about its origins and nature, despite more than a century of anthropological debate.

Definitions of incest and its associated behaviors are often implicit and frequently at odds. Deploying analytical criteria, students of sociobiology commonly define incest as heterosexual intercourse between consanguineal relatives who share twenty-five percent or more of the same genes. Other anthropologists class this as "close inbreeding" and define incest in cultural terms, as sexual activity proscribed on the basis that the partners are classed as kin of some kind. Incest avoidance is sometimes defined as the circumvention of incestuous activity by unconscious processes, and incest taboos as explicit cultural rules prohibiting incestuous activity. More commonly, however, incest avoidance is used simply to refer to the practice of avoiding incestuous activity, and incest taboos refer to the processes that result in this avoidance, be they conscious, unconscious, or both. Here, the cultural definition of incest and the latter definitions of avoidance and taboo will be used, with "proscription" and "prohibition" used synonymously with "taboo."

However defined, incest has traditionally formed a core topic in kinship studies. Many theorists see its avoidance as constitutive of the family and some go so far as to implicate it in the emergence of culture itself. Outside anthropology, incest has been of longstanding interest to students of biological evolution and within the last two decades has become a focus of sociobiological theorizing. It has formed the core of Freudian psychoanalysis; it has attracted attention from feminist scholars, some of whom implicate it, along with rape, in the reproduction of patriarchal society; and it constitutes a recurrent theme in Western literature, drama, and news media, in connection with the controversial "recovered memory" movement of the last decade. Incest is also a prominent concern of psychology, psychiatry, and social work professionals because, quite apart from whatever dysfunctional genetic consequences it may have, it can have serious psychological effects, particularly on unwilling participants, and it can precipitate family break-up and imprisonment of offenders. The psychological consequences of incest in non-Western societies are poorly documented, but social consequences range from ridicule to corporal, and even capital, punishment.

Despite the enormous interest in incest and a plethora of ethnographic data, its psychocultural complexity, ethnographic difficulties in probing what can be a delicate if not repressed topic, and descriptive and analytical ambiguities that include the definitional vagaries mentioned above have left quite basic deficiencies in our knowledge of incest's global manifestations. However, certain broad characteristics can be sketched. Most, if not all, societies have proscribed sexual activity between consanguineal nuclear kin. The most celebrated exceptions were marriages between royal family members in places such as Hawaii, the Inca Empire, and Central Africa. In these cases, however, it is often unclear whether the parties involved were actually full siblings, whether the marriages necessarily entailed intercourse, and, if they did, whether the acts were viewed as incest. Illicit nuclear-family incest occurs in every society, but establishing its incidence is difficult because of the subject's sensitivity and related difficulties in obtaining unbiased samples. In the Western world, the incidence of heterosexual intercourse between postpubertal, nuclear-family consanguines has been estimated at less than one percent, but the incidence of sexual advances to nuclear consanguines of any age is probably well over ten percent (for summaries see

Leavitt 1990; van den Berghe 1983). With the exception of the colonial Greek settler-class of Roman Egypt, next to nothing is reliably known of the incidence of incest in the non-industrial world. In the Egyptian case, perhaps one sixth or more of all marriages involved full siblings, who clearly indulged in intercourse even though this was apparently regarded as incestuous. Shaw (1992) suggests that racist ideologies, intense economic pressures, and the precedent of incest within the local royal family may have overcome whatever inhibitions were involved. Anecdotal evidence indicates that, in most societies, incestuous activity between young siblings and between father and daughter is probably more common than between mother and son. Reactions to these different forms of incest differ widely: in some societies, incest between father and daughter provokes the most intense reactions; in others, that between mother and son; in yet others, that between brother and sister.

With very few exceptions, incest proscriptions are not confined to the nuclear family, though no specific extension applies universally beyond it. There is a strong tendency to class sexual activity with non-nuclear family kin referred to by a nuclear-kin term as incest. As kinship "distance" from the nuclear family increases, there is commonly a slippage between incest proscriptions and incest aversion—between the aversion that society dictates people should feel and what they actually feel. Concomitantly, the incidence of incest usually increases with kinship "distance." Contrary to some early anthropological assumptions, incest prohibitions are not always coterminous with marriage rules: the fact that marriage with a distant clan member is prohibited, for example, does not necessarily mean that intercourse is also prohibited.

Theories accounting for incest aversion, avoidance, and taboo are frequently classified by whether they construe these phenomena as primarily biological or cultural. Cultural theories argue that incest taboos are cultural in nature, instituted because of the social benefits they confer. Alliance or Cooperation Theory is commonly attributed to a comment by Edward B. Tylor (1888), who stated that early humans were faced with a simple practical alternative between marrying out and being killed out. Subsequently elaborated by Leslie White (1948), it asserts that incest proscriptions enhance survival by forcing humans to form marriage alliances beyond their immediate kin, thereby securing the economic, political, and military benefits

of intergroup cooperation. The renowned scholar of marital alliance, Claude Lèvi-Strauss (1969), went so far as to claim that incest taboos constitute the very transition between nature and culture. For him, everything that is universal and instinctive in humans belongs to the natural order; everything subject to a rule is cultural. Human incest avoidance is unique, he claims, because it is simultaneously universal, instinctive, and rule governed; alone among human institutions, it is therefore both natural and cultural, representing the first step between the two. Commonly, Alliance Theory is criticized for erroneously equating marriage rules and incest proscriptions; logically, societies could allow intrafamily incest and yet still insist that children marry out to gain the benefits of alliance.

Family Disruption or Family Socialization Theory draws on Sigmund Freud's psychoanalytic thesis that incest taboos are reactive defenses by offspring against a recognition that the expression of Oedipal desires would disrupt the family. Bronislaw Malinowski (1927) transformed this idea into anthropological terms, arguing that incest subverted family organization in three ways: it is socially and emotionally incompatible with the non-sexual character of family relationships; it engenders sexual jealousies, competition, and hostile rivalry among family members; and it upsets age and generational distinctions within the family and produces disruptive exchanges of roles. Consequently, a society that failed to proscribe incest could develop neither a stable family unit nor, as a result, a secure social order. Critics of this argument commonly ask why societies could not simply deal with whatever disruptions incest causes by instituting rules of sexual access within the family—as occurs in fraternal polyandry and sororal polygyny, where siblings share a sexual partner without destabilizing the family.

Cultural theories share a presumption that incest aversion and avoidance are primarily learned rather than biologically inherited. Humans are innately inclined toward, or at the very least not averse to, sexual activity with close kin, but they proscribe it culturally because of the disastrous social consequences to which it supposedly leads. These premises are questionable. It is difficult to explain, without resorting to functionalist assumptions, how incest avoidance could be instituted and maintained when, as is often the case, people appear to have no explicit awareness of the social benefits that theorists claim for it. In addition, many ethologists now accept that inbreeding avoidance is common among non-human species. How many of these instances are actually analogous to incest avoidance in humans is debatable. In many if not most species it is not the individual organism that avoids inbreeding, but processes that depress or prevent the opportunity—for example, large breeding formations, high mortality, or the dispersal or expulsion of offspring before puberty. In these instances, the depression of close inbreeding may be less the product of attempts to avoid it than a side effect of dominance behavior, competition for food resources or mates, or some other process. Nonetheless, there remain species as diverse as prairie-deer mice, greylag geese, and non-human primates in which close inbreeding opportunities exist but are partially or wholly avoided, indicating that incest avoidance in humans has a biological foundation.

Biological theories attribute the core of incest aversion and avoidance to biology. In contrast to cultural theorists, they presume that humans are innately inclined against—or at the very least are not inclined toward— sexual activity with close kin, and this disinterest is culturally reflected in incest taboos. Demographic Theory argues that incest avoidance is a consequence of the effects that biological parameters had on early human mating patterns. Because early human life spans were so short, parents customarily died before their offspring became sexually active. Because birth spacings were prolonged, moreover, older siblings usually had chosen a sexual partner by the time their younger, opposite-sex siblings were old enough to mate. Consequently, intrafamilial mating was unlikely for demographic reasons, and this state of affairs was later codified and perpetuated as incest avoidance and taboo. Demographic Theory is commonly criticized for failing to explain why an act that was once rare should subsequently be codified as a proscription: early humans were unable to travel faster than about fifteen miles an hour, but this did not result in a prohibition against rapid mechanical transport. In addition, if incest avoidance has phylogenetic precursors in non-human species, then the relevance of early human demographics becomes moot.

Most other biological theories derive from Edward Westermarck's (1922) hypothesis that, because close inbreeding is genetically harmful for offspring, natural selection has resulted in persons who live "closely together from the childhood of one or both of them"

and are therefore likely to be close kin, experiencing an aversion to sexual activity with one another. These theories claim support from studies of Israeli *kibbutzim*, Chinese *sim-pua* marriages, and Lebanese patrilateral parallel cousin marriages, which appear to show that children raised in close association experience sexual disinterest or aversion to one another in later life, even though they are subject to no formal incest taboo. The genetic basis to this argument has caught the attention of sociobiologists, but is a contentious issue in anthropology. Earlier in this century, many anthropologists dismissed the idea that close inbreeding had any net genetic consequences. Today, a number of empirical studies seem to demonstrate such an effect (e.g., Shepher 1983), but contemporary opponents detect serious methodological flaws in this work and point to other studies that find no such linkage. Critics concede that close inbreeding *can* be genetically deleterious, but they argue that this depends on social and environmental circumstances and that, under those prevailing in the early history of humanity, inbreeding may have had no net effect or might actually have been advantageous in ridding the gene pool of harmful recessives (Leavitt 1990).

Other theorists have effectively disengaged Westermarck's hypothesis from its genetic roots, arguing that incest avoidance is a by-product of some property of childhood socialization. Suggested candidates include: childhood punishment and pain, which becomes associated with family members and produces a psychological aversion to sexual relations; repeated sexual stimulation between young siblings that eventually results in stimulus saturation and sexual disinterest or, because it goes unconsummated, frustration and aversion; and a cognitive dissonance between the erotic passion of sexual partners and the amity that family members feel for one another.

Biological theorists do not deny a cultural component to incest avoidance; indeed, given its cultural variability, they would be hard-pressed to do so. Yet, they tend to set aside, and leave unanalyzed, aspects, such as the variable extensions of incest avoidance, that they are unable to reduce to biology. If incest avoidance does have a biological component, however, these extensions seem particularly important to understanding how biology and culture interact.

Classifying incest theories as cultural or biological unavoidably oversimplifies a complicated debate: incest theories are considerably more nuanced than this outline suggests. In addition, they often address logically different levels of explanation and therefore may be less opposed than they seem. Incest phenomena can be explained at a proximate level (what is the mechanism in humans responsible for incest aversion, avoidance, and taboo?), an ultimate level (what is the adaptive significance of this mechanism?), an ontogenetic level (how does the mechanism develop during the life of the individual?), and a phylogenetic level (through what evolutionary progression did the mechanism emerge and develop?). Contrary to common opinion, for example, Freud's and Westermarck's theories are not necessarily opposed since Westermarck primarily addressed proximate and ultimate explanatory levels while Freud focused mainly on the ontogenetic and phylogenetic dimensions.

To judge from the tenor of recent publications, some version of the Westermarck hypothesis is currently considered the strongest explanation of incest avoidance and taboo, though alliance theory still has its champions. After more than a century of debate, however, this most prominent of human issues is still far from settled, and a number of questions merit closer research. There is surprisingly little fine-grained information on the way incest avoidance and taboos are conceptualized in non-Western societies. How is incest talked about? How are attitudes to incest within different family dyads expressed, and how do they vary? How do people express the extension of incest avoidances beyond the nuclear family, and what reasons do they give for these extensions? Although the term "taboo" carries connotations of horror, few reports specify in detail whether incest is actually avoided because people consider it disgusting or dangerous, or because they find it ridiculous, funny, or whatever.

More attention could profitably be directed to the broader contexts of meaning in which incest is embedded. In particular, how is it related to other areas of sexuality and sexual aversion? Little ethnographic attention has been directed, for example, to whether, and in what degree, attitudes expressed toward, and sanctions imposed on, sexual activity between kin actually stem from its incestuous nature as opposed, say, to the marital status of those involved, generational differences between them, or, in the case of same-sex activity, abhorrence of homosexuality. Reports that sexual activity with an in-law is considered incestuous often fail to document that the liaison is indeed avoided because of the kin link involved rather than because it constitutes adultery or fornication.

Finally, closer attention could be paid to what precisely is meant when it is reported that a society avoids incest or observes an "incest taboo." Definitional ambiguities often obscure whether the reference is to a consciously entertained cultural rule, an unconscious avoidance, or some more complex cognitive process. Perhaps because of this, analytical treatments of the nature of incest taboos also incline to the perfunctory. Taboos are treated as simple regulations prohibiting a sexual activity to which humans are "naturally" inclined, as straightforward reflections of a sexual aversion that humans "innately" feel, or both, depending on the context. Almost certainly, however, incest taboos and the aversion and avoidance that accompany them are manifestations of much more complex cognitive processes than currently is imagined.

PAUL B. ROSCOE

SEE ALSO: Alliance, Conflict, and Exogamy; Functionalism; Marriage; Sociobiology

ARENS, WILLIAM. *The Original Sin: Incest and its Meaning.* New York: Oxford University Press, 1986.

FOX, ROBIN. *The Red Lamp of Incest.* New York: Dutton, 1980.

LEAVITT, GREGORY C. "Sociobiological Explanations of Incest Avoidance: A Critical Review of Evidential Claims." *American Anthropologist* 92 (1990): 971–993.

LÈVI-STRAUSS, CLAUDE. *The Elementary Structures of Kinship.* 1949. Translated by James H. Bell, John R. von Sturmer, and Rodney Needham. Boston: Beacon Press, 1969.

MALINOWSKI, BRONISLAW. *Sex and Repression in Savage Society.* New York: Meridian, 1927.

MURDOCK, GEORGE PETER. *Social Structure.* New York: MacMillan, 1949.

SHAW, BRENT D. "Explaining Incest: Brother-Sister Marriage in Graeco-Roman Egypt." *Man* (n.s.) 27 (1992):267-299.

SHEPHER, JOSEPH. *Incest, A Biosocial View.* New York: Academic Press, 1983.

TYLOR, EDWARD B. "On a Method of Investigating the Development of Institutions, Applied to Laws of Marriage and Descent." *Journal of the Royal Anthropological Institute* 18 (1888): 245-272.

VAN DEN BERGHE, PIERRE L. "Human Inbreeding Avoidance: Culture in Nature." *Behavioral and Brain Sciences* 6 (1983):91-123.

WESTERMARCK, EDWARD. *The History of Human Marriage,* vol II. 1891. Revision. New York: Allerton, 1922.

WHITE, LESLIE A. "The Definition and Prohibition of Incest." *American Anthropologist* 50 (1948):416-435.

INDIGENOUS PEOPLES

Conventionally, "indigenous peoples" is a polite label replacing "tribes," "aborigines," and similar terms which carry, for many, connotations of "primitive," "primeval," "stone age," and other unwarranted and negative attributes. Societies that are categorized as "indigenous peoples" have relatively small populations, and ancestral cultures of their own—even if much has since been displaced through acculturation—and typically occupy the status of minority group within a nation-state controlled by others.

There are many groups who can comfortably be called "indigenous" who do not quite fit the above set of criteria. Some indigenous societies have large populations: the Tarahumara of northern Mexico, for instance, number perhaps sixty thousand people. Then, too, some indigenous societies have acculturated so thoroughly to the dominant surrounding society that they exist mainly in name and as a political faction. Finally, there are some indigenous societies that have formed separate nation-states with full membership in the United Nations, and, thus are no longer minorities within a nation-state.

We need not be too concerned about the exceptions. Human societies are not like animal species that fall into clearly bounded sets, commonly without gradations in between. When we talk about "peasants," "industrial societies," "urban societies," "hunter-gatherers," and other societal types, what we are doing is positing a set of features that many societies illustrate exactly, but which also includes societies around the edges of the category to which our conclusions about the type may apply only to some extent, or not at all.

Thus, while it is tempting to argue endlessly about definitions and criteria and the exceptions to those definitions, the category "indigenous peoples" is useful and usable. We need it in order to talk about these societies, to identify the needs indigenous societies have in common, and to act on those needs. The category is as much needed by indigenous societies themselves as by the rest of us. As long as we recognize that there are many societies for which our generalizations will be suspect, and that applying policies and programs to indigenous societies will therefore be "messy," the term can be used honestly and usefully.

Indigenous peoples are members of the human community; they have been, are now, and will be in the future. Indigenous peoples have a past that has included a time of social and political independence. They have a more recent history that chronicles the loss of that independence to colonial states. During this period they were converted into enclaves in nations controlled by others, and they experienced a growing intrusion, often forced, into their lifeways of the cultural and economic ways of the surrounding society. Today, indigenous societies find themselves under escalating cultural assault, but energized by surging ethnic pride and an acute sense of jeopardy. Most certainly, indigenous peoples have a future.

THE DESTRUCTION AND THE CREATION OF INDIGENOUS PEOPLE

While empires have been established many times and in many regions over the past five thousand years, trampling indigenous societies in their path, in global terms nothing equals the expansion of Europeans that began about five centuries ago. By 1600 Europeans had beachheads on every continent except Australia and Antarctica, and everywhere they sought to expand, control, and convert. Europeans' opportunism, and their attitudes toward themselves and toward the peoples they encountered, disrupted more indigenous societies in more areas than ever before. Indeed, the cultural and commercial onslaught of European-derived populations on indigenous societies around the globe broadens and intensifies year after year.

For most of the period since the European expansion began, the dominant view has been that indigenous peoples were intriguing, but ultimately undeserving, relics. They were peoples who needed to be religiously enlightened, politically neutralized so that their lands and resources could be safely appropriated, culturally changed to become marginal precincts of the dominant culture, and, if necessary, exterminated. Indeed, large numbers of indigenous societies disappeared physically and culturally, particularly where the dominant society had conscripted the entire land base, occupied it densely, and afforded its indigenous occupants neither isolation nor refuge.

At the same time, one cannot help but be astonished at the number of indigenous societies that persist. In the United States, for instance, there are over five hundred federally recognized tribes in thirty-two states, and still others seeking recognition. Canada has a similar number. In most of the world's other continental areas and Oceania the number of indigenous peoples is also large. Nonetheless, indigenous peoples remain largely invisible to most members of the world's dominant societies and are thought to be mainly a phenomenon of the past.

Indigenous peoples range from a small number still practicing traditional life ways in remote areas, to groups occupying reservations apart from the dominant society, to groups whose social reality revolves around bars and clubhouses in cities. Where governments have allotted reservations or reserves, as in North America, these places are often plagued by severe poverty, early mortality, undereducation, substance abuse, family dysfunction, and other deprivations. The poorest county in the United States, Shannon County, South Dakota, is an Indian reservation. At the same time, these reservations are psychologically and spiritually central to the peoples who occupy them.

What is remarkable among indigenous peoples, especially since the mid-1980s, is the resurgence of ethnic pride, the spread of effective means of political assertion, and, in a significant number of cases, substantial improvement in their financial resources. This has been true on a global scale. Notable examples may be found in Australia and New Zealand, the Amazon, eastern Asia, the Pacific islands, and North America. In Africa this combination of changes has thus far been disrupted, although political assertiveness and ethnic pride are elements contributing to much news, good and bad.

Strange as it may seem, indigenous societies are not only surviving, many are being created. While the process can be seen in many parts of the world, it is especially visible in North America. For example, by the 1960s almost all of the approximately 260 tribal members of Connecticut's Mashantucket Pequot, who suffered a calculated massacre by European settlers in 1637, were working and living in cities. Only one family lived full time on a small parcel of reservation land. In the 1980s Mashantucket entrepreneurial and political acumen led to the establishment of a full-blown gambling casino on the reservation which by 1994 had become the largest single gambling facility in the hemisphere with gross revenues of perhaps 600 million dollars. In 1993 the Mashantuckets declared and financed a powwow that brought some twelve hundred native dancers and competitors from across the United States. Through these ceremonies, performances, and consultations the Mashantuckets sought to better acquaint themselves with features of American indigenous cultures and from that knowledge build a Mashantucket culture, recreating what had been almost entirely lost. Through the powwow and other initiatives the Mashantucket Pequot are intentionally building anew a cultural tradition that will be theirs.

The 1980s and 1990s brought forth an intense process of cultural creativity, led by native artists writing poetry and novels, choreographing dance and costume, writing music, and painting and sculpting. These artists are not simply replicating traditional art, they are creating new cultural expressions. They use traditional materials and forms, but also canvas, musical scores, the theatrical stage, and the printed page. Like all artists, they draw from the traditional, but create and respond to the present. We are witnessing building on the ancient, we are witnessing the creation of new forms of indigenous culture built on old roots.

THE PRESENT AND THE FUTURE OF INDIGENOUS PEOPLES

Indigenous societies, like all societies, respond culturally to the changing circumstances they encounter. Only by doing so can a culture survive and supply a viable life way to the people who practice it. Arctic Inuit use snowmobiles and outboard motors in place of dog sleds and skin kayaks. Amazonian Kayapos use two-way radios, camcorders, and fax machines. Guatemalan Mayan women weave their stunning wraparound skirts using color-fast acrylic thread. The pickup truck is virtually an icon of Native American males in reservation communities. Does this mean these people are no longer indigenous?

Indigenous societies continue to draw on a traditional cultural core of values and practices that link them with their past and set them apart from others. Often members of the dominant society are unaware of these differences and may not even be aware that a person they work with or pass on the street is a member of an indigenous group. This is partly because indigenous persons tend to keep their distinctiveness to themselves, but it is also due to the bi-cultural skills they often have. In dominant society they adopt those behaviors that work for them; back home their traditional cultural framework holds sway. Consequently, people of the dominant society commonly conclude that if an indigenous person does not act like their distorted stereotype from a past era, that the person no longer "qualifies" and is an undeserving pretender if he or she claims to be indigenous. Their conclusion is shortsighted.

What we see in many parts of the world are indigenous societies taking great pride in their distinctiveness, led by knowledgeable and determined leaders who are conversant with the levers of influence within the dominant society's political system and who know how to use them to make gains for their communities. As mentioned above, native artists are also a critically important force. Other factors are: (1) careful use of the media to mobilize support among the voters of the dominant society; (2) joining the indigenous cause to the campaigns of heavy-weight advocacy organizations, especially those committed to the environment and human rights; (3) using modern communication technologies such as telephone, fax machine, and electronic mail to mobilize support, to advance their political efforts, and to share experience with other groups; (4) favorable outcomes in court decisions and litigation; and (5) the judicious use of more abundant financial resources.

The victories being won by indigenous societies are striking. The Amazonian Kayapo have thwarted a Brazilian Amazonian development project worth half a billion dollars. Ecuador's Amazonian groups marched on the capital and won ratification of land claims and limits on oil exploration without their consent. The Eastern Cree have frustrated the intent of Canada's largest power company to complete a massive hydroelectric project at James Bay, Quebec. Canadian Inuit will soon control Nunavut, a new political unit comprising one fifth of Canada's land surface. Native Americans in the United States are finally gaining a meaningful level of political sovereignty within their reservations, are now able to reclaim skeletal material and funerary objects from the archeological collections of museums and universities, and have opened more than one hundred casinos, many of them extremely profitable. It is tempting to conclude that in the Western hemisphere indigenous peoples have begun to reverse a pattern of defeat, subordination, and deprivation that has lasted five centuries.

Setbacks are inevitable. The Guatemalan Maya suffered at least one hundred thousand deaths since 1980 in a war of extermination conducted largely by Guatemala's government and military leaders. In much of the Amazon basin, peoples are still killed for their land. African indigenous societies are caught up in ghastly civil conflicts that threaten their very existence. These disasters will continue to occur, perhaps even intensify, as the underdeveloped world explodes over its deepening poverty, as the elites and the common people of dominant societies see an erosion of their power over an indigenous underclass, and as indigenous societies claim long-neglected rights.

Despite the battles and defeats that lie ahead, indigenous societies have a future. They will be political and social groups of significance within the nation-states in which they are found. Sovereignty will be broadened. International and intercontinental alliances between indigenous groups will expand. There will be a widening recognition of indigenous peoples at the United Nations, among its agencies, and in other international bodies. And as all this moves ahead, indigenous cultures will become stronger, more visible, and more prideful.

In 1971, a "stone age" society, the Tasaday, was reported in the remote mountains of the Philippines. Banner headlines trumpeted the discovery, news helicopters descended, and photos of people who reportedly had never been contacted by the outside world appeared in Sunday supplements. Since then many have concluded that the Tasaday were a hoax, but the high level of interest is significant and the episode raises an important question: why the all-out pursuit of a last-remaining stone age society?

Westerners strongly desire the opportunity to know and learn from societies with truly different life ways and world views. Given the ongoing resurgence of our indigenous contemporaries, we will have ample opportunity to fulfill that interest. At the same time, we will have to accustom ourselves to a new reality. Indigenous peoples are not oddities from the past, marginal to the present. Rather they are increasingly masters of their own destinies and full partners with the rest of us.

THOMAS C. GREAVES

SEE ALSO: Indigenous Rights

BODLEY, JOHN H. *Tribal Peoples and Development Issues: A Global Overview.* Mountain View, Calif.: Mayfield, 1988.

BURGER, JULIAN. *The Gaia Atlas of First Peoples: A Future for the Indigenous World.* New York: Anchor, 1990.

CRAWFORD, JAMES, ed. *The Rights of Peoples.* New York: Oxford University Press, 1988.

CULTURAL SURVIVAL. *State of the Peoples: A Global Human Rights Report on Societies in Danger.* Boston: Beacon Press, 1993.

ECHO-HAWK, WALTER R., and ROGER C. ECHO-HAWK. "Repatriation, Reburial, and Religious Rights." *Handbook of American Indian Religious Freedom,* edited by Christopher Vecsey. New York: Crossroad Publishing, 1991.

Indian Country Today (Newspaper). Rapid City, S.D.: Native American Publishing, Inc. [published since 1981].

SUAGEE, DEAN B. "Human Rights and Cultural Heritage, Developments in the United Nations Working Group on Indigenous Peoples." In *Intellectual Property Rights for Indigenous Peoples, A Sourcebook,* edited by Tom Greaves. Oklahoma City: Society for Applied Anthropology, 1994.

TAYLOR, WILLIAM B. and FRANKLIN PEASE, eds. *Violence, Resistance, and Survival in the Americas.* Washington: Smithsonian Institution Press, 1994.

WILMSEN, EDWIN N., ed. *We Are Here: Politics of Aboriginal Land Tenure.* Berkeley: University of California Press, 1989.

INDIGENOUS RIGHTS

Indigenous rights have long been an area of dispute, since it is not easy to define exactly who indigenous people are, what rights they have, and how these rights should be protected. In the Americas, Australia, the Philippines, and other regions where invaders arrived from elsewhere, subjugated the natives, and settled in the new territories, it is relatively easy to distinguish between indigenous peoples and their conquerors. In other parts of the world, such as the mainland of Asia, population migrations and patterns of land use dating back thousands of years make it hard to distinguish between indigenous peoples and the rest. The government of India, for example, insists that it is meaningless to speak of the rights of its indigenous peoples, since it considers all the people of India to be indigenous. It does however recognize the existence of what it terms "scheduled tribes," of peoples who are sometimes referred to as "tribal." Such peoples have normally been remote from the mainstream, having their own separate languages and cultures. They claim their lands by virtue of lengthy occupancy. Characteristically, indigenous or tribal peoples have been subjugated by alien states, whose inhabitants regard them as inferiors and outsiders. Historically, therefore, their rights have neither been much considered nor respected.

In 1550–1551 King Charles V of Spain sponsored a famous debate on the proper treatment of indigenous peoples. He summoned a council of fourteen learned men to Valladolid to hear bishop Las Casas, recently returned from America, and Juan Ginés de Sepúlveda discuss whether it was lawful to wage war on the indigenous peoples of the Americas as a means of converting them to the Catholic faith. They also discussed whether it was lawful for Spaniards to hold indigenous people in slavery. Sepúlveda used Aristotle's doctrine of "natural slavery," according to which some people were destined to be slaves, to justify enslaving the Indians. He believed that the Indians were savages who needed to be civilized, forcibly if necessary, by incorporation into the Catholic faith and the Spanish empire. Las Casas argued that the Indians were rational beings who were capable of living in civilization and should neither be enslaved nor forcibly converted. Above all, he insisted that they should not receive the inhuman treatment that the earliest conquistadors meted out to them. The debate was inconclusive and the Spanish colonialists continued to treat the Indians much as before. When enlightened opinion gained the upper hand at court and the Crown issued edicts to protect the Indians or abolish indigenous slavery, the colonists ignored the laws or threatened rebellion. When conservatives were more influential at court, the colonists continued to exploit the Indians, secure in the knowledge that learned opinion was on their side.

This process was not peculiar to the Americas. In the heyday of western imperialism, indigenous peoples were conquered and dispossessed all over the world and always in the name of civilization. In the nineteenth century their imperial masters adopted evolutionary justifications for their rule, claiming that it was both inevitable and justifiable for more advanced nations to rule over other peoples and to introduce them to civilization. These imperialist justifications are no longer taken seriously, but many of the old arguments still persist. Since indigenous peoples are always subordinate to alien states, their rights are defined by those states. States have been reluctant to recognize the rights of indigenous peoples for a number of reasons.

Firstly, indigenous societies, which are often considered "tribal" or "traditional," are thought to be obsolescent. It is supposed that they cannot adjust to the modern world and should therefore be helped to disappear, so that their members can individually pass into the modern mainstream. Secondly, indigenous societies are thought to stand in the way of economic development. States are therefore reluctant to recognize their rights to land or resources, arguing that this will hamper economic progress nationally.

Self-determination for indigenous peoples is likewise routinely opposed by states, on the grounds that this would undermine the state itself. Self-determination is thought to lead to separatism, with the danger that parts of the state will break off or that the state itself may break up. Alternatively, self-determination is thought to undermine the state by isolating ethnic groups within it.

All of these arguments are seriously flawed. Indigenous peoples have shown remarkable resilience and ingenuity in adapting to modernization while maintaining their own cultures and traditions. In the Americas, the region of the oldest European colonialism, a five-hundred-year assault on indigenous cultures has not succeeded in eradicating them. Indigenous societies have shown an extraordinary capacity to adapt. In fact the indigenous peoples of the Americas are very active in the worldwide movement for indigenous rights. Such societies are not doomed, as is often claimed, by the march of progress. When indigenous societies disappear, they have not fallen victim to abstract laws of history or nature, but they have been destroyed by the political choices of the powerful.

The contention that indigenous peoples stand in the way of development implies that development can only proceed in a certain way, which entails depriving indigenous peoples of their resources. In fact, there are many different ways of pursuing economic development and the only defensible ones are those that take into account the interests of all people, indigenous or other, who live in the area to be developed. Since indigenous peoples are by definition different from those who control the states in which they live,

their interests are normally ignored when development is planned in their areas. This is not a necessity of development. It is power politics.

Meanwhile the demand of indigenous peoples for self-determination does not necessarily mean that they wish to secede from the states in which they reside. The majority of indigenous societies making this demand are asking for local autonomy, not a separate state. It does imply that states should be willing to tolerate the presence of indigenous populations who have no intention of blending into the mainstream, but demand the right to maintain their own languages and cultures, without therefore being treated as second-class citizens.

Now that ethnic conflict has broken out in so many parts of the world, states are more reluctant to grant even limited autonomy to ethnic groups that reside within their borders and this reluctance extends to indigenous peoples, who are considered to be a special kind of ethnic minority. Traditionally, authoritarian states have tried to suppress the expression of ethnicity, as for example in Spain under Franco and in the former Yugoslavia under Tito. Meanwhile liberal democracies, such as in western Europe and the United States, have striven to discourage ethnicity, in the hope that it would become irrelevant and evaporate in the course of modernization. The former Soviet Union was an anomaly. Its several republics were ethnically defined, but in fact were all controlled by Moscow in an authoritarian and multiethnic empire. When that empire broke up, the newly independent republics were left to their own power struggles, and to face the consequences of being defined as ethnic states.

In fact, ethnic differences within a state do not invariably lead to conflict. There have been long periods of history where ethnic groups have lived peaceably side by side—in Central Asia, India, and even in the Balkans. Ethnic conflicts have erupted where ethnicity was suppressed, where some ethnic groups felt oppressed by others, or where unscrupulous leaders incited them in order to enhance their own power. Meanwhile the traditional antidotes have not worked very well. Authoritarian states that tried to stifle ethnicity and liberal democracies that tried to dissipate ethnicity by encouraging their citizens to identify only with the state have been equally unsuccessful. Both of these solutions depended on the denial of ethnicity. A third possibility, which depends on the acceptance of ethnicity in a form that does not undermine the state, is the plural solution sought by a few avowedly multiethnic states, such as Indonesia or modern Spain.

Although acceptance of multiethnic solutions is a necessary condition for the recognition of indigenous rights it is not a sufficient one. Indigenous peoples insist that they are different from other ethnic minorities and that they therefore deserve different consideration. First, indigenous people claim rights of priority, which are reflected in their names. Those in the United States call themselves "Native Americans," as distinct from all other Americans whose ancestors came from overseas; those in Canada refer to themselves as the "First Nations," and so on. Second, indigenous peoples claim rights to land because of their prior occupancy of it. Third, indigenous groups claim that they were once sovereign peoples, whose sovereignty was extinguished by force of conquest. In fact some Native American spokespeople take the position that the sovereignty of their groups has been suppressed but never extinguished. Fourth, in line with the theme of involuntary subjection to alien rule, indigenous peoples now demand that the wrongs done to them be taken into consideration as their rights are recognized and protected.

It is not easy, either theoretically or practically, to determine what indigenous rights are, or should be, and how they ought to be protected. When the United Nations promulgated the Universal Declaration of Human Rights, this charter was intended to protect the rights of individuals. Meanwhile the United Nations, which is an organization of member states, has had to be solicitous of the rights of states. It has been notoriously reluctant to protect the rights of groups that do not control states. This was assumed to be an internal matter for the states themselves to resolve.

This left indigenous peoples totally without recourse, since their rights were normally not recognized by the states which had subjugated them and the injustices they suffered were also inflicted or permitted by those states. In the past twenty years, a movement has been gathering momentum worldwide to have indigenous rights recognized and protected. Indigenous and pro-indigenous organizations forced the issue onto the agenda of the United Nations, which declared 1993 to be the "Year of Indigenous People." This was done to counterbalance the recognition by the United Nations of Christopher Columbus in 1992,

the quincentenary of his first voyage to the Americas. Many member states, who did not wish to extend any international recognition to groups within their states, strongly opposed this special year. These member states succeeded in eliminating the final *s* in People(s), so that the formal title of the year referred to People—individuals rather than to groups. More important was the creation of a Working Group on Indigenous Populations within the U.N. Commission on Human Rights, which has been charged with defining the nature of indigenous rights and persuading the international community to recognize and protect them.

DECLARATION ON INDIGENOUS RIGHTS

This declaration, drafted by the U.N. Working Group on Indigenous Populations, stresses that indigenous peoples have the right of self-determination. This clearly refers to autonomy *within* states rather than separation *from* them. The draft goes on to specify the rights of indigenous peoples within the state and the duties of the state toward indigenous peoples. The remainder of the declaration deals with various classes of rights and protections, as follows:

1. Indigenous peoples should be free from genocide (physical annihilation) and ethnocide (cultural extinction). They should also be freed from dispossession, discrimination, and hostile propaganda.

2. An indigenous people should have the right to maintain its own culture, including its own language, religion, and customs. It should control the education of its children, and should have programs in its own language available through the media.

3. An indigenous people should have the right to maintain its own social institutions and form of governance. It should also have the right to decide on membership within the group and on the responsibilities of individuals in its own communities.

4. An indigenous people should have the right to maintain its traditional economic activities and land use patterns. In this connection its rights to its own land and resources should be recognized and protected. There should be just compensation for resources taken away by force in the past.

5. The special relationship of indigenous peoples to their land should be recognized. Their environments should therefore be protected or rehabilitated, if necessary.

6. Indigenous peoples should be represented in all government bodies that make decisions concerning them. They should also be consulted about development projects planned in their areas, to ensure that the indigenous groups concerned also benefit from such projects.

This declaration presents a number of theoretical problems. What happens if the traditions and customs of an indigenous people include activities that are repugnant to or illegal in the rest of the state? What happens if the state insists on institutions and practices that are repugnant to an indigenous people? The difficulties are symmetrical in theory but not in practice, for it is normally only the state that can veto indigenous customs, not the other way round. There may be a hierarchy of differences, some of which the state will tolerate and others which it will not. The state may or may not feel compelled to intervene if it considers that indigenous procedures do not guarantee fair trials or fair elections. It is more likely to insist that indigenous custom not be permitted to infringe on the human rights of individuals, for example, by discriminating against certain classes of people or by mutilating women, as among those peoples of Africa who practice female circumcision. The most difficulty is likely to be caused by customary activities that are held to infringe the rights of individuals, which are protected by the state. Here the collectivist traditions of many indigenous peoples may clash with the individualist focus of much thinking and legislation concerning human rights.

These theoretical difficulties are not however the major obstacles to the implementation of the Declaration on Indigenous Rights. The obstacles are political. In all states there are powerful interests that profit economically and politically from the denial of indigenous rights. Their representatives will continue to argue that the recognition of indigenous rights would hamper economic development and undermine the state. They will continue to insist that it is absurd to try and guarantee the rights of inferior outsiders at the expense of the majority of the population. Their arguments are known to be false, but their political influence will only be diminished, and indigenous rights adequately protected, when world opinion decides that infringing the human rights of minorities is as unacceptable as enslaving individuals.

DAVID MAYBURY-LEWIS

SEE ALSO: *Cultural Survival Inc.; Indigenous Peoples*

BODLEY, JOHN. *Tribal Peoples and Development Issues: A Global Overview.* Mountain View, CA: Mayfield Publishing Company, 1988.

BURGER, JULIAN. *Report from the Frontier: The State of the World's Indigenous Peoples.* London, Atlantic Highlands, N.J.: Zed Books and Cambridge MA; Cultural Survival, 1987.

———. *The Gaia Atlas of First Peoples: A Future for the Indigenous World.* New York: Doubleday Anchor, 1990.

MAYBURY-LEWIS, DAVID. *Millennium: Tribal Wisdom and the Modern World.* New York: Viking Penguin, 1992.

INDUSTRIAL AGRICULTURE

Industrial agriculture is a method of food production characterized by high investments of capital in machinery and inputs, less use of labor than in other agricultural systems, and a reliance on the products of industry for part of the production process. Characteristic of industrial societies in many parts of the world, industrial agriculture is increasingly studied by anthropologists because of the growing trend toward research in industrial societies and because the methods of this food system are often held as a goal for developing countries by ministries of agriculture and international development agencies.

Industrial agriculture represents a deviation from the trend in agricultural evolution through most of human history, in which shifting cultivation is made permanent and yields increased per land unit by the addition of labor, both animal and human (Netting 1977). Industrial agriculture usually involves the heavy use of irrigation systems, harvesters, and other machinery. On-farm tasks, such as manuring and crop storage, are replaced by industrial products and services, such as petroleum-based fertilizers and storage in grain elevators. Farmers rely on industries that manufacture tires, make airplanes for aerial spraying, develop new herbicides, and provide such services as insurance and tax accounting. These industries all extract a profit in provisioning farmers and often are internationally based, making an industrially based food system very complex and interdependent.

Industrial agriculture is also ecologically volatile (Barlett 1987). The use of large equipment has increased soil compaction and erosion, while monocropping and chemical use have dramatically altered soil structure and ecosystems in many regions. Some experts argue that industrial agriculture is not sustainable, although increasing international concern has led to a range of new techniques designed to ameliorate ecological damage (Chibnik 1987). Industrial agriculture depends heavily on the use of fossil fuels to run machinery and to fertilize the soil, and ecological study often emphasizes that the high yields of modern agriculture are due in part to the energy subsidy of petroleum. For some crops industrial agriculture permits massive breakthroughs in yields and improvements in animal husbandry, although some of this increase is due simply to heavier fertilizer use and abandonment of poorer lands. Industrial agriculture is characterized by a growth ethic and rapid technological change, both of which present challenges to farm management.

The contrast between a more labor-intensive and a more capital-intensive system in the production of the same crop can be seen in the contrast of rice production in the state of Arkansas and in Japan in the 1950s. Both systems produced about fifty bushels per acre, but the Japanese invested ninety human-days of work, compared with fourteen in Arkansas. In contrast, the Japanese used only ninety horsepower-hours of energy in the year's production, while the U.S. farmers used 805 (Hardesty 1977).

The role of the state in industrial agriculture is complex and central. Crops, credit, and markets are regulated, as are production methods, chemical use, and worker safety. State intervention can shift the entire use of land in certain areas by subsidizing or prohibiting land uses. During the 1980s in Nebraska, tax laws encouraged nonfarm investors to finance irrigation systems for semiarid lands, which in turn led to a shift in land use from pasture to corn. The increased grain production contributed to a national glut and low prices, while medium-scale farmers were disadvantaged in competition with large irrigated farms.

Industrial agriculture in the United States evolved in a unique historical combination of plentiful fertile land, cheap energy, abundant capital, competition with industry for available labor, and an economy that encouraged technological development. Most anthropological research has concentrated on two variants of farm organization in U.S. agriculture: family farms and corporate farms. Although these terms can have diverse meanings, family farms are generally understood to be owner-operated agricultural units, in which management is combined with family labor on the farm (Barlett 1989). Most family farmers own some of the land they work, and some may hire labor on a part-time or full-time basis. Family farms are the most widespread organization of production in the United States, both in numbers and geographical extent.

Corporate farms, also known as industrial-type farms or the factory-in-the-field, are large-scale enterprises, in which management is separated from ownership and labor, generally represented by three different groups of people (and sometimes by different ethnic groups, as well). Owners may be families or corporations, but they usually delegate production decisions to a management specialist or company. Laborers on corporate farms are wage workers, sometimes temporary, sometimes part-time. In one Arizona study of lettuce, cotton, and citrus production, researchers found six ranks of farm workers, from the technological elite to transient day laborers (Padfield and Martin 1965). The industrial-type variant thus is more bureaucratic and hierarchical in the daily rhythms of the labor process.

Reliable, skilled labor, at a price that does not threaten profits, is the basis on which corporate farming in the United States has been built, and during the twentieth century the government has cooperated with landowners, particularly in the Southwest, to provide a flow of immigrants and temporary workers from China, the Philippines, Mexico, Japan, and Caribbean nations (Padfield and Martin 1965). The organization of labor on corporate farms is affected by the state and by the characteristics of each crop produced. Miriam J. Wells (1984) explored the strawberry industry in California, where the delicate nature of the plants and the constant care needed puts special requirements on labor and prevents full mechanization. When faced in the 1970s with pressures from the United Farm Workers Union and with increased labor protection legislation, large-scale strawberry growers introduced a modern form of sharecropping to solve their labor problems. As independent contractors, workers lost certain legal protections, including union rights, unemployment insurance, and minimum wages. Independent contractors were usually legal Mexican immigrants who controlled small sections of a larger farm. When extra labor was needed, it was their responsibility to recruit workers from among kin and friends and to pay them from their profits. This system generated a cheap, high-quality labor force and protected the landowners, for a time at least, from union pressure.

Social science theorists have been predicting for more than a century that corporate farms will outcompete family farms and that family farms ultimately will not survive in an industrial context. Although it is true that the numbers of owner-operated units have greatly declined because of mechanization and increasing farm size, the continued prominence of family farms in both the United States and Europe seems to show a stable accommodation with industrial society. The expectation of full differentiation of family farms into farm workers and large corporate owners has taken insufficient account of the diseconomies of scale of agriculture and the difficulties of farm management under normal growing conditions (Reinhardt and Barlett 1989). Farming is a high-risk business, in which the payoffs are in part nonpecuniary, but the persistence and efficiency of family units—and the passion with which young people wish to continue them—bodes well for the future survival of a diverse structure of production within industrial agriculture. On the other hand, corporate farms have spread rapidly into developing countries, as the production of luxury fruit and vegetable crops has expanded in Africa, Asia, and Latin America. Many of these new crops are grown under contract or on plantations owned outright by foreign corporations, often with agronomic techniques and patterns of social organization imported from industrial countries.

Family farms are distinctive in the way they combine the goals of two units, the farm and the family, each with its own life cycle (Bennett 1982). Each unit has its process of formation, development, and decline, and many of the management challenges for family farms come from the discordant pace of change in the two units. In Dodge County, Georgia, these conflicting demands caused painful dilemmas for parents during the recession and the farm crisis of the 1980s (Barlett 1993). Parents wanted to treat all their children alike in the matters of college opportunities or the gift of a vehicle, but the sudden decline in farm incomes made inequities necessary. Some parents agonized about getting out of farming altogether, if the standard of living during that decade was too low to conform to life-style expectations. Men and women, often with different personal goals and definitions of a successful life, weighed their financial well-being in the long and short run, the quality of their daily work life, the risks of farming, their enjoyment of the autonomy of self-employment, their status as property owners, and the satisfactions of an agrarian life. Farming is seen as meaningful work with important spiritual dimensions, providing a good environment for children, but if consumption standards fall too low, families are torn between agrarian and industrial definitions of success.

Sonya Salamon's (1992) research on seven communities of Illinois farmers illuminates the role of ethnic origins in different family goals and farm management styles. Although "the farmer" is often seen as a solitary male decision-maker, her research and that of numerous others incorporates a focus on women and the importance of complex family ties, within the household and across generations. Salamon distinguishes two ethnic traditions that persist in Illinois agriculture: Germans and Yankees (of Protestant British Isles origins and by way of the Northeast U.S.). Although industrial agriculture's rapid change since World War II has left corn fields, barns, and equipment looking identical from the windshield of a passing car, distinct family practices and values prevail. For the German families, land is a sacred trust, which allows continuity of farm ownership and an agrarian way of life. For Yankees, land is a commodity and farming is a business that allows a family to increase its wealth and power. The implication of these divergent values is that a Yankee farmer may be willing to sell the farm and move to a larger location if an opportunity arises. Yankee children are schooled in independence and are encouraged to seek off-farm careers. A Yankee farm son may emphasize that it is the challenge of farming that draws him to the career, while the German son may emphasize the continuity of family ties to a particular plot of land. Yankee communities are more stratified and less socially cohesive.

Yankee families are more likely to exhibit an entrepreneurial, ambitious management style, with a willingness to take risks through expansion and debt. The average farm size of the group is larger, and the risks of farm loss are greater. The German farmers follow a more cautious management style, preferring to own all the land they cultivate, expand the farm slowly, and minimize debt. German communities are close-knit, revolving around the social and religious activities of the church. In both ethnic traditions, males as landholders and primary decision- makers exert some dominance over women and children, but the family hierarchy is stronger and more developed in the German family.

The survival of family farms and a continuation of a diverse structure of industrial agriculture has been shown to be connected to the overall community welfare of rural regions (Goldschmidt 1978; Lobao 1990). When many farms are reduced to a small number of large farms relying on poorly paid hired labor, rural communities are more likely to suffer declining business districts, weakened schools and hospitals, and fewer churches and civic organizations. Counties with these conditions show higher levels of rural poverty, less democratic political participation, and greater unemployment. In these ways, the organization of industrial agriculture has social, economic, political, and ecological consequences and plays a growing role in rural development around the globe.

PEGGY F. BARLETT

SEE ALSO: Agriculture and Farming Systems; Irrigation Systems

BARLETT, PEGGY F. "Industrial Agriculture in Evolutionary Perspective." *Cultural Anthropology* 2 (1987): 137–154.

——— . "Industrial Agriculture." In *Economic Anthropology*, edited by Stuart Plattner. Stanford, Calif.: Stanford University Press, 1989.

——— . *American Dreams, Rural Realities: Family Farms in Crisis.* Chapel Hill, N.C.: University of North Carolina Press, 1993.

BENNETT, JOHN W. *Of Time and the Enterprise.* Minneapolis: University of Minnesota Press, 1982.

CHIBNIK, MICHAEL, ed. *Farm Work and Fieldwork: American Agriculture in Anthropological Perspective.* Ithaca, N.Y.: Cornell University Press, 1987.

GOLDSCHMIDT, WALTER. *As You Sow: Three Studies in the Social Consequences of Agribusiness.* Montclair,

N.J.: Allanheld, Osmun,1978.

HARDESTY, DONALD L. *Ecological Anthropology.* New York: John Wiley and Sons, 1977.

LOBAO, LINDA M. *Locality and Inequality: Farm and Industry Structure and Socioeconomic Conditions.* Albany: State University of New York Press, 1990.

NETTING, ROBERT MCC. *Cultural Ecology.* Menlo Park, Calif.: Cummings, 1977.

PADFIELD, HARLAND, and WILLIAM E. MARTIN. *Farmers, Workers, and Machines: Technological Social Change in Farm Industries of Arizona.* Tucson: University of Arizona Press, 1965.

REINHARDT, NOLA, and PEGGY BARLETT. "The Persistence of Family Farms in United States Agriculture." *Sociologia Ruralis* 29 (1989): 203–225.

SALAMON, SONYA *Prairie Patrimony: Family, Farming and Community in the Midwest.* Chapel Hill: University of North Carolina Press, 1992.

WELLS, MIRIAM J. "What Is a Worker? The Role of Sharecroppers in Contemporary Class Structure." *Politics and Society* 13 (1984): 295–320.

INFANTICIDE

Infanticide refers to the killing of an infant or young child, technically "pedicide," by a conspecific. Across human societies, infanticide tends to be an uncommon event, regarded with discomfort and grief by the parents, even if they are the perpetrators. People are often reluctant to discuss infanticide—except to attribute it to their enemies or supposed moral inferiors. Indeed, the majority of reports involve rumors of genocide accompanying political oppression and war, circumstances which render it difficult to obtain precise information. For example, in Exodus 1:16, King Herod orders the midwives to kill all sons born to Hebrews.

Except in the case of literate bureaucracies that outlaw infanticide, documentation is usually poor. Furthermore, some anthropologists are reluctant to report infanticide for fear of stigmatizing their study populations or subjecting them to sanctions. With few reliable, quantitative reports, infanticide has proved difficult to study in a scientific manner.

Moral issues raised by infanticide are complicated by ethnocentric values. For example, in many parts of the modern world, an impoverished mother faced with rearing a child she is unable to support would be punished for smothering her infant at birth—"direct infanticide," while infant handling practices that lead to death through starvation or "natural" causes are tolerated—"indirect infanticide." Populations of European descent who condemn the "savage" practice of eliminating an ill-timed infant at birth, often ignore their own recent histories of child abandonment. Throughout the seventeenth and eighteenth centuries, infant mortality rates rose as a result of the common European practice of sending infants away to distant wet nurses, or depositing them in foundling homes (Hrdy 1992).

INFANTICIDE ACROSS CULTURES

In the absence of other means of birth control, infanticide may be used to space births to ensure maternal survival and the needs of existing offspring, as well as to eliminate defective or unviable offspring. These practical functions are summed up by the Japanese peasant's term for infanticide, "mabiki," or "thinning out." One percent of live births are terminated by the mother for such practical reasons by the !Kung San people of Southern Africa (Howell 1979). High rates of infanticide were probably common among our Pleistocene hunting and gathering ancestors where women's productive labor would constrain the number of children they could simultaneously care for should offspring be born too close together.

Across cultures, higher rates of child abandonment and infanticide are found where the mother lacks alternative means for alleviating the costs of child rearing (Hrdy 1992). As in all mammals, until the invention of baby bottles, survival of an infant required suckling by either the mother or another lactating female, to nurse the baby. In many environments, a mother must rely on support from her mate, kin, or other surrogate caretakers. Among Ache foragers in Paraguay, Hill and Hurtado (1996) report that nine percent of boys and sixteen percent of girls are killed by conspecific adults before they reach the age of five years. Since male hunters are critical for providing food among the Ache, children whose fathers leave or die are most at risk. Fatherless infants may be killed by other group members or by the mother herself, since unprotected children are very vulnerable. In groups such as the Ayoreo of Bolivia, where women become pregnant before establishing stable relationships, young mothers have been reported to kill as many as six offspring before settling into a relationship and

successfully rearing children who are then much loved (Bugos and McCarthy 1984).

Protection and provisioning of human infants, in contrast to most other mammals, continues long past weaning, sometimes into adulthood where offspring depend on parentally provided resources to marry. Even when intact families have the resources available to rear offspring, such prolonged and sometimes costly dependence can prejudice parents against diverting resources to children considered unlikely to contribute in terms of either production or reproduction to the prosperity and continued survival of the lineage or socially defined "house." Particularly in highly stratified societies, maintenance of social rank may require limiting the number of heirs. In one of the most extreme such cases, among various elite Rajput clans, such as the Jharejas in precolonial Northern India, almost all daughters born to the highest-ranking families were killed to avoid diverting family resources to provide for their dowries. A dearth of daughters at the top meant that wives had to be obtained from lower-status families, who competed among themselves to accumulate large dowries, or more nearly "groom prices," to marry their daughters into these elite "daughter-slaying" families. Although they could expect no granddaughters, grandsons of hypergamously married daughters would be advantaged. Dickemann (1979) has argued that where high rank permits male polygyny (either multiple wives or concubines), it would be adaptive for those families who could do so to make high rank and its attendant advantages available to sons. By contrast, low-ranking families, whose sons would be unlikely to obtain consorts, should rear daughters who would be more valuable to them both reproductively and materially since at the lowest ranks no dowry was required. Among the poorest, the parents might receive some payment for their daughter.

Even in less stratified societies, traditions of warfare and raiding for women may make sons critical for protection and hence explain preferential female infanticide in groups where daughters would be vulnerable to abduction by other clans if there were no sons to protect them. As pointed out by Divale and Harris (1976), there is an association between warfare and the practice of female infanticide. Their initial explanation for discrimination against daughters in a "male supremacist complex"—that parents eliminated future mothers in order to reduce population growth and resulting pressure on resources in the local environment—relies on the assumption that infanticidal parents sacrifice their own interests to benefit the group or population as a whole. More probably, such parents were eliminating daughters in the hopes of conceiving a son sooner. Whatever their motivation, the highest reported rates of direct infanticide derive from those groups where powerful preferences for sons exist. Among the horticultural Eipo people of highland central New Guinea, forty percent or more of live births ended in infanticide, due primarily to the elimination of daughters (Schiefenhövel 1989).

Due to the traditional Asian preference for sons, combined with state-imposed limitations on family size, high rates of female infanticide persist in parts of rural China. In India, female infanticide has been outlawed for over a century, but amniocentesis followed by selective abortion has created new opportunities to bias investment toward sons. Unwanted daughters who survive may suffer severe neglect.

THE PARADOX OF INFANTICIDE: GROUP VS. INDIVIDUAL SELECTION

Since offspring are vital to the continued survival of any species, it seems odd from an evolutionary perspective to find behaviors that so markedly decrease infant survival. Partly for this reason, anthropologists tended to dismiss early reports of infanticide, especially among animals, as accidents or unnatural "pathological" behaviors brought about through crowding or human disturbance, or else attributed infanticide to some group benefit such as population control. Anthropologists from the Radcliffe-Brownian school were convinced that individuals behave as they do so as to preserve, not disrupt, a fundamentally integrated social structure.

While those influenced by Radcliffe-Brown focused on the role played by each individual in the survival of the group, anthropologists influenced by new trends in evolutionary biology focused on selection for traits that enhance the reproductive success of individual lineages—even at the expense of weaker individuals, groups, or even species. By the 1980s, most field biologists, but not all anthropologists (Bartlett et al. 1994) were convinced that infanticide in animals, even when it led to high rates of infant mortality, was not an aberration and was, in fact on average, adaptive for perpetrators, increasing their own relative reproductive success (Hausfater and Hrdy

1984). Infanticide is a widespread and protean phenomenon among fish, insects, birds, and mammals. It has been reported as a reproductive strategy for all the major primate groups, including prosimians, new-world monkeys, old-world monkeys, and apes, as well as humans.

FUNCTIONAL CLASSES OF INFANTICIDE

Infanticide is not a unitary phenomenon, the only constant being the vulnerability of the victim. Nevertheless both in animals, where infanticide is an evolved adaptation, and in humans, where it results from some combination of evolved predispositions and conscious, culturally mediated decisions, infanticide tends to fall into five categories. Four of the five are functional solutions to problems routinely confronted by organisms in environments where resources are finite (Hausfater and Hrdy 1984).

Exploitation of the Infant as a Resource

The infant itself becomes a resource when individuals responsible for an infant's death directly benefit from use or even consumption of the infant through cannibalism. Not surprisingly, consumption of the infant as a food resource turns out to be most common among carnivorous predators and is reported for humans under only the most dire circumstances.

Resource Competition

The death of the infant increases access to resources by the killer or his or her lineage. Infanticide by human stepparents would fall into this category. In particular, children whose mothers live with a man unrelated to them are at much higher risk of being abused or killed than children in the population at large. Even though it is virtually never advantageous for stepparents to kill infants in post-industrial societies, and child homicide in the United States is rare, an American child living in a home with one or more substitute parents is statistically one hundred times more likely to be fatally abused than a child living with natural parents only (Daly and Wilson 1988). Substitute parents, especially those who did not deliberately choose to adopt a child, are less likely than natural parents to experience emotional rewards in exchange for the tremendous demands on time, energy, and resources that children make. As in the classic European folk stereotypes about wicked stepparents, lethal tension may arise over diversion of resources to unrelated children that might otherwise benefit the stepparent's own current or future children.

Sexually Selected Infanticide

Individuals improve their own opportunities to mate by eliminating dependent offspring of a rival. Typically, a male entering the breeding system from outside it eliminates an unweaned infant, thereby circumventing continued suppression of ovulation through lactation by the mother. The mother therefore becomes reproductively available to the incoming male sooner, compressing her reproductive career into the brief window of opportunity during which that male controls access to her before he himself is usurped by another male. The complex genetic, endocrinological, and developmental basis for sexually selected infanticide, as well as specialized mechanisms by which males avoid killing their own offspring have only been well studied among laboratory rodents (Parmigiano and vom Saal 1994). In this "sexually selected" form of infanticide, competition between males leads not to death of the defeated rival, but—as Charles Darwin noted in 1871—to few or no offspring.

Although a rare event, difficult to observe, and still regarded as controversial among some anthropologists (Bartlett et al. 1994), sexually selected infanticide has been reported for over a dozen primate genera (Hausfater and Hrdy 1984). In species characterized by male takeovers, the longer the study, the more cases of infanticide are reported (Sommer 1994). Long-term studies for wild mountain gorillas in Rwanda indicate that around 14 percent of infants born are likely to be killed by an unrelated adult male during their first three years of life (Watts 1989). Based on a twenty-five year study of langur monkeys around Jodhpur, in Rajasthan, North India, one-third of all infants are killed by males invading the breeding unit from outside it (Sommer 1994).

For many primate populations, the threat of infanticide by unrelated males must have been a major selective pressure on mothers. The threat of infanticide is critical for understanding gorilla and common chimpanzee breeding systems: mothers need males to protect their offspring from other males. Some primatologists are therefore beginning to wonder if protection of infants from conspecifics may also have been an important function of early hominid families.

Parental Manipulation of Progeny

Parents on average increase their own lifetime reproductive success by eliminating particular offspring. The most usual circumstance is that of a mother terminating investment in an infant with poor prospects of survival and reproduction. An infant may also be terminated if its birth jeopardizes the mother's own survival or future reproductive options, or jeopardizes the survival of other current or future offspring, who due to age, sex, ecological conditions, or likelihood of paternal investment, are more likely to survive and reproduce. Infanticide to cull litters is well documented for rodents, and other mammals, but nowhere is this strategy for family planning more varied or elaborate than among humans who consciously calculate probable outcomes, and base decisions on past histories known to them. Whether or not reduced maternal motivation to invest in infants leads to infanticide or merely causes a mother to deny caregiving in other ways, depends on ecological, social, and cultural variables, as well as life-historical attributes of the mother. For example, young mothers near the peak of their reproductive potential are more likely than older ones to commit infanticide (Daly and Wilson 1988; Bugos and McCarthy 1984).

Daly and Wilson (1984) reviewed a representative sample of sixty cultures from the Human Relations Area Files. Infanticide was reported in thirty-nine of these cultures, and in thirty-five the circumstances were known. By and large, the infant tended to be one of a pair of twins, defective in some way, or otherwise considered to be of poor quality; there was often a problem with timing such that the birth interval was too short, or else inadequate parental resources for rearing the child were anticipated. In some cases, the infant was sired by a man other than the woman's current mate.

"Pathological" Infanticide

Pathological infanticidal behavior is not advantageous to the perpetrator. Most contemporary Western cases of lethal child abuse by parents or stepparents are obviously nonadaptive. Other options, such as foster homes, are available and, if detected, perpetrators are punished. However, some "Darwinian psychologists" argue that the disinterest in nurturing that characterizes abusive parents would in fact have been adaptive in an "environment of evolutionary adaptedness" where parents terminated investment in infants under adverse circumstances.

SUMMARY

Infanticide predates the origin of *Homo sapiens*. Sexually selected infanticide is widespread among other primates, and it has been suggested that protection of infants from conspecifics may have been integral to the evolution of the human family. Among modern humans, however, infanticide by parents is far more commonly documented than is infanticide by invading males. Elimination of infants is most often practiced where alternative means for mitigating the enormous investment needed to rear each human infant are unavailable. In the absence of birth control, infanticide has traditionally been a widely used tool for family planning.

SARAH BLAFFER HRDY

BARTLETT, THAD Q., ROBERT W. SUSSMAN, and JAMES M. CHEVERUD. "Infant Killing in Primates: A Review of Observed Cases with Specific Reference to the Sexual Selection Hypothesis." *American Anthropologist* 95(4) (1994): 958-990.

BUGOS, PAUL and LORRAINE MCCARTHY. "Ayoreo Infanticide: A Case Study." In *Infanticide: Comparative and Evolutionary Perspectives*, edited by Glenn Hausfater and Sarah Blaffer Hrdy. New York: Aldine/de Gruyter, 1984.

DALY, MARTIN and MARGO WILSON. "A Sociobiological Analysis of Human Infanticide." In *Infanticide: Comparative and Evolutionary Perspectives*, edited by Glenn Hausfater and Sarah Blaffer Hrdy. New York: Aldine, 1984.

———. *Homicide*. New York: Aldine/de Gruyter, 1988.

DICKEMANN, MILDRED FEMALE. "Infanticide, Reproductive Strategies and Social Stratification." In: *Evolutionary Biology and Human Social Behavior*, edited by Napoleon Chagnon and William Irons. North Scituate, Mass.: Duxbury Press, 1979.

DIVALE, WILLIAM T., and MARVIN HARRIS. "Population, Warfare, and the Male Supremacist Complex." *American Anthropologist* 78 (1976): 521-538.

HAUSFATER, GLENN and SARAH BLAFFER HRDY. *Infanticide: Comparative and Evolutionary Perspectives*. New York: Aldine, 1984.

HILL, KIM, and M. HURTADO. *Ache Life Histories and Demography*. New York: Aldine/de Gruyter, 1996.

HOWELL, NANCY. *Demography of the Dobe !Kung*. New York: Academic Publishers, 1979.

HRDY, SARAH BLAFFER. "Fitness Tradeoffs in the History and Evolution of Delegated Mothering with Special Reference to Wet-Nursing, Abandonment and Infanticide." *Ethology and Sociobiology*. 13(5-6) (1992): 409-442.

PARMIGIANI, S. and F. VOM SAAL, eds. *Infanticide and Parental Care*. Switzerland: Harwood Academic Publishers, 1994.

SCHIEFENHÖVEL, W. "Reproduction and Sex Ratio Manipulation Through Preferred Female Infanticide, Among the Eipo in the Highlands of Western New Guinea." In *The Sociobiology of Sexual and Reproductive Strategies*, edited by Anne Rasa, Christian Vogel, and Eckart Voland. London: Chapman and Hall, 1989.

SOMMER, VOLKER. "Infanticide Among the Langurs of Jodhpur: Testing the Sexual Selection Hypothesis with a Long-term Record." In *Infanticide and Parental Care*, edited by S. Parmigiani and F. vom Saal. Switzerland: Harwood Academic Publishers, 1994.

WATTS, DAVID. "Infanticide in Mountain Gorillas: New Cases and a Reconsideration of the Evidence." *Ethology* 81 (1989):1-18.

INHERITANCE

Inheritance of wealth includes the transfer of rights, roles, authority, property, and money from one individual to another. Most commonly, inheritance occurs across generations and serves as a link between periods of time as well as between individuals. Although inheritance usually refers to the transfer of culturally significant valuables at death, it has been extended to include pre-mortem transfers of material or other assets between generations; for example, dowry to daughters and bride-price provided to sons are often considered forms of inheritance in the anthropological literature.

Patrilineal inheritance (father to son) is most prevalent on a worldwide basis; however, concentrations of matrilineal inheritance (mother's brother to sister's son) occur in southeast Asia, the Pacific, and across the matrilineal belt of Africa. Bilineal inheritance, by which sons and daughters inherit from parents, is most prevalent in the European regions and is often associated with limited heirship (i.e., a limited subset, usually in which one child of each sex inherits from parents). Variations in classes of beneficiaries are compounded by variation in the partibility of inheritance; for example, primogeniture, where the majority of parental wealth goes to the first born, has intrigued not only anthropologists but historians, demographers, and economists.

Forms of unigeniture are associated with stem family structure, wherein one beneficiary child retains residence at the parental home, marries, and produces the subsequent generation while his/her siblings seek fortunes and mating opportunities elsewhere. Partible inheritance is associated with joint family structure in which all children of one sex stay in the parental home with their spouses and when the parental generation dies the family estate is split more or less equally among them. Whether inheritance practices are causal to family structure or merely correlated with specific family forms is a topic of current debate.

The importance and meaning of such variation in inheritance has been approached from a variety of theoretical perspectives. Anthropological literature focuses on two main themes: that of social replication, in the sense of roles, obligations, and social structure; and genetic replication, the successful production of biological descendants. In the former view, regional clustering of patterns is assumed to reflect similarities in culture due to sharing and borrowing of cultural norms. The latter view ascribes more biologically functional explanations to observed patterns of inheritance, such that regional concentrations of patterns may reflect either historical ties or convergent ecological conditions.

INHERITANCE AS A MEANS OF SOCIAL REPLICATION

Social anthropologists have traditionally focused on normative patterns of inheritance that result in a new generation mirroring the previous generation in terms of social status and interfamilial social connections. Pierre Bourdieu views replication of the "lineage" or "patrimony" as the corpus that is reproduced over generations as both a result and a cause of the replication of the larger social structure. Inheritance strategies then are an inseparable part of a larger set of biological and social mechanisms of replication by groups to further the aims of the group in the next generation. The various strategic paths undertaken by families, including the specifics of inheritance, "[arise] from systems of demands that are not automatically

compatible, have their common origin in the habitus, which is the product of the structures that it tends to reproduce and which implies a 'spontaneous' submission to the established order and to the orders of the guardians of that order." (Bourdieu 1990).

The "habitus" is the "whole system of predispositions inculcated by the material circumstances of life and by family upbringing" (Bourdieu 1976) through which the social structure replicates itself. Members of lineages act so as to perpetuate the material and social distinctions of their lineage because they are imbued with the principles of that same social structure which is thereby reproduced from one generation to another. The system produces individuals that are socialized to reproduce that system through inheritance and other practices.

British anthropologist Jack Goody focuses similarly on the socially defined family with its material and social position as the unit replicated through the process of inheritance of wealth and status. Utilizing selected and broad cross-cultural comparisons that span geographical concentrations of normative practices, for example, African patrilineal and European bilineal inheritance, he links patterns of inheritance to modes of production—specifically associating male-biased inheritance with labor-intensive modes of production, whereas the development of capital-intensive production is associated with the inclusion of female heirs (Goody 1969). Goody clearly places the nature and importance of specific property as primary to systems of marriage and kinship (Goody 1976) and links intensive agricultural economies to class hierarchies and subsequently to familial strategies to maintain the status of daughters as well as sons—and so, to bilineal inheritance. Thus, modes of production are associated with development of hierarchical classes and result in patterns of inheritance and strategies for the maintenance of familial status from generation to generation. The vagaries of births and of sex-specific mortality of children in conjunction with strategies to maintain familial status result in conflicts between parental desire to provide for children and a desire to retain the unity of familial wealth and status (Hrdy and Judge 1993). With Goody's focus on familial status as the trans-generational goal, familial strategizing and invocation of ecological and economic influences on inheritance patterns, his perspective is poised between cultural anthropologists' primary focus on culture and sociobiologists' focus on the individual's genetic self-interest as a determinant of individual behavior.

INHERITANCE AS A MEANS OF GENETIC REPLICATION

While many of the variables of interest to social anthropologists are also invoked by those employing biological perspectives, the explanatory framework differs substantively. In contrast to the family-systems approaches, anthropologists using evolutionary biology as an organizing principle have conceptualized inheritance as a tool that is employed by individuals to increase the reproductive success of their direct descendants and other biological kin, as distinct from replication of the society in which they are members. The evolutionary framework provides an approach for cross-cultural analyses of inheritance because it predicts that the direction of inheritance parallels the greatest probabilities of genetic replication (Alexander 1974). Contrary to some explications, the evolutionary framework does not posit a genetic determination of inheritance practices; rather, it posits that inheritance patterns will differ with varying social structures, ecologies, and technologies in predictable ways—all of which conform to individual fitness criteria, and none of which require differences in gene frequencies that correspond to differences in inheritance practices.

From an evolutionary framework, normative patterns are compared relative to socioecological variability among cultures and culture groups. The cross-generational replication of social order is viewed as an incidental and probabilistic product of individuals transferring property in ways that increase the relative survival, mating, and reproductive success of their individual relatives and descendants. That is to say, individuals that expend time and energy to accumulate property, social status, knowledge, and so forth will leave greater genetic representation in future generations if such wealth can be left to individuals with close genetic relationships and used to increase the reproductive success of those relatives. It follows from the law of natural selection that where wealth helps parents to successfully raise children and to find mates for those children, people who leave wealth to these closest relatives will leave more descendants.

Direct Descendants and Other Heirs

Observing that parents leave wealth to their children does not distinguish the evolutionary perspective from

that of the social theorists. However, viewing the investment of wealth in descendants as a specific form of kin investment (Hamilton 1964), that is, parental investment (Trivers 1972), has allowed the elaboration of more precise predictions regarding patterns of variability in inheritance practices in relation to social and ecological conditions. Testing these predictions using cross-cultural and other comparative methodologies has resulted in the development of more precise hypotheses as well as elucidation of what might be referred to as human universals.

Sex Bias Among Potential Heirs

In an early application of sociobiological theory to cross-cultural differences in humans, Hartung (1976) proposes that son-biased inheritance of wealth results from the greater reproductive benefit to which men can employ wealth than can women, that is, men in many societies use wealth to obtain additional mates and thus additional children, whereas wealthy females could increase their number of children by relatively little regardless of the number of their mates. As predicted, cross-cultural data confirms that male-biased inheritance is more prevalent in polygynous marriage systems, as is the payment of bride-price, and thus male relatives, especially sons, are preferred heirs in those systems wherein inherited wealth can be used to increase male reproduction (Hartung 1982).

Borgerhoff-Mulder (1989) builds on Hartung's cross-cultural findings with a case study of the relationship of parental wealth, inheritance, and reproductive success of Kipsigis daughters and sons. She found that parental wealth in terms of cattle was reproductively more beneficial to sons than to daughters, whereas parental wealth in terms of land, a culturally more novel form of wealth for these historically pastoralist people, benefited sons and daughters equally. Contrary to the prediction that resources that benefited offspring equally would be allocated equally, Kipsigis bestowed both land and cattle wealth solely on sons.

Trivers and Willard (1973) proposes that the sex difference in reproductive variance which typifies mammals could result in natural selection for gender-biased production of offspring within populations, such that individual females with ample resources produce more male offspring and those with fewer resources produce more females. Applying this hypothesis to human data and focusing on investments in, rather than production of, daughters and sons,

Smith et al. (1987) analyzed summaries of one thousand probated wills from British Columbia and found that wealthier decedents favored sons in their wills while poorer decedents favored daughters. While those results support the hypothesis of Trivers and Willard (1973), Hrdy and Judge (1992) analyzes a large sample of wills in the United States and find that a higher variance among males in reproductive success than among females, and stronger relationships for males between wealth and number of surviving children, were insufficient to generate son-biased inheritance.

In Hrdy and Judge's case study of inheritance, the total estate value of the majority of sampled estates was insufficient to elevate a son into the wealth region associated with larger numbers of surviving children, and inheritance to sons and to daughters was equal. The reproductive returns to investment via inheritance in daughters and sons was not significantly different. That these results can be predicted by family systems theory, by Goody's mode of production explanation, and by ecologically informed sociobiological hypotheses indicates that these various approaches are not mutually exclusive but rather invoke different levels of explanation of inheritance phenomena.

Matrilineal Inheritance

Using Murdock's (1967) cross-cultural codes, Hartung (1976) demonstrates that in the vast majority of societies, a man's wealth is inherited by his children or by close patrilineal relatives. Evolutionary theory predicts that inheritance by individuals other than children should occur only under certain limited conditions. Alexander (1974) predicts that matrilineal inheritance will be normative when low probability of paternity prevails.

Cross-cultural analyses indicate that transfer of resources from a man to the children of his wife or wives is associated with a high probability that those children are genetic descendants of their jural father, while the normative inheritance practices of husbands in societies in which women's sexual behavior is less restricted, and thus paternity less certain, do not favor their putative children (Gaulin and Schlegal 1980; Hartung 1985).

Flinn (1981) suggested that pressure or coercion by uterine kin may result in inheritance practices favoring sister's children even when probability of paternity is sufficiently high that men might be expected to favor their own children. If there is any paternity uncertainty, a man will be more closely related on average to his sister's children than to the putative children of his brother. The summed coercion by uterine kin for investment might overcome direct fitness interests. Such a conflict-based model is particularly interesting as it suggests that matrilineal inheritance should be relatively unstable over time, which appears to be the case within the historical record.

Hartung (1985) expanded the discussion of matrilineal inheritance noting that when probability of paternity is low, daughter inheritance would increase the relatedness of future beneficiaries to ego more directly than does inheritance to sister's children. However, such a solution is rare, if extant, and Hartung developed a model illustrating the fitness advantage that accrues to a man's uterine kin across several generations when he bequeaths wealth to his sister's offspring rather than his putative offspring. Hartung also put forth the hypothesis that low probability of paternity and matrilineal kinship, reckoning relatives predominantly through female lines, may be concomitant results of ecological and social factors that cause male lineages to be chronically short-lived as a consequence of a high death rate among adult men.

CONCLUSION

One of the major differences between human society and that of most other organisms is the importance in a majority of known cultures of acquiring, accumulating, and transferring resources across generations. The relationship of inheritance patterns to family structure, social structure, and class hierarchies has caused inheritance practices to be of intellectual interest to social anthropologists, archaeologists, and evolutionary anthropologists. Identifying the nature of "human universals" in inheritance practice and discovering empirically valid explanations of cross-cultural and inter-individual variability in inheritance practices has been important in sociocultural and evolutionary anthropology.

Inheritance—the transmission of acquired property, roles, and status from one individual to another across time—functions to increase the relative differences among members of a population in terms of wealth, status, and reproductive success across generations. Inherited wealth provides a mechanism for promoting and stabilizing social hierarchies, increasing cultural and economic inertia, and decreasing economic mobility and equality of opportunity (Hartung 1988). Accordingly, it is a subject of contemporary relevance which has been well informed by anthropological research.

DEBRA S. JUDGE

ALEXANDER, RICHARD D. *The Evolution of Social Behavior. Annual Review Ecology and Systematics* 5 (1974): 325-383.

BORGERHOFF-MULDER, M. "Reproductive Consequences of Sex- biased Inheritance for the Kipsigis." In *Comparative Socioecology: The Behavioural Ecology of Humans and Other Mammals,* edited by V. Standen and R. A. Foley. Oxford: Blackwell Scientific Publications, 1989.

BOURDIEU, PIERRE. "Marriage Strategies as Strategies of Social Reproduction." In *Family and Society: Selections from the Annales,* edited by Robert Forster and Orest Ranum. Baltimore: Johns Hopkins Press, 1976.

———. *The Logic of Practice.* Palo Alto: Stanford University Press, 1990.

FLINN, MARK. "Uterine vs. Agnatic Kinship Variability and Associated Cousin Marriage Preferences: An Evolutionary Biological Analysis." In *Natural Selection and Social Behavior,* edited by Richard D. Alexander and Donald W. Tinkle. Chiron Press, 1981.

GAULIN, S., and A. SCHLEGAL. "Paternal Confidence and Paternal Investment: A Cross-cultural Test of a Sociobiological Hypothesis." *Ethology and Sociobiology* 1 (1980): 301-309.

GOODY, JACK. "Inheritance, Property, and Marriage in Africa and Eurasia." *Sociology* 3 (1969): 55-76.

———. *Production and Reproduction: A Comparative Study of the Domestic Domain.* Cambridge: Cambridge Univ. Press, 1976.

HAMILTON, W. D. "The Genetical Evolution of Social Behavior Parts I and II." *Journal of Theoretical Biology* 7 (1964):1-52.

HARTUNG, JOHN. "On Natural Selection and the Inheritance of Wealth." *Current Anthropology* 17 (1976): 607-613.

———. "Polygyny and Inheritance of Wealth." *Current Anthropology* 23 (1982): 1-7.

———. "Matrilineal Inheritance: New Theory and Analysis." *The Behavioral and Brain Sciences* 8 (1985): 661-688.

———. "Deceiving Down: Conjectures on the Management of Subordinate Status." In *Self-deceit: An Adaptive Mechanism,* edited by Joan Lockard and Delroy Paulus. Englewood Cliffs, N.J.: Prentice-Hall, 1988.

HRDY, SARAH B., and D. S. JUDGE. "Allocation of Resources Among Close Kin, Sacramento California 1890-1984." *Ethology and Sociobiology* 13 (1992): 495–522.

———. "Darwin and the Puzzle of Primogeniture: An Essay on Biases in Parental Investment After Death." *Human Nature* 4 (1993): 1-45.

MURDOCK, GEORGE P. *Ethnographic Atlas.* Pittsburgh: Univ. of Pittsburgh Press, 1967.

SMITH, S., B. KISH, and C. CRAWFORD. "Inheritance of Wealth as Human Kin Investment." *Ethology and Sociobiology* 8 (1987): 171-182.

TRIVERS, ROBERT. "Parental Investment and Sexual Selection." In *Sexual Selection and the Descent of Man,* edited by Bernard Campbell. Chicago: Aldine, 1972.

TRIVERS, ROBERT, and D. WILLARD. "Natural Selection and Parental Ability to Vary Sex Ratio of Offspring." *Science* 179 (1973): 90-92.

INITIATION RITES

Most initiation rites accompany admission to an age group, such as adolescence or full adulthood. Other admissions are to secret societies or special statuses, such as for a priest, magician, or king. The ceremonies mediate three phases: separation from the former status, transition, and incorporation in the new status.

Adolescent initiation ceremonies constitute the most frequent type of initiation rite described in the anthropological literature. Arnold Van Gennep (1909), a frequently cited source on rites of passage, gave examples in a wide variety of societies. These ceremonies are found in many, although not all, human societies and are associated with the conspicuous physiological and behavioral changes during the transition from childhood to adolescence. Alice Schlegel and Herbert Barry III (1979) provide information on many attributes of adolescent initiation ceremonies in the standard world sample of 186 societies, which includes all known types of preindustrial societies. The ceremony is defined as social recognition of the transition from childhood to adolescence.

FEATURES OF THE CEREMONY

A general purpose of the adolescent initiation ceremony is to establish different roles for men and women. Schlegel and Barry found that none of the

652

reported ceremonies was for initiates of both sexes together. Although the ceremonies are exclusively for boys or girls, an initiation ceremony for one sex is compatible with a corresponding ceremony for the opposite sex. Among 182 societies with information on absence or presence of a ceremony, 102 have a ceremony for one sex or both sexes. This custom is therefore present in the majority of societies (56 percent). The sample of 182 societies includes forty six (25 percent) with a ceremony for both sexes, thirty nine (21 percent) with a ceremony for girls only, seventeen (9 percent) with a ceremony for boys only, and eighty (44 percent) with no ceremony. A statistical analysis shows that a ceremony for one sex predicts presence more often than absence of a ceremony for the opposite sex. In the majority of societies, other participants are exclusively males in ceremonies for boys and exclusively females in ceremonies for girls. The physical components usually include activities the initiate must perform or manipulations of the initiate, such as massage, sweat baths, bathing, body painting, or painful procedures. The ceremony is interpreted by members of the society as a marker of the initiate's change in status, physical characteristics, or behavior.

SOCIETIES WITH CEREMONIES

Schlegel and Barry (1980) report several cultural conditions associated with presence of adolescent initiation ceremonies. A ceremony is present in 84 percent of thirty-one societies where the principal source of food is gathering or fishing and in 74 percent of thirty-eight societies with matrilocal or other uxorilocal residence. The average contribution of women to the subsistence economy is higher in societies where a ceremony is present. These cultural attributes are usually found in small communities in societies with low or medium levels of technological complexity.

Barry and Schlegel (1980) report that in societies where an adolescent initiation ceremony is present, differentiation between the sexes is emphasized in early childhood. Large differences are more likely to be reported between young boys and girls in the traits inculcated, and authority figures are more likely to be adults of the same sex. The adolescent initiation ceremony also emphasizes the differentiation between men and women. Cultural continuity, which underlies the prominent sex differentiation both in early childhood and in the adolescent initiation ceremony,

might help boys and girls to adapt to the physical changes in adolescence.

An initiation ceremony can be a mechanism for permitting more freedom and privileges in adolescence than in childhood. In most societies with a high degree of social stratification, there is no initiation ceremony and a low degree of sexual freedom for adolescents. Barry and Schlegel (1986) found that the mean sexual freedom of adolescents is higher among the few stratified societies with an initiation ceremony for either sex. The ceremony appears to counteract the restrictive effect of social stratification on sexual behavior.

CEREMONIES FOR BOYS

The ceremonies for boys are generally larger and more conspicuous events than the corresponding ceremonies for girls. The ceremonies for boys, therefore, have attracted more attention from observers and theorists. Attributes that are found more often in adolescent initiation ceremonies for boys than for girls include a large gorup of initiates and participants, a genital operation, and a focus on responsibility, wisdom, or valor. The information is from the study of pre-industrial societies by Schlegel and Barry (1979).

John M. Whiting et al. (1958), in a study of fifty-six societies, reported that an initiation ceremony for boys was present in most societies in which infants sleep exclusively with their mothers and where this sleeping arrangement is prolonged by a postpartum sex taboo of nine months or longer. They proposed a psychogenic interpretation of the ceremony as a technique for counteracting the boy's emotional dependence on his mother and hostility toward his father. A subsequent modification of this interpretation is that the child identifies with the male or female figure who has superior status. The initiation ceremony helps the boy to shift from a primary feminine to a secondary masculine identification (Burton and Whiting 1961).

Frank Young (1965), in a study of a partially different sample of fifty-four communities, concluded that a high degree of adult-male solidarity characterizes most societies with initiation ceremonies for boys. He proposed the sociogenic interpretation that the initiation ceremony has the function of dramatizing and perpetrating male solidarity. The rival psychogenic and sociogenic interpretations are compatible with each other and difficult to test separately. Most societies with a high degree of solidarity among adult males also have infrequent contact of the young child with the father. The boy therefore must shift from an initial identification with the mother to strong bonding with the father and other men. A dramatic initiation ceremony may help the boy to make this major change in social orientation and self-identity.

CEREMONIES FOR GIRLS

Attributes that are found more often in adolescent initiation ceremonies for girls than for boys include occurrence at the time of genital maturation, a single initite, with participation limited to the immediate family, seclusion of the initiate, and a focus on fertility or sexuality (Schlegel and Barry 1979). In most societies, the ceremony is for a single girl, participation is limited to the immediate family, and the initiate is secluded. These attributes indicate why ceremonies for girls are less conspicuous and have been studied less than the corresponding ceremonies for boys. Young (1965) reported that adolescent initiation ceremonies for girls are more likely to be present in societies with polygyny and extended families. The ceremony is interpreted as having the function of dramatizing solidarity among the multiple adult women in these households. This is similar to Young's sociogenic interpretation of the function of initiation ceremonies for boys. The more limited scope of female than male solidarity may explain why the ceremonies are generally less elaborate for girls than for boys.

Judith K. Brown (1963), in a study of seventy-five societies, found that an adolescent initiation ceremony for girls is more likely to be present in societies in which the girl does not leave the domestic unit of her parents after marriage and in which women make important contributions to the food supply, such as by foraging or agriculture. The ceremony was interpreted as having the function of dramatizing the girl's genital maturity in societies in which she will remain in the same residence after marriage or make an important contribution to the subsistence economy. Schlegel and Barry (1980), using a larger sample, also found these two cultural characteristics associated with presence of a ceremony for girls.

A further finding by Schlegel and Barry is that initiation ceremonies for girls occur predominantly in tribal societies with low technological complexity. An important source of food is generally the meat of herbivorous wild animals. These animals might be frightened away by the odor of menstrual blood. The spread of this odor is restricted by seclusion and observance of taboos, which are usually components of the initiation ceremonies for girls. Michio Kitahara (1984) found that societies with initiation ceremonies for girls are more likely to have highly developed menstrual taboos, which are compatible with the need to avoid frightening away animals that constitute part of the food supply. Another suggestion by Kitahara is that the initiation ceremony may contribute to inhibition of subsequent sexual activity by the female initiates. Too many young children may hinder a small band of nomadic hunters or gatherers, which is consistent with a finding by Barry and Schlegel (1986). Mean sexual freedom in adolescence is lower in foraging societies in which an initiation ceremony for girls is present than in foraging societies in which a ceremony for girls is absent.

PAINFUL CEREMONIES

The adolescent initiation ceremony in some societies inflicts pain on the initiates. These practices have attracted great interest because they are unusual examples of seemingly maladaptive harsh treatment of children. Pain as a component of the adolescent initiation ceremony is generally believed to be inflicted mainly on boys rather than girls. This is true of pain in the form of a genital operation. It is reported for boys in twenty societies and for girls in only seven societies. The operation is usually circumcision or subincision for boys, clitoridectomy for girls. Painful procedures without a genital operation are reported as components of the ceremony with similar frequency for boys (in twenty societies) and for girls (in twenty-one societies). These painful procedures include beating, tattooing, tooth extraction, and eating of obnoxious substances.

Whiting, Kluckhohn, and Anthony (1958) reported that the initiation ceremony for boys includes painful hazing or genital operations or both in each of fourteen societies with long duration of exclusive mother-son sleeping arrangements and postpartum sex taboos. These procedures are assumed to make the ceremony more effective. Yehudi A. Cohen (1964) suggested that male bonding is strengthened by the painful procedures in the initiation ceremony for boys. Brown (1963) reported that initiation ceremonies for girls are more likely to include painful procedures in societies where the infant sleeps exclusively with the mother. The proposed explanation is based on a conflict of sex identity for girls in these societies. The girl has a primary feminine identification owing to the exclusive sleeping arrangement with her mother, but in early childhood she develops a secondary masculine identification because the domestic unit is dominated by males. The pain inflicted in the initiation ceremony helps the girl to accept her female role in a society that is dominated by men.

SOCIETIES WITHOUT CEREMONIES

Schlegel and Barry (1980) identify several cultural conditions associated with the absence or the presence of adolescent initiation ceremonies in the world sample of preindustrial societies. Ceremonies are absent in 64 percent of fifty-five societies with intensive agriculture and in 62 percent of fifty societies in which the mean size of the local community is 400 or more. A high degree of cultural complexity generally appears incompatible with adolescent initiation ceremonies.

Adolescent initiation ceremonies do not occur in contemporary industrial nations, which have an extremely high degree of cultural complexity. Several other characteristics of social life in these nations might contribute to the absence of ceremonies. Special recognition of the onset of adolescence might interfere with school, which begins several years before genital maturity and continues during adolescence. Ceremonial differentiation between boys and girls would conflict with the general policy of providing the same education to both sexes. The multiplicity of religious, occupational, and residential groups might conflict with ceremonies that pertain to the entire local community.

OTHER RECOGNITIONS OF GENITAL MATURITY

The onset of genital maturity is a major physical change that begins the distinctive developmental stage of adolescence. Some societies recognize the beginning of this stage in ways that do not fulfill the definition of an initiation ceremony. These alternative observances might be adequate substitutes for initiation ceremonies. In some tribes in North America, boys go on a solitary spirit quest, seeking a dream or vision that will define their adult status. The typical procedures include food deprivation and self-inflicted pain. Because these activities are solitary, away from the family and community, they are not defined as initiation ceremonies.

Some religious ceremonies in contemporary nations are associated with the onset of genital maturity. These include the Jewish bar mitzvah for boys and bas mitzvah for girls. In some Christian churches, baptism or confirmation ceremonies coincide with adolescence. These are not defined as initiation ceremonies because they involve a religious group rather than the entire community.

CEREMONIES AT OTHER STAGES OF LIFE

Adolescence is only one of the successive stages of life. Ceremonies may be associated with each stage. Examples are ceremonies for naming an infant, weddings, and funerals.

Cohen (1964) distinguishes between two stages of puberty. The first, at age 8 to 10 years, initiates sleeping away from the natal home and brother-sister avoidance. These changes in relationships with family members are defined as initiation ceremonies. The second stage of puberty coincides more closely with genital maturation. The rituals in this later stage correspond to the prevalent definition of adolescent initiation ceremonies. The first stage is regarded as a more important and stressful social change. An initiation ceremony for boys is present in more societies in the first stage of puberty than in the second stage. In contemporary nations, a ceremonial event that may substitute for an adolescent initiation ceremony is graduation from high school or college, which coincides with a later stage of youth or full social adulthood rather than genital maturity. Some ceremonies are associated with entry of an individual or group into a special status. These ceremonies include initiation in a college fraternity or sorority or in an adult social or occupational group. The inauguration of the president of the United States or other public official is a ceremony for a single initiate, but television makes possible the participation of millions of viewers.

CONCLUSION

Initiation rites constitute one type of rites of passage. The most extensively studied type of initiation rite is the adolescent initiation ceremony. This ritual observance of genital maturity has an important role in many societies, indicated by conspicuous features, such as genital operations and other painful procedures. Because these ceremonies are absent from contemporary nations, information about them requires anthropological descriptions of other types of societies. Adolescent initiation ceremonies emphasize sex differentiation. Ceremonies for boys appear to encourage bonding of groups of adult males. Ceremonies for girls appear to emphasize readiness of the individual to procreate children. Several cross-cultural studies of adolescent initiation ceremonies have generated interesting but inconclusive interpretations. Future research should analyze selected aspects of the ceremonies, such as painful procedures, in addition to comparisons of societies in which the ceremony is present and absent. Research on adolescent initiation ceremonies can be expanded by studying other types of initiation rites and other rites of passage.

HERBERT BARRY III

SEE ALSO: Adolescence; Genital Mutilation

BARRY, HERBERT, III, and ALICE SCHLEGEL. "Early Childhood Precursors of Adolescent Initiation Ceremonies." *Ethos* 8 (1980): 132–145.

———. "Cultural Customs that Influence Sexual Freedom in Adolescence. *Ethnology* 25 (1986): 51–62.

BROWN, JUDITH K. "A Cross-Cultural Study of Female Initiation Rites." *American Anthropologist* 65 (1963): 837–953.

BURTON, ROGER V., and JOHN W. M. WHITING. "The Absent Father and Cross-Sex Identity." *Merrill-Palmer Quarterly of Behavior and Development* 7 (1961): 85–95.

COHEN, YEHUDI A. *The Transition from Childhood to Adolescence: Cross-Cultural Studies of Initiation Ceremonies, Legal Systems, and Incest Taboos.* Chicago: Aldine, 1964.

KITAHARA, MICHIO. "Female Physiology and Female Puberty Rites." *Ethos* 12 (1984): 132–150.

SCHLEGEL, ALICE, and HERBERT BARRY III. "Adolescent Initiation Ceremonies: A Cross-Cultural Code." *Ethnology* 18 (1979): 199–210.

———. "The Evolutionary Significance of Adolescent Initiation Ceremonies." *American Ethnologist* 7 (1980): 696–715.

VAN GENNEP, ARNOLD. *Les rites de passage.* Paris: Librarie Critique Emil Nourry (1909). Translated by Monika B. Vizedom and Gabrielle L. Caffee as *The Rites of Passage.* Chicago: University of Chicago Press, 1960.

WHITING, JOHN W. M., RICHARD KLUCKHOHN, and ALBERT S. ANTHONY. "The Function of Male Initiation Ceremonies at Puberty." In *Readings in Social Psychology,* edited by Eleanor E. Maccoby, Theodore M. Newcomb, and Eugene L. Hartley. New York: Holt, Rinehart & Winston, 1958.

YOUNG, FRANK W. *Initiation Ceremonies: A Cross-Cultural Study of Status Dramatization.* Indianapolis, Ind.: Bobbs-Merrill, 1965.

INTENTIONAL COMMUNITIES

The term "intentional communities" is increasingly used to refer to the small-scale social formations also known as utopian communities, sectarian societies, collective settlements, communes, socialistic experiments, cooperative colonies, and alternative communities. It provides a convenient umbrella under which the other terms can be subsumed, each with its own emphasis. An intentional community is defined as a group of people who associate by choice and out of shared convictions in a cooperative and usually coresidential living arrangement, with active fellowship as an explicit goal. The notion of voluntarily chosen fellowship is central, and it serves to distinguish intentional communities from those arising from traditional, accidental, or purely pragmatic association. By convention, the term is restricted to communities that exist within a context of state-level polities. Scholarship on intentional communities is interdisciplinary, engaging the efforts of anthropologists, economists, geographers, historians, political scientists, psychologists, sociologists, and students of religion.

Intentional communities in this sense of the term have an uneven temporal and spatial distribution. The earliest generally acknowledged exemplar is the Essene community of the second century B.C. to the second century A.D., a messianic Jewish sect known from the writings of Flavius Josephus and Pliny the Elder and that is known in the Dead Sea Scrolls. At least some Essenes apparently lived in a separatist community and held their possessions in common. The apostolic community described in the Bible can be considered another early example, as can the various monastic communities of medieval Europe. The latter's connection to powerful institutions of the wider society, however, has led many students of intentional communities to consider them a separate phenomenon, and the same can be said of monastic communities in other religious traditions. On the other hand, some of the Beguine and Beghard communities dating from the twelfth century, as well as other similar lay associations throughout Europe, would seem to qualify. The Hussite Rebellion and the Protestant Reformation of the sixteenth century spawned historically important intentional communities, some of which survive to the present. From Anabaptism, the left wing of the Reformation, came the Mennonites, Amish, and Hutterites, the latter especially committed to communitarianism. From the defeated remnant of the Hussites emerged the Moravian Brethren, who also had communitarian inclinations. Two hundred years after the Reformation, religious reformers in Central Europe known as Radical Pietists preached separation from the established church, leading to the formation of a large number of communities. In England, communities were formed in the seventeenth century by Diggers, Quakers, and Philadelphians, among other groups.

The communitarian impulse was transmitted to the Americas by many of these sectarians. The Moravians established several important communities during the American colonial period, from 1735 to 1753, as did various groups of Radical Pietists (1742). Historians have even interpreted the Puritans as initially engaged in creating utopian communities. On the eve of the American Revolution, a group of breakaway Quakers arrived from England in 1774 to establish what is probably the best-known religious communal society in U.S. history, the United Society of Believers in Christ's Second Appearing, better known as the Shakers. Twenty Shaker communities were founded before the 1840s, and the group's peak population of about 4,000 (Brewer 1986; Bainbridge 1984) was achieved in the 1820s or 1830s. Several other Pietist groups arrived in the first half of the nineteenth century, including the Harmonists, who built communities in Pennsylvania and Indiana; the Separatists of Zoar, Ohio; and the Inspirationists of Amana, Iowa. In the 1870s a small number of Hutterites emigrated to North America and settled on the northern plains of the United States and Canada, where in 1994 they numbered roughly 35,000 living in about 300 colonies. Except for the Shakers, the membership of these religious communities has remained largely immigrant.

Nonsectarian communitarian movements began to appear in the first half of the nineteenth century, and once again, Europe was often the seedbed, but the communitarian aspects were fully realized in the United States. The earliest was the utopian scheme of the Scottish industrialist and philanthropist Robert Owen, who purchased the site of New Harmony, Indiana, and established a model community there in 1825. Other Owenite colonies followed, including the interracial Nashoba Community founded in 1826 by Frances Wright. The ideas of the French utopian visionary Charles Fourier stimulated the formation of more than thirty intentional communities from Massachusetts to Iowa in the 1840s. The followers of another Frenchman, Étienne Cabet, champion of the egalitarian state, attempted to model his ideas in several communities in the United States, the first in 1848. All of these efforts were criticized by Karl Marx and Friedrich Engels as utopian socialism, in contrast to their own scientific socialism, in which reform would come through class struggle rather than through the formation of experimental communities.

From the 1840s on, hundreds of intentional communities appeared in the United States based on a dazzling variety of ideologies. Among the most famous were Brook Farm, Massachusetts, founded in 1841 by New England Transcendentalists (but converted to Fourierism in 1843); Oneida, New York, where, beginning in 1848, John Humphrey Noyes tried to implement his perfectionist ideas, including mutual criticism, complex marriage, and a system of eugenics; the Brotherhood of the New Life, begun in 1861, one of four communities founded by the spiritualist and mystic Thomas Lake Harris; the all-female Women's Commonwealth of Belton, Texas, started in the late 1860s by Martha McWhirter, who preached Methodist leader John Wesley's doctrine of sanctification, according to which the sanctified should separate themselves from the sinful; Kaweah Cooperative Commonwealth, established in 1885 in the Sequoia forest area by members of California's labor union movement; the Christian Commonwealth in Georgia, where in 1898 adherents of the Social Gospel movement combined Marxian socialism with Christian doctrine for the sake of social action; Fairhope, Alabama, founded in 1898 by supporters of Henry George's single-tax plan; and Point Loma, California, one of three Theosophical communities organized around 1900. Clearly, quite diverse social movements have chosen communitarianism as the social form with which to advance their visions.

In the twentieth century, as new communities continued to appear in Europe and North America, communitarianism took root in other countries as well, often but not always as the result of Western influence. Two especially important developments occurred in Japan and in Palestine and Israel. Japan's oldest commune, Ittoen (Garden of the One Light), was founded in 1905 in Kyoto, based on Buddhist principles of self-denial and service. Dozens of other intentional communities formed in Japan during the twentieth century, some based at least partly on Western ideas (Marxian socialism, anarchism) and others on indigenous philosophies. The Robert Owen Association has existed in Japan since 1958 to promote Owen's cooperative program, although it has not formed any communities. The Israeli kibbutzim, which in 1987 numbered nearly 300 with a total population of 127,000, represent the largest category of intentional communities with the greatest number of members. The first kibbutz began in 1909 as an agricultural experiment. Additional kibbutzim formed under the influence of Zionism and a youth movement among East European Jews who hoped to escape the oppressive life of the shtetl. Glorifying collective agricultural labor, the movement also experimented with collective childrearing and more egalitarian gender roles. The kibbutzim played an important role in the Jewish settlement of Palestine. In 1947 they were the residences of more than 7 percent of the Jewish population; in 1987, 3.5 percent of Israeli Jews lived in kibbutzim. In the last twenty years many kibbutzim have moved toward manufacturing and mainstream lifestyles.

The U.S. counterculture movement of the 1960s spawned a large number of communes based on an ever-widening array of ideologies, including Eastern philosophies, environmentalism, liberation theology, social action, and the human-potential movement. The 1990 edition of the *Directory of Intentional Communities* lists more than 300 extant communities in North America, but many others are not listed, including the Hutterian communities. Estimates by some scholars place the total number of intentional communities in North America in 1995 as high as 3,000. The directory also lists more than fifty communities in other countries (Colombia, India, England, Australia, New Zealand, Japan, Denmark, France, Sweden, Uruguay, Guatemala, Ecuador, Scotland, Germany, South Africa, Wales, and Ireland); again, many others exist but are not listed, including the Israeli kibbutzim. Many of the communities located outside Europe and North America were founded by Euro-Americans.

The fact that intentional communities are primarily a Western phenomenon has several explanations. A sense of society as dynamic is deeply rooted in both the Judeo-Christian tradition (the Edenic myth that looks backward and millenarian convictions that look forward) and the Greco-Roman tradition (the lost golden age and the progressive evolution of society). Accordingly, Westerners find it comparatively easy to imagine society other than it is and especially to imagine a better society. Although this notion languished during the Middle Ages, the Renaissance and the Reformation reawakened utopian thought and enhanced it with a growing emphasis on individualism and a theme of righteous separation from the whole. The rise of industrialism in the West created ever more visible social problems that intensified the reform impulse. Many intentional communities attempt to avoid or ameliorate the evils of industrialism as part of their programs. In this view, it is not surprising that communitarianism has taken root in Japan, the most industrialized non-Western country. It is often argued that the United States, in particular, is fertile ground for communitarianism because of the freedoms guaranteed by its political system, the traditional importance of voluntary association, and (historically) abundant land.

Intentional communities demonstrate diverse demographic profiles, economic arrangements, social and political organizations, and ideological bases. The very largest have as many as 2,000 persons at a single location, although few communities surpass 1,000 members. Most of the communities are autonomous, but in the Shaker, Hutterite, and kibbutz cases, among others, the individual community is part of a larger federation, with a common history and belief system and, in some instances, even centralized administrative functions. At the time of formation, most intentional communities are eager to attract new members, although they vary widely in their degree of selectivity, from the virtually unrestricted admission policy at Owen's New Harmony or the 1960s commune of Drop City to the highly selective policy, often with a probationary period, characteristic of many religious communities. Some communities choose to remain smaller than their resources would permit, usually by limiting new admissions. In the face of high birth rates, the Hutterites require each colony to divide when it reaches approximately 125 members. Thus, whereas many intentional communities at some level think of themselves as models for the wider society, most do not wish to grow indefinitely, valuing face-to-face intimacy among their members for practical and ideological reasons.

Economic arrangements nearly always include a more intensive sharing of resources than is found in the wider society. In many cases this sharing extends to common ownership of land, resources, capital, and products. Those who join relinquish their property to the community. Members labor for the common good without compensation and in return receive food, clothing, shelter, medical care, and child support. Dormitory or apartment-style residence is typical, meals are taken collectively, and members may be expected to wear uniforms. Such a high degree of sharing was more common in eighteenth- and nineteenth-century groups, although it still occurs. Other communities function as cooperatives, leaving more room for individual ownership, but have some collective dimensions. All communities develop businesses in which their members work. Although job options are usually limited, a system of job rotation can increase the variety. Community members may even be allowed to hold employment outside the community and either tithe or contribute to a general fund that supports community activities.

The political structure of intentional communities varies considerably. Many form around the teachings of a charismatic leader and consequently develop a hierarchical structure in which obedience and commitment to the rules are rewarded with advance. This need not result in marked inequities, but more than one community has been undermined by resentment from the majority over privileges taken by the few. Communitarians are likely to be sensitive to this issue, because most communities are putatively egalitarian in terms of material benefits, even if they acknowledge gradations in spirituality. Not surprisingly, then, many communities create democratic or consensual political systems in which all full members participate equally in making important decisions; experience in these instances quickly teaches the advantage of small size.

Reinforcing the material egalitarianism of most intentional communities is the emphasis on fellowship. The social organization usually fosters togetherness in work, dining, and recreation. The metaphor of family is often present, with members using the terms "brother" and "sister" for one another and occasionally "father" or "mother" for a charismatic leader (e.g., Father [George] Rapp, Mother Ann [Lee]). Implied is a boundary separating the community from the outside, although the strength of the boundary varies considerably; some groups seek to minimize social contact with the wider society, whereas others are much more engaged. The family metaphor is often accompanied by modifications of traditional sexual arrangements. A number of groups, especially those stemming from Pietist or monastic traditions, require or at least esteem celibacy. The Shakers are famous but by no means unique in this regard. Others experiment with nonmonogamous sexuality, ranging from the free love of some hippie communes to more formal group marriage practices. At Oneida, where marriage was proscribed, any man or woman could sexually proposition another member of the community through an intermediary, but exclusive affection was not permitted. The contemporary Kerista community in San Francisco went even further by instituting a sleeping rotation. The majority of intentional communities retain a traditional pattern of sexual relations.

The egalitarian ethos may extend to gender roles, although this is more common in twentieth-century communities and in those without a traditional religious basis. The Shakers, with their dual male-female leadership structure, have often been cited as early advocates of gender equality, but scholarship in the last decade has cast strong doubt on the degree to which this was actually practiced. In newer communities gender equality seems to be more easily attained in decision-making than in division of labor, especially in agrarian-based communities. Some students of kibbutz life report a reassertion of the family and traditional gender roles compared to the earlier "pioneer" period.

The diversity of ideological bases of intentional communities has often been cited, and most scholars resolve these differences into two types—religious and secular. Those categories must be used cautiously, however, because some communities are difficult to classify and because researchers may use different definitions. Nevertheless, important differences between the two have been claimed, notably the longer life span of religiously based communities, the usual explanation being that religion provides a unifying bond that allows communities to overcome divisive forces. This finding must be qualified in two ways. First, religion may not in fact be the key variable that ensures longevity; other researchers have claimed primacy for ethnicity, particular economic arrangements, and number of commitment mechanisms. Second, although the long-lived communities nearly all have a religious base, a sizable majority of intentional communities, whether religious or secular, lasted less than thirty years.

Communities founder for various reasons. They fail to indoctrinate the second generation, lose cohesiveness after the founder's death, are poorly organized or financed, use inadequate criteria for admission, cannot compete materially with the wider society, or cannot defend themselves against attempts to be undermined by the wider society. Intentional communities tend to arise when economic or social conditions are stressful and to decline when conditions improve in the wider society. Some scholars conclude that intentional communities are inherently short-lived, although the 450-year history of the Hutterites belies this conclusion. Others believe that the issue of longevity has received too much attention and that emphasis should be placed instead on the existence of social problems that elicit a communitarian response, the benefits that individuals accrue from membership, and the contributions in new technology, alternative-lifestyle models, and social service that these communities have made to the wider society.

JONATHAN G. ANDELSON

BERRY, BRIAN J. L. *America's Utopian Experiments: Communal Havens from Long-Wave Crises.* Hanover, N.H.: University Press of New England, 1992.

BREWER, PRISCILLA. *Shaker Communities, Shaker Lives.* Hanover, N.H.: University Press of New England, 1986.

CHMIELEWSKI, WENDY, LOUIS J. KERN, and MARLYN KLEE-HARTZELL, eds. *Women in Spiritual and Communitarian Societies in the United States.* Syracuse, N.Y.: Syracuse University Press, 1993.

BAINBRIDGE, WILLIAM SIMS. "The Decline of the Shakers: Evidence From the United States Census." In *Communal Societies—Journal of the Communal Studies Association.* University of Southern Indiana, Evansville, Ind. vol. 4, 1984.

ERASMUS, CHARLES. *In Search of the Common Good.* New York: Free Press, 1977.

HOSTETLER, JOHN A. *Hutterite Society.* Baltimore: Johns Hopkins University Press, 1974.

KANTER, ROSABETH MOSS. *Commitment and Community: Communes and Utopias in Sociological Perspective.* Cambridge, Mass.: Harvard University Press, 1972.

KRAUSZ, ERNEST, ed. *The Sociology of the Kibbutz.* New Brunswick, N.J.: Transaction Books, 1983.

PETER, KARL A. *The Dynamics of Hutterite Society.* Edmonton, Can.: University of Alberta Press, 1987.

ZABLOCKI, BENJAMIN. *Alienation and Charisma: A Study of Contemporary American Communes.* New York: Free Press, 1980.

INTERNATIONAL UNION OF ANTHROPOLOGICAL AND ETHNOLOGICAL SCIENCES

The International Union of Anthropological and Ethnological Sciences (IUAES) is a world organization of social and biological anthropological scientists and institutions working in the fields of anthropology and ethnology, but it is also of interest to archaeologists, linguists, and human biologists, among others. It aims to enhance professional exchanges and communication among scholars throughout the world in a collective effort to expand knowledge and understanding of human diversity, with the goal of contributing to a better understanding of humankind and to a sustainable future based on harmony between nature and culture.

Various anthropological congresses were held in different parts of the world from the mid-nineteenth century onward. The first International Congress of Anthropological and Ethnological Sciences (ICAES) was held in London in 1934, the second in Copenhagen in 1938. In August 1948 the International Union of Anthropological and Ethnological Sciences was founded as a concomitant of the ICAES held in Brussels that year. Other congresses followed, in Vienna (1952), Philadelphia (1956), Paris (1960), Moscow (1964), and Tokyo (1968). In the latter year the ICAES and the IUAES were united, de jure, into one organization, and subsequently other Congresses have been held every five years—in Chicago (1973), Delhi (1978), Quebec and Vancouver (1983), Zagreb (1988), and Mexico City (1993).

The president of the congress is chosen by the anthropological and ethnological community in the host country and also serves as the president of the union until the next congress. The president is supported by an executive secretary and an executive committee chosen by the anthropologists in the host country, for a five-year term. The executive committee of the union, chaired by the president, includes the immediate past-president, seven vice presidents, and six members-at-large, all of whom collectively represent the international anthropological community as well as the major subdisciplines of anthropology. To ensure a measure of continuity, the vice presidents have a maximum ten-year term of office (i.e., two five-year periods), and the members-at-large are appointed for five years but may be reelected for one additional five-year period, either as a vice president or as a member-at-large. The secretary-general is appointed by the permanent council, on the recommendation of the executive committee and serves for an indefinite period.

The permanent council is the supreme governing body of the IUAES, and the recommendations of the executive committee become effective only after acceptance by the permanent council, which consists of the national delegations, any one of which has a maximum of six members plus honorary members from a particular country. Each national delegation has one vote, and all decisions of the permanent council are by a majority of the national delegations present and voting at a meeting or represented at the meeting by proxy. The permanent council meets at each of the world congresses and at least once during the intervening five-year periods, usually at an intercongress, a small congress dedicated to a single theme, with attendance by invitation only. World congresses may be attended by anyone who cares to do so. A general assembly is convened at the union's major congresses. It is advisory to the president, the permanent council, and the executive committee and consists of all members of the union and, in the case of institutions or associations in good financial standing at the time of the meeting, one representative.

In practice, the affairs of the IUAES are organized by the executive committee and, in particular, by the secretary-general, who is the senior administrative officer of the union and responsible for the general oversight and administration of all activities under the authority of the president, the permanent council, and the executive committee. The secretary-general maintains records of the affairs of the union, minutes of the general assembly, the permanent council, and the executive committee, and statements of accounts. The secretary-general maintains membership records, administers the funds and property of the union, gives notices of meetings, and produces three issues per year of the IUAES newsletter. Given the widespread, scattered locations of the executive committee members at any one time, the secretary-general therefore serves as the hub of IUAES activities on an ongoing basis.

The task of organizing a congress or intercongress is undertaken by the president and the executive secretary working in close association with the secretary-general and the executive committee and the permanent council. The congresses and inter-congresses, characterized by formal presentations and discussions and often followed by publication of the proceedings, require substantial planning and funding to ensure their success.

The union also supports the endeavors of several commissions, each of which is composed of internationally based experts who collectively investigate one anthropological topic of mutual interest. Commission members meet periodically, at world congresses, intercongresses, or elsewhere. Most of the commissions produce newsletters, books, and other major publications and generally serve as clearinghouses for the exchange of ideas and for academic innovations. They are required to report regularly to the secretary-general and to the permanent council and may be terminated by the latter body if their work becomes unsatisfactory or no longer relevant. In 1994 there were eighteen commissions: Commission on Aging and the Aged, Commission on the Anthropology of AIDS, Commission on Documentation, Commission on Folk Law and Legal Pluralism, Commission on Food and Food Problems, Commission on Human Ecology, Commission on Medical Anthropology and Epidemiology, Commission on Museums and Cultural Heritage, Commission on Nomadic Peoples, Commission for the Anthropological and Ethnological Study of Peace, Commission on Urban Anthropology, Commission on Urgent Anthropological Research, Commission on Visual Anthropology, Commission on Anthropology of Women, Commission on Cultural Dimensions of Global Change, Commission on Anthropology in Policy and Practice, Commission on the Anthropology of Tourism, and Commission on Theoretical Anthropology.

Anthropologists who have made outstanding contributions to scholarship may be appointed as honorary members of the union, with due regard to a balance of regional and disciplinary representation. Honorary members may not exceed twenty in number.

The IUAES may, either through its commissions or as a single body, affiliate with other organizations with broadly similar interests and concerns. The IUAES has, since 1953, been a member organization of the International Social Science Council and, since 1949, the International Council for Philosophy and Humanistic Studies, both of which are international nongovernmental organizations based in Paris. In 1993 the IUAES became a member of the International Council of Scientific Unions and, as such, looks forward to playing an increasingly important role in the work of the international scientific community. Each of these bodies systematically supports the IUAES with funding that may be used for various stipulated anthropological activities. Financial constraints limit the effectiveness of the IUAES, but it is determined to promote the study of the anthropological sciences throughout the world and thereby play its part in making the world a better place in which to live.

ERIC SUNDERLAND

INTERPRETATIVE ANTHROPOLOGY

SEE: Discourse Analysis; Narrative; Postmodernism; Reflexive Anthropology; Structuralism and Post-structuralism; Symbolic Anthropology; Thick Description; Writing Culture

IRRIGATION SYSTEMS

Irrigation may be defined as those physical and social arrangements by which humans deliberately supply fresh water to crop plants. All irrigation systems require sources of water, means of conveyance from the source to the field, and field delivery means. Some systems move water by gravity, and others—lift systems—move water by means of lifts or pump sets.

Sources for gravity systems include water flowing on the surface and in horizontal wells often called qanats. Gravity conveyance is achieved by open ditches dug in the dirt, and sometimes by pipes. Field delivery includes flooding the whole field, or flooding just the plowed furrows. In either case the field must be carefully graded so that water flows in the right direction and at the right speed.

Irrigation systems may have one or more points where water is lifted. If the water source is underground and a vertical well-shaft is used, then the water must be lifted to the surface. This lift can be buckets, animal-driven lifts, human- or animal-driven pumps, wind- or current-driven pumps, or pump-sets driven by electricity or engines. Once on the surface the water can be moved around in closed pipes. Field delivery can be done by sprinklers above the surface of the field, or by drip lines buried in the soil, which require pressurized conveyance systems and thus industrial pump-sets.

There are some strong correlations among the various features. Gravity systems tend to supply large areas, have complex social organization, and demand little non-human energy and technology. Lift systems tend to supply smaller areas, have simple social organization, demand large amounts of energy, and are technologically complex with long chains of relationships to suppliers of energy, machinery, spare parts, and information. The water and energy efficiencies are inversely related. Gravity systems use little industrial energy, and are not terribly efficient in their use of water. Lift systems use large amounts of energy, and are highly efficient in their use of water.

The major purpose of irrigation is to relieve water stress on crop plants. Every plant has periods of relative sensitivity to moisture stress. Increasing, or even ensuring, some yield from the plant requires that water stress be minimized or eliminated. Water stress can be produced when there is simply not enough rain during a wet season for that particular kind of plant (as in a desert), or when plants are cultivated during the dry season. Irrigation systems provide the water that relieves water stress on the plant. Irrigation water can also be used to relieve temperature stress. Humans have moved crop plants around the earth for a variety of reasons. Moving them east-west is usually not problematic, but moving them on the north-south gradient, or trying to change altitude often causes temperature concerns. Frost that extends for the length of the growing season is a major concern. Irrigation water can be used to prevent a freeze, thereby extending the growing season. Virtually every crop plant is now being irrigated.

INTERNAL ORGANIZATION

All irrigations systems must be constructed, and then must be operated; these processes are usually called Operation and Maintenance or, O and M. Construction requires knowledge, effective planning, and the application of labor and materials to the task. Construction is typically a relatively short process, perhaps taking at most two to three years. There is a short burst of intense activity at the end of which there is a visible accomplishment. For more than four millennia, rulers have bragged about major hydrologic construction projects.

O and M involves tasks and roles. There are a small number of tasks to be performed in every irrigation system. Acquisition is the social and physical act of abstracting water, at a head-gate, from its natural location. Distribution is the social and physical act of moving water from the head-gate to its destination. Maintenance is the necessary counter-entropic activity to keep the physical system in working order. Conflict resolution is the universal response to the universal opportunity for conflict over water. Accounting is the process of keeping track of performance of rights and duties.

All multiple-farm irrigation systems have a number of roles to perform the tasks. Farmer, or consumer of water, is universally found. Someone must pay attention to acquisition, distribution, maintenance, accounting, and conflict resolution. In small systems the farmers do all of this. In large systems with a high division of labor, all the work on the system is performed by teams of specialists that do not include farmers. There is a manager (CEO), subordinates who distribute the water (usually called ditch-riders in the U.S.), and workers (primarily concerned with maintenance). In virtually every irrigation system known a single set of roles are responsible for all the O and M tasks. There may be a division of labor within the role set, but the tasks are linked to one another by a single role set. Many systems require farmers to fill most of the worker and managerial roles.

Operation, unlike construction, can be expected to last for the lifetime of the system, and some systems have lasted for two thousand years or more. Allocation of water, maintenance, accounting, and conflict resolution take place in small units, and must constantly be done. It is not glamorous work. Usually at best the worker is no worse off at the end of the day than at the beginning. Nobody ever installs a monument bragging about the operation of an irrigation system. The work involved is either drudgery (maintenance), or dangerous (balancing the conflicting interests of two or more passionate parties).

There are clear incentives and rewards for construction. However, the incentives and rewards for operation are far less clear, and sometimes the rewards are negative. Clearly, construction demands enough labor, materials, and knowledge, and the social organization to mobilize all three. As the size of the construction project increases, so will the need for labor, materials, and knowledge, and so also will the demands on the social organization increase.

Operation also requires labor, materials, knowledge, and the social organization to mobilize and apply them. It does not require a great deal of labor, generally speaking, but that labor is very hard to motivate. The task of cleaning a canal is one of the least interesting and enjoyable jobs in agriculture. It is miserable work. Simply requiring it is usually not enough; a substantial number of workers may prefer to pay a money fine rather than work, meaning that the work may not be finished. Some systems link the annual canal cleaning to sacred duty, as in the Andes (Guillet 1992) or in Bali (Lansing 1991), and/or make a party out of the affair, with a feast and alcohol as a bonus at the end. A major problem for the leaders of the system is to motivate labor for maintenance.

The task of allocating the water to the farmers, and operating the gates and canals so that the water arrives in sufficient quantity and on the right timetable does not require much in the way of labor or materials. However, it is a delicate task, and frustration on the part of farmers may well turn into violence. Nature usually provides either too little water, or too much water, both of which pose serious problems for farmers, and for the operators of the system.

A good manager of allocation has to know the system very well, understand the needs of the farmers and of the system itself, and balance all the conflicting pressures. A successful manager must be calm, flexible, honest, willing to listen, knowledgeable, and have excellent judgment. The manager must also earn the respect of large numbers of farmers. There must be incentives to do the job, and they only sometimes include increased wealth. In farmer-managed systems these ditch riders/managers are only sometimes among the wealthier and more powerful in the local stratification system, but in centralized systems the occupants of these roles often have significant opportunities to convert public assets into private benefits.

Conflict is potentially present in every unified irrigation system. There appear to be substantially different amounts of theft and non-performance of duties in different irrigation systems, although no one has succeeded in discovering how to measure these differences. One likely hypothesis is that this difference might be the product of quality of distribution of water.

Theft, fines, disputes over water rights, peculation, and so on are handled at the irrigation system level first. The most famous and exclusive conflict- resolution procedures occur in Valencia, Spain, where the water court meets at the north door of the Cathedral every Thursday morning at 10:00 to adjudicate conflicts within the system. There is no appeal from this court to any other court, which makes Valencia unique (Glick 1970). Where the state exists and is effective in rural justice, interpersonal violence over irrigation matters automatically involves the justice system of the state.

For most of the twentieth century the social science literature has distinguished between "centralized" and "traditional" irrigation systems (Wittfogel 1957; Millon 1962). More recently the distinction has been phrased as that between agency-managed and farmer-managed systems (Coward 1980). For most scholars the crucial fact in these distinctions is the location of the source of authority over the roles performing the tasks necessary for running the system. Several sources can be distinguished: the national government, provincial government, local government, participating farmers, a single owner of the system, or no source of authority at all. National and provincial sources of authority represent centralized authority. Farmer-managed or traditional systems are those run by local government or the farmers themselves.

For decades anthropologists have focused on the difference between "large" and "small" systems. "Large" systems have been held to require centralized authority, to be complex, and to be technically demanding. "Small" ones, on the other hand, are thought to be managed by the farmers, or by "traditional" means, are simple, and are not technically demanding.

There are several conceivable ways of defining the size of a system, and probably the most effective and easiest way is to measure the area of the fields that receive water from the source conveyance system. There is information on systems that vary from a few hectares to more than 700,000 hectares.

An empirical study of the relationship of size and structure of authority has shown that (1) there are "small" systems (700 ha) with centralized authority, (2) there are "large" systems (458,000 ha) run by farmers, and (3) that in between these two extremes there is as yet no basis for predicting whether the system will have a centralized or a farmer-based authority structure (Hunt 1988). In consequence the old general rule about size and centralized authority must be rejected.

EXTERNAL EFFECTS

Scholarship on the external effects of irrigation systems inevitably invokes the name of Karl Wittfogel, author of *Oriental Despotism* (1957). According to Wittfogel, the control over construction leads to control over most of the rest of society, or "oriental despotism." Wittfogel's argument was based on the fact that the construction of large systems is very demanding of resources, and of control over resources. Wittfogel is thought to have presented an irrigation hypothesis. In fact, Wittfogel was writing about hydraulic matters, which included productive works such as irrigation, but wherein protective works, such as flood-control systems, were far more important. Most scholars have ignored both the size criterion of "oriental despotism," and the hydraulic rather than irrigation foundation of the argument.

Investigating what difference an irrigation system makes in social, economic, or environmental terms is surprisingly difficult. Comparing irrigated areas with unirrigated ones almost always involves a major difference in natural resource endowment as well. Disentangling the sources of variance is therefore extremely difficult. We are reduced to imagining what a given valley would support without irrigation. While not impossible, it is very hard to generate knowledge with this research design.

The economic effects of irrigation include increased production of food and fiber, increased productivity of both land and labor, and therefore an increase in agricultural surplus. Agricultural surplus is the amount of agricultural product which is greater than the consumption of the agricultural sector. The increased production is a consequence of moving, or removing, the constraint of water supply on agricultural production. The greater primary productivity results in increased labor and land productivity.

There are social effects of irrigation resulting from increased production. The effects include a larger population, and an increase in the division of labor in society. Childe (1950) held that the surplus of irrigation was important in the invention of the state. There are claims for organizational implications of irrigation systems as well, (Wittfogel 1957) but there is good reason to be skeptical of the law-like basis for such observation.

Irrigation is strongly, but not perfectly, correlated with the existence of cities. The surplus production effect is stronger where the rainfall is lower. Irrigation is not strongly associated with stratification. There are a number of non-state societies with irrigation that are not stratified and a number of communities with irrigation within states where there is minimal stratification within the community. As pointed out above there is, within a broad range of size, no correlation between size and structure of authority.

The question of the association between irrigation and the evolution of the state is widely regarded as settled. Irrigation did not cause the state, and the most that can be said now is that irrigation, and state institutions, often co-evolved (Service 1975). It is probable that the surplus function was more important than the labor function.

There are environmental consequences of irrigation systems. The banks of major rivers are primary productivity zones. With irrigation one is extending the water regime over a much wider zone, thereby changing the topography, and the plant and animal communities. The human population is much larger, and the habitat for other plants and animals is often changed radically. The habitat for some microorganisms relevant for humans is expanded. Malaria, schistosomiasis, and other water-related diseases have opportunities for major expansion. The habitat for some small animals (rats, squirrels, monkeys, birds—those living in and around the vegetation on the banks of canals) may expand, and they are in competition with man for man's food crops. Finally, the habitat for large animals (elephant, deer, pig, hippo, etc.) is probably expanded, due to greater primary productivity, but humans attempt to prevent them from living in the zone. With herds of wild elephant there may not be much to be done. But humans do a great deal to discourage tigers, lions, and ungulates from using the irrigated zone. Humans vastly prefer to be the only macro-predator, and to limit large animals to the domesticated ones.

There is also the issue of environmental degradation. There are some who hold that any irrigation system produces environmental degradation (Reisner 1986). Many of these systems are formed by draining wetlands. It is certainly the case that irrigation systems are a change in the environment. It is not so clear that all such changes can reasonably be called degradation.

The most often noted degradational changes are salinization and waterlogging. The physics is well established and well understood. Irrigation can cause the water table to rise, waterlogging the root zone. When it gets close enough to the surface, water will rise by capillary action and evaporate, leaving behind the salts, now no longer in solution. The salt inhibits plant growth, thereby promoting soil degradation.

The existence of such salinated zones is by no means as well established. The Aswan High Dam is reputed to have produced such salination in the Nile Valley. There is no evidence for such salination on the old agricultural lands in the Nile Valley (Hunt 1987). The Imperial Valley in California is also supposedly a major site of salination, but research conducted by Hunt in 1992 found less than 0.001 percent of the land surface to be salinated. The Indus Basin in India and Pakistan, and the zone around the Aral Sea, are reportedly seriously degraded due to waterlogging and salinity.

The solution to the salination problem, discovered early on, is drainage. Drainage systems (in parallel with the water delivery system) lower the water table, thereby preventing the capillary rise of water and salt accumulation due to evaporation. The large areas of serious salination in the world are a consequence of irrigation without adequate drainage.

WHAT WE DO NOT KNOW

A great deal is known about the physics and the sociology of irrigation. There are some topics that have received very little attention, producing clear gaps in our knowledge.

Local or folk knowledge of irrigated agriculture (soils, moisture stress, hydraulics, environmental effects) is virtually totally uninvestigated. Those who have done fieldwork in irrigation systems (cultural anthropologists, geographers, rural sociologists) are convinced that the irrigators are highly skilled, and in effect know a great deal about the systems they are operating. However, systematic and detailed attempts have not been made to describe the structure of local knowledge, how it is transmitted, how it varies from one person to another, or how it relates to the actions that must be taken to operate an irrigation system.

The local belief system would also include much of what we call religion (temples, priests, rituals, cosmology, congregations, etc.). There has been very little attention paid to the relationship between religion and the organization and operation of irrigation systems, with the exception of Bali. On the island of Bali there are Hindu kingdoms and temple territories. Lansing (1991) indicates that the priests of the major temples are deeply involved in both construction and operation of irrigation systems, particularly with inter-system regulations.

Most who write about irrigation systems refer to water rights. There are a few studies of national water codes, and there is extensive literature in jurisprudence concerning conflict over water rights, at least as seen through the lens of litigation and legislation. However, there are virtually no local studies of water rights. The connection (if any) between the national and legal concepts, and local practice, is unknown.

Most social scientists who study irrigation systems have a sense that some systems are run more effectively than others. It has been very difficult to be explicit and precise about quality of management. As a consequence it has been impossible to empirically study the relationship of quality to other features, such as structure of authority, design of the physical system, crop discipline, and so forth.

Wittfogel's "oriental despotism" was based on a hydraulic, not an irrigation, hypothesis. If irrigation is the management of water shortage, the other side is management of water surplus (drainage, flood control). Students of irrigation have almost totally neglected flooding and how humans have engineered the environment to cope with it. Irrigation and flood control very often go hand in hand, and in many river valleys both must be present if the agricultural system is to reliably produce a surplus.

DISTRIBUTION IN TIME AND SPACE

The distribution of irrigation systems in time and space is not very clearly known. The invention of irrigation cannot have been very difficult. The relationship between soil moisture and plant wilting is extremely obvious, and closely connected in time. The delay in the plant response to soil dryness is very rapid (a matter of a few days for small plants; trees are another matter).

Our knowledge of early irrigation systems is extremely fragmentary. Most of the attention has been focused on early states. Many have suspected a strong connection between irrigation and early civilizations, and there is good reason for doing so. Lower Mesopotamia, Egypt, and the Indus Valley civilizations all occupied the banks of large rivers in arid areas. There was not sufficient rainfall to grow the food and fiber necessary to provide for the population, and irrigated agriculture is not only the obvious solution, it is the only visible solution. For two hundred years, Western scholarship on irrigation has focused on early states, but there is no necessary connection between states and irrigation. States can arise without it and can perhaps even exist without it. The other side of the coin is that far simpler societies can have irrigation, and almost certainly had it long before the state crystallized. There is some evidence that irrigation existed in New Guinea at about 7,000 B.C.

It can be very difficult to find direct evidence for early irrigation systems. The high-potential environments tend to remain so over millennia. The earliest irrigation facilities are often used for a very long time, and if improved will simply be enlarged, often destroying early evidence. In any case, irrigation is very hard to date archaeologically. The activities of use and maintenance move a great deal of earth back and forth in a small space. The environment alternates between wet and dry, making preservation of organic datable materials quite unlikely. Because there is so much disturbance of the soil, stratigraphic dating using pottery is extremely problematic.

Some indirect dating is possible when there is excavation or good survey data on settlement pattern and food consumption. In some cases irrigation is demonstrably necessary to support other activities at the site, but there are other cases where irrigation is possible but not demonstrable. In short, irrigation is conceivably nearly as old as domesticated plants, but it is very hard to demonstrate. Most early states were profoundly involved with water management, usually with irrigation, and always with drinking water.

Our knowledge of the distribution of irrigation systems in space is somewhat less patchy. In the tropics and temperate zones, where there is an industrial economy there is almost certainly some irrigation. In the less-developed world irrigation is quite widely found, although not so often dependent upon industrial lifting technology. The distribution among non-state cultures is, according to the ethnographic record, not very wide-spread. Irrigation is very rare in Melanesia and sub-Saharan Africa and confined to the southwest of Native North America. It is often found where taro and volcanic islands coincide in Polynesia and Micronesia but not elsewhere and it is rare in insular Southeast Asia. It is widely found where states have existed for millennia (the Andes and the West coast of South America, highland Mesoamerica, Eastern Asia, peninsular and insular Southeast Asia, South Asia, Southwest Asia, North Africa, and the north shore of the Mediterranean).

Our knowledge of spatial distribution is constrained by three biases prominent in fieldwork by cultural anthropologists. First, most are natives of relatively urban and non-arid cultures of origin. They tend not to be alert to water-related issues at home, and this opacity extends to fieldwork. Second, most fieldworkers have spent most of their time within or close to a settlement where relatively few irrigation systems are located. Third, for many decades anthropologists have wanted to do fieldwork among the most "indigenous" or "unacculturated" populations available, which has meant going up into the hills, rather than working down in the valleys where irrigation is far more likely to occur. These three conditions combine to generate ethnographies and field reports that are silent on irrigation. In many cases irrigation is not present. But there are some cases where irrigation is demonstrably present, and ignored in the monograph.

It is safe to say that there is no contemporary nation in the tropics or the or temperate zones that is without significant irrigation activity. Irrigation systems are widely found, and are of substantial importance to the economic and social dimensions of life for the majority of humans now alive. The more arid the climate the more important irrigation is. Every nation reports total irrigated area, and has done so for over thirty years. What is not reported are numbers and sizes of irrigation systems. There are probably more than three million, but we have substantial information on less than one hundred of them in the anthropological literature.

ROBERT C. HUNT

CHILDE, VERE GORDON. "The Urban Revolution." *Town Planning Review* 21 (1950): 3–17.

COWARD, E. WALTER, JR. *Irrigation and Agricultural Development in Asia.* Ithaca, NY: Cornell University Press, 1980.

GLICK, THOMAS. *Irrigation and Society in Medieval Valencia.* Cambridge: Harvard University Press, 1970.

GUILLET, DAVID. *Covering Ground: Communal Water Management and the State in the Peruvian Highlands.* Ann Arbor, MI: University of Michigan Press, 1992.

HUNT, ROBERT C. "Agricultural Ecology: The Impact of the Aswan High Dam Reconsidered." *Culture and Agriculture* 31 (1987): 1–6.

———. "Size and the Structure of Authority in Canal Irrigation Systems." *Journal of Anthropological Research* 44 (1988): 335–355.

LANSING, STEPHEN. *Priests and Programmers: Technologies of Power in the Engineered Landscape of Bali.* Princeton: Princeton University Press, 1991.

MILLON, RENÈ. "Variations in Social Responses to the Practice of Irrigated Agriculture." In *Civilization in Arid Lands,* edited by R. Woodbury. University of Utah Anthropological Papers, #62, 1962.

REISNER, MARC. *Cadillac Desert: The American West and its Disappearing Water.* New York: Penguin Books, 1986.

SERVICE, ELMAN R. *Origins of the State and Civilization: The Process of Cultural Evolution.* New York: W.W. Norton, 1975.

WITTFOGEL, KARL. *Oriental Despotism.* New Haven: Yale University Press, 1957.

J

JUDICIAL PROCESS

Judicial process is a concept that has been used in anthropology with a striking lack of precision and uniformity. Given its long history in Western legal theory and sociology, it is best approached by first taking up its common meaning in those fields. Judicial process, sharply distinguished from either the legislative or the administrative process, is used by lawyers and sociologists to denote the resolution of a case (or dispute) through a determination of the facts at issue and the application to those facts of the relevant laws and precedent by an adjudicator. Judicial process in this sense also encompasses the operation of civil law, which does not necessarily involve a conflict or a breach. Supreme Court Justices Oliver Wendell Holmes and Benjamin Cardozo both defined law in terms of the judicial process; in their view, law itself is to be found in the working of the judicial process.

In the context of societies with an established jurisprudence and centralized court systems, judicial process is located in the operation of those court systems within an accepted jurisprudential framework. Broadly speaking, and with much procedural variance, judicial process as an ideal type is found wherever an adjudicator reaches a binding decision after all parties to the dispute have been heard, the evidence has been presented and the facts determined, and relevant precedent considered.

Historically, many, if not all, non-Western state-organized societies also had centralized court systems with an established jurisprudence; judicial process, as commonly understood in Western law and sociology, reasonably can be used to describe the operations and processes found in, for example, Islamic and traditional Chinese court systems. Moreover, each of the postcolonial nation-states has some form of judicial process in this strict sense.

Thus, the object of the strictly defined judicial process is necessarily judicial decision-making. One critical perspective views judicial decision-making as rationalization, or justification, for decisions reached, rather than a clear deduction from the actual facts and precedent at issue. As a consequence, the actual decision can never be approached analytically—only its justification. In this view, judicial process is purely discourse about decisions. A related and classic debate is that of rules versus principles; some theorists posit the existence of rules and of law as a body of rules; others believe that there are no absolute rules and that law is best seen as discourse; for example, there is no absolute rule about property, merely a way of talking about property. The critical legal studies movement should also be noted. Simply put, the movement takes the view that there is no law beyond politics and ideology; in opposition are those who hold that there is a realm of legal principles existing beyond the reach of ideology. These arguments are important in any discussion of judicial process because they all, in some way, call into question the common use of the term in Western jurisprudence and sociology.

The term "judicial process" is also widely used in anthropology (Gluckman 1955; Epstein 1973; Moore 1979), but its use and its meaning are much more difficult to pin down. We bear in mind but attempt to move beyond the endless disputes in anthropology over the definitions of law, custom, and norm; over whether "primitive" law is even "law"; and over the very use of Western jurisprudential terms to describe that which occurs in stateless societies.

Anthropologists seeking to use the concept of judicial process for comparative purposes face a number of choices, foremost among them the necessity of deciding whether and how much to broaden the definition. If judicial process is narrowly defined in Western jurisprudential terms, its utility for cross-cultural comparison will be restricted to that universe of societies that have courts, but within that universe it can produce crisp and highly focused generalizations. On the other hand, the ethnographic record is replete with societies that clearly have no judicial process that falls within the scope of this narrow definition. A looser definition can bring many of those societies within the comparative frame, but at the cost of an increasing imprecision.

If judicial process is taken to be located at the intersection of some obligatory norm, custom, or social relationship and the process used to determine its breach or the consequences of its breach, then the concept may have broad analytic usefulness. There are, however, many other threshold questions that must be considered. Does judicial process require a court, an adjudicative process, and an adjudicator with the power of enforceability? Many small groups process disputes through something more closely resembling, in Western terms, arbitration and/or mediation, and the decisions reached are not always necessarily binding on the parties. Is it useful to speak of a judicial process in the absence of a court? Processing of disputes in "courtless" societies may be directed more to the maintenance of order and social harmony than to the enforcement of rules. Sanctions may involve political or supernatural agents. Are there in fact structural similarities between the judicial process, if broadly defined, of small groups and that of state-organized societies? Last, it is arguable whether in small noncentralized groups one can speak at all of judicial process (however broadly defined) without considering social life as a whole. Judicial process, here, is not to be found in a narrow context.

Nevertheless, there is a vast body of ethnographic literature, some of it of very high quality, that does reference judicial process. Particularly influential in anthropology are the writings of Max Gluckman (1955) on the law of the Barotse in Africa. Simply put, Gluckman took the position that the judicial process in Barotse courts was similar to that found in Western courts and that most forensic institutions are based on the same general principles. He defined the judicial process as "the specification of general concepts, with moral implications, in order to apply them to specific circumstances so as to defend established and emergent values of rightdoing." Judicial process in this sense has comparative utility, as Gluckman himself forcefully pointed out.

The use of this concept in anthropology has been accompanied by much controversy, in large part because of the failure to distinguish strict and loose usages of the term. One such example is the long-running dispute over whether Gluckman's hypothesis of the "reasonable man" can be applied with analytic usefulness cross-culturally. Briefly, and in Gluckman's (1963) words, the reasonable man "was the means by which the judges applied the fixed rules of general law and morality to the varied circumstances of Barotse life." The reasonable man is, of course, a central concept of Western jurisprudence. Within anthropology, Gluckman's notion that the reasonable man is a central concept in a universally posited judicial process remains a center of controversy.

More recently, interpretive anthropologists have argued that without a full understanding and explication of the culture from which it arose and of which it is a part, there can be no useful analysis or understanding of any society's judicial process. In this view, there is no such construct as the reasonable man in the absence of culture. Judicial reasoning, so central to the judicial process, here is seen as arising out of and informed by culture. The judicial process and culture are inextricably fused and neither can be analyzed or understood in the absence of the other. This approach to the judicial process, exemplified by Clifford Geertz (1983), may have less immediate comparative value but allows a much richer description and deeper understanding.

A related issue, and one that remains ripe for further research, involves the self-conscious attempts to bring custom into the judicial process in colonial and postcolonial regimes. These attempts necessarily involve "finding" custom in the tangled skeins of indigenous, colonial, and postcolonial legal systems. In addition, because one dimension in which societies differ is the degree of self-consciousness with which they view their own norms, a degree that changes over time, this process of "finding" custom tends to involve, among many other things, a theory of judicial process that may or may not be appropriate.

The question of whether there are in fact general principles to be found in the judicial process cross-culturally, notwithstanding variations in social and political organization, remains a potent issue in anthropology. The question also remains of whether judicial process as commonly understood in Western jurisprudence can in fact be usefully applied cross-culturally. The definition and use of the concept of judicial process within anthropology remains unsettled.

PETER WESTON BLACK
BARBARA WEBSTER BLACK

See also: Conflict Resolution; Legal Anthropology

EPSTEIN, A. L. "The Reasonable Man Revisited: Some Problems in the Anthropology of Law." *Law and Society Review* 7 (1973): 643–666.

FORTES, MEYER. "Towards the Judicial Process: A Tallensi Case." *Social Analysis* 22 (1967): 132–146.

GEERTZ, CLIFFORD. "Local Knowledge: Fact and Law in Comparative Perspective." In *Local Knowledge: Further Essays in Interpretive Anthropology*. New York: Basic Books, 1983.

GLUCKMAN, MAX. *The Judicial Process Among the Barotse of Northern Rhodesia*. Manchester: Manchester University Press, 1955.

———. *Order and Rebellion in Tribal Africa*. New York: Free Press, 1963.

LOH, WALLACE D. *Social Research in the Judicial Process*. New York: Russell Sage Foundation, 1984.

MOORE, SALLY FALK. "Archaic Law and Modern Times on the Zambezi: Some Thoughts on Max Gluckman's Interpretation of Barotse Law." *International Journal of the Sociology of Law* 7 (1979): 3–30.

ROSEN, LAWRENCE. *The Anthropology of Justice: Law as Culture in Islamic Society*. Cambridge: Cambridge University Press, 1989.

K

KIN GROUPS, RESIDENCE, AND DESCENT

The overwhelming bulk of human history and evolution has taken place in small scale band and tribal societies. Kin groups, marital residence, and descent reckoning is the way people in small scale societies are grouped together and organized. In modern industrial societies the use of kin groups as the primary mode of social organizaiton has given way to organizations based on geographical propinquity or special interests, for example, political wards, corporations, labor unions, and professional associations—what anthropologists call sodalities or voluntary organizaitons. But even in industrial society the nuclear family and, to a lesser extent, the extended family is important. In pre-industrial society kinship was paramount. People were either relatives by blood or marriage, or they were strangers which usually meant enemies.

Choice of residence by a newly married couple is important in understanding the kinship organization of a society, because the sum of these choices creates local groups composed of different aggregations of kin. In about 95 percent of the world's societies, couples choose to live with or near relatives rather than nonrelatives. In addition, in the vast majority of instances, couples prefer to reside with close kin rather than distant kin. Descent refers to criteria that are relevant within a society for establishing special groups or categories of kinsmen. Kinship organization is always an important component of social organization in societies.

The most common form of postmarital residence in cultures is unilocal residence. In matrilocal societies the married couple takes up residence with relatives of the wife, while in patrilocal ones couples reside with relatives of the husband. Similarly, the most common form of descent ideology in cultures is unilineal. When descent group recruitment is unilineal, only kinship links traced through a single sex are utilized to determine membership. Patrilineal groups, for example, occur in about 50 percent of the world's societies and membership is traced exclusively through male kin links. Included are the immediate offspring of one's father, one's father's brother, one's father's brother's son, one's father's father, and so forth. In addition to males, females in patrilineal societies are members of their father's group and usually remain so after marriage. In a few instances, however, inclusion of females in their natal group is terminated at marriage and they acquire rights of membership in their husband's group. In other instances, female rights in their father's group become attenuated and they acquire limited rights of membership in their husband's group.

Approximately 14 percent of societies in the ethnographic record possess matrilineal descent, where membership is traced exclusively through female kinship links, with children belonging to their mother's group. Both patrilineal and matrilineal groups exist in about 3 percent of societies. In these cultures individuals belong to both their mother's and their father's group. When both types of groups exist in a society they typically have different functions.

A few cultures possess very unusual descent principles. For example, in several societies sons belong to their father's descent group while daughters belong to their mother's group or, vice versa, sons belong to their mother's group and daughters to their father's. In at least two cultures, odd-numbered children (first born, third born, and so on) belong to their mother's group while even-numbered children belong to their father's group.

MAIN SEQUENCE KINSHIP THEORY

Differential subsistence contribution has been linked to the development of unilocal residence. It is thought that if males contribute predominantly to the food supply of a society they will be in patrilocal residence, with closely related males living near each other. The wives of these men will be recruited from outside neighborhoods or communities. Similarly, if females contribute predominantly to subsistence, they will be in matrilocal residence and their husbands will move to join them after marriage. Unilocal residence, in turn, is thought to influence the presence of unilineal descent groups, patrilocality leading to the formation of patrilineal groups and matrilocality to matrilineal groups. Unilocal residence and unilineal descent will then influence the semantic patterns found in the kin terminology systems of societies.

Interestingly, the proposed relationship between matridominant and patridominant contribution to subsistence and residential localization does not hold for worldwide samples. In food collecting societies, however, a modest association exists between subsistence contribution and unilocal residence. For example, in plant-gathering societies this primarily female activity is associated with matrilocal residence. Similarly, in societies in which fishing, a primarily male activity, is especially important, residence tends to be patrilocal. When hunting is especially important, however, this primarily male activity does not lead to patrilocality as expected; instead, there is actually a weak tendency toward matrilocality. This suggests that the modest association between subsistence contribution and unilocal residence in food-collecting societies is not a meaningful one. It appears that warfare factors are the operative ones and subsistence contribution in foraging societies is only secondarily associated with these conflict variables.

The remainder of the sequence claims that unilocally aggregated kin will coalesce into unilineal descent groups and that both residential proximity and descent group participation will be reflected in the semantic lumping and splitting characteristic of a society's kin categorization system. Numerous kin terminology practices, however, are not related to residential proximity and kin group participation in the predicted way. In addition, the mere aggregation of certain kin does not directly cause the formation of unilineal descent groups in a society. Hence, unilocal residence is only a necessary but not a sufficient condition for the development of unilineal kin groups. For example, societies may practice unilocal residence for as long as one thousand years without developing unilineal descent groups.

Unilocal residence rules, unilineal descent group recruitment rules, and certain kin classification and naming practices are indeed related, but underlying factors such as residential proximity and kin group participation play, at most, a very restricted role in determining these relationships. Instead, the presence of warfare seems to be instrumental in the formation of descent groups in a society, and this variable also plays an important role in determining patterns of residential localization. Unilocal residence, while not directly causing descent group formation, strongly influences the form of recruitment rule adopted if descent groups do arise: patrilocality leading to a patrilineal rule and matrilocality to a matrilineal one. Symbolic features of kinship organization such as residence rules and descent group recruitment rules are in turn related in very limited ways to certain semantic patterns found in kin terminology systems.

POSTMARITAL RESIDENCE

Unilocal residence is extremely common cross-culturally, with approximately 70 percent of societies practicing patrilocality and 12 percent practicing matrilocality, but there are other forms of residence. For example, in about 1 percent of cultures husbands and wives live separately and do not establish a common household; this is called duolocal residence. Another residence practice is neolocal, which occurs in about 5 percent of the world's cultures. This pattern is common in large-scale societies that de-emphasize kin relationships and where market exchange is present. With neolocal residence married couples typically live apart from relatives of both the husband and the wife. Another pattern found in about 7 percent of the world's cultures is bilocal. Between one-third and two-thirds of couples reside with the wife's relatives in bilocal societies and the remainder with the husband's. Couples with this residence practice locate their household according to the opportunities and advantages presented by residing with relatives of one spouse or the other. Another residence form is avunculocal, which is found in about 5 percent of the world's cultures. This unilocal residence practice occurs only in matrilineal societies and involves a couple taking up residence with the husband's mother's brother, which brings into residential proximity the closely related male members of a matrilineal descent group.

Other types of residential choice exist besides bilocality. For example, about 1 percent of societies allow a choice between matrilocal and avunculocal residence. In addition, about the same number allow a choice between avunculocal and patrilocal residence. Other patterns involve a few couples living matrilocally in patrilocal societies, or the reverse, a few living patrilocally in matrilocal societies. In addition, in neolocal societies a few couples may be living unilocally, and, similarly, in unilocal societies a few may be living neolocally. A different type of variation can occur during the early years of marriage. It is not uncommon in patrilocal societies for the first few years of marriage to be spent in matrilocal residence. Another type of residential switch can occur in bilocal societies. Couples sometimes change from residence with one spouse's relatives to residence with the other's.

DESCENT GROUPS

While unilineal principles of descent are found in almost two-thirds of the world's cultures, other descent principles and corresponding types of groups and social categories occur. For example, some societies have nonunilineal descent groups. These groups do not emphasize kinship links traced exclusively through a single sex and membership is not assigned at birth. An individual is usually eligible for membership in more than one nonunilineal group. Choice of membership will depend on the opportunities and advantages associated with belonging to one group or another. In societies with unilineal or nonunilineal descent principles, certain groups of relatives are considered especially important and are singled out for special treatment. In cultures with bilateral descent principles, but no descent groups, individuals acknowledge both mother's and father's relatives more or less equally. These bilaterally related relatives comprise an individual's personal kindred.

While all societies have descent principles not all societies have descent groups. Even when descent groups exist, they may be strong corporate groups with important political, legal, economic, and ritual-religious functions or very weak groups with few functions. Hence, the intracultural importance of these groups varies greatly across cultures. Descent groups almost always require marriage outside the group, implying that husbands and wives in most societies come from different groups. These intergroup marriages are important in forming alliances of various sorts between descent groups.

Sometimes descent groups are based on demonstrable kinship links that trace through specified ancestors to one in the past. These are usually called "lineages." Descent groups are also based on nondemonstrable descent from a presumed common ancestor. Sometimes this is an animal or a place. Presumed common ancestor groups are usually called "clans" or in the older literature "sibs." Groups based on demonstrated, as opposed to presumed, common ancestry, are more common in societies of medium scale than in small-scale ones. Descent groups are typically arranged into a hierarchy of units of greater or lesser inclusiveness. For example, several small descent groups may be included in a larger, more inclusive group. This larger descent group may, in turn, be linked with others into a yet larger group. Maximal descent groups are the largest ones in a culture not themselves encompassed in a more inclusive group and are usually based on presumptive common ancestry. They range in size from about 100 members in very small-scale societies to several tens of thousands of members in very populous ones. Sometimes an entire culture is divided into two maximal descent groups. This type of dual organization is characteristic of unilineal societies with small populations. Unilineal cultures with medium to large populations tend to be divided into more than two maximal descent groups.

DETERMINANTS OF POSTMARITAL RESIDENCE

Patrilocal residence is the norm in more than 70 percent of all societies, except for very large-scale ones that have predominantly neolocal residence. Similarly, patrilineal descent groups are found in about half of the world's cultures. Groups of residentially aggregated and very closely related males tend to form fraternal interest groups that are very effective in intrasocietal conflict situations. Fighting within a community and between separate communities belonging to the same cultural unit is endemic in patrilocal societies. Thus, where internal conflict is common, societies find it advantageous to aggregate groups of closely related males. Alternatively stated, by residentially aggregating closely related males, fraternal interest groups are created and these groups often engage in intrasocietal conflict. Internal conflict can cause a community to fission and split and separate communities within a single culture to move apart, ensuring that a population is spread more or less evenly over a given geographic area.

Most small- and medium-scale societies studied by anthropologists have been pacified by colonial regimes or by incorporation into large-scale cultures, giving a misleading impression of peacefulness and docility. In addition, as societies increase in size, warfare and feuding are controlled to an increasing extent by centralized political elites and are less a function of fraternal interest groups. The actual activities involved in warfare in nonstate societies might sometimes be better described as skirmishing, raiding, and ambushing. These activities are not, however, inconsequential. The overall mortality rate of these conflict practices can be quite high, often higher than for modern warfare.

Matrilocal residence acts in several ways to lessen the quarrelsome tendencies found in patrilocal societies. Internal conflict, for example, is almost nonexistent. Instead, if matrilocal societies fight, they engage in external warfare with different cultural units. Matrilocal societies also tend to be either recent migrants to the area they occupy or to be neighbors of recent migrants. In addition, they are usually relatively small in terms of total population size. Migration of societies into a new region can put great pressure on the local resource base, resulting in severe intercultural competition which may lead to external warfare. This form of warfare is particularly harsh, because peacemaking mechanisms are weaker and less prevalent compared to those for internal warfare. In short, migrating societies tend to engage in external warfare where peacemaking mechanisms are weak, which is all the more threatening because they tend to have relatively small populations. As a result, these cultures find it advantageous to avoid the extra rigors of feuding and internal warfare. How does matrilocality help them to achieve this goal?

In taking up matrilocal residence, a husband may move to his wife's community. In addition, his brothers may move to their wives' communities. The result of this moving is that closely related males are geographically dispersed, and it is difficult for them to operate as solidary units and to pursue quarrels with other such units within their cultural group. Matrilocal residence, then, can break up fraternal interest groups and, thus, defuse intrasocietal quarrels.

This dispersal does not always occur, however, as many matrilocal marriages are contracted between men and women from the same community; thus, closely related males are not always geographically separated as implied above. Matrilocal communities tend to practice intracommunity marriage when they have matrilineal descent groups or other institutions that involve matrilineal succession to authority. Since formal decision-making positions in a society are in most instances occupied by males, if they move to another community after marriage they are not readily available to make or carry out the decisions of their kin groups.

If closely related males are not always located in separate communities, how does matrilocal residence in these cultures serve to discourage feuding and internal warfare? Although males are not usually physically dispersed in societies with matrilineal descent groups, their interests are. A man's interests in his own descent group are somewhat muted because his sister's sons will inherit the material resources and leadership positions in this group. As a corollary, his sons will inherit resources and assume leadership positions in his wife's descent group. Through his children a man acquires a sort of derivative interest in his wife's group. Similarly, his brothers acquire derivative interests in the descent groups of their wives. This disperses the loyalties of closely related and potentially solidary males.

Matrilocal residence, therefore, either geographically scatters closely related males or disperses their interests and in this way weakens the solidarity of fraternal interest groups. This serves to dampen internal warfare and feuding tendencies. A secondary consequence is the likely creation of a larger group of solidary males. Such males are solidary to the extent that they have cross-cutting loyalties and interests that promote cooperation beyond their individual descent groups. Matrilocal residence thus decreases feuding and internal warfare tendencies within societies and increases overall male solidarity in the face of external threats.

Average house size in terms of floor space is at least twice as large in matrilocal societies than in patrilocal societies. Large average house size, in turn, enables more families to live together, often bringing males who are not closely related into intimate association with each other. This close contact can serve to create countervailing interests on the part of these males in each other's descent groups. In short, living in intimate association with males from other descent groups may serve to decrease tendencies for intra-societal quarrels to break out between members of different descent groups.

In summary, matrilocal residence and associated matribased arrangements, such as matrilineal descent groups and matrilateral extended households, are found where there is severe competition for resources due to migration, where external but not internal war exists, and where the population size of societies is relatively small. Patrilocal societies, on the other hand, tend to have high rates of feuding and internal warfare. In addition, they also tend to engage in external warfare, which may serve a boundary maintenance and spacing function between neighboring cultures. Patrilocal societies, therefore, tend to engage in both internal and external conflict, while matrilocal cultures engage in only external warfare. In short, both types of societies fight externally, while only patrilocal cultures regularly fight internally.

Matrilocal societies, by dampening intracultural conflict and creating pan-societal groupings of cooperative males can usually hold their own in competition with patrilocal cultures. As levels of sociocultural integration increase, the importance of residence and descent practices and associated warfare activities decreases, and the importance of more formal political and bureaucratic organization increases.

An additional correlate of patrilocality is polygyny, or the concurrent marriage of one man to two or more women. Polygyny is common cross-culturally, occurring in more than three-fourths of societies in the ethnographic record. The number of men polygynously married, however, varies greatly. In some of these cultures a majority of married men have more than one wife, while in others only a few do. A strongly polygynous marriage system requires mechanisms such as warfare for creating a surplus of marriageable females. By disproportionately killing adult males, warfare produces an excess of marriageable females. A more important cultural mechanism that can greatly multiply the number of marriageable females is the practice of delaying the marriage of men while encouraging women to marry at an early age. This practice can as much as double the number of females of marriageable age and is very common in polygynous societies.

Polygynous marriage is difficult in matrilocal cultures, because a man can reside with only one set of matrikin at a time. This limits his choice of a second wife to close relatives of his first wife who are residing nearby, typically her sisters or matrilateral parallel cousins (i.e., mother's sister's daughters). Co-wives who are sisters or cousins occupy a single dwelling in more than 90 percent of cultures. When co-wives are unrelated they live together in the same house in only about 36 percent of cultures. Because co-wives are sisters or cousins more commonly in matrilocal than patrilocal societies, this feature also contributes to the large house size that characterizes these cultures. Occasionally a man will alternate his residence, living for a time with one wife and her kin, then switching to residence with a second wife and a different set of matrikin. This practice, however, is rare, and polygyny is uncommon in matrilocal societies, occurring in less than 20 percent of them.

Approximately 80 percent of patrilocal cultures are associated with polygyny, at least in part, because their residence practices are compatible with this custom. Polygyny in turn tends to cause early marriage for females and delayed marriage for males, with the result that young adult males in these societies are seldom married and consequently have few family and domestic responsibilities. Therefore, they are readily available to serve as warriors and to contribute to the feuding and internal warfare that characterizes patrilocal cultures. Also, polygyny may contribute directly to an increase in the intensity of conflict in these societies because of quarrels over women. Hence, patrilocality, internal warfare, polygyny, and delayed marriage for males form a feedback network in which an increase in one variable reverberates through the system, causing an increase in the other variables. This produces two polar types of societies: one which is polygynous, patrilocal, and internally and externally quarrelsome; and another which is nonpolygynous, matrilocal, and peaceful internally but not externally.

About two-thirds of patrilocal societies possess patrilineal descent groups while fewer than half of matrilocal societies possess matrilineal descent groups. Avunculocal cultures, however, always possess matrilineal descent groups, which suggests that they develop from formerly matrilocal-matrilineal ones. Aggregation of closely related male matrilineal kinsmen in avunculocal residence may occur when the threat of external warfare decreases in formerly matrilocal societies. These matrilineally aggregated males will then tend to form fraternal interest groups and begin to war with other such groups within these societies and, indeed, feuding and internal conflict are common in these cultures. Alternatively, the development of internal war, itself, may encourage the development of avunculocal residence and the consequent formation of fraternal interest groups in formerly matrilocal-matrilineal societies.

When sister's sons reach adulthood in avunculocal societies, they move into residence with their mother's brother. This aggregates a core of matrilineally related males who are optimally located for making and carrying out the decisions of their kin groups. Since a wife joins her husband and his matrilineal male relatives after marriage, avunculocal residence is also compatible with polygyny and more than 50 percent of these cultures practice this marriage custom. Avunculocal societies thus tend to be intermediate in societal type, possessing some of the features characteristic of patrilocal societies and some characteristic of matrilocal ones.

Control over formal decision-making processes in societies by males may also help to explain the pervasiveness of patrilocality and associated patribased arrangements such as patrilineal descent groups cross-culturally. The fraternal interest groups that result from patrilocal residence may be more effective in intracommunity decision-making contexts in small- and medium-scale societies than are the somewhat less solidary groupings of males that result from avunculocal residence, while matrilocal residence seems especially designed to break up groups of closely related males by dispersing them geographically or by dispersing their interests and sentiments. Avunculocal males are somewhat less solidary than patrilocal males, because they do not live their entire lives in one residential group.

Bilocal residence occurs most often in societies that have suffered severe depopulation and disruption because of the introduction of epidemic diseases. Bilocality is also common in hunting and gathering bands where rainfall variability is great, a factor that can cause variability in the food supply. A variable food supply thus promotes residential variability in these foraging societies. In addition, bilocality is common in hunting and gathering bands when local group size is less than fifty. Small local group size in these cultures can produce a highly unbalanced sex ratio in the marriage age population because of chance factors of birth and death, which leads to bilocality in an attempt to preserve the existing size and distribution of local groups.

Bilocal residence may also serve to dampen internal warfare tendencies by geographically dispersing many closely related males. Indeed, at least in foraging societies, internal conflict is somewhat less common in bilocal cultures compared to patrilocal ones. Finally, bilocal societies are less frequently and less strongly polygynous compared to patrilocal societies, because many men are residing with their wives' relatives, making polygyny difficult. In short, bilocal societies are also intermediate in type between matrilocal and patrilocal cultures but in a different way than avunculocal societies.

RESIDENCE AND DESCENT IN TEMPORAL PERSPECTIVE

Unilocal residence, including avunculocality, is by far the most common type of residence pattern found in the world today. It occurs in almost 90 percent of the societies in the contemporary ethnographic record and may have been even more prevalent in the past. Since neolocality is found disproportionately in large-scale societies with commercial exchange, this residence pattern has become much more frequent in the last few thousand years. Bilocality is also associated with recent depopulation in societies exposed to new epidemic diseases through European expansion and colonialism. Thus, bilocality has increased in frequency over the last several hundred years. It follows that unilocal residence was even more frequent in the past than it is today. In the very distant past, however, before the domestication of plants and animals, when only food collecting bands existed, unilocal residence was probably slightly less frequent than it is today, because of the moderate tendency on the part of foraging societies to practice bilocality.

Unilineal descent groups occur in almost two-thirds of all societies today but only in about one-third of hunting and gathering cultures. Descent groups, therefore, are about twice as frequent in contemporary food-producing cultures compared to food-collecting ones. Because unilineal descent groups develop in societies with unilocal residence where warfare is also frequent, this suggests that warfare increased greatly following the domestication of plants and animals, which commenced about 11,000 years ago. Thus, the huge increase in world population that accompanied the agricultural revolution may have led to an increase in the frequency and intensity of warfare in food-producing societies. This increase in its turn may have led to a great increase in the formation of unilineal descent groups in these cultures.

The inference above assumes that contemporary food-collecting cultures are representative of those of the preagricultural past. Because the foraging societies of today differ in several ways from those of the remote past, this inference may not be valid. One difference is that contemporary foraging cultures often live adjacent to populous food producers. Foragers may adapt to the presence of strong food-producing neighbors by becoming more docile and less warlike, at least externally. Another difference is that the food-collecting cultures of today often occupy environments such as deserts and tundras, which are, at best, only marginally suitable for food production. These environments may also be marginal for food collectors, which would result in a very sparse population of foragers. Low population density, in turn, would tend to spread local foraging groups out so that they less often come into contact, decreasing the likelihood of conflict. In short, contemporary hunters and gatherers differ in several ways from those of the distant past and these differences may have dampened warfare tendencies among them, with the consequence that the formation of unilineal descent groups may be less frequent. Thus, rather than warfare increasing among food producers, it may have decreased in frequency and intensity among contemporary hunters and gatherers compared to those of the remote past.

The modern study of kinship, residence, and descent was begun by George P. Murdock (1949), although his comparative approach builds on the field data collected by earlier anthropologists (Murdock 1962-1971). Murdock's Main Sequence Kinship Theory formed the staring point of much of the later research. Much of the work on warfare and fraternal interest groups was done by Otterbein (1970) and Van Velzen and Van Wetering (1960). Much of the work on marital residence was done by Melvin and Carol Ember (1983), while the work on matrilocal and matrilineal societies was done by Divale (1984), Schegel (1972), and Kloos (1963).

The findings of systematic comparative research reviewed, although obtained relatively recently, address themselves to a set of questions concerning residence and descent posed some time ago. In the meantime, the attention of field anthropologists has shifted in several ways. One shift has been toward different questions involving kinship and social organization. These new problem areas offer many opportunities for systematic comparative research. Another shift has been toward more fine-grained and more processually oriented treatments of residence and descent. These newer treatments and descriptions point the way toward more sensitive and revealing comparative research.

STANLEY R. WITKOWSKI
WILLIAM T. DIVALE

BOHANNAN, PAUL, and JOHN MIDDLETON, eds. *Marriage, Family, and Residence.* Garden City, N.Y.: Natural History Press, 1968.

DIVALE, WILLIAM T. *Matrilocal Residence in Preliterate Society.* Studies in Cultural Anthropology No. 4. Ann Arbor, Mich.: UMI Research Press, 1984.

EMBER, MELVIN, and CAROL R. EMBER. *Marriage, Family, and Kinship: Comparative Studies of Social Organization.* New Haven, Conn.: HRAF Press, 1983.

GOODENOUGH, WARD H. *Description and Comparison in Cultural Anthropology.* Chicago: Aldine, 1970.

KLOOS, PETER. "Marital Residence and Local Endogamy: Environmental Knowledge or Leadership." *American Anthropologist* 65 (1963): 923–928.

LEVINSON, DAVID, and MARTIN J. MALONE. *Toward Explaining Human Culture.* New Haven, Conn.: HRAF Press, 1980.

MARSH, ROBERT M. *Comparative Sociology.* New York: Harcourt Brace, and World, 1967.

MURDOCK, GEORGE P. *Social Structure.* New York: Macmillan, 1949.

———. "Ethnographic Atlas." In *Ethnology.* Several installments 1962-1971.

OTTERBEIN, KEITH F. *The Evolution of War: A Cross-Cultural Study.* New Haven, Conn.: HRAF Press, 1970.

PASTERNAK, BURTON. *Introduction to Kinship and Social Organization.* Englewood Cliffs, N.J.: Prentice-Hall, 1976.

SCHLEGEL, ALICE. *Male Dominance and Female Autonomy.* New Haven, Conn.: HRAF Press, 1972.

TEFFT, STANTON K., and DOUGLAS REINHARDT. "Warfare Regulation: A Cross-Cultural Test of Hypotheses Among Tribal Peoples." *Behavior Science Research* 9 (1974): 151–172.

Van den Berghe, Pierre L. *Human Family Systems: An Evolutionary View.* New York: Elsevier, 1979.

Van Velzen, H. U. E. T., and W. Van Wetering. "Residence Power Groups and Intra-Societal Aggression." *International Archives of Ethnology* 49 (1960): 169–200.

Witkowski, Stanley R. "A Cross-Cultural Test of the Proximity Hypothesis." *Behavior Science Notes* 7 (1972): 243–263.

KIN RELATIONS

See: Alliance, Conflict, and Exogamy; Feuding; Kin Groups, Residence, and Descent

KIN SELECTION

Natural selection describes the statistical outcome of competition between alternatives. Charles Darwin (1859) argued that traits vary within populations and that variants aiding reproduction will, by virtue of being passed on more frequently, characterize a larger proportion of individuals in successive generations. In this way any variant yielding reproductive advantages will spread through a population over time. This suggests that organisms will come to exhibit traits that are fundamentally self-serving. Any trait that aided an individual's reproduction would spread, regardless of its impact on the individual's neighbors.

This self-serving view of organisms, however, is oversimplified. While organisms do exhibit traits that aid their own reproduction, they also sometimes exhibit traits that augment the reproduction of others while diminishing their own. If such altruistic traits are happenstance, there is nothing to be explained. If they are not, the critical question arises of how the evolutionary process can explain the existence of such traits. Altruistic traits can be considered the proverbial double-edged sword in evolutionary terms; not only do they decrease their bearer's reproduction, but they simultaneously increase the reproductive output of the bearer's competitors. Such traits might be expected to perish almost immediately.

The theory of kin selection was advanced in 1964 by W. D. Hamilton, resolving this seeming paradox of evolved altruism. Hamilton's key insight was that genes have two possible routes into the next generation. First, a gene could aid its bearer's own repro-duction, thereby increasing its own frequency in the next generation. Alternatively, it could cause its bearer to aid the reproduction of others carrying the same gene. While the latter type of gene imposes the burden of costly aid on its bearer, Hamilton recognized that such a gene could still spread evolutionarily if a sufficiently large benefit accrued to other bearers. From the standpoint of the gene, this indirect strategy has the same net effect as the direct strategy: it increases the gene's frequency in the next generation. Hence, giving aid to others at one's own expense can, indeed, be favored by the evolutionary process if the net effect on an underlying gene is positive.

Hamilton's model is constructed at the level of genes rather than of whole individuals. It is genes that are perpetuated and persist evolutionarily, not whole individuals (Lewontin 1970), and it is the potential net benefit to genes that explains the evolution of altruism. Therefore, the mathematical understanding of altruism between whole individuals must take into account the fact that, monozygotic twins excepted, no two individuals are genetically identical in sexual species. Essential to this model, then, is that individuals target altruism toward others likely to bear the same genes. Heredity itself provides a statistically reliable method of discriminating between those who are likely to share genes and those who are not. The proportion of genes shared in common by a dyad represents the chance that a given gene present in one individual is likewise present in the other. For example, if a pair of individuals have half of their genes in common (as exemplified by full siblings), then the chance that a gene found in one of them also exists in the other is one-half. Because genetic relatives share higher proportions of genes in common than unrelated individuals, evolutionarily favored altruism is expected to be preferentially targeted at kin.

Also essential to Hamilton's model of kin selection is that altruists only accept costs and bestow benefits that are weighed appropriately. In terms of social behavior between whole individuals, it is a particular cost-benefit relation that characterizes altruism, but in Hamilton's evolutionary model altruism is only expected where a net benefit accrues to an underlying gene. In mathematically equivalent terms, the cost incurred by a whole altruist must be less than the benefit received by a whole recipient when devalued by the chance that the recipient actually carries the same gene. If these conditions are met, the net effect on the gene will be positive; the behavior will have the effect of increasing the frequency of the underlying gene in the next generation. Thus, the gene is evolutionarily favored. If the cost were greater or the benefit smaller than this, the net effect on the gene would be negative. In such a case, the gene would be better evolutionarily by causing its bearer to withhold the benefit and redirect what would have been the cost of its own reproduction; this is equivalent to the direct route to the next generation.

For example, consider an actor faced with the following situation. He has a chance to aid his full sibling in a manner that would augment the sibling's reproduction by two units. Under what conditions would he be evolutionarily favored to do so? Because the chance that the sibling actually possesses the same underlying gene is one-half, the actor should only act if the cost to himself is less than one unit. Similarly, an actor should only be willing to spend one reproductive unit performing an altruistic act for a half-sibling if the resultant augmentation of the half-sibling's reproduction is greater than four units, because the chance that the gene is shared in common by a pair falls to one-quarter in half-siblings. As the degree of relatedness, equal to the chance that a gene is shared in common between a dyad, decreases, altruism will only be favored evolutionarily if the ratio of the cost to the benefit decreases proportionately.

There are two major issues that must be considered in understanding kin selection. First, is behavior affected by genes? Hamilton's model explains social behavior by appealing to selection acting on genes, but it does not claim that all genes affect behavior nor that there is a one-to-one correspondence between any gene and any specific behavior. All that is required for Hamilton's model to be consistent is that behavior has a genetic basis; in other words, changing an individuals' genetic makeup can change his behavior. Richard C. Lewontin (1974) notes, with respect to *Drosophila*: "There appears to be no character—morphogenetic, behavioral, physiological, or cytological—that cannot be selected." Moreover, S. J. C. Gaulin (1987) notes: "For animals, the data are overwhelming; virtually every behavioral trait that has ever been investigated has shown marked and rapid response to selective breeding."

The other common criticism of kin selection has been that organisms cannot possibly be expected to carry out such complicated mathematical computa-

tions in behavioral decision-making (Sahlins 1977). Figuring the probabilistic degree of relatedness might be difficult, and approximating costs and potential benefits in terms of the actors' and recipients' reproduction would be nearly impossible at the conscious, intelligent level. The evolution of altruism under kin selection, however, requires neither computational intelligence nor conscious thought. Compared to an organism whose behavior violated these mathematical rules, any organism that behaved in a manner consistent with them would transmit to the next generation relatively more copies of the genes underlying its behavior. As this process continues across generations, a larger and larger proportion of the population will come to possess the genes that caused their ancestors to behave in accordance with the mathematical prescriptions of kin selection. Thus, individuals in the population will come to be characterized by behaving as if they actually did understand and perform such calculations, even if they are entirely unaware of them.

Kin selection theory can be useful in understanding small-scale social interactions between individuals. For example, P. W. Sherman (1980) has shown that the dangerous and costly behavior of alarm calling in ground squirrels is correlated with the number and degree of relatedness of genetic relatives within hearing distance. Similarly, Napoleon A. Chagnon (1980; Chagnon and Bugos 1979) has shown that, among Yanomamo involved in a high-risk encounter (specifically, an ax fight), factions tended to be constructed along biological kin lines. This suggests that when threats present themselves, kin preferentially aid kin in accordance with Hamilton's model.

Kin selection theory can also be useful in predicting and understanding complex, large-scale cultural phenomena. For example, Chagnon's research on the Yanomamo has found that when large villages fission, genetic relatives remain in cohesive groups. The degree of relatedness among members of small, postfission groups was found to be higher than that among the original group. This demonstrates that even in complex social restructuring, individuals ally themselves with kin.

Kin selection also can be useful in understanding cultural kinship systems and the behaviors generated by them. Where cultural and biological kinship categories are alike, altruistic behavior could arguably be a result either of cultural norms preferring kin or of kin selection. Where cultural and biological kin systems apparently diverge, however, critical tests of kin selection arise. K. Hawkes (1983) has shown that among Binumariwen sweet potato farmers, gardening help is more closely correlated with social distance between individuals than with genetic distance. This is not in violation of kin selection predictions, however, since "pairs of individuals who are socially nearest will tend, on the average, to be genetically nearest" (Hawkes 1983); that is, culture weighs social kin categories in precisely the manner expected by kin selection, when average biological relatedness between an individual and members of particular kin categories are considered. Even more powerful are cases in which behavior favors biological kin at the expense of cultural kin. Chagnon's (1980) data on Yanomamo indicate that genetic rather than social distance determines cohesion during a village fissioning; fictive brothers scatter among groups, and genetic brothers do not.

Kin selection is simply a special case of natural selection operating on the genes underlying behavior in social organisms. The operation of this mechanism is well documented in several organisms (Trivers and Hare 1976; Sherman 1980). The complex and diverse cultural traditions and institutions that we as humans construct do not suggest that we are above or beyond the evolutionary influences. Rather, they provide unique chances to rigorously test kin selection theory under a wide range of circumstances, as well as to gain valuable insights into the whole operation of and interaction between culture and biology.

CHRISTINE REIBER MILBERG

CHAGNON, NAPOLEON A. "Mate Competition, Favoring Close Kin, and Village Fissioning Among the Yanomamo Indians." In *Evolutionary Biology and Human Social Behavior: An Anthropological Perspective,* edited by Napoleon A. Chagnon and W. Irons. North Scituate, Mass.: Duxbury Press, 1979.

——— . "Kin Selection Theory, Kinship, Marriage, and Fitness Among the Yanomamo Indians." In *Sociobiology; Beyond Nature/Nurture?,* edited by G. W. Barlow and James Silverberg. Boulder, Colo.: Westview Press, 1980.

CHAGNON, NAPOLEON A., and BUGOS, P. "Kin Selection and Conflict: An Analysis of a Yanomamo Ax Fight." In *Evolutionary Biology and Human Social Behavior: An Anthropological Perspective,* ed-

ited by Napoleon A. Chagnon and W. Irons. North Scituate, Mass.: Duxbury Press, 1979.

DARWIN, CHARLES R. *On the Origin of Species.* London: John Murray, 1859.

GAULIN, S. J. C. "A Logical Structure for Human Sociobiology." In *Proceedings of the 1986 Biennial Meeting of the Philosophy of Science Association,* edited by A. Fine and Peter K. Machamer. East Lansing, Mich.: Philosophy of Science Association, 1987.

HAMILTON, W. D. "The Genetical Evolution of Social Behavior." *Journal of Theoretical Biology* 7 (1964): 1–52.

HAWKES, K. "Kin Selection and Culture." *American Ethnologist* 10 (1983): 345–363.

LEWONTIN, RICHARD C. "The Units of Selection." *Annual Review of Ecology and Systematics* 1 (1970): 1–18.

——— . *The Genetic Basis of Evolutionary Change.* New York: Columbia University Press, 1974.

SAHLINS, MARSHALL D. *The Use and Abuse of Biology.* Ann Arbor: University of Michigan Press, 1977.

SHERMAN, P. W. "The Limits of Ground Squirrel Nepotism." In *Sociobiology: Beyond Nature/Nurture?,* edited by G. W. Barlow and James Silverberg. Boulder, Colo.: Westview, 1980.

TRIVERS, R. L., and H. HARE. "Haplodiploidy and the Evolution of the Social Insects." *Science* 191 (1976): 249–263.

KINSHIP TERMINOLOGY

Kinship terms (kinterms) are a set of words (Saussurean "signs") in some given language that label the specific categories of relatives or kinfolk (often spoken of as "Alters") of some reference person (often spoken of as "Ego"). The set of kinterms in any particular terminologeced system partitions the universe of positions on Ego's genealogy ("kintypes," such as mother's brother's son, father's sister's daughter, sister's daughter, etc.), such that each kintype falls into one and only one kinterm category (e.g., in English, cousin, niece, etc.). Each kinterm category, on the other hand, can and typically will include more than one kintype. A given language/culture can have several related alternative systems of linking kinterms to kintypes.

The "universe" centers on Ego and includes Ego's consanguineal ("blood," i.e., by shared descent) and affinal (by marriage) relatives. "Lineal" kin—relatives on Ego's direct line of ancestors and descendants—are often distinguished from "collateral" kin—consanguines, such as siblings, parents' siblings, or siblings' children, who are not on Ego's direct line. With increasing genealogical distance from Ego (measured by more links in the string of relatives through whom Ego is linked to Alter), the sense of relatedness often attenuates. In many systems, the likelihood of a kinterm being applied to a distant relative decreases with genealogical distance, often more rapidly for affines than for consanguines. On the other hand, in some societies all members of some bounded social unit (such as, for example, a *Jati* [an Indian caste grouping], a tribe, or a group of lineages) to which Ego belongs are considered kin, and so kinterms are applied (in their strict denotative sense) to all members of that unit but not outside it.

Kinterm category membership is designated by a statement of the form "Z is X's Y": for example, "Bill is Joe's uncle"—that is, someone is not an uncle per se but, rather, is some particular Ego's uncle. From the fact that a kinterm's application depends on a string of relatives linking Ego to Alter, it follows that each kinterm has a reciprocal kinterm (based on tracing the string in the opposite direction); if Bill is Joe's uncle, then Joe will be Bill's nephew (in English), and "nephew" is a reciprocal of "uncle." In English, another reciprocal of "uncle" is "niece," and "nephew" and "niece" are also reciprocals of "aunt"; the minimal set of terms that contains all the reciprocals of all terms in the set—such as {uncle, aunt, nephew, niece}—is sometimes spoken of as a "range set."

Kinterms are normally understood as lexemes—that is, as words or phrases whose meaning cannot be predicted from the meanings of their parts—but, more properly, they are "segregates" (Frake 1962), that is, units with conventional meanings within a culture. Thus, in English, "grandfather" is understood as a separate term from "father," and "great uncle" is understood as a kind of "uncle" (uncle plus modifier).

Attending to conventional kinterm expressions serves well in understanding the functioning of these terms within a language. When one looks for the kinship categories that express underlying social relations or cognitive categorizations, however, the situation becomes more complicated. Many languages apply various of their ordinary stock of everyday inflections or modifiers to kinterms. Thus, although

English (which does not have grammatical gender) uses separate words to distinguish brother from sister, Spanish (which has grammatical gender) automatically distinguishes them (outside of the system of kinterm lexemes) as *hermano vs. hermana*. Does one conclude, then, that sibling gender is more important to English speakers than to Spanish speakers? Alternatively, does one conclude that sibling gender is equally important to both but that English, lacking an automatic grammatical way of recognizing the distinction, has been forced to maintain contrasting lexemes, whereas Spanish has not been so forced? How is Fanti (a West African language) to be understood? In this West African language there is only one sibling term, *nua*, but very general age and sex modifiers (*panyin vs. kakraba; banyin vs. besia*) are routinely applied to that sibling term.

GENEALOGY AND METAPHOR

The relevance of biological relatedness to kinterm categories has been debated. On the nonbiological side of the debate, some anthropologists see kinterm categories in many cultures (including the modern United States) as having nothing to do with genealogy, whereas others see them—even where there is genealogical reckoning—as being based on social roles that might or might not correlate with actual biological facts.

The opposed view claims that the biological model of descent, in which each child is produced by the union of a father with a mother, is universally present, even in cultures that ostensibly deny it (e.g., the Trobriand) or socially avoid it (e.g., polyandrous groups in Tibet). According to this view, the biological model underlies most cultures' primary expectations about socialization wherein children are normally expected to be raised in a household unit that includes their father and their mother, even if that unit may be embedded in some kind of more extended unit. In this view, the normal default (and, hence, focal or kernel) reference of "father" and "mother" kinterms is to the biological parents who raise a child, even if the terms also are applied to many other people—and even if, in every society, there are other routes (e.g., adoption, subsequent parental marriages, etc.) by which people can assume parental roles for children. Secondary kinds of parental roles are sometimes terminologically recognized in terms such as "stepfather" or in terms for adoptive mothers; often such people are simply spoken of as fathers or mothers.

The argument regarding the biological basis of kinterm categories also applies to children (as the reciprocal relations to parents), to siblings (others with whom Ego shares her or his parents), and to other kin categories related through one's parents, siblings, spouses, or children.

Related to the question of whether kinship terminologies universally have a biological base, and particularly associated with Edmund Leach (1958), is a questioning of the validity or the usefulness of the traditionally understood kinship domain itself. When one term (such as *tabu* in the Trobriand system) refers both to a kin class (father's sisters) and to some significant nonkin referents (roughly, the state of items that are taboo, sacred, forbidden), is that term to be understood as having the kin referent as its primary sense, from which the term is to be seen as extending out metaphorically to other areas? Alternatively, is the term to be seen as having a primary sense—not specific to the kin universe—that embraces the common elements of its various applications? At issue is not just the priority of genealogy but also whether or not (or to what degree) a term such as "tabu" can even be compared validly to kinterms with similar genealogical referents in other systems.

Since in all known cultures the distribution of specific kinterms (when used in what native speakers consider a strictly "correct" denotative sense) maps well onto genealogically defined categories, there has to be some logical relationship between kinterms and genealogy, and thus some cultural recognition (whether direct or indirect) of a genealogical basis for kinterms. On the other hand, in every culture kinterms are often applied metaphorically to nongenealogical kin. The debate about genealogy does serve to emphasize the fact that, apart from whatever their primary definitions might be, the normal communicative information carried by kinterms in normal conversational usage in most cultures has much more to do with affect and behavioral expectations than it does with genealogical relatedness per se.

In most cultures, kinterms form a rich source of metaphor. Metaphoric usage of kinterms can range from the narrowest sense in which a particular kinterm is applied to some technically inappropriate relative on the basis of behavioral interactions or feeling tone (e.g., in English, addressing an older cousin as "uncle"), through the still narrower sense in which the kinterm is applied to neighbors or friends who act like the cat-

egory of kin in question or who are "felt" to be like such a relative (e.g., the common use of "uncle" and "aunt" for nonrelatives in small-town America), to the broader sense in which a priest can be a "father" or some politician can be the "father of his country," and to the even broader sense in which we can speak of "the mother lode" or "the thought being father to the deed."

CLASSIFICATION OF KINSHIP TERMINOLOGIES

Kinterm systems have been classified in several ways. Morgan (1871) distinguished "classificatory" from "descriptive," referring, according to one reading of his work, to systems in which specific kinterms include both lineal and collateral kin versus those in which specific kinterms can include one or the other but not both. According to another reading, Morgan's distinction referred to that between systems whose kinterm categories each contain more than one kintype and those whose categories each contain only one kintype. Murdock (1949) offered a four-way distinction: "generational" terminologies (in which no lineal/collateral nor mother's side/father's side [and its reciprocal] distinctions are made); "lineal" (in which no side of family distinction is made but in which lineal relatives are distinguished from collaterals); "bifurcate merging" (in which no lineal/collateral distinction is made but in which the father's side/ mother's side [and its reciprocal] distinction is made); and "bifurcate collateral" (in which both side and lineality distinctions are made). Building on the distinction between "cross cousins" (the children of opposite-sexed siblings) and "parallel cousins" (the children of same-sexed siblings), Murdock also introduced the widely used classification of types of kinship terminologies based on the terminological assignment of Ego's "cousins" (i.e., parents' siblings' children): in the "Hawaiian" type, cross cousins are not distinguished from parallel cousins, and both are called by the same terms as Ego's siblings; in the "Eskimo" type, cross cousins are not distinguished from parallel ones, but cousins are terminologically distinguished from siblings; in the "Iroquois" type, cross cousins are distinguished from parallel cousins, and parallel cousins are called by the same terms as siblings; in the "Sudanese" type, paternal cross cousins are distinguished from maternal ones, and both are distinguished from parallel cousins; in the "Omaha" type, cross cousins are distinguished from parallel cousins and siblings, and (consistent with patrilineal kingroups) Ego's paternal cross cousins are classified cross-generationally with Ego's sisters' children, and Ego's maternal cross cousins are, reciprocally, classified with Ego's mother's siblings; and in the "Crow" type, cross cousins are distinguished from parallel cousins and siblings, and (consistent with matrilineal kingroups) Ego's paternal cross cousins are classified cross-generationally with Ego's father's siblings, and Ego's maternal cross cousins are, reciprocally, classified with Ego's brothers' children.

LANGUAGE AND SOCIETY

Kinship studies have provided one locus in which anthropologists have explored the relationship among language, culture, and society. Kinship studies have played a crucial role in the development of anthropological approaches to the study of the semantics of natural language and to the exploration of culturally shared, structured knowledge systems. At the same time, socially oriented kinship theorists have raised important issues concerning the relationship of kinterm categories to various social phenomena. These phenomena include rules for inheritance and succession, social roles (and, thereby, role theory), and social groupings—whether domestic groups such as households, or descent groups such as lineages, clans, moieties, sections, and the like.

The discussion of the relationship of kinship terminology to society takes place at two levels. One level concerns the correlational issue—what terminological patterns or types are found to co-occur with what social forms (such as unilineal descent, cross-cousin marriage, levirate or sororate, and so forth). Bifurcate-merging terminologies tend to go with some sort of sociocentric, corporate unilineal groupings, whereas lineal terminologies tend more to go with bilateral descent and Egocentric kin groupings.

The second level concerns the relationship of particular kinterms (or kinterm contrasts) within a system to other relevant cultural information. Contrasts among kinterm categories are generally felt by anthropologists to represent information that is important in the culture of the terms' users. Debate has long continued, however, concerning whether the important information at issue is social (concerning social relations, social groups, or social rules) or something else. For those who see social information as at issue, and who see kinterms as labeling social

roles, there still remains the problem of whether the kinship terminology is to be seen as directly reflecting the social information in question or as only indirectly reflecting such—through a filter imposed either by systemic constraints within the terminology or by speakers' cognitive constraints. There remains also the question of whether the external information relevant to some given kinterm category is to be seen as pertaining to all relatives in the category or only to some subset (e.g., focal vs. extended ones).

The relationship of kinterm categories to social features additionally concerns the relationship, within a given system, of particular kinterm categories to particular social groupings. For societies that have descent groups (lineages), there has been some interest in sorting kin into a domestic sphere (household) and a descent-group sphere (Schneider 1962). There is concern with whether kinterm categories reflect such groupings—and, if so, which groupings, under what conditions, and in what manner. Some anthropologists have wanted to restrict the recognition of kinship (in societies with unilineal descent groups) to members of the descent groups and thus have considered the parent to whose descent group Ego did not belong not to be kin to Ego; sometimes (e.g., Trobriand Islands, as described by Bronislaw Malinowski 1929) the native speaker's characterization of his or her own kin relations has encouraged such a view. In a few extreme matrilineal cases, such as the Nayar of south India, there do arise special questions concerning the interaction among marriage, paternity, and the socialization role normally expected to be exercised by fathers. A weaker version of descent-group emphasis is seen in the tendency of many anthropologists to assume a primacy (relative to kinterms as well as other kinship issues) of descent groups over domestic groupings. Conversely, other anthropologists consider that kinterms always primarily represent domestic roles (of socialization) and that descent-group roles (where they enter in at all) only constitute a secondary subdivision.

DAVID B. KRONENFELD

SEE ALSO: Cognitive Anthropology; Componential Analysis; Family and Household Structure; History of Anthropology; Kin Groups, Residence, and Descent; Language; Linguistic Anthropology; Marriage; Semiotics

FRAKE, CHARLES O. "The Ethnographic Study of Cognitive Systems." In *Anthropology and Human*

Behavior, edited by T. Gladwin and W. C. Sturtevant. Washington, D.C.: The Anthropological Society of Washington, 1962.

KEESING, ROGER M. *Kin Groups and Social Structure.* Holt, Rinehart & Winston, 1975.

LEACH, EDMUND. "Concerning Trobriand Class and Kinship Category Tabu." In *The Developmental Cycle in Domestic Groups,* edited by Jack Goody. Cambridge: Cambridge University Press, 1958.

———. *Rethinking Anthropology.* London School of Economics Monographs in Social Anthropology, no. 22. London: Athlone, 1961.

LOUNSBURY, FLOYD G. "Another View of Trobriand Kinship Categories." In *Formal Semantic Analysis,* edited by E. A. Hammel. American Anthropologist Special Publication 67 (No. 5, Part 2) 1965: 142-85.

MALINOWSKI, BRONISLAW. *The Sex Life of Savages.* New York: Harcourt, Brace & World, 1929.

MORGAN, LEWIS HENRY. "Systems of Consanguinity and Affinity of the Human Family." In *Smithsonian Contributions to Knowledge*, no. 218. Washington, D.C.: Smithsonian Institution, 1871.

MURDOCK, GEORGE PETER. *Social Structure.* New York: Macmillan, 1949.

SCHNEIDER, DAVID M. and KATHLEEN GOUGH, eds. *Introduction to Matrilineal Kinship.* Berkeley and Los Angeles: University of California Press, 1962.

L

LANGUAGE

Anthropologists estimate that more than 6,000 different languages are spoken in the world today, but within the next several hundred years at least 90 percent of these languages no longer will be spoken. Because most languages have either very scanty or no documentation, the descriptive task facing language scholars is immense. Every language is of inestimable value, and each is a collaborative work of art of a people and a precipitate of thousands of years of human history. In addition, each language gives invaluable information concerning the range of possibilities that human speech can embody. Access to the full range of this variation is essential to achieving a complete understanding of our shared linguistic humanity.

FULL HUMAN LANGUAGE

All known languages are full and complete; no language lacks anything essential or central to human speech. They all have vocabularies containing thousands of lexical items and syntax, that is, principles for combining words into phrases, sentences, and ultimately into discourse. In addition, they all have devices for combining morphemes, the minimal units of meaning and grammatical distribution, into words. Furthermore, they all have a means of giving physical substance to morphemes, either auditorily or gesturally.

Pidgin languages are an exception. These languages have a greatly reduced lexicon and grammar; their vocabularies contain hundreds of lexical items, rather than thousands, with similarly reduced grammars. Pidgins sometimes develop in situations where adult speakers do not share a common language. When pidgins are acquired by children as a first language they expand in a relatively short period of time into full languages called Creoles.

Every full human language (FHL) is an immensely complex and elaborate whole. There is no conceiv-

able way that FHL could have sprung into existence all at once. Thus, forms of language that were not full and complete must have existed prior to the development of FHL. In short, a series of more rudimentary forms of speech formed developmental stages on the way to FHL. Surely many such stages over as much as several million years are implied.

SIGN LANGUAGES

The sign languages of the deaf are FHLs. These manual languages contain thousands of lexemes, meaningful speech forms that are items of the vocabulary of a language, and full grammars. While their gestural-visual mode of transmission differs radically from the vocal-auditory channel utilized by speakers of vocal language, other differences involve mostly a greater emphasis on simultaneity and the overlapping of gestures, compared to the strictly linear nature of vocal speech. Physically, speech is composed of a sequence of ineluctably linear and non-overlapping sound segments, with the exception that suprasegmental phenomena such as stress, pitch, and other intonational features are coextensive with, or form an overlay on, the main segmental stream. Supra-segmental knowledge is the first aspect of language a child acquires and the last mastered by an adult learning a second language.

A gestural morpheme takes about twice as long as a vocal morpheme to produce, yet average rates of sentence production and discourse for sign language are comparable to those for spoken language, implying that gestural compression is common. For example, the concept "bruise" in American Sign Language (ASL) is conveyed by compounding the sign for "blue" and the sign for "spot." Production of this compound, however, takes only the time necessary for a single sign, thus the two signs are compressed by means of abbreviation and overlapping into a much shorter time period. ASL grammar provides another means of compression by varying slightly a sign or sign phrase to convey grammatical information. This modulation of sign production is usually simultaneous with emission of the sign or sign phrase itself.

The ASL gestures that correspond to the morphemes of speech are not composed of a series of gestures equivalent to the series of consonants and vowels that are strung together to produce phonological morphemes. Gestural signs utilize a range of handshape configurations, body locations, and hand movements, the place, configuration, movement (PCM) system, but these basic elements of a holistic gestural sign occur for the most part simultaneously. Again sign language is less strictly linear than vocal language. In summary, the striking modality difference between these two language forms produces only the most minor and nonessential structural differences.

ANIMAL SIGNALING SYSTEMS

One way to define or characterize human language is to compare it to animal signaling systems. Animals utilize a range of modalities for signaling purposes. One is vocalization or calling, another involves gestures and displays (various body postures and positions), and another involves the emission of specialized scents called pheromones. Signals occur in situations involving food, danger, mating, and reproduction, identification of parent and offspring, group aggregation, dominance/submission encounters, territorial marking and defense, and so forth.

While social species of animals possess larger signaling systems than nonsocial species, even social signaling systems are extraordinarily small by human standards. The average number of signals ranges from fifteen for a sample of social insect species, to seventeen for a sample of fish, to twenty-one for birds, to twenty-five for mammals. If we compare the vocabulary size of FHLs to the size of animal signaling systems, we are comparing tens to thousands. If the appropriate comparison is with sentences then the difference is virtually an infinite one, since the number of sentences that can be constructed using the lexical and grammatical resources of any FHL are so numerous as to be not easily countable.

Another difference is that animal signals are not combined into larger units comparable to the phrases and sentences of FHL. A rare exception occurs in the signaling system of the chickadee. For this bird species, ten percent of signaling situations elicit combined calls.

These compounds unite the essential features of two calls such as "danger-food" into a single more elaborate vocalization unit. Signals such as threat displays which can be produced with varying degrees of forcefulness might also form exceptions. These displays can be analyzed as compounds composed of a basic threat signal combined with an emphasis signal which varies in strength by continuous degrees.

Animal signals are essentially holistic units and, as such, are not easily decomposable into constituent elements which can be used over and over again to construct additional signals. On the other hand, the morphemes of speech, with only minor exceptions, can be readily decomposed into a linear sequence of sound segments. These phonological units are used again and again in different combinations to label the thousands of different semantic referents or basic concepts found in all FHLs. The number of functionally different sound segments (themselves classes of sounds called phonemes) ranges from about ten to 120 in languages, with an average inventory consisting of approximately thirty phonemes. The universe of phonemic possibilities from which all languages draw their segment inventory consists of approximately 600 different phonological units. Certain consonants and vowels occur very frequently in languages, while others occur very infrequently.

Perhaps the most striking characteristic of animal signals is that they are typically nonsemantic while the morphemes of human language are virtually always richly meaningful. FHL is essentially a bipartite system at all levels except the strictly phonological level, consisting of a series of phonological strings of varying lengths associated with a series of semantic referents or meanings. The twofold structure of language in which meanings are paired with sound sequences occurs at the level of the morpheme, the word, the phrase, the sentence, and ultimately at the level of discourse itself.

One social ant species has a pheromone that is emitted when an individual dies. Other ants respond to this scent signal by dragging the dead ant from the nest and discarding the body. An investigator chemically synthesized the pheromone and daubed it on a captured ant. This ant was repeatedly dragged from the nest by conspecifics, that is, its same-species nest mates, all the while struggling and kicking with its legs and waving its antennae. The nondaubed ants were responding automatically to the presence of the scent, ignoring the obvious evidence that the "dead" ant was very much alive. Thus, responses to signals are largely stereotyped and involuntary. In addition, signals are usually triggered automatically by an appropriate stimulus situation. In summary, animal signaling systems are designed in such a way that decisions are not required on the part of the animals giving the signal and those responding to it.

Animal signals are also for the most part biologically innate. For instance, the songs of many bird species will appear in mature birds that have had no exposure to the calls of their species. While the basic songs are innate, a polished performance of the songs is dependent on exposure during maturation. Thus, experience transforms a tyro into an expert performer, but this environmental input has to occur during an especially receptive period early in a bird's life well before singing starts.

Animal signaling systems are thus designed to operate without recourse to meaning or understanding. In addition, since the signals are innate, a new one can be added only through a lengthy process of evolutionary natural selection. Because these systems are deeply embedded within the biological substance of the animal, they operate automatically without the necessity for decision- making. Thus, they render meaning or semanticity irrelevant to their functioning.

FHLs, of course, are learned and are entirely voluntary in their functioning. Human speakers, in any situation, can choose from a virtually limitless supply of possible utterances. Animal signals automatically elicit a fixed external response by conspecifics, while human speech elicits a fundamentally fixed internal response, namely interpretation of the speech message. Internal semantic decoding is so automatic that humans seem incapable of choosing not to decode a speech message they have heard. Thus, understanding is the goal of human speech while automatic external response by conspecifics is the goal of animal signals.

Recent research has demonstrated that birds and mammals, and perhaps other organisms to a lesser extent, are capable of constructing semantically based categories. Thus animals are able, to some degree at least, to reduce their specific experience to a set of more general semantic categories. For example, some semantic learning and volition has been observed in the signaling system of the vervet monkey. Vervets

have several danger calls including a snake alarm, a carnivorous bird alarm, and a carnivorous mammal alarm, each with correspondingly different evasive actions. Juvenile vervets emit many false alarms. As they mature they give fewer false alarms, seemingly learning to be more specific in recognizing environmental dangers. This suggests some degree of volition is involved in adult production of alarms. When what looks like a snake turns out to be only a stick, for example, an alarm call is suppressed. Volition is also evidenced in adults who for the most part do not respond automatically to juvenile alarms but check first to determine whether the danger is real.

Semanticity is also entering the vervet signaling system. Because vervets cease giving false alarms to snake-like sticks and cease giving predatory bird alarms to falling leaves, this suggests they are forming from their experience a set of semantically based categories that might be broadly characterized as leaf versus bird and snake versus stick. These acquired semantic categories then supplant the innate stimulus configurations which originally triggered the alarms. Thus, the vervet signaling system is developing some dependence on the environmental experience of individual vervets, some dependence on decision-making, and some recourse to meaning.

It seems likely that early humans, in a similar manner, altered a pure signaling system and moved it closer to FHL. The amount of change involved, however, should not be exaggerated. If a pure signaling system represents the first step on a thousand-step journey toward FHL, adding some learning, volition, and semanticity to such a system represents only a few additional steps on this long journey.

APE LANGUAGE PROJECTS

Several projects have attempted to teach a form of human language, namely ASL, to our closest phylogenetic relatives, the great apes. These projects have demonstrated that chimpanzees, gorillas, and orangutans can acquire a small portion of FHL. Ape language systems provide a plausible model for communication systems early humans may have possessed. Washoe, a mature female chimpanzee has been exposed intensively from ten months of age to ASL. (Actually she has been taught Signed English, a hybrid system that utilizes the gestural signs of ASL combined with the syntax or word order principles of spoken English.) She has acquired about 240 signs and produces them in sequences that have a mean length of utterance (MLU) of fewer than two signs, approximating the language skills of a two-year-old child.

Koko, a mature female gorilla has been exposed intensively to Signed English since she was one year old. She has acquired about 500 ASL signs and produces them in strings that have an MLU of 2.7 signs, which is roughly equivalent to the language skills of a two-and-a-half-year-old child. Both Washoe and Koko have comprehension vocabularies that are much larger than their production vocabularies and can "understand" strings of ASL signs that are longer than they typically produce. Human language users, both children and adults, also have comprehension vocabularies that are larger than their production vocabularies and can understand sentences longer than they typically produce.

Loulis, Washoe's adopted "son," acquired more than fifty ASL signs during a five-year period in which only Washoe and three other chimpanzees signed in his presence. Washoe was observed forming Loulis's hands into ASL signs in the presence of appropriate objects and actions. Another, less explicit form of teaching, is modeling or intentionally providing an example of behavior that can form the basis for observational learning. Washoe engaged in much modeling behavior. She would make eye contact with Loulis and then produce an ASL sign in the presence of the object it referred to. She would sometimes make the sign on the object itself. When it was appropriate she would make the sign on Loulis, that is, she made the "gum" sign on his cheek and the "hat" sign on his head. Deaf parents also engage in these shaping and modeling behaviors when teaching their children.

Intentional teaching may be an indication that an animal possesses conscious awareness of itself. Formal instruction suggests the attribution of mental operations to a conspecific based on some degree of conscious awareness of the operation of mental processes in one's own mind. Mentation is attributed to a conspecific and an assessment is made of the knowledge possessed by this individual. Information that would augment this knowledge then is provided through formal tuition.

All critics agree that apes have acquired gestural names or labels for semantically based categories. These projects have demonstrated that apes have a modest symbolic capacity, an ability to associate an arbitrary or conventional gesture with an idea or concept. In the Russian language scholar Vygotsky's terminology, apes are capable, to some degree at least, of associating "units of social exchange" or conventionalized gestures with "units of generalized thought" or semantically based categories.

Humans are biologically specialized to produce the sounds of vocal speech and combine them into a flowing speech stream. This kinesthetic skill, which all normal humans possess, is probably our most impressive motor accomplishment. Motor capacities for speech production as detailed as these take a considerable time to develop and become biologically embedded in a species. Apes do not have similar innate motor capacities; therefore attempts to teach them spoken language have failed utterly.

Chimpanzees and gorillas have demonstrated, however, a considerable ability to decode spoken language. For example, in the Koko project, if the investigators using vocal language mention something in which Koko is especially interested, such as candy, she becomes excited and starts signing to ask for sweets. To obviate this, investigators have begun vocally spelling out words referring to sensitive topics, a system adopted by many parents of young children. Similarly, Kanzi, a male pygmy chimpanzee, is able to carry out, without trial-and-error fumbling, relatively complicated behavioral tasks when given only vocal instructions, for example, "Go look under the bed [which may be several rooms away] and find the doll [one object among many] and bring it here."

Recent research demonstrates that the sound differences used to distinguish similar phonemes from each other in languages are also utilized to distinguish general environmental or ambient non-language sounds from each other. It has also been discovered that human infants at a very young age are able to perceive, accurately and almost flawlessly, virtually all the sound contrasts that occur in all the world's languages. Between six months and one year of age they lose the ability to distinguish sound differences that their native language does not utilize. This seems to suggest that human offspring do not learn to hear the sound contrasts that are important in their native language, instead they learn to suppress those not utilized, but only in a linguistic context because these same contrasts remain important in distinguishing ambient sounds. In short, we seem to be relatively unspecialized and perhaps not too different from apes in our sound perception capacities, while we are extraordinarily specialized in terms of our sound production capabilities.

CHILD LANGUAGE ACQUISITION

Children in a few short years acquire the basics of FHL with almost no formal tuition and with a brain that does not reach adult dimensions until language acquisition is largely complete. How is it that children can acquire FHL so easily, so quickly, and so effortlessly?

Much of our linguistic knowledge, especially of phonology and grammar, is implicit or tacit. Bringing this knowledge into conscious awareness so that it can be examined and explicitly formulated is often very difficult. The ability of native speakers to produce and understand a literally endless stream of well-formed sentences, many of which are novel and have never been produced before, provides ample evidence of their knowledge of the principles which underlie the phonological, grammatical, and lexical components of their native language. The relative inability of speaker-hearers to bring this knowledge into conscious awareness, and to articulate it in an explicit manner, is evidence only of its tacit nature and explains why language, for the most part, is not formally taught to children. How can adults explicitly teach what they cannot readily formulate?

Intentional modeling can provide explicit linguistic patterns for a child to observe and imitate, but intentional modeling seems to have little influence on acquisition of syntax. Children cannot even mechanically repeat sentences that their current grammar cannot independently produce. One child produced the sentence "Nobody don't like me," which his mother corrected by providing the intentional model: "No. Say nobody likes me." This exchange was repeated a full eight times before the child produced the sentence, "Oh, nobody don't likes me." Although the child finally acknowledged and added the third person singular suffix to the word "like", he was unable to alter the double negative construction produced by his internalized grammar. While it is undoubtedly helpful to expose children to a rich sample of language behavior, intentional modeling as a syntactic teaching tool seems largely to be ineffective.

Study of language acquisition has also shown that simple reinforcement models are incapable of explaining children's language learning. Thousands of hours of observation have demonstrated that parents pay almost no attention to the grammatical well-formedness of a child's statements. Caretakers are much more likely to say "Yes, that's right" when an utterance is true even if it is grammatically ill-formed by adult standards, than they are to endorse a false, but grammatically well-formed, statement. It has been noted that this training regimen of ignoring grammatical correctness but rewarding true statements, produces adults who speak grammatically flawlessly but who are not notably truthful.

Because the number of sentences that can be formed using the lexical and grammatical resources of any FHL is virtually infinite, children cannot simply memorize sentences. They have to extract the principles which underlie regularities in sentence formation. The first principles a child forms tend to be very broad and nonspecific and, usually, very different from those of adult language. Thus, early combinations produced by children are typically very different from adult models. For example, one child said "allgone milk" as he finished drinking his milk and "allgone sticky" after washing his hands. When the front door was closed he produced the string "allgone outside." Over time children's early syntactic principles are altered, refined, and brought into conformity with the detailed regularities of adult syntax. Children also have to induce the regularities of word formation, morpheme structure, phonological organization, and semantic understanding which are operative in their native language. To accomplish these tasks in a few short years is a momentous undertaking.

Children seem to possess an elaborate capacity for forming hypotheses to account for the regularities they observe in the linguistic data to which they are exposed. These hypotheses are then tested against additional language data and, if necessary, are revised and altered. Children use their preliminary hypotheses, and those that survive testing, to guide their linguistic behavior to produce the words, phrases, and sentences of their native language. In summary, children have an elaborate and extraordinarily powerful hypothesizing capacity that aids them in formulating, to a great extent implicitly, the principles that underlie the regular patterns in the phonological system, grammatical system, and lexicon of their native language.

Children's early grammars are communicatively quite effective, raising the question of why they continue acquisition until the adult model is attained. As speakers they can easily make their relatively uncomplicated needs and wants known with their preliminary grammars. On the other hand, adults and other caretakers persist in producing complicated grammatical constructions that children as hearers ultimately decode and acquire. We can imagine children deciding to stop language acquisition halfway through but they never do. In fact, if children are presented with two FHLs during these early years, they will acquire both of them with no apparent difficulty.

Children the world over proceed through a similar set of steps in the acquisition of language. The first word appears at about one year of age and the first word combination at about one year and nine months. Early strings tend to leave out functional morphemes and thus are telegraphic. Regular increases in average utterance length occur with increasing age until the basics of FHL are mastered by five or six years of age, although vocabulary continues to be added after this age and grammatical understanding continues to deepen. Children within individual language communities possess widely varying intellectual capacities and are exposed to widely varying linguistic inputs, but all proceed through these steps at more or less the same rate. Children with serious intellectual disabilities may proceed through these steps at a slower pace, and for those with severe deficits, acquisition may cease before the adult model is attained. These maturational regularities in acquisition suggest that while language is learned by children, they seem biologically primed and prepared to learn it.

Although deaf children proceed through the same acquisition steps as hearing children the early milestones are accomplished somewhat sooner. Chimpanzees acquiring ASL pass the early milestones of the first sign and the first sign combination even earlier than deaf children. This suggests that manual motor skills mature more rapidly than vocal motor skills, and that chimpanzees mature, manually, faster than deaf children. Early vocabulary acquisition seems more dependent on development of manual or vocal motor skill than on maturation of semantic categorization skills. Indeed, there is abundant independent evidence that children acquiring vocal language begin to construct semantically based categories well before they produce their first word.

Children's grammars, at two to three years of age, are extraordinarily similar across languages. This has led to the proposal that a "basic child grammar" is

innate. If so, this initial rudimentary grammar provides a stepping stone or a means for children to bootstrap their way toward the highly complex and widely divergent grammars that characterize the adult languages they are acquiring. An alternative suggestion is that a single complete grammar is innate, the one that surfaces when pidgin languages expand into Creoles. Indeed, there are some similarities between "basic Creole grammar" and "basic child grammar."

Another proposal claims that a highly constrained innate design pattern underlies the surface diversity of all FHLs. It is indeed true that FHLs could be vastly more diverse than they in fact are. Powerful limitations on diversity characterize all components of language: phonology, grammar, and lexicon. These constraints need not in every instance be innate; some may be attributable to communicative efficacy principles. In short, the majority of possible language variabilities is not empirically observed, thus it seems to be ruled out by either biologically innate or communicative efficacy constraints.

It has become clear since the 1960s that the human species is language adapted. There are a host of biological devices wired into our neurocircuitry that imply this. This innate foundation for FHL testifies to a long history of language use in the human species. Possession of innate language capabilities, it should be emphasized, does not in any way lessen the overwhelming importance of learning as a mechanism of language acquisition and use. The great preponderance of detailed and very extensive knowledge that characterizes each FHL has to be painstakingly learned.

At least two specialized cognitive mechanisms are highly important to language acquisition and use. The first is an elaborate symbolic capacity which allows us to capture and encode the richness of our specific experience in a set of more general semantic categories to which names or labels can then be attached. That we share this cognitive capacity to some degree with the great apes is interesting but in no way lessens its importance to our species. The second is that we have an elaborate hypothesizing capacity and some evidence exists that apes also possess this capacity to a modest degree. This cognitive capacity is used to extract language regularities and regularities in other realms of experience. We use it, for example, to induce principles underlying our social behavior, many of which we know only implicitly. We also use it to extract regularities that characterize our initial knowledge of the external physical world. These cognitive capacities seem more general and more widely shared with other animal species than the more specific innate capabilities which underlie full human language.

STANLEY R. WITKOWSKI

BERLIN, BRENT, and PAUL KAY. *Basic Color Terms.* Berkeley: University of California Press, 1969.

BICKERTON, DEREK. *Language and Species.* Chicago: University of Chicago Press, 1990.

BROWN, ROGER. *A First Language: The Early Stages.* Cambridge, Mass.: Harvard University Press, 1973.

CHENEY, DOROTHY L., and ROBERT M. SEYFARTH. *How Monkeys See the World.* Chicago: University of Chicago Press, 1990.

DEMOPOULOS, WILLIAM, and AUSONIO MARRAS, eds. *Language Learning and Concept Acquisition: Foundational Issues.* Norwood, N.J.: Ablex Publishing, 1986.

GARDNER, R. ALLEN, BEATRIX T. GARDNER, and THOMAS E. VAN CANTFORT, eds. *Teaching Sign Language to Chimpanzees.* Albany, N.Y.: State University of New York Press, 1989.

GREENBERG, JOSEPH HAROLD. *Language Universals with Special Reference to Feature Hierarchies.* The Hague: Mouton, 1966.

GREENBERG, JOSEPH H., ed. *Universals of Language.* Cambridge, Mass.: MIT Press, 1963.

KLIMA, EDWARD S., and URSULA BELLUGI. *The Signs of Language.* Cambridge, Mass.: Harvard University Press, 1979.

LENNEBERG, ERIC H. *Biological Foundations of Language.* New York: Wiley, 1967. Reprint. Malabar, Fla.: R.E. Krieger. 1984.

LIEBERMAN, PHILIP. *The Biology and Evolution of Language.* Cambridge, Mass.: Harvard University Press, 1984.

PATTERSON, FRANCINE G. "Creative and Innovative Uses of Language by a Gorilla." In *Children's Language,* vol. 2, edited by K. E. Nelson. New York: Gardner Press, 1980.

SAVAGE-RUMBAUGH, E. SUE, JEANNINE MURPHY, ROSE A. SEVCIK, KAREN E. BRAKKE, SHELLY L. WILLIAMS, and DUANE M. RUMBAUGH. *Language Comprehension in Ape and Child.* Monographs of the Society for Research in Child Development, vol. 58, nos. 3–4 (1993).

SLOBIN, DAN ISSAC, ed. *The Crosslinguistic Study of Language Acquisition,* vol. 2 of *Theoretical Issues.*

Hillsdale, N.J.: Lawrence Erlbaum Associates, 1985.

WANNER, ERIC, and LILA R. GLEITMAN, eds. *Language Acquisition: The State of the Art.* New York: Cambridge University Press, 1982.

LEADERSHIP

The term "leadership" is usually defined in terms of group decision-making, protection, or dispute settlement, but it is often confused with the concepts of "dominance," "power," "authority," "influence," and "prestige." In part, this confusion simply reflects the fact that leaders often do exhibit one or more of these different qualities. Still, these concepts do not always coincide, so anthropologists have been careful to distinguish among them in the many different societies they have examined. Anthropologists have also been careful to distinguish different domains of leadership. An individual might wield a great deal of influence in spiritual matters but have little influence over decisions about war, politics, economics, or the family. A man might be extremely powerful over men's activities but have little or no power over women. In some societies, leadership may be closely tied to wealth, but elsewhere leaders may actually have fewer goods than their followers. The personal characteristics required of a leader and the rewards for leadership also vary cross-culturally.

The most common explanations for why leadership varies have been evolutionary. As Carneiro demonstrates (1973), not all cultural variation in leadership can be attributed to unilineal evolution, but some characteristics are clearly scalable in evolutionary terms. Societies generally have special religious practitioners before they have formal political leadership. A regular rule of leadership succession occurs before societies have installation ceremonies for political leaders, which occurs before they have special residences for political leaders, which occurs before their rulers have bodyguards. Simpler societies tend to have fewer leadership roles. For example, Werner (1981) showed that among Brazil's Mekranoti Indians, the same people are recognized as especially good or influential in most areas of life. In complex societies, leadership is much more specialized. Perhaps in recognition of this phenomenon, most anthropological attention has been devoted to characterizing leadership in groups representing different levels of social complexity: animal societies, band-level and tribal societies, chiefdoms, and states.

LEADERSHIP IN ANIMAL SOCIETIES

Studies of animal behavior have concentrated more on dominance hierarchies than on leadership per se. Wilson (1980) distinguishes between "despotic" systems, in which one dominant individual presides over others equal in rank, and systems of multiple ranking, in which there is a more or less linear sequence of dominance. Commonly, the dominant individuals are privileged with regard to access to females (in the case of males), or egg laying (in the case of many female arthropods), and with regard to access to food or other resources. Phylogenetic comparisons show a loose correlation between larger brain size and more flexible behavior on the one hand, and more complex and orderly dominance chains on the other. Arthropods as well as many fish, amphibian, and reptile species have despotic systems, short-chain hierarchies, or systems in which dominance must be established anew on each encounter. In addition, dominance is established through more directly aggressive means. In contrast, social birds and mammals generally show long-chain hierarchies and may demonstrate dominance through more "ritualistic" displays, especially body posturing and homosexual mounting and insertion, as occurs among dolphins and many primates. In addition, many monkeys and apes have coalitions of peers and "nested hierarchies," in which groups may be dominant over other groups, but individuals within a group show internal dominance hierarchies.

De Waal (1982) observed many truly "Machiavellian" maneuvers among our closest relatives, the chimpanzees. For example, in one group, a subordinate male gained the support of a group of females by protecting them against attacks, and used this support to overthrow the dominant male. One of the techniques used to maintain dominance was to gain the support of losers instead of winners in conflicts within the group. As observed by Machiavelli, the losers then feel more grateful toward the dominant individual and are more likely to support him.

Although the dominant chimpanzees assume a leadership role in their policing of intragroup conflicts, they are not necessarily leaders in other senses. As with other species, it is often more subordinate individuals who most explore their environment and innovate, possibly because they have more to gain and less to lose by exploration. In a series of experiments

with captive chimpanzees, Menzel (1992) demonstrated that chimpanzees soon learn to follow the leads of a chimpanzee with knowledge about the location of food, but dominant individuals continue to lead by closely observing the knowledgeable individual for subtle, often deliberately deceptive clues about the food's location.

LEADERSHIP IN BAND AND TRIBAL SOCIETIES

Although variation in leadership patterns among different species may at least partially be attributed to biology, differences among human societies are attributed primarily to cultural and social factors.

The Mbuti pygmies of Zaire have been described as virtually leaderless, but most societies have more or less clearly defined leadership roles. In analyzing Brazil's Nambikwara Indians, Lévi-Strauss (1944) suggested that all societies have leaders because there are always some individuals who enjoy prestige more than others. What needs to be explained is not why leaders exist but rather why societies differ in their acceptance of leaders. In the simplest societies, such as the Nambikwara or the !Kung (of Botswana), leaders complain that they receive only the blame if things go wrong and must generally work harder than the others. If leaders become overly proud, they are humiliated to keep them in their place. Otherwise their followers simply abandon them by moving somewhere else. In effect, people "vote" with their feet.

Fried (1967) gave the name "egalitarian" to the world's simplest societies. He recognized that status differences do exist in egalitarian societies but wished to emphasize that access to this status depends on ability rather than family ties or wealth. Still, all known societies also restrict access to leadership on the basis of age and sex, although not always to the same degree. Simmons (1945) showed that the aged are more likely to participate in government in societies with group responsibility for crimes, recognized judicial authority, and permanent residence. These factors permit elders to exercise their social wisdom but do not tax them physically. Women are somewhat more likely to exercise leadership roles where they are less burdened by child-care tasks and where they control the distribution of resources.

"BIG MEN"

Although most band-level societies discourage arrogance in their leaders, some egalitarian societies

encourage exaggerated ambition. Harris (1974) suggests that hunters and gatherers, such as the !Kung, generally discourage overly zealous leaders because their excessive ambition would result in over-exploitation of wild game and other food resources. In some societies, such as many Melanesian groups and the North American northwest-coast Indians, highly ambitious "big men" succeed in making everyone work harder to produce excess goods. The surplus production is used to sponsor elaborate feasts for rival groups. The feasts act as a kind of regional insurance policy against local food shortages owing to drought, hurricanes, or other factors. In bad years a group suffers the humiliation of being invited to another village's feast but does not die of hunger. The sponsoring group is rewarded for its excess production by acquiring greater pride and prestige. According to Harris, without the "big man's" ambitious incentives, people would not be able to muster the will necessary to produce more than they needed at the moment.

RELIGIOUS LEADERS

Most egalitarian societies have religious specialists who, through visions induced by such means as fasting, torture, or hallucinogens, travel to the spiritual world and communicate their visions to the community. Commonly, the shamans carry out ritual cures, and, frequently, through their visions of witchcraft and other phenomena, they also deal with relations between different communities and clarify their community's cosmology. Based on the results of psychological projective tests, Shweder (1972) found that Zinacanteco shamans in Mexico were more creative in explaining and interpreting things than were other community members.

Many egalitarian societies have also experienced religious movements inspired by charismatic leaders. These movements have generally been explained as a response to oppression after contact with Western society.

LEADERSHIP IN CHIEFDOMS AND STATES

Carneiro (1991) defines a chiefdom as "an autonomous political unit comprising a number of communities under the permanent control of a paramount chief." Chieftainships occurred in several Polynesian islands, Africa, and the Americas, especially in the Circum-Caribbean region. Chiefs generally inherited their positions, were wealthy, and were treated with great deference. In some places, their power was described as "absolute."

Although some anthropologists have linked the concept of chieftainship to the notion of unequal access to leadership, this link is not well established. Many band and tribal societies also give members of certain kin groups privileged access to leadership or have rules of leadership inheritance within families, even though the leaders do not have the powers or the wealth of a chief. Also, many state-level societies, such as the early civilizations of the Middle East and of the Americas, had leadership inheritance. Werner (1984) showed that the tendency for a chief's son to inherit his father's position among Brazil's tribal Mekranoti Indians may result from his personal ties to other communities, acquired through travels with his father or through visits from foreign dignitaries. Such "influence mongering" may be most common in societies, such as many Pacific-island societies, where contacts between communities are important but sporadic, so that the leaders' families come to know each other well, but other contacts with outsiders are not common.

Clastres (1974) and Carneiro (1970) have offered similar explanations for how chiefdoms and social stratification arose. In simple societies people do not need to follow leaders who fail to please them. They can simply move away. When population density increases, however, especially in more circumscribed areas, the "fight" option becomes more costly. When more exploitative leaders impose themselves in these situations, people can no longer flee (the easiest option) but must either fight or accept the exploitation. The more costly the flight and flight options, the more likely people are to submit to the authority of a chief. In state-level societies the alternatives to submitting to the leader's authority are very costly indeed.

State-level societies have more specialized leaders—leaders for each of the different levels of the political hierarchy and for many specialized tasks, such as military pursuits, religion, judicial decisions, or technology.

LEADERSHIP IN THE CONTEMPORARY WORLD

In their studies of contemporary societies, anthropologists have traditionally concentrated on smaller communities, especially communities in developing

LEADERSHIP

countries. Consequently, most leadership studies have dealt with community leaders in the Third World.

Political patronage is one of the most common forms of leadership in developing countries, especially in Latin American and Mediterranean cultures. In return for votes during political elections, patrons provide their clients with government jobs or other public services and protect them against legal problems. Forman (1975) distinguishes between "patron-dependency," in which dependents cannot choose their political patron, and "patron-clientship," in which clients may have more than one patron and may switch loyalties if convenient. Patron dependency is most common in less-developed, rural areas run by "bosses" with more absolute power, whereas patron clientship is more characteristic of urban society.

Elaborating on others before him, Da Matta (1987) suggests that the political patronage system in Brazil has its origins in Brazil's historic lack of regional integration and of a middle class. Because of these factors, the elites had little knowledge of the country they ruled and invented many unrealistic laws that could not be followed. As a result, virtually everyone became "illegal." With this situation, application of the law becomes a question of political connections. Individuals must have patrons in order to protect them against the laws and against those who disobey the laws. Personal alliances become much more important than contractual/legal relations. This facilitates political corruption and rewards those best able to circumvent the laws. Of course, the system also helps the elites remain in power, so there is little incentive to change the system.

BECOMING A LEADER

Anthropologists usually cite a combination of personal characteristics to account for how leaders rise to their positions. Although different types of leadership may require somewhat different traits, overall, the similarities seem much more striking than the differences. Compared to followers, leaders are usually more intelligent, more knowledgeable, more aggressive, more popular, older, and taller. This is true in both simple band and tribal societies and in contemporary industrial societies, and in the United States it applies to leaders in such diverse areas as the military, business, education, and government. Most of these

characteristics are easily understandable as traits that would help a leader exercise authority. Still, the fact that leaders tend to be taller than their followers in practically all known societies needs additional explanation. Gregor (1979) suggests that the greater respect accorded to taller people may result from the childhood habit of literally "looking up" to adults. The importance of early childhood experiences is also emphasized by Kracke (1978). Based on his psychoanalysis of leaders and followers among the Amazonian Kagwahiv Indians, Kracke suggests that "the essence of leadership is willingness to take a parental role." He argues that leaders tend to have a strong identification with their parents, whereas followers generally have an insecure identification with parents.

Although they are similar in many respects, different types of leaders also exhibit some contrasts. Limited studies suggest that Western leaders may be more competitive than leaders in simpler societies. In simpler societies, everyone already knows everyone else very well, so competition is less important in evaluating people's capacities. The greater importance of visibility in complex societies may also be related to the lack of knowledge of others. Also, generosity may be more important in simpler societies. Economic providers in complex societies are those who own the most capital, but in simpler societies it is the most generous who can best provide for the others.

In complex societies, different types of leaders also have contrasting personal traits (Stogdill 1974). For example, compared to leaders in other areas, leaders in the arts and sciences are less likely to be older than their followers. Perhaps this is related to the greater importance of innovation and originality in these fields.

Recently, anthropologists have turned their attention to the world's governing elite, but just what direction this research will eventually take remains to be seen.

DENNIS WERNER

SEE ALSO: Chiefdoms and Nonindustrial States; Cultural Evolution; Redistribution; Religious Practitioners; Shamanism

CARNEIRO, ROBERT L. "A Theory of the Origin of the State." *Science* 169(1970):733-738.

————. "Scale Analysis, Evolutionary Sequences, and the Rating of Cultures." In *A Handbook of Method in Cultural Anthropology,* edited by Raoul Naroll and Ronald Cohen. New York: Columbia University Press, 1973.

————. "The Nature of the Chiefdom as Revealed by Evidence from the Cauca Valley of Colombia." In *Profiles in Cultural Evolution,* edited by A. T. Rambo and K. Gillogly. Ann Arbor: University of Michigan, 1991.

CLASTRES, PIERRE. *La société contre l'état.* Paris: Éditions de Minuit, 1974. *Society Against the State,* translated by Robert Hurley. Urizen Books, 1977.

DA MATTA, R.A. *Casa e a Rua.* Rio de Janeiro: Ed. Guanabara, 1987.

DE WAAL, FRANS B. "Power & Sex Among Apes." In *Chimpanzee Politics.* New York: Holt & Rineholt, 1982.

FORMAN, SHEPARD. *The Brazilian Peasantry.* New York: Columbia University Press, 1975.

FRIED, MORTON H. *The Evolution of Political Society.* New York: Random House, 1967.

GREGOR, T. "Short People." *Natural History* 88 (1979):14-23.

HARRIS, M. *Cows, Pigs, Wars, and Witches.* New York: Random House, 1974.

KRACKE, W. and H. KRACKE. *Force and Persuasion: Leadership in an Amazonian Society.* Chicago: University of Chicago Press, 1978.

LÉVI-STRAUSS, CLAUDE. "The Social and Psychological Aspects of Chieftainship in a Primitive Tribe." *Transactions of the New York Academy of Sciences* 2 7(1944): 16-32.

MENZEL, E. W. *Machiavellian Intelligence.* Oxford: Clarendon Press, 1992.

SHWEDER, R. "Aspects of Cognition in Zinacanteco Shamans." In *Reader in Comparative Religion,* edited by William A. Lessa and Evon Z. Vogt. New York: Harper and Row, 1972.

SIMMONS, LEO W. "Attitudes Toward Aging and the Aged." *Journal of Gerontology* 1 (1945):72-95.

STOGDILL, RALPH M. *Handbook of Leadership.* New York: Free Press, 1974.

WERNER, DENNIS. "Are Some People More Equal Than Others?" *Journal of Anthropological Research* 37 4(1981): 360-373.

————. "Leadership Inheritance and Acculturation among the Mekranoti of Central Brazil." *Human Organization* 41 4 (1984): 342-345.

WILSON, EDWARD O. *Sociobiology.* Cambridge, Mass.: Harvard University Press, 1980.

LEGAL ANTHROPOLOGY

The law is one of the most impressive and most complex achievements in the history of human cultural development—a fact that sometimes makes it difficult to understand its simpler forms. There are at least three subjects in the comparative study of legal systems. First, there is the substantive law of many different societies, including the degree to which codification as a specific cultural attainment is recognized, and the methods for deriving such laws. The second subject includes the procedures and institutionalization of dispute settlement by which disputes are recognized or "named" and lifted out of the context in which they occur, then are systematically and predictably put into a settlement context, are heard (or judged) in this protected context by agreed procedure, and then the result is reinserted into the context from which the disputes were originally taken. The third subject is the way law fits in with other control mechanisms and values of society, that is, the processes by which some aspects of custom, morality, and usage are recontexted into a jural realm and the consonance of such law with other dimensions of culture.

Legal anthropology covers those three subjects (and others) ethnographically and comparatively. Legal processes and the way that those processes fit into the rest of culture are the primary foci of the discipline of legal anthropology. Three seldom-mentioned ideas that underlie the subdiscipline of legal anthropology should also be noted. One involves the human biological heritage, the second involves the tendency to take one's own system as a model for judging others, and the third involves the scale of society.

One way to understand the law is to call it a system of third-party interference in two-party disputes. All legal systems depend on the validity and effectiveness of such third-party interference. Such interference also appears to have biological roots; it is also found among chimpanzees and orangutans, both of whom interfere in disputes in order to reestablish a peaceful social situation and may then comfort the loser. The genius of human law is not just that it

systematically brings a third party into two-party disputes, but that it regularizes the process in the name of justice. Once a legal system has developed, the law may be used for some purposes that do not specifically involve a third party.

No specific legal system, including that of the United States, serves adequately as a model for comparative studies of legal systems. To merely apply theory or generalizations from U.S. society, instead of searching for theory in other societies and seeing how they correspond, is the single most lethal trap in legal anthropology. The Western legal model enlightens ideas found in other cultural arrangements, but those other arrangements also illuminate Western practices. Indeed, there is no branch of comparative anthropology in which a model from any single society serves as an adequate model for comparison. Thus, all theory in legal anthropology must include insights from many legal systems. Such metatheory, so derived, is not an adequate device for judging any single specific legal system—just as no single system is an adequate basis for creating such metatheory. Legal systems can be compared on the basis of what people say they should do (substantive law), on the basis of what they are observed to do in fact, which provides the view of the institutionalization of jural process, and on methods for deriving law and on the consonance of the law with the other dimensions of culture.

The scale of society is an integral consideration for legal anthropology, although it has not been adequately studied. The idea of scale has two branches—on the one hand it has to do with size, and on the other, with complexity. Although increased complexity usually accompanies increase in size, complexity may be increased or decreased with no change in size. As the social group gets bigger or more complex or both, social principles that work adequately in small or simple groups fail to work very well; specialized organizations to subserve specific purposes are developed. The larger and more diverse a culture becomes, the more necessary it becomes to create and maintain a specialized legal system.

Disputes are solved in hunting-and-gathering societies by self-help and by families and bands. Such small-scale societies have no need for specialized institutions to do the job. When specialized jural institutions come into play, self-help does not disappear, although some of its characteristics change. With the enlarged community that results from fixed settlement or agriculture, moots emerge. In a moot, the people of the community, or some significant portion of them, give themselves a special role and a special context for settling disputes. History is rife with attempts to make institutions for interfering in disputes concordant with other aspects of the culture. In medieval Europe, for example, "hard cases" were handed over to the religious institutions where they were settled by ordeal or by "wager of battle."

Once a specialized jural institution is founded, it can be called a court. There are forerunners of courts: the leopard-skin chief of the Nuer uses mediation to help settle disputes between the principals. If everyone wants the dispute settled, such mediation works. Arbitration is another mode of settling disputes without a fully organized court. Efforts in the United States to use mediation and arbitration to relieve the courts have met with some success. Courts, as agencies of government, share with the religious institutions the task of creating standards of behavior and seeing to it that they are followed. In some systems, such as those of Western Europe, church and state have been separated more or less successfully. In Islamic law, the two have purposefully not been separated.

The history of legal anthropology is long and impressive. Other than such outstanding exceptions as Sir Henry Sumner Maine's *Ancient Law* (1861) and George Lawrence Gomme's *Primitive Folk Moots* (1880), most of the early work on the subject (before legal anthropology as a subdiscipline emerged) consisted of attempts to codify the laws of various early historical groups, using the Western idea of a code of law. Perhaps the most obvious examples of such early fieldwork are those of Roy F. Barton among the Ifugao (1919) in the Philippines and Bruno Gutmann (1926) and R. S. Rattray (1929) in Africa. Bronislaw Malinowski (1926), during the same period, broadened the definition of law to include social rules and obligation based on reciprocity.

The study of legal anthropology was given a new format and organization by jurist Karl Llewellyn and anthropologist E. Adamson Hoebel in *The Cheyenne Way* (1941). Llewellyn, in this and other publications, created a new set of principles and a new vocabulary for examining law across cultures. Hoebel had done extensive fieldwork among the Cheyenne, talking at great length with old people about disputes they remembered and how their grandparents and other ancestors handled settlement of those disputes. (Such

study of so-called memory cultures of Native Americans was standard in Hoebel's time.) Among the many significant aspects of their book was recognition of the case method as the best way to study the law of non-Western peoples.

The year 1954 was a watershed for legal anthropology. In England, Max Gluckman published *The Judicial Process Among the Barotse,* which set an enviably high standard for reporting cases, this time observed while they were actually being tried. In the United States, Hoebel published *The Law of Primitive Man.* Two other important books—Watson Smith and John M. Roberts's *Zuni Law* and Paul Howell's *A Manual of Nuer Law* were published the same year. With these studies, the emphasis shifted from substantive law to the processes by which law operated. The focus on process is still dominant.

Two debates, the first over the insider-outsider perspective and the second over the definition of law, marked the next period and established some of the central questions, approaches, and techniques of comparison. Gluckman and Paul Bohannan (1957) engaged in a lively exchange in the 1950s over the issue of the "reasonable man." Gluckman had used this term from Western law to describe a standard for judicial reasoning among the Lozi. He also said it could be used in studying law cross-culturally. Bohannan objected that using such Western-oriented ideas not only deemphasized but falsified the legal folk culture. This debate has never been settled. Those who are interested primarily in the niceties of ethnography tend to agree with Bohannan. Others, especially those lawyers who value precision in their own terms or are interested in comparison at the substantive rather than the process level, tend to agree with Gluckman. Comparison is indeed made more difficult if legal ideas from Western culture are made part of the data instead of part of the theory, but it is essential that the data not be confused with theoretical scaffolding. The second debate, which continued through the 1970s, concerned the nature of law. Leopold Pospisil (1967) and others debated the elements of a correct definition of law—rules, principles, intention of universal applicability, territoriality, sanction, authority, symbols, commands, and social control. By the 1980s inquiry into a universal nature of law had been abandoned.

The collection of data on processes of dispute resolution in U.S. and other cultural traditions has always been a central focus of legal anthropology.

Several approaches have been taken to the collected material. Some authors provide compendia of examples, others look into typologies of factors that distinguish one type from another, while still others detail evolutionary typologies, or the catharsis and entertainment value, or the community consensus aspects of dispute settlement. Carol Greenhouse (1986), for example, studied a group of Southern Baptists who specifically eschewed the courts because of their principle that an adequately Christian life could be led only by following the law of God; on the other hand, the Zapotec studied by Laura Nader (1990) said that harmony must be achieved through systematic confrontation with the nonharmonious.

In the 1980s leading areas of interest were legal language or discourse, the historical dimension, hierarchy and domination-resistance, and new methodologies for approaching folk conceptualizations of law. Although most of the innovative work in previous years had been done on data from non-Western societies, many good studies were begun by legal anthropologists on conflict and courts in the United States. The work in the area of legal language has focused on how language is used in the courts, what kind of "work" that language does, how identities and categories get constructed through legal language, and how routines, repertoires, and types of discourse determine outcome. The gendered basis of legal language is an intriguing aspect of these studies.

Several recent collections, including *History and Power in the Study of Law: New Directions in Legal Anthropology* (1989) and *Ethnography and the Historical Imagination* (1992), in legal anthropology have engaged the historical dimension—the change in legal institutions, ideas and processes through time—and the ways in which the law encodes hierarchy and domination. Viewing law as nonneutral and full of asymmetrical power relations, these works study the forms of resistance to such encoding. Hierarchy, boundary creation, and appropriation questions with respect to ethnicity have also been taken up as ethnic cultural traditions move into courts questioning the "ownership" of certain cultural items that have been taken over by other subcultural units. Another way to configure hierarchy and boundaries is through consideration of the differences between the local, intermediate, state, and transnational levels of legal systems, a very new area of interest in legal anthropology.

An emerging interpretive and hermeneutic approach to law suggests that law is a distinctive way of "imagining the real," rather than positing law as a separate field to be studied as a distinct entity. This approach focuses on discourse and translation, as well as on what law shows us about culture, particularly the similarities between ordinary and judicial concepts. The discretion of the *qadi* judge in Morocco does not focus on development of a consistent body of doctrine but rather on the fit between decisions of Muslim judges and social relations in the specific case (Rosen 1989). The role of legal documents within a cultural tradition and the way they are produced, used, and reproduced have provided new insights. Work on Yemeni legal documents (Messick 1986) and on Tibetan law codes (French 1994) has centered on questions about the social status of documents, the relationship between oral and written, the role of documents in legal transactions, and the cultural characteristics of documents. Document specialists, documentary practice, and legal interpretation can be viewed as windows to social process.

In summary, the theories of legal anthropologists about the general nature of legal systems have begun to add up into a consistent set of propositions. Multiplex relationships are to be contrasted with single-interest relationships (Gluckman 1954). Multiplex relationships are diffuse, multidimensional, and moral; they are most commonly found in small face-to-face societies. Single-interest relationships are specialized, functionally specific, instrumental, and goal-oriented; they are common in large urban areas. This dichotomy has been redefined and reinterpreted many times. For example, it has been reworked into proposals that "multiplex" means mediation, whereas "single-interest" is said to mean the opposition involved in legal conflict. It has also been postulated that conflict in multiplex settings is actually about defining relationships. This bipolar model is complicated (Yngvesson 1985) by the fact that formal legal conflict may actually be useful in defining multiplex, continuing relationships and that parties recognize that the use of law in one setting may enhance nonlegal solutions in others.

Pospisil (1967) set out the multiplicity of legal levels, a theory that every functioning group or subgroup of a society possesses a legal system of its own. According to this theory, each individual in a society stands within several concentric circles of legal systems—family, church, community, workplace, state—

each of which has distinct rules, sanctions, and procedures. Bohannan (1965) postulated that customary rules become law when they are reinstitutionalized within the legal system. Such double institutionalization guarantees both the legal process and its fit with other institutions.

Sally Merry (1990) and John Conley and William O'Barr (1990) have been working with another dichotomy found in the United States between "true law," involving rules associated with male professionals, rule-orientation, high-status, and "clean," resolvable, unambiguous cases, and "dirty law," involving relationships, with female mediators handling unresolvable, interpersonal relationship-oriented disputes.

Publications in legal anthropology are widely scattered, but in the early 1990s, the Association for Political and Legal Anthropology upgraded its newsletter to become the journal POLAR (Political and Legal Anthropology Review). Legal anthropology is a small field, but its influence is growing in legal studies as well as in anthropology.

PAUL BOHANNAN
REBECCA FRENCH

BARTON, ROY F. *Ifugao Law.* Berkeley: University of California Press, 1919.

BOHANNAN, PAUL. *Justice and Judgment Among the Tiv.* London: Oxford University Press for International African Institute, 1957.

——— . "The Differing Realms of the Law." *American Anthropologist Special Publication: The Ethnography of Law,* edited by Laura Nader. *American Anthropologist* 67 (1965): 33–42.

COMAROFF, JOHN L., and JEAN COMAROFF. *Ethnography and the Historical Imagination.* Boulder, Colo.: Westview Press, 1992.

CONLEY, JOHN, and WILLIAM O'BARR. *Rules versus Relationships: The Ethnography of Legal Discourse.* Chicago: University of Chicago Press, 1990.

FRENCH, REBECCA. *The Golden Yoke: The Legal System of Buddhist Tibet.* Ithaca, N.Y.: Cornell University Press, 1994.

GLUCKMAN, MAX. *The Judicial Process Among the Barotse of Northern Rhodesia.* 1954. 2nd ed. Manchester, Eng.: Manchester University Press, 1967.

GOMME, GEORGE LAWRENCE. *Primitive Folk Moots.* London: S. Low, Marston, Searle & Rivington, 1880.

GREENHOUSE, CAROL J. *Praying for Justice: Faith, Order, and Community in an American Town.* Ithaca, N.Y.: Cornell University Press, 1986.

GUTMANN, BRUNO. *Das Recht der Dschagga.* Munich: Beck, 1926. Translated as *Chagga Law,* New Haven: HRAF Publishing, 1953.

HOEBEL, E. ADAMSON. *The Law of Primitive Man: A Study in Comparative Legal Dynamics.* Cambridge, Mass.: Harvard University Press, 1954.

HOWELL, PAUL. *A Manual of Nuer Law.* Oxford: Clarendon Press, 1954.

MAINE, HENRY SUMNER. *Ancient Law,* repr. of 1861 ed. Boston: Beacon, 1963.

MALINOWSKI, BRONISLAW. *Crime and Custom in Savage Society.* London: Routledge & Kegan Paul, 1926.

MERRY, SALLY. *Getting Justice and Getting Even: Legal Consciousness Among Working-Class Americans.* Chicago: University of Chicago Press, 1990.

MESSICK, BRINKLEY. "The Mufti, the Text, and the World: Legal Interpretation in Yemen." *Man* 21 (1986): 102–119.

NADER, LAURA. *Harmony, Ideology, and the Construction of Law, Justice, and Control in a Zapotec Mountain Village.* Stanford, Calif.: Stanford University Press, 1990.

POSPISIL, LEOPOLD. "Legal Levels and Multiplicity of Legal Systems in Human Societies." *Journal of Conflict Resolution* 9 (1967): 2–26.

RATTRAY, R. S. *Ashanti Law and Custom.* London: Oxford University Press, 1929.

ROSEN, LAWRENCE. *The Anthropology of Justice: Law as Culture in Islamic Society.* New York: Cambridge University Press, 1989.

SMITH, WATSON, and JOHN M. ROBERTS. *Zuni Law.* Cambridge, Mass.: Peabody Museum, 1954.

STARR, JUNE, and JANE COLLIER. *History and Power in the Study of Law: New Directions in Legal Anthropology.* Ithaca, N.Y.: Cornell University Press, 1989.

YNGVESSON, BARBARA. "Re-examining Continuing Relations and the Law." *1985 Wisconsin Law Review* (1985): 623–646.

LEISURE

During the first half of the twentieth century, several prominent anthropologists called for more attention to leisure as a cultural phenomenon. Bronislaw Malinowski (1931), for example, referred to leisure and recreation as creative elements in culture wherein cultural progress may take place. Similarly, Alfred L. Kroeber (1948) and Felix Keesing (1960) described leisure as a common context for cultural innovation and creativity. Keesing urged anthropologists to engage in a systematic analysis of leisure. Others, such as Franz Boas (1940) and V. Gordon Childe (1951), accorded leisure an even more prominent role in the dynamics of culture. In their view the adoption of sedentary agriculture provided an increase in the food supply that permitted increased leisure, a larger population, and the rise of craft specialization. In turn, a larger population could use its newfound leisure to think and invent devices that would provide even more food and leisure. Thus, leisure was implicated in a cumulative process of cultural development. Indeed, this surplus theory was prominent in anthropological thinking about culture change and elaboration from the 1930s through the mid-1950s. In the 1950s and later, however, evidence began to accumulate that refuted the assumptions that food collectors have little free time, that sedentary agriculture provides a more dependable and nutritious diet, or that any increases in leisure are utilized for thinking or invention (Just 1980).

The relationship of leisure to the evolution and elaboration of culture is one of two principal areas pursued by anthropologists when they consider leisure; the adaptive character of leisure is the other. Leisure per se, however, has attracted little attention from anthropologists, although much of what is often termed expressive culture—including art, music, play, games, festivals, literature, dance, performance, and other symbolic productions—clearly overlaps with leisure.

WHAT IS LEISURE?

When leisure has been considered by anthropologists it has almost universally been treated as free or unobligated time. Recreation, a related concept, usually denotes activities that take place during free time, such as games, sports, reading for pleasure, camping, or watching television, although recreation and leisure are often conflated, as in the term "leisure-time activities." On one hand, such apparently straightforward and objective definitions are useful, because it is uncertain whether anthropologists, who may be limited in cultural and linguistic competence in the society they are studying, can accurately assess the deeper meanings that leisure or recreation may have for their informants. On the other hand, simplistic notions of leisure as either free time or a particular kind of activity effectively obscure the fact, well known to ethnographers, that what appears to be leisure often takes place within the context of productive activity. This can be particularly true for women, whose leisure has traditionally been bound to the home and the domestic economy. As women wash clothes, work in fields, or go to market, they often can engage in social leisure with friends that is otherwise unavailable in the confines of the home. In these examples, neither free time nor type of activity delineates leisure, as the overall contexts are those of work, whereas the activities are multiple.

The young and the old, the infirm, or the incarcerated, for example, also may have much unobligated time, but such time would not normally be thought of as leisure. Similarly, many early reports by missionaries, colonial officials, and other travelers characterized members of various indigenous populations as leisured to the point of indolence. Such a view reflects both an ethnocentric imposition of a Western cultural value ("time is money") on others and a failure to understand that the alleged indolence may be part of an appropriate cultural response to local techno-environmental conditions. For example, it is now obvious that there is little point for food collectors to acquire resources much beyond their immediate needs if they have no way to store or transport those resources effectively. Their alleged indolence is merely the result of having considerable free time left over after the food quest is satisfied, a situation that Marshall Sahlins (1972) referred to as Zen affluence but which Peter Just (1980) characterized as forced idleness.

Because of such factors many current sociological definitions of leisure incorporate the notion of its meaning for partakers, generally stressing relative freedom of choice, intrinsic motivation, enjoyment, and self-expression. Such subjective definitions, although attractive, present their own peculiar difficulties, especially for anthropologists. It is difficult enough to determine what "leisure" means for members of one's own cultural and linguistic group, let alone to understand what it means for members of other cultures who speak unfamiliar languages.

LEISURE AND CULTURAL EVOLUTION

In modern industrial societies in which time is scarce, time acquires economic value and must be used with care. Just (1980) hypothesized that under such conditions, technological changes would be directed toward increasing free time, making a scarcity of free time, rather than an abundance (as in the surplus theory), instrumental in cultural elaboration. Research during the 1980s suggested that neither the surplus theory nor Just's (1980) time-scarcity hypothesis adequately explains the relationship between cultural complexity and the availability of free time. Ruth Munroe et al. (1983) compared productive inputs of labor of !Kung San, Machiguenga, Canchino, Kikuyu, Logoli, and U.S. women. The !Kung San and the Machiguenga are primarily food collectors, and the others, with the exception of the U.S. women, are horticulturists and herders. The sample of U.S. women was from Los Angeles County. Munroe et al. found that the time spent in a combination of food preparation, garden labor, chores, animal care, and wage labor was much higher for the three horticultural societies than for either the food collectors or the U.S. sample. If leisure is assumed to vary inversely with work time, it can then be concluded that members of societies at the extremes of cultural complexity may have substantially more free time than members of societies at moderate levels of cultural complexity.

Kim Hill et al. (1985) suggested yet another alternative, that cultural complexity and the amount of time devoted either to work or to leisure are unrelated. They observed that when the sum of productive effort is considered—including travel to food sources, bringing food home, processing it, and miscellaneous related activities—food collectors and subsistence horticulturists expend roughly the same amount of time in food acquisition.

Garry E. Chick (1986) reviewed these competing positions and attempted to test the relationship between free-time availability and cultural complexity (1992) using cross-cultural data from the Human Relations Area Files (HRAF). Efforts to code leisure were unsuccessful owing to the paucity of information on the topic, even though HRAF has categories devoted to recreation, recreation facilities, labor and leisure, and leisure-time activities. Hence, leisure was treated as time left over after labor. Societies in the Standard Cross-Cultural Sample were coded for hours of productive labor per day (for adult males) and these data were compared with codes for cultural complexity. The nature of the relationship was assessed with polynomial regression to determine whether the data were best fit by a straight line or a parabola. Societies at both the lower and upper ranges of cultural complexity appeared to have slightly more free time than those in the middle, but, instead of being distinctly parabolic, the relationship could be described nearly as well by a straight line as by a curve. Further, the large amount of variance observed among societies at all levels of complexity suggested that either the data contain high levels of error or that the hypothesized relationship is weak or nonexistent.

Related hypotheses, however, were more promising. If, in fact, free time is a scarce, but desirable, commodity, there are several ways to attempt to increase its availability. Children can be inexpensive sources of labor if their net work output is greater than the net input needed to raise them. Thus, where there is a need for high levels of adult subsistence labor, it may be possible to augment the available labor pool by having many children. In addition, children may be put to productive labor at an earlier age in societies where free time is relatively scarce for adults. Therefore, Chick (1992) further hypothesized that societies at low and at high levels of cultural complexity would have both low levels of fertility and relatively extended periods of nonproductive childhood and adolescence when compared with societies of moderate cultural complexity.

HRAF sources were coded for the number of children who reach the age of economic productivity per female and the age at which children begin to contribute to household production. Plots of these data with cultural complexity were best fit by inverted U and U-shaped curves (Chick 1992). Although the hypotheses were supported, the data upon which they are based must be viewed with caution, because HRAF sources on the variables in question are often nonexistent, vague, or contradictory. Nevertheless, case studies of hunter-gatherers (e.g., Lee and DeVore 1968) indicate that such groups have relatively small families and that childhood and adolescence are relatively unconstrained by work. Similarly, families

in westernized, industrialized societies tend to have low levels of fertility and extended periods of childhood and adolescence. Even in Western history, however, during the early parts of the industrial revolution, when working-class adults labored long hours in order to make a living, child labor was rampant. Thus, there is reason to believe that the availability of free time depends upon subsistence conditions. There is evidence to suggest that the same is true for the way in which leisure is experienced.

ADAPTIVE ASPECTS OF LEISURE

Joshua Rubin et al. (1986) used time-allocation data from four Amazonian groups to determine if the way in which leisure is experienced contributes to adaptation to environmental conditions. The four groups are linguistically and culturally similar and reside in similar habitats in central Brazil. Each of the four groups subsists primarily by slash-and-burn horticulture, but each augments its diet by hunting and fishing. They differ, however, in terms of the length and intensity of their contact with Brazilian society, and two of the groups, the Kanela and the Bororo, live in habitats that are substantially degraded in comparison with those of the other two groups, the Xavante and the Mekranoti. Rubin et al. suggested that a comparison of the leisure of the four groups would show that adaptation to habitat conditions occurs through the adjustment of patterns of consumption. They further indicated that energy may be conserved both in consumption and in production. They defined leisure as activities that did not directly contribute to either production or reproduction and noted that some leisure activities can be costlier than others in terms of energy. Thus, more energy is required for vigorous play or dancing than for sitting quietly or sleeping, and the choice to do one or the other may be culturally favored and related to habitat degradation. Therefore, they hypothesized that the proportion of time spent in low-cost leisure activities should increase while the rate of return on subsistence activity declines.

An analysis of their time-allocation data supported this hypothesis and distinguished two patterns of leisure consumption. To produce numbers of calories similar to those obtained by the Xavante and the Mekranoti from their relatively abundant habitats, the Kanela and the Bororo, living in their relatively degraded environments, allocate their labor differently among subsistence activities than the other two groups but do not actually spend more hours working. Similarly, the groups utilize their leisure time differently. The Xavante and the Mekranoti spend nearly twice as much of their leisure in active, high-energy-cost pursuits (47.4 percent and 48.6 percent, respectively) than either the Kanela or the Bororo (25.3 percent and 33.4 percent, respectively). The results are most striking for children under the age of fifteen. Kanela children spend more than twice as much time sleeping and resting than playing actively. Bororo children also spend more time in low-energy-cost activity than in high-cost play. The opposite is true of Xavante and Mekranoti children, who spend significantly more time playing actively than resting or sleeping. Thus, Rubin et al. found that the degree of habitat degradation and the energy spent in leisure are related for these four groups. In particular, the activity levels of children appear to be adjusted according to the effort needed to obtain adequate nutrition from the habitat. Members of the groups need not be aware of these energy-allocation strategies or their benefits, and conscious decisions to intensify production are not made. Instead, members of the two groups living in relatively degraded habitats reduce their needs. This strategy has also been observed among primates in degraded habitats where the animals spend little if any time in play and apply their energy resources instead to the quest for food (Baldwin and Baldwin 1972).

Whether such adaptive constraints on leisure occur in other societies is unknown. It would be informative, for example, to compare economically marginal groups and members of the middle class in modern Euro-American culture to see if adjustments in active versus inactive leisure are apparent. The evidence suggests that the amount of leisure, in terms of free time, may be relatively constant across cultures, regardless of their complexity or their habitat, but the degree to which that free time is utilized actively or passively may differ.

Intracultural variation in leisure activity is similarly related to production by the spillover and compensation theories (Wilensky 1960). The spillover theory suggests that the nature of leisure derives directly from the nature of work—active work leads to active leisure and passive work to passive leisure. The compensation theory presents the opposite perspective, that active, hence tiring, work engenders passive, recuperative leisure but passive, thus enervating, work leads to active, invigorating leisure. Considerable research has been devoted to the work-leisure relationship since the 1950s, but neither the spillover nor the compensation theory has been found to adequately account for how leisure is experienced. It is likely that choices of both work and leisure are products of a complex of ecological, enculturative, and idiosyncratic variables.

SUMMARY

Although the amount of free time available may be related to cultural complexity, and the distribution of active and passive leisure activities may be related to the ease or difficulty of making a living, neither the free-time nor the type-of-activity conceptualizations of leisure deal in any substantive way with what free-time activities mean to participants. Ultimately, the understanding of leisure as a pancultural phenomenon will require the simultaneous incorporation of all of its constituents, including unobligated time, activity type, and the meaning of the actions for those at leisure.

Garry E. Chick

See Also: Feasts and Festivals; Games; Play; Sports

Baldwin, John D., and Janice I. Baldwin. "The Ecology and Behavior of Squirrel Monkeys (*Saimiri oerstedi*) in a Natural Forest in Western Panama." *Folia Primatologica* 18 (1972): 161–184.

Boas, Franz. *Race, Language, and Culture.* New York: Free Press, 1940.

Chick, Garry E. "Leisure, Labor, and the Complexity of Culture: An Anthropological Perspective." *Journal of Leisure Research* 18 (1986): 154–168.

——— . "A Cross-Cultural Perspective on Leisure." Paper presented at the annual meeting of the Society for Cross-Cultural Research, Santa Fe, N.Mex., February 1992.

Childe, V. Gordon. *Man Makes Himself.* New York: New American Library, 1951.

Hill, Kim, Hillard Kaplan, Kristen Hawkes, and Ana Magdelena Hurtado. "Men's Time Allocation to Subsistence Work Among the Ache of Eastern Paraguay." *Human Ecology* 13 (1985): 29–47.

Just, Peter. "Time and Leisure in the Elaboration of Culture." *Journal of Anthropological Research* 36 (1980): 105–115.

KEESING, FELIX. "Recreative Behavior and Culture Change." In *Men and Cultures,* edited by Anthony F. C. Wallace. Philadelphia: University of Pennsylvania Press, 1960.

KROEBER, ALFRED L. *Anthropology.* New York: Harcourt Brace, 1948.

LEE, ROBERT B., and IRVEN DEVORE, eds. *Man the Hunter.* Chicago: Aldine, 1968.

MALINOWSKI, BRONISLAW. "Culture." In *Encyclopedia of the Social Sciences,* vol. 2, edited by R. A. Seligman. N.Y. Macmillan, 1931.

MUNROE, RUTH H., ROBERT L. MUNROE, CAROL MICHELSON, AMY KOEL, RALPH BOLTON, and CHARLENE BOLTON. "Time Allocation in Four Societies." *Ethnology* 22 (1983): 355–370.

RUBIN, JOSHUA, NANCY M. FLOWERS, and DANIEL R. GROSS. "The Adaptive Dimensions of Leisure." *American Ethnologist* 13 (1986): 524–536.

SAHLINS, MARSHALL. *Stone Age Economics.* New York: Aldine, 1972.

WILENSKY, HAROLD L. "Work, Careers, and Social Integration." *International Social Science Journal* 12 (1960): 543–560.

LIFE HISTORY

The life history is an ethnographic method used to study cultural phenomena by focusing on the personal experiences over time of one or more individuals. Life histories are distinguished from biographies in fields other than anthropology such as history or literature by choice of subject (usually ordinary people, rather than public figures, often nonliterate members of traditional societies, ethnic minorities, or urban sub-cultures); by fieldwork methods involving face-to-face interaction (collaboration with a living subject through interviews that are usually tape-recorded and transcribed and the use of observations and sometimes personal documents, such as diaries or historical records); and formal attention to topics of theoretical interest in the discipline (such as how individuals acquire a particular cultural, gender, or political identity).

Gathering material for a life history is a relatively time-consuming and repetitive method, one better suited to exploring the meaning of an individual's life than to the collection of straight ethnographic information. As Ruth Benedict (1959) observed in her closing address as president of the American Anthropological Association in 1947: "The unique value of life histories lies in the fraction of the material which shows that repercussions the experiences of a man's life—either shared or idiosyncratic—have upon him as a human being molded in that environment." Benedict argued that the humanities would provide more adequate models of understanding life histories than the social sciences, particularly psychology, then dominated by a positivist approach. Since Benedict's time, life histories have been used increasingly to understand how persons conceive of themselves and their lived experiences. This is due in part to a disciplinary and interdisciplinary shift occurring since the 1970s toward narrative analysis, reflexivity, interpretation or hermeneutics, phenomenology, psychoanalysis, and cultural critiques rooted in Marxism and feminism. Thus, Benedict's call for humanistic models to interpret life histories has been increasingly realized.

HISTORY OF THE METHOD IN THE UNITED STATES

According to Lewis L. Langness (1965), life histories became an integral part of cultural anthropology in the United States from about 1925 through 1945. The first full-length publication was *Crashing Thunder* (1926), an account edited by Paul Radin from interviews he conducted with a middle-aged Winnebago man. The fluorescence of life histories as a self-conscious method arrived in the 1930s and 1940s with the rise of culture-and-personality studies (DuBois 1944; Simmons 1942). Key works on the use of life histories and other personal documents were sponsored at this time by the Social Science Research Council (Allport 1942; Dollard 1935; Kluckhohn 1945).

Dollard (1935) listed the following criteria for judging the techniques used in life histories: the subject must be viewed as a specimen in a cultural series; the organic motors of action ascribed must be socially relevant; the peculiar role of the family group in transmitting the culture must be recognized; the specific method of elaboration of organic materials into social behavior must be shown; the continuous related character of experience from childhood through adulthood must be stressed; the "social situation" must be carefully and continuously specified as a factor; and the life-history material itself must be organized and conceptualized. Applying these criteria to *Crashing Thunder*, Dollard concluded that the work "should be taken as an inside view of the Winnebago culture rather than as a careful analysis of a human life."

Gordon Allport (1942), Clyde Kluckhohn (1945), and Lewis L. Langness (1965) added useful discussions of field techniques and methods for collecting life histories, the use of such personal documents as diaries and projective tests, problems of reliability and validity, new topics for cultural analysis, and suggestions for presenting biographical data. As indicated by the term "anthropological science" used by Kluckhohn and Langness, these authors tried to blend the demands of positivism (representative sampling, attention to truth-telling, triangulation of sources) with an appreciation of the humanistic potential of the method. Kluckhohn argued that greater numbers of life histories of women should be collected to provide more balanced understandings of cultures. He proposed the collection of topical life histories in addition to the standard episodic type; he also suggested that preoccupation with getting subjects to recall past events diverted anthropologists from the possibility of collecting rich "contemporaneous" life histories, that is, accounts of lives in progress.

Kluckhohn anticipated a radical phenomenological approach that would include methods and genre, as well as the content of the subject's lived experience: "Anthropologists have also clung too closely to the conception of the life record in strictly sequential or chronological terms. This is reflected in the manner in which they have presented their materials and probably channeled the interviewing too. . . In many cultures which conceive time so very differently from the manner which Western culture regards as 'natural,' too much pressure upon the subject to specify absolute dates or even sequences must mean that all of his recollections or comments are forced through a very artificial screen." An entire subgenre of the life history could be developed simply by putting this one insight of Kluckhohn's into practice.

Expanding upon Kluckhohn's work, Langness (1965) contributed an historical analysis of the literature, a more comprehensive bibliography, new suggestions for the analysis of life history documents, and an introduction to ethical problems such as protection of the subject's identity that were only just becoming evident under changing social conditions of anthropological research. Kluckhohn and Langness found the life history literature weakest where systematic analysis and interpretation were concerned.

LIFE HISTORIES AND LIFE STORIES: THE INTERPRETATIVE TURN

It has been difficult to distinguish between anthrobiographies and biographies in the anthropological literature due to the manner in which most life histories are produced. An extremely popular model has been that of Oscar Lewis (1961), who composed complex first-person accounts that read like autobiographies or life stories, without an explicit record of the contribution made by the interviewer/editor. A new emphasis on life stories that distinguishes them from life histories has emerged, partly through the influence of European philosophical traditions (Bertaux 1981). In terms of genre, life story research does not create the illusion of a naturalistic unfolding of an individual's development. Rather, life stories are treated more as distinct speech acts elicited under particular circumstances and illuminating particular issues of the subject's lived experience.

Explicit concerns with phenomenology (attempts to understand the lived experience of subjects) and hermeneutics (attempts to elucidate how understandings of lived experiences are constructed textually) entered the life history literature in the mid-1970s (Langness and Frank, 1981; Watson and Watson-Franke, 1985). Strategies used to address phenomenological and hermeneutic concerns include a turn away from totalizing life histories constructed according to anthropologists' agendas, as in Dollard's criteria, and toward the incorporation of partial self-narratives or life stories within more open texts (Crapanzano 1980; Ginsburg 1989); and reflexive reports of the elicitation frame or context, including analyses of the power relations between life historian and life history subject, with the goal of producing not only texts but analyses in a more collaborative way than before (Myerhoff 1978; Personal Narratives Group 1989; Shostak 1981). As with other ethnographies, there is also a new playfulness in the writing of life histories that often involves including autobiographical material by the anthropologists, a biography in the shadow (Behar 1993; Kondo 1990). There is a vitality in this writing reminiscent of the exciting mood of self-discovery and coming to consciousness of certain popular autobiographies, particularly by authors who have struggled against racism and other forms of oppression (Langness and Frank 1981).

Promising studies of life stories have also begun to appear in phenomenologically influenced fields overlapping anthropology, such as linguistics (Linde 1993), sociology (Rosenthal 1993), and psychology (Rosenwald and Ochberg 1992). Most employ a strict methodological stance of neutral listening, with subsequent analysis of the life stories in terms of the formal organization of discourse rather than in terms of theories or data external to the text. These newer studies objectify the subject's discourse rather than the subject as a person. They do not necessarily presuppose a coherent psychic unity or personality of which the life story is a "reflection." Rather, linguistic and cultural practices are studied as strategies used by subjects to lend narrative coherence to disparate, conflicted, and contradictory life experiences.

To describe the life history as a fixed method exclusive to cultural anthropology would be unduly limited. Life histories by culture-and-personality theorists in the 1930s and 1940s were similarly part of a zeitgeist that cut across academic fields. Dollard's criteria continue to provide a strong foundation for life history studies, with three additional guidelines: life story materials should be presented whenever possible in textual forms that distinguish the subject's discourse from that produced by the life historian; the subject's self-analysis should be an object for interpretation, the life history document should in most cases be reviewed by the subject, and the subject's critique should be included in the text; the historical context of the life history and life story discourses should be specified, including an analysis of power and other relations between the life historian and subject.

The following trends may also be noted: The term "the subject" is being replaced by other terms, such as "the narrator," that are free from hierarchical and scientific connotations. Numerous critiques of the ethnocentrism and gender bias of the humanities, as traditionally construed, may require a term other than "humanistic" to refer to interpretative approaches to life histories. Better representation in the profession of anthropology of peoples traditionally studied but excluded from elite academic positions is needed to broaden the interpretation of life histories and life

stories, to increase their usefulness to the communities who have a stake in the research, and to keep vital the liberating potential of autobiography and life history as creative genres associated with the transformation of individual consciousness and cultures.

GELYA FRANK

ALLPORT, GORDON. *The Use of Personal Documents in Psychological Science*. New York: Social Science Research Council, Bulletin 49, 1942.

BEHAR, RUTH. *Translated Woman: Crossing the Border with Esperanza's Story*. Boston: Beacon Press, 1993.

BENEDICT, RUTH. "Anthropology and the Humanities." In *An Anthropologist at Work: Writings of Ruth Benedict*, edited by Margaret Mead. Boston: Houghton Mifflin, 1959.

BERTAUX, DANIEL. *Biography and Society: The Life History Approach in the Social Sciences*. Beverly Hills, Calif.: Sage Publicatios, 1981.

CRAPANZANO, VINCENT. *Tuhami: Portrait of a Moroccan*. Chicago: University of Chicago Press, 1980.

DOLLARD, JOHN. *Criteria for the Life History, With An Analyses of Six Notable Documents*. New Haven, Conn.: Yale University Press, 1935.

DUBOIS, CORA A. *People of Alor*. Minneapolis: University of Minnesota Press, 1944.

GINSBURG, FAYE D. *Contested Lives: The Abortion Debate in an American Community*. Berkeley: University of California Press, 1989.

KLUCKHOHN, CLYDE. *The Personal Document in Anthropological Science*. In *The Use of Personal Documents in History, Anthropology and Sociology*, edited by Louise Gottschalk, Clyde Kluckhohn, and Robert C. Angell. New York: Social Science Research Council, Bulletin 53, 1945.

KONDO, DORINNE K. *Crafting Selves: Power, Gender, and Discourses of Identity in a Japanese Workplace*. Chicago: University of Chicago Press, 1990.

LANGNESS, LEWIS L. *The Life History in Anthropological Science*. New York: Holt, Rinehart and Winston, 1965.

———, and GELYA FRANK. *Lives: An Anthropological Approach to Biography*. Novato, Calif.: Chandler and Sharp, 1981.

LEWIS, OSCAR. *The Children of Sanchez: Autobiography of a Mexican Family*. New York: Vintage Books, 1961.

LINDE, CHARLOTTE. *Life Stories: The Creation of*

Coherence. New York: Oxford University Press, 1993.

MYERHOFF, BARBARA G. *Number Our Days*. New York: E.P. Dutton, 1978.

PERSONAL NARRATIVES GROUP. *Interpreting Women's Lives: Feminist Theory and Personal Narratives*. Bloomington: Indiana University Press, 1989.

ROSENTHAL, GABRIELE. "Reconstruction of Life Stories: principles of Selection in Generating Stories for Narrative Biographical Interviews." In *The Narrative Study of Lives*, vol. 1, edited by Ruthellen Josselson and A. Lieblich. Newbury Park, Calif.: Sage Publications, 1993.

ROSENWALD, GEORGE C. and RICHARD L. OCHBERG, eds. *Storied Lives: The Cultural Politics of Self-Understanding*. New Haven, Conn.: Yale University Press, 1992.

SHOSTAK, MARJORIE. *Nisa: The Life and Words of a !Kung Woman*. Cambridge, Mass.: Harvard University Press, 1981.

SIMMONS, LEO W. *Sun Chief: The Autobiography of a Hopi Indian*. New Haven, Conn.: Yale University Press, 1942.

WATSON, LAWRENCE C., and MARIA-BARBARA WATSON-FRANKE. *Interpreting Life Histories: An Anthropological Inquiry*. New Brunswick, N.J.: Rutgers University Press, 1985.

LINGUISTIC ANTHROPOLOGY

"Linguistic anthropology" is the label applied to one of the four major subfields of anthropology, the subfield that has language as its primary subject matter and that has deep affinities with the discipline of linguistics. The subfield is also sometimes called "anthropological linguistics," and the two labels can cause confusion, because they are often used interchangeably but actually refer to somewhat different types of inquiry. When a distinction is drawn between linguistic anthropology and anthropological linguistics, the difference is part disciplinary focus, part history. For linguistic anthropology, the focus is on anthropology. The research questions are anthropological, and the subject matter studied to answer the questions is language or linguistics. Linguistic anthropologists may, for example, be interested in the social consequences of the difference in the ways that men and women speak. They would thus use linguistics to document the speech differences, which could

then be investigated anthropologically. By contrast, anthropological linguistics is the study of linguistic questions and issues, using anthropological techniques and procedures. A scholar who planned, for example, to record and describe a previously unstudied language, say in the highlands of New Guinea or in the Amazon Basin, would need to do the research in the people's home areas—in the field—following interview and recording procedures essentially as an anthropologist would but concentrating specifically on the structure of the language.

The difference in focus has historical foundations. Anthropological linguistics is historically older, emerging from field research in the first two to three decades of the twentieth century. The field research was on American Indian languages, a subject that came to be central to linguistics in the Americanist tradition. Anthropological linguistics represented the fieldwork tradition within linguistics, especially if the research was done by linguists who were members of departments of anthropology. Linguists in anthropology pursuing research on Native American languages were the prototypical anthropological linguists. Linguistic anthropology emerged as the name for the subfield when the interests in language began to move significantly beyond description, comparison, and classification of languages based on structural features. Especially prominent in that emergence was the question of how language, as a part of culture, is both revealing of culture and structuring of culture.

EARLY HISTORY

Anthropology and linguistics have separate but intertwined histories. Anthropology traces its origins to social philosophy of the eighteenth century, which was itself heavily influenced by the body of information on people in non-Western societies that had resulted from European exploration. Linguistics grew primarily out of the classics and from philological interests in European languages. The major long-term intersection of the fields began in the early twentieth century in the study of Native American societies in the New World. The sheer diversity of Native American societies and their radically different characteristics compared with Old World European societies eventually led to serious study of them. An academic discipline, in fact, arose to carry out the studies. American anthropology emerged as a discipline dedicated to an understanding of the origins, distribution, and characteristics of the people and societies who were the original inhabitants of the Western Hemisphere. Unlike anthropology in European countries, which tended to be primarily or exclusively ethnological (the comparative study of societies and cultures), several traditionally distinct disciplines joined into one in the United States to form an integrated approach to research on American Indians. Those disciplines included ethnology, archaeology, physical anthropology, and anthropological linguistics.

EARLY TYPES OF RESEARCH

The scholarship produced by the early anthropological linguists was of three major types. The primary one was descriptions of the linguistic structure and linguistic characteristics of individual languages, produced by such scholars as Franz Boas, Edward Sapir, Leonard Bloomfield, Morris Swadesh, and Mary Haas. That genre of research is known as the Americanist Tradition (Hymes 1983). The research was conducted as fieldwork, largely the recording of texts from native speakers, linguistic description of language form in the text, and analyses of the form in linguistic terms. Much of the work was salvage in nature, to record as much as possible before the language disappeared.

A related and second type of scholarship in the first decades of research on American Indian languages was the comparison of the linguistic features of languages with the ultimate goal of classification. The idea was to identify degrees of genetic relationship among languages and to build relationships into larger clusters of language families. The first classification was produced by John Wesley Powell in 1891, and it contained fifty-eight major taxa. Sapir produced two classifications, the earlier one recognizing twenty-three major taxa and a more carefully considered one in 1929 that recognized six major taxa. The genetic classification of Native American languages contributed substantially to a variety of anthropological concerns about the origins and distribution of Native American societies. Perhaps most important, the linguistic classifications served as an organizing framework for the large and initially chaotic mass of information that was accumulating about Native American populations. The language family groups provided obvious, first-order units for systematizing and ordering other types of anthropological information.

The third type of scholarship produced in anthropological linguistic anthropology in the early part of the twentieth century is more abstract and more methodological than the other two types. At the time linguistic analyses were strictly structural in nature. Language form was systematically divided into constituent parts, which were considered to be the inventory of units from which the language could be built. The procedures for the discovery of the basic units were well established and rigorous, making them attractive as models for analysis of other types of social and cultural information. The first-order objective of the research was identification of invariant patterns. Social and cultural behavior, however, operates at a more or less direct level of consciousness, and thus the informational base can be fairly easily manipulated. Boas (1911) and Sapir (1927) recognized, however, that linguistic patterning is largely unconscious to the speakers of a language. The value of the insight is that linguistic patterning is less susceptible to secondary rationalization and thus valuable for accurate insights into cultural process.

THE SAPIR-WHORF HYPOTHESIS

Each of the three types of research has continued in linguistic anthropology. Linguistic description and genetic reconstruction, however, have become more and more the province of linguistics and have, correspondingly, diminished in linguistic anthropology. The implications of linguistic patterns for culture structure and process, by contrast, have continued to grow in importance. The idea that linguistic patterning is unconscious and thus reflective of invariant cultural patterns has a corollary that is even more important for anthropology. If the patterning is given some directive force, then the structure of language may have a constraining or even controlling influence on the pattern of one's thoughts. A clear expression of that idea can be found in Sapir's famous book *Language*, published in 1921. One of Sapir's students, Benjamin Lee Whorf, made the idea the cornerstone of his work, culminating in his well-known "The Relation of Habitual Thought and Behavior to Language" (1941). In both cases, the fundamental ideas are that individuals adapt to their social environments through the languages they speak and that the social environments are thus not isomorphic with each other. The similarity of their ideas led Harry Hoijer (1956) to christen them the Sapir-Whorf hypothesis.

The Sapir-Whorf hypothesis has intrinsic interest, because it addresses the question of the extent to which the language one speaks influences the way one thinks. It has been the subject of a considerable amount of discussion. Much of the literature has been critical, attempting to reject the hypothesis altogether. The issue, however, is not simple, and it is compounded by the question of what Whorf, in particular, actually meant in his writings. A wide variety of claims have been attributed to him, some not supported by the evidence. A consistent misinterpretation is that Whorf proposed that the structure of language an individual speaks actually determines the thought patterns and thus the worldview of the individual.

John Lucy (1985) has clarified some of the worst misconceptions. A central part of Whorf's argument is that the ontological categories on which important language distinctions are based, such as tenses and classifiers, are habitually used by speakers and that the habitual use itself predisposes them to see their physical and cultural world through the categories. For example, the basis on which spatial distance is conceptualized can vary considerably from one society to another. A distance may be thought of as long or short, depending on the number of units of measurements involved, as in kilometers or in units of time required to traverse the distance. As is well known among anthropologists, however, in many small-scale societies the unit of measurement seems to be based on social distance. A specific location is near or far, depending on the social distance in the relationship between the speaker and an individual at that "distant" location.

Linguistic anthropologists have remained interested in Sapir's and Whorf's ideas since they were first proposed, but two new developments in the early 1960s took center stage away from the extreme relativism of the 1940s and 1950s. The new developments, however, were both direct departures from the Sapir-Whorf hypothesis. In one case, interest was focused on the commonalities underlying the diversity of language and thought across societies. That area of inquiry has been referred to by a variety of names, principally ethnoscience or ethnographic semantics. The second development extended the idea of relativity from language structure to language use, thereby opening up a new subfield of inquiry, the ethnography of speaking.

ETHNOGRAPHIC SEMANTICS

The fundamental idea in ethnographic semantics is that the phenomena that are particularly important to a society will be organized into a structured domain and named (Conklin 1962; Frake 1962). The names of the items in a domain, the words themselves, can each stand alone and refer to some specific referent, such as a type of kinsman. The words, however, also have membership in a larger collective, a domain, and the meaning of a word is thus reflexive of the domain. The lexical item, "uncle," for example, might name a particular type of individual (or an individual), but it also is reflective of the larger domain of kinship. The characterization of a domain can be made in terms of the shared elements of the words, in effect the semantics of the lexical units. Linguistic anthropologists interested, for example, in types of relatives, would select kinship as a domain to be investigated, elicit the inventory of lexical items that named types of relatives, and then seek to discover the features, or components, from which the meaning of the lexical items were constructed. In English kin terms, "father" would be constructed from the features "male," "ascending generation one," and "lineal relative," whereas "mother" would be the same except for female gender and "son" would be the same except for "descending generation one." The idea behind the analysis was that it would provide an account of how native speakers organized their culture into domains and how they used the components of the domains to structure meaning.

Ethnographic semantics was best applied in cases in which domains were relatively clear in their scope and were elaborated lexically. In several of those areas, kinship for example, the results eventually proved to be of limited value, largely because the analyses tended to focus on how the semantics of words could be organized rather than on how members of societies actually organized their cultural knowledge. An analysis might be thorough but devoid of psychological reality, that is, without shedding any direct light on how speakers actually organized the components. The two domains in which ethnographic semantics have been the most successfully applied are ones in which the problem of psychological reality could be most directly addressed. One of these is in color term research and the other is the nomenclature and classification of botanical and zoological phenomena.

The classic work on color terms was by Brent Berlin and Paul Kay (1969). They began their research with a comparison across twenty languages of the lexical terms for basic colors (colors that are primary, salient, and singly-named [monolexemic], such as red, blue, yellow, green). The sample has now been extended to more than 100 languages in an ongoing project, the World Color Survey. Among the major findings of the study are that the appearance of basic color terms across societies follows an implicational scale. If a society has only two color terms, they will be light (white) and dark (black); if a society has three terms, the third one will be red; if there are four terms, the fourth one will be green or blue, and so forth through seven terms. The database is now rich enough that variation has been documented in the paths that are taken in the "unfolding" of basic color terms in the blue, green, and yellow regions of the color spectrum.

Research on folk terminology and classification of plants and animals has been recently summarized by Berlin (1992). Relatively small-scale societies that continue to live in close association with their traditional environments appear to name and classify the flora and fauna in highly similar ways. The total number of names for native plants and animals in any such society is approximately 500, and 80 percent of those, more or less, are at a particular level of classification, the folk generic level. That level includes plants and animals, such as oak, pine, rose, eagle, raccoon, and lizard. Generics, however, occupy a position in a hierarchy. At the next highest level, directly above generics, is life form, which in English would include bird, mammal, reptile, tree, and flower. Up the taxonomic hierarchy another level are the unique beginners, animal and plant. Coming back down the hierarchy to one rank below folk generics, are varietals, such as white pine, pin oak, bald eagle, and striped lizard, and down one level further are specifics, such as kinds of white pine, kinds of pin oak, and so on. Although the actual names of plants and animals vary, of course, from society to society, the basic hierarchic structure is very much the same across all of the societies.

The remarkable similarity across societies of ethnobiological nomenclatural and classificational systems is apparently due to the similar ways that members of the societies perceive their local biota. Perception of morphological form and of salience seem to be the bases of the similar taxonomies. People perceive morphological traits of different types of plants and animals in much the same way, regardless of the language they speak or their particular geographical location, and the common perception and perceptual strategies produce the similar hierarchic structures.

THE ETHNOGRAPHY OF COMMUNICATION

A second type of ethnographic inquiry, the ethnography of speaking, began at about the same time as ethnographic semantics. The basic objective of each was similar, to improve the way ethnography was done in order to produce descriptions of societies more in their own terms and categories. In ethnographic semantics the new approach was to produce descriptions that were more focused and fine-grained; in the ethnography of speaking, the new element was the research topic itself, speech. The consequence was a major shift in the study of language, culture, and society. Throughout its history, linguistic anthropology tended to analyze language structure and then to use structure to discover patterns of association with other phenomena, such as gender and social class. In the ethnography of speaking, however, speech behavior rather than language structure became the subject matter, the topic to be investigated.

Dell H. Hymes (1962) produced the theoretical framework for the ethnographic study of speaking. The ultimate objective of the ethnography of speaking was a complete description of the speech resources available in a speech community and the patterns and functions that ensued from their systematic utilization. Actual speech behavior was described and analyzed in order to detect patterns of speech use within specific communities, which involved looking at types of speakers and situations, genres of speech, variant functions of speech, and interrelationships among those factors. The shift from relativity of language structure to relativity of speech use literally opened up a broad, exciting new area of research, liberating researchers from the limitations of studying language only through linguistic structure. In time, the ethnography of speaking was also expanded to cover types of signs and symbols other than spoken language, such as gesture, and the name was also expanded to the ethnography of communication.

SOCIOLINGUISTICS

During the early to mid-1960s, another area of research began to develop, deriving from a variety of sources in linguistics, philosophy, and sociology (Gumperz and Hymes 1972; Ervin-Tripp 1969). The subject matter was the social nature of speech, especially the socially organized use and consequences of speech. The approach was microlevel, looking at the interplay of the social characteristics of the speaker, the speech recipient, and the form of speech employed. Seemingly minor variations in any of the characteristics could completely alter the meaning of the speech. An utterance by one speaker to a hearer could have a particular meaning if the dyad was characterized as friendship, whereas the same utterance could have a radically different meaning if the dyad was characterized as enmity. This area of inquiry was referred to as sociolinguistics, based on the recognition that language is fundamentally social in its function. Language use is not simply correlated with social features such as class and gender but is intrinsically social itself.

In time, a number of subareas of sociolinguistics arose, most of them areas of inquiry in their own right today. These include conversational analysis, social interaction, discourse analysis, pragmatics, speech act theory, and ethnomethodology. The period of the 1960s and 1970s saw rapid development in these and other areas of sociolinguistics through cross-disciplinary and cross-cultural research. The ultimate objective was increased understanding of how social actors construct meaning in their interactions with one another.

CURRENT DIRECTIONS

The innovative research agendas in the 1960s and 1970s laid the foundation for a flowering of research topics in the 1980s and 1990s. The databases for studies of color terms have grown considerably and new issues have emerged. Particularly intriguing is the possibility that the term "yellow" has "wild card" status in the evolutionary sequence. Studies of ethno-biological nomenclature and classification have continued to expand, with new issues also arising there. One of the central ones is the ultimate motivation for the taxonomies and their form. The bulk of evidence supports the intellectualist position: that people name and classify the living world simply because they are confronted perceptually by them, as opposed to the utilitarian position that the basis for naming and classifying is the utility served by the plant or animal. Part of the difficulty in resolving the issue is that multiple taxonomies exist for the same plants or animals. A given plant may, for example, be a representative of a type of plant, a kind of food, or a type of medicine but have only one "name." In general, the name appears much more likely to be based on perception than on function, which means that universalist cognitive processes appear to be involved.

Developments within other areas of language, culture, and society have become so numerous and diversified as to preclude easy and succinct summary. Themes can be identified, but even here studies do not fall easily into clear-cut categories. One fairly evident theme is that ethnography continues to be a mainstay for productive characterizations of language and speech behavior in selected communities, such as William Hanks's study of Yucatec Mayan (1990). A major goal of ethnographic studies is to show how language form and behavior are used to construct social identity, especially in public places. The establishment of an identity must be to some degree through ritualized, traditionally sanctioned, and publicly approved forms, necessarily involving language use.

Another emergent theme is pragmatics. Just as the linguistic units of language must be related to each other in structured ways in order to form larger units, such as sentences and paragraphs, units of language use must be related to each other in structured, discernible ways in order to allow participants to construct and reconstruct social identities. To discern the structures, linguistic anthropologists have to attend to the unfolding of social interaction, to look at the patterning of speech behavior in terms of the interrelationships of its units or components. An additional consideration, one that substantially increases the complexity of the task of pragmatics, is the question of how the units or forms are tied in form and function to the broader context in which the behavior is constructed.

The grounding of language use in behavior and of the behavior in specific contexts is, however, only the first part of the analytic endeavor. Contexts themselves are interactive. Features that are present in a setting, such as particular objects or even audiences, may not be merely backdrops to serve as anchors for speech but may be selectively and strategically interwoven into the stream of behavior. In a sense, features of contexts can be activated or deactivated, as the speech circumstances and objectives warrant. Grounding of speech in context is often not a one-time, straightforward matter, but a shuttling back and forth, according to the nature of the social interaction.

The multilayer view of language use, social interaction, and the construction of meaning tied to time and space considerations requires mechanisms to move between and among layers, to mediate between units and across functions. The search for mechanisms and for an understanding of how they work constitutes a central part of contemporary linguistic anthropology. A leading figure in that enterprise is Michael Silverstein (1976), whose classic work on shifters helped initiate inquiry into the question of mechanisms (shifters being devices that cast or recast language from one dimension or domain to another, e.g., verbal tense). Much current focus is on indexicals, a language form that is tied to meaning not through direct naming (reference) but through association of specific and general, as the characteristics of an individual's speech indexing his or her gender or social class. Indexicality is not an occasional feature of language form; it is inherent in form-function relationships (Gumperz and Levinson 1991).

Indexicality itself must be based on underlying cognitive capacity and process, although the specific nature of the bases are not well worked out (except perhaps for color terminology). Along with a much more complete account of the mechanisms of mediation, the specification of how language behavior is related to underlying principles of thought and meaning is a contemporary challenge for linguistic anthropology. The two tracks of the subdiscipline, nomenclatural/classificational and ethnographic/sociolinguistic may be closer to each other in orientation and goals than might appear to be the case. In the categories most studied, color terms and folk biology, names and categories, despite their enormous surface linguistic diversity, appear to have universalist bases. Pragmatic studies of language use, which shows even greater diversity, must also have common, underlying bases, toward which mechanisms such as indexicals must point. This is where linguistic anthropology is likely to make its advances and contributions in the future. We may eventually be in a position to fully develop and understand linguistic relativity in all its complexity.

BEN G. BLOUNT

SEE ALSO: *Color Terminology; Descriptive (Structural) Linguistics; Historical Linguistics; Naming; Sociolinguistics*

BERLIN, BRENT. *Ethnobiological Classification.* Princeton, N.J.: Princeton University Press, 1992.

BERLIN, BRENT, and PAUL KAY. *Basic Color Terms.* Berkeley: University of California Press, 1969.

BLOUNT, BEN G., ed. *Language, Culture, and Society: A Book of Readings.* Prospect Heights, Ill.: Waveland Press, 1995 (originally published 1974).

BOAS, FRANZ. "Introduction." In *Handbook of American Indian Languages, Part 1.* Washington, D.C.: Smithsonian Institution, 1911.

CONKLIN, HAROLD. "Lexicographical Treatment of Folk Taxonomies." In *Problems in Lexicography*, edited by F. W. Householder and S. Saporta. Indiana University Research Center in Anthropology, Folklore, and Linguistics Publication 21, 1962.

ERVIN-TRIPP, SUSAN. "Sociolinguistics." In *Advances in Experimental Social Psychology*, edited by L. Berkowitz. New York: Academic Press, 1969.

FRAKE, CHARLES. "The Ethnographic Study of Cognitive Systems." In *Anthropology and Human Behavior*, edited by T. Gladwin and W. C. Sturtevant. Washington, D.C.: Anthropological Society of Washington, 1962.

GUMPERZ, JOHN J., and DELL H. HYMES, eds. *Directions in Sociolinguistics: The Ethnography of Communication.* New York: Holt, Rinehart, Winston, 1972.

GUMPERZ, JOHN J., and STEPHEN C. LEVINSON. "Rethinking Linguistic Relativity." *Current Anthropology* 32 (1991): 613–623.

HANKS, WILLIAM. *Referential Practice: Language and Lived Space Among the Maya.* Chicago: University of Chicago Press, 1990.

HOIJER, HARRY, ed. *Language in Culture.* Chicago: University of Chicago Press, 1956.

HYMES, DELL H. "The Ethnography of Speaking." In *Anthropology and Human Behavior*, edited by T. Gladwin and W. C. Sturtevant. Washington, D.C.: Anthropological Society of Washington, 1962.

——— . *Essays in the History of Linguistic Anthropology.* Amsterdam: John Benjamins, 1983.

LUCY, JOHN. "Whorf's View of the Linguistic Mediation of Thought." In *Semiotic Mediation: Sociocultural and Psychological Perspectives*, edited by E. Mertz and R. J. Parmentier. Orlando, Fla.: Academic Press, 1985.

SAPIR, EDWARD. *Language: An Introduction to the Study of Speech.* New York: Harcourt Brace and World, 1921.

——— . "The Unconscious Patterning of Behavior in Society." In *The Unconscious: A Symposium*, edited by E. S. Dummer. New York: Knopf, 1927.

SILVERSTEIN, MICHAEL. "Shifters, Linguistic Categories, and Cultural Description." In *Meaning in Anthropology*, edited by K. Basso and H. Selby. Albuquerque: University of New Mexico Press, 1976.

WHORF, BENJAMIN LEE. "The Relation of Habitual Thought and Behavior to Language." In *Language, Thought, and Reality: Selected Writings of Benjamin Lee Whorf,* edited by J. B. Carroll. Cambridge, Mass.: Massachusetts Institute of Technology Press, 1941.

LINGUISTICS

SEE: Descriptive (Structural) Linguistics; Historical Linguistics; Linguistic Anthropology; Sociolinguistics

LITERACY

In the social sciences the terms "literate" and "literacy" occur in a variety of contexts. Most generally a contrast is drawn between those preliterate or nonliterate (and therefore in one sense prehistoric) societies that do not have a full-fledged system of writing for transcribing language and those that do. More frequently the terms refer not to societies but to individuals, the percentage of people who can read and write in a particular society, which is therefore divided into the literate and the illiterate. Even among those who can read, competence obviously varies, so that literacy becomes a measurable quality, with some individuals being more literate than others.

In most societies with writing, until 100 years ago only a minority could read and write; the rest were illiterate and hence were themselves dependent on the oral or visual transmission of knowledge. They were not, however, dependent on knowledge originating in the oral or visual registers, and, consequently, their traditions differed in kind from those of a society without writing because they would be indirectly influenced by the written forms; illiterates would imbibe Christian or Buddhist book learning through stories, sermons, paintings, and sculpture. Equally, they might learn to conduct cognitive operations invented by the written culture (such as the arithmetic tables learned by heart). The same is true of technological advances developed through the medium of written operations; illiterates may benefit from living in a literate culture, although the inability to read and write will place them in a disadvantageous position regarding others who can. Even cultures without writing may be influenced by contact with literate outsiders in a similar manner. The radio could stand as one example, because literacy was clearly a prerequisite of its invention but not its operation. Today, however, there is probably no society in the world that does not have some literates who are capable of gaining access to written knowledge produced elsewhere (Cipolla 1969).

If one understands writing and reading to refer to full-fledged methods of transcribing language, then they appear first in Mesopotamia around 3100 B.C.E. The words "reading" and "writing" have been used by some (for example, by Jacques Derrida) to refer to such activities as "reading" the stars. In European languages (although it is not otherwise very widespread) it is possible to employ the verbs to refer metaphorically to universal processes of understanding or interpretation (the writing on the wall), but it seems more profitable to adopt the more usual restricted usage.

Research on literacy has been of three main types. First, there are the attempts to assess the long-term cultural effects of introducing writing to societies in the past and in the present, including an assessment of its impact on the economy, the polity, religion, and even on the family (Goody 1986). Second, there have been the studies of particular societies at specific times, carried out in the past mainly by historians (Clanchy 1979; Stock 1983). Third, there are the observational studies on the present undertaken by anthropologists and sociologists as well as the experimental and physiological work done by psychologists (Scribner and Cole 1981; Street 1984).

Cultural studies emphasize the significant effect of this addition to society's means of communication. In Mesopotamia writing seems first to have been used as a way to certify the distant transfer of goods, a kind of labeling device, the equivalent of sending an accompanying letter, but it soon proved its utility for recording transactions, whether by merchants, royal servants, or temple administrators. Some of the most interesting developments arose in the context of teaching, because temple schools were essential to the training of scribes. Just as lists developed for economic and administrative purposes, word lists were critical to learning and the organization of knowledge (Gelb 1963).

For anthropology, a consideration of the role of literacy affects many basic issues, such as the distinction between "advanced" and "primitive" societies, between scientists and bricoleurs, between the domesticated and the savage mind, between types of logic and rationality, forms of exchange (reciprocal and commercial), types of government (bureaucratic and simple states), legal procedures (the fixity of codes, the role of precedent), and forms of religions (of the book as distinct from the more eclectic varieties). The hypothesis that those differences are affected by the long-term presence of writing avoids having to deny their significance, or having to seek dubious explanations of a physical or cultural genetic kind. It points instead to a precise mechanism.

Observations on the acquisition of writing by contemporary societies strengthen this claim. Learning to read and write, as well as the acquisition of the knowledge this opens up, has dramatic effects, enabling societies' members to quickly find their way around the world with ease. Individuals from tribal backgrounds may easily find themselves on the national or even world stage, receiving prizes for political, scientific, or literary achievement. That is one indication of how literacy has not only changed the world but changed people's ability to participate in it, changing their understanding of that world (Olson 1994).

At another level, psychological tests have proved disappointing in the search for overall literacy effects, partly because each form of writing has different cognitive implications, depending on the character of the script, its relationship to natural language, and the content of the written tradition. No effects are unmediated. The absence of a historical perspective is critical to the results of these tests (Goody 1987). Psychological tests of writing may point to schooling rather than literacy per se as the important variable, but then schooling is virtually essential to the acquisition of literacy (and vice versa) and certainly to much (but not all) of the products of a written tradition. The basic problem with such tests is that they look at what is internal to the organism and tend to decontextualize mental abilities, instead of seeing them from an interactive perspective, which would include the book itself as part of the cognitive operations encompassed by writing.

Writing or literacy is neither a simple nor a single variable. Forms of script differ individually and can be seen as predominantly logographic, syllabic, or alphabetic, displaying increasing accessibility for most

purposes in that order. They also vary in the instruments (stylo and surface) used for the inscription and in the mode of mechanical reproduction that followed the invention of printing, first in the East, then some centuries later in the West.

There can be no doubt that the mechanical reproduction of writing marked another important stage in the development of literacy. It meant that more people could buy books at lower cost; it encouraged writing in the vernacular and gave individuals direct access to the written word, including the word of God, rather than the mediated access on which the priesthood of the Catholic church insisted. It encouraged the Reformation, just as Protestantism encouraged literacy and education; a significant percent of the cases heard by the Inquisition in Malta had to do with reading "heretical" books. In fifteenth-century England about 10 percent of men could read; by the Cromwellian period that had risen to 30 percent (and 10 percent for women), although rates were even higher in urban than in rural areas. In Protestant Sweden rates were much higher—almost 100 percent by 1750. In England the dramatic change only took place after 1870 with the beginning of compulsory education.

The role of writing in promoting or encouraging changes in the social system depends on the power of this medium to store linguistic acts in visual form, which enables them to be communicated at a distance over space and over time, but it is not simply the new form of storage but the shift in channel from mouth and ear to hand and eye that changes the nature of linguistic acts in significant ways. For example, spelling affects pronunciation, as in the reinstatement of the English "h" in the eighteenth century with all its class implications; the letter had been visually present much earlier but in speech it had been universally dropped as in the French *herbe* and the American *herb*. More generally, the flow of speech becomes reorganized in such a way that it can be understood without the presence of the speaker, so that the conventions of punctuation become a necessary part of language. Words are separated one from another and nouns become separable from verbs and even from sentences; in early writing systems they are often incorporated in lists that present the terms belonging to a single category, such as trees or vegetables, in a row or column, treating language in a way that would be virtually impossible in an oral culture and raising problems of the inclusion or exclusion of items that generate questions, sometimes interesting, sometimes idiotic, concerning the units or the category.

The first achievement of writing is to ensure the storage and communication over time and space of linguistic messages. This is its prime role in transforming social organizations, but the process of setting down such messages, whether or not they are then communicated to anyone, leads to changes in human understanding itself (Havelock 1976; Senner 1990). In terms of the mechanics of reading and writing, these involve the development of secondary skills, the coordination of the eye with the brain, the inner ear, and the silent voice, by which linguistic thoughts are expressed in visual formulae and vice versa. The process of learning to read involves the deliberate cultivation of exact memory and verbatim recall right from the start. The memorizing of hundreds of basic shapes is crucial to any logographic writing such as Chinese; syllabic scripts make fewer initial demands, and alphabetic ones fewer still. The verbatim learning of arbitrary letters in an arbitrary order, the abc's, is as intrinsic now as it was to the ancient Syrians who invented it (Diringer 1968). Moreover the recall of the shape and composition of words, of the often conventional association of phonemes and graphemes, remains a feature of rapid reading and accurate writing, that is, spelling. The fact that the process is at once so arbitrary and so powerful means that this instrument of information retrieval also provides a model for certain forms of learning, and of learning to learn—at least the sort of learning that psychologists and educationalists often understand by the term. In addition, writing entails the development of manual dexterity of the kind involved in handling a paint brush (indeed the activities are closely related in terms of cultural history) and to a lesser extent in sewing and in the use of eating implements, especially chopsticks.

What are the consequences of such procedures, once established? The process of writing, which even in correspondence is often one of speaking about rather than speaking to, involves the deliberate, artifactual use of language, not simply for special purposes (as with oratory in oral societies) but for a whole range of activities where we are engaged in a conscious struggle with words and meanings, which is also a struggle with words and things.

The deliberate visual recording of language means not only a search for words but a search for genres.

Discourse, even when not informal, often trails off into another activity, being punctuated by a drink of water, a mouthful of food, the rustle of paper, the closing of a door, or, in other words, by another nonlinguistic activity. Written composition, however, has to have a formal beginning and an end; "Dear Christine" is completed by "Yours sincerely, Stephen," laid out in a particular format, with the specification of place and date. Apart from the letter, there is a gamut of genres from the report to the passport, as well as the literary genres ranging from the novel to the sonnet. These developments appear gradually over time, but eventually not only each composition but each subunit takes on a specific form; each topic requires the paragraph, each sentence a capital letter and full stop, each word its break. Syntax and punctuation become more precise and more formal as a result of becoming visual. Part of the reason behind these changes is that whereas speech operates as one of a cluster of channels in face-to-face communication, writing as a register stands on its own. It is "decontextualized," or rather the context is highly restricted. Hence, clarity of expression and precision of genre, syntax, and punctuation are encouraged by the visual representation of language.

Not only is language decontextualized but because of the permanency of writing, which materializes the flow of speech, words can be rearranged more freely in composition and also taken out of the sentence structure as individual items and grouped with others of the same "class." Such an activity is not impossible in oral converse, but its use is enormously developed in early literate cultures where the reading and copying of lists, as in Mesopotamia, is one of the basic methods of instruction. Listing has other implications, because it means placing items in unambiguous categories, giving each one a position, leading to consolidation on the one hand and reconsideration on the other (Goody 1976). The list is a component of the table or matrix, an important instrument of intellectual operations. It is also intrinsic to recordkeeping of a multitude of kinds, from trading operations to administrative personnel to astronomical observations. It is the relative permanency of writing that makes it valuable as a means of storing information, whether in the form of note-taking, of the more deliberate recording of the Nile floods over time, of the history written for future generations, or of the accidental survival of personal letters.

So much for writing. While reading aloud is necessarily an individual task, and a frequent feature of early literacy, especially when only a small proportion of the population had the skills, it involved an immediate audience, the physical presence of hearers. So, too, did a parallel feature of early literacy, the repetitive reading to oneself of a piece, then its subsequent recitation, as if produced purely orally, to a collected audience. Such a process involves rereading, that is, going over for a second or a third time the linguistic message, in a fashion that is virtually impossible without writing. The backward look facilitates not only verbatim memorizing but also understanding and critical analysis, as well as enabling the writer to construct and present more complex sentences than would otherwise be possible. Such reviewing is the counterpart of comparing several versions of the same incident, poem, or account and of evaluating their differences, a procedure that gave birth to history in the technical sense.

Literacy not only encourages such deliberate perusal of the text, it also makes possible the opposite, that is, the highly selective forms of retrieval that are involved in consulting a dictionary (or even a library), as well as the skipping and the speed reading that takes place when we read a detective story rather than a poem. The potential results of such procedures are vital to the growth of knowledge. In the first place, the deliberate perusal of a text facilitates the search for inconsistencies, for contradictions, while the ability to set side by side different texts referring to the same events or notions leads to the cultivation of criticism and of skepticism. It allows not only for criticism of the texts but also their further elaboration by commentary, which can in its turn be stored away for future reference, leading to the building up of libraries of stored knowledge. These libraries encapsulate "objective knowledge" in the sense that this information has become theoretically independent of specific human teachers, except teachers in the technique of literacy itself, which now becomes the critical technology of the intellect, that is, apart from language itself. Indeed, it could be argued that intellectuals and ideologies, in the sense in which these words are often used, begin with literacy.

The development of criticism is also the development of logic, but there is another element that derives from the formalization of the procedures themselves, which in turn arises from the laying out of propositions in the summary visual form. The syllogism does not represent an oral way of ordering one's thoughts but a written one that lies at some remove from ordinary discourse. Such formalization is also a type of abstraction, of generalization. We are not primarily concerned with particular propositions embedded in a concrete situation but with a paradigm, a model, a type of argumentation. As such, the expressions, propositions, and premises, are decontextualized in a meaningful sense. Indeed, this is true of much literate communication. Even if I write a letter to a particular individual (and most literate communications are not addressed to such a limited audience), I cannot visualize the precise situation, above all the mood, in which it will be received. Hence, neither context nor tone can be the same as in a face-to-face situation; I have to allow for more contingencies and make my request more precise. On the other hand, if I am giving a legal decision or reacting to some misdemeanor, I have to reckon that my words will be used as a precedent and applied in many different situations, so they have to be more general in their import and less tied to the specific situation. In other words, I cannot assume a context and it has to be specified, or I have to work on a plane of greater abstraction and generalization, a fact of considerable importance in the growth of knowledge.

The use of writing enables us to accumulate knowledge and at the same time to formalize, summarize, and generate it by means of paralinguistic devices, such as diagrams (including Euclidean geometry), lists, and tables. Such devices not only facilitate comprehension, their creation advances understanding by grouping material in new or question-raising ways. The telephone directory and the dictionary are important developments from the simpler forms, powerful instruments of knowledge and communication. At the same time the shopping list or railway timetable enables one to plan one's future action, and the critical value of such tables for the allocation of time, for teaching, for work, in calendars, and in daily diaries needs no stressing. Once again, while planning is intrinsic to all human communities, such action can be greatly enhanced by the use of literacy.

JACK GOODY

CIPOLLA, D. R. *Literacy and Development in the West*. Harmondsworth: Penguin, 1969.

CLANCHY, M. T. *From Memory to the Written Record: England 1066–1307*. Cambridge, Mass.: Harvard University Press, 1979.

DIRINGER, DAVID. *The Alphabet: A Key to the History of Mankind,* 3rd ed. New York: Funk and Wagnalls, 1968.

EISENSTEIN, ELIZABETH L.. *The Printing Press as an Agent of Change*. New York: Cambridge University Press, 1979.

GELB, IGNACE J. *A Study of Writing,* 2nd ed. Chicago: University of Chicago Press, 1963.

GOODY, JACK. *The Domestication of the Savage Mind*. New York: Cambridge University Press, 1976.

——— . *The Logic of Writing and the Organization of Society*. New York: Cambridge University Press, 1986.

——— . *The Interface Between the Written and the Oral*. New York: Cambridge University Press, 1987.

HAVELOCK, E. *Origins of Western Literacy*. Toronto: OISE Press, 1976.

OLSON, DAVID R. *The World on Paper: The Conceptual and Cognitive Implications of Writing*. Cambridge: Cambridge University Press, 1994.

OLSON, DAVID R., and N. TORRANCE, eds. *Literacy and Orality*. Cambridge: Cambridge University Press, 1991.

ONG, WALTER J. *Orality and Literature: The Technologizing of the Word*. London: Methuen, 1982.

SCRIBNER, SYLVIA, and MICHAEL COLE. *The Psychology of Literacy*. Cambridge, Mass.: Harvard University Press, 1981.

SENNER, WAYNE M., ed. *The Origins of Writing*. Lincoln: University of Nebraska Press, 1990.

STOCK, B. *The Implications of Literacy*. Princeton, N.J.: Princeton University Press, 1983.

STREET, B. *Literacy in Theory and Practice*. Cambridge: Cambridge University Press, 1984.

LOVE

The anthropological study of romantic (or passionate) love is virtually nonexistent because of the widespread belief that romantic love is unique to Euro-American culture. This belief is by no means confined to anthropology. Historians argue that affection was of secondary importance to more utilitarian ambitions throughout much of European history. Lawrence Stone (1988) goes further, insisting that "if romantic love ever existed outside of Europe, it only arose among the nonwestern nations' elite who had the time to cultivate an aesthetic appreciation for subjective experiences." Underlying these Eurocentric views is the assumption that modernization and the rise of individualism are directly linked to the appearance of romantic notions of love.

The validity of an affectionless past is challenged by some historians, who draw upon the insights of an earlier generation of anthropologists to argue that European preindustrial courtship was neither cold and aloof nor devoid of affection. Nevertheless, much of this revisionist work continues to explain instances of romantic passion as a basis for marriage, ignoring the role romantic love plays in extramarital affairs. Consequently, little has been done to alter the prevalent opinion that romantic love is a European contribution to world culture.

Psychologist Paul Rosenblatt (1967), in a pioneering series of cross-cultural investigations, correlated modes of cultural transmission and social organization to the emergence of romantic love as a basis for marriage. Writing within the 1960s functionalist milieu, he assumed, as did almost everyone else, that the social construction of reality had a corresponding impact on the construction and expression of private sentiment. In effect, one assumed the other. The premise of much of this research is apparent—cultural traditions bind the individual emotionally into a web of dependency with others, thereby rechanneling or defusing the intensity of an individual's emotional experience. This web of dependency, in turn, undermines the individual's proclivity to fantasize about a lover or the erotic. From these and related studies, it has often been inferred that the non-Western cultures are incapable of or are closed to feelings and desires that are independent of the social context or customary expectation. By this logic the social context circumscribes an individual's experience and a simplistic one-to-one correspondence is assumed, implying that the internal life of the non-Westerner is one-dimensional, inhibited, and heavily dependent on societal values.

Since the 1980s, evolutionary-oriented anthropologists and psychologists have explored the possibility that romantic love constitutes a human universal. These researchers point out that romantic love may constitute the sort of psychological mechanism that promotes reproductive success by increasing the likelihood of frequent sexual intercourse. From the evolutionary perspective, humans have evolved the propensity to experience romantic love, which can be recognized as a sudden, unrestrained passion that often results in an immediate, if short-term, commitment. In this view, romantic love centers on a biological core that is expressed as love and enacted in courtship. Concurring, Michael Liebowitz (1983) draws upon biochemical research that suggests that the giddiness, euphoria, optimism, and energy that lovers experience in the early stages of infatuation is caused by increased levels of phenylethylamine, an amphetamine-related compound that produces mood-lifting and energizing effects. In effect, romantic love arises from forces within the human brain that are independent of the socially constructed mind.

Romantic or passionate love can be defined as having three components: the idealization of the other, its occurrence within an erotic context, and the expectation of its enduring into the future (Lindholm 1988). Romantic passion may constitute a psychological mechanism in the service of mating-effort strategies that are oriented toward either long-term or short-term reproductive success. Romantic passion stands, therefore, in sharp contrast to the companionship phase of love (sometimes referred to as attachment), which is characterized by the growth of a more peaceful, comfortable, and fulfilling kind of love relationship; it is a strong and enduring affection built upon long-term association.

In the past, when anthropologists focused on romantic love, they tended to concentrate on the presence or absence of a formal ideology of romance; left unexamined were those instances in which individuals, despite cultural rules denying the existence of such a relationship, still fall in love. In a cross-cultural study of romantic love, William Jankowiak and Edward Fischer (1992) found evidence of romantic love's presence in 88.5 percent of 166 sample cultures. They concluded that romantic love is a human universal, or, at the least, a near universal. Their study also suggests that romantic love and its distant relative lust are the two most powerful panhuman emotions. These two emotions are organized around different cultural and psychological criteria, which puts them in several ways in direct competition with one another, and this competition raises important implications for understanding some of the turmoil often found in male-female relationships.

Choice in mating is not a European invention and has always been an integral part of many human cultures. Numerous tribal societies allow individuals to choose their own mates. Even in polygamous societies in which parents arrange marriages, men in subsequent marriages often "follow their heart" and marry for love. There is tremendous variation in the way cultures encourage or discourage the expression of romantic passion. In some, romantic passion is rejected as an evil and frightening emotional experience; in others, it is tolerated but not admired; in still others, it is glorified as one of the culture's highest ideals. To date, no researcher has explored this intriguing topic.

Numerous studies have explored the relationship between the expansion of the global economy and the origins of the ideology of romantic love as a basis for marriage. William Goode (1959), for example, argues that the presence of a love culture, as opposed to a culture that tolerates love, depends on the family economy's transformation from a unit of production to a unit of consumption, a transformation that also increases the degree of adolescent freedom. No longer bound to the survival of the family economy, marriage becomes a personal matter. The shift in the family economy also contributes, at least in the short run, to the effectiveness of romantic love as a discourse of defiance, whereby lovers circumvent the arrangements of their parents and choose their own marriage partners. In time, romantic love—an ideology of subversion—is recast not only as a justification for marriage but also as an admired and cherished life goal.

In sum, romantic passion may in fact be muted, although never entirely repressed, by other cultural variables. The capacity to experience romantic passion is not related to whether a particular society is sexually repressed or open, field dependent (i.e., oriented toward how others will respond) or field independent (i.e., oriented toward self or individuality) as to psychological orientation to the group or to the self, or bilateral or unilineal as to rules of descent. The different degrees of frequency and intensity with which individuals from different cultures experience romantic passion is not clear. Because researchers have rarely studied the relative frequency with which a person falls in and out of love, it is unclear if romantic love is experienced with less frequency in the cultures that deny or disapprove of the emotional experience.

WILLIAM JANKOWIAK

BUSS, DAVID. "Love Acts: The Evolutionary Biology of Love." In *The Psychology of Love,* edited by Robert

Sternberg and Michael Barnes. New Haven, Conn.: Yale University Press, 1988.

CANCIAN, FRANCESCA. *Love in America: Gender and Self-Development.* New York: Cambridge University Press, 1987.

ENDLEMAN, ROBERT. *Love and Sex in Twelve Cultures.* New York: Psychic Press, 1988.

FISCHER, HELEN. *The Anatomy of Love.* New York: Norton, 1992.

GOODE, WILLIAM. "The Theoretical Importance of Love." *American Sociological Review* 24 (1959): 38–47.

JANKOWIAK, WILLIAM, ed. *Romantic Passion: A Universal Emotion?* New York: Columbia University Press, 1995.

JANKOWIAK, WILLIAM, and EDWARD FISCHER. "Romantic Love: A Cross-Cultural Perspective." *Ethnology* 31 (1992): 149–156.

LIEBOWITZ, MICHAEL. *The Chemistry of Love.* Boston: Little, Brown, 1983.

LINDHOLM, CHARLES. "Lovers and Leaders: A Comparison of Social and Psychological Models of Romance and Charisma." *Social Science Information*, vol. 8 (1988): 1–27.

MELLEN, SYDNEY. *The Evolution of Love.* San Francisco: W. H. Freeman, 1981.

ROSENBLATT, PAUL. "A Cross-Cultural Study of Child Rearing and Romantic Love." *Journal of Personality and Social Psychology* 4 (1966): 336–338.

———. "Marital Residence and the Functions of Romantic Love." *Ethnology*, vol. 6 (1967): 471–480.

STONE, LAWRENCE. "Passionate Attachments in the West in Historical Perspective." In *Passionate Attachments*, edited by W. Gaylin and E. Person. New York: Free Press, 1988.